The Greenwood Encyclopedia of Science Fiction and Fantasy

Advisory Board

The Greenwood Encyclopedia of Science Fiction and Fantasy

Themes, Works, and Wonders

EDITED BY GARY WESTFAHL

FOREWORD BY NEIL GAIMAN

GREENWOOD PRESS
Westport, Connecticut • London

Library of Congress Cataloging-in-Publication Data

The Greenwood encyclopedia of science fiction and fantasy : themes, works, and wonders / edited by
Gary Westfahl ; foreword by Neil Gaiman.
   p. cm.
   Includes bibliographical references.
   ISBN 0–313–32950–8 (set : alk. paper)—ISBN–0–313–32951–6 (v. 1 : alk. paper)—
ISBN 0–313–32952–4 (v. 2 : alk. paper)—ISBN 0–313–32953–2 (v. 3 : alk. paper)
   1. Science fiction, American—Encyclopedias. 2. Fantasy fiction, American—
Encyclopedias. 3. Science fiction, English—Encyclopedias. 4. Fantasy fiction,
English—Encyclopedias. I. Westfahl, Gary.
PS374.S35.G74   2005
813′.0876203—dc22   2005013677

British Library Cataloguing in Publication Data is available.

Library of Congress Catalog Card Number: 2005013677
ISBN: 0–313–32950–8 (set)
     0–313–32951–6 (vol. 1)
     0–313–32952–4 (vol. 2)
     0–313–32953–2 (vol. 3)

First published in 2005

Greenwood Press, 88 Post Road West, Westport, CT 06881
An imprint of Greenwood Publishing Group, Inc.
www.greenwood.com

Printed in the United States of America

The paper used in this book complies with the
Permanent Paper Standard issued by the National
Information Standards Organization (Z39.48–1984).

10 9 8 7 6 5 4 3 2 1

Contents

Alphabetical List of Themes

VOLUME 1

VOLUME 2

■

Alphabetical List of Classic Works

A.I.: Artificial Intelligence (2001)
Alice's Adventures in Wonderland by
  Lewis Carroll (1865)
Alien (1979)
Alphaville (1965)
Animal Farm: A Fairy Story by George
  Orwell (1945)
Babylon 5 (1993–1998)
Back to the Future (1985)
Batman (1989)
Beauty and the Beast (1946)
Blade Runner (1982)
Blakes 7 (1978–1981)
Blood Music by Greg Bear (1985)
The Book of the New Sun by Gene
  Wolfe (1980–1983)
Brave New World by Aldous Huxley
  (1932)
Brazil (1986)
Bring the Jubilee by Ward Moore
  (1953)
The Brother from Another Planet
  (1984)
Buffy the Vampire Slayer (1996–2003)
A Canticle for Leibowitz by Walter M.
  Miller, Jr. (1959)
Cat's Cradle by Kurt Vonnegut, Jr.
  (1963)
Childhood's End by Arthur C. Clarke
  (1953)
A Christmas Carol by Charles Dickens
  (1843)
City by Clifford D. Simak (1952)
The Clan of the Cave Bear by Jean
  Auel (1980)
A Clockwork Orange (1971)

A Clockwork Orange by Anthony
  Burgess (1962)
Close Encounters of the Third Kind
  (1977)
The Colour of Magic by Terry Pratchett
  (1983)
Conan the Conqueror by Robert E.
  Howard (1950)
*A Connecticut Yankee in King Arthur's
  Court* by Mark Twain (1889)
Consider Phlebas by Iain M. Banks
  (1987)
Dawn by Octavia E. Butler (1987)
The Day of the Triffids by John
  Wyndham (1951)
The Day the Earth Stood Still (1951)
*Deathbird Stories: A Pantheon of Mod-
  ern Gods* by Harlan Ellison (1975)
The Demolished Man by Alfred Bester
  (1953)
The Difference Engine by William
  Gibson and Bruce Sterling (1990)
*The Dispossessed: An Ambiguous
  Utopia* by Ursula K. Le Guin (1974)
Do Androids Dream of Electric Sheep?
  by Philip K. Dick (1968)
Dr. Jekyll and Mr. Hyde (1931)
Doctor No (1962)
*Dr. Strangelove, or How I Stopped
  Worrying and Learned to Love the
  Bomb* (1964)
Doctor Who (1963–1989)
Dracula (1931)
Dracula by Bram Stoker (1897)
Dragonflight by Anne McCaffrey
  (1968)

Guide to Related Topics

THEMES ENTRIES BY CATEGORY

Abstract Concepts and Qualities

Absurdity
Androgyny
Anxiety
Beauty
Chivalry
Colors
Courage
Darkness
Decadence
Destiny
Eternity
Evil
Force
Freedom
Friendship
Gender
Guilt and Responsibility
Hubris
Identity
Illusion
Individualism and Conformity
Intelligence
Invisibility
Knowledge
Light
Love
Madness
Magic
Memory
Mystery
Names
Nature

Nudity
Old Age
Optimism and Pessimism
Pain
Paranoia
Personification
Progress
Secret Identities
Sense of Wonder
Sexism
Sexuality
Social Darwinism
Sublime
Taboos
Talents
Time
Virginity
Vision and Blindness
Wisdom
Xenophobia
Yin and Yang

Animals

Animals and Zoos
Apes
Birds
Cats
Dinosaurs
Dogs
Dragons
Fish and Sea Creatures
Horses
Insects

Lions and Tigers
Parasites
Rats and Mice
Snakes and Worms
Supernatural Creatures
Talking Animals
Unicorns

Characters

Adam and Eve
Aliens in Space
Aliens on Earth
Amazons
Androids
Angels
Apprentice
Arthur
Astronauts
Babies
Barbarians
Children
Clones
Clowns and Fools
Computers
Cyborgs
Demons
Detectives
Doppelgänger
Dwarfs
Elder Races
Elves
Fairies
Family
Fathers
Frankenstein Monsters
Ghosts and Hauntings
Giants
Goblins
Gods and Goddesses
Golem
Heroes
Hive Minds
Humanity
Kings
Last Man
Mad Scientists

Mentors
Mermaids
Messiahs
Monsters
Mothers
Native Americans
Pirates
Queens
Robots
Satan
Scientists
Shakespeare
Shapeshifters
Superheroes
Superman
Temptress
Trickster
Vampires
Villains
Werewolves
Witches
Wizards
Writing and Authors
Youth
Zombies

Disciplines and Professions

Advertising
Anthropology
Architecture and Interior Design
Art
Biology
Business
Cosmology
Divination
Ecology
Economics
Education
Eschatology
Espionage
Ethics
Fashion
Feminism
Genetic Engineering
History
Hypnotism

Illustration and Graphics
Journalism
Language and Linguistics
Mathematics
Medicine
Music
Philosophy
Physics
Poetry
Politics
Psychology
Religion
Technology
Theatre
Writing and Authors

Events and Actions

Apocalypse
Betrayal
Birth
Carnival
Christmas
Communication
Crime and Punishment
Curses
Cycles
Death
Disaster
Disguise
Divination
Dreams
Enlargement
Escape
Estrangement
Evolution
Exile
First Contact
Flood
Flying
Halloween
Invasion
Marriage
Metamorphosis
Miniaturization
Mutation
Nuclear War

Pantropy
Perception
Plagues and Diseases
Possession
Promise
Reading
Rebellion
Rebirth
Reincarnation
Revenge
Rituals
Role Reversals
Sacrifice
Sin
Sleep
Suicide
Survival
Teleportation
Terraforming
Theft
Time Travel
Timeslips
Torture
Touch
Trade
Transportation
Uplift
Violence
Work and Leisure

Games and Leisure Activities

Art
Carnival
Chess
Christmas
Clowns and Fools
Disguise
Dreams
Drugs
Escape
Fashion
Food and Drink
Games
Gifts
Halloween
Home

Humor
Labyrinth
Music
Pastoral
Poetry
Puzzles
Riddles
Sleep
Sports
Stories
Taverns and Inns
Theatre
Toys
Virtual Reality
Work and Leisure

Horror

Aliens on Earth
Blood
Borderlands
Curses
Dark Fantasy
Darkness
Death
Decadence
Demons
Divination
Doppelgänger
Dreams
Elder Races
Estrangement
Evil
Frankenstein Monsters
Ghosts and Hauntings
Goblins
Golem
Guilt and Responsibility
Halloween
Hell
Horror
Hypnotism
Illusion
Invasion
Invisibility
Labyrinth
Mad Scientists
Madness

Monsters
Mutation
Omens and Signs
Pain
Paranoia
Parasites
Possession
Prisons
Psychic Powers
Puzzles
Reincarnation
Rituals
Sacrifice
Satan
Sin
Skeletons
Sublime
Supernatural Creatures
Torture
Vampires
Violence
Voodoo
Werewolves
Witches
Zombies

Literary Concepts

Absurdity
Allegory
Alternate History
Arcadia
Bildungsroman
Books
Carnival
Chivalry
Clichés
Comedy
Cyberpunk
Cycles
Dark Fantasy
Decadence
Deus ex Machina
Doppelgänger
Dystopia
Escape
Fables
Fairy Tales

Love and Sexuality

Magical Beings

Wizards
Zombies

Magical Places

Arcadia
Atlantis
Borderlands
Carnival
Dimensions
Heaven
Hell
Hollow Earth
Imaginary Worlds
Labyrinth
Lost Worlds
Parallel Worlds
Rings
Shared Worlds
Threshold
Virtual Reality
Wilderness

Objects and Substances

Antimatter
Automobiles
Blood
Books
Clocks and Timepieces
Computers
Dolls and Puppets
Drugs
Elements
Fire
Flowers
Food and Drink
Gifts
Gold and Silver
Inventions
Machines and Mechanization
Magical Objects
Maps
Mirrors
Money
Omens and Signs
Plants
Rings

Rockets
Skeletons
Statues
Swords
Television and Radio
Toys
Treasure
UFOs
Water
Weaponry

Religions and Religious Concepts

Adam and Eve
Apocalypse
Christianity
Christmas
Demons
Divination
Eschatology
Evil
Golem
Halloween
Heaven
Hell
Islam
Judaism
Messiahs
Mythology
Omens and Signs
Reincarnation
Religion
Rituals
Sacrifice
Satan
Sin
Voodoo
Witches
Yin and Yang

Social and Political Concepts

America
Anthropology
Australia
Business
Carnival

China
Chivalry
Cities
Civilization
Class System
Community
Crime and Punishment
Cultures
Decadence
Dystopia
Economics
Education
Ethics
Exile
Family
Freedom
Friendship
Future War
Galactic Empire
Globalization
Governance Systems
Guilt and Responsibility
Habitats
History
Humanity
Individualism and Conformity
Japan
Kings
Nuclear War
Overpopulation
Planetary Colonies
Politics
Postcolonialism
Post-Holocaust Societies
Prisons
Progress
Race Relations
Rebellion
Rituals
Russia
Secret History
Slavery
Social Darwinism
Space War
Taboos
Taverns and Inns
Trade
Urban Fantasy

Utopia
Violence
War
Work and Leisure
Xenophobia

Sciences and Scientific Concepts

Air Travel
Alien Worlds
Aliens in Space
Aliens on Earth
Alternate History
Androids
Antimatter
Astronauts
Biology
Black Holes
Clones
Comets and Asteroids
Computers
Cosmology
Cyberspace
Cyborgs
Dimensions
Earth
Ecology
Elements
Eschatology
Evolution
Far Future
First Contact
Force
Future War
Galactic Empire
Generation Starships
Gravity
Immortality and Longevity
Inventions
Machines and Mechanization
Mad Scientists
Mars
Mathematics
Medicine
Mercury
The Moon
Mutation
Near Future

Nuclear Power
Nuclear War
Pantropy
Parasites
Physics
Plagues and Diseases
Planetary Colonies
Predictions
Psychic Powers
Psychology
Robots
Rockets
Scientists
Sea Travel
Social Darwinism
Space Habitats
Space Opera
Space Stations
Space Travel
Space War
The Sun
Superman
Suspended Animation and Cryonics
Symbiosis
Technology
Technothrillers
Teleportation
Television and Radio
Terraforming
Time Travel
UFOs
Uplift
Venus
Virtual Reality
Vision and Blindness
Weaponry
Weather

Settings

Africa
Alien Worlds
America
Arcadia
Asia
Atlantis
Australia

Black Holes
Borderlands
Castles
Caverns
Cemeteries
China
Cities
Comets and Asteroids
Community
Cultures
Cyberspace
Desert
Dimensions
Earth
Egypt
Europe
Farms
Forests
Frontier
Galactic Empire
Gardens
Generation Starships
Habitats
Heaven
Hell
Hollow Earth
Home
Hyperspace
Imaginary Worlds
Islands
Japan
Jungles
Jupiter and the Outer Planets
Labyrinth
Landscape
Latin America
Libraries
Lost Worlds
Mars
Mercury
Microcosm
The Moon
Mountains
Parallel Worlds
Planetary Colonies
Polar Regions
Prisons

Rivers
Russia
Shared Worlds
South Pacific
Space Habitats
Space Stations
Stars
The Sun
Taverns and Inns
Threshold
Venus
Virtual Reality
Wilderness

Space

Alien Worlds
Aliens in Space
Aliens on Earth
Astronauts
Black Holes
Comets and Asteroids
Cosmology
Dimensions
Earth
First Contact
Force
Galactic Empire
Generation Starships
Gravity
Hyperspace
Invasion
Jupiter and the Outer Planets
Mars
Mercury
The Moon
Pantropy
Parallel Worlds
Planetary Colonies
Rockets
Sense of Wonder
Space Habitats
Space Opera
Space Stations
Space Travel
Space War
Stars

The Sun
Terraforming
Venus

Subgenres and Narrative Patterns

Air Travel
Allegory
Alternate History
Bildungsroman
Comedy
Cyberpunk
Dark Fantasy
Deus ex Machina
Dystopia
Exploration
Fables
Fairy Tales
Fin de Siècle
Future War
Gothic
Hard Science Fiction
Heroic Fantasy
Horror
Magic Realism
Metafiction and Recursiveness
Mythology
Pastoral
Postmodernism
Prehistoric Fiction
Quests
Romance
Ruritanian Romance
Satire
Sea Travel
Secret History
Space Opera
Space Travel
Space War
Steampunk
Surrealism
Sword and Sorcery
Technothrillers
Tragedy
Underground Adventure
Underwater Adventure
Urban Fantasy

Utopia
War
Westerns

Time

Alternate History
Clocks and Timepieces
Cycles
Cosmology
Dimensions
Divination
Eschatology
Eternity
Evolution
Far Future
Fin de Siècle
Future War
Generation Starships

History
Hyperspace
Immortality and Longevity
Medievalism and the Middle Ages
Memory
Near Future
Omens and Signs
Parallel Worlds
Post-Holocaust Societies
Predictions
Prehistoric Fiction
Progress
Seasons
Social Darwinism
Speed
Suspended Animation and Cryonics
Time
Time Travel
Timeslips

CLASSIC WORKS BY CATEGORIES

∎

Books

Alice's Adventures in Wonderland by Lewis Carroll (1865)
Animal Farm: A Fairy Story by George Orwell (1945)
Blood Music by Greg Bear (1985)
The Book of the New Sun by Gene Wolfe (1980–1983)
Brave New World by Aldous Huxley (1932)
Bring the Jubilee by Ward Moore (1953)
A Canticle for Leibowitz by Walter M. Miller, Jr. (1959)
Cat's Cradle by Kurt Vonnegut, Jr. (1963)
Childhood's End by Arthur C. Clarke (1953)
A Christmas Carol by Charles Dickens (1843)
City by Clifford D. Simak (1952)
The Clan of the Cave Bear by Jean Auel (1980)

A Clockwork Orange by Anthony Burgess (1962)
The Colour of Magic by Terry Pratchett (1983)
Conan the Conqueror by Robert E. Howard (1950)
A Connecticut Yankee in King Arthur's Court by Mark Twain (1889)
Consider Phlebas by Iain M. Banks (1987)
Dawn by Octavia E. Butler (1987)
The Day of the Triffids by John Wyndham (1951)
Deathbird Stories: A Pantheon of Modern Gods by Harlan Ellison (1975)
The Demolished Man by Alfred Bester (1953)
The Difference Engine by William Gibson and Bruce Sterling (1990)
The Dispossessed: An Ambiguous Utopia by Ursula K. Le Guin (1974)
Do Androids Dream of Electric Sheep? by Philip K. Dick (1968)

Dracula by Bram Stoker (1897)

Dragonflight by Anne McCaffrey (1968)

The Drowned World by J.G. Ballard (1962)

Dune by Frank Herbert (1965)

Earth Abides by George R. Stewart (1949)

Ender's Game by Orson Scott Card (1985)

The Eye of the World by Robert Jordan (1990)

Fahrenheit 451 by Ray Bradbury (1953)

The Female Man by Joanna Russ (1974)

Flatland: A Romance of Many Dimiensions by Edwin A. Abbott (1884)

Flowers for Algernon by Daniel Keyes (1966)

The Forever War by Joe Haldeman (1975)

Foundation by Isaac Asimov (1951)

Frankenstein, or The Modern Prometheus by Mary Shelley (1818)

From the Earth to the Moon by Jules Verne (1865)

Galapagos by Kurt Vonnegut, Jr. (1985)

The Gate to Women's Country by Sheri S. Tepper (1988)

Gateway by Frederik Pohl (1977)

Gulliver's Travels by Jonathan Swift (1726)

The Handmaid's Tale by Margaret Atwood (1986)

Harry Potter and the Sorcerer's Stone by J.K. Rowling (1997)

Helliconia Spring by Brian W. Aldiss (1982)

Herland by Charlotte Perkins Gilman (1915)

The Hitchhiker's Guide to the Galaxy by Douglas Adams (1979)

The Hobbit by J.R.R. Tolkien (1937)

Hospital Station by James White (1962)

Hyperion by Dan Simmons (1989)

I, Robot by Isaac Asimov (1950)

Interview with the Vampire by Anne Rice (1976)

The Island of Doctor Moreau by H.G. Wells (1896)

Islandia by Austin Tappan Wright (1942)

Jurassic Park by Michael Crichton (1990)

Jurgen: A Comedy of Justice by James Branch Cabell (1919)

Kindred by Octavia E. Butler (1979)

The King of Elfland's Daughter by Lord Dunsany (1924)

Last and First Men by Olaf Stapledon (1930)

The Last Man by Mary Shelley (1826)

The Last Unicorn by Peter S. Beagle (1968)

The Left Hand of Darkness by Ursula K. Le Guin (1969)

Lilith by George MacDonald (1895)

The Lion, the Witch, and the Wardrobe by C.S. Lewis (1950)

Little, Big by John Crowley (1981)

Looking Backward, 2000–1887 by Edward Bellamy (1887)

Lord Foul's Bane by Stephen R. Donaldson (1977)

Lord of Light by Roger Zelazny (1967)

Lord of the Flies by William Golding (1954)

The Lord of the Rings by J.R.R. Tolkien (1954–1955)

Lost Horizon by James Hilton (1933)

The Lost World by Arthur Conan Doyle (1912)

The Man in the High Castle by Philip K. Dick (1962)

The Martian Chronicles by Ray Bradbury (1950)

Mary Poppins by P.L. Travers (1934)

The Mists of Avalon by Marion Zimmer Bradley (1982)

More Than Human by Theodore Sturgeon (1953)

The Narrative of Arthur Gordon Pym by Edgar Allan Poe (1838)

Neuromancer by William Gibson (1984)

Nineteen Eighty-Four by George Orwell (1949)

Norstrilia by Cordwainer Smith (1975)

Out of the Silent Planet by C.S. Lewis (1938)

The Owl Service by Alan Garner (1967)

The Past Through Tomorrow by Robert A. Heinlein (1967)

Pawn of Prophecy by David Eddings (1982)

Perdido Street Station by China Miéville (2000)

Peter and Wendy by J.M. Barrie (1911)

The Picture of Dorian Gray by Oscar Wilde (1891)

A Princess of Mars by Edgar Rice Burroughs (1917)

The Purple Cloud by M.P. Shiel (1901)

Red Mars by Kim Stanley Robinson (1992)

Rendezvous with Rama by Arthur C. Clarke (1973)

She by H. Rider Haggard (1887)

The Shining by Stephen King (1977)

Slaughterhouse-Five, or The Children's Crusade: A Duty-Dance with Death by Kurt Vonnegut, Jr. (1969)

Snow Crash by Neal Stephenson (1992)

Solaris by Stanislaw Lem (1961)

The Space Merchants by Frederik Pohl and C.M. Kornbluth (1953)

A Spell for Chameleon by Piers Anthony (1977)

Stand on Zanzibar by John Brunner (1968)

Star Maker by Olaf Stapledon (1937)

The Stars My Destination by Alfred Bester (1956)

Starship Troopers by Robert A. Heinlein (1959)

Startide Rising by David Brin (1983)

The Story of Doctor Dolittle by Hugh Lofting (1920)

Strange Case of Dr. Jekyll and Mr. Hyde by Robert Louis Stevenson (1886)

Stranger in a Strange Land by Robert A. Heinlein (1961)

The Sword of Shannara by Terry Brooks (1977)

Tarzan of the Apes by Edgar Rice Burroughs (1914)

The Time Machine by H.G. Wells (1895)

Timescape by Gregory Benford (1980)

Titus Groan by Mervyn Peake (1946)

Triplanetary by E.E. "Doc" Smith (1948)

Triton by Samuel R. Delany (1976)

Twenty Thousand Leagues under the Sea by Jules Verne (1870)

2001: A Space Odyssey by Arthur C. Clarke (1968)

Utopia by Thomas More (1551)

A Voyage to Arcturus by David Lindsay (1920)

The War of the Worlds by H.G. Wells (1898)

The Water Babies by Charles Kingsley (1863)

We by Yevgeny Zamiatin (1921)

A Wizard of Earthsea by Ursula K. Le Guin (1968)

Woman on the Edge of Time by Marge Piercy (1976)

The Wonderful Wizard of Oz by L. Frank Baum (1900)

The Worm Ouroboros by E.R. Eddison (1922)

The Years of Rice and Salt by Kim Stanley Robinson (2002)

Films

A.I.: Artificial Intelligence (2001)

Alien (1979)

Alphaville (1965)

Back to the Future (1985)

Batman (1989)

Beauty and the Beast (1946)

Blade Runner (1982)

Brazil (1986)

The Brother from Another Planet (1984)

A Clockwork Orange (1971)

Close Encounters of the Third Kind (1977)

The Day the Earth Stood Still (1951)

Dr. Jekyll and Mr. Hyde (1931)

Doctor No (1962)

Dr. Strangelove, or How I Stopped Worrying and Learned to Love the Bomb (1964)

Dracula (1931)

E.T.: The Extra-Terrestrial (1982)

Field of Dreams (1989)

Forbidden Planet (1956)

Frankenstein (1931)

Godzilla, King of the Monsters (1954)

Heaven Can Wait (1978)

The Incredible Shrinking Man (1957)

Invaders from Mars (1953)

Invasion of the Body Snatchers (1956)

The Invisible Man (1933)

Island of Lost Souls (1933)

It's a Wonderful Life (1946)

Jason and the Argonauts (1962)

La Jetée (1962)

King Kong (1933)

The Lord of the Rings: The Fellowship of the Ring (2001)

Mad Max (1979)

The Man Who Fell to Earth (1976)

The Matrix (1999)

Metropolis (1926)

Planet of the Apes (1968)

Snow White and the Seven Dwarfs (1937)

Solaris (1972)

Star Trek: Generations (1994)

Star Trek: The Motion Picture (1979)

Star Wars (1977)

Stargate (1994)

Superman (1978)

The Terminator (1984)

The Thing (from Another World) (1951)

Things to Come (1936)

Topper (1937)

Total Recall (1990)

A Trip to the Moon (1902)

2001: A Space Odyssey (1968)

The Wizard of Oz (1939)

Television Series

Babylon 5 (1993–1998)

Blakes 7 (1978–1981)

Buffy the Vampire Slayer (1996–2003)

Doctor Who (1963–1989)

Farscape (1999–2003)

Futurama (1999–2003)

Hercules: The Legendary Journeys (1994–2000)

The Outer Limits (1963–1965)

The Prisoner (1967–1968)

The Quatermass Experiment (1953)

Red Dwarf (1988–1998)

The Simpsons (1989–)

Star Trek (1966–1969)

Star Trek: Deep Space Nine (1993–1999)

Star Trek: Enterprise (2001–2005)

Star Trek: The Next Generation (1987–1994)

Star Trek: Voyager (1994–2001)

The Twilight Zone (1959–1964)

Wonder Woman (1976–1979)

The X-Files (1993–2002)

Xena: Warrior Princess (1995–2001)

Volume 3,
Classic Works A–Z

A.I.: ARTIFICIAL INTELLIGENCE (2001)

They made us too smart, too quick, and too many. We are suffering for the mistakes they made because when the end comes, all that will be left . . . is us.

—Steven Spielberg
A.I.: Artificial Intelligence (2001)

Summary

In a bleak future when global warming has submerged much of the world, advanced countries maintain their standard of living by rigid population control (see **Overpopulation**). **Robots** abound. A **scientist** proposes to build a robot that can **love**. David is such a child-robot, programmed to unconditionally love his owner, Monica, whose own child is in suspended animation awaiting treatment for a possibly incurable disease. When the real child recovers and comes home, the result is sibling rivalry until, with only slight justification, David is perceived as a threat. When Monica abandons him in a **forest,** he sets out on a **quest** for the Blue Fairy from the **fairy tale** *Pinocchio* so he can become a real boy and regain his "**mother's**" love. After a narrow **escape** from a demolition derby in which robots are destroyed to amuse bigoted crowds, and accompanied by an adult sex robot called Gigolo Joe (see **Sexuality**), David meets his creator, who praises his uniqueness but plans to market a line of similar "Davids," to which David responds with **violence.** Eventually David encounters a **statue** of the Blue Fairy in a submerged amusement park. Trapped there, both by falling debris and his own programming, he waits two thousand years while **Earth** freezes and **humanity** becomes extinct. Advanced robots excavate David from the ice and compassionately resurrect Monica, but their science can only keep her alive for one day. So, David enjoys a day of perfect happiness, goes to **sleep** with his "mother," and shuts down forever.

Discussion

A.I: Artificial Intelligence is an unlikely blending of talents. It takes its initial concept (and one recognizable scene) from Brian W. Aldiss's "Super-Toys Last All Summer Long" (1969); the screen treatment is by Ian Watson, who worked extensively with Stanley Kubrick before his death; the project was then inherited and filmed by Steven Spielberg. But the marriage of Kubrick's bleakness with Spielberg's sentimentality is uneasy, resulting in a film that sometimes seems like a collision between *A Clockwork Orange* and *E.T.: The Extra-Terrestrial.*

Asked about humanity's responsibility to its robot creations, the scientist glibly compares himself to God. The theme of the story is set, as the scientist places himself in the long tradition of blasphemous usurpers of God's powers launched by Mary Shelley's *Frankenstein* (see **Hubris**). When David reaches his maker's office, it is a moment of mythic intensity, but behind the glass door he finds just a salesman, and in an adjoining room, rows of robots identical to himself, packaged for shipping, belying any hope he may have in his uniqueness, or his being anything more than a product (see **Identity**). The scene recalls key encounters in other films, that of the killer **android** Roy Batty with his designer in ***Blade Runner*** and between any number of **Frankenstein monsters** and their creators, but, precisely because David seems harmless, the vision here is even darker. When David is trapped underwater (see **Underwater Adventure**) in a submarine helicopter, accompanied by his robot teddy bear and begging the statue to make him a real boy, the spectacle is both pathetic and horrifyingly nihilistic.

The story line never quite comes to terms with the **absurdity** and cruelty of David's situation. Early in the film, he asks Monica if she will die, a disconcerting question from any child, much less a mechanical one. If she dies, what will happen to him? The chilling answer: no one cares what will happen to the robot fifty years in the future; he will simply be an obsolete product. Of course, there is no possibility for Monica to have a normal relationship with David, since he will not age as she does.

Since David is sentient, but unable to break his programming, he is therefore doomed. The ending is the only possible one—a happy **death**, through **illusion**—but even here possibilities are evaded. Monica—waking up from death two thousand years after the extinction of humanity, with only one day to live, and her memories selectively edited (so she has no husband or natural son to draw her attention away from David)—is in a poignant, horrifying predicament, but it is hardly touched upon. The film lurches sharply one way, then another, as sentimental hope gives way to cynical despair.

Uneven and imperfectly fitted-together as it is, *A.I. Artificial Intelligence* remains a powerful, sometimes beautiful film. While Kubrick would have made the film differently, it is better to have it as a Kubrick-Spielberg collaboration than not at all. The visual quality is first-rate, as are many performances. The satirical elements are compelling when they are on-target (see **Satire**), like the all-knowing **computer** that David and Gigolo Joe consult, "Doctor Know," depicted as an animated caricature of Albert Einstein. Visions of the apocalyptic last days of human **civilization** are made all the more effective by their routine flash and glitter (see **Apocalypse**). The **city** of the future seems like a gigantic amusement park, entertaining humans who do not realize that they are on the verge of extinction. To them, it is **business** and pleasure as usual up to the end. Their successors will not be their own descendants, but descendants of the robots they cheerfully neglect and abuse. Overall, *A.I.: Artificial Intelligence* is certainly one of the finest Hollywood treatments of the robot theme.

Bibliography

Brian W. Aldiss. *The Twinkling of an Eye, or, My Life as an Englishman.* New York: St. Martin's
    Press, 1999.

Philip J. Hefner. *Technology and Human Becoming.* Minneapolis: Fortress Press, 2003.

T. Kreider. "*A.I.: Artificial Intelligence.*" *Film Quarterly,* 56 (December, 2002), 32–39.

Frederic Raphael. *Eyes Wide Open.* New York: Ballantine Books, 1999.

Lucius Shepard. "AIeeeeeee!" *The Magazine of Fantasy and Science Fiction,* 101 (December,
    2001), 112–117.

Phillip Strick. "*A.I.: Artificial Intelligence.*" *Sight and Sound,* 11 (October, 2001),
    38–39.

J. Tibbetts. "Robots Redux." *Literature/Film Quarterly,* 29 (2001), 256–261.

Ian Watson. "My Adventures with Stanley Kubrick." *Playboy,* 46 (August, 1999), 82–85, 90,
    158–159.

—Darrell Schweitzer

ALICE'S ADVENTURES IN WONDERLAND
BY LEWIS CARROLL (1865)

■

> *She generally gave herself very good advice (though she very seldom followed it).*
>
> —Lewis Carroll
> *Alice's Adventures in Wonderland* (1865)

Summary

Alice's Adventures in Wonderland is a classic example of a **children's** fantasy whose **humor** appeals to all ages. During her **underground adventure,** the severely reasonable child Alice is repeatedly contrasted (see **Role Reversals**) with "adult" figures whose behavior varies from logic-chopping **absurdity** to **violence** and outright **madness.** These include animated playing cards (see **Games; Kings; Queens**), figures from proverbs and sayings, and talking **animals** like the vanishing Cheshire **cat** (see **Invisibility**).

Alice grows to **giant** form (see **Enlargement**) and undergoes **miniaturization** thanks to magic **food and drink,** including mushrooms (suggesting **drugs**). Her trifling **quest** is to enter a magic **garden.** During wanderings she weeps a literal **flood** of tears, forming a body of **water** large enough for swimming; recites and listens to nonsense **poetry;** sees the **metamorphosis** of a baby into a pig; and plays a croquet game with hedgehog balls and flamingo mallets (see **Birds**).

The haphazard story line climaxes with a hilariously lunatic parody of a criminal trial (see **Crime and Punishment**), at which Alice finds herself both physically and morally large enough to protest at the legal absurdity. After one fleeting instant of **horror**, the whole farrago dissolves into the safety and distance of a **dream**.

Discussion

This vein of playful humor continues in the superior sequel *Through the Looking-Glass* (1871), which uses a **mirror** as Alice's gateway to her second **imaginary world** and makes some play with mirror reflections: the famous nonsense verse "Jabberwocky," which all by itself inspired a 1977 film, is first seen in reversed print. (The warped language of "Jabberwocky" reappears in Carroll's epic nonsense poem *The Hunting of the Snark* [1876], involving **sea travel** in quest of the title's elusive **monster**.)

Living **chess** pieces replace the cards; the checkered **landscape** becomes the board for a demented chess game. The Red Queen is a paradigm of super-**speed** in a land where "it takes all the running *you* can do, to keep in the same place"; the Red King offers a metafictional paradox, since the entire action supposedly takes place in *his* dreams; the White Queen is wildly disorganized; the melancholy White Knight with his bizarre **inventions** is unusually sympathetic and may represent the author.

Additionally there are talking **flowers** and **insects**, nursery-rhyme characters like the Lion and the Unicorn (see **Lions and Tigers; Unicorns**) and Humpty Dumpty (an insufferable abuser of language who claims to pay words extra after overworking them), a Griffin from **mythology**, and even talking food. Wordplay, paradox, logical quibbles and mathematical jokes litter the text (see **Mathematics**). Alice attains the eighth rank of the chessboard and undergoes metamorphosis from pawn to Queen. As this second dream fades, the terrifying Red Queen—seized by Alice in a "capture" that delivers checkmate—dwindles to Alice's own pet cat.

Both books were definitively illustrated by Sir John Tenniel (see **Illustration and Graphics**); many other artists have made the attempt, most interestingly Mervyn Peake (see *Titus Groan*). Tenniel balked at drawing the eponymous "The Wasp in a Wig," a *Looking Glass* chapter which was deleted and published separately in 1977.

"Lewis Carroll," in real life the staid Oxford mathematician Charles Lutwidge Dodgson, improvised the first *Alice* story aloud for girl children—one named Alice—during a **river** outing on July 4, 1862. He rewrote it from **memory** with his own illustrations as *Alice's Adventures Under Ground* (published in facsimile, 1886), later revised and expanded as the book generally referred to as *Alice in Wonderland*. This has frequently been filmed and televised, the best known though not the best production being a 1951 Disney animated movie.

Amateur **psychology** sees a riot of symbolic **sexuality** in *Alice*, beginning with her fall down a rabbit-hole and including scenes like the engulfing, amniotic Pool of Tears or her development of a hugely elongated, flexible neck resembling a snake (see **Snakes and Worms**). Such exegesis of nonsense is all too easy. Even when being ejaculated from a chimney, sometimes a lizard is just a lizard.

More alarming are the **death** jokes, such as Humpty Dumpty's sinister suggestion, at first glance related to **immortality and longevity**, that "with proper assistance" Alice might have stopped growing older at seven. However, mildly sadistic violence was commonplace, even expected, in Victorian **fairy tales** for children. The innocent, personified, talking oysters (see **Fish and Sea Creatures**) in the *Looking Glass* poem "The Walrus and the Carpenter" are, without exception, eaten by the title characters.

Carroll had a gift for quotable coinages, puns, zanily literal misunderstandings of idiomatic phrases, and games and **puzzles** of mathematics and logic that he made palatable with whimsical humor. *A Tangled Tale* (1885) presents tough "word problems" as charming nonsense stories. Even the educational Dodgson treatise *Symbolic Logic* (1896) is full of comic premises: "Guinea-pigs are hopelessly ignorant of music." This aspect of *Alice* is extensively documented in Martin Gardner's *The Annotated Alice* (2000) which also explains now-forgotten contemporary allusions and prints the original, morally uplifting poetry that Carroll parodied.

With James Branch Cabell's *Jurgen* and James Joyce's *Finnegans Wake* (1939), the *Alice* books are among the most celebrated of all literary dreams, and certainly the best loved and most quoted. Extensive homage is paid to them in John Crowley's *Little, Big*.

Bibliography

G.K. Chesterton. "Lewis Carroll." Chesterton, *A Handful of Authors*. London and New York: Sheed and Ward, 1953, 112–119.

Morton N. Cohen and Roger Lancelyn Green, eds. *The Letters of Lewis Carroll*. London: Macmillan, 1979.

Martin Gardner, ed. *The Annotated Alice: The Definitive Edition*. New York: W. W. Norton, 2000.

Jean Gattégno. *Fragments of a Looking-Glass*. 1974. Trans. Rosemary Sheed. London: George Allen & Unwin, 1977.

Douglas Hofstadter. *Gödel, Escher, Bach*. New York: Basic Books, 1979.

Francis Huxley. *The Raven and the Writing Desk*. London: Thames and Hudson, 1976.

Florence Becker Lennon. *The Life of Lewis Carroll*. Third Edition. New York: Dover, 1972.

Robert Phillips, ed. *Aspects of Alice*. New York: Vanguard Press, 1971.

Edmund Wilson. "C.L. Dodgson." Wilson, *The Shores of Light*. New York: Farrar, Straus and Young, 1952, 540–550.

—David Langford

ALIEN (1979)

∎

Summary

Alien is a **horror** story, set in space, about a cargo ship's discovery of an alien that is physically superior to humans. The *Nostromo*'s crew is roused from **sleep** on a long journey to investigate a call for help from an **alien world**. On the planet they find an alien ship containing preserved eggs. A crew member investigates and an egg precipitates a creature onto his face. The face-hugger's **blood** is an acid that can eat through the steel decks of the ship. It seems to die, but it has deposited a further creature within its victim that bursts from his chest and runs away. The crew hunts for the creature, unsuccessfully. One by one, crew members are killed. The last survivor, Ripley, destroys the *Nostromo* to **escape**, but then discovers the **monster** aboard her escape pod. She finally rids herself of it by blowing it out an airlock into space.

Discussion

Alien indicts big **business** for sending the crew to the planet where the monster is discovered. The **android** medical officer, Ash, is aware of the potential the creature has and wants it for the Company that owns *Nostromo*. He attempts to keep it alive and return it to Earth, but is destroyed. This theme of keeping the alien alive for Company use recurs, more blatantly, in the three sequels to *Alien*.

The evocative setting of the *Nostromo* is claustrophobic, a freighter designed for cargo. The oppressively enclosed sets are made even moodier and threatening by the gloomy lighting used in much of the film. This adds to the feeling of danger, where shadows may be hiding places for the creature. The bright scenes are made threatening, as in the scene where the second-stage creature literally erupts from a man's chest while he sets at the dinner table.

Instead of a male hero, Ripley, the lieutenant played by Sigourney Weaver, is the protagonist who eventually destroys the creature. She is strong, decisive, and suspicious of the situation. She attempts to keep the crew who visited the planet out of the *Nostromo*, but is foiled by Ash. She takes the lead thereafter in every attempt to deal with the danger that destroys everyone but her. She seems an ideal feminist hero, as is even more observable in the sequels, particularly *Aliens* (1986) (see **Feminism**).

The film involves **first contact** with an alien species. Other films like *E.T.: The Extra-Terrestrial* and *Close Encounters of the Third Kind* advance the notion that such is to be sought and conducted delicately. *Alien* seems to regress to the older style of film, where aliens are a threat. But here, the alien does not represent another race that has its own qualities and values; rather it is purely **evil**, like a **vampire**. This makes *Alien* more horror than science fiction, despite its future setting.

The use of **suspended animation and cryonics** is prominent in all films. In *Alien* the eerie beginning is of a completely still, almost ghostly, ship, woken into life by the **computer** as it flicks the lights on and begins the arousal process. At the end of the film the process is reversed, and we see Ripley sleeping quietly as her escape pod heads for Earth. The vulnerability displayed contrasts strongly with her previously active and decisive role. She discovers the monster just as she has prepared for cold-sleep, stripped to her underwear without even the symbolic armor of clothes. She defeats the creature by evacuating the pod of air, firing a grapnel to leave it hanging in space, and then firing the rockets to destroy it utterly.

The defeat of the creature at the last minute, *after* it has already been supposedly been beaten, is common in the sequels as well. In *Aliens* a hive of aliens is discovered on the original planet, where a colony has been established. Ripley is sent, with troops and a Company representative, to find out why the colony has ceased **communication**. Soon, the troops have nearly all been killed, the Company representative has betrayed them all, the hive is destroyed, and Ripley, with three companions, escapes back to the main ship. There she learns that the hive **queen** has followed. Ripley defeats the queen by putting on an exoskeleton used for loading ships, fighting it hand to hand, and again sending it out an airlock.

Aliens is considered more an action movie than *Alien*. Ripley is once more left alone to save the day, but this time she must save a small child, the sole survivor of the colony. To do this she must survive attacks by hundreds of creatures and then enter into the hive to perform the rescue.

Alien3 (1992) sees Ripley deposited on a **prison** planet where she must defend herself and inmates from an alien and ends when she jumps into a smelter because she has discovered she has an alien in her. The fourth film, *Alien Resurrection* (1997), has a **clone** of Ripley combined with some features of the alien creature, who is also resurrected. Ripley becomes quasi-**mother** to the alien, which is once more defeated by being sucked out a broken window into space. (An additional film, the inferior *Alien vs. Predator* [2004], is essentially unrelated to the previous films except for the presence of the now-familiar monster.)

Bibliography

Anthony Ambrogio. "*Alien.*" Donald E. Palumbo, ed., *Eros in the Mind's Eye*. Westport, CT: Greenwood Press, 1986, 169–179.

Rebecca Bell-Metereau. "Woman: The Other Alien in *Alien*." J.B. Weedman, ed., *Women Worldwalkers*. Lubbock: Texas Tech Press, 1985, 9–24.

Barbara Creed "*Alien* and the Monstrous-Feminine." Annette Kuhn, ed., *Alien Zone*. London: Verso, 1990, 128–141.

Thomas Doherty. "Genre, Gender, and the *Aliens* Trilogy." Bary K. Grant, ed., *The Dread of Difference*. Austin: University of Texas Press, 1996, 181–199.

T.J. Matheson. "Triumphant Technology and Minimal Man." *Extrapolation*, 33 (Fall, 1992), 215–229.

Stephen Neale. "Issues of Difference." James Donald, ed., *Fantasy and the Cinema*. London: BFI Publishing, 1989, 213–223.

Mary Pharr. "Synthetics, Humanity, and the Life Force in the *Alien* Quartet." Gary Westfahl and George Slusser, eds., *No Cure for the Future*. Westport, CT: Greenwood Press, 2002, 133–140.

Janice H. Rushing. "Evolution of the New Frontier in *Alien* and *Aliens*." *Quarterly Journal of Speech*, 75 (February, 1989), 1–24.

John Trushell. "Material Interest." *Vector*, No. 224 (July/August, 2002), 11–17.

—Ian Nichols

ALPHAVILLE (1965)

Summary

Lemmy Caution, secret agent 003 of the Outerlands, drives his car (see **Automobiles**) through space and arrives after midnight in Alphaville, capital of a distant galaxy. His mission is to extract Professor von Braun, inventor of the Alpha 60 **computer** that controls the **city** and its inhabitants. Two agents have already failed in the attempt, Dick Tracy and Guy Leclair (the French Flash Gordon). Lemmy finds that Alphaville is peopled by a tranquilized, emotionally numb citizenry who docilely follow the dictums of Alpha 60 and its **scientist** minions. Disguised as a reporter (see **Disguise; Journalism**), he meets Natasha von Braun, daughter of his target. With her help, Lemmy eventually uncovers Aleph 60's "Grand Omega Minus" plan to insert brainwashed men into other galaxies to foment social unrest. He survives assassination, car chases, and an interrogation prior to destroying the computer and driving off through space with Natasha. As the young woman awakens to **love**, Alphaville and its occupants taste **freedom**.

Discussion

Originally entitled *Tarzan versus IBM*, *Alphaville* is the brainchild of writer-director Jean-Luc Godard. A fixture of French New Wave cinema, Godard helped to transform international filmmaking during the 1960s and 1970s through innovative use of hand-held cameras, editing, narrative and generic experimentation, explicit sexual content, and non-studio financial sources. The epitome of *auteur* cinema, wherein the director's unique personal vision is evident in each film, Godard infuses *Alphaville* with his trademark mix of pop **art** bravado and highbrow erudition.

Like many French New Wave directors, Godard appropriates elements from different genres and reassembles them to unique effect. *Alphaville*'s generic provenance is first and foremost science fiction, with a setting at once referencing the totalitarian **dystopia** of George Orwell's **Nineteen Eighty-Four** and the technological **utopia** of Aldous Huxley's **Brave New World**. Against a backdrop of ridiculous sci-fi place names like Heisenberg Boulevard, Mathematics Park, and Rue Enrico Fermi, the protagonist is grafted from **detective** fiction. Sporting a trenchcoat and hat, Lemmy, while a character introduced in the novels of Peter Cheyney, also recalls Raymond Chandler's iconic private eye, Philip Marlowe. His hard-boiled sensibility is tempered by moral scruples not unlike those of other fictional detectives like Mike Hammer or Sam Spade, and in one self-referential shot, Lemmy reads a copy of Chandler's *The Big Sleep* (1939).

The central thematic conflict of *Alphaville* is that of **individualism and conformity**. Lemmy, an outsider to the city, struggles against the automaton inhabitants under Alpha 60's control: **technology** is equated with totalitarianism. Lemmy is a romantic loner, whereas Alphaville's populace are forbidden from saying "Why?" and consume tranquilizers and Bibles (i.e. dictionaries) that list only words approved for use. In a scene that exemplifies the absurd ambiance of the film, Lemmy witnesses a "water ballet gala" where people who fail to conform are executed. Stalwart individuals are placed on a diving board and shot by a soldier with a sub-machine gun; when victims topple into the **water** shouting defiant last words, bikini-clad women wielding knives stab them to **death**.

These issues are shaped by Godard's usual array of references to **writing and authors**. Lemmy is on a self-described "journey to the end of night," alluding to Louis-Ferdinand Céline's vitriolic **satire** by the same name, *Journey to the End of the Night* (1932), in which the protagonist experiences the **horrors** of modernity in the first half of the twentieth century. When Lemmy helps Natasha rediscover her emotions, he has her read aloud from the surrealist (see **Surrealism**) Paul Éluard's collection of poems *The Capital of Pain* (1926). When Lemmy is interrogated by Alpha 60, he offers quotations from philosophers Henri Bergson and Blaise Pascal (see **Philosophy**).

Just as quotations shape the central thematic conflict, so does **architecture and interior design**. Godard and cinematographer Raoul Coutard transform Paris locations into what can be termed an intergalactic capital of **pain**. Lemmy navigates a black-and-white metropolis of blinking **lights**, gloomy high-rise buildings, and long, gray highways. Luminous surfaces contribute to the glacial emotional atmosphere, and Coutard's underlighting and choice of grainy film stock create a drab environment suggesting Eastern **Europe** under Soviet control. A general **darkness** engulfs intermittent pools of light, with Godard accentuating the sharp, disturbing contrast through straight cuts from dark scenes to bright ones. This high-contrast style typifies film noir, and befits the generic heritage of *Alphaville*'s protagonist.

If *Alphaville* is self-consciously constructed from previous texts and genres, it also serves as a touchstone for later films. The eerie voice of Alpha 60 echoes in the computer nemeses of *2001: A Space Odyssey* and *WarGames* (1983), and presages a string of films that trade on the fear of ubiquitous, silicon villainy (e.g., *The Terminator* series and *The Matrix* series) (see **Villains**). Godard's acerbic depiction of a futuristic totalitarian bureaucracy similarly anticipates *Brazil*, while his hard-boiled mix of science fiction and film noir provides a model for *Blade Runner*. As a result, *Alphaville* transcends its French New Wave context and emerges as a key development in the history of science fiction cinema.

Bibliography

Keith M. Booker. "Detectives in Dystopia." Georgia Johnston, ed., *Essays on Transgressive Readings*. Lewiston, ME: Mellen, 1997, 187–208.

Wheeler Winston Dixon. *The Films of Jean-Luc Godard*. Albany: State University of New York Press, 1997.

Jean-Luc Godard. *Alphaville*. Trans. Peter Whitehead. London: Faber and Faber, 2000.

Lee Hilliker. "The History of the Future in Paris." *Film Criticism*, 24 (Spring 2000), 1–22.

Margo Kasdan. "Eluard, Borges, Godard." *Symposium*, No. 30 (1976), 1–13.

Kaja Silverman and Harun Farocki. *Speaking about Godard*. New York: New York University Press, 1998.

David Sterritt. *The Films of Jean-Luc Godard*. Cambridge: Cambridge University Press, 1999.

Allen Thiher. "Postmodern Dilemmas." *Boundary 2* (Spring, 1976), 947–964.

Robin Wood. "*Alphaville*." Charles Barr, ed., *The Films of Jean-Luc Godard*. New York: Praeger, 1970, 83–93.

—*Neal Baker*

ANIMAL FARM: A FAIRY STORY BY GEORGE ORWELL (1945)

■

*All animals are equal
but some animals are more equal than
others.*

—George Orwell
Animal Farm (1945)

Summary

In the guise of a beast **fable**, George Orwell (the pseudonym of Eric Arthur Blair) wrote *Animal Farm* specifically as a political **satire** on Revolutionary and post-Revolutionary **Russia** but, more broadly, to warn of the dangers implicit in all revolutions (see **Politics**). Mr. Jones, the owner of Manor Farm, ill-treats his animals. At the prompting of the ancient boar, Old Major, they decide to revolt against their human master and succeed in expelling him and achieving **freedom** from tyranny. Their original, idealistic **governance system** based on equality, mutual help, and denial of all things human is soon overthrown by the pigs, who re-establish a **class system** with themselves as leaders. Corrupted by power, they privilege themselves and enslave the other animals. Their leader, Napoleon, ousts rival Snowball with the help of propagandist Squealer, who persuades the animals that whatever Napoleon says is right. A new tyranny replaces the old one and to the original slogan, "All animals are equal" is added, "but some animals are more equal than others." In a final **betrayal** of the revolution, Napoleon negotiates an entente between pigs and humans to oppress the lower classes. But violent argument dissolves the alliance and the watching animals can no longer distinguish pigs from humans.

Discussion

Although influenced by Jonathan Swift's satires (see *Gulliver's Travels*) and Rudyard Kipling's animal stories, Orwell said the specific trigger for *Animal Farm* came from seeing a small boy whipping a huge cart-horse. "It struck me that if only such animals became aware of their strength we should have no power over them. . . . The concept of a class-struggle between humans was pure illusion, since whenever it was necessary to exploit animals, all humans united against them: the true struggle is between animals and humans."

Animal Farm was written to expose the betrayal of the Russian Revolution by Joseph Stalin who, Orwell believed, had introduced a tyranny as extreme as the Tsarist regime. In his detailed **allegory**, humans are capitalists; animals are socialists, inspired by Old Major (Marx) to develop animalism (Socialism); wild creatures are the recalcitrant *muzhiks*; and pigs are Bolsheviks. Jones is the Tsar and the Rebellion the October Revolution. Neighboring farmers are the Western powers that initially support the Tsarists; the hoof and horn flag is the hammer and sickle and the pig committee is the *Politbureau*. Napoleon (Stalin), protected by his aggressive **dogs**, ousts Snowball (Trotsky) to become dictator of a totalitarian state. The purges of Stalinist Russia are represented by forced confessions exacted by Napoleon and subsequent executions of enemies. Napoleon's dealings with the lawyer and local markets represent the Treaty of Rapallo (1922) that ended the capitalist boycott of Soviet Russia and enabled **trade** to occur.

When Orwell wrote the book in 1943 he was also attacking contemporary Britain for its alliance with Stalinist Russia against Germany—the basis for the final meeting between pigs and humans, reflecting Orwell's disgust at the respect Britain was according Stalin, despite the regime he presided over. Squealer the propagandist represents not just Soviet and Nazi indoctrination but British pro-Stalinist censorship: hence the strikingly English name, Manor Farm. The violent argument that quickly destroys the animal–human rapport was prophetic: by the time the book was published, the Western–Soviet alliance was already unraveling. Orwell was antitotalitarian and mistrusted all revolutions because they allowed new leaders to become dictators in their turn. Because his didactic fable concerns morality, not just politics, it retains universal relevance. In this **microcosm**, where the **talking animals** represent the gamut of human stereotypes and reactions, he produced an important political analysis of how high-principled revolution against tyranny turns to dictatorship and a reign of terror.

In plotting this process Orwell starts with the idealistic theory that justifies revolution. Old Major tells the animals they lead lives of misery because they are exploited by Man, who consumes without producing; only get rid of Man and all the **evils** of life will disappear. But he warns them: "Remember that in fighting against Man, we must not come to resemble him. Even when you have conquered him, do not adopt his vices. Weak or strong, clever or simple, we are all brothers. All animals are equal." To ensure his message, his seven Commandments are painted on the barn wall.

After evicting Jones, the animals live in **pastoral** freedom, but this egalitarian system is soon subverted by greed. The pigs seize power by exploiting the political "weaknesses" of the others. Led by Napoleon, they argue that, having more **intelligence**, they are natural leaders and deserve special rights. They assume all the habits and privileges of humans and modify the rules of the revolution to exempt themselves, using the machinery of oppression, terror, bribes, propaganda, and lies. **History** (the laws on the barn wall) is perpetually rewritten until no one is sure what actually happened. Under the new regime, animals work harder and remain hungry. The loyal altruistic draughthorse Boxer, representing the simplicity of the common man, is sent to the knackery.

Animal Farm made Orwell the most influential English novelist of his day. His even bleaker novel, **Nineteen Eighty-Four**, about totalitarianism, developed many of the same ideas: the pervasive "Doublethink," compulsory worship of the party head, the slogans with which people are brainwashed, and the blackening of opponents' reputations.

Bibliography

Jenni Calder. *Huxley and Orwell*. London: Edward Arnold, 1976.

J.R. Hammond. *A George Orwell Companion*. New York: St. Martin's Press, 1982.

Christopher Hollis. *A Study of George Orwell*. London: Hollis and Carter, 1956.

Robert Lee. *Orwell's Fiction*. Notre Dame: University of Notre Dame Press, 1969.

Jeffrey Myers. *A Reader's Guide to George Orwell*. London: Thames & Hudson, 1975.

Jeffrey Myers, editor. *George Orwell*. London: Routledge & Kegan Paul, 1975.

Edward Thomas. *Orwell*. Edinburgh: Oliver and Boyd, 1965.

Raymond Williams. *George Orwell*. London: Fontana/Collins, 1971.

Raymond Williams, ed. *George Orwell*. Upper Saddle River, NJ: Prentice Hall, 1974.

—*Roslynn Haynes*

B

BABYLON 5 (1993–1998)

Summary

The brain child of writer–creator J. Michael Straczynski, *Babylon 5* was a landmark television series, recounting a **space war** of galactic scale as seen by characters from five species, who live and interact on a **space station** thrust into prominence by unfolding **history**. Heavily influenced by written science fiction and fantasy, particularly Frank Herbert's *Dune*, J.R.R. Tolkien's *The Lord of the Rings*, and Isaac Asimov's *Foundation*, as well as the American Revolutionary War, Civil War (see **America**), and World War II, the story was structured to show the buildup to **war**, war itself, and the aftermath of war.

The setting of *Babylon 5* is a diplomatic space station, brokering an uneasy harmony between **humanity**, the declining empire of the Centauri, the warrior-priest Minbari, the vengeful Narn, and the mysterious, powerful Vorlons. The fragile peace is threatened when an ancient race out of legend, the Shadows, returns and offers the Centauri a chance to reclaim their lost glory. The resulting galactic war finds humanity caught between warring **elder races**, until, with the help of a being of supreme power (see **Gods and Goddesses**), the station's captain leads humanity out from under the interference of older beings to a position of galactic prominence and self-determination. By the series' conclusion, we have also witnessed a coup d'etat on **Earth**, a war of independence on **Mars**, and the establishment of a galactic government (see **Governance Systems**).

Discussion

Babylon 5 displayed knowledge of and respect for literary science fiction, which is rare in television, as well as an admirable attention to scientific detail. The station itself, a huge rotating cylinder positioned at a Lagrange point between a moon and a neighboring planet, is patterned after the work of **scientists** like Gerard K. O'Neill (see **Space Habitats**). The frequent space battles initially featured no sound effects, until scientific realism gave way to dramatic necessity. The typical **clichés** of **hyperspace** and other means of achieving faster than **light** travel were eschewed in favor of "jump gate" technology, a means of **space travel** similar to **teleportation**. Furthermore, artificial **gravity**, though found on alien spacecraft, was noticeably absent from Earth ships, as humans had not yet mastered the **technology**. These and other details evidenced a commitment to the accuracy of **hard science fiction** absent in most televised science fiction.

Likewise, the series incorporated a multitude of classic science fiction scenarios and themes, most utilized to expert effect. In contrast to the *Star Trek* series, where **time travel** provides a frequent excuse for inconsequential adventure stories, a single instance of time travel in *Babylon 5* (first experienced in the episode "Babylon Squared" [1994]) forever alters the course of galactic history, gives birth to an entire alien **religion**, and provides the impetus for numerous cultural movements and societal upheavals on multiple worlds (see **Alien Worlds**). The episode "In the Shadow of Z'ha'dum" (1995) sees a new Earth agency created called the "Ministry of Peace." This Orwellian nomenclature is deliberate (see George Orwell's *Nineteen Eighty-Four*), as it starts a chain of events that sees Earth grow increasingly totalitarian. The episode "Severed Dreams" (1996) finds Captain Sheridan forced to severe the station's diplomatic ties with Earth, which thrusts protagonists into an unusual opposition with the homeworld, recalling the British series *Blakes 7* (see **Politics; Rebellion**).

The mysterious elder race of the Shadows was not dissimilar to the Elder Gods of H.P. Lovecraft's **horror** stories. Discovery of one of their biotechnological spacecraft lying dormant under the sands of Mars is certainly reminiscent of his classic novella "At the Mountains of Madness" (1936). When Vorlons are themselves revealed to be another of these "First Ones," they appear to the younger races as **angels**. Later, it is learned that early encounters with their race deliberately seeded these impressions in our ancestors, much as aliens of Arthur C. Clarke's *Childhood's End* were responsible for humanity's notion of **demons**. The ensuing conflict between good and **evil** owes much to Babylonian **mythology**, as creator Straczynski has frequently attested.

In a nod to the film *Forbidden Planet*, the two-part episode "A Voice in the Wilderness" (1994) has characters discover, inside a nearby planet, a "Great Machine" built by a now-vanished race and capable of enormously powerful acts (see **Inventions**), while a recurring character, Psi Cop Alfred Bester, is a tip of the hat to the well-known author of *The Demolished Man*. "The Deconstruction of Falling Stars" (1997), which leaps forward to witness events one hundred, five hundred, one thousand, and one million years in the future, includes a deliberate allusion to Walter M. Miller, Jr.'s *A Canticle for Leibowitz*, as a time five hundred years after the events of the series sees an order of the Catholic Church secretly working to preserve humanity's technological knowledge after a "Great Burn" similar to that novel's "Flame Deluge."

Although it has not been widely commented on, *Babylon 5* was deliberately framed as a historical narrative, a slice of the future recounted from a position even further ahead in time, with a rich history both before and after the specific events of the series. This awareness of the narrative as narrative shows up strongly in the telemovie *In the Beginning* (1998), the episode "And Now for a Word" (1995), and "The Deconstruction of Falling Stars" (see **Metafiction and Recursiveness**). Although the series ended at the culmination of its planned five-season arc, the universe of *Babylon 5* was rich enough to continue in made-for-television movies and a short-lived spin-off (*Crusade* [1999]), as well as various books and other media.

Bibliography

David Bassom. *The A-Z Guide to Babylon 5*. New York: Dell, 1997.
Edward James and Farah Mendlesohn, eds. *The Parliament of Dreams*. Reading, UK: Science Fiction Foundation, 1998.
Jane Killick. *Babylon 5 Season by Season, 1: Signs and Portents*. London: Boxtree, 1998.
———. *Babylon 5 Season by Season, 2: The Coming of Shadows*. London: Boxtree, 1998.
———. *Babylon 5 Season by Season, 3: Point of No Return*. London: Boxtree, 1998.
———. *Babylon 5 Season by Season, 4: No Surrender, No Retreat*. London: Boxtree, 1998.
———. *Babylon 5 Season by Season, 5: The Wheel of Fire*. London: Boxtree, 1998.
Kurt Lancaster. *Interacting with Babylon 5*. Austin: University of Texas Press, 2001.
Andy Lane. *The Babylon File*. London: Virgin, 1997.

—*Lou Anders*

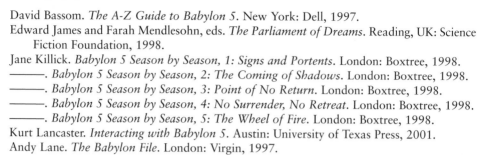

BACK TO THE FUTURE (1985)

Summary

Seventeen-year-old Marty McFly comes from a **family** of losers: his **mother** is a quiet drunk; his **father** is so spineless that he is still bullied by the same lout, Biff, who bullied him in high school; his brother and sister have failure written all over them. But Marty is determined to make good; his best friend may be the **mad scientist** Dr. Emmett Brown ("Doc"), but his girlfriend is the lovely Jennifer.

One night Doc shows Marty the time machine he has invented (see **Time Travel**), a DeLorean **automobile** powered by plutonium. The Libyan terrorists from whom Doc stole the plutonium appear and gun him down; Marty **escapes** in the car, but is transported back thirty years to 1955. There he must persuade the younger Doc to "pre-invent" time travel to send him back to the future. He also meets his parents George and Lorraine as teenagers and must persuade the attractive Lorraine to fall for the gawky misfit George, a complicated matter because Lorraine seems sexually attracted to Marty. Soon chance conspires with Marty's own efforts to force George into a situation where he stands up to Biff, duly impressing Lorraine. After Marty inadvertently introduces rock'n'roll **music** to the 1950s, Doc sends him back to his own era. There, Marty discovers his formerly deadbeat family members are now loving, confident, and successful; his father, a recognized writer (see **Writing and Authors**), awaits publication of his first science fiction novel. However, Doc then reappears and persuades Marty and Jennifer to travel with him thirty years into the **near future**.

Discussion

Back to the Future seemed in many respects a typical teen **comedy**, following the lead of *Grease* (1977) and the series *Happy Days* (1974–1984) in recalling the **America** of the 1950s as a **utopia** of lost innocence and harmless teenage hijinks carried out under the noses of indulgently befuddled parents, a time before the turbulent 1960s when families were functional and the biggest problem teenagers might face was a bully's fists.

Nothing about the film prepared audiences for the first sequel, *Back to the Future, Part II* (1989), a more serious exercise in exploring the potential paradoxes of time travel; its roots lie less in the accepted simplicities and **clichés** of screen science fiction, more in the joyous time-travel convolutions of written science fiction. Again using the DeLorean, Doc whips Marty from 1985 into 2015 to deal with difficulties Marty's **children** are causing his somewhat seedy self there. There is a nostalgic feel to this future, as if it were the world of *Things to Come* filtered through several lenses (see **Architecture and Interior Design**). But there is a larger crisis further back in the timeline, so back the pair go to another 1985, a **parallel world** and **dystopia** spun into existence when Biff in 1955 obtained information about the future. To nip this dystopia in the bud, Doc and Marty must indulge in further time travel.

Part II was not much liked by the critics and public, in part because it ended with a cliffhanger and exhortation to see the next movie—causing many viewers to feel cheated—and also because it eschewed the teen-comedy coziness of its predecessor. Audiences expecting another jolly family outing, laden with **humor**, were treated instead to a chilling dose of thought provocation. Time travel was no longer a **game** leading to frivolous fun and a foreordained happy ending; instead it was serious business with potentially grievous consequences. Also unsettling was the absence of resolutions to the dilemmas it outlined, all postponed to the next installment. This adverse reception does not explain why *Back to the Future, Part III* (1990) returns to the safety of *Back to the Future*'s ambience of light-hearted action adventure, since *Part II* and *Part III* were shot together; thus, the changes of mood were clearly part of director Robert Zemeckis's master-plan from the outset.

The third film is as much a **western** as time-travel adventure, its story essentially beginning with the closing scenes of *Part II*: after Doc is shot back to 1885, Marty comes across Doc's gravestone, which informs him that his friend will be shot in the back on September 7, 1885. Using the DeLorean, Marty embarks upon a **quest** to save him. Marty finds that in 1885 his hometown of Hill Valley (whose various incarnations in the three films can be read as a portrait in **microcosm** of the "matter of America") is a raucous **frontier** community tyrannized by outlaw Buford Tannen, ancestor of Biff, the bully of the two earlier films. Giving himself the handle "Clint Eastwood," the first cowboy-style name that comes to mind, Marty must right wrongs amid a western milieu and near-anachronisms reminiscent of the series *The Wild, Wild West* (1965–1969). In the finale, a huge railway steam engine is converted into a device capable of **flying** through both space and time. Essentially, this film brightens the darkness of *Part II* by returning to America's roots—the individuality, **freedom**, and can-do spirit represented by the western genre—to demonstrate that even the most complex of time-travel problems can be resolved with good old-fashioned Yankee ingenuity, grit, and determination.

While this sequence of films might seem, thanks to the somberness of *Part II*, an ill-matched collection, the trilogy does tell a coherent story, its unity strengthened by countless minor cross-references between the three, so that only by the end of the third film is the story of the first fully told. Such structural integrity, with all possible loose ends neatly tied off, is expected—or at least hoped for—in written science fiction. In terms of the screen, it is a rare achievement.

Bibliography

Ilsa J. Bick. "*Back to the Future* I and II." *Psychoanalytic Review*, 85 (December, 1998), 909–930.

Jody Duncan. "Back to *Back to the Future*." *Cinefex*, No. 43 (August, 1990), 34–67.

Andrew Gordon. "*Back to the Future*." *Science-Fiction Studies*, 14 (November, 1987), 372–385.

Norman Kagan. *The Cinema of Robert Zemeckis*. Dallas: Taylor Trade Publishing, 2003.

Michael Klastorin and Sally Hibbin. *Back to the Future*. London: Hamlyn, 1990.

Fred Pfeil. "Plot and Patriarchy in the Age of Reagan." Pfeil, *Another Tale to Tell*. London: Verso, 1990, 227–242.

Janine Pourroy. "Backyard Adventures: Spielberg Style." *Cinefex*, No. 24 (November, 1985), 38–67.

Elizabeth A. Richardson. "*Back to the Future*." *Extrapolation*, 29 (Summer, 1988), 128–139.

Jay Ruud. "Back to the Future as Quintessential Comedy." *Literature/Film Quarterly*, 19 (1991), 127–133.

—*John Grant*

BATMAN (1989)

∎

[Bruce Wayne:] First I must have a disguise. Criminals are a superstitious cowardly lot. So my disguise must be able to strike terror into their hearts. I must be a creature of the night, black, terrible . . . a . . . a . . .

[Caption:] As if in answer, a huge bat flies in the open window!

[Bruce Wayne:] A bat! That's it! It's an omen . . . I shall become a BAT*!*

—Bill Finger
"The Legend of the Batman—Who He Is
and How He Came to Be!" (1940)

Summary

Debuting in 1939 in *Detective Comics* No. 27, the Batman was a masked avenger of the night. Driven by the murder of his parents, Bruce Wayne dedicated his life and vast financial resources to pursue criminals. Like contemporary Dick Tracy, Batman evolved a colorful rogue' gallery of **villains**, chief among them the Joker, the Penguin, the Riddler, Catwoman, and Two-Face. Although he starred in two 1940s serials (*Batman* [1943] and *Batman and Robin* [1949]), Batman only achieved worldwide notoriety in the 1960s by means of a "camp" television series, *Batman* (1966–1968), starring Adam West. Tim Burton's 1989 film offered a grimmer interpretation of the character, retelling his origin story with a focus on his conflict with the Joker.

Discussion

Observing that criminals were a "superstitious cowardly lot," millionaire Wayne sought an image to strike terror into their hearts and drew inspiration for his costume from the timely appearance of a bat. A vast **cavern** beneath his **family** estate provided an appropriate headquarters where he stored an arsenal of vehicles, chief among them the Batmobile (see **Automobiles**), and special **weaponry** such as the Batarang.

Influenced by pulp precursors like the Shadow, Batman was originally a dark vigilante who had little compunctions about killing criminals (see **Crime and Punishment**). Initially hunted by police, he soon developed an alliance with Police Commissioner James Gordon. His guns discarded, Batman relied instead on a combination of brains, fists, and high-tech gadgetry, and the stories were revised to include a code against killing. Batman was further softened in 1940 by the addition of a sidekick in the person of **apprentice** Dick Grayson, an orphaned acrobat who became Wayne's ward and Batman's partner Robin.

In the 1940s and 1950s, tales of this "dynamic duo" became increasingly light-hearted. The pair were deputized by the police and stories shifted from vigilantism to the solving of elaborate **puzzles** and traps staged by increasingly outlandish villains and even **aliens on Earth**. This came to a head with the 1960s series, which sought to couple Batman with the Pop Art movement of artists like Andy Warhol. Widely criticized for its silliness, the television show nonetheless ensured the survival of the Caped Crusader at a time when **superheroes** were falling out of fashion.

In the 1970s, writer Denny O'Neil sought to rescue Batman from his camp degeneration. Teaming with artist Neal Adams, known for realistic portrayal of superheroes, O'Neil stripped Batman of his sidekick and most traditional foes. This Batman was a serious **detective** who used the latest forensic techniques as a modern-day Sherlock Holmes battling corrupt politicians, international terrorists, and organized crime. Those colorful villains O'Neil retained were transformed from silly pranksters to serious threats. Chief among these was the Joker, a criminal disfigured as a result of an encounter with Batman, which immersed him in a bath of chemicals. Initially conceived as a ghastly murderer, the Joker had become a buffoon obsessed with perpetrating elaborate pranks (see **Clowns and Fools; Trickster**). The recast Joker was a homicidal maniac who frequently escaped, not from **prison**, but from newly created Arkham Asylum (named for **horror** scribe H.P. Lovecraft).

Most of the rogue's gallery returned in the 1980s, and the comics found themselves in the contradictory position of presenting the character as serious, adult entertainment while simultaneously embracing the cartoonish aspect of colorful opponents and their elaborate **games**. *The Dark Knight Returns*, a 1986 graphic novel by writer/artist Frank Miller, not only revolutionized the comic field but played up the **darkness** of the Batman character. The story of an aging **hero** ending his retirement for one final showdown, it remains a definitive examination of the character.

In 1989, Batman came to film in a production focusing on both the darkness and **surrealism** of the crimefighter's world. Originally only a fictional New York, the Batman's home city of Gotham was re-envisioned as a nightmarish environment of twisted skyscrapers and crumbing **Gothic** cathedrals (see **Architecture and Interior Design**). The film added to Batman's origin story the notion that it had been the Joker, in the years before his disfigurement, who had murdered the Batman's parents. In doing so, it emphasized the oft-recurring theme that the Batman and his chief nemesis were two sides of the same coin (see **Yin and Yang**). Sadly, the next two films, *Batman Returns* (1992) and *Batman Forever* (1995) increasingly emphasized the surrealism and played down the seriousness, so that by the fourth and last film in the series, *Batman and Robin* (1997), the franchise had degenerated into a decadent, overblown version of the camp series.

Fortunately, a new television project, *Batman: The Animated Series* (1992–1995), launched in the wake of the film franchise, drew its inspiration not from cinema but from comics. The brainchild of producers Paul Dini and Bruce Tim, *Batman: The Animated Series* (later *The Adventures of Batman and Robin*) accomplished the daunting task of synthesizing six decades of comic material into a coherent narrative. Another series, *Batman Beyond* (1999–2001) recast the aging Wayne as **mentor** to a new incarnation of the Dark Knight, who fought for justice against the backdrop of a futuristic Gotham City inspired by the science-fictional Los Angeles of *Blade Runner*. A 2005 film, *Batman Begins*, returns the character to its more realistic, 1970s interpretation, emphasizing Wayne's **humanity** and portraying Gotham City as a credible, real-world metropolis.

Bibliography

Scott Beatty. *Batman*. London: DK Publishing, 2001.

Will Brooker. *Batman Unmasked*. New York: Continuum, 2000.

Tim Burton and Mark Salisbury. *Burton on Burton*. London: Faber and Faber, 1995.

Les Daniels. *Batman*. San Francisco: Chronicle Books, 1999.

Joel Eisner. *The Official Batman Batbook*. Chicago: Contemporary Books, 1986.

Michael L. Fleisher. *The Encyclopedia of Comic Book Heroes Volume 1: Batman*. New York: Collier Books, 1976.

Bob Kane. *Batman and Me*. Forestville, CA: Eclipse Books, 1989.

John Marriott. *Batman: The Official Book of the Movie*. New York: Bantam Books, 1989.

Robert E. Pearson and William Uricchio. *The Many Lives of the Batman*. New York: Routledge, 1991.

—*Lou Anders*

BEAUTY AND THE BEAST (1946)

■

My heart is good. But I am a monster.

—Jean Cocteau
Beauty and the Beast (1946)

Summary

A bankrupt merchant has three daughters: two are cruel and vain, but the youngest, Belle, is so devoted to her **father** that she refuses a **marriage** offer from a handsome man for his sake. The father goes on a journey to salvage his **business**. He asks each daughter what gift she would like on his return. While the older sisters ask for finery. Belle requests only a rose. The father, caught in a storm, seeks refuge in a haunted **castle**, where he plucks a rose from the **garden**, only to incur the wrath of the castle's beast-like inhabitant, who insists that the merchant must die unless one of his daughters agrees to take his place. Belle, insisting that it is all her fault (see **Guilt and Responsibility**) agrees, expecting to die. But the Beast does not devour her. He proves to be gentle, except when his animal nature overcomes him. Belle sees the **humanity** in him and falls in **love**. Ultimately, Belle must save the Beast from **death**, and he is transformed into a handsome prince, even as her former suitor (who has come to kill the Beast and steal his **treasure**) dies and becomes bestial himself (see **Metamorphosis**).

Discussion

The work of the French **surrealist** artist, playwright, and director Jean Cocteau, this film remains of the most exquisite and most adult of the many adaptations of the famous **fairy tale** by Marie LePrince de Beaumont (1756). While specifically evoking the naive beliefs of **children** in its prologue (for example, that love will transform, that a beast's bloody hands will smoke and he will be ashamed if confronted by a pure maiden), *Beauty and the Beast* rapidly moves into darker, eerier territory, with none of the comforting prettiness of the 1991 Disney animated musical version. The Beast's castle is a genuinely scary place, highlighted by the film's most famous image—a hall lined with candelabras held by living human arms affixed to the walls. The castle is alive, brilliantly presented on the screen with deft use of **light** and shadow and simple yet sufficient special effects. Plaster faces in the walls open living, human eyes and turn to follow Belle as she passes; doors open of their own accord; sheets slither off her bed like serpents; disembodied hands serve her at the table. The battlements and gardens are filled with grotesque animal **statues**.

A **magic** place, like the realm of Faerie itself, has strange and arbitrary **taboos**. A rose must not be plucked; Belle, when sent to visit her father, must return in a week lest the Beast die of grief; she must never look into the Beast's eyes; she must never see him eat, though she glimpses him lapping **water** out of a pool like a **dog**. The Beast's gifts are **illusions**: a string of pearls turns into a dead vine.

But gradually Belle's perspective changes. The Beast's castle is the safe place, where she lives in comfort. When she returns **home** to visit her ailing father, she encounters only treachery and hypocrisy, as her **family** and wastrel former lover Avenant plot to trick her into betraying the Beast (see **Betrayal**). Beastliness, she learns, is more than a matter of fur and fangs.

Ultimately the story itself may be interpreted as an **allegory** of sexual maturity (see **Sexuality**). Belle, reluctant to leave her father and get married, is afraid of adulthood. The Beast surely personifies, in particular, the fears of every underage girl about to marry a man she hardly knows. Her relations with him, which she expects to be terrible, turn out to be not so bad after all. Through love, she discovers the humanity in him, even while becoming unable to return to her former, Cinderella-like life at home.

For all these reasons, *Beauty and the Beast* is not a children's film. It is very Freudian, deeply influenced by psychoanalysis (see **Psychology**). While there is no explicit sex, there is much sexual tension, as the Beast is barely able to control his lust, but at the same time he becomes the object of Belle's sympathy and unacknowledged desire as she finds herself increasingly drawn to him. Everything in the Beast's castle—shadows, flowing draperies, rich, soft, but animate bedcovers—is dark and sensual, both frightening and inviting. Avenant, too, lusts after Belle, but it becomes clear that he is merely greedy, seeking one more conquest even as he schemes to acquire the Beast's **treasure**. Their love or marriage would never have worked out. Yet he is the handsome one, even as the Beast is outwardly ugly. In the climactic scene, as Avenant dies, he turns into the Beast, even as the handsome Prince looks very much like Avenant.

Beauty and the Beast is a high-point of fantastic cinema, like a vivid **dream** of great psychological depth. As in all his works, Cocteau uses the techniques of **surrealism** to delve into the human subconscious and into myth.

Bibliography

Silvia Bryant. "Reconstructing Orpheus Through 'Beauty and the Beast.' " *Criticism*, 31 (Fall, 1989), 439–453.

Jean Cocteau. *Beauty and the Beast*. New York: Dover Books, 1972.

Margaret Crosland. *Jean Cocteau*. New York: Knopf, 1956.

D. Galef. "A Sense of Magic." *Literature/Film Quarterly*, 12 (April, 1984), 96–106.

Rene Gilson. *Jean Cocteau*. New York: Crown Publishers, 1969.

Lynn Hoggard. "Writing with the Ink of Light." Wendell Aycock and Michael Schoeneche, eds., *Film and Literature*. Lubbock, TX: Texas Tech University Press, 1988, 123–134.

Elizabeth Sprigge and Jean-Jacques Kihm. *Jean Cocteau*. London: Gollancz, 1968.

Francis Steegmuller. *Cocteau*. Boston: Little, Brown, 1970.

Cornelia A. Tsakiridou, ed. *Reviewing Orpheus*. Lewisburg, PA: Bucknell University Press, 1977.

—*Darrell Schweitzer*

BLADE RUNNER (1982)

■

I've seen things you wouldn't believe. Attack ships on fire off the shoulder of Orion. I watched C-beams glitter in the dark near the Tannhausen gate. All those moments will be lost in time, like tears in rain. Time to die.

—Hampton Fancher and
David Webb Peoples
Blade Runner (1982)

Summary

In the Los Angeles of 2019, Blade Runner Rick Deckard is assigned to track down and eliminate five **androids**, or "replicants," who have illegally returned to **Earth**. His mission is made more difficult by Rachel, a replicant with whom Rick falls in **love**.

The escapees are searching for Tyrell, their creator, hoping that he can extend their fixed, four-year lifespan. After refusing to help them, he is blinded and killed by the replicants' leader, Roy Batty. Having retired the other replicants, Rick goes head to head with Roy and nearly falls to his **death**; but at the last moment, Roy finds his **humanity** and rescues Rick before dying. Rick and Rachel leave the **city** together.

Discussion

Despite being a financial disaster on initial release, Ridley Scott's heavily designed 1982 film—along with *Alien,* which he also directed—has come to dominate discourse about science fiction movies. It offered a striking vision of **near future** cities, suffering from rain (see **Weather**) and **overpopulation**, saturated with **advertising** (Scott had a background in commercials) and all sorts of **fashion**. The film was a dark **dystopia**, a **cyberpunk** world when the term had barely been conceived, and the most visually impressive science fiction epic since *Metropolis*. Influenced in part by comic books and film noir, the film would be a visual influence on anime and manga—Scott's *Black Rain* (1989), filmed on location in **Japan**, looks much like *Blade Runner*—and science fiction imagery.

In adapting Philip K. Dick's novel, scriptwriters Hampton Fancher and David Peoples stripped out many of the themes of *Do Androids Dream of Electric Sheep?* as well as the motivation of central character Rick, leaving him as a noirish **detective** tracking down criminals (see **Crime and Punishment**) who are coded as having escaped from **slavery** (see **Escape**). Harrison Ford's downbeat performance as Rick persuaded some viewers to assume that he too is a replicant who perhaps does not realize what he is—leading to a sense of **paranoia** over the **identity** of the characters. This was augmented by continuity errors in dialogue caused by editing a replicant out of the film, leaving one of the original six escapees unaccounted for. It is claimed that, in a late scene, Rick's eyes glow like the other androids, indicating that he is a replicant.

Eyes form a leitmotif throughout the film, from an early shot of an eye looking out from a skyscraper to a visit to the manufacturer of replicant eyes. Roy's blinding of Tyrell before killing him suggests an Oedipal reading of the film that draws upon the **psychology** of **fathers** and sons—it is certainly a confrontation between a creator **scientist** and his **Frankenstein monster**, searching for **survival** beyond his allotted four years. Aside from this fatal flaw, Roy is a **superman**, physically and intellectually superior to humans and gifted with **memories** of marvels—assuming these are genuine of course.

Balancing the replicants' problem with aging, there is the designer who aids them, J.F. Sebastian—a less interesting character than the novel's J.R. Isidore—who has reached a premature **old age**. Despite the overpopulation visible elsewhere in the film, Sebastian appears to be the only person living in his building. His fate is only apparent from careful listening to background dialogue, but even if he was not killed by Roy he would soon wear out. Roy's own death is also ambiguous; he still has more than a year to go of his allotted four, although at one point the film was to be set in 2020. In the end he seems to just accept his **destiny** and engages in willful **suicide**.

The film exists in a number of different versions, with the voice-over and flying off into the sunset added after previews left audiences baffled. The voice-over adds to the noir feel of the film and gives Rick ownership of the point of view even when he is absent from scenes. The international cut of the film had stronger language and slightly more **violence** than the U.S. version. The accidental showing at a festival of one preview version led to the release of the so-called "director's cut," which removed the voice-over—making Rick and Roy more equal in narrative status— excised the ending of flying off into the sunset, and added Rick's **dream** of a **unicorn**, taken as further evidence that he is an android. Additional scenes have been included on DVDs and in a documentary.

By the time these alternate versions had become available, the film—like William Gibson's *Neuromancer*—had been confirmed as central to the canon of **postmodernism** in vividly portraying a world dominated by **globalization**, multiculturalism, and consumerism. Also celebrated and analyzed by critics were the film's deconstruction of notions of **identity** and nostalgia for the 1940s, not to mention moments of pastiche and parody, especially of the films *The Maltese Falcon* (1941) and *The Big Sleep* (1946).

Bibliography

Joe Abbott. "The Monster Reconsidered." *Extrapolation*, 34 (Winter, 1993), 340–350.
Mark Bould. "Preserving Machines." Jonathan Bignell, ed., *Writing and Cinema*. Harlow, Essex: Longman, 1999, 164–178.
Guliana Bruno. "Ramble City—Postmodernism and *Blade Runner*." *October*, 41 (1987), 61–74.
Scott Bukatman. *Blade Runner*. London: BFI, 1997.
Peter Fitting. "Futurecop." *Science-Fiction Studies*, 14 (November, 1987), 340–354.
Judith B. Kerman, ed. *Retrofitting Blade Runner*. Bowling Green, OH: Bowling Green State University Popular Press, 1991.
Kevin R. McNamara. "*Blade Runner*'s Post-Individual Worldspace and Philip K. Dick's *Do Androids Dream of Electric Sheep?*" *Contemporary Literature*, 38 (1997), 422–446.
Paul M. Sammon. *Future Noir*. New York and London: HarperCollins, 1996.
Vernon Shetley and Alissa Ferguson. "Reflections in a Silver Eye." *Science Fiction Studies*, 28 (March, 2001), 66–76.

—Andrew M. Butler

BLAKES 7 (1978–1981)

∎

Summary

This fifty-two-episode television series begins on a future **Earth**, capital of a totalitarian regime, the Federation, which rules much of the galaxy. Blake, previously a resistance leader, has been brainwashed by the Federation and now lives as a model citizen. When resistance members remind Blake of his past, Federation troopers gun them down. Blake is sentenced to **exile** on the bleak Cygnus Alpha colony. En route, the shuttle encounters a deserted alien spaceship, the *Liberator*, which is commandeered by Blake and fellow transportees Jenna, Avon, Vila and Gan. In addition to the ship's **computer**, Zen, they are soon joined by a humanoid telepath, Cally. The *Liberator* is an enormously powerful ship, faster than any used by the Federation, and equipped with a **teleportation** system. Over the next forty-nine episodes, the crew opposes the Federation in increasingly desperate forms of resistance, their fight gradually losing ground. Midway through the second season, Gan is killed, and at the end of this series Jenna and even Blake disappear after a disastrous attempt to destroy the Federation's center of operations. The end of the third season sees the destruction of the *Liberator*, replaced by the less impressive *Scorpio* in the final season. In a shockingly nihilistic final episode, the crew re-encounters Blake. Believing he has been betrayed (see **Betrayal**), Avon shoots Blake dead, following which he and other surviving crew members are massacred by Federation troopers.

Discussion

The brainchild of Terry Nation, creator of the Daleks for *Doctor Who*, *Blakes 7* (the apostrophe is strangely omitted in the series titles) reflects a number of his preoccupations. The Earth-based Federation (see **Galactic Empire**) is an **evil**, corrupt, and utterly ruthless regime (see **Politics**). Indeed, Nation's Orwellian vision of the future is perhaps the most dystopian ever seen in television science fiction (see **Dystopia**). Even the purported **heroes** of the series are, initially at least, mainly petty criminals on the run. Over the course of the series, their resistance to the Federation becomes a more conventional fight for **freedom**, and in the final season they are reduced to merely fighting for **survival**, another typical obsession of Nation's.

Nation was not the only link with *Doctor Who*. The producer of the first three seasons of *Blakes 7*, David Maloney, had directed numerous stories, while script editor Chris Boucher had been a writer. Similarly, many directors, designers, and visual effects personnel had learned their craft on *Doctor Who*. *Blakes 7* was created in response to the growing popularity of film and television science fiction in the mid-1970s. On British television, *Doctor Who* was at the height of its popularity, and *Star Wars* was taking the world by storm when *Blakes 7* entered production.

One impressive aspect of the series is the way in which it combines a narrative arc over fifty-two episodes—the fight against the Federation (see **Quests**)—with a diverse set of individual stories. In the first season, episodes tend to alternate between battles against the Federation and more staple, if often imaginative, science fiction fare. In the former category, "Seek-Locate-Destroy" (1978) introduces the characters of Servalan, the female Commander of the Federation, and her sidekick Travis, for whom extermination of the rebels becomes an obsession. In the latter category, the first season includes explorations of **alien worlds** ("The Web" [1978]) and mixtures of genres like "Mission to Destiny" (1978), combining a murder **mystery** with **space opera**. The second season continues Blake's increasingly desperate fight against the Federation, culminating in season finale "Star One" (1979) with his attempted destruction of the Federation's nerve center, even though he learns this will leave millions of people at risk from invading forces of the Andromeda galaxy. In the ensuing conflict (see **Space War**), Blake, suffering ever more from **paranoia**, disappears until the last episode of the series, and Avon becomes the rebels' leader. Increasingly, the series resorted to **cliché**, as writers struggled to avoid repetitiveness in the conflict between the rebels and the Federation or in the exploration of the science fiction genre. For example, in the third season Cally, the telepath (see **Psychic Powers**), is overused as a hackneyed plot device, frequently susceptible to being taken over by alien forces ("Sarcophagus" [1980], "Ultraworld" [1980]).

The destruction of the *Liberator* in "Terminal" (1980), the final story of the third season, was originally meant to signal the series' end. After a hiatus, however, *Blakes 7* returned, albeit still without its eponymous leader. With a weaker ship, suffering increasing setbacks in the fight against the Federation, and with Avon as leader, the final series is significantly more pessimistic (see **Optimism and Pessimism**). In the final episode, "Blake" (1981), the crew discovers Blake working as a bounty hunter on a **planetary colony**. Here, the rebels are finally caught and killed by the Federation. Although bleak, this ending is consistent with the series mood, which had frequently shocked audiences with graphic **violence** and the **deaths** of regular characters.

The series is also notable for its now-dated attempts to display futuristic **technology**. Both rebel ships are equipped, unlike any owned by the Federation, with teleportation devices. Likewise, the means of **space travel** available to inhabitants of the galaxy are diverse, although executed within a tight television budget. Finally, and consistent with the series' exploration of power and totalitarianism, preoccupation with the futuristic **weaponry** of both the rebels and the Federation is evident.

Bibliography

Jean Airey. "The Man Who Killed *Blakes 7*." *Starlog*, No. 193 (February 1991), 42–44, 70.
Jean Airey and Laurie Haldeman. "*Blake's 7*: The Complete Episode Guide, Part One." *Starlog*, No. 147 (October 1989), 75–80.
———. "*Blake's 7*: The Complete Episode Guide, Part Two." *Starlog*, No. 148 (November 1989), 54–57.
Tony Attwood. *Blake's 7: The Programme Guide*. London: Virgin, 1994.
Sue Jenkins. "Spock, Avon and the Decline of Optimism." *Foundation*, No. 25 (June 1982), 43–45.
John Kenneth Muir. *A History and Critical Analysis of Blake's 7*. Jefferson, NC: McFarland, 2000.
Joe Nazzaro and Sheelagh Wells. *Blake's 7*. London: Virgin, 1997.
Patrick O'Neill. "Terry Nation." *Starlog*, No. 106 (May 1986), 34–35.
Adrian Rigelsford. *Terry Nation's Blakes 7*. London: Boxtree, 1995.

—*Alan Gibbs*

BLOOD MUSIC BY GREG BEAR (1985)

■

Summary

Blood Music is expanded from Bear's 1983 novelette of the same title, which won both Hugo and Nebula Awards. Both versions extrapolate a simple premise of **near future biology**—specifically, **genetic engineering**—into a devastating **metamorphosis** of **Earth**'s biosphere.

With obsessed, geekish **hubris**, a U.S. genetic researcher works to **uplift** white cells from his own blood, producing "noocytes" that can outperform mice (see **Rats and Mice**) in maze-solving tests (see **Labyrinth**). Ordered to discontinue this work, he defiantly saves his creations by injecting them into his own bloodstream. The noocytes become a **hive mind** entity with real **intelligence**, which colonizes its creator's body, attempts to improve its environment by making "helpful" physiological changes, and then learns of other human bodies—other worlds—that are potential **planetary colonies** for this intelligent plague. Soon the entire biomass of North America (with a few immune exceptions) is melted down into a single noocyte superorganism. Yet nothing essential is lost in this **disaster**, since noocytes revere their human creators and lovingly preserve each individual **memory** and personality in biological **virtual reality**. All this perhaps is disturbing to our prejudices, but nevertheless it is arguably a **utopia**.

Discussion

The **horror** of such indiscriminate, devouring biological transformation was popularized in **monster** movies like *The Blob* (1958) and more intelligently exploited in Theodore L. Thomas and Kate Wilhelm's *The Clone* (1965)—whose all-assimilating eponym is mindless but nigh irresistible—and Brian Stableford's *The Walking Shadow* (1979)—which develops the concept of "third-phase life" ultimately monopolizing the biosphere. The nanotechnological equivalent is the "gray goo" to which—in a worst-case scenario—unrestrained nano-machines might reduce all available matter, as in Wil McCarthy's *Bloom* (1998). Bear's innovation, which has in turn been imitated, was the adroit **role reversal** whereby a menace becomes a marvel—in fact a route to mass **immortality and longevity** without the usual **cyberspace** discontinuity of personality copying/transfer from flesh to **computer** media. (An interesting science fiction forerunner is Damon Knight's more modestly scaled "Four In One" [1953]: here the routine horror of being swallowed by an amorphous blob and digested—all but one's nervous system—is reinterpreted as a route to life-enhancing metamorphosis, though not of entire populations.)

The events of *Blood Music* are grounded in plausible, commercial genetic engineering, with cutting-edge experimentation conducted by an obsessive geek working in "Enzyme Valley" (by analogy with computing's Silicon Valley), not the traditional lone **mad scientist**. This stands in contrast to the deployment of similar **technology** as a home bathtub project in Frank Herbert's more conventional disaster novel *The White Plague* (1982).

Following that initial biological meltdown, the noocyte assimilation deliberately confines itself to North America for the time being. Much of the later story of *Blood Music* thus deals with the attempts of Earth's other countries, and of an infected but unassimilated human, to understand, communicate with, and respond appropriately to the threat and promise of the gestalt entity. The concept of "**blood** music" forms part of Bear's poetic evocation of noocyte cells' attempts to establish **first contact** (see **Communication; Language and Linguistics**) with a human host, as individual humans might struggle to attract and hold the attention of Earth's metaphorical ecosphere intelligence, "Gaia"—or of God or the universe itself.

Meanwhile, there is much inevitable **paranoia** in the world of **politics**. One perhaps inappropriate reaction is the still-unreconstructed Russian attempt (see **Russia**) to erase the problem through **nuclear war**. With a touch of ingenious mysticism, Bear here suggests that the sheer number of individual noocyte consciousnesses—the North American total being calculated at a billion trillion or 10^{20}, "neglecting, of course, the entirely negligible human population"—can affect quantum mechanics by the fantastic density of Heisenbergian observation they can bring to bear. The theoretical interaction between consciousness and physical law becomes an active, practical tool as local distortions of **physics** make nuclear chain reactions temporarily impossible, so that the Russian missile strike fizzles.

There is also a remarkable virtual-reality **exploration** of the interior of the noocytes' biological computer universe. This realm is a science fiction reification of Teilhard de Chardin's metaphorical universe of mind, the "Noosphere" (see **Philosophy**), as an organic **microcosm**. Here communication and understanding are near-perfect; personalities can be copied and multiplied; new **freedoms** abound; there need be no more loneliness.

In final scenes of transcendence that deliberately and successfully echo the concluding **apocalypse** of Arthur C. Clarke's *Childhood's End*, the entire Noosphere (first absorbing the remaining unassimilated humans) tears itself free from Earth and the hampering confines of matter, consumes the solar system, and launches itself into the unknowable. A female **last man** viewpoint witnesses the end.

Throughout the book, Bear is laudably careful to create complex, memorable personalities for his human characters, forcing favorable comparisons with the stiffness and limited emotional range found in *Childhood's End*. While several critics felt that the original 1983 novelette was more perfectly formed, the novel expansion of *Blood Music* not only consolidated the author's reputation but won the leading (and highly prestigious) French science fiction award, the Prix Apollo.

Bibliography

Gene DeWeese. "Once Over Lightly." *Science Fiction Review*, 56 (Fall 1985), 19.

Gregory Feeley. "Greg Bear: Interview." *Interzone*, No. 37 (July, 1990), 25–27.

John Foyster. "*Blood Music*." *Australian Science Fiction Review* (Second Series), 4 (September 1986), 27–28.

Colin Greenland. "*Blood Music*." *Foundation*, No. 37 (Autumn 1986), 86–88.

Len Hatfield. "Galaxy Within." *Extrapolation*, 31 (Fall, 1990), 240–257.

Len Hatfield. "Getting a Kick Out of Chaos." Nicholas Ruddick, ed., *State of the Fantastic*. Westport, CT: Greenwood, 1992, 133–140.

Elisabeth Kraus. "Biotech Bodies, Identity and Power in Works by Rebecca Ore, Pat Cadigan, Greg Egan and Greg Bear." Domna Pastourmatzi, ed., *Biotechnological and Medical Themes in Science Fiction*. Thessaloniki, Greece: University Studio Press, 2002, 323–332.

Nik Morton. "*Blood Music*." *Vector*, No. 133 (August/September 1986), 10–11.

—*David Langford*

THE BOOK OF THE NEW SUN BY GENE WOLFE (1980–1983)

∎

Summary

Though conceived as a single work, *The Book of the New Sun* was published as four novels: *The Shadow of the Torturer* (1980), *The Claw of the Conciliator* (1981), *The Sword of the Lictor* (1982), and *The Citadel of the Autarch* (1983); a later sequel was *The Urth of the New Sun* (1987). In a **far future** so remote that our planet has changed its name to Urth and the **Sun** is dying, former torturer Severian (see **Torture**) describes how he became Autarch of the Commonwealth, a great country in what was once South America. He calls this story, which he composes a decade after attaining the throne, *The Book of the New Sun* (see **Books**). His motives for writing his confession are primarily to justify both the **governance system** of the Commonwealth and the strangeness of his life.

Superficially, that life is simple to tell. Adopted as an orphan **apprentice** by the Guild of Torturers, Severian matures in the huge, labyrinthine capital of Nessus (see **Labyrinths**); after breaking the rules by letting a beautiful prisoner kill herself, he goes into **exile** and begins a long journey towards his **destiny**, which has been foretold in various ways (see **Divination**). At first that journey seems picaresque, but we soon learn that very little on Urth is what it seems. Darkening and shaping his consciousness is the fact that he, as Autarch, will become involved in the continuing crisis of Urth's very existence, for unless he is found worthy to bring a New Sun to Urth, all will perish in an entropic night of the universe. The New Sun is, in fact a white hole (see **Black Holes**)—everything here which reads like fantasy is ultimately explicable in science fiction terms—and *The Urth of the New Sun*, in which Severian travels to the universe of Yesod to undertake his test, reveals that this **ritual** is sham, that Severian had already been selected and the white hole will soon impact Urth. The seemingly happy ending is that Urth is saved.

Discussion

No synopsis can fully unsort the complexities of this greatest work to date by the most daunting literary craftsman ever to use science fiction from the inside, that is, as a writer whose every text is deeply shaped by an overwhelming affinity with the fantastic. *The Book of the New Sun* stands at a profound distance from almost all science fiction in that it is a text which gives delight—and true understanding of at least some of its innumerable puzzles—only when it is read with the most minute attention to detail and nuance. Wolfe never exactly lies—though his creature Severian, who claims to have an infallible **memory**, is by no means a reliable narrator—but he almost never speaks clearly.

Still, the text offers many immediate pleasures of the text. The bustling, multi-colored fantasy-like texture of life on Urth is dazzlingly portrayed; miracles and marvels proliferate; a **sense of wonder** pervades throughout. But *The Book of the New Sun* must be unlocked before it can give its full joy and reveal its full depth and **darkness.**

Severian himself embodies aspects of both Christ (see **Christianity, Messiahs**) and Apollo, and is being groomed for his ultimate role by the Hierogrammates (see **Aliens on Earth**) whose representatives move backward in time (see **Time Travel**) and shape events the same way that a puppeteer shapes the stories played out by the toy players. None of the people Severian meets along his way are what they seem at first (see **Secret Identities; Shapeshifters**). Some are members of his own **family** (whom he is reluctant to identify in his narrative); some are aliens; some are manufactured creatures (see **Androids; Robots**). As numerous episodes involving the **theatre** continually hint, they are all under the control of (almost always) unseen masters. Severian himself may be no more than a puppet.

Overall, there are two fundamentally opposed readings of *The Book of the New Sun*, or, one might say, two radically different universes in which its story takes place. If Severian's intuitions about his nature are to be believed, Wolfe has created a profoundly Christian vision of the nature of reality, one in which Severian's progress is towards something like godhead and the world is ultimately saved. If Severian, on the other hand, is both a liar and tool of alien shapers, then the universe of *The Book of the New Sun* is a cold place indeed; and Severian—like all other mortals in the book—is a mere strutter on the stage.

In the end, almost certainly, like a great **yin and yang**, these contrasting readings inform each other. And as the universe turns within the Book, each may be true—until the next turning of Severian's pages.

Bibliography

Michael Andre-Driussi. *Lexicon Urthus*. Albany, CA: Sirius Fiction, 1994.
———. *A Quick and Dirty Guide to the Long Sun Whorl*. Albany, CA: Sirius Fiction, 1997.
Robert Borski. *Solar Labyrinth*. New York: iUniverse, Inc, 2004.
John Clute. "Moses Supposes" and "Fisher." Clute, *Scores*. Harold Wood, Essex: Beccon Publications, 2003, 140–144, 248–255.
Joan Gordon. *Gene Wolfe*. Mercer Island, WA: Starmont House, 1986.
Lillian Heldreth. "The Mercy of the Torturer." Robert A. Latham and Robert A. Collins, eds., *Modes of the Fantastic*. Westport, CT: Greenwood, 1995, 186–194.
Peter Malekin. "Remembering the Future." Donald E. Morse, ed., *The Fantastic in World Literature and the Arts*. Westport, CT: Greenwood, 1987, 47–57.
Norman Talbot. "Audience and the Narrators in Gene Wolfe's *Book of the New Sun*." Jenny Blackford, ed., *Contrary Modes*. Melbourne: Ebony, 1985, 38–60.
Peter Wright. *Attending Daedalus*. Leeds: Liverpool University Press, 2003.

—John Clute

BRAVE NEW WORLD BY ALDOUS HUXLEY (1932)

∎

> *"But cleanliness is next to fordliness," she insisted."*
> *"Yes, and civilization is sterilization,"* Bernard went on, concluding on a tone of irony the second hypnopaedic lesson in elementary hygiene.
>
> —Aldous Huxley
> *Brave New World* (1932)

Summary

Aldous Huxley pictures a world state in the seventh century AF (after Ford). His **dystopia** depends on a scientific caste system (see **Class System**) in which embryo components of the social machine are hatched in incubators, then brought up in communal nurseries where they are conditioned to fulfill social roles on a scale from intellectuals (Alphas) to manual workers (Epsilons). This hierarchical society is founded on immediate gratification, consumerism, and mindless happiness for all. Society maintains control by giving or withholding the **drug** soma. All members are conditioned to be perfectly adapted and happy in their appointed niches, except Bernard Marx, a misfit Alpha-Plus resulting from an accident in the quality control of embryos.

As therapy, Marx is sent to visit the Reservation, where recalcitrant Mexican Indians live a pre-technological life of superstitious primitivism. Here Marx meets John Savage, also a misfit in his society, and brings him back to London as his protégé. Initially enchanted by this world, Savage becomes its most outspoken critic. In a dialogue with World Controller Mustapha Mond, he argues that a scientifically controlled state is incompatible with individualism and demands the human right to be unhappy (see **Individualism and Conformity**). Eventually, after succumbing to Fordian temptations, he commits **suicide** in self-disgust.

Discussion

Aldous Huxley believed that science, while not necessarily **evil**, must be made to serve **humanity**. Science and **technology**, despite their disadvantages, help to feed people and the Reservation is no model society; but material well-being is not enough for human fulfillment. Although this novel has elements of fantasy it represents a warning about a possible "real" state, not escapist fiction.

Anticipating **clones** and **genetic engineering**, Huxley warned against importing techniques from science into sociology and assuming that technology can deliver more satisfying lives. Specifically he targets the scientific **utopias** of H.G. Wells, who had repeatedly depicted society being rescued from poverty, waste, disease, and **wars** through science-based efficiency and order. Huxley, however, shows that efficiency and control comes at the price of human **freedom** and, like Yevgeny Zamiatin, he associates scientific rationalism with totalitarianism, since both require subjection of the individual to the system. The reward for such conformity is security, which has great appeal to mass **culture**; part of the irony of the title, taken from William **Shakespeare**'s *The Tempest* (c. 1611), is that this society is not brave but totally disempowered.

Huxley extends the external conformity imposed in Zamiatin's *We* to include the level of psychological conditioning (see **Psychology**), thereby criticizing the contemporary fads of hypnopaedia, behaviorism, consumerism, and instant self-gratification. Characters in the novel represent key figures that Huxley blamed for the descent of his own society into hedonism and state control: Rudolf Diesel, Friedrich Engels, Thomas Malthus, Karl Marx, Vladimir Lenin, Alfred Mond (founder of ICI), Ivan Pavlov, Hermann von Helmholtz, behaviorist psychologist J.B. Watson, and those "gods" of Brave New World, Our (Henry) Ford and Our (Sigmund) Freud. Ford is deified for promoting the assembly line and of consumerism, Freud for insights into psychological control. The ultimate ordering and efficiency of a society based on mindless universal happiness is achieved through manipulation of self-indulgence and fake stimulation by the drug soma. Mustapha Mond, Director of various institutes and soma-dispensers, admits that, for perfect health, men and women must have their adrenals stimulated periodically. V.P.S. (Violent Passion Surrogate) treatments are therefore compulsory, providing "all the tonic effects of murdering Desdemona and being murdered by Othello without any of the inconveniences."

As in E.M. Forster's story "The Machine Stops" (1909), the antithesis to this regulated urban world is provided by **nature**. For John (Noble) Savage, who comes from a desert **wilderness** and is devoted to Shakespearean **tragedy**, the right to be unhappy is a criterion of humanity. In *The Island of Doctor Moreau* H.G. Wells had foreshadowed many of these motifs, including the speeding up of **evolution** by a megalomaniac **scientist**; but whereas Moreau demanded that all his creatures suffer, Huxley asks: is happiness inversely proportional to great **art** and literature? Does perfect happiness equate to subhuman stupor?

The presentation of just two possibilities, Brave New World and the Reservation, neither of which is really desirable, is a limitation of the novel, and in his preface to the 1950 edition and in *Brave New World Revisited* (1958) Huxley conceded that there should have been a third alternative to scientific dystopia and primitivism. He subsequently addressed this in his utopia, *Island* (1962).

Samuel Butler's *Erewhon* (1872) provided the model for inversion on which this **satire** depends. Huxley condemns the virtues of Brave New World society (efficiency or "Fordliness," cleanliness, consumerism, stability, psychological control), and affirms contrary values (solitude, truth, heroism, responsibility, self-denial). There is wordplay on the deification of Ford (By Ford! Oh Fordey!). "Ts" are worn as decoration instead of the Christian cross (see **Christianity**) and nursery rhymes are Fordized. **Birth**, motherhood, and **families** are so repulsive that only under the respectability conferred by scientific discussion can they be mentioned, and even then only with much embarrassment. Conversely, sexual experiences and promiscuity produce no blushes; only chastity and fidelity are matters of shame.

In *Brave New World Revisited* Huxley suggested that his prophecies were eventuating sooner than he had feared. *Brave New World* foreshadowed George Orwell's ***Animal Farm*** and ***Nineteen Eighty-Four*** and totalitarian dystopias of the 1950s such as Kurt Vonnegut, Jr.'s *Player Piano* (1952) and Ray Bradbury's ***Fahrenheit 451***.

Bibliography

Robert S. Baker. *Brave New World*. Boston: Twayne, 1990.

Peter Bowering. *Aldous Huxley*. London: Athlone Pres, 1968.

Lawrence Brander. *Aldous Huxley*. London: Rupert Hart-Davis, 1969.

Jenni Calder. *Huxley and Orwell*. London: Edward Arnold, 1976.

Katie de Koster, ed. *Readings on Brave New World*. San Diego: Greenhaven, 1999.

Peter Firchow. "Brave at Last." *Aldous Huxley Annual*, 1 (2001), 157–174.

Jerome Meckier. "Aldous Huxley." *Utopian Studies*, 7 (1996), 196–212.

James Sexton. "Background to *Brave New World*." *Aldous Huxley Annual*, 3 (2003), 1–9.

W. J. Stankiewicz. "Aldous Huxley Our Contemporary." *Aldous Huxley Annual*, 1 (2001), 31–41.

—*Roslynn Haynes*

BRAZIL (1986)

Summary

In a gloomy **city**, simultaneously futuristic and old-fashioned, monumental, and run-down (see **Architecture and Interior Design**), a swatted fly falls into a teletype, transforming the name Tuttle into Buttle on a printout. Consequently, the innocent Buttle is arrested. His neighbor Jill tries to report the wrongful arrest to the Ministry of Information, where she is recognized by lowly bureaucrat Sam Lowry—at night, he dreams of **flying** above the city in winged armor and rescuing an ethereal maiden (see **Beauty**). Jill is the woman of his **dreams,** so he sets out to find her in reality. However, Sam's life is complicated by his efforts to redress the Buttle/Tuttle error, and by Tuttle, a rogue duct-engineer, who performs illegal repairs on Sam's air-conditioning, incurring Central Services' wrath. In Sam's dreams, Jill is captured and he is attacked by **giants;** in reality, her **knowledge** of the Buttle/Tuttle error puts her life at risk. Sam alters her **computer** records to show that she is already dead. After a night of passion, Sam is arrested. About to be tortured by his old friend Jack, Sam is rescued by Tuttle. Reunited, Jill and Sam **escape** the city, and settle in the countryside, but this **pastoral** idyll is a delusion—Sam is still strapped into the **torture** chair.

Discussion

Brazil is a difficult film to categorize. Its moments of **comedy** and **satire,** its ill-disciplined and sometimes self-indulgent **humor,** are clearly related to the **absurdity** and **surrealism** of *Monty Python's Flying Circus* (1969–1974), for which director Terry Gilliam produced animated sequences. It follows the narrative pattern of many **dystopias,** interweaving political **rebellion** with **romance** and sexual dissidence, culminating with a flight from the city. There is, however, no green world outside, only a post-holocaust wasteland, concealed by massive billboards (see **Advertising**). *Brazil* can, then, be understood as a mournful **allegory** about **individualism and conformity,** in which dreams of liberation are destined to be thwarted, **freedom** is delusory, and **madness** and **illusion** are preferable to sanity and the real.

This generic blending might be best understood as a variety of postmodern intertextuality (see **Postmodernism**). There are allusions to the Odessa Steps sequence from Sergei Eisenstein's *Battleship Potemkin* (1925) and George Orwell's ***Nineteen Eighty-Four*** (in one shot only, the office next to Lowry's is room 101), and in one dream sequence, Lowry's enemy is revealed to be himself, as in ***The Prisoner,*** Irvin Kershner's *The Empire Strikes Back* (1980) (see ***Star Wars***) and John Boorman's *Excalibur* (1981). Lowry's malfunctioning automated kitchen seems like something from a novel by Philip K. Dick, while a grim apartment block is ironically named Shangrila Towers, after the **utopia** of James Hilton's ***Lost Horizon.*** *Brazil* develops imagery and ideas recognizable from Gilliam's *Jabberwocky* (1977), *Time Bandits* (1981) and, especially, his short *The Crimson Permanent Assurance* (1983), in which aged accountants convert their office building into a **pirate** vessel, literalizing "corporate raiding"; and Gilliam would further develop *Brazil's* imagery in *The*

Adventures of Baron Munchausen (1989), *The Fisher King* (1991), and *Twelve Monkeys* (1995) (see **La Jetée**). This sense of a patchwork intertext is exacerbated by the random-seeming targets of its satire: advertising for Mellowfields Top Security Holiday Camps, **mothers** obsessed with cosmetic surgery, the inverted snobbery of the *maître d'hotel*, gourmet food reduced to variously-flavored gunk (see **Food and Drink**), the consumers for Christ organization, a child who wants a credit card for **Christmas,** and so on.

Alternatively, *Brazil* might be understood as a differently conceived **cyberpunk,** although one that demonstrates the same **paranoia** about **Japan**'s economic growth (the dream-Lowry is attacked by a samurai whose costume is decorated with computer chips). If **Blade Runner** is a British director's vision of a future United States, then *Brazil* could be seen as an American's vision of a future Britain—or, more accurately, as a depiction of 1980s Britain as it existed in the Thatcherite imagination—a nightmare of centralization and nationalized industries, of constraining dinosaurs that needed to be killed by and for brave little entrepreneurs like Tuttle (and like Gilliam himself, who famously had to battle with Universal to get even a recut version of the movie released in the United States). Perhaps, like William Gibson and Bruce Sterling's **The Difference Engine**, *Brazil* is a **steampunk** revisioning of cyberpunk, an **alternate history** extrapolated not from Victorian times but from the late 1940s and early 1950s. Set, as an opening title indicates, "somewhere in the 20th century," it envisions an information economy controlled by a repressive state bureaucracy (see **Governance Systems**) in which, as in Gwyneth Jones's *Escape Plans* (1986), working with computers is labor, not liberation. While certain of its propaganda slogans—"Information is the key to prosperity"—recall cyberpunk and seem proleptic of the dot.com boom, many of the others—"Loose talk is noose talk," "Don't suspect a friend, report him," "Suspicion breeds confidence"—allude to both World War II and Orwell's anti-Stalinist satire, demonstrating that information need not be factual to be a powerful instrument of social control. As one character remarks, "Information Retrieval—they never tell you anything."

Ultimately, despite a frequently astonishing visual sensibility and nicely judged performances from a cast packed with familiar faces from British TV and theatre, *Brazil* lacks the intellectual coherence of dystopias like Orwell's **Animal Farm,** *Nineteen Eighty-Four* and Yevgeny Zamiatin's **We**. Rather, its ability to be both pointed in its satire and incoherent in the targets it selects places it alongside Frederik Pohl and C.M. Kornbluth's **The Space Merchants,** Neal Stephenson's **Snow Crash,** and **Futurama.**

Bibliography

Ian Christie, ed. *Gilliam on Gilliam*. London: Faber and Faber, 1999.

John Erickson. "The Ghost in the Machine." *Utopian Studies*, 4 (1993), 26–34.

Regian-Mihal Friedman. "Capitals of Sorrow." *Utopian Studies*, 4 (1993), 35–43.

Terry Gilliam, Charles Alverson, and Bob McCabe. *Brazil*. London: Orion, 2001.

W. Russell Gray. "Taking *Nineteen Eighty Four* Back to the Future." *Utopian Studies*, 2 (1991), 147–156.

Jack Mathews. *The Battle of Brazil*. New York: Applause Theatre Book Publishers, 1998.

Janet Staiger. "Future Noir." Annette Kuhn, ed., *Alien Zone II*. London: Verso, 1999, 97–122.

David Sterritt and Lucille Rhodes, eds. *Terry Gilliam Interviews*. Jackson: University Press of Mississippi, 2004.

Linda Ruth Williams. "Dream Girls and Mechanic Panic." I.Q. Hunter, ed., *British Science Fiction Cinema*. London: Routledge, 1999, 153–168.

—Mark Bould

BRING THE JUBILEE BY WARD MOORE (1953)

■

> *Adults smile, but can any of them be sure the memories they cherish were the same yesterday? Do they* know *that a past cannot be expunged? Children know it can. And once lost, that particular past can never be regained. Another and another perhaps, but never the same one. There are no parallel universes—though this one may be sinuous and inconstant.*

> —Ward Moore
> *Bring the Jubilee* (1953)

Summary

A classic of **time travel** and **alternate history**, Ward Moore's novel begins in the mid–twentieth century, after the South won the American Civil War. The Confederacy is now a great nation, although blacks are still enslaved (see **Race Relations**); the United States is backwards and largely rural (see **America**). Young Hodge Backmaker sets off in 1938 to the big **city**, New York, a place of ten-story skyscrapers, paved streets, and chaotic bicycle traffic. An obvious mark, he is immediately mugged but eventually makes his way to Haggershaven, Pennsylvania, a center of learning near Gettysburg, established by Major Herbert Haggerwells, a Confederate officer who settled there after the **war**. Hodge becomes an historian specializing in the Civil War, convinced that the pivotal moment came when (in his timeline) the Confederate forces occupied the hill called Little Round Top at the Battle of Gettysburg. A descendant of the Major, Barbara Haggerwells, with whom Hodge has a **romance**, invents a time machine (see **Time Travel**). Given the chance to verify his thesis, Hodge goes back in time to 1863 to observe and inadvertently prevents the Confederates from taking the hill, thus restoring **history** to the version the reader knows. Ironically, this proves Hodge correct, but it cancels out his own future, Haggershaven, and Barbara. He lives out his life in the past and leaves his account behind in a manuscript.

Discussion

As simple as a **fable** but a book of considerable complexity, *Bring the Jubilee* is one of the first books to ponder the **ethics** of changing the past. Though Hodge recognizes that the new world he has created is better than the old, he must also consider the countless **deaths** he caused by prolonging the war beyond the Confederate victory of 1863.

We see here one of the major roots of the alternate history story. While there have long been novels that are essentially political tracts—such as Saki's *When William Came* (1914), about the Kaiser invading an ill-prepared Britain—the science-fictional origins of such stories are found in pulp magazines, where the logical consequences of time travel were considered in great detail. Nat Schachner's "Ancestral Voices" (1933) explores the impact on subsequent history of removing one person from the past. Murray Leinster's "Sidewise in Time" (1934) suggests that if the past is changed, a whole new history will result, either canceling out the former future or, as in Leinster's story, "forking" time so that alternate time lines come into being. Turning points of history are often battles or wars. Alternative versions of the Civil War have become standard for American writers, even as British writers examine alternatives to the Reformation, as in Keith Roberts's *Pavane* (1968), about the repressive, Catholic Britain that resulted when the Spanish Armada won.

Coming out of this science fiction tradition, *Bring the Jubilee*, intriguingly, does not begin at the pivotal point of change, but from the perspective of the alternate world long after the change has happened. The generic context—that this book was written as science fiction, not a political tract—further enriches the story's meaning. It partakes of the tropes of the post-holocaust novel of the period (see **Post-Holocaust Societies**). The **hero** is an ignorant young man who goes out into the ruined world to learn how things got to be this way (see **Knowledge**) and ultimately to seek some redoubt of hidden learning to improve the lot of **humanity**. As such, it recalls Poul Anderson's *Vault of the Ages* (1952), John Wyndham's *Re-Birth* (1955), or Leigh Brackett's *The Long Tomorrow* (1955). That Moore should see a Confederate victory as a catastrophe might offend a few Southern chauvinists, but surely the stunted world he depicts, in which **slavery** still exists in North America, is not to be preferred. Yet the conclusion of the book strikes a subtle note, as Hodge realizes that his "brave new world is not so brave," and that, in a corrupt deal to resolve the Hayes–Tilden election of 1876, the politicians (see **Politics**) have betrayed the victory of the Civil War, condemning blacks to inferior status as Reconstruction ends. So his bold (if accidental) stroke has not solved all the country's problems, as, indeed, in real life, one act seldom does. It merely sets things on a different course. As Hodge changes the battle's outcome by unintentionally killing none other than Major Herbert Haggerwells, it is a question, not merely of making things different, but of **guilt and responsibility**. He is left a forlorn **exile** in the new world. There is a classic paradox here: if Hodge caused the death of the ancestor of the woman who built the time machine, how was he able to go back in time and do so? The answer seems to be one of a balance between free will (see **Freedom**) and **destiny**. If Hodge pushes against the fabric of history, it has a way of pushing back.

Bibliography

Jon K. Adams. "Science Fiction in Pursuit of History." Bernd Engler and Kurt Muller, eds., *Historiographic Metafiction in Modern American and Canadian Literature*. Munchen: Schoningh, 1994, 147–161.

Robert Geary. "The Ironical Mysteries of Time." Edgar L. Chapman and Carl B. Yoke, eds. *Classic and Iconoclastic Alternate History Science Fiction*. Lewiston, NY: Edward Mellen Press, 2003, 39–48.

Harry Harrison. "Worlds Beside Worlds." Peter Nicholls, ed., *Science Fiction At Large*. New York: Harper & Row, 1976, 105–114.

Karen Hellekson. *The Alternate History*. Kent, OH: Kent State University Press, 2001.

Larry Niven. "The Theory and Practice of Time Travel." Niven, *All the Myriad Ways*. New York: Ballantine Books, 1971, 110–123.

David Pringle. "*Bring the Jubilee* by Ward Moore (1953)." Pringle, *Science Fiction: The 100 Best Novels*. New York: Carroll and Graf, 1985, 41–42.

Robert Reginald. "A Stitch in Time." Reginald, *Xenograffiti*. San Bernardino, CA: Borgo Press, 1996, 19–23.

Gavriel Rosenfeld. "Why Do We Ask 'What If?'" *Theory and History*, 41 (December, 2002), 90–103.

—Darrell Schweitzer

THE BROTHER FROM ANOTHER PLANET (1984)

Summary

The Brother, a mute black human-like alien, crashes his spaceship in the **water** between the Statue of Liberty and Ellis Island. After recovering in the derelict Immigration Center, he wanders into New York City, receiving an ambivalent welcome from habitués of Odell's bar in Harlem, who persuade a social worker to find him lodgings and work. The Brother is being pursued by two white alien Men in Black. After wry, underplayed comic adventures, the Brother finds a dead junkie and shoots up. Virgil takes him on a nighttime tour of the decaying **city** and explains the intertwined workings of capitalist (see **Economics**) and racist (see **Race Relations**) logics in **America**. The Brother falls for Malverne (see **Romance**), a night-club singer, and they spend the night together. When she leaves, the Brother traces the supplier of the **drugs** plaguing the neighborhood, a white businessman dabbling in narcotics to balance his company's books. The Brother suffocates him. The Men in Black capture the Brother, but he is rescued by other aliens who emerge from the city (see **Aliens on Earth**). The Men in Black self-destruct, and the Brother returns to Harlem.

Discussion

As even cursory examination of the *Star Wars* and *Star Trek* franchises indicates, science fiction and fantasy—and particularly visual science fiction—tend to imagine species difference in terms of racial difference, taking physical characteristics and behavioral traits from stereotyped images of non-whites and constructing essentialized alien species from these fragments. **Alien**, *Predator* (1987), and *Lost in Space* (1998) have specifically black killer aliens (see also **King Kong**), and the **heroes** of *Men in Black* (1997) are paramilitary immigration officials dedicated to the exclusion of aliens.

Within this general trend, *The Brother from Another Planet* can be considered as riposte to **Blade Runner**. It has been argued that the latter's replicants are only ironically Aryan, their whiteness foregrounding racial oppression in contemporary America; their plight recalls that of escaped slaves, while the police hover overhead, deciding who counts as human. In contrast, *The Brother from Another Planet* directly confronts the legacy of **slavery** and contemporary racism, individual and structural, through the simple mechanism of casting a black actor as an escaped alien slave and setting him loose in New York. While his initial situation might resemble those of alien visitors in **The Day the Earth Stood Still**, *E.T.: The Extra-Terrestrial*, and *Starman* (1984), the Brother has no mission; he has not come to offer either global or individual redemption. Instead, his presence serves to indicate how far we still are from the dream of **freedom**. As the movie regularly informs us, Harlem signified the Promised Land not only for slaves but also for subsequent generations of African-Americans; and despite its images of **community**, however depleted, the movie is at pains to demonstrate that Harlem—indeed America—remains a long way from being the Promised Land.

The Brother from Another Planet should also be considered in the context of other early 1980s science fiction movies like *Born in Flames* (1983), *Liquid Sky* (1983), and *Repo Man* (1984). Not only do they repudiate spectacular effects and the aesthetics of distraction—dominant in science fiction cinema since the success of *Star Wars* and **Close Encounters of the Third Kind**—in favor of credible characters and narrative and thematic complexity, but they also attempt to utilize science fiction imagery and ideas to explore and critique alienation in contemporary urban settings. And as its not-unsympathetic portrayals of racist characters in Harlem—a nervous rookie cop and two lost guys from Indiana—suggest, *The Brother from Another Planet* argues that the pervasive racism it identifies is not the sole cause of oppression, impoverishment, and alienation.

By repeatedly drawing attention to the falsely utopian discourses of **advertising**, alcohol, drugs, and the visceral pleasure of being fast enough to beat video games, the movie emphasizes the processes by which desires are transformed into commodities. This commodification of desire is foregrounded by Virgil, who evokes images of racial and **gender** oppression within a broader context of the extraction of labor and, thus, of profit.

The alienation consequent on such commodification is exemplified in the Brother's relationship with Malverne. He is initially drawn to her because of her image, the cover of her new album replicated all over the city. Before making love, she removes false eyelashes and hair extensions and reminds the Brother that she is a real person, not a figure on a stage, not an image. After a night of passion and tenderness, she is forced to leave because she has no more bookings in New York. The Brother's desire for Malverne was prompted by her commodified image, but unlike all the other images of women the Brother sees in a montage sequence of advertisements for beer, holidays, strip shows, porn movies, and covers of fashion and lifestyle magazines, Malverne briefly becomes three-dimensional, a person; but like these other women, she, too, is subject to her own commodification.

Bibliography

Mark Bould. "The False Salvation of the Here and Now." Diane Carson and Heidi Kenaga, eds., *Sayles Talk*. Detroit: Wayne State University Press, 2005, 112–141.

Melba J. Boyd. "But Not the Blackness of Space." *Journal of the Fantastic in the Arts*, 2 (1989), 95–107.

Diane Carson, ed. *John Sayles Interviews*. Jackson: University of Mississippi Press, 1999.

Ed Guerrero. *Framing Blackness*. Philadelphia: Temple University Press, 1993.

Chris Henderson. "*Starlog* Interview: Joe Morton." *Starlog*, No. 90 (January, 1985), 16–18.

Gerry Molyneaux. *John Sayles*. Los Angeles: Renaissance Books, 2000.

Jack Ryan. *John Sayles, Filmmaker*. Jefferson, NC: McFarland, 1998.

Gavin Smith, ed. *Sayles on Sayles*. London: Faber and Faber, 1998.

Linda Trefz. "*Brother from Another Planet*." *American Cinematographer*, 65 (1984), 43–48.

—*Mark Bould*

BUFFY THE VAMPIRE SLAYER (1996–2003)

Summary

Buffy the Vampire Slayer was originally produced as a feature film (1992) in which a ditzy cheerleader learns she is the Vampire Slayer, the latest of an ancient line of girls with supernatural ability to fight **vampires** and other **monsters**. Though a critical and box office failure, the film's premise was developed as a television series.

In the series premiere, Buffy and her divorced **mother** have just moved to Sunnydale, California, where Buffy hopes to put her Slaying behind her and lead a normal life. Instead, she learns that Sunnydale High School sits on a demonic portal called the Hellmouth; that school librarian Rupert Giles is her Watcher, a specially trained **mentor**; and that a vampire lord called The Master is planning a massacre. She also befriends social outsiders Willow and Xander, snobbish Cordelia, and the mysterious but noble vampire Angel. With their help and that of other characters who later join the ensemble cast, Buffy continues her Slaying career through high school and into college.

While *Buffy* uses both episodic and serialized storytelling, larger story arcs predominate as each season builds towards an apocalyptic confrontation with the year's major **villain**. The series concludes with Buffy leading her friends and a band of Potential Slayers in a **war** against the First Evil. In this war, the First is defeated, Sunnydale and the Hellmouth are reduced to a huge crater, and the power of the Slayer is released not to one girl in each generation, but to every Potential Slayer, thus freeing Buffy from her lonely responsibility.

Discussion

Although the imagery of *Buffy*, with vampires, **werewolves**, and **demons**, has its roots in **horror** stories, *Buffy* itself is the antithesis of horror. Creator Joss Whedon often explained that he created *Buffy* because he felt sorry for that blonde girl who always gets killed by monsters in horror movies, and wanted to see her kill the monster instead. Hence **feminism** is a central theme of this **urban fantasy**, which stands out among contemporary action–adventure series in having not only a female lead but a true **gender** balance with complex female characters equaling the number of male characters. Later seasons explore topics associated with more radical aspects of feminism, as Willow becomes a powerful **witch** and has two homosexual relationships (see **Homosexuality**).

Various characters tell the Slayer that **Death** is her gift, and Buffy wrestles constantly both with the dehumanizing effects of **violence** and the likelihood of her own early death, raising issues of heroism and **sacrifice** (see **Heroes**). Her death, burial, and revival by Willow's witchcraft ("The Gift" [2001], "Bargaining" [2001]) lead to an exploration of Willow's abuse of power in playing God and the consequences of reversing death for Buffy, who realizes that death was indeed a **gift**, freeing her from the hardships of her calling. However, the series' most outstanding treatment of death concerns Buffy's mother, Joyce, whose death of completely natural causes becomes a profound expression of the inevitability of mortality ("The Body" [2001]).

Almost every major character has at least one significant **romance**, which nearly always ends unhappily, either through the violent death of one partner or through a failure of commitment. Buffy's relationship with Angel is an extreme example of this pattern. When the two consummate their love, a **curse** turns Angel into his demonic alter-ego, Angelus, whom Buffy is forced to kill just as Willow's spell restores his soul ("Becoming" [1998]).

Buffy is above all a **Bildungsroman**, as characters mature from young high school students to adulthood. In the first season, they are concerned as much with grades and popularity as with monsters. By the final season the mundane issues confronting them include careers, **marriage**, and being a surrogate parent for an orphaned younger sister. Many of the series' strongest dramatic moments arise not from encounters with monsters, but from the juxtaposition of these monsters with young adult conflicts, as when Buffy first encounters Angelus, the morning after giving Angel her virginity, in an extraordinary depiction of teen fears of post-coital rejection ("Innocence" [1998]).

In the course of its run, *Buffy* acknowledged many classic horror icons, including **ghosts and hauntings**, demons, **zombies**, **doppelgängers**, **Frankenstein monsters**, werewolves, and even an encounter with Bram Stoker's *Dracula*. Many homages were done with tongue in cheek, and **humor** is a major element of the series. Horror aspects of the stories were constantly leavened with humorous moments, like the vampire Spike being comforted by his intended victim Willow when he discovers he is unable to "perform" by biting her ("The Initiative" [1999]).

Buffy's tackling of issues like teen **sexuality**, lesbianism, witchcraft, addiction, and **religion** often provoked controversy in print and on the Internet. The episode "Earshot" (1999) was postponed after the shootings at Columbine High School in April 1999, because a similar event was a plot point of the episode.

From an inauspicious beginning, *Buffy the Vampire Slayer* became a major cultural icon, whose popularity spawned a successful spinoff series, *Angel* (1999–2004), as well as the accessories of cult TV, including books, merchandise, and countless fan websites; its dramatic and thematic sophistication led to critical acclaim and a considerable body of academic analysis.

Bibliography

Vivian Chin. "Buffy? She's Like Me, She's Not Like Me—She's Rad." Frances H. Early and Kathleen Kennedy, eds., *Athena's Daughters*. Syracuse: Syracuse University Press, 2003, 92–102.

Lynn Schofield Clark. *From Angels to Aliens*. New York: Oxford University Press, 2003.

Christopher Golden and Nancy Holder, with Keith R. A. DeCandido. *Buffy the Vampire Slayer*. New York: Simon & Schuster, 1998.

Roz Kaveney, ed. *Reading the Vampire Slayer*. New York: Tauris Parke, 2002.

James B. South, ed. *Buffy the Vampire Slayer and Philosophy*. Peru: Open Court, 2003.

Gregory Stevenson. *Televised Morality*. Lanham: Hamilton Books, 2004.

Rhonda V. Wilcox and David Lavery, eds. *Fighting The Forces*. Lanham: Rowman & Littlefield, 2002.

Glenn Yeffeth, ed. *Seven Seasons of Buffy*. Dallas: BenBella Books, 2003.

—Karen Stoddard Hayes

C

A CANTICLE FOR LEIBOWITZ
BY WALTER M. MILLER, JR. (1959)

The trouble with being a priest was that you eventually had to take the advice you gave to others.

—Walter M. Miller, Jr.
A Canticle for Leibowitz (1959)

Summary

Taking a cue from the Dark Ages, the Catholic Church becomes the sole repository for human **knowledge** after the great "Simplification" which followed a **nuclear war**. In the novel's first section, a novice monk finds an old fallout shelter containing writings of the legendary founder of his order, Leibowitz, who was actually a "security risk," a blacklisted **scientist** of the twentieth century. His grocery list and circuit designs are lovingly copied by monks who have no idea of their meaning. Six hundred years later, a Renaissance has occurred. St. Leibowitz's writings have been interpreted and the electric light is rediscovered. Technological **progress** speeds up (see **Technology**). Six hundred years after that, the world has reached a level far beyond the twentieth century. But **nuclear war** again threatens. The monks of St. Leibowitz **escape** by spaceship (see **Space Travel**) to another solar system, taking the treasured writings of their founder, so the Catholic Faith (see **Christianity**) and **civilization** might endure.

Discussion

This is a beautifully written, richly ironic novel, which captures all the fears (see **Anxiety**) of the Cold War era: that nuclear war might be inevitable, that technological progress leads to the downfall of civilization, and that **history** itself may be cyclical (see **Cycles**). It is a meditation on the limitations of human free will and good will, the first of its ironies being that St. Leibowitz wasn't even Catholic, or religious, but a victim of McCarthy Era purges, and that the future of civilization seems to depend on complete misapprehension of his life and work. When genuine knowledge is extracted from his papers, the results are a mixed blessing. The increased technology empowers warlords, ultimately leading to civilization's **rebirth**, but just as inevitably to its demise. The role of the Church, then, is not to change the world, but to preserve worthwhile scraps of it against the unstoppable forces of human nature.

A Canticle for Leibowitz, though its three sections were originally published in *The Magazine of Fantasy and Science Fiction,* was not labeled science fiction when published in hardcover. It was one of the genre's first break-out books, able to reach a wider audience of people who did not even know that they were reading science fiction. Within the field, its influence was considerable, starting a fashion for post-technological, medieval futures (see **Medievalism and Middle Ages**) of which Richard Cowper's *The Road to Corlay* (1978) is a notable example. Much of the atmosphere and structure of the book is also replicated in Keith Roberts's *Pavane* (1968), an **alternate history** in which the Spanish Armada won, and a medieval, Catholic Britain of the 1960s stirs with revolt. Roberts shares Miller's loving concern with the close textures of such a world and has the same sense of tragic irony about the cyclical nature of history (see **Tragedy**).

Indeed this theme is central to science fiction, and can be found written on a galactic scale in Isaac Asimov's ***Foundation*** and its sequels, which follows the same model as Miller did, with compilers of the *Encyclopedia Galactica* endeavoring to carefully replicate lost fragments of the past. The balance between the benefits and liabilities of scientific knowledge is also pivotal to the entire discourse of science fiction. If no one ever investigated the universe, we would all still be living in caves. But if the flawed nature of **humanity** leads inevitably a new **apocalypse**, is progress worth it? Do we have any choice? Miller offers no easy answer, just the hope that some good individuals (perhaps inspired by **religion**) will be around to salvage something. A further irony occurs in the book with the elusive figure of the Wandering Jew (see **Judaism**), who seems to imply that he has seen all this before and knows better.

A Canticle for Leibowitz is Miller's most significant work. While he published some distinguished short fiction during the 1950s, after 1959 he devoted himself to what was for him the insoluble problem of writing a sequel, *St. Leibowitz and the Wild Horse Woman* (1997), which actually takes place during the time of the middle section of the original book, in the era of feudal warlords on the American plains and the rediscovery of electricity. It is a more massive, less entrancing book than the original, although with profound depths. Miller could not bring himself to finish the last chapter. He described his struggle as being like "spitting through a screen," then killed himself. The book was completed by Terry Bisson and published to good reviews, but it has had nowhere near the impact of *Canticle*—which remains one of the great classics of science fiction, and one of the finest examples of core science fiction themes treated from a religious perspective. The motifs of future barbarism (see **Barbarians**) and rebuilding civilization after a catastrophic war had existed in the literature before, but seldom had they been handled with such artistry and intelligence.

Bibliography

Thomas P. Dunn. "To Play the Phoenix." Carl B. Yoke, ed., *Phoenix from the Ashes.* Westport, CT: Greenwood Press, 1987, 105–115.

R.M. Griffin. "Medievalism in *A Canticle for Leibowitz*." *Extrapolation,* 14 (May, 1973), 112–125.

Dominic Manganiello. "History as Judgement and Promise in *A Canticle for Leibowitz*." *Science-Fiction Studies,* 13 (July, 1986), 159–169.

Walker Percy. "Walter M. Miller, Jr.'s *A Canticle for Leibowitz*." *Southern Review*, 7 (Spring, 1971), 572–578.

William H. Roberson and Robert L. Battenfeld. *Walter M. Miller: A Bio-Bibliography*. Westport, CT: Greenwood Press, 1992.

David Seed. "Recycling the Texts of the Culture." *Extrapolation*, 37 (Fall, 1996), 257–271.

William A. Senior. "From the Begetting of Monsters." *Extrapolation*, 34 (Winter, 1993), 329–342.

Judith A. Spector. "Walter M. Miller's *A Canticle for Leibowitz*." *Midwest Quarterly*, 22 (Summer, 1981), 337–345.

Susan Spencer. "The Post-Apocalyptic Library." *Extrapolation*, 32 (Winter, 1991), 331–342.

—*Darrell Schweitzer*

CAT'S CRADLE BY KURT VONNEGUT, JR. (1963)

∎

All of the true things I am about to tell you are shameless lies.

—Kurt Vonnegut, Jr.
Cat's Cradle (1963)

Summary

Cat's Cradle is a satirical commentary on amoral **scientists**, more comic than the author's *Slaughterhouse-Five* but as trenchant in its implications (see **Satire**). The narrator, John, researching a book on what famous people were doing when the first atomic bomb was dropped on Hiroshima, encounters the **children** and acquaintances of Dr. Felix Hoenikker, a "father of the atomic bomb." Hoenikker is an emotionally retarded physicist for whom everything is a **game**: turtles, atomic weapons, a piece of string. Typically, Hoenikker was playing cat's cradle as the bomb was dropped. Hoenikker has also discovered a crystalline substance, ice-nine. Having a melting point of 114.4°F one crystal will freeze all **water** in contact with it, thereby destroying the **Earth** by ice. When Hoenikker dies his three children divide the lethal ice-nine crystals between them. It is only a matter of time before a crystal is let loose from its thermos flask into a body of water.

The narrator tracks Hoenikker's elder son Franklin to San Lorenzo, a barren island in **Latin America** ruled by a dictator, Papa Monzano. Here he encounters the hedonistic **religion** of Bokononism, which teaches its devotees to "live by foma, the harmless untruths that make you kind and healthy and happy."

Discussion

Vonnegut can be considered an early New Wave science fiction writer. Skeptical and pessimistic about the role of science and **technology** in American **culture** (see **America**), these writers reject unquestioning belief in scientific **progress**. Their stories focus on the amorality or immorality of scientists, who had been the **heroes** of earlier science fiction. Like Romantic poets, many New Wave writers reject rationalism for a mystical, emotional response to the world. *Cat's Cradle* is a classic example of such novels. It expresses pessimism about **humanity** and the universe, but is fatalistic rather than despairing, using **humor** as its weapon.

After failing a science course at Cornell and flunking a training program in military engineering, Vonnegut studied **anthropology**. Subsequently he spent three years as a publicist for the General Electric Company, which prided itself on its commitment to progress, and where his brother worked as an atmospheric scientist. All these factors had an impact on *Cat's Cradle*. The inspiration for Felix Hoenikker was Irving Langmuir, Head of GEC research laboratories. Langmuir had contributed to developing the atom bomb and many of Hoenikker's actions and comments, including the idea of ice-nine, were derived from him. Through Hoenikker, Vonnegut satirizes the notion that the "absent-minded" scientist is "innocent" just because he is unconcerned about wealth or fame. Hoenikker has a child-like **sense of wonder** but, without responsibility, he is highly dangerous. His room is littered with cheap **toys** and his research interests are arbitrary—whatever he comes across—with no thought for social consequences. Vonnegut's attack on scientists includes the suggestion that, to ordinary people, they wield a form of **magic**, beyond comprehension but frightening in its power.

Like the atom bomb itself, the invention of ice-nine is a scientific–military collaboration, requested by U.S. Marines who want to avoid sinking into mud. Hoenikker takes up their problem as an intellectual game and invents the most lethal substance in the world with no thought of its logical outcome. In this, recalling Mary Shelley's *Frankenstein* he is in the tradition of **mad scientists** and amoral scientists abrogating responsibility. After Alamogordo a fellow scientist remarked that science had now known **sin**, to which Hoenikker replied: "What is sin?" We learn that **Russia**, America, and Papa Monzano have all obtained crystals of ice-nine from Hoenikker's children. Ending the world through ice-nine instead of a nuclear holocaust is an appropriate Cold War **apocalypse**. Ironically it is precipitated by not the superpowers but a petty dictator: his corpse, frozen as ice-nine, plunges into the sea, thus freezing the Earth's oceans. Vonnegut emphasizes that Hoenikker is not unique. The head of his research laboratory, the generically named Dr. Asa Breed, is equally unable to relate to people.

The alternative to this scientific materialism is the mystical religion of Bokononism, which flourishes illicitly on San Lorenzo. Vonnegut thus sets up a dichotomous situation not unlike that of Aldous Huxley's *Brave New World*—an inhumane technological society and a primitive society, with no third option. Bokononism itself is a combination of opposites—a mystical religion but one that cynically ridicules itself; it has no essential beliefs unlike most religions, including the religion of science. The epigraph to *Cat's Cradle* includes the quotation from the Books of Bokonon: "Nothing in this book is true." Bokononism supports **illusion**, which is allegedly anathema to science but which Vonnegut suggests is the unadmitted basis of science. In contrast to Hoenikker and Breed is the Bokononist Koenigswald, a former Nazi doctor, who tries to atone for his activities at Auschwitz by spreading kindness, making people feel better, even if by unscientific means.

While hard science privileges rationality over emotions, New Wave writers often defend irrationality against the tyranny of logic, **knowledge**, and the **politics** of bureaucrats and technocrats. So Vonnegut puts forward the flexible, humanist tenets of Bokononism, practiced on the easy-going island of San Lorenzo, as an alternative to the ordered technocracy of America.

Bibliography

William Rodney Allen. *Understanding Kurt Vonnegut.* Columbia: University of South Carolina Press, 1991.

Harold Bloom, ed. *Kurt Vonnegut.* Philadelphia: Chelsea House Publishers, 2000.

David H. Goldsmith. *Kurt Vonnegut.* Bowling Green, OH: Bowling Green State University Popular Press, 1972.

Jerome Klinkowitz. *Kurt Vonnegut.* London, NY: Methuen, 1982.

Jill Krementz, ed. *Happy Birthday, Kurt Vonnegut.* New York: Delacorte, 1982.

James Lundquist. *Kurt Vonnegut.* New York: Ungar, 1977.

Robert Merrill, ed. *Critical Essays on Kurt Vonnegut.* Boston: G K Hall, 1990.

Leonard Mustazza, ed. *The Critical Response to Kurt Vonnegut.* Westport, CT: Greenwood Press, 1994.

Daniel L. Zins. "Rescuing Science from Technocracy." *Science-Fiction Studies,* 13 (July, 1986), 170–181.

—*Roslynn Haynes*

CHILDHOOD'S END BY ARTHUR C. CLARKE (1953)

■

> *The opinions expressed in this book are not those of the author.*
>
> —Arthur C. Clarke
> *Childhood's End* (1953)

Summary

Although Arthur C. Clarke is best known to the world for the 1968 book and film *2001: A Space Odyssey*, his most influential science fiction novels appeared in 1953: *Against the Fall of Night* (revised 1956 as *The City and the Stars*) and *Childhood's End*. Like Olaf Stapledon's *Last and First Men*—which Clarke praised—both offer uncomfortable perspectives on the future of **humanity**.

Childhood's End opens with human dreams of **space travel** and pioneering **exploration** destroyed by the arrival of alien Overlords (see **Aliens on Earth**), who bloodlessly and benevolently take over the **Earth**. For much of the book, their motives, and reasons for concealing their physical appearance, are obscure.

The true role of the Overlords is as metaphorical midwives to the **birth** of humanity's successors. A new generation of Earth's **children** is born with **psychic powers,** soon becoming fused via telepathy into a gestalt (see **Hive Minds**) that effortlessly feeds itself through telekinesis, the end-point of physical **evolution**. No longer comprehensible to older humans, this group entity leaves Earth like a butterfly emerging from its pupa after **metamorphosis**—destroying the planet in the process—and flies away to join an equally incomprehensible galactic Overmind.

Discussion

Like H.G. Wells's *The War of the Worlds*, this novel applies a **role reversal** twist to the British colonialist ethos (see **Postcolonialism**), with Earth on the receiving end of benign takeover. One of the Overlords' major interventions in human affairs is a show of force—locally blotting out the **Sun**—that warns South Africa to cease maltreatment of its white minority (see **Race Relations**). The spectacle of colossal alien ships looming above all major cities has had many science fiction echoes, for example in the film *Independence Day* (1996).

The Overlords' coyness about their appearance provided the single surprise of Clarke's earlier story "Guardian Angel" (1950), which was expanded to become the first segment of *Childhood's End*. It is assumed that prehistoric racial **memory** of **first contact** with the Overlords long influenced **religion** and even now would trigger **xenophobia**, for these kindly visitors have the horns, wings and barbed tails traditionally ascribed to **demons** and **Satan**. Later it is proposed that race memory defies **time**, and that the ominous aura of this physical shape arises from its association with humanity's cataclysmic end.

This demonic aspect, with its implication of soullessness, resonates usefully with the Overlords' true racial flaw. Despite being intellectual **superman** figures, they themselves lack the potential for psychic powers needed to follow the races they shepherd into post-human transcendence. As one says, "we shall always envy you."

With overt associations of **evil** dispelled, the aliens nevertheless prove inimical to human religion. The **gifts** of **technology** with which they nurture a new "Golden Age" (see **Utopia**) include **time** viewers that confirm Clarke's own belief that **Christianity** and other faiths have purely human origins. These devices were revisited in Clarke's later collaboration with Stephen Baxter, *The Light of Other Days* (2000). The Golden Age has several unconvincing aspects, such as the erasure of irrational (in the author's view) puritanism by the introduction of reliable contraceptives and infallible DNA identification of paternity, and of national boundaries and differences by ubiquitous personal air cars (see **Air Travel**). Global generalizations like "Man had lost heart" are frequent.

Partly anticipating William Golding's *The Lord of the Flies*, the posthuman children (segregated for humanity's protection) abandon **civilization** and engage in mysterious **rituals**, "naked and filthy." Their mental processes become incomprehensible and their physical abilities are feared even by the Overlords. Perhaps implausibly, many of the dead-end remnants of old humanity opt for **suicide** over the loss of their children and their future.

A digression involving a whale/squid exhibit (see **Fish and Sea Creatures**) for the Overlords' homeworld museum allows a human stowaway—aided by a new **drug** for suspended animation (see **Suspended Animation and Cryonics**)—to skip ahead eighty years thanks to a round trip at relativistic velocity, and to report the end of Earth as the **last man**. The scenes of destruction are spectacular and effective. A coda shows us the pathos and stoicism of the "superhuman" Overlords who are left behind, excluded from merging into the unknowable gestalt which they serve, and which is Clarke's secular equivalent of **Heaven** or even God.

Despite some prior narrative clumsiness, the apocalyptic finale of *Childhood's End* had an impact on genre science fiction that is still remembered, as shown by the book's appearance in the 2004 "Retro Hugo" shortlist of novels deemed worthy of a Hugo Award had these been presented in 1954. Its ultimate theme of an intellectual and parapsychological, rather than technological, "Singularity" in human **progress**, transcending matter and the need for Earth itself, is deliberately homaged in Greg Bear's *Blood Music*. Alarmingly gifted children are linked with upheaval or **apocalypse** in later works like Neil Gaiman and Terry Pratchett's *Good Omens* (1990) and Stephen Baxter's *Time* (1999).

Clarke's bleakly Stapledonian vision and **philosophy** are memorable in a way that transcends the more routine—even, to modern eyes, clichéd—plot aspects of *Childhood's End*.

Bibliography

Merritt Abrash. "Utopia Subverted." *Extrapolation*, 30 (Winter, 1989), 372–379.

Bruce A. Beatie. "Arthur C. Clarke and the Alien Encounter." *Extrapolation*, 30 (Spring, 1989), 53–69.

Russell Blackford. "Technological Meliorism and the Posthuman Vision." *New York Review of Science Fiction*, No. 159 (November 2001), 1, 10–12.

Elisabeth S. Frisby. "Nietzschean Themes in Clarke's *Childhood's End*." *Philosophy in Context*, 11 (1981), 71–80.

Elizabeth A. Hull. "Fire and Ice." *Extrapolation*, 24 (Spring, 1983), 13–32.

John Huntington. "The Unity of *Childhood's End*." *Science-Fiction Studies*, 1 (Spring, 1974), 154–164.

Lucy Menger. "The Appeal of *Childhood's End*." Dick Riley, ed., *Critical Encounters*. New York: Ungar, 1978, 87–108.

David N. Samuelson. "*Childhood's End*." *Science-Fiction Studies*, 1 (Spring, 1973), 4–17.

Eugene Tanzy. "Contrasting Views of Man and the Evolutionary Process." Joseph D. Olander and Martin H. Greenberg, eds., *Arthur C. Clarke*. New York: Taplinger, 1977, 172–195.

—David Langford

A CHRISTMAS CAROL BY CHARLES DICKENS (1843)

■

Summary

Ebenezer Scrooge, a miserly businessman, particularly refuses to celebrate **Christmas**. He gives his clerk, Bob Cratchit, the minimum amount of holiday time off with which to celebrate it (in addition to paying him a pittance), refuses a dinner invitation from his nephew, and vehemently declines to contribute to charitable funds. On Christmas Eve he is visited by the ghost of his former partner, Jacob Marley, bound in a chain made of cashboxes, who tells him that he will be visited, on three successive days, by three further spirits, who will endeavor to save him from Marley's fate. In turn, Scrooge is visited by the Spirits of Christmas Past, Present, and Future, who respectively show him how Scrooge's life was warped by past experiences; how those connected with him through **business** and **family** relationships keep Christmas; and how their lives and his own life will likely end if he does not change his ways. Scrooge awakes to discover that the visitations have been compressed into one night, and it is now Christmas Day. He celebrates his deliverance by sending a large goose to the Cratchit family, promising charitable donations to others, and dining with his nephew, before giving Bob Cratchit a raise in salary and promising to help his family further.

Discussion

A Christmas Carol is the first of Charles Dickens's five **Christmas** books, and still the best loved. Of the five, four deal with **ghosts and hauntings**, using supernatural means to transform a central character who has lost faith in human dignity, bringing each to a new appreciation of the indomitable nature of the human spirit. In this instance, Scrooge is taken to the past and future (see **Time Travel**) so he can learn the error of his ways, and also see their effects.

The key to Scrooge's redemption is **memory**. The Spirit of Christmas Past causes Scrooge to revisit his childhood and early years of employment, recalling the pleasant Christmases he spent until, driven by fear of poverty and need to make **money**, Scrooge puts business before all else and alienates his fiancée, who releases him from their agreement.

The Ghost of Christmas Present shows Scrooge how even the poorest contrive in some way to celebrate Christmas. **Food and drink** and general hospitality play a great part in this spirit's visit; when he appears in Scrooge's quarters he is seated on a throne constructed of food. We are given lyrical descriptions of the contents of grocers' and fruiterers' stores and an elaborate description of the Cratchit family's anticipation of its Christmas meal, although it is clear, reading between the lines, that it is more meager than one might suppose, particularly when juxtaposed with the description of Scrooge's nephew's dinner. It is significant that Scrooge's first act of repentance is to send the Cratchit family the largest goose he can find.

The visits made by all three spirits place great emphasis on the importance of family. It is particularly emphasized that Scrooge was not present at Marley's deathbed and that he is now alone in the world. This resonates with the picture provided by the Ghost of Christmas Future of Scrooge's own death, also alone. More shocking still is the way in which Scrooge is robbed of literally everything he owns (see **Theft**), even the shirt off his back, because there is no one to care for him. By contrast, in portrayals of the Cratchit family and Scrooge's former fiancée, great emphasis is laid upon the role of **children** within families and the joy they are perceived as bringing, no matter what the economic condition of the family. This is subtly underlined by the fact that for Belle's children there are **gifts**, while the matter is not touched upon in the Cratchit household. It is also striking that Ignorance and Want, who accompany the Ghost of Christmas Present, are shown as starving children.

As his journeys proceed, Scrooge becomes ever more stricken with **guilt and responsibility**—recognizing that, as Marley observed, the common welfare should also have been his business. Dickens's portrait of the wrongs of his society is comprehensive, and the message is clear: Scrooge, as a wealthy man, has a duty to those less fortunate than himself (see **Class System; Ethics**).

At least fourteen films have been based on Dickens's story. One of the best-known and most successful is the 1951 version directed by Brian Desmond-Hurst, starring Alastair Sim as Scrooge. The 1984 version, directed by Clive Donner and starring George C. Scott, has been memorably described as lacking in squalor, although scenes involving the Spirits are noteworthy. *Scrooged* (1988), directed again by Donner and starring Bill Murray as Frank Cross, Scrooge's modern-day equivalent, proved to be a successful and imaginative updating of the story. *The Muppet Christmas Carol* (1992), directed by Brian Henson, remained faithful to the original story, with Michael Caine unexpectedly successful as Scrooge.

Bibliography

Chris Baldrick. *In Frankenstein's Shadow*. New York: Oxford University Press, 1991.
Simon Callow. *Dickens' Christmas*. New York: Harry N. Abrams, 2003.
Joseph D. Cusumano. *Transforming Scrooge*. New York: Llewellyn, 1996.
Paul Davis. *The Lives and Times of Ebenezer Scrooge*. New Haven: Yale University Press, 1990.
Ruth Glancy. "Introduction." Charles Dickens, *Charles Dickens Christmas Books*, ed. Glancy. Oxford: World Classics, 1988, ix–xxii.
Fred Guida. *A Christmas Carol and Its Adaptations*. Jefferson, NC: McFarland, 2000.
Michael Patrick Hearn, ed. *The Annotated Christmas Carol*, by Charles Dickens. New York: W. W. Norton, 2003.
Gary Westfahl. "A Christmas Cavil, or, It's a Plunderful Life." *Interzone*, No. 151 (January, 2000), 40–41.

—*Maureen Kincaid Speller*

CITY BY CLIFFORD D. SIMAK (1952)

■

> *These are the stories that the Dogs tell when the fires burn high and the wind is from the north. Then each family circle gathers at the hearthstone and the pups sit silently and listen and when the story's done they ask many questions:*
> *"What is Man?" they'll ask.*
> *Or perhaps: "What is a city?"*
> *Or: "What is war?"*

> Clifford D. Simak
> *City* (1952)

Summary

In the **far future,** human **civilization** is merely a myth—**stories** told by **dogs** throughout the multiverse of "cobbly" worlds (see **Parallel Worlds**). The tales handed down through generations are so outlandish—speaking of **space travel** to other planets, impossibly large permanent settlements called "**cities,**" and the unfathomable concept of **war**—that they can be little more than parables and **fables** invented by earlier ages as cautionary tales. Still, enough clues and tantalizing **mystery** remains in the eight recorded stories to give canine scholars more than enough incentive to argue over the fall of **humanity**, its **uplift** of dogs, the creation of **robots**, the opening of the cobbly worlds, and the Websters—a family whose legacy is at the epicenter of the momentous changes. These scholarly discussions frame and link the tales, illuminating future doggish society as much as the stories under examination.

Discussion

According to Clifford D. Simak, the stories that comprise *City* were written in response to the **horrors** of World War II, with later stories particularly reacting to the atomic age opened by destruction of Hiroshima and Nagasaki (see **Nuclear War**). Nuclear weapons were only effective against concentrated populations, he reasoned; therefore cities must become obsolete and diminish.

The novel can be divided into three episodic sequences: Twilight of Humans, Transition, and Dogs Ascendant. The first sequence offers an amiable, nostalgic opening, focusing on a conflation of circumstances—personal aircraft (see **Air Travel**), cheap **nuclear power** and hydroponic tank **farms**—that devalue land and prompt a great migration away from cities. Municipal politicians struggle with their growing irrelevancy even as displaced farmers become squatters in abandoned neighborhoods and conflicts between human rights and property rights ensue. Years later, the human race has become increasingly isolated and agoraphobic. The trend goes unnoticed in this **pastoral** society until Jerome Webster is called to **Mars** to perform emergency brain surgery on his close friend, Juwain, a Martian philosopher on the verge of a monumental breakthrough (see **Philosophy**). Jerome faces overwhelming **anxiety** at the thought of leaving his estate and ultimately fails to do so, themes which Isaac Asimov expanded on in his **robot** mystery novel *The Naked Sun* (1957). The sequence concludes with a census-taker encountering a descendent of Jerome, whose experiments on dogs have given them speech and heightened **intelligence** as an atonement of sorts for Jerome's failure (see **Guilt and Responsibility**). The census-taker also encounters a mutant human (see **Superman**), advanced in intelligence and longevity but devoid of compassion and empathy, who has casually uplifted a colony of ants (see **Insects**) to a nearly industrial level of **technology**, only to callously destroy their **civilization**. He also discerns the solution to the incomplete Juwain philosophy, but refuses to share it.

The transition section of the novel establishes the mechanism by which Simak removes the human race as an obstacle to dogkind's ascendance: to colonize Jupiter (see **Jupiter and the Outer Planets**), humans must undergo **metamorphosis** to take the form of the native loper (see **Pantropy**), which is similar to the solution for **Mars** colonization used by Frederik Pohl in *Man Plus* (1976). The loper form is so superior to the human body, however, that transformed subjects refuse to revert back. This **knowledge** is exploited by mutants, who finally disclose the Juwain philosophical breakthrough—clear understanding of opposing viewpoints—to normal humans. The result is a mass migration to Jupiter, with **Earth**'s disaffected population eagerly shedding its humanity for better lives as lopers.

In the final act, dog civilization has greatly progressed in the absence of humans. When another Webster visits the old estate, dogs greet him as a god. Fearful that humans could exploit and corrupt this **utopia**, the Webster returns to the last human enclave and seals it off from the rest of the world behind an impenetrable barrier. Only the robot servant Jenkins is left to represent the Websters and serve as **mentor** to the infant doggish society, which grows to include other species and evolves into a benevolent version of George Orwell's ***Animal Farm***. In the ironically titled tale "Aesop," however, Simak deliberately muddies the waters with a fable full of ambiguity. A vicious, invisible predator crosses the **dimensions** from the cobbly worlds, and the doggish congress of **talking animals** is helpless before it. The utopia is saved only through the violent intervention of a few remnant humans. The fact these humans retain enough savagery to defend doggish society also makes them a looming danger to that same society. Jenkins addresses both threats by leading the last humans into the cobblies' homeworld (see **Exile**).

A millennia later, Jenkins returns to Earth after the extinction of both humans and cobblies to find the uplifted ants usurping control of the dogs' helper robots and overrunning the Earth. Rather than poison the ants as humans would do, dogs and their followers abandon the Earth to the insects, migrating throughout the cobbly worlds instead. In the 1970s, Simak added an unexpected "Epilog" in which Jenkins, now alone on Earth, discovers the ants' mechanistic society has collapsed—a final parting shot at the corrupt human legacy. The tale ends on an optimistic note with Jenkins leaving Earth to mentor the troubled, space-faring robot civilization.

Simak's condemnation of *Homo sapiens* is thorough and complete, in stark contrast to most science fiction of the time, and the human race meets with an ignoble, rather than glorious, end. Even when humanity's **courage** and potential are acknowledged, they are irrevocably tainted by innate violent and destructive tendencies.

Bibliography

Thomas D. Clareson. "Clifford D. Simak." Clareson, ed., *Voices for the Future, Volume 1.* Bowling Green, OH: Bowling Green State University Popular Press, 1976, 64–88.

Robert A. Heinlein. "To Read SF Is to Read Simak." *Algol*, 14 (Summer/Fall 1977), 11.

Dennis Jarog. "The Trap of the Frontier." *Lan's Lantern*, 11 (July, 1981), 41–44.

George Laskowski. "Interview With C. D. S." *Lan's Lantern*, 11 (July 1981), 14–24.

Sam Moskowitz. "Clifford D. Simak." Moskowitz, *Seekers of Tomorrow*. Cleveland and New York: World Publishing Company, 1966, 266–282.

John Ower. "Aesop and the Ambiguity of Clifford Simak's *City*." *Science-Fiction Studies*, 6 (July, 1979), 164–167.

Robert Silverberg. "*City*: Clifford D. Simak." Silverberg, *Reflections and Refractions*. Grass Valley, CA: Underwood Books, 1997, 323–329.

Clifford D. Simak. "Author's Foreword." *City*. New York: Ace Books, 1976, 1–4.

—*Jayme Lynn Blaschke*

THE CLAN OF THE CAVE BEAR BY JEAN AUEL (1980)

■

Summary

The Clan of the Cave Bear, the first novel in Jean Auel's Earth's Children series, takes place in the Pleistocene Epoch, 25,000–35,000 years ago, on the northern coast of the Black Sea in what is today the Ukraine. An earthquake separates a young modern human, Ayla, from her **family**. A Neanderthal tribe, the Clan of the Cave Bear, discovers the child and adopts her. Brought up in the Neanderthal **culture**, Ayla is subjugated, as are all Neanderthal women, under the Clan's inflexible patriarchy. Although the modern Ayla is genetically superior to the Neanderthals, benefiting the tribe, her skills, ingenuity, and dexterity threaten the primitive males. Eventually, she rebels against male dominance. Her evolutionary endowment forces her to leave the Clan without her son, conceived when Broud, a Neanderthal antagonist, raped her. Ayla searches for her own kind, thus beginning the Earth's Children saga.

Four works followed: *The Valley of the Horses* (1983), *The Mammoth Hunters* (1985), *The Plains of Passage* (1990), and *The Shelters of Stone* (2002). The sequels, which tell the story of Ayla's odyssey across Pleistocene **Europe** and her encounters with other Cro-Magnons, lack the cultural and scientific interest of *The Clan of the Cave Bear* since they portray the interactions, not of early-modern humans, but of human sub-species, one of which was disappearing from the **Earth**.

Discussion

The novel is an extraordinary work of **prehistoric fiction**. Auel incorporated contemporaneous scientific theories into recreating prehistoric life, beginning her research in 1977. She traveled to archaelogical sites in Europe, recreating everyday prehistoric activities, making tools, tanning hides, and preparing food from wilderness resources. A cave discovery in Shanidar, Iraq, had the greatest emotional impact on the author (see **Caverns**). Excavated from 1957 to 1961, it contained the 50,000-year-old remains of Neanderthal adults and **children**. Since one adult **skeleton** was buried with **flowers**, scientists believed this evidenced Neanderthal **ritual** practice and belief in an afterlife (see **Religion**). Although theories about Neanderthal **anthropology** remain contentious, Auel brought the ancient drama of Shanidar Cave to life in her novel.

The novel is notable for its theoretical content, which enlivens her story. Auel treats the **evolution** of hominid language (see **Language and Linguistics**), tool **technology**, and the relationship between modern **humanity** and Neanderthals. Neanderthal speech patterns, for example, exhibit phonemic traits consistent with theories on voice anatomy. In addition, Auel portrays the Neanderthals as communicating through sign language, an inference drawn from the fossil record and experimentation on primates. With respect to technology, Auel consulted authorities: thus, in the story, the craftsman Droog expertly manufactures spear points and specialized tools. Auel contributes to the theme of the genetic and cultural relationship between human groups and reflects on the human proclivity for ethnic, racial, and **gender** prejudice. The Neanderthals and early–modern humans are both human beings, but the former is a distinct (and soon to be extinct) sub-species. She asserts this when Ayla is raped by the Neanderthal Broud and bears a child exhibiting features of both forms. The Clan's shaman, describing these children as "mixed spirits," suggests that, though the Clan is dying out, it will survive through interbreeding with the dominant human group. In the spring of 1999, Auel's fiction may have been corroborated scientifically: Portuguese **scientists** discovered the 24,500-year-old remains of a human child apparently having both Neanderthal and modern human features, suggesting that the two groups interbred and were genetically mixed.

Auel's reconstruction of Neanderthal life and the relationship between co-extensive human groups is an exercise in imaginative ethnography. She creates an **ecological** religion for the Clan, illustrating the development of ritual and religion among primitive peoples. Revering Ursus, the spirit of the cave bear, the Clan recognizes a pantheon of natural entities governing climatic processes and animal behavior (see **Gods and Goddesses**). Adoration of Ursus culturally unites all Neanderthal clans. The Clan observes a talismanic system: they carry amulets of red ochre and bear fat (see **Magical Objects**). Cave **fires** have both practical and spiritual meaning, warding off predators, cooking meat, warming the clan, and driving away **evil** spirits. The physical and spiritual lives of the Neanderthals are interrelated: each person has a totem spirit. Even procreation is understood spiritually: the protective spirit being defeated in conception. But religion also ratifies Neanderthal social structure: male domination over women maintains the balance of physical and spiritual **forces** in the Clan's world. The highlight of the Clan's religious life is the invocation ceremony: garbed in animal skins, anointed with paint, playing drums and flutes, and using symbolic gestures, the Clan invokes the protection of Ursus (see **Supernatural Creatures**) as they face extinction.

The Clan of the Cave Bear is an extraordinary resource for academics, Auel capably researched the subject in the library and the field, recreating a critical era in human **history**: the ascendancy of modern humanity and parallel descent of Neanderthals into extinction. Along with its scientific content, the novel treats an abundance of modern themes (issues of gender, **race relations**, and **old age**), giving it universal appeal and providing opportunities for humanistic study. However, to read the novel in the context of science also reveals questionable assumptions: why does Auel endow her Neanderthals with **psychic powers**? Is there any basis to assume that language deficiency would somehow stimulate nonverbal communication, beyond signing? Another question worthy of discussion concerns Neanderthal natural **medicine**: did Auel study **Native American** pharmacology and bring that into her novel? These and other questions reflect the intellectual depth of her fiction.

Bibliography

Tracy Cochran. "The View from Mount Auel." *Publisher's Weekly*, 249 (April 22, 2002), 35–37.

Charles De Paolo. "Wells, Golding, and Auel." *Science Fiction Studies*, 27 (November, 2000), 418–438.

———. *Human Prehistory and Fiction*. Jefferson, NC: McFarland, 2003.

Bill Feret. "Interview: Jean M. Auel." *Starlog*, No. 107 (June, 1986), 50–51, 63.

Nicholas O'Connell. "Jean M. Auel." O'Connell, *At the Field's End*. Washington: Madrona, 1987, 208–219.

Heather Schell. "The Sexist Gene." *American Literary History*, 14 (Winter, 2002), 805–827.

Clyde Wilcox. "The Not-So-Failed Feminism of Jean Auel." *Journal of Popular Culture*, 28 (Winter, 1994), 63–70.

Clyde Wilcox. "Prehistoric Gender Politics." *Extrapolation*, 40 (Winter 1999), 325–333.

Diane S. Wood. "Female Heroism in the Ice Age." *Extrapolation*, 21 (Spring, 1986), 33–38.

—*Charles De Paolo*

A CLOCKWORK ORANGE (1971)

Summary

A Clockwork Orange paints a picture of a decadent, spiritually and morally bankrupt Britain (see **Decadence**). A gang of **youths** led by Alex de Large routinely rape, mug, and murder while under the influence of **drugs**. One evening, while on a rampage, Alex's leadership is challenged by his cohort, Dim. Alex is arrested, having knocked unconscious the Cat Lady, his third victim so far. She later dies in a hospital and Alex receives a long **prison** sentence. The Home Secretary visits Alex in prison and selects him for rehabilitation through a form of aversion therapy believed to "recondition" subjects through controlled exposure to sexual and violent images. The treatment is successful and Alex is released back into society, a model citizen. However, Alex is unable to defend himself against the wrathful **revenge** of former friends and victims: he inadvertently stumbles into the residence of a former victim, Mr. Alexander, who seeks vengeance by locking up Alex and playing Beethoven at high volume, causing in Alex the same nausea provoked by the idea of sex or **violence**. Alex jumps from the upstairs window in a desperate attempt to end his suffering and wakes up in a hospital bed. The home secretary bribes Alex to conceal this public relations disaster, and the effects of the therapy are reversed. After making a full recovery, Alex is again released into society and reverts to violent behavior.

Discussion

Unanimously accepted by commentators as science fiction set in the **near future**, Stanley Kubrick's film, like similar works, also functions as a commentary on present-day society. With the exception of the vehicle that Alex and his crew use in their second attack, many of the film's visuals—its **fashion** and the futuristic **architecture and interior design**—as well as the experimental aversion therapy (see **Psychology**) and political background (see **Politics**) seem drawn from the time of the film's production.

This cinematic **dystopia** thus reflects the social realities of early 1970s Britain. The dissolution of inner **cities** and the extended **family** that inform the film's social background were already topical in 1962 when the film's source, Anthony Burgess's *A Clockwork Orange*, was published. The dilapidated council estates and drug joints, the pervasiveness of violence, and Alex's precarious family situation are expressions of these developments. The wealthy (the majority of Alex's victims) live in villas outside the city, reinforcing the image of a strongly determined **class system**.

This society's **governance system** is authoritative and corrupt, as illustrated by the government-run council estates. The rehabilitation of violent prisoners is, the interior minister admits, primarily intended to secure political power and advance the minister's career: cells must be freed up for "political offenders," an election is nearing, and the right-wing government hopes to capitalize on a successful law and order record. The nature of the aversion therapy (brainwashing) expresses the authoritarian flavor of the political backdrop through strong allusions to Nazi methods, while the minister's attempts to bribe Alex concretize the image of political corruption.

In this examination of **individualism and conformity**, the rebellious Alex displays a greater life force than any of his compatriots. His methods of getting ahead reflect perverted ideas of personal furtherance (see **Social Darwinism**) through natural selection and procreation (rape), representing a clear breach of Jean-Jacques Rousseau's Social Contract (see **Philosophy**) as a basis for human **civilization**. The aversion therapy is designed to enforce conformity with social norms defined by the very political establishment responsible for the social decay that informs the backdrop to this film.

The prison padre makes the moral case against brainwashing prisoners as a way of controlling crime (see **Crime and Punishment**) (and of turning "**evil**" citizens into "good" ones). Reflecting the traditional science fiction Frankenstein theme (see **Frankenstein Monsters**), the "clockwork orange" of the film's title is precisely what Alex turns into as a result of the therapy: he is left still an organic being, yet without the ability to assert free will in certain situations. Alluding to the imperative of every human being making a moral choice—a **freedom** Alex has been deprived of through the therapy—the padre argues that free will and moral choice, even if used for evil, are better than a will programmed to meet the needs of the state. For, apart from representing a chilling hypothesis on the **ethics** and principles of crime and punishment, this "cure" also cements Alex's entrenchment in the state with more disciplinary controls than when he was in prison or undergoing the therapy. The provocative implication of Burgess's novel and the film is that free will is a good above the moral jurisdiction of the state—even at the risk of social decay—and that such decay can also result from the actions of a state built upon a spirit of democratic consensus. Still, the film remains controversial not because of its message, but because of the way Kubrick conveyed it—choreographing violence to the sound of Gene Kelly's "Singin' in the Rain," filling scenes with **blood** and **nudity**, and seeming at times more interested in celebrating the colorful decadence of Alex's lifestyle than in opposing the steps his society takes to suppress it.

Bibliography

James Chapman. "A Bit of the Old Ultra-Violence." I.Q. Hunter, ed., *British Science Fiction Cinema*. New York: Routledge, 1999, 128–137.

Mario Falsetto, ed. *Perspectives on Stanley Kubrick*. London, New York: G.K. Hall, 1996.

David Hughes. *The Complete Kubrick*. London: Virgin Books, 2000.

Doris Hunter and Howard Hunter. "*Siddhartha* and *A Clockwork Orange*." P.E. Richter, ed., *Utopia/Dystopia?* Cambridge, MA: Schenkman, 1975, 125–142.

Samuel McCracken. "Novel into Film; Novelist into Critic." *Antioch Review*, 32 (June, 1973), 427–436.

Stuart Y. McDougal, ed. *Stanley Kubrick's A Clockwork Orange*. Cambridge: Cambridge University Press, 2003.

Colin Odell and Mitch Le Blanc. "The Return of *A Clockwork Orange*." *Vector*, No. 211 (May/June, 2000), 10–11.

Vivian C. Sobchack. "Decor as Theme: *A Clockwork Orange*." *Literature/Film Quarterly*, 9 (1981), 92–102.

Alexander Walker. *Stanley Kubrick*. New York: W. W. Norton and Co., 1999.

—*Alexander Graf*

A CLOCKWORK ORANGE
BY ANTHONY BURGESS (1962)

When a man cannot choose he ceases to be a man.

—Anthony Burgess
A Clockwork Orange (1962)

Summary

Alex, a fifteen-year-old hooligan, begins his narration by describing a typical day in his life in a **near future** England. He and his *droogs* drink "milk plus" in a *moloko* bar, then head out for a night of "ultra-violence": they beat up an elderly professor and a drunkard, raid a shop, defeat a rival gang, and steal an **automobile** (see **Theft**). In the countryside, they invade a **home**, attack a writer, and rape his wife. After ditching the car in a canal, Alex caps the evening by listening to classical **music**. The next morning Alex defies his parents by skipping school (see **Education**) and instead rapes two preteens. That evening, due to Alex's brutal leadership his *droogs* abandon him in the midst of another robbery, their victim dies, Alex is convicted of murder, and he is sentenced to fourteen years of **prison** (see **Crime and Punishment**). There, Alex feigns good behavior but kills an inmate who makes advances on him (see **Homosexuality**). In return for **freedom**, Alex volunteers to be subjected to aversion therapy promoted by the government as a means of controlling crime. Now sickened by violence, Alex is helpless at the hands of his former *droogs*, who are now policemen, and a series of his previous victims. The writer drives him to attempt **suicide**, which causes a political scandal, leading the government to reverse the therapy (see **Politics**). In the final chapter of the British edition, Alex, still a hooligan a decade later, sees that his former *droogs* have become mature adults and considers having a **family**.

Discussion

"Clockwork orange" refers to making the natural artificial, in this case, Burgess's warning of the dangers of social conditioning imposed by an overbearing government (see **Governance Systems**). Bereft of his capacity to commit **evil**, Alex is dehumanized by his consequent inability to exercise free moral choice. Perhaps mischaracterized as a **dystopia**, given that little is said about the larger social structure, Alex's England clearly presents a grim future (see **Decadence**): streets are yielded to **youth** gangs, the family is emasculated, moral standards are gutted, and the government is willing to recruit thugs as policemen. There are no **heroes**, not even among figures of authority or dissidents. Ironically named "defender of mankind," the lawless psychopath Alex seems relatively sympathetic.

The recovery of his power to commit evil thus may be read as somewhat positive inasmuch as he regains his autonomy and, almost uniquely in his society, his individuality (see **Individuality and Conformity**). On the other hand, Alex's narrow range of moral choice (see **Ethics**) derives not just from Ludovico's Technique (see **Psychology**) but also his previous life as a hoodlum; he has always been a "clockwork orange" whereby his recurrent question, "What's it going to be then, eh?" is answered by more "ultra-violence." Lacking nurturing family structures, future England denies its youth the capacity for moral growth. Following the author's wishes, American editions now include the twenty-first chapter, which suggests Alex's late-developing impulse to settle down as a family man (see **Bildungsroman**).

Some commentators claim Alex's tale would be uninteresting but for the unusual language (see **Language and Linguistics**) of his narration. Except when citing statements by others, Alex uses an artificial argot devised by him and other *nadsats* (the Russian root "-teen"). While a few terms are of uncertain provenance, the great majority are derived from Russian (see **Russia**). Alex and his *droogs* do not speak or understand Russian, although there is a suggestion that the Russian government is subliminally influencing English youth. The plural *droogs* ("friends"), for example, should be *droozya* and Russians do not use *viddy* ("to see") in the sense of "to understand." *Ptisia* ("bird") for "woman" and *koshka* ("cat") for "man," moreover, reflects English, not Russian, slang of the early 1960s. Alex's account amounts to a remarkable example of *skaz*, a narrative language discernibly different from that of the perceived author, which serves to describe the narrator. Burgess places demands on the reader to figure out what Alex is saying, although he often either sets *Nadsat* in a self-explanatory context ("Dim yanked out his false zoobies, upper and lower") or simply accompanies a term with its English equivalent ("bandas or gruppas or shaikas"). Stanley Edgar Hyman prepared a glossary for the first American edition.

Many readers have noted how Alex's distorted language serves to shield him from the **violence** he commits. Giving a *veck* (short for *cheloveck*, "person") a *tolchock* ("blow") with his *rooker* (*ruka* = "hand") in the *gulliver* (*golova* = "head") and causing the "red, red *krovy*" to flow (*krov* = "blood") is for him "real horrorshow" (*harasho* = "good"). Clearly it is his language of choice, except when he addresses authorities, a device that gives him and other hoodlums a sense of power and group solidarity (see **Identity**), an antidote for their social alienation. The language is shared by the consequently complicit reader. *Nadsat* develops into a poetic idiom that provides the only positive outlet for Alex's misapplied creativity for, besides Russian borrowings, Alex's narration includes many forms of expressive linguistic innovation.

Bibliography

Geoffrey Aggeler. *Anthony Burgess*. Tuscaloosa: University of Alabama Press, 1979.

Robert Bowie. "Freedom and Art in *A Clockwork Orange*." *Thought*, 56 (December, 1981), 402–416.

Todd F. Davis and Kenneth Womack. "O My Brothers." *College Literature*, 29 (Spring, 2002), 19–36.

Robbie B.H. Goh. "'Clockwork' Language Reconsidered." *JNT: Journal of Narrative Theory*, 30 (Summer, 2000), 263–280.

Michael Gorra, "The World of *A Clockwork Orange*." *Gettysburg Review*, 3 (Autumn, 1990), 630–643.

Thomas L. Mentzer. "The Ethics of Behavior Modification." *Essays in Arts and Sciences*, 9 (May, 1980), 93–105.

Patrick Parrinder. "Updating Orwell? Burgess's Future Fictions." *Encounter*, 56 (January, 1981), 45–53.

Rubin Rabinovitz. "Ethical Values in Anthony Burgess's *Clockwork Orange*." *Studies in the Novel*, 11 (Spring, 1979), 43–50.

Philip E. Ray. "Alex Before and After." *MFS: Modern Fiction Studies*, 27 (Autumn, 1981), 479–487.

—*Brett Cooke*

CLOSE ENCOUNTERS OF THE THIRD KIND (1977)

Summary

A blackout hits the heartland of America and Roy Neary, a power company employee, sets out to investigate the problem. While on the road he witnesses what he believes to be a **UFO** and subsequently meets others who have had similar experiences, including Jillian, a woman whose young son is abducted by the **aliens on Earth**. Neary becomes obsessed with finding out the truth behind his experience and ends up getting fired from his job, alienating his wife and **children** in the process. After his **family** abandons him, he regresses to a child-like state of primitivism wherein the artistic impulse becomes the only way for him to deal with the mystery of the UFO. Neary inexplicably constructs a towering **mountain** made of trash, household products, mud, and **plants,** inside his living room. He then spots a news story on the television reporting on a chemical spill in rural Wyoming, near the Devil's Tower National Monument. Convinced that the two mountains are the same and the extraterrestrials are psychically communicating with him, Neary journeys to Wyoming where he believes the aliens will make definitive contact. Once there, Neary and Jillian are apprehended by the military and interrogated by Lacombe, a benevolent **scientist** who has devised a means to communicate with the aliens by use of sign language and **music**. Neary and Jillian escape from custody and journey to the mountain where the visitation will occur. After a spectacular show of **light** and music, the aliens' gigantic mothership lands and actual communication between humans and extraterrestrials is made. Neary is then invited by the aliens to board their ship and travel into the unknown.

Discussion

Released in 1977, the same year that George Lucas's *Star Wars* reinvented the cliffhanger serials of the 1930s and 1940s for a new generation, Spielberg's film had firm roots in the science fiction films of the 1950s. But unlike films like *The Thing (from Another World)* and *Invasion of the Body Snatchers*, *Close Encounters* eschewed the **paranoia** and **xenophobia** (see **Invasion**) that defined the Cold War science fiction film.

What sets the film apart from its cinematic peers as well as its antecedents, is its approach to the subject of contact with the extraterrestrials. Instead of fearing the outsider, Neary cannot wait to make further contact with them. Although his **first contact** is decidedly frightening and ends up destabilizing his entire life, his eventual interaction with the aliens during the finale is unquestionably optimistic (see **Sense of Wonder**). Neary's entrance into the mothership and ascent to the stars (see **Escape**) mirrors a religious experience (see **Religion**). In many ways, all the characters who come into contact with the aliens undergo similar spiritual transformations.

Spielberg's take on the military is also different from many of his contemporaries, as well as television shows like *The X-Files*, which consistently viewed the military as a nefarious tool utilized by a malicious shadow government. In *Close Encounters* the military is controlled by the watchful eyes of the scientists preparing the contact in Wyoming. Treachery, subterfuge, and willful misinformation by the military is not perpetrated for malicious reasons, but because the scientists and aliens have to be shielded from danger. In one sense, this peculiar benevolent and paternal view of the government—especially in the wake of the 1973 Nixon/Watergate scandal that subsequently permeated many of the American films of the era—is refreshing yet ultimately unrealistic. This is unfortunate, since the film's startling and complex examination of Neary's regression into sometimes horrifyingly child-like behavior and his subsequent "spiritual" **rebirth** is unforgettable.

This quasi-religious sentiment also mimics the creative/artistic impulse. Both Neary's and Jillian's lives fall apart after their initial alien encounters, yet they mend their lives through **art**—sculpture and painting, respectively. Neary will risk all that he holds dear—his family and their **love** and understanding—in order to comprehend the deeper truth behind his contact with aliens. In many respects, Spielberg's interpretation of Neary's fall from grace, and his eventual ascent into the heavens, is akin to the idea that there is no one closer to the divine than the artist.

Spielberg's film was such a huge success for Columbia Pictures that in the summer of 1979 the studio re-released it into theaters as a "Special Edition." Under pressure to complete the original version for a late 1977 release, Spielberg had been unable to fine-tune the editing and several major special effects shots were abandoned to make the release date. The "Special Edition" was intended to be the director's definitive cut. Sixteen minutes of footage from the original version was deleted, seven minutes of new footage were added (including a new ending showing Neary inside the spaceship), and a few scenes were entirely re-edited. Although the new finale was generally viewed as a disappointment, the "Special Edition" was another big hit for the studio and helped spawn the compulsion for directors to re-edit their films after the initial theatrical release. Spielberg subsequently released a "director's cut" of *Close Encounters* onto DVD, which combined both previous versions minus the footage showing the interior of the mothership.

Bibliography

Algis Budrys. "The Empire Talks Back." *Isaac Asimov's Science Fiction Magazine*, 4 (November, 1980), 44–59.

Thomas M. Disch. "A Closer Look at *Close Encounters*." *Foundation*, No. 15 (January, 1979), 50–53.

Charlene Engels. "Language and Music of the Spheres." *Film/Literature Quarterly*, 24 (1996), 376–384.

Clara Maria Henning. "*Star Wars* and *Close Encounters*." *Theology Today*, 35 (July, 1978), 202–206.

Herb Lightman. "Spielberg Speaks About 'Close Encounters.'" *American Cinematographer*, 59 (January, 1978), 39–42, 58–59, 95.

Joseph McBride. *Steven Spielberg*. New York: Simon & Schuster, 1997.

John Pym. "The Middle American Sky." *Sight and Sound*, 47 (Spring, 1978), 99–100.

Garrett Stewart. "Close Encounters of the Fourth Kind." *Sight & Sound*, 47 (Summer, 1978), 167–174.

Robert Torry. "Politics and Parousia in *Close Encounters of the Third Kind*." *Literature/Film Quarterly*, 19 (1991), 188–196.

—Derek Hill

THE COLOUR OF MAGIC BY TERRY PRATCHETT (1983)

■

> *An ancient suitcase was coming to eat him.*
>
> —Terry Pratchett
> *The Colour of Magic* (1983)

Summary

This episodic fantasy is set on Discworld, which is flat and—following Hindu mythic **cosmology**—supported by four elephants, which stand on a vast spacefaring turtle. In its major **city** Ankh-Morpork, the terminally inept **wizard** Rincewind stumbles into a job as native guide to Twoflower, this world's first international tourist. Farcical **humor** and **disasters** follow. Ankh-Morpork is set on **fire** by hopeful speculators after Twoflower introduces the concept of fire insurance (see **Money**). Next, helped by a dim **barbarian** hero with a talking **sword**, the obscene Lovecraftian god Bel-Shamharoth is comically routed in its temple.

In episode three, Rincewind and Twoflower are involved with political in-fighting among riders of magical **dragons**, parodying Anne McCaffrey's *Dragonflight*. Finally, following much **sea travel**, they are captured by the cruel Kingdom of Krull, which dominates a third of Discworld's rim, where the sea spills over in an eternal waterfall. Destined for **sacrifice**, they contrive to replace Krull's "chelonauts" (see **Astronauts**) on a mission over the edge to probe such cosmic **puzzles** as the turtle's sex. The story ends in literal free fall, with an outrageous **deus ex machina** rescue in the sequel *The Light Fantastic* (1986).

Discussion

The Colour of Magic is an engaging though relatively slight picaresque **comedy**, significant as the opening of Terry Pratchett's phenomenally popular Discworld sequence, now well past its thirtieth volume.

Discworld began as a haphazard playground in which **clichés** of **heroic fantasy** and **sword and sorcery** were mercilessly spoofed (see **Satire**). **Gods and goddesses**, in their retirement home Dunmanifestin, play **games** with the world and cheat repeatedly. **Magic** itself has a flavor of **physics** and of Pratchett's former employment in the **nuclear power** industry: thaumaturgical contamination tends to leak from spell **books** and linger upon battlefields, with alarming effects on the **ecology**.

Rincewind is a relatively formulaic comic character, a total coward usually seen on the run, who later develops a self-justifying **philosophy** of cowardice. Pratchett uses him as a familiar humorous foil in exotic settings, such as parodic equivalents of **China/Japan** and **Australia** in *Interesting Times* (1994) and *The Last Continent* (1998), respectively, and a rare instance of fantasy **space travel** (powered by **dragons**) in *The Last Hero* (2001).

Other Discworld subseries handle darker themes with greater maturity than Rincewind's romps. **Death**, personified as a robed, scythe-bearing **skeleton** speaking in capital letters, appears throughout—an eternally humorless straight man who is somehow on **humanity**'s side against things worse than himself. His kinder aspect first appears when he takes on an inept apprentice in *Mort* (1987). Repeatedly he opposes the antilife Auditors of Reality, who object to the messiness of life and plot against it: pensioning off our compassionate Death in *Reaper Man* (1991), assassinating the equivalent of Father **Christmas** in *Hogfather* (1996), and stopping **time** itself with a doomsday clock in *Thief of Time* (2001) (see **Clocks and Timepieces**).

A major subseries features **witches** and hence, often **feminism**. Redoubtable witch Granny Weatherwax challenges the **sexism** of the wizards' Unseen University (see **Education**) in *Equal Rites* (1987). With a tiny, ill-assorted coven, she works to give malformed stories their proper ending: William **Shakespeare**'s *Macbeth* (c. 1606), for example, begins as a propaganda play (see **Theatre**) commissioned by the usurping **villain** in *Wyrd Sisters* (1988). A warped **fairy tale** in *Witches Abroad* (1991) threatens to marry Cinderella to a transformed frog (see **Metamorphosis**). Elsewhere Granny tackles malign **elves** (echoing *A Midsummer Night's Dream* [c. 1594]), garlic-immunized **vampires**, and a warped version of the film *The Phantom of the Opera* (1926) (see **Music**).

Stories of **detectives** and **crime and punishment** dominate the Ankh-Morpork City Watch subseries, beginning in *Guards! Guards!* (1989) with a plot to overthrow the city's unloved though efficient leader, the "Patrician," using a summoned dragon, and to reinstate a **king**. In a delicious parody of noir thrillers, a drunken Captain Vimes and his seedy, inept Watchmen save Ankh-Morpork. Their further exploits involve an assassin carrying the world's only rifle (see **Weaponry**) in *Men at Arms* (1993)—also showing **race relations** between humans, **dwarfs**, trolls, etc.—a murder plot involving **golems** in *Feet of Clay* (1996), and **war** in **Egypt**-like **deserts** in *Jingo!* (1997).

Unusually in fantasy, Ankh-Morpork is undergoing an industrial revolution. Long-range **communication** by semaphore is central to Vimes's diplomatic mission in *The Fifth Elephant* (1999); printing presses and newspapers convulse the city in *The Truth* (2000) (see **Journalism**); and *Going Postal* (2004) describes the struggle between the semaphore Internet (with hackers) (see **Cyberspace**) and a revived Post Office. Amid increasingly dark comedy, the Ankh-Morpork sequence features much thought on practical modern **politics**, contrasting with the bad old days that Vimes revisits by **time travel** in *Night Watch* (2002).

Additionally there are stand-alone novels. The strongest is *Small Gods* (1992), unsparingly dissecting fundamentalist **religion;** the most endearingly silly is *Moving Pictures* (1990), recounting the rise and fall of Discworld's cinema industry, with tiny **demons** painting very fast inside each camera. *Pyramids* (1989) spoofs ancient Egypt. *Monstrous Regiment* (2003) shows **war** from the viewpoint of cross-dressing girl soldiers. Shorter Discworld books for **children** began with *The Amazing Maurice and His Educated Rodents* (2001), with a **cat** and a troupe of rats (see **Rats and Mice**) operating the Pied Piper swindle. Pratchett continues to extract humor from fantasy tropes by treating them with ingeniously skewed common sense. He is a regular British best-seller.

Bibliography

Martin Brown. "Imaginary Places, Real Monuments." Miles Russell, ed., *Digging Holes in Popular Culture.* Oxford, UK: Oxbow Books, 2002, 67–76.

Andrew M. Butler, *Terry Pratchett.* Harpenden, Hertfordshire, UK: Pocket Essentials, 2001.

Andrew M. Butler, Edward James, and Farah Mendlesohn, eds., *Terry Pratchett: Guilty of Literature.* Reading, Berkshire, UK: Science Fiction Foundation, 2000.

John Clute. "The Big Sellers, 3: Terry Pratchett." *Interzone*, No. 33 (January/February, 1990), 24–27.

Colin Greenland. "Death and the Modem." *Fear*, 19 (July, 1990), 23–26.

Peter Hunt. "Terry Pratchett." Hunt and Millicent Lenz, eds., *Alternative Worlds in Fantasy Fiction.* New York: Continuum, 2001, 86–121.

David Langford. "*Equal Rites*" and "*Moving Pictures*." Langford, *Up Through an Empty House of Stars.* Holicong, PA: Cosmos, 2003. 87–89, 156–158.

John Newsinger. "The People's Republic of Treacle Mine Road Betrayed." *Vector*, No. 232 (November/December, 2003), 15–16.

Stan Nicholls. "Terry Pratchett Leaves the Furniture Alone." Nicholls, *Wordsmiths of Wonder.* London: Orbit, 1993, 340–347.

—*David Langford*

CONAN THE CONQUEROR
BY ROBERT E. HOWARD (1950)

∎

"I think of Life!" he roared. "The dead are dead, and what has passed is done! I have a ship and a fighting crew and a girl with lips like wine, and that's all I ever asked. Lick your wounds, bullies, and break out a cask of ale. You're going to work ship as she never was worked before. Dance and sing while you buckle to it, damn you! To the devil with empty seas! We're bound for waters where the

seaports are fat, and the merchant ships
are crammed with plunder!"

—Robert E. Howard
"The Pool of the Black One" (1933)

Summary

Conan, having wandered far from his homeland in the remote **wilderness** of Cimmeria, and having gained much experience from serving in the armies of various **civilized** countries, is now **king** of Aquilonia, a major country in the western Hyborian world. He is a successful monarch, but his enemies resurrect an ancient, Sauron-like **wizard** from the remote past, Xaltotun of Acheron, with whose help Conan is deposed and captured. He later **escapes**, venturing to far Khitai (see **China**) and Stygia (see **Egypt**), finally obtaining the Heart of Ahriman, a magical gem that can destroy the wizard (see **Magical Objects**). The wizard had, meanwhile, betrayed all his confederates and is on the verge of magically turning back **time**, restoring the world to the era when Acheron ruled over all—before Conan stops him.

Discussion

Through the imagery of Frank Frazetta paintings, comic books, and Arnold Schwarzenegger movies, Robert E. Howard's Conan the Barbarian has become as much an icon as Robin Hood in Lincoln green, with his fur loincloth, often worn with heavy boots, his bare but hugely muscled chest, arms, and thighs, drawn **sword**, grimacing face, and, very likely, a horned helmet. Readers of Howard, however, know that the hero was a lot more complex than that—and dressed more sensibly.

Newcomers may be surprised to learn that Howard wrote only one Conan novel, serialized in *Weird Tales* in 1935 and 1936 as "The Hour of the Dragon," referring to the time of chaos unleashed by the events in the story; the title was changed for obvious commercial reasons to *Conan the Conqueror* for book publication, though restored to Howard's original title in some later editions. It is also, chronologically, the final Conan story, at least as written by Howard, though pastiche-writers have extended the saga beyond it.

The entire story is absolutely archetypal, and has been replayed again and again in comic books, pastiches, and **heroic fantasy** generally. The character of Conan is likewise an archetype: the almost feral man, born outside **civilization** with primitive strengths and attributes civilized people have lost. Thus he is an outsider and misfit, although he is superior to most of the men around him, in strength, cunning, and a rugged sense of honor.

While it is always dangerous to read biographical details into fictional characters, Conan does seem an idealized version of his creator. Howard, too, felt out of place in the Texas backcountry where he lived. His letters are filled with arguments about the superiority of barbarism over civilization and the idealization of certain types of **barbarians**, particularly Celts. At the same time, Howard was no "noble savage" sentimentalist. He was well aware that barbaric life is brutish, nasty, and short, but at least in the **dreams** of his fiction, he preferred the **freedom** of a wandering Conan to the dull life of a modern man tied down to **family** and job. Howard's own life, as is evident from numerous sources, was quite unsatisfactory. He was stifled by small-town life, cultural isolation, and a family situation that included an overbearing **father** and a clinging, invalid **mother** to whom he was by all accounts devoted. He committed **suicide** at age thirty, as soon as he learned that his mother was in her final coma, perhaps because he could not bear to go on without her, or because he felt that now his duty to her had been discharged, and he was no longer obligated to endure the misery of existence. In any case, Howard was clearly in need of escape and emotional release. His stories seethe with rage and passion.

Once the Conan stories, novelettes, and novellas, most originally published in *Weird Tales*, began to appear in book form in the 1950s, and, more importantly, in mass-market paperbacks edited by L. Sprague de Camp in the 1960s, Howard became enormously popular, leading to volumes featuring incomplete Howard stories finished by other writers as well as non-Conan stories about other **heroes** rewritten to feature Conan. More recent editions, however, endeavor to present Howard's works in their original form. The Conan books also created a whole new market niche in which any number of other such barbarian heroes battled wizards and **monsters** in mock-antique worlds very much like Howard's. As such, Howard was one of the two major forces in the creation of modern fantasy, the other being J.R.R. Tolkien (see *The Lord of the Rings*). To them, writers of **imaginary world** fantasies owe virtually everything.

Howard's Hyborian Age is not a model of world-building. Certainly it lacks the meticulous consistency of Tolkien's Middle-earth and is a riot of anachronisms and undigested influences. Indeed, some Conan stories pastiche **pirate** movies, Harold Lamb's stories of Cossacks, or even Robert W. Chambers's novels of Indian Wars in upstate New York. Yet ultimately it does not matter. Each individual Conan story is vivid, poetic, and emotionally intense enough to sweep aside any such objections. Howard imagined that Conan crouched down by his side and began to regale him with tales of wild adventures, out of sequence, as they occurred to him, without much regard for any intellectual or scholarly constructs—and that is how Howard wrote them. The Conan stories may be naive art, but they are still, in their own way, great art.

Bibliography

Marc A. Cerasini and Charles Hoffman. *Robert E. Howard*. Mercer Island, WA: Starmont House, 1987.

L. Sprague de Camp. *The Conan Reader*. Baltimore: Mirage Press, 1968.

L. Sprague de Camp, with George H. Scithers, eds. *The Conan Swordbook*. Baltimore: Mirage Press, 1969.

———. *The Conan Grimoire*. Baltimore: Mirage Press, 1972.

Novalyne Price Ellis. *One Who Walked Alone*. West Kingston, RI: Donald M. Grant, 1986.

Don Herron, ed. *The Dark Barbarian*. Westport, CT: Greenwood Press, 1984.

Robert E. Howard. *Selected Letters, 1923-1930*. Ed. Glenn Lord with Rusty Burke and S.T. Joshi. West Warwick, RI: Necronomicon Press, 1989.

———. *Selected Letters, 1931-1936*. Ed. Glenn Lord with Rusty Burke, S.T. Joshi, and Steve Behrends. West Warwick, RI: Necronomicon Press, 1991.

E. Hoffman Price. "Robert Ervin Howard." Price, *Book of the Dead*. Sauk City, WI: Arkham House, 2001, 70–93.

—Darrell Schweitzer

A CONNECTICUT YANKEE IN KING ARTHUR'S COURT BY MARK TWAIN (1889)

Summary

When Hank Morgan, a foreman at the Colt arms plant in Hartford, receives a blow to the head, he is transported back in **time** to the days of King **Arthur**. Using modern scientific **knowledge**, Hank saves his own life by presenting himself as a powerful **wizard**, and becomes Arthur's all-powerful factotum, Sir Boss, while beginning a long-term feud with rival wizard Merlin. Convinced of the superiority of modern ways, Hank begins to transform the kingdom, introducing such modern ideas as **journalism, advertising,** and advanced **technology** starting with explosives. He goes on knightly **quests**, marries the lady Alisande, and has a child named Hello Central after his **memories** of a telephone girl back home.

Disturbed by the feudal **governance system**, he persuades Arthur to join him in traveling incognito, to demonstrate the faults of the system. After they are sold into **slavery** and then rescued, reform is finally in sight, but Hank's hopes are dashed when the church turns the kingdom against him. In a final battle with the massed knight errantry, Hank slaughters thousands of opponents and blows up all his factories. Put to long-term **sleep** by the dying Merlin, Hank awakes in his own time, exiled from his wife and child and all he has come to **love**.

Discussion

Twain's novel is the precursor of **time travel** stories, the first story in which the protagonist travels physically back in time, and it is arguably an **alternate history** in depicting a medieval world altered by Hank's intervention. It has spawned parallel tales of anachronistic encounters like L. Sprague de Camp's *Lest Darkness Fall* (1941), a optimistic revision in which a traveler to the past—here the late Roman Empire—successfully "improves" **history**, and Poul Anderson's *The High Crusade* (1960), in which medieval knights defeat an alien **invasion** and proceed to conquer the galaxy.

The work is a blend of **comedy, satire** and **tragedy**, which sometimes confuses readers. At the simplest level (which has influenced film adaptations), it is a comedy of two **cultures** meeting—American slang contrasted with prose lifted from Thomas Malory's *Le Morte d'Arthur* (1485), knights in armor riding bicycles. Twain himself reported that the idea for the novel stemmed from an incongrous mental image of a knight smoking a cigar. However, even this humorous juxtaposition of past and present evolves into serious interrogation, as Twain satirizes **medievalism and the Middle Ages** to attack the **romanticism** of Walter Scott: it turns out that **castles** are drafty, suits of armor uncomfortable, and people far too credulous. Even **humor** itself is mocked, as bad jokes from Twain's time appear in the time of Arthur.

Twain's satire also becomes a critique of the differences between old **Europe** and new **America**, as Hank objects to the **class system**, lectures middle-class Englishmen on **economics**, and tries to mitigate Morgan le Fay's use of **torture**. The concept of **chivalry** is challenged when the knights are revealed to be lacking in **ethics** and utterly uncaring about people below their class, although Arthur does show great moral **courage** when he helps a sick family in a plague house. **Christianity** is gently spoofed at first, as when a hermit's **ritual** bowing in prayer is used to run a sewing machine, but later the church is shown as devoted to its own power.

Hank himself is no modern saint. He claims to want to root out superstition, but he masks his technology as **divination** and **magic** to maintain his power, behaving precisely like the colonialists that Twain despised. As Merlin's final **revenge** plays out, Hank destroys the modern **civilization** he has created simply to keep it out of the hands of his enemies. The final **absurdity** is that the only lasting impact of the reign of Sir Boss is a bullet-hole in a suit of armor, which moderns blame on Cromwell's troops.

Richard Rodgers and Lorenz Hart adapted Twain's novel as a Broadway musical, *A Connecticut Yankee* (1927), and there have also been many film adaptations, though these are typically comic, playing off the contrast of American and medieval cultures while giving little or no attention to Twain's more biting satire or the tragedy of the conclusion. The relatively straightforward adaptations are the silent *A Connecticut Yankee in King Arthur's Court* (1921), *A Connecticut Yankee* (1931) with Will Rogers, Bing Crosby's musical *A Connecticut Yankee in King Arthur's Court* (1949), and a television movie, *A Connecticut Yankee in King Arthur's Court* (1989). More extravagant fantasy elements appear in the Bugs Bunny television cartoon *A Connecticut Rabbit in King Arthur's Court* (1978) and *The Spaceman and King Arthur* (1979), while other, more recent versions replace Hank Morgan with a teenage protagonist: *A Kid in King Arthur's Court* (1995), *A Young Connecticut Yankee in King Arthur's Court* (1995), and, on television with Whoopi Goldberg, *A Knight in Camelot* (1998). However, as is also the case with Twain's *The Adventures of Huckleberry Finn* (1884), no adaptation to date has really done justice to Twain's original vision.

Bibliography

Lawrence I. Berkove. "*Connecticut Yankee.*" James S. Leonard, ed., *Making Mark Twain Work in the Classroom*. Durham, N.C.: Duke University Press, 1999, 88–109.

William J. Collins. "Hank Morgan in the Garden of Forking Paths." *Modern Fiction Studies*, 32 (1986), 109–114.

Bud Foote. *The Connecticut Yankee in the Twentieth Century*. Westport, CT: Greenwood Press, 1991.

Jane Gardiner. "A More Splendid Necromancy." *Studies in the Novel*, 19 (1987), 448–458.

Roger George. "The Road Lieth Not Straight." *ATQ*, 5 (1991), 57–67.

Kevin J. Harty. "Cinematic American Camelots Lost and Found." Harty, *Cinema Arthuriana*. Revised. Jefferson, NC: McFarland, 2002, 96–109.

Donald L. Hoffman. "Mark's Merlin." Sally K. Slocum, ed., *Popular Arthurian Traditions*. Bowling Green, OH: Bowling Green State University Popular Press, 1992, 46–55.

Lee Clark Mitchell. "Lines, Circles, Time Loops, and Mark Twain's *A Connecticut Yankee in King Arthur's Court*." *Nineteenth-Century Literature*, 54 (1999), 230–248.

Thomas D. Zlatic. "Language Technologies in *A Connecticut Yankee*." *Nineteenth-Century Literature*, 45 (1991), 453–477.

—A. William Pett

Consider Phlebas by Iain M. Banks (1987)

■

Summary

Iain Banks had immediate British success with the grotesque **horror** and **humor** of his debut *The Wasp Factory* (1984), followed by the increasingly fantastical, metafictional *Walking on Glass* (1985) and *The Bridge* (1986). *Consider Phlebas* surprisingly applied the same exuberant narrative energy to **space opera**, for which Banks uses his middle initial.

The background is an immense **space war** between the vaguely communist Culture and the more conventional Idiran **galactic empire**. Exotic **weaponry** abounds (see **Antimatter; Hyperspace**) and many **space habitats, planetary colonies** and even **stars** are destroyed. The protagonist is a humanoid "Changer" capable of **disguise** through limited **metamorphosis**. Fighting for the **religion**-driven Idirans, he see much **violence, torture,** and spectacular action on his freewheeling interstellar **quest** for a valuable Culture AI "Mind" (see **Computers**). The destructive climax occurs deep underground in a dead world's railway **transportation** system.

The enemy Culture is a genuine if ambiguous **utopia** with an economy of abundance, thanks to **technology** that extracts free energy from hyperspace. It has flaws, notably an **America**-like tendency to meddle with less developed **civilizations**, but it is far preferable to the hidebound, bellicose Empire. With dark irony, the Changer—who ultimately fails—has chosen the wrong side.

Discussion

Banks's initial strategy for importing narrative tension into utopia was to show the Culture in conflict. **War** with the Idirans in *Consider Phlebas* was followed by the subtler undermining of an unpleasant though much smaller galactic empire in *The Player of Games* (1988). Here the Empire of Azad is an oppressive maelstrom of unchecked market forces (some **satire** on Thatcherite Britain was inferred by critics), riddled with sadism, racism against aliens (see **Race Relations**), and **sexism** complicated by three-gendered **sexuality**. But advancement is theoretically possible to anyone through victory in the complex **game** of azad, whose tension and savagery precisely **mirrors** Empire **culture**. Special Circumstances, the Culture's dirty-tricks department, therefore manipulates the human games-master **hero** into challenging the system by entering the latest Azad tournament. Neither the Empire nor the Culture (in the shape of the hero's **robot** drone assistant) plays fair; the hero is pushed to his limits and beyond. All ends satisfyingly despite **betrayal, fire,** and **apocalypse**.

Less cheerfully, *The State of the Art* (1989) shows **Earth** from the viewpoint of a covert Culture observation team. There is Kiplingesque horror in the portrayal of a visitor who goes native, accepting the local afflictions of disease (see **Plagues and Diseases**) and **death**. Our society cannot, in Culture terms, be called civilization.

But a less savory side of the Culture is highlighted in *Use of Weapons* (1990), whose interwoven story lines move forward and backward in **time**. A weaponry-loving Special Circumstances mercenary, veteran of all too many botched wars and messy interventions, is reactivated for a new mission. Meanwhile, deeper and deeper flashbacks home in on a major early trauma of his whose symbols (a woman, a chair, immobilized transportation) resonate throughout. At the book's disturbing core, confusions of **memory** and **identity** are resolved by a dazzling **role reversal**. The Culture must share the **guilt and responsibility** of its tool.

The discovery of a huge, powerful and enigmatic artifact from another universe in *Excession* (1996) serves as a catalyst to expose factionalism within the Culture. A splinter group of spaceship Minds seizes the opportunity to foment "just" war against the Affront, **aliens in space** who revel in outrageous acts. Other powerful Minds are concerned for the status quo. Human participation, though consistently entertaining, is chiefly in spectator roles. There is a sense that Culture Minds regard **humanity** as pets and indulge their whims, though one eccentric Mind-ship has the hobby of thoroughly punishing human war criminals (see **Crime and Punishment**). Wisps of unease are almost lost in extravagant large-scale action and Banks's characteristic inventiveness.

Reverting to a human scale, *Inversions* (1998) is another tricky novel, part of whose deception is that it is a Culture book in disguise. Two obscurely linked outsiders, a female doctor and a male bodyguard, serve rival countries—a kingdom (see **Kings**) and a Cromwellian protectorate—on a backward world. There is much small-scale violence, skullduggery, torture, poison, intrigue, and assassination. The mirror-image relationship between the outsiders is slowly made clear (with several surprises), while the tussle of local **politics** resolves unexpectedly. To readers unfamiliar with significant references to "Culture" and "special circumstances," the disguised robot weapon that saves one emissary must seem **magic**—a **deus ex machina**.

Previous hints of Culture **decadence** are reinforced in *Look to Windward* (2000)—another title taken from T.S. Eliot's *The Waste Land* (1922). Humans with little purpose in life are seen vapidly enjoying extreme sports, usually with a hidden technological safety-net (see **Teleportation**). A significant occasion looms on the **habitat** where the action is mostly set: the arrival of the dying **light**-flare of a sun detonated in the Idiran war 800 years before. From an alien world where Culture intervention went badly and much more recently went wrong, a terrorist strike is planned. The conclusion features multiple **suicides**, a shocking **revenge**, and a segue into the very **far future** where the Culture itself may be long gone. Banks's exhilarating style and wit often hides dark abysses.

Bibliography

Sara M. Alegre. "Consider Banks." *Revista Canaria de Estudios Ingeleses*, 41 (November, 2000), 197–205.

Carolyn Brown. "Utopias and Heterotopias." Derek Littlewood and Peter Stockwell, eds. *Impossibility Fiction*. Amsterdam: Rodopi, 1996, 57–74.

Colin Greenland. "*Use of Weapons*." *Foundation*, No. 50 (Autumn 1990), 91–94.

Simon Guerrier. "Culture Theory." *Foundation*, No. 76 (Summer, 1999), 28–38.

William H. Hardesty. "Mercenaries and Special Circumstances." *Foundation*, No. 76 (Summer, 1999), 39–47.

———. "Space Opera Without the Space." Gary Westfahl, ed., *Space and Beyond*. Westport, CT: Greenwood Press, 2000, 115–122.

Ronnie Lippens. "Imachinations of Peace." *Utopian Studies*, 13 (2002), 135–147.

Stan Nicholls. "Iain M. Banks." Nicholls, *Wordsmiths of Wonder*. London: Orbit, 1993, 137–142.

Lawrence Person. "The Culture-D Space Opera of Iain M. Banks." *Science Fiction Eye*, No. 6 (February 1990), 33–36.

—David Langford

D

DAWN BY OCTAVIA E. BUTLER (1987)

For a moment, she saw Nikanj as she had once seen Jdahya C as a totally alien being, grotesque, repellant beyond mere ugliness with its night crawler body tentacles, its snake head tentacles, and its tendency to keep both moving, signaling attention and emotion . . . . She stared at it for a moment longer, wondering how she had lost her horror of such a being. Then she lay down, perversely eager for what it could give her.

—Octavia E. Butler
Dawn (1987)

Summary

Dawn, the first novel in Octavia E. Butler's Xenogenesis trilogy, is set in the future and depicts the adaptation of Lilith Iyapo, a survivor of a **nuclear war** on **Earth**, to life with an alien species, the Oankali. Lilith awakens from stasis on an organic Oankali spaceship and learns that the aliens have rescued her and other human survivors of the nuclear catastrophe. The Oankali are an ever-changing, nonviolent, egalitarian species who depend on **genetic engineering** and the collection of new genetic material. They expect **humanity** to either join them and be healed or live out its remaining days left sterile by the nuclear war. The Oankali refuse to let healed humans repopulate Earth on their own because the aliens have identified the essential contradiction in the human condition—**intelligence** paired with the drive to create hierarchies—as the cause of human **violence**. In *Dawn*, Lilith becomes a mediator between Oankali and humans and eventually lives with the aliens, though secretly hoping to **escape**. At the end of the novel, she finds herself pregnant with a human-Oankali daughter.

The second novel in the trilogy, *Adulthood Rites* (1988), narrates the kidnapping of Lilith's human-Oankali son, Akin, by human resisters. Through Akin's eyes the novel depicts the violent behavior of humans who value their genetic purity above all other considerations. The third novel, *Imago* (1989), portrays the adventures of Jodahs, Lilith's first human-Oankali ooloi child. Ooloi are the genetic engineers among the Oankali who are neither male nor female but form a group of their own.

Discussion

The Xenogenesis trilogy questions traditional concepts of **family**. Oankali families have multiple parental members: an ooloi, a male and a female Oankali and, when in **symbiosis** with humans, a male and female human. The ooloi intermediary is needed to facilitate procreation as well as the blending of genes, eventually implanting a carefully designed fertilized egg in a female family member. The ooloi use only their own complex bodies to accomplish this, and they control precisely which characteristics a child will have. Ooloi who live in a five-member, human-Oankali family design constructs, beings with human and Oankali characteristics and abilities. Ooloi can also cause controlled **mutations** in their environment.

Love, **sexuality**, and desire in Oankali society are governed largely by biochemical processes instead of human concepts of attraction, **friendship**, or adherence to **taboos**. When undergoing a **metamorphosis** in its life, an adolescent ooloi must set out to find a couple with whom to mate. The ooloi then biochemically bonds with the man and woman. This bond makes the couple dependent on the ooloi, preventing mates from leaving the symbiosis. The Oankali world contradicts human **biology** and **psychology**. Couples cannot mate or procreate on their own: paired nonooloi experience revulsion should they try to approach one another without the ooloi's facilitation. At the same time, the ooloi can amplify feelings of pleasure in its mates, rewarding them for the symbiosis. When needing to find a couple and complete metamorphosis, the ooloi must bond with a man and woman at all cost: Jodahs, for example, seduces a human brother-sister pair and heals them of diseases caused by radiation. Ironically, for all their ability to exert peaceful restraint, the ooloi have drives they cannot resist, drives that can lead to deceitful, coercive, or violent acts.

Additionally, the Xenogenesis trilogy focuses on the themes of health, healing, and biological and genetic change. The Oankali are able to connect with any organism by **touch** and then analyze its genetic makeup; in fact, they have a drive to constantly collect new genetic information and construct new generations with new abilities and traits. Additionally, they are able to alter the genetic characteristics of any organism if they are able to establish physical contact. The Oankali can practice organic **medicine** (i.e., without **technology**) effectively in all but the gravest of cases (such as fatal injuries). Their promise to humanity is a very long life without illnesses in an egalitarian society without violence. The Oankali's strictly benevolent use of their healing abilities could benefit all humans.

However, humanity in this trilogy—as in other Butler novels—is violent, unrestrained, and cruel. Most humans are repulsed by the Oankali and believe that the only form of acceptable **survival** requires living outside of Oankali society and maintaining human genetic purity. However, this is impossible without Oankali help, as almost all humans are sterile and ill. The main objective for many humans is to resist what they see as an alien **invasion**. Overall, the trilogy asks if the Oankali are taking their efforts—which recall the eugenicist movement—too far, or if humans are going too far in their stubborn insistence on unadulterated genetic purity. The novels can at once be understood as a commentary on humanity's history of **race relations** and **xenophobia** as well as on humanity's experiments with eugenics.

Bibliography

Frances Bonner. "Difference and Desire, Slavery and Seduction." *Foundation*, No. 48 (Spring, 1990), 50–62.

Amanda Boulter. "Polymorphous Futures." Tim Armstrong, ed., *American Bodies*. New York: New York University Press, 1996, 170–185.

Gregory Jerome Hampton. "Octavia Butler and Virginia Hamilton." *English Journal*, 96 (July, 2003), 70–74.

Rebecca J. Holden. "The High Cost of Cyborg Survival." *Foundation*, No. 72 (Spring, 1998), 49–56.

Naomi Jacobs. "Posthuman Bodies and Agency in Octavia Butler's Xenogenesis." Raffaella Baccolini and Tom Moylan, eds., *Dark Horizons*. New York: Routledge, 2003, 91–112.

Nancy Jesser. "Blood, Genes and Gender in Octavia Butler's *Kindred* and *Dawn*." *Extrapolation*, 43 (Spring, 2002), 36–61.

Michelle Osherow. "The Dawn of a New Lilith." *NWSA Journal*, 12 (Spring, 2000), 68–83.

Stephanie A. Smith. "Morphing, Materialism, and the Marketing of Xenogenesis." *Genders*, No. 18 (Winter, 1993), 67–86.

Eric White. "The Erotics of Becoming." *Science-Fiction Studies*, 20 (November, 1993), 394–408.

—*Éva Tettenborn*

THE DAY OF THE TRIFFIDS BY JOHN WYNDHAM (1951)

Summary

Recovering in a hospital from damage to his eyes, Bill Masen is prevented from seeing the green **light** of a meteor shower. Awakening, he discovers that the rest of the hospital, perhaps the world, is blind (see **Vision and Blindness**). He rescues another sighted person, Josella Playton, but the world has descended into chaos. This **disaster** has been made worse by **humanity**'s new vulnerability to triffids, biologically engineered carnivorous **plants** raised for their oil and possessors of lethal stings. At first the few survivors squabble about strategies for **survival**. Bill and Josella are captured by a group led by the populist Coker and forced to help groups of blind people scavenge among the ruins of London. When plague strikes, Bill **escapes** and again encounters Coker, who has changed his mind about the practicality of saving as many blind people as possible before rescue arrives. Becoming friends, they join a survivor group in the country, but Bill decides to continue his search for Josella, whom he finds with several others in an isolated **farm**. A visit from a semi-fascist group intent on establishing a feudal regime makes them accept an invitation to join another set of survivors on the Isle of Wight, but they seem to be developing a stable basis for regaining some sort of **civilization**.

Discussion

A **near future** extrapolation of 1950s **anxiety** about **invasion, nuclear war,** and social breakdown, *The Day of the Triffids* expresses this anxiety through a sense of impending **apocalypse**. Wyndham's attempt to expand from a traditional science fiction audience toward a more mainstream one made the novel a best-seller. It has remained in print since publication and has been dramatized several times for radio, television, and film.

The collapse of society, and Masen's exposure to several groups of survivors, make it clear that all agreed bases for **community** have been changed: but what are the new ones? What responsibility do the sighted have to the blind? Do traditional **gender** roles and questions of sexual behavior have relevance in a world where female fertility has become a prize? The novel explores rather than definitively answers these questions. Masen's companions Josella and Coker are quicker on the uptake than he is—there is sly **humor** in the way Josella understands the need for polygamy and insists on choosing Masen's "other" wives before he has worked out the implications—but his detachment makes these themes integral to the plot, not separate discussions. It is Masen, however, who insists that, in a world with satellite **weaponry** and international tensions, the blinding cannot necessarily be plausibly explained as the result of a "comet" or "meteor shower." Masen himself is rescued sometimes too easily from moral dilemmas by turns in the plot, but the dilemmas are hard and real.

While there are scenes that suggest a kind of reveling in the Crusoe-like state of being a survivor able to live off the wreckage of civilization (see **Last Man**), Wyndham satirizes this stance as much as he gives in to it (see **Satire**). Masen and Josella at one point take refuge in a luxury apartment, where she dresses in finery. But their idyll is soundtracked by the noise of panic and **suicides**, and Masen's sexual nervousness underlies the occasion's sybaritic qualities.

Although Masen narrates, Wyndham distributes viewpoint through several characters, including the illegitimate working-class Coker who is in some ways more dominant. Coker leads questions about survival, and criticizes—sometimes crassly—the refusal of some female characters to step out of their conditioned roles. His class background also allows one criticism of the novel—that it is in some way a metaphor for fear of the changing British **class system**, threatening the increasingly precarious position of middle-class people like Masen (or Wyndham)—to be addressed, if not comprehensively refuted. Through Coker and Josella (author of a sexually provocative novel), Wyndham's proto-**feminism**, although crude, also becomes a genuine topic for debate. The coming-together of Masen, Josella, and two (unrelated) **children** among the survivors suggest ideas about **family** and metaphorical **islands** of safety in juxtaposition with the real island to which the group retreats.

The strength of the plot is the way it allows *two* disasters to combine and reinforce one another as if through a series of feedback loops. The triffids are only harmful *when* the advantage humanity has over them—sight—is removed. But the potential danger is in allowing humanity to be dominated by the benefits of **genetic**

engineering without considering the malign possibilities. We pay the price. Both triffids and—if Masen is to be believed—blindness are caused by *metaphorical* myopia that prevents us from foreseeing consequences. It is this metaphorical element that makes the 1963 film version as interesting as it is, unfortunately, unsuccessful. A scene (not from the novel) in an airliner after the blinding shows us crew and passengers attempting to deal with the disaster with an air of repressed normality. It is when a child innocently asks whether the pilot is blind, too, that all the suppressed panic is released. A 1981 televised version by the BBC is more successful but has never been re-released.

Bibliography

Thomas D. Clareson and Alice S. Clareson. "The Neglected Fiction of John Wyndham." Rhys Garnett and R.J. Ellis, eds., *Science Fiction Roots and Branches*. London: Macmillan, 1990, 88–103.

David Ketterer, "John Wyndham and 'the Searing Anguishes of Childhood.'" *Extrapolation*, 41 (Summer, 2000), 87–103.

David Ketterer. "Questions and Answers." *New York Review of Science Fiction*, No. 187 (March, 2004), 1, 6–10.

Colin Manlove. "Everything Slipping Away." *Journal of the Fantastic in the Arts*, 4 (1991), 29–53.

Sam Moskowitz. "SF Profile: John Wyndham." *Amazing Stories*, 38 (June, 1964), 29–40.

Andy Sawyer. "John Wyndham on Screen." I.Q. Hunter, ed., *British Science Fiction Cinema*. London: Routledge, 1999, 75–87.

Maureen Kincaid Speller. "Skiffy Stuff." *Banana Wings*, 11 (1998), 53–58.

Owen Webster. "John Wyndham as Novelist of Ideas." *Science Fiction Commentary*, No. 44/45 (December, 1975), 39–58.

Rowland Wymer. How 'Safe' Is John Wyndham?" *Foundation*, No. 55 (Summer, 1992), 25–36.

—Andy Sawyer

THE DAY THE EARTH STOOD STILL (1951)

I'm impatient with stupidity. My people have learned to live without it.

—Edmund H. North
The Day the Earth Stood Still (1951)

Summary

When a **UFO** lands in Washington DC its occupant, Klaatu, is not treated with ambassadorial respect but is shot by a trigger-happy soldier mistaking his **gift** for a weapon. Taken to a hospital, Klaatu heals quickly. He requests an audience with all the world's leaders but is informed that this would be impossible in the current political climate. This, however, is precisely the reason for his visit—**humanity**'s propensity towards **violence** poses a grave threat to the future safety of the known universe. The choice is stark: the world must police its arms or there will be no alternative but to destroy **Earth** for the greater good. To show he has the power to realize this, Klaatu has briefly allowed his hulking **robot** Gort to unleash deadly rays on military hardware. Adopting a disguise, Klaatu **escapes** the authorities and rents a room at a boarding house, where he meets Helen Benson and her son Bobby, from whom he learns the nature of humanity. With the help of Professor Barnhardt he plans to gather together the world's scientific community to deliver his message and implements a grandiose scheme that will stop all the world's machines from working for half an hour. However, the authorities close in on him and he is killed. With Helen's help, Gort revives Klaatu long enough to deliver his ultimatum.

Discussion

Robert Wise's *The Day the Earth Stood Still* presents a twist on the usual **aliens on Earth** scenario because the film portrays a **first contact** involving aliens that neither require our help nor threaten **invasion**. Describing himself as a neighbor, probably from **Mars** or Venus, Klaatu represents a genuine threat to humanity because of the reluctant necessity he feels in unleashing **disaster** upon the world if it does not comply with his requests. This paradox is one of many that typify the film—the threat of unimaginable violence as a means to prevent **war**. Klaatu's **technology** may be far ahead of ours but it stems from known principles—the **nuclear power** that poses such a threat to the universe is also the benevolent fuel behind his **space travel**. Similarly Gort, a robot built for ultimate force, is an instrument of peace; the fragile **cycle** of **war** and peace will need to be curtailed when Earth has realized its place in the greater universe.

Klaatu's interaction with the everyday folk when he is in **disguise** shows the extent of his technological and intellectual superiority. His adoption of Bobby as his guide is deliberate not only in the perceived use of **children** as honest but naïve voices, but because, in some respects, we are all children to Klaatu. This manifests itself both in a physical sense because, despite his looks, he is well into his seventies due to advancements in **medicine** (see **Immortality and Longevity**) and also in his paternal attitude towards humans. He approaches the world's top **scientists** as his allies but treats their knowledge as no different than Bobby's, correcting Professor Barnhardt's equations in a manner not dissimilar to helping the boy with his **mathematics** homework. By becoming a **mentor** for Bobby he ultimately becomes both a surrogate **father** and a confidant of Helen, showing that fatherhood involves interaction and compassion, two traits her current beau lacks.

His separation from human primitivism has made him naïve in his own way: he expects all the world leaders to acquiesce to his request for an audience without understanding the nature of world **politics**. He can communicate because he has been monitoring Earth's activities and, although his motives are discussed by the media (see **Journalism; Television and Radio**), he fails to exploit the global potential that it offers him. His only opportunity for media exposure is an abruptly curtailed sound-bite, delivered when standing in the crowd with Bobby, gazing speculatively at his own spaceship.

Despite his apparent role as an intergalactic emissary, Klaatu begins to become a messianic (see **Messiahs**) figure as his life becomes a metaphor for **Christianity**. He comes to bring peace to the people of Earth but must endure hardship and **sacrifice** to get that message across. Eventually he is executed only to be reborn (see **Rebirth**) before delivering his final dictum and ascending once more into the heavens.

Wise's film differs substantially from its source, "Farewell to the Master" by Harry Bates (1940). Here Klaatu is killed on arrival and the robot Gnut attempts to reverse engineer him from tape recordings of his voice. There is also an implication that Gnut is perhaps a time traveler rather than a space traveler (see **Time Travel**), and the concern about dire consequences resulting from Klaatu's death is not the result of an explicit threat.

The Day the Earth Stood Still remains a key film in the science fiction genre. Although influential, its success has paradoxically resulted in few imitators, probably because themes of invasion and war are more proven box-office draws than peace and reconciliation.

Bibliography

Allan Asherman. "Man Who Was Klaatu: Michael Rennie." *Filmfax*, 17 (November, 1989), 74–79.

Leroy W. Dubeck, Suzanne E. Moshier and Judith E. Boss. "*The Day the Earth Stood Still*." Dubeck, Moshier, and Boss, eds., *Science in Cinema*. New York: Teacher's College Press, 1988.

Krin Gabbard. "Religions and Political Allegory in Robert Wise's *The Day the Earth Stood Still*." *Literature/Film Quarterly*, 10 (July, 1982), 150–154.

Cyndy Hendershot. "The Atomic Scientist, Science Fiction Films, and Paranoia." *Journal of American Culture*, 20 (Spring, 1997), 31–41.

Laura Long. "Klaatu, Gort & I." *Starlog*, No. 151 (February, 1990), 26–27.

Steve Rubin. "Retrospect: *The Day the Earth Stood Still*." *Cinefantastique*, 4 (Winter, 1976), 4–23.

Al Taylor and Doug Finch. "Director Robert Wise Remembers *The Day the Earth Stood Still*." *Fantastic Films*, 4 (April, 1982), 20–21, 54.

Gary Westfahl. "Martians Old and New, Still Standing Over Us." *Interzone*, No. 168 (June, 2001), 57–58.

Michael J. Wolff. "After the Earth Stood Still." *Starlog*, No. 211 (February, 1995), 19–23, 69.

—*Michelle Le Blanc and Colin Odell*

DEATHBIRD STORIES: A PANTHEON OF MODERN GODS BY HARLAN ELLISON (1975)

■

The Deathbird closed its wings over the Earth until at last, at the end, there was only the great bird crouched over the dead cinder. Then the Deathbird raised its head to the star-filled sky and repeated the sigh of loss the Earth had felt at the end. Then

> *its eyes closed, it twitched its head care-*
> *fully under its wing, and all was night.*
>
> —Harlan Ellison
> "The Deathbird" (1973)

Summary

Harlan Ellison's *Deathbird Stories: A Pantheon of Modern Gods*, often considered one of his best books, collects nineteen stories published between 1960 and 1974. Ellison's most thematically unified collection, *Deathbird Stories* deals, as the introduction indicates, with the ideas that **gods and goddesses** exist only if people believe and that modern times elicit modern deities. While many stories concern various modern-day gods, the theme is not obvious in all stories, which range from science fiction to fantasy to **horror** to, in some cases, combinations of these modes.

Clearly science fiction is "Along the Scenic Route" (1969), about legalized duels between drivers of **automobiles** loaded with advanced **weaponry**. Three stories— "Paingod" (1964), "The Place with No Name" (1969), and "The Deathbird" (1973)—concern **aliens in space** and **aliens on Earth** who possess god-like attributes. Another story, "Neon" (1973), features a **cyborg**. Both "Shattered Like a Glass Goblin" (1968) and "Bleeding Stones" (1973) are horror.

Fantasy dominates the collection, as the remainder of the stories includes characters and creatures such as ghosts (see **Ghosts and Hauntings**), **unicorns,** supernatural snakes (see **Snakes and Worms**), **dragons,** and assorted deities and **supernatural creatures**, with situations that include other realms, **magic** shops, and **metamorphoses**, almost all of which are set in **cities** in contemporary **America**. Most stories are traditional in form, though "At the Mouse Circus" employs **surrealism** and "The Deathbird" **postmodernism**.

Discussion

Ellison treats the central theme of *Deathbird Stories*, the nature of gods and their relationship to humanity, in various ways. Sometimes the gods or god figures are benevolent, like the snake-like alien whose enemy demonized her as **Satan** in "The Deathbird" and the well-intentioned aliens known as Jesus and Prometheus in "The Place with No Name." More often, Ellison's deities are malevolent, like the god-like computer in his "I Have No Mouth, and I Must Scream" (1967). Examples here include the deranged god to whom an alien race grants control of Earth in "The Deathbird"; the god who feeds on urban **violence** in "The Whimper of Whipped Dogs" (1973); Mars, the god of war from Roman **mythology**, in "Basilisk" (1972); the vengeful gods of machines in "Corpse" (1972) and "Ernest and the Machine God" (1968); the pagan gods who create a supermodel succubus in "The Face of Helene Bournouw" (1960); and the deity of "Rock God" (1969). The god-like alien who dispenses **pain** throughout the universe in "Paingod" also seems malevolent, but after learning about pain directly through **possession** of a human he comes to see it as something that can help people.

Other stories also deal with characters whose fates are determined within supernatural circumstances, often through moral tests. The ghost in "On the Downhill Side" (1972) can **escape** his fate if another ghost chooses to **love** him; he is aided by his unicorn's **sacrifice**. In "O Ye of Little Faith" (1968) a man who cannot believe in anything visits a fortuneteller; when he attacks her he is plunged into a realm of supernatural beings who cannot believe in *him*. Both "Pretty Maggie Moneyeyes" (1967) and "The Place with No Name" involve characters being supernaturally trapped until they can find others to take their places, while in "Delusion for a Dragon Slayer" (1966) a dying man is transported to a realm of **heroic fantasy** to earn the **Heaven** he desires. Industrial pollution causes stones to bleed and animates gargoyles, who embark on a bloody killing spree in "Bleeding Stones," while **drugs** and spiritual emptiness transform a group of counterculture **youth** into **vampires, werewolves,** and **goblins** who destroy themselves and each other in "Shattered Like a Glass Goblin."

Moral tests are also central to the two longest and best stories. In "Adrift Just Off the Islets of Langerhans: Latitude 38° 54′ N, Longitude 77° 00′ 13″ W‴" (1974), Lawrence Talbot, the werewolf from the film *The Wolf Man* (1941), enlists the help of a magically located business and a descendent of Mary Shelley's *Frankenstein* to locate his soul and break the **curse** of his immortality. He accomplishes this by having his **intelligence** transferred to a miniaturized simulacrum to explore his own psyche (see **Miniaturization**); ultimately he chooses life when he sees how he can help others achieve psychic healing as well. In "The Deathbird," which inverts the mythologies of **Judaism** and **Christianity, humanity**'s alien protector aids its savior, originally Adam but reincarnated many times (see **Adam and Eve; Reincarnation**), in a final confrontation with Earth's mad God. Finally, this savior must summon the title's cosmic **bird** to put Earth out of its self-inflicted ecological misery (see **Ecology**).

In addition to destructive supernatural forces, machines and **technology** are also depicted negatively in *Deathbird Stories*, from the killer cars of "Along the Scenic Route" to the industrial pollution in "Bleeding Stones" and "The Deathbird." While his implants and prostheses aid the protagonist of "Neon," they also make him a freak who is then open to seduction by a being who communicates through electric signs. A more positive presentation of technology can be found in "Adrift Just Off the Islets of Langerhans," where Talbot's friend Victor employs his scientific genius to enable Talbot's quest.

Bibliography

Oscar De los Santos. "Clogging Up the (In)Human Works." *Extrapolation*, 40 (Winter, 1999), 5–20.

Joseph Francavilla. "Mythic Hells in Harlan Ellison's Science Fiction." Carl D. Yoke, ed., *Phoenix from the Ashes*. Westport, CT: Greenwood Press, 1987, 157–164.

Darren Harris-Fain. "Created in the Image of God." *Extrapolation*, 32 (Summer, 1991), 143–155.

Peter Malekin. "The Fractured Whole." *Journal of the Fantastic in the Arts*, 1 (1988), 21–26.

Joe Patrouch. "Harlan Ellison's Use of the Narrator's Voice." Donald M. Hassler, ed., *Patterns of the Fantastic*. Mercer Island, WA: Starmont, 1983, 63–66.

Philip M. Rubens, "Descents into Private Hells." *Extrapolation*, 20 (Winter, 1979), 378–385.

George E. Slusser. *Harlan Ellison*. San Bernardino, CA: Borgo Press, 1977.

Ellen R. Weil. "The Ellison Personae." *Journal of the Fantastic in the Arts*, 1 (1988), 27–36.

Ellen Weil and Gary K. Wolfe. *Harlan Ellison*. Columbus: Ohio State University Press, 2002.

—Darren Harris-Fain

THE DEMOLISHED MAN BY ALFRED BESTER (1953)

Summary

This classic treatment of **psychic powers**—specifically telepathy—won the first-ever Hugo award for best novel in 1953, on the strength of its 1952 *Galaxy* magazine serialization.

Anti-**hero** Ben Reich is an obsessed **business** tycoon troubled with bad **dreams** of a "Man With No Face." Convinced that his company Monarch Inc. is losing control of **transportation** to the D'Courtney Cartel, Reich resolves to murder D'Courtney (see **Crime and Punishment**). He must evade the "Esper" **detectives** of 2301, or face erasure of **memory** and **identity**, also known as Demolition.

Reich has many resources: natural killer instinct, **money** to recruit an Esper henchman, ingenuity to infect himself with an obsessive, thought-concealing jingle (see **Poetry**), and Monarch's corporate might to destroy evidence. His nemesis Powell, the telepathic Police Prefect, sees Reich's guilt but despairs of a conviction; unsupported Esper evidence is inadmissible.

The key lies in Reich's **psychology**. An Oedipus complex drives him to kill not for gain but because the hated rival is his **father**—a fact, like D'Courtney's acceptance of a peaceful merger offer, that Reich's mind refuses to register. His self-**betrayal** is actualized in a psychodrama of **apocalypse**, telepathically orchestrated by Powell. Demolition follows as both defeat and healing (see **Medicine**).

Discussion

The real strength of *The Demolished Man* lies in Bester's constant flow of science fiction invention, stylistic energy, and compelling prose tempo. The narrative drive is relentless, hypnotic.

Concealed by a hide-and-seek **game** played in **darkness** at a house party awash with **decadence**, Reich stuns D'Courtney's guards with advanced optical **weaponry** and savagely, needlessly, commits his ingenious murder of an old, dying man (who, it later emerges, was contemplating **suicide** anyway). There is a witness, a girl driven to near-**madness** by this **violence** and sent into a **cycle** of hysterical re-enactment of the scene. Reich must silence her but cannot kill this woman who, not *consciously* known to him, is his half-sister Barbara. The post-crime story becomes a duel between Reich, unscrupulously covering his tracks, and Powell's police (handicapped by rules of evidence) struggling to outwit him. Further killings ensue.

A clue to Reich's state of denial follows his merger offer to D'Courtney, a code **communication** to which the reply is WWHG—seized on with angry triumph as "Refused," although the codebook seen a few pages earlier translates it as ACCEPT OFFER. Another hint is that the police **computer**, assessing the case against Reich, initially reports a passion rather than a profit motive (assumed by Powell to be a machine error).

Echoing the pop-psychological insights, the text contains various knowing sub-Freudian jokes. On the first page, Reich's liquid bed of "carbonated glycerine" at just over **blood** temperature is an almost ludicrously obvious symbol of the womb (see **Birth**) to which Demolition brings metaphorical return. His impregnable safe exists out of phase with normal **time**: a literal time vault. A minor character is a blind voyeur (see **Vision and Blindness**). Reich's first major slip is to reveal awareness of Barbara's near-**nudity** during the crime: thus, punningly, he too exposes himself.

Indeed, Reich becomes literally his own worst enemy. When he seems triumphant, with the police case in ruins, an unknown assassin begins to set deadly booby-traps for him. The unknown is himself, a rejected, denied aspect of personality: the Man With No Face.

Incidental decoration includes Bester's trademark use of typographical patterns, giving the flavour of complexly patterned telepathic conversations. Some characters have shorthand names, anticipating **cyberspace** conventions: "kins, 3maine." The climactic vision of dissolution breaks into incantatory capitals: "ABOLISH. / DESTROY. / DELETE. / DISBAND. / ERASE ALL EQUATIONS. / INFINITY EQUALS ZERO . . . ."

Powell and Reich emerge as oddly linked counterparts, with Reich the metaphorical **evil** twin, though Powell too indulges in minor crime by telling fanciful lies. Balancing Reich's Monarch-developed weaponry, Powell also has the ability to stun foes, via an Esper trick called Basic Neuro Shock. Eventually Reich the loner **villain** is overwhelmed by, literally, the power of the **community**: a mental fusion of telepaths, dangerously channelled by Powell, whose vision is that all **humanity** will one day share his talent. There will be no more lone sociopaths.

All these disparate features combine, synergetically, into a novel of sustained pace and dazzlement that is ultimately—despite a too-portentous closing paragraph—very moving.

Bester's other great science fiction novel *The Stars My Destination* has many significant parallels with *The Demolished Man*. Again the anti-hero, Foyle, is a driven, obsessed man (here motivated by **revenge**) who goes to **war** against an entire Solar **civilization** transformed by the harnessing of psychic powers, in particular **teleportation**. His tools include copious money and unusual weaponry; he is expensively remade into a **cyborg** killer. Decadence abounds, as do Grand-Guignol gestures. Late in the book Foyle, like Reich, faces his own **guilt and responsibility** and undergoes—here voluntarily—spiritual **metamorphosis**.

None of Bester's other book-length work was to match these two early masterpieces. *The Deceivers* (1981), clearly a late attempt to match *The Stars My Destination*, is an embarrassingly pale reiteration of its themes. Bester wrote many fine short stories, but as a novelist he peaked early.

Bibliography

Alfred Bester. "Science Fiction and the Renaissance Man." Basil Davenport, ed., *The Science Fiction Novel*. Chicago: Advent, 1959, 77–96.

Alfred Bester. "Writing and the Demolished Man." Bester, *Alfred Bester Redemolished*. New York: iBooks, 2001, 505–513.

Harold Bloom. "Alfred Bester." Bloom, ed., *Science Fiction Writers of the Golden Age*. New York: Chelsea House, 1995, 47–62.

W.L. Godshalk. "Alfred Bester: Science Fiction or Fantasy?" *Extrapolation*, 16 (May, 1975), 149–155.

Jane Hipolito and Willis E. McNelly. "The Statement is the Self." M.J. Tolley and Kirpal Singh, eds., *The Stellar Gauge*. Carleton, Australia: Norstrilia, 1980, 63–90.

Charles Platt. "Alfred Bester." Platt, *Who Writes Science Fiction?* Manchester, UK: Savoy, 1980, 108–118.

David Pringle. "*The Demolished Man* by Alfred Bester." Pringle, *Science Fiction: The 100 Best Novels*. London: Xanadu, 1985, 33–34.

Jeff Riggenbach. "Science Fiction as Will and Idea." *Riverside Quarterly*, 5 (August, 1972), 168–177.

—David Langford

THE DIFFERENCE ENGINE BY WILLIAM GIBSON AND BRUCE STERLING (1990)

Summary

It is London in the year 1855. A generation ago Lord Byron had become prime minister of Britain, a Britain transformed by Charles Babbage's difference engines, mechanical **computers**. Edward Mallory, a savant, finds himself embroiled in a web of deception and libelous rumors when he rescues Ada Byron at a race course and comes into possession of a box of programming cards. With the aid of Fraser, a policeman, Mallory tries to clear his name and stay alive. One of Mallory's acquaintances, Laurence Oliphant, a writer, diplomat and secret agent (see **Espionage**), searches for Sybil Gerard, daughter of murdered rebel Winstanley Gerard, in order to discredit an enemy of the regime, Charles Egremont. Meanwhile a difference engine, infected with a particular program, grows to sentience.

Discussion

In the 1980s battle lines were drawn in the science fiction genre between the **cyberpunk** writers and the rest—sometimes referred to as humanists. The works of one subgroup, based in Orange County and including Tim Powers, James Blaylock, and K.W. Jeter, were referred to as **steampunk**, and so it was perhaps confusing to see the chief two novelists of cyberpunk collaborating on a steampunk novel. As typical of the subgenre, we find ourselves in a Victorian London, with characters drawn to Whitechapel and the East End, a **city** of horse-drawn carriages and thick fogs, scientific societies and **scientists** at each others' throats, and more advanced **technology** than was present in the nineteenth century.

In this **alternate history** Charles Babbage has succeeded in manufacturing mechanical computers, which were not made in the real world until a century and a half later. This has led to an information society with much **intelligence** gathered about individuals. Lord Byron has not died as a result of battle wounds but has become the leader of a group of radicals and, in time, prime minister of Britain; his opposition comes from Percy Shelley (see **Poetry**), which seems counter to our Shelley's interest in scientific exploration. Other changes are sketched in: the political geography of the United States is vastly different, with Manhattan for example being a communist stronghold under the rule of Karl Marx (see **Governance Systems**).

The great changes are largely offstage, though, even in the tapestry of documents and impressions that make up the epilog, a history of the world between 1830 and 1991. The focus is upon the (imaginary) Edward Mallory, the (real life) Laurence Oliphant (1829–1888), and the (intertextual) Sybil Gerard (from Benjamin Disraeli's *Sybil, or The Two Nations* (1845), which also features the novel's villain, Charles Egremont (see **Metafiction and Recursiveness**). Sybil is one of the weaker elements in the book, being absent for the greater part of its duration, and whilst Edward's experiences fill much of the book, Laurence becomes central to the penultimate sections. None of these characters seems aware of the greater significance of their actions, which is to say the emergence of the sort of Artificial Intelligence (AI) seen in Gibson's *Neuromancer*.

A major impact of the speeded-up **progress** of technology is an increase in the pollution levels of London unabated by Joseph Bazalgette's sewer projects. This gives an image of a **dystopia** in **Europe** and **America**, rather than the **utopia** that a technocratic meritocracy might have produced in more traditional science fiction. Brunel succeeds Byron in the premiereship, and one wonders whether his political career has impeded his engineering feats. There is no sense of there having been a Great Exhibition in 1851, which helped fund the national museums in Kensington that are clearly expanded upon here. The new technology, with its sense of greater speed—steam driven cars and underground trains—brings fear and disconcertion rather than pleasure.

The playfulness of the tiny, alternative details and the literary references give a sense of **postmodernism** to the novel, although it never quite becomes a convincing parody of the Victorian novel, in which the sex scene between Mallory and Hattie could never have been included. The postmodernism is further served by the disembodied form of the narrator, which appears to be the 1991 (fictional) version of the difference engine, looking back a century and a half to its origins. The story can be read as a fantasy of a computer's earliest memories, attempting to boot itself up into consciousness. However, there is also nothing to stop these being false **memories** and the engine being an unreliable narrator.

Bibliography

M. Keith Booker. "Technology, History, and the Postmodern Imagination." *Arizona Quarterly*, 50 (Winter, 1995), 63–87.

Lewis Call. "Anarchy in the Matrix." *Anarchist Studies*, 7 (1999), 99–117.

Dani Cavallaro. *Cyberpunk and Cyberculture*. London: Athlone Press, 2000.

David Fischlin, Veronica Hollinger, and Andrew Taylor. "'The Charisma Leak'": A Conversation with William Gibson and Bruce Sterling." *Science-Fiction Studies*, 19 (March, 1992), 1–16.

Steffan Hantke. "Difference Engines and Other Infernal Devices." *Extrapolation*, 40 (Fall, 1999), 244–254.

Christine Kenyon Jones. "SF and Romantic Biofictions." *Science-Fiction Studies*, 24 (March, 1997), 47–56.

Nicholas Spencer. "Rethinking Ambivalence." *Contemporary Literature*, 40 (Fall, 1999), 403–429.

Francis Spufford. "The Difference Engine and *The Difference Engine*." Francis Spufford and Jenny Uglow, eds., *Cultural Babbage*. London: Faber & Faber, 1996, 266–290.

Herbert Sussman. "Cyberpunk Meets Charles Babbage." *Victorian Studies*, 38 (Fall, 1994), 1–23.

—Andrew M. Butler

THE DISPOSSESSED: AN AMBIGUOUS UTOPIA BY URSULA K. LE GUIN (1974)

■

The way to see how beautiful the earth is, is to see it as the moon. The way to see how beautiful life is, is from the vantage point of death.

—Ursula K. Le Guin
The Dispossessed (1974)

Summary

This novel portrays an anarchist **planetary colony** (Anarres) founded on a **desert** world by refugees from a moderately capitalist neighboring one (on Urras) through the eyes of a theoretical **scientist** named Shevek. Although Anarresti attitudes are generally hostile to Urras, Shevek's rebel streak and intellectual curiosity leads him to contact and ultimately meet with Urrasti to explore new **knowledge** in **physics**. The real function of his intellectual journey, however, is to learn how thoroughly Anarresti values permeate his thinking and to appreciate both their limits and their worth. The novel is told in alternating chapters beginning with Shevek's departure for Urras, flashing back to his earliest childhood, then continuing the story of his voyage, his growth and maturation, and ultimately, his return **home**. The next-to-last chapter leads us back to the beginning, explaining why he decided to leave in the first place.

Discussion

Plot and character are less important than setting in this work, which is one of the best-known 1970s **utopias**. Inspired by such anarchist thinkers as Peter Kropotkin and Paul Goodman, Le Guin portrays the **economics** of a society in whose ultrademocratic, decentralized **governance system money** has no function, and unforced cooperation and extreme personal **freedom** are constrained only by a sense of social obligation and shame. Like most utopian writers of the 1970s, Le Guin avoids depicting a perfect society, preferring to perform a thought experiment by depicting a system that had been designed to function well in a wealthy world and that is then forced to try to live up to its ideals on a desert planet with few material resources. It can be compared with the Soviet experience that catastrophically failed to provide the benefits of socialist liberty and abundance in an underdeveloped economy (see **Russia**). The people of Anarres may not have luxury, but they have many comforts, and enjoy their freedom.

A-IO, the capitalist society on Urras—though clearly meant to show the superficial qualities of elite **culture**—is no **dystopia**, and has its attractions for Shevek; but the planet is also home to a contrasting Soviet Russian-style dictatorship—Thu—which exists mainly to show how radical ideals can be perverted. Contemporary readers, conditioned by living in an economy dominated by ideas of the market, often fail to grasp the ideals being presented through the portrait of Anarres, and some background reading on anarchist political theory can be useful.

One of the concerns of the novel is to explore the question of whether a thoroughly egalitarian society can also foster genius. Shevek's originality makes him an outcast, but the novel suggests that he can combine elements of the social freedom of Anarres with the individual freedom of Urras to promote a healthier society. The physics in the novel is a purely romantic invention meant to reflect the themes of unity and circularity that underlie Anarras' ideology, developed originally by the philosopher and activist Laia Odo, who is movingly depicted in "The Day Before the Revolution" (1974).

The Dispossessed appeared during the early years of the modern feminist movement (see **Feminism**), and reflects many of its concerns, including the rejection of **gender** stereotyping, insistence on equal job opportunity for women, equal parenting responsibility for men, a deemphasis on physical **beauty**, preference for cooperative, non-hierarchical modes of decision-making, and various forms of sexual freedom, including equal rights for homosexuals (see **Homosexuality**). It was attacked by some critics on rather narrow grounds for making its central figure male and being sexist in various regards (see **Sexism**); but others disagree. Samuel R. Delany wrote an influential detailed critique of the work, "To Read *The Dispossessed*" (1977), and his *Triton* is commonly regarded as, in part, a reply to Le Guin's novel, placing much more stress on individual freedom and less on the value of cooperation.

Toward the end of the novel Le Guin ties this work into her larger body of fiction involving the galaxy-roaming Hainish who have seeded numerous worlds with **humanity**, including **Earth**. One result of their intellectual exchange is the combination of Albert Einstein's relativity theories with Shevek's variation on Odonian physics, suggesting that humanity is improved by being tolerant and open to a variety of cross-fertilizing ideas.

Bibliography

Marleen Barr and Nicholas D. Smith, eds. *Women and Utopia*. Lanham, MD: University Press of America, 1983.

Barbara Drake. "Two Utopias." Sheila Roberts, ed., *Still the Frame Holds*. San Bernardino, CA: Borgo Press, 1993, 109–128.

Thomas P. Dunn. "Theme and Narrative Structure in Ursula K. Le Guin's *The Dispossessed* and Frederik Pohl's *Gateway*." Michael Collings, ed., *Reflections on the Fantastic*. Westport, CT: Greenwood, 1986, 87–96.

Neil Easterbrook. "State, Hererotopia." Donald M. Hassler and Clyde Wilcox, eds., *Political Science Fiction*. Columbia: University of South Carolina Press, 1997, 43–75.

Lillian M. Heldreth. "Speculations on Hetereosexual Equality." Donald E. Palumbo, ed., *Erotic Universe*. Westport, CT: Greenwood Press, 1986, 209–220.

Mario Klarer. "Gender and 'The Simultaniety Principle.'" *Mosaic*, 25 (Spring, 1992), 107–121.

Joseph D. Olander and Martin Harry Greenberg, eds. *Ursula K. Le Guin*. New York: Taplinger, 1979.

M.T. Tavormina. "Physics as Metaphor." *Mosaic*, 13 (Spring/Summer, 1980), 51–62.

Victor Urbanowicz. "Personal and Political in *The Dispossessed*." Harold Bloom, ed., *Ursula Le Guin*. New York: Chelsea, 1986, 145–154.

—Paul Brians

DO ANDROIDS DREAM OF ELECTRIC SHEEP? BY PHILIP K. DICK (1968)

> *You will be required to do wrong no matter where you go. It is the basic condition of life, to be required to violate your own identity. At some time, every creature which lives must do so. It is the ultimate shadow, the defeat of creation; this is the curse at work, the curse that feeds on all life. Everywhere in the universe.*

—Philip K. Dick
Do Androids Dream of Electric Sheep? (1968)

Summary

Rick Deckard, a police department bounty hunter in the **post-holocaust society** of 1992, must kill six technologically advanced Nexus-6 **androids** who have escaped their **Mars** colony and fled to **Earth** (see **Escape**). Deckard hopes the **money** can resurrect a failing **marriage** and improve his **community** status by allowing him to purchase a real animal, most of which have died from radioactive dust. Since androids appear human, Deckard must detect empathy; the Rosen Association, which manufactures "andys," tries to discredit the empathy test, but Deckard exposes trial subject Rachael as a Nexus-6. Confident in the test's reliability, he "retires" one android, then tracks a second (an opera singer), who has him arrested by an alternate (android) police force that also has bounty hunters, such as Phil Resch. Resch kills the android police captain (the third name on Deckard's list), and after escaping together they laser the opera singer. Deckard subsequently tests Resch, who is clearly human but almost without compassion. Now anxious about his own **identity**. Deckard buys a Nubian goat, an expense outrageously beyond his means. Overjoyed, his wife Iran insists they share their happiness through the empathy box; reluctantly, Deckard mentally connects with the religious leader Mercer, who remarks he must "violate his own identity." Feeling he hasn't been "given" anything by Iran or Mercer, Deckard contacts Rachael, who bribes him with sex. A parallel plot concerns a "special"—the dust-damaged J.R. Isidore. In his apartment building, he finds the android Pris, soon joined by Roy and Irmgard Baty. Following a tip, Deckard arrives and kills the three androids, then in exhilarated psychological fugue flees to the **desert** where he has a **vision** of Mercer and finds a toad, the most sacred of animals. Returning home exhausted, Iran gently reveals that the toad is artificial, and Deckard collapses into **sleep**.

Discussion

Among the most accomplished and subtly complicated of Dick's fictions, the book has had an enormous impact, especially following release of the film adaptation ***Blade Runner***. Most readings link it to his other works of the 1960s, especially *The*

Man in the High Castle, The Simulacra (1964), "The Little Black Box" (1964), and *Ubik* (1969), though its themes resonate with almost everything Dick wrote. Dick became famous for concocting labyrinthine convolutions and gymnastic reversals of conceptual dichotomies—authentic/inauthentic, reality/**illusion**, sanity/**paranoia**, hope/despair, **sublime**/kitsch, and dozens more. The vacillations between alternatives estrange readers (see **Estrangement**), forcing our careful contemplation of the daily difficulties of an ethical life (see **Ethics**)—rather than, as many novels and moralists do, rushing readers toward simple conclusions. Dick tries neither to assign guilt to Deckard's decadent culture (see **Decadence**), nor to praise him for his insight that "electric things have their lives, too." Rather, he disrupts readers from the comfortable assumption that we do in fact know what we think we know, producing a profitable cognitive dissonance to shake us from dogmatic slumbers. Confirmed by the scholarly criticism, Dick's brilliant textual tactics produce as many incompatible conclusions as William **Shakespeare**'s *Hamlet* (c. 1601).

For instance, the novel vividly and powerfully asks what makes individuals *authentically* human, rendering problematic the fundamental categories of human identity (autonomy, **biology**, etc.). Deckard's culture reveres animals, even arachnids, but kills humanoid androids; "specials"—humans of diminished physical, psychological, or intellectual capacity—are regarded as quasi-human, and while not "retired" they do not receive the empathy that allegedly marks humanness, denoting a morally discriminatory **class system**. Despite this fact, Isidore appears the sole character fully capable of a full empathetic life.

Similarly, the novel hovers on the possibility of biographical **allegory** or political prophecy (see **Politics**); parts directly parallel Dick's life while others indict current cultural trends. The book's society teeters at the **threshold** of total collapse into "kipple" (Dick's neologism for entropic decay). As synecdoche for the entire **culture**, Deckard fears two things: an elided boundary between human and android, and possible ascendancy of another species, with humans losing dominance over androids; this boundary ambiguity produces a pathology typically associated with the legitimation **anxiety** of postmodernity (see **Postmodernism**).

Another of the novel's controversial features concerns the status of its single **religion**, Mercerism, which preaches the sanctity of all life and invites solitary humans to find communal unity in a **virtual reality** of Mercer's "ascent." Iran follows Mercer's agonizing climb by means of a black box that shares empathy in the physical body, leaving stigmata that signify an authentic merging. Capitalism easily corrupts Mercerism and empties empathy into ownership—the conspicuous display of "moral" wealth (animals) replicating ethical authenticity. Deckard shares this commodity fetishism, perhaps one reason he has never found empathetic fusion easy; yet in his wasteland vision he claims complete and permanent fusion, even without the machine device. Since we also learn Mercerism is an elaborate hoax, coupled with the possibility of a covert government strategy to contain political dissent, all the religion's features and functions seem suspicious.

The conclusion presents special intricacies: Does Deckard's epiphany in the desert constitute a true **metamorphosis**, revealing profound empathy for all life, or is it hallucinatory, a rationalization that bespeaks complete denial and false consciousness? Even astute critics argue that Deckard has acquired compassion from hard experience and thereby achieved harmonious unity with both wife and world. But surely this **cliché**—that despite horrific **violence** husband and wife find renewal with a resurrected **love**, a formula common in bourgeois melodrama—remains inconceivable within Dick's anticonventional cosmos.

Two salient contrasts with the theatrical release of *Blade Runner* provide a key insight into Dick's project: *Blade Runner* concerns whether or not the replicants are human; the novel asks if Deckard is human. *Blade Runner* foregrounds the replicants' ontology; the novel addresses Deckard's ethical behavior and the philosophical status of readers' **perception** (see **Philosophy**). While film commonly exteriorizes inner psychology, it also shifts the novel's generic mode. In classical terms, *Blade Runner* constitutes **comedy**—since we end with redemption and symbolic marriage (although this is more ambiguous in the "Director's Cut"). The novel instead offers ironic **tragedy**—since we remember the etymology of the Greek word, which means "goat-song."

Bibliography

Philip K. Dick. *The Shifting Realities of Philip K. Dick*. Ed. Lawrence Sutin. New York: Pantheon, 1995.

Jill Galvan. "Entering the Posthuman Collective in Philip K. Dick's *Do Androids Dream of Electric Sheep?*" *Science-Fiction Studies*, 24 (November, 1997), 413–429.

N. Katherine Hayles. *How We Became Posthuman*. Chicago: University of Chicago Press, 1999.

Judith B. Kerman, ed. *Retrofitting Blade Runner*. Bowling Green, OH: Bowling Green State University Popular Press, 1991.

Patrick A. McCarthy. "Do Androids Dream of Magic Flutes?" *Paradoxa*, 5 (1999–2000), 344–352.

R.D. Mullen, Istvan Csicsery-Ronay, Jr., Arthur B. Evans, and Veronica Hollinger, ed. *On Philip K. Dick*. Terre Haute: SF-TH, 1992.

Christopher Palmer. *Philip K. Dick*. Liverpool: Liverpool University Press, 2003.

William Schultz. "How Is Genetic Engineering a Sign and a Cause of the Deterioration of Human Nature?" Domna Pastourmatzi, ed., *Biotechnological and Medical Themes in Science Fiction*. Thessaloniki, Greece: University Studio Press, 2002, 361–370.

—Neil Easterbrook

DR. JEKYLL AND MR. HYDE (1931)

Summary

Benevolent Dr. Jekyll is eager to marry his fiancée Muriel, but her **father** insists that matters should not progress so quickly. One of his concerns is that Jekyll's theories are regarded as outrageous by the medical establishment (see **Medicine**). Jekyll believes that the human id and ego can be released from each other by **drugs**. One day Jekyll defends Ivy, a young chanteuse of dubious virtue, from an assailant, and is smitten by her charms; he is disturbed to be so aroused by Ivy despite his **love** for Muriel. Jekyll then drinks the potion he has prepared to release the id and transforms into a toothy, shambling, hirsute travesty of himself—in effect, an evolutionary throwback (see **Evolution**). When Jekyll's butler discovers this brute, Jekyll claims it is a friend of his, Hyde.

When Muriel goes on vacation with her father, Jekyll realizes this gives him a chance to indulge his baser instincts. Once more becoming Hyde, he brutalizes various people and tracks down singer Ivy at her workplace, a disreputable dance hall. She prefers the animalistic Hyde to the genteel Jekyll, despite his brutality, and they set up a domicile together. When Muriel returns, however, Jekyll resolves to forsake Ivy. By now, though, he cannot control his **metamorphoses** into Hyde and, as Hyde, he murders Ivy. When the butler refuses to allow Hyde into Jekyll's laboratory, Hyde gets Jekyll's friend Dr. Lanyon to retrieve the antidote, and Lanyon witnesses his transformation back into Jekyll. During another spontaneous metamorphosis, Hyde assaults Muriel. This time Lanyon, aware of his friend's **secret identity**, leads the police to his refuge. Shot dead, Hyde reverts to Jekyll's physical form.

Discussion

When MGM released its 1941 remake of this movie, it managed very successfully to suppress all copies of the 1931 version, and not until 1994 was a complete copy discovered, allowing the film to once more be fully appreciated. It is not hard to understand MGM's attempt to erase the 1931 version from **history**, for all comparisons favor the earlier film: Fredric March's performance as Jekyll/Hyde is sensational in contrast to Spenser Tracy's stodgier effort, and Robert Mamoulian's direction is far more imaginative than Victor Fleming's, filled with effective uses of shadows, split images, and **mirrors** to suggest the two sides of Jekyll's personality. The film's opening sequence is often commented on, as audiences learn about Dr. Jekyll by seeing the world through his eyes as he carries on with his daily routine and observing his face only in a mirror. The scene in which Jekyll first becomes Hyde—a centerpiece in any Jekyll and Hyde film—was ingeniously achieved by applying layers of different-colored makeup to March's face, then using a series of color transparencies to reveal stages in the transformation. The effect of **horror** was further heightened by the sound of a human heartbeat in the background.

More so than Robert Louis Stevenson's novel *Strange Case of Dr. Jekyll and Mr. Hyde*, this film invites consideration as a fable of repressed **sexuality** and its tragic consequences (see **Tragedy**). Jekyll's desire to immediately marry Muriel is clearly rooted in sexual desire, which may be one reason why her father resists the suggestion. It is clearly sexual frustration that then impels Jekyll to transform himself into Hyde and satisfy his lust in the arms of Ivy. In turn, a sense of self-loathing over this sexual indulgence, driven by the Victorian sense of morality that he cannot **escape**, leads Jekyll to murder Ivy, threaten Muriel, and ultimately doom himself. Jekyll's sexual urges are also interestingly linked to his love of **music**: the film opens with Jekyll playing his organ (perhaps recalling the similar keyboard habits of *The Phantom of the Opera* [1926]), he is attracted to a beautiful singer, and Hyde chillingly instructs Ivy to sing to him right before he murders her. These powerful psychological depths make this film more disturbing than its remake, even though the later version paradoxically struggles to bring the story's sexuality more to the forefront.

Overall, there have probably been over fifty other film adaptations of Stevenson's novel, most of them forgettable, but a few merit some discussion. A notable precursor of the 1931 film was the 1920 silent version starring John Barrymore. Here, the father of Jekyll's fianceé, an amoral society doctor, is the person who leads Jekyll into the path of **evil**; this story has much in common with Oscar Wilde's *The*

Picture of Dorian Gray, with the father playing the part of Wilde's Henry Wooton. Barrymore's performance is a curiously effective mixture of subtlety and atrocious melodrama, conveying that Jekyll is both a benevolent seeker after truth and a **mad scientist**; he portrays Hyde's viciousness by either the quirk of an eyebrow or a histrionic fit. Also noteworthy is *Mary Reilly* (1996), based on the 1990 novel by Valerie Martin, which probes the character of Jekyll's maid as she is simultaneously repelled, fascinated, and lured by both Jekyll and Hyde. This complex female reaction to Jekyll/Hyde, a subtext in other versions of the story, becomes the focus of this version. *I, Monster* (1971), starring Christopher Lee, bizarrely renames the central duo Dr. Charles Marlowe and Edward Blake, but is otherwise a straightforward and credible adaptation. There was also a stage musical, *Jekyll & Hyde* (1997), which was later filmed for television and released on video in 2001.

Bibliography

Richard J. Anobile, ed. *Dr. Jekyll and Mr. Hyde.* New York: Avon, 1976.

Thomas G. Aylesworth. "Self-Made Monsters." Aylesworth, *Monsters from the Movies.* Philadelphia: J.B. Lippincott, 1972, 46–68.

Ivan Butler. "Three Early Sound Horror Classics." Butler, *Horror in the Cinema.* New York: Paperback Library, 1971, 59–75.

Albert S. D'Agostino. "Mamoulian on His *Dr. Jekyll and Mr. Hyde.*" *Cinefantastique*, 1 (April, 1971), 36.

William K. Everson. "*Dr. Jekyll and Mr. Hyde.*" Everson, *Classics of the Horror Film.* Secaucus, NJ: Citadel Press, 1974, 73–76.

Alan Jones. "Dr. Jekyll and the Maid." *Cinefantastique*, 26 (April, 1995), 12–13, 61.

Patricia Moir. "The On-Screen Evolution of Dr. Jekyll and Mr. Hyde." *Cinefantastique*, 28 (October, 1996), 59–60.

Mark Spergel. *Reinventing Reality.* New York: Rowman & Littlefield, 1993.

—*John Grant*

DOCTOR NO (1962)

Summary

The James Bond phenomenon began with Ian Fleming's novels detailing the exploits of England's most famous fictional spy, and a British television adaptation of the first, *Casino Royale* (1953), appeared in 1954. However, most people know Bond through the movies, perhaps the most successful film series of all time. *Doctor No*, the first film, was produced by "Cubby" Broccoli and Harry Saltzman, whose Eon Productions have made all the "official" Bond films. Agent 007, played by Sean Connery, is assigned to Jamaica to investigate problems with **America's rocket** launches. Working with an American agent, Bond learns that the mysterious Doctor No is responsible. Along the way, Bond repeatedly seduces women, one of whom helps him defeat the **villain**, who is part of an international organization seeking world power.

Although the Bond formula was not fixed until *Goldfinger* (1964), *Doctor No* includes the basic elements of later films: international intrigue, power-hungry villains, and Bond's conquests of beautiful women, all within a framework of **espionage**-related action and **violence**. Also, *Doctor No* introduces the ambiguous role of **technology** within these films. Bond uses a variety of clever gadgets and vehicles throughout the series, beginning with *From Russia with Love* (1963), but so do his enemies, who employ high-tech devices for **evil** ends. In *Doctor No*, the villain dabbles with **nuclear power**, uses an unspecified technology to drive American rockets off course, and possesses a set of superstrong mechanical hands (see **Cyborgs**), the result of his radioactive experiments.

Discussion

Essentially *Doctor No* and other James Bond movies are **technothrillers**, spy stories wherein the **heroes** and villains combat one another with sophisticated **weaponry**, clever **inventions**, and other machines, including Bond's specially adapted **automobiles**. As a spy, Bond often works as a **detective**, trying to solve the **mystery** assigned to him and avert problems such as man-made **disasters** or **nuclear war**. His nemeses are often **mad scientists**, whose operations are frequently hidden on **islands**, as in *Doctor No*. Typically Bond is captured and often endures **torture** before making his **escape** and ending the villain's plans. Sometimes his villains are after **money** rather than power, as in *Goldfinger*, which involves a villain who attempts to corner the world's gold market (see **Gold and Silver**).

Bond is a British agent but usually works in conjunction with agents from America, **Europe**, and elsewhere (see **Globalization**) as he travels the world. Early films reflect Cold War **politics** in that **Russia** is often on the other side, as in *From Russia with Love*, though in later films Russia is an ally. In *You Only Live Twice* (1967) international villains try to pit the United States and the Soviet Union against each other for their own purposes.

In addition to his fellow agents, Bond works with many of the women he seduces, who are sometimes the villains' partners and sometimes **family** members of their victims seeking **revenge**. While Bond's many conquests have led to frequent charges of **sexism** against the series, most women in the Bond movies are competent and independent, and sometimes formidable foes. Other figures against whom Bond often fights are henchmen, who generally possess powerful weapons as well as considerable strength.

While all of the Bond films feature advanced technology, some are closer to science fiction than others. For instance, in the opening sequence of *Thunderball* (1965)—remade with an older Connery in an "unofficial" Bond film called *Never Say Never Again* (1983)—Bond escapes his pursuers using a rocket pack, while in *You Only Live Twice* the villains capture American and Soviet spacecraft and their **astronauts** to provoke war between the superpowers. In *The Man with the Golden Gun* (1974) the superweapon is a device to control solar radiation, while *Moonraker* (1979) involves the **theft** of a space shuttle and **genetic engineering**, with much of the action set on the villain's **space station**. The title of *GoldenEye* (1995) refers to a powerful space weapon that threatens the **Earth**, and *Die Another Day* (2002) includes another weapon in space, along with hovercraft tanks and an invisible car. Fantasy elements are almost entirely absent from the films, although *Live and Let Die* (1973) includes **voodoo** and a Tarot card reader with magical abilities.

The Bond films have appealed to a variety of audiences both for their stylish synthesis of **sexuality** and violence and for the ways in which they touch on contemporary concerns yet remain escapist entertainment, part of which is related to the films' **humor**. The movies have also adapted somewhat to the times, and **fashion** and glamour have always been an important part of the Bond films. Perhaps the most important aspect of the series' success, besides its popular formula, is the casting of James Bond. Each actor—Connery, George Lazenby, Roger Moore, Timothy Dalton, and Pierce Brosnan—brought a slightly different interpretation to the role, but despite the unevenness of the series each actor has had his fans.

The series has also proven ripe for parody. *Casino Royale* (1967), with David Niven as James Bond, was made with legally purchased rights to Fleming's novel but spoofed the popular Bond films, while Mike Myers's Austin Powers movies, beginning with *Austin Powers: International Man of Mystery* (1997), are an affectionate parody of the series. The films have also inspired numerous others, both in their depiction of espionage and their increasingly amazing stunts.

Bibliography

Tony Bennett and Janet Woollacott. *Bond and Beyond*. London: Macmillan, 1987.

Jeremy Black. *The Politics of James Bond*. Westport, CT: Praeger, 2001.

John Brosnan. *James Bond in the Cinema*. London: Tantivy, 1981.

James Chapman. *License to Thrill*. New York: Columbia University Press, 2000.

John Cork and Bruce Scivally. *James Bond*. New York: Abrams, 2002.

Oreste Del Bueno and Umberto Eco, eds. *The Bond Affair*. Trans. R.A. Downie. London: Macdonald, 1966.

Christopher Lindner, ed. *The James Bond Phenomenon*. Manchester: Manchester University Press, 2003.

Steven Jay Rubin. *The James Bond Films*. Norwalk: Arlington House, 1981.

—Darren Harris-Fain

DR. STRANGELOVE, OR HOW I STOPPED WORRYING AND LEARNED TO LOVE THE BOMB (1964)

> *Gentlemen, you can't fight in here! This is the War Room.*
>
> —Stanley Kubrick, Terry Southern, and Peter George
> *Dr. Strangelove, or, How I Learned to Stop Worrying and Love the Bomb* (1964)

Summary

At Burpelson Airforce Base, General Jack D. Ripper instructs the 843rd bombing wing to strike targets in the Soviet Union (see **Russia**). In his B-52, Major Kong welcomes the chance to conduct "nuclear combat toe-to-toe with the Rooskies." In

Washington, General Turgidson is summoned to the War Room, where President Merkin Muffley is trying to regain control of the situation. Ripper, however, has taken advantage of systems in place to launch an attack that can only be recalled by using a code he will not reveal, hoping to force Muffley to launch a full-scale attack to avoid annihilation by Soviet retaliation. Instead, Muffley contacts the drunken Soviet Premier Kissoff to co-ordinate the destruction of the bombers, only to learn that the Soviets have built a doomsday weapon which will destroy the world once a bomb hits the country. As Burpelson is attacked by U.S. troops, Ripper commits **suicide**, but Group Captain Mandrake works out the code to recall the planes. After all but Kong's plane are destroyed or turn back, Kong rides a nuclear bomb down to its target. In the War Room, Dr. Strangelove advocates establishing shelters in deep mines to survive the clouds of radioactive fallout that will be produced by the doomsday machine. (Mandrake, Strangelove and Muffley are all played by Peter Sellers.)

Discussion

Alongside Sidney Lumet's *Fail-Safe* (1964) and James B. Harris's *The Bedford Incident* (1965), Stanley Kubrick's first science fiction movie, based very loosely on Peter George's *Red Alert* (1958), sets out to expose the problems inherent in any system carefully designed to both prevent and, if necessary, launch a successful nuclear war. Unlike those earnest, tense melodramas, *Dr. Strangelove* is a **satire**, relying on deadpan **comedy** to establish and elaborate upon the **absurdity** of the nuclear arms race; as Herbert Marcuse once pointed out, the problem with nuclear deterrence is that it is based on a logic that does away with the need to do away with the most likely cause of **nuclear war**—nuclear weapons. Stylistically, the movie switches between formal shot-constructions for interiors and jerky hand-held cameras during the attack on Burpelson and in some of the plane interiors, and between documentary and fictional footage. Similarly, its **humor** ranges from comical character names and wordplay (spoofing the significantly named characters in *Strategic Air Command* [1955], such as Hawkes and Hope) to ironic disjunctions between the image and **music** on the soundtrack, most obviously in Vera Lynn's rendition of "We'll Meet Again" during the climactic **apocalypse**. The movie's allusions, ranging from Jonathan Swift's *Gulliver's Travels* (Kong's primary target is Laputa) to the film *King Kong*, also seem to follow no coherent pattern. However, this apparent confusion might be interpreted as an attempt not to succumb to the kind of systematizing logic that the film criticizes.

   Dr. Strangelove continues the critique of dehumanzing **technology** familiar from such 1950s science fiction as Bernard Wolfe's *Limbo* (1952) and Kurt Vonnegut, Jr.'s *Player Piano* (1952), while articulating, like Peter Watkin's *The War Game* (1966), an **anxiety** about nuclear war that was given fresh impetus and a sense of imminence by the Cuban Missile Crisis in 1962. (The film *Matinee* [1993] provides a science-fictionalized evocation of that period.) Along with *The Manchurian Candidate* (1962), it constitutes a culmination of the treatment of **paranoia** in such 1950s movies as *Invasion of the Body Snatchers* and *Invaders from Mars*. It ridicules rabid postwar anticommunism through the ludicrous Turgidson and insane Ripper (see **Madness**), who believes there is a Communist conspiracy to pollute his "precious bodily fluids" by fluoridating drinking water. Christian fundamentalism (see

Christianity) is mocked, and American national identity is lampooned through Kong's hopelessly anachronistic cowboy image (see **Westerns**).

Throughout the movie, **violence** and aggression are linked to male **sexuality**. An airman ogles a *Playboy* centerfold. Turgidson describes sex with his secretary in terms of rocket launches. Ripper, whose name recalls Jack the Ripper and who seems coded as a latent homosexual (see **Homosexuality**), launches a nuclear war ostensibly to eliminate a problem that causes his impotence, but implicitly to compensate for it. This connection culminates in the plan of Strangelove, a character modelled on whitewashed Nazi rocket scientist Wernher von Braun and *Metropolis*'s Rotwang (see **Mad Scientists**), to build a subterranean civilization (see **Post-Holocaust Societies**) comprised of the leading military and scientific men, with ten women, selected for stimulating sexual characteristics, to every man. A movie whose opening self-conscious eroticization of a mid-air refuelling of a B-52, spoofing *Strategic Air Command*'s techno-porn, ends with an orgy of destruction.

The scenario of an apocalypse potentially resulting from a faulty system was updated for the **computer** age in the juvenile adventure movie *WarGames* (1983), wherein a schoolboy nerd playing games with a NORAD computer almost triggers a nuclear war. The consolatory suggestion that the situation is a fluke anticipates the tendency in films like *Enemy of the State* (1998) to replace the amoral, manipulative governments of conspiracy thrillers like *The Parallax View* (1973) and *Three Days of the Condor* (1975) with rogue elements in otherwise functional **governance systems**. Not only did *Dr. Strangelove* anticipate the imagery that mapped together bodily **invasion** and national invasion in paranoia about hackers, immigrants, and viruses of both sorts since the 1980s, but it also had the insight to reject the ameliorative complacency of other films, recognizing that the problems it imagined were not exceptions, but rather arose from even the most carefully structured cybernetic and corporate systems themselves.

Bibliography

Merritt Abrash. "Through Logic to Apocalypse." *Science-Fiction Studies*, 39 (July, 1986), 129–138.

M. Keith Booker. *Monsters, Mushroom Clouds, and the Cold War*. Westport, CT: Greenwood Press, 2001.

H. Bruce Franklin. *War Stars*. Oxford: Oxford University Press, 1988.

Jonathan Kirshner. "Subverting the Cold War in the 1960s." *Film and History*, 31 (2001), 40–44.

George W. Linden. "*Dr. Strangelove, Or: How I Learned to Stop Worrying and Love the Bomb*." Jack G. Shaheen, ed., *Nuclear War Films*. Carbondale: Southern Illinois University Press, 1978, 58–67.

Dan Lindley. "What I Learned Since I Stopped Worrying and Studied the Movie." *PS: Political Science and Politics*, 34 (September, 2001), 663–667.

Randy Rasmussen. *Stanley Kubrick: Seven Films Analyzed*. Jefferson, NC: McFarland, 2000.

David Seed. "Absurdist Visions." Seed, *American Science Fiction and the Cold War*. Edinburgh: Edinburgh University Press, 1999, 145–156.

Jerome F. Shapiro. *Atomic Bomb Cinema*. London: Routledge, 2002.

—Mark Bould

DOCTOR WHO (1963–1989)

∎

Summary

Debuting on November 23, 1963, the day after the assassination of President Kennedy, *Doctor Who* began as a **children**'s show about a mysterious gentleman and his granddaughter who traveled through **time** and space in a machine disguised as a police box (see **Time Travel**). The granddaughter was soon ditched for a succession of companions, and the Doctor himself quickly evolved from an absent-minded professor adrift in an out-of-control time machine into an increasingly **heroic** figure personally compelled to fight **evil** wherever and whenever he encountered it. The show grew in sophistication across its three decades as fans learned that the Doctor was not human, had the ability to regenerate his form when mortally wounded (see **Rebirth**), was equipped with two hearts, and was a renegade Time Lord from the **alien world** of Gallifrey.

Discussion

The Doctor was first portrayed by William Hartnell, who played the time traveler as a stern old man capable of both capriciousness and cruelty. In fact, in the initial story line ("An Unearthly Child" [1963]), the Doctor selfishly sets his time machine in motion with visitors aboard, knowing that he will be incapable of returning them to their own time. At this time, the program was seen mostly as an educational series of historical (and pre-historical) adventures (see **History**). *Doctor Who* became an overnight success, however, when it took a step into the future and introduced the **evil** Daleks, mutant organisms housed inside individual miniature tanks.

The real innovation came in 1966 when Hartnell's ailing health forced the actor into retirement. Rather than casting another actor of a similar type or introduce a new character in his place, the producers created the notion that the character was capable of self-renewal (later known as regeneration) and replaced him with polar opposite actor Patrick Troughton (see **Metamorphosis**). This introduced the notion of change as a staple concept of the series, perhaps a key component of its longevity. Troughton's Doctor was younger, shorter, friendlier, and funnier, and he became a genuine **hero**, actively seeking to better the plight of those worlds he encountered in his journeys. At the end of his tenure, fans learned he was a renegade Time Lord, a member of an ancient and powerful race who were the self-appointed arbiters of the fourth **dimension**.

Caught and tried by his own people for interfering in the affairs of other worlds (see **Crime and Punishment**), the third Doctor (Jon Pertwee) found himself exiled to **Earth** (see **Exile**). Taking a page from *The Quatermass Experiment*, he served as a scientific advisor to a worldwide military organization called U.N.I.T. formed to combat a series of alien **invasions**. This Doctor was a dashing combination of James Bond (see *Doctor No*) and *Batman*, working for a United Nations Intelligence Task-force and employing an arsenal of high-tech **inventions**. Like Batman, he also drove a customized **automobile**, albeit an antique yellow roadster christened "Bessie." A reoccurring nemesis was introduced in the person of the Master, another renegade Time Lord with a proclivity for evil.

For many people, the series achieved its peak with fourth Doctor Tom Baker, who spent a record seven years in the role. His exile previously dispensed with for services rendered, this Doctor left U.N.I.T., returning the character to his roots as a traveler in time and space. No longer hunted by his own kind, he traveled for the joy of **exploration**, a restless nature, and desire to do good. Foppish and eccentric, this was the most alien portrayal of the Doctor thus far. The series achieved a new degree of sophistication under producer Philip Hinchcliffe, who sought to counterbalance the **humor** of the Doctor against quality storytelling and production values. A particularly effective episode was "Robots of Death" (1977), which drew inspiration from Frank Herbert's *Dune* and Isaac Asimov's *I, Robot,* as well as borrowing plot details from an Agatha Christie play. It was during Tom Baker's tenure that Douglas Adams, author of *The Hitchhiker's Guide to the Galaxy*, served as script editor. Adams penned the acclaimed episode "City of Death" (1979).

M.C. Escher's drawing of the same name inspired "Castrovalva" (1982), which presented the most handsome and human Doctor to date in the person of Peter Davison, who saw the most **violence**. Typically, the Doctor's companions would leave when they fell in **love**, but Davison's companions left under much more tragic circumstances. One exited when she felt overwhelmed by all the **blood**, one left to help the victims of plague, and one actually died—the only companion to do so in the series' history ("Earthshock" [1982]).

Colin Baker's Doctor was a return to William Hartnell's tetchiness. Crass, arrogant, at times cowardly, his Doctor took a while to catch on with fans. It was also during his tenure that the program was put on the only hiatus of its twenty-six year run. The series sought to reinvigorate itself during Sylvester McCoy's period as the Seventh Doctor. Mysterious, powerful, and moody, his Doctor was a **chess** master plagued by feelings of **guilt and responsibility** who appeared in seemingly pre-staged conflicts to play out the winning hand. McCoy returned in a 1996 Fox/BBC co-produced telefilm, which saw Paul McGann take the role of the Time Lord in a single appearance.

Following the series' demise, the character survived in books and audio books, until being revived in a 2005 BBC production starring Christopher Eccleston, with additional episodes planned.

Bibliography

Jeremy Bentham. *Doctor Who: The Early Years*. London: Allen, 1986.

Andrew M. Butler. "British National Identity and the Phenomenon of *Doctor Who*." *Vector*, No. 232 (November/December, 2003), 9–15.

John Fiske. "Popularity and Ideology." W.D. Rowland, ed., *Interpreting Television*. Beverly Hills: Sage, 1984, 165–198.

Peter Haining. *Doctor Who: A Celebration*. London: Virgin/Doctor Who Books, 1995.

David J. Howe. *Doctor Who: The Television Companion*. London: BBC Worldwide, 1998.

Jean-Marc L'Officier. *Doctor Who: The Universal Databank*. London: Doctor Who Books, 1992.

John K. Muir. *A Critical History of Doctor Who on Television*. Jefferson, NC: McFarland, 1999.

John Tulloch and Manual Alvarado. *Doctor Who: The Unfolding Text*. New York: St. Martin's, 1983.

John Tulloch and Henry Jenkins, eds. *Science Fiction Audiences*. New York: Routledge, 1995.

—Lou Anders

DRACULA (1931)

■

Summary

The 1931 *Dracula*, directed by Tod Browning, is the most important, though not the best, **vampire** film ever made. It established the iconography of the vampire, complete with cape and coffins, firmly in the public mind. Most of what the public "knows" about vampires comes from this film, not from Eastern European folklore. Through this film the likeness of Bela Lugosi has been forever wedded to that of the undead Count.

The film was based, not directly on Bram Stoker's *Dracula*, but on the stage play by Hamilton Deane and John Balderston (1927). The screenplay for the film is by Garrett Fort, though it may have been heavily rewritten by Tod Browning. The story line is now familiar to everyone: Dracula, first observed in his **castle** in Transylvania, travels to London in search of fresh victims. While the count is first regarded as suave and sophisticated by his new neighbors, the wise Van Helsing deduces that he is a vampire, responsible for the mysterious illness of a young woman. Van Helsing eventually manages to drive a stake into the heart of the vampire while he lies dormant in his coffin, ending the menace.

Discussion

The Dracula of the novel is a horrible old man with a white moustache, who grows younger (see **Immortality and Longevity**) as he drinks **blood**. He climbs down castle walls head-first, as an **insect** might. Since a vampire must be invited into a house before he can enter, Dracula must hypnotize the madman Renfield to gain access to his beautiful victim (see **Hypnotism**). He is not the sort of person you would invite to a cocktail party. Only a lunatic (see **Madness**), and a mind-controlled lunatic at that, would ever ask him inside (see **Psychic Powers**). Yet in the film, Dracula is actually seen at a party, and Van Helsing must resort to a **mirror** to determine that the otherwise charming Count is a vampire.

Furthermore, in the book Dracula is rarely seen after the first few chapters, yet gains even greater potency as the unseen menace manipulating events. For stage and screen, Dracula had to be made more presentable, more human. Bela Lugosi, with his strange accent and unusual delivery, made a fine Dracula, and could impart sinister meaning into such now famous lines as "I never drink . . . wine." But he is already far removed from the Stoker creation. This process of humanizing Dracula was to continue until, by the 1979 version with Frank Langella, the Count had become a romantic antihero, what one unimpressed critic termed a "cuddly Dracula."

Lugosi's Dracula is at least convincingly **evil**, opposed by the stalwart Van Helsing and served by the memorably cackling, fly-eating Renfield. After a promising opening, however, the film seems to almost purposely avoid all the best cinematic possibilities in the story. It looks like a filmed stage-play. Many of the effects are unsatisfactory, such as a patently fake vampire bat. Still, for the longest time it was the best Dracula film, particularly for audiences who had not seen the considerably more horrific German silent version, F.W. Murnau's *Nosferatu* (1922), which Bram Stoker's widow tried to destroy.

For a while after 1931, Bela Lugosi refused to play the role of the Count. In 1935, he played a Dracula-like character in *The Mark of the Vampire*, but he is an impostor, pretending to be a vampire to frighten criminals. The 1936 film *Dracula's Daughter* with Gloria Holden, is an unwatchable mess. A thinly disguised Dracula (as "Count Alucard") appeared in 1943's *Son of Dracula* with Lon Chaney, Jr. struggling in the title role. Dracula (John Carradine) then made his way into two "monster rallies," films featuring as many Universal monsters as possible, for maximum box-office, if minimum plot logic: *House of Frankenstein* (1944) and *House of Dracula* (1945). Lugosi finally reprised his filmic Dracula in *Abbott and Costello Meet Frankenstein* (1948), after which his career deteriorated rapidly.

It remained for the British actor Christopher Lee to revitalize the role in 1958's *The Horror of Dracula*. While Lee has no trace of Lugosi's foreign accent, his Dracula is in many ways more authentic, a brutal predator rather than a suave charmer. Like the Dracula in Stoker's book, he is always *present* but seldom actually seen. In exactly seven minutes of on-screen time, Lee achieved a performance so dynamic that he is, like Lugosi, forever wedded to the role in the public mind. Sequels followed, of descending quality. In 1970's *Count Dracula*, Lee actually resembles the Stoker character in appearance, right down to the white moustache which darkens as he regains his youth, but the film suffered from a low budget and muddled direction. Numerous other adaptations range from the ridiculous, in *Billy the Kid vs. Dracula* (1966), to good-natured spoofing, in *Love At First Bite* (1979), to considerably more creditable versions starring Jack Palance (1973) and Louis Jordan (1978). This last is in many ways the most authentic adaptation of Stoker's book ever done, though Dracula himself is still more a romantic than monstrous figure. Among the most bizarre adaptations is Francis Ford Coppola's inappropriately entitled *Bram Stoker's Dracula* (1992), which is in many ways the most variant of all. Hundreds of Dracula or Dracula-related films have been made over the years, including a Turkish series, beginning with *Drakula Istanbulda* (1953). The Count even had a brief run-in with the protagonist of **Buffy the Vampire Slayer**.

Through these films, the figure of Dracula has become one of the best-known characters in popular culture, ranking with Sherlock Holmes, Tarzan, Robin Hood, and very few others. For all he has been repeatedly staked, impaled, and destroyed by sunlight, we have not seen the last of him.

Bibliography

Ivan Butler. "Dracula and Frankenstein." Butler, *Horror in the Cinema*. New York: Paperback Library, 1979, 39–58.

Alan G. Frank. "The Count." Frank, *Horror Movies*. 1974. Secaucus, NJ: Derbibooks, 1975, 40–75.

Alan G. Frank. *The Movie Treasury: Monsters and Vampires*. London: Octopus Books, 1976.

James Craig Holte. *Dracula in the Dark*. Westport, CT: Greenwood Press, 1997.

Bob Madison, ed. *Dracula, The First Hundred Years*. Baltimore: Midnight Marquee Press, 1997.

David J. Skal. *Hollywood Gothic*. New York: W.W. Norton & Co., 1990.

Montague Summers. *The Vampire*. New Hyde Park, NY: University Books, 1960.

Montague Summers. *The Vampire in Europe*. New Hyde Park, NY: University Books, 1961.

—Darrell Schweitzer

DRACULA BY BRAM STOKER (1897)

∎

> *[Dracula:] Welcome to my house! Enter freely and of your own will!*
>
> —Bram Stoker
> *Dracula* (1897)

Summary

The plot of Bram Stoker's **Gothic** novel *Dracula* would be too well-known to need summary, save that, due to many movie versions, most people's conceptions of the novel's content are incorrect. Jonathan Harker, a real estate agent, is sent to Transylvania to negotiate with Count Dracula, who desires to acquire property in England. He encounters the Count, a repulsive, white-haired man with a long moustache, hairy palms, and clawed fingers, in the Count's half-ruined **castle**. Harker soon learns that Dracula is an undead **vampire** intent on spreading his power to England. Harker escapes the castle, but not before the Count has departed for England, along with numerous boxes of his native earth, in which he can find refuge. Dracula, in England, begins to prey upon Lucy Westenra, a friend of Harker's fiance, Mina, growing younger as he does. Dr. Van Helsing, a Dutch specialist, is brought in to investigate Lucy's situation, but cannot prevent Lucy from becoming a vampire and being destroyed. Van Helsing, Harker, and others team up to drive the Count from England. Dracula forces Mina to drink his **blood**, establishing a telepathic link with her. Dracula's earth-boxes are discovered and destroyed. He retreats to Transylvania, with the **heroes** in pursuit. Dracula is cornered in the courtyard of his castle just as the sun goes down, and is slain.

Discussion

A great deal has been made of the sexual undertones in *Dracula* (see **Sexuality**). Interpretations range as far as an **allegory** of the plight of Victorian women (see **Feminism**) to Dracula as a disease vector, a walking personification of the great nineteenth-century unmentionable, syphillis. Fantasy author Tim Powers has responded, "No, it's about a guy who lives forever by drinking blood. Don't take my word for it. Read the book." While there is undeniably sexual tension below the surface of the story, Powers is more correct than not, and the romantic and erotic elements brought out in later Hollywood retellings of the story are barely hinted at in Stoker's text.

Stoker's Count, unlike the later versions of the character, is anything but a suave charmer. Since it is one of the limitations of the vampire that he cannot enter a place until invited inside, this is the function of the gibbering, fly-eating madman Renfield in the story (see **Madness**). Through Renfield, Dracula gains access to Mina. Dracula is wholly predatory, not given to romantic musings or moments of self-pity. His most human trait is a fierce pride in his **family**'s **history**, with which he tries to impress Jonathan Harker at their first meeting.

Dracula's only mention of the subject of **love** occurs at the end of the third chapter. The Count has returned to the castle with a child in a sack. He confronts his three "wives," female vampires, who are threatening Jonathan, and drives them off. "You yourself never loved!" the vampires protest. Dracula answers that he understands love, and that they can love Jonathan all they like when he is no longer useful. Meanwhile, there is the child for them to devour. When Dracula forces Mina to drink his blood, many chapters later, the scene is told in terms of rape. For Mina, the encounter causes extreme revulsion and despair. If Stoker's vampires can project a sexual allure, it is only as bait. Dracula is purely **evil**. When Mina briefly expresses pity for Dracula, she is immediately shouted down by the shocked heroes.

Certainly the fears *Dracula* exploits *are* sexual fears, and they do relate to disease and **death.** The Count is the unclean, foreign *thing* that invades modern, scientific England. He is the remnant of medieval **darkness**, which the modern world hopes it has moved beyond, but, in its heart of hearts, fears it has not.

Unlike H.P. Lovecraft's **monsters,** which come from outer space and are "supernatural" only in the sense that no human can comprehend them, Dracula is a part of the older, spiritual world. Stoker's vampires are literally damned souls, who fascinate us by their ability to move between the worlds of life and death. Vampires in eastern European folklore are more unruly ghosts than re-animated immortals (see **Immortality and Longevity**). Stoker's Dracula is a mixture of both, solid enough to tear out someone's throat, but capable of turning into a mist—a thing both of physicality and shadow.

Against this ancient menace is pitted the very modern Dr. Van Helsing, who keeps his diary on a wax-cylinder recorder, the height of 1897 **technology**. Even though he may resort to older **magic,** his approach is closer to that of a **scientist** than an exorcist, defeating Dracula by means of experience and research. The other heroes win their victory largely through raw **courage** and moral outrage. Reason and righteousness fight side by side against Dracula.

Vampirism, in Stoker's book, is not a "dark gift," as it is in the work of Anne Rice (see *Interview with the Vampire*). It is a **curse,** to be extirpated for the good of **humanity** and very likely because God demands it. The novel's furious, melodramatic action is all directed toward the driving of this evil from the sunlit, mortal world. The definitive vampire novel, *Dracula* has spawned countless adaptations, imitations, and spin-offs. Very likely it will outlive them all.

Bibliography

Paul Barber. *Vampires, Burial, and Death.* New Haven: Yale University Press, 1988.

Belford Belford. *Bram Stoker.* London: Weidenfeld and Nicolson, 1996.

Bob Madison, ed. *Dracula: The First Hundred Years.* Baltimore, MD: Midnight Marquee Press, 1997.

Raymond McNally and Radu Florescu. *In Search of Dracula.* Greenwich, CT: New York Graphic Society, 1972.

Phyllis A. Roth. *Bram Stoker.* Boston: Twayne, 1982.

Darrell Schweitzer. "Count Dracula and His Adaptors." Schweitzer, *Windows of the Imagination.* San Bernardino, CA: Borgo Press, 1998, 129–142.

David J. Skal. *Hollywood Gothic.* New York: Norton, 1990.

Leonard Wolf, ed. *The Annotated Dracula*, by Bram Stoker. New York: Clarkson N. Potter, 1975.

—Darrell Schweitzer

DRAGONFLIGHT BY ANNE MCCAFFREY (1968)

∎

Summary

Dragonflight and *Dragonquest* (1971), the first two books of a series of novels set on the **alien world** of Pern, follow young Lessa as she transforms herself from a ugly, outcast servant into the **hero** who saves her people from seemingly inevitable destruction. In the first book, which begins the story many thousands of years after humans had first landed on Pern, Lessa has survived the **invasion** of her family's **castle** holding by hiding her **identity** from the invaders for a decade. In the course of manipulating a visiting dragonrider, F'lar, to kill the usurping lord-holder, she is selected to participate in a "dragon impressing" ceremony in the last dragon-weyr left on the planet. She succeeds with one of the very few gold queen-dragon eggs, which also makes her the mate of F'lar when his bronze **dragon** mates with her queen. At the time of the first novel, dragons and their riders have been neglected by lord-holders because of an unusually long delay in the reappearance of the "thread"—dangerous substances that fall out of the skies for decades at a time and then disappear. Lessa and F'lar, who still believes their planet is threatened by the thread, must first revalidate the importance of preparations for threadfall and then, in *Dragonquest*, find some way to increase their numbers quickly as thread begins to fall. Both make heroic efforts to save the often ungrateful people.

Discussion

McCaffrey's early Pern novels were so popular that their many sequels, exploring different subcultures of Pern's society, have been embraced by readers and attracted critical attention. McCaffrey also created a subseries for children, the Harper Hall books of *Dragonsong* (1976), *Dragonsinger* (1977), and *Dragondrums* (1979), which focused on a young girl and the dragon's precursors, fire-lizards.

The dragons of Pern satisfy universal human fantasies of **flying** and perfect **communication** between humans and animals. They also make literal the myths of dragons found in the literature of a wide range of **cultures**. Dragons are generally friendly to humans, but bond only with individual men. A very few women are chosen to bond with queen dragons. These bonds, called "impressions," are created when one human of many possible candidates is able to link with the dragon as it emerges from its egg (see **Psychic Powers**). Humans must ride dragons to protect the planet during attacks of threadfall.

Dragons are genetically engineered scions of small "fire lizards" and essential to human **survival** on this alien planet in a far off galaxy. The secret of their origin is explored in subsequent volumes, especially the "prequel" called *Dragonsdawn* (1988). Although the **fire** lizards introduced in the Harper Hall children's trilogy are the creatures of Pern's original **ecology**, humans long ago created a new ecological system and social system to survive on this alien planet as they eventually lost their advanced **technology**. Thus, McCaffrey gradually reveals how dragons were created and provides a broad cultural context to support them.

McCaffrey's **culture** has late medieval references (see **Medievalism and the Middle Ages**). The majority of Pern's human inhabitants live in feudal holdings on its small northern continent, protected inside either **caverns** or buildings of stone from intermittent falls of thread; during the times when it falls, any life that is not protected—human, animal or plant life—is devoured, producing more deadly "thread." The human culture is a vast feudal caste system, with three kinds of hierarchy: one with the dragonrider at the top, another with a Lord-holder who is responsible for overseeing the work of his people, and the third with a Master in charge of one of various crafts halls patterned after late medieval guilds. Each of these groups has responsibilities to each other, as well as loyalties within their **communities**. Dragonriders live in weyrs, usually built inside caves high up off the ground so their dragons can live inside with them. Lords live in stone, castle-like buildings often built out from ground-caves and with room for all their people to subsist within their safety during threadfall. Master crafters have holdings where **youth** are trained and crafts perfected, but they spend much of their lives as individuals in holdings and weyrs as their function is both **education** and entertainment.

The **family** is thematically central to the survival of this **class system**. Children are usually raised into the caste of their parents, and the majority of Pern's human inhabitants are farmers (see **Farms**), fishermen, and workers who support them (cooks, cleaners, etc.). They receive their education both through working with their elders and through ballads taught them by harpers and designed to reinforce their place in that society. The crafts people are sometimes born into the profession and sometimes chosen from talented children in holdings. Dragonriders could be the chosen children of other dragonriders, but they have to also be chosen by a dragon as it hatches, so male children of the weyrs cannot be sure they will grow into dragonriders. Women who might become companions of queen dragons are traditionally selected from outside the weyrs. This provides the mechanism by which Lessa becomes a Dragonrider of Pern and a place for individual nonconformity to an otherwise rigid social structure. The introduction of dragons and their riders into an otherwise recognizable historical culture creates the complexity that makes McCaffrey's imaginative vision so compelling.

Bibliography

Marleen S. Barr. "Science Fiction and the Fact of Women's Repressed Creativity." *Extrapolation*, 23 (Spring, 1982), 70–76.

Mary T. Brizzi. *Anne McCaffrey*. Mercer Island, WA: Starmont House. 1986.

Anne Crany-Francis. *Feminist Fictions*. New York: St. Martin's, 1990.

Patricia Harkins. "Myth in Action." C.W. Sullivan, ed., *Science Fiction for Young Readers*. Westport, CT: Greenwood, 1993, 157–166.

Anne McCaffrey. "Retrospection." Denise Du Pont, ed., *Women of Vision*. New York: St. Martin's Press, 1988, 20–28.

Jody Lynn Nye with Anne McCaffrey. *The Dragonlover's Guide to Pern*. New York: Ballantine, 1989.

Robin Roberts. *Anne McCaffrey: A Critical Companion*. Westport, CT: Greenwood Press, 1996.

Kay E. Vandergrift. "Meaning-Making and the Dragons of Pern." *The Children's Literature Association Quarterly*, 15 (Spring, 1990), 27–32.

Carolyn Wendell. "The Alien Species." *Extrapolation*, 20 (Winter, 1979), 343–354.

—Janice M. Bogstad

THE DROWNED WORLD BY J.G. BALLARD (1962)

> *So he left the lagoon and entered the jungle again, within a few days was completely lost, following the lagoons southward through the increasing rain and heat, attacked by alligators and giant bats, a second Adam searching for the forgotten paradises of the reborn Sun.*
>
> —J.G. Ballard
> *The Drowned World* (1962)

Summary

Sometime in the **near future** the **Earth** undergoes a **disaster:** solar storms have led to rising temperatures, the melting of polar ice caps, and the flooding of much of the planet (see **Flood**). Surrounded by reptiles and previously unfamiliar **fish and sea creatures**, a group of survivors, including biologist Dr. Kerans and Beatrice Dahl, explore London and avoid being evacuated to safer ground, surviving an encounter with marauding **pirates** and other hazards. At the end of the novel, instead of logically heading north for cooler climates, Kerans instead elects to head further south into the lagoons and the **jungle**.

Discussion

New Wave in its approach rather than its form, this is one of three early novels by Ballard—the others being *The Drought* (1964) and *The Crystal World* (1966)—in which the **apocalypse** is embraced rather than battled, and in this case the ingenuity of **humanity** will certainly not save the planet from flood. It could be contrasted with the disaster and apocalyptic novels of a decade earlier, notably John Wyndham's *The Day of the Triffids*, among others, and before that H.G. Wells's *The War of the Worlds*. On the face of it, Ballard's novel thus rejects the optimism of genre science fiction and expresses **anxiety** about the **survival** of the race (see **Optimism and Pessimism**). Despite the **estrangement** caused by the ending, within the context of the novel it marks a psychic fulfillment on the part of the protagonist—who realizes that humanity is superfluous in this phase of the Earth's **ecology**.

London under **water** is a **landscape** of **surrealism**, a place out of the imaginations of Max Ernst and Salvador Dalí, whose paintings seem to have seeped into the **dreams** of Kerans (see **Absurdity**). The re-emergence of flora and fauna from the Triassic period conveys the sense that **time** is going backwards rather than forward—an echo, perhaps, of the trajectory in Joseph Conrad's "Heart of Darkness" (1899), although Ballard claims not to have read it at the time of writing the novel. Colonel Riggs, the lingering representative of the government's diminishing authority, resets all the clocks he finds in an attempt to reinstate time (see **Clocks and Timepieces**).

The surreal **underwater adventure** of Kerans diving down into a flooded plane-tarium is a traveling back in time on a bodily level, the building being described as a womb. This also forms part of the **death** instinct of Kerans that permeates the novel: he seeks to survive only to die at the appropriate time, because he has already faced a number of inappropriate deaths. The death instinct traces the trajectory of the restoration of the organism to its original state—salmon swimming upstream to spawn and die, or Kerans as both the **last man** and new Adam (see **Adam and Eve**). The death is another **rebirth**.

Kerans's fulfillment is threatened by the somewhat stereotyped **villain** Strangman, who invades London seeking to steal its works of **art** and becomes the one person standing against the flooding of the city. Strangman mocks and nearly drowns Kerans; he even quotes the "Death by Drowning" sequence of T.S. Eliot's *The Waste Land* (1922), scavenging **poetry** as his does art, as fragments shored against his ruin. After he drains a lagoon to unveil the former streets of London, they become the scene for acts of **violence** (see **Crime and Punishment**) which further threaten Kerans's life until he is rescued by Riggs. (This, along with other sequences in the novel, recalls William Golding's *Lord of the Flies*, depicting humanity's reversion to savagery.) It becomes necessary for Kerans to flood the **city** once more, to side with the apocalypse, before heading south.

The sole significant female character in the novel is Beatrice Dahl, whose clearly allusive name points the reader to Dante Alighieri's guide in *Paradiso* (c. 1306–1321), although it is perhaps designed as much to contrast with Dante as to express similarities. Beatrice leads Dante to Paradise; Kerans is also heading for par-adise of sorts, but in the end he goes without his Beatrice, although she is clearly in his mind on the journey. Beatrice is alternately an image of revelation—of the col-lective unconsciousness that the characters all seem to be dreaming—and of danger and trouble—she is also seen as Pandora.

With the exception of the potboiler *The Wind from Nowhere* (1962), Ballard's science fiction novels are all explorations of inner landscapes as much as they are of external spaces. This impulse was already there in Ballard's essay "Which Way to Inner Space?" (1962) wherein he called for the exploration of inner rather than outer space. The journey through the landscape represents the inner state of the traveler, and the surreal, apocalyptic terrain of Ballard's novels can be seen to rep-resent the traumas of contemporary men (and, less often, contemporary women). The Earth's latitudes represent a spectrum, from the ultimate in primeval at the equator to decadent civilization at the poles, and the characters Ballard is interested in are those who are heading south, not north.

Bibliography

Brian W. Aldiss. "The Wounded Land." Thomas D. Clareson, ed., *SF: The Other Side of Realism*. Bowling Green: Bowling Green State University Popular Press, 1971, 116–129.

K.V. Bailey. "There Are No Nightmares At the Ritz." *Vector*, No. 121 (August, 1984), 24–28.

Peter Brigg. *J.G. Ballard*. Mercer Island, WA.: Starmont House, 1985.

Paul Di Filippo. "Twenty-Five Years of Drowning." *Quantum*, 37 (Summer, 1990), 13–15.

Colin Greenland. *The Entropy Exhibition*. London: Routledge and Kegan Paul, 1983.

Roger Luckhurst. *The Angle Between Two Walls*. Liverpool: Liverpool University Press, 1997.

Patrick A. McCarthy. "Allusions in Ballard's *The Drowned World*." *Science-Fiction Studies*, 24 (July, 1997), 302–310.

David Pringle. *Earth Is the Alien Planet*. San Bernardino, CA: Borgo Press, 1979.

Umberto Rossi. "Images from the Disaster Area." *Science-Fiction Studies*, 21 (March, 1994), 81–97.

—*Andrew M. Butler*

DUNE BY FRANK HERBERT (1965)

> *I must not fear. Fear is the mind-killer. Fear is the little-death that brings total obliteration. I will face my fear. I will permit it to pass over me and through me. And when it has gone past I will turn the inner eye to see its path. Where the fear has gone there will be nothing. Only I will remain.*
>
> —Frank Herbert
> *Dune* (1965)

Summary

Dune is a seminal novel that inspired five sequels by author Frank Herbert, additional sequels by other hands, a theatrical film, and two television mini-series. Set in the **far future** on the **desert** world of Arrakis, it tells the story of Duke Leto Atreides and his son, Paul. Leto is sent to rule Arrakis by the Emperor Shaddam but is destroyed by him and Baron Harkonnen. Paul survives to become leader and **messiah** of the native Fremen **culture**. When Arrakis is invaded by Harkonnen and Imperial troops, the Duke is killed. Paul and his mother, Jessica—the Duke's mistress and priestess in an ancient order called the Bene Gesserit—**escape** into the sands. They are discovered by Fremen, who believe Paul may be the Lisan al-Gaib, a prophet who will change Arrakis. Paul is already aware he may be the Bene Gesserit messiah figure, or Kwisatch Haderach. Paul's leadership grows and his plans for revenge mature. These are based on control of the melange longevity spice upon which the spacer guild relies to navigate. Arrakis is its source. Using giant sandworms (see **Snakes and Worms**), the martial skills of the Fremen, and his **psychic powers**, Paul storms the Harkonnen capital. He captures the Emperor and kills the Baron's son, regaining control of the planet.

Discussion

Dune takes a serious view of **ecology**. Liet-Kynes, the Imperial Planetologist, plays a crucial part in creating the hope the Fremen have for a different world. Everything about the Fremen reflects this. All their efforts, from giant underground reservoirs to the code of **water** preservation, go towards creating a green and fruitful world. Paul's arrival causes this dream to be realized centuries earlier than hoped, and part of the series that follows, particularly *Children of Dune* (1976), is set on the remodelled Arrakis.

Dune is set in a Universe where a **galactic empire** is ruled by three interlocking forces (see **Governance Systems**). The Imperium is the governing body, in the person of the Emperor. The Great Houses are the equivalent of a parliament, without legislative power. The Space Guild is the third force, controlling interstellar **space travel**. All three support the Great Convention, a set of rules that enforces, among other things, a ban on the use of nuclear weapons against people. **Betrayal** and scheming are constant as houses attempt to gain more power, which leads to the vendetta between the Harkonnens and the Atreides.

Religion is a powerful force in the universe of the novel. It is based on the Orange Catholic Bible—a compromise text, originally reviled, written with the intent of uniting the disparate sects—which has many elements of **Islam**. Created by conference, it became the text that formed the basis of the Fremen's belief system. The Bene Gesserit use it as their own text and quote from it to serve their own purposes: to inflict superstitions on primitive worlds which will protect members of their order, and to leave worlds open for exploitation.

The Bene Gesserit wish to breed a superior male psychic. Members of the order are female and aware of a group mind, which contains knowledge of the past and future (see **Hive Minds**). Their abilities are limited by an unapproachable area within this mind, which is the male part of human experience. Through a breeding program and primitive **genetic engineering** they hope to produce a male with the same powers as a Bene Gesserit. This Kwisatch Haderach would be able to see future possibilities in their entirety, not partially. Paul's powers are developed by this breeding program, but finally brought into flower by his use of a powerful extract of melange in a Fremen ritual.

The **alien world** of Arrakis is particularly well visualized. Herbert is meticulous in constructing a background that is believable and detailed. There are two main settings; the courts in the **city** and the deserts. Both cultures are intricate; the Machiavellian plots and devious **politics** of the city are finely drawn and the **technology** is believably different, as are the explanations of why some things work and some do not. In the wastelands, the culture of the Fremen, with its complex system of **taboos** and laws, is as finely drawn and detailed. The world around them has every detail in place, from the tiny sand-mice to the immense sandworm **monsters**.

Dune creates a future without **computers**. Two generations of humans revolted against the machines and destroyed them in the Butlerian Jihad. The tenet after the Jihad became "man may not be replaced." Instead, individuals were trained and conditioned to be superior in calculating and making decisions. These are mentats, and Thufir Hawat, the Atreides mentat, plays a significant part in the novel. It was out of the Jihad that the conference which developed the Orange Catholic Bible came, with the support of the Bene Gesserit. The Spacers Guild also supported the revolt against the machines, since it gave them even more control over space travel.

The rich background and setting of *Dune*, together with the loose ends left at the end of the first novel, demanded a sequel, and Herbert produced five of them: *Dune Messiah* (1968), *Children of Dune*, *God-Emperor of Dune* (1981), *Heretics of Dune* (1984), and *Chapterhouse: Dune* (1987). Of these, *Children of Dune* is by far the most interesting in the ways that it extends the complexity of the original novel. In addition, Herbert's son Brian Herbert and Kevin J. Anderson have collaboratively produced additional sequels after Herbert's death.

Bibliography

Michael R. Collings. "Epic of Dune." William Coyle, ed., *Aspects of Fantasy*. Westport, CT: Greenwood Press, 1986, 131–139.

Lorenzo DiTommaso. "History and Historical Effect in Frank Herbert's *Dune*." *Science-Fiction Studies*, 19 (November, 1992), 311–325.

Brian Herbert. *Dreamer of Dune*. New York: Tor, 2003.

Frank Herbert. "Dune Genesis." *Omni*, 2 (July, 1980), 72–74.

Susan McLean. "Psychological Approach to Fantasy in the Dune Series." *Extrapolation*, 23 (Summer, 1982), 150–158.

Willis E. McNelly. *The Dune Encyclopedia*. New York: Berkley, 1984.

Tom O'Reilly. *Frank Herbert, The Maker of Dune*. New York: Berkley, 1987.

Donald E. Palumbo. *Chaos Theory, Asimov's Foundations and Robots, and Herbert's Dune*. Westport, CT: Greenwood Press, 2002.

Susan Stratton. "The Messiah and the Greens." *Extrapolation*, 42 (Winter, 2001), 303–316.

—*Ian Nichols*

Ɛ

EARTH ABIDES BY GEORGE R. STEWART (1949)

Summary

While charting the **ecology** of a remote region of rural California, Isherwood Williams is bitten by a rattlesnake. He recovers to find that the United States and almost certainly the world has been devastated by a plague (see **Plagues and Diseases**). Journeying across **America** to New York and back, Ish finds scattered, traumatized individuals. Gradually, a **community** coalesces around him. Concerned that his "Tribe" should not simply exist as scavengers, Ish tries to educate the **children**, but only his youngest son Joey accepts literacy as the way to access the stored **wisdom** of **civilization**. When the predatory, amoral Charlie arrives and makes sexual advances to a mentally retarded girl who has become **taboo** to the other males, the problem of social control becomes acute: they have no alternative but to kill him. Shortly afterwards, fever strikes and Joey is among those who die. Realizing that the old ways cannot be restored, Ish takes advantage of his status as the "Last American" and the numinous image of the hammer he has carried almost by accident since his days as a researcher. He introduces "primitive" tools like the bow and arrow that will survive among the children when the guns and cartridges run out. The Tribe will perhaps survive, closer to **nature**. All Ish can tell is that the old world will pass away, but **Earth**, for a time, will abide.

Discussion

The novel's early images of a deserted America are effective echoes of displaced **anxieties** of post-Hiroshima or Cold War destructions, but call up much earlier visions of **apocalypse**. Ish begins as the **last man** in a devastated world, thrown Crusoe-like upon his own resources. As a workable community gathers around him—loving, maternal Em, who gives him the emotional strength to continue; solid, dependable George; wise Ezra—the question of building upon simple **survival** in order to return to the best of the old ways comes to the fore.

Linking Jack London's *The Scarlet Plague* (1915) with later novels like John Wyndham's *The Day of the Triffids*, *Earth Abides* is one of science fiction's most effective studies of **post-holocaust societies**. Ish's dilemma is how far a tiny group, or collection of tiny groups, can really aspire to return to the vast range of specialized **technologies** and ways of life developed in modern times. As Stewart interpolates sections describing the fates of those animals that depend on **humanity** for survival—**dogs**, **cats**, sheep, cattle—we realize that civilization is a process by which humanity domesticates itself. Survival, once the conditions that allow such domestication are removed, is a matter of chance. Joey, the "Child of the Promise," is too frail to carry upon his shoulders the burden of restoring twentieth-century America. The societies with the best chance are those that, close to the land, have always depended upon subsistence existence. Almost consciously, Ish guides his Tribe to a romanticized version of a Native American relationship with the land as hunter-gatherers (Ish's name recalls Ishi, name given to the last survivor of a Native American tribe in the early twentieth century (see **Native Americans**).

The novel, therefore, may be said to dramatize retreat from a society that has grown too big, too specialized, and too menacing. **Disaster** wipes the slate clean, and a neo-primitive society can begin again. But it is more than a simple **escape** into a tribal ideal. Ish, as an ecologist, is deeply concerned about the relationship of species to their environments. Humanity is a species that specialized in social roles, but the "chance" element of survival has meant that some "social roles" have vanished. One of them, Ish seems constantly to worry, is that of "leader." Very early in the book, he justifies to himself his isolation in the **wilderness** as an escape from the problems of dealing with people. There are scenes in which his harangues about things the group must do, or items of **technology** that could be restored to make their lives better, are greeted with good-natured ridicule. *Earth Abides*, then, is not a "blueprint for survival" but a study of a man who has to re-invent *himself* as much as his civilization. It explores tensions between individual and group (see **Anthropology**) and past and future (see **Time**), but above all between human civilization and the wider biosphere and physical world.

Biblical cadences and a tone of melancholy add to its **pastoral** qualities, which become even more apparent as we see the diseased Charlie, challenging the established sexual mores of Ish's Tribe, as the serpent in Eden or as proof that death does lurk in **Arcadia**. With no external legal resources to appeal to, or internal methods of social control other than mild ostracism, the group can only take an action, which their personal moral codes abhor. By voting for Charlie's execution, Ish knows that he may be bringing into existence all the brutal and oppressive ways of the old world, and casting his ballot is in part an act of cowardice, done in the hope that the others may outvote him. It is not surprising, then, that he questions whether Joey's death, caused by a disease that Charlie may have brought into the community, is in some way a punishment for his **sin**. Ish's (almost) final thought is that he no longer desires that the cycle of **slavery** and **war** that had brought modern civilization should continue. We realize then that the novel's title (from the Book of Ecclesiastes) is ambiguous. Perhaps the Tribe is the beacon for a new human ecology. Perhaps it, too, will pass away.

Bibliography

Brian W. Aldiss. "*Earth Abides*." *Vector*, No. 15 (Spring, 1962), 10–11.
Elizabeth Cummins Cogell. "The Middle-Landscape Myth in Science Fiction." *Science-Fiction Studies*, 15 (July, 1978), 134–142.
P. Schuyler Miller. "*Earth Abides*." *Astounding Science-Fiction*, 46 (October, 1950), 129–130.
David Pringle. "Apologies to Ishi." *Interzone*, No. 130 (April, 1998), 56–57.
———. "*Earth Abides* by George R. Stewart (1949)." Pringle, *Science Fiction: The 100 Best Novels*. New York: Carroll and Graf, 1985, 23–24.

Leon Stover. "Anthropology and Science Fiction." *Current Anthropology*, 14 (1973), 471–474.

———. "Benevolent Catastrophe." Stover, *Science Fiction from Wells to Heinlein*. Jefferson, NC: McFarland, 2002, 155–158.

———. "Social Science Fiction." Jack Williamson, ed., *Teaching Science Fiction*. Philadelphia: Owlswick, 1980, 137–144.

Gary K. Wolfe. "The Remaking of Zero." Eric Rabkin, Martin H. Greenberg, and Joseph Olander, eds., *The End of the World*. Carbondale: Southern Illinois University Press, 1983, 1–19.

—*Andy Sawyer*

ENDER'S GAME BY ORSON SCOTT CARD (1985)

Welcome to the human race. Nobody controls his own life, Ender. The best you can do is choose to be controlled by good people, by people who love you.

—Orson Scott Card
Ender's Game (1985)

Summary

Ender Wiggin is a genetically engineered child genius taken from his **family** (see **Genetic Engineering**) by the military to fight a **space war** against an **insect** race, a **hive mind** known as the Buggers, that has already attacked **humanity**. Ender trains with other brilliant **children** in an orbiting battle school where he becomes a commander. Through the Giant's Drink, a **computer** game, Ender unknowingly makes contact with the Buggers. Ender is repeatedly presented with two options: fight and win, or lose and die. On **Earth** Valentine and Peter, Ender's two equally brilliant siblings, assume internet identities through which they guide public opinion. In command school Ender comes under the tutelage of Mazer Rackham, previous victor over the Buggers. Ender and his child army conquer the Buggers in a **cyberspace** simulation when he destroys the alien home planet. It is then revealed to him that what he thought was a **game** has been real all along. In human eyes he is a great **hero**, but in his own he is the perpetrator of xenocide (elimination of an alien race). Valentine and Ender leave for the stars; he is guided to the sole surviving Bugger queen whom he carries with him while he seeks a place for her to flourish.

Discussion

Two sets of sequels follow *Ender's Game*: the first (*Speaker for the Dead* [1986], *Xenocide* [1991], *Children of the Mind* [1996]) concerns Ender and Valentine as they voyage into the universe; the second (*Ender's Shadow* [1999], *Shadow of the Hegemon* [2000], *Shadow Puppets* [2002], *Shadow of the Giant* [2005]) is about children from the battle school (Bean, Petra, Alai) and Peter Wiggin, who become commanders in **wars** on Earth. As Speaker for the Dead (a person who investigates, bears witness to, and honors the dead), Ender travels to the planet Lusitania where another race of aliens, the Pequeniños (or "piggies") has been discovered. Ender's friend Jane, an **intelligence** that has come to inhabit the faster-than-light human **communication** network, now assumes vast importance in human life. In the next two novels Ender, his family, Valentine (now a famous historian), and Jane derail a series of human plots to destroy the Buggers, Piggies, and Lusitanians. The second set of sequels follows Bean, Ender's most talented commander from the battle school, as he and Petra, together with Peter Wiggin and his parents, join to bring some form of peace to Earth's warring nations. Unlike Ender, Bean has known all along that the children are engaged in a real war, perhaps Bean is more powerful than Ender.

Ender's Game is both philosophical text and action novel, about spirit and mind, reality and simulation. As in Frank Herbert's *Dune* and its sequels, all action is rooted in **philosophy**. As in the typical **Bildungsroman**, the young must learn to distinguish what the truth is—here, however, the world is under a military **governance system** where all information is thoroughly controlled. As a child in the army Ender must fit himself into the war machine without losing himself: the word "loss" is key. Ender has been drilled to believe that loss means death, that he is only a tool for the military's use. He also learns that "following orders" is an insufficient excuse for his acts; he must assume responsibility and atone for what he has done (see **Guilt and Responsibility**). Almost a Christ figure, Ender is as knowing and compassionate as he has been murderous (empathy gives him the ability to see into his enemies and destroy them). In part the novel explores the individual's duties during times of **community** crisis: it is not good enough simply to submit or resist; one must work carefully at each decision.

Card confronts the paradox that the military, an authoritarian structure, is often used to protect **freedom**. As in Joe Haldeman's *The Forever War* (but unlike Robert A. Heinlein's *Starship Troopers*), the only thing that can successfully defeat a hive mind is a more powerful hive mind. The battle school makes Ender into a hive commander in charge of his child army's unitary intelligence. Unlike Heinlein, Card refuses to romanticize the military: they "requisition" Ender, control his parents, use Valentine when it suits them, and lie as they please. The book presents the reader with moral questions about a world prepared to **sacrifice** children to save a race. The military is not the benevolent **father** protector we see in *Starship Troopers*, but a much more jaded role-playing, self-serving force.

Gaming is key to the text. Ender drifts into solipsism because his existence is governed by a string of meaningless wins and losses. Into a secular universe of **social Darwinism** Card introduces spiritual underpinnings that will become paramount in the sequels. Communication, family, honesty, trust, and faith will all be put forward as answers to militarism. While the series can be read in the context of the Church of the Latter Day Saints (Card is a devout Mormon), such a reading may conceal the texts' richness. The series is about being Other even when one is at **home**. Ender is doomed never to be at home, never to be anything but alien, even to the three alien races (especially humanity) that he saves.

Bibliography

Brian Attebery. "Godmaking in the Heartland." Donald E. Morse, ed., *The Celebration of the Fantastic*. Westport, CT: Greenwood Press, 1992, 61–69.

Tim Blackmore. "Ender's Beginning." *Extrapolation* 32 (Summer, 1991), 124–142.

Michael R. Collings. *In the Image of God*. Westport, CT: Greenwood, 1990.

Bernie Heidkamp. "Responses to the Alien Mother in Post-Maternal Cultures." *Science-Fiction Studies*, 23 (November, 1996), 339–354.

Anne D. Jordan, "*Ender's Game*." *Teaching and Learning Literature*, 4 (May/June, 1985), 26–28.

John Kessel. "Creating the Innocent Killer." *Foundation*, No. 90 (Spring, 2004), 81–97.

Elaine Radford. "Ender and Hitler." *Fantasy Review*, 10 (June, 1987), 11–12, 48–49.

George Slusser. "The Forever Child." Gary Westfahl and George Slusser, eds., *Nursery Realms*. Athens: University of Georgia Press, 1999, 73–90.

Edith S. Tyson. *Orson Scott Card*. Lanham, MD: Scarecrow, 2003.

—Tim Blackmore

E.T.: THE EXTRA-TERRESTRIAL (1982)

∎

How do you explain school to higher intelligence?

—Melissa Mathison
E.T.: The Extra-Terrestrial (1982)

Summary

An alien is stranded on **Earth** when its spaceship must evacuate to **escape** detection (see **Aliens on Earth**). "E.T." is later found and protected by Elliott, child of a dysfunctional **family**. As the two become **friends**, they form an empathic link: Elliott becomes drunk and then ill in sympathy with the alien. Meanwhile a hunter of **UFOs** (called Keys in the credits, referring to those hanging on his belt—only the central family and their friends are named in the film) is on their trail and has almost tracked them down. The homesick alien constructs a **communication** device out of **toys** and other household objects, enabling E.T. to "phone home" and request rescue. It seems that this will come too late—E.T. falls ill and is captured, along with Elliott, by Keys and **scientists**. E.T. comes back from the dead—or has been playing dead—and with the aid of Elliott, his brother, and friends, they manage to rendezvous with the mothership. Elliott is given the chance to accompany E.T. but remains behind at **home**.

Discussion

While marked—even marred—by the sentimentality that afflicts too many of Steven Spielberg's later films, this is far more than a version of a **first contact** narrative, like *Close Encounters of the Third Kind*, retold for **children**, although the camerawork does largely operate at a child's height. The mist, smoke, smog, and night which envelop much of the film lend an air of both **mystery** and **beauty** as flashlights and other **light** cut through the gloom. At points Spielberg resorts to jumpcuts, to tremendous effect.

At the same time—as Andrew Gordon among others has observed—the film is a **fairy tale**, a **Bildungsroman** in which an isolated boy (a middle child, neither having friends as his older brother Michael does nor receiving maternal attention as his younger sister Gertie does) finds a friend with magical powers (see **Magic**) and reaches a new maturity. This is enhanced by various references to Peter Pan and Wendy (see J.M. Barrie's *Peter and Wendy*)—in the story of Tinker Bell's **rebirth** told to Gertie by the **mother**, in the sense of the teens as lost boys, in Keys as a latter-day Hook, in the quasi-magic ability of E.T. and the boys fly, and then in E.T., Tinker Bell-like, coming back from the dead.

The alien can also be read as a **messiah** in an **allegory** of **Christianity**: having descended from the heavens he is found in a humble place. He performs miracles with **touch**, healing the sick and bringing **plants**, at least, back from the dead. He is persecuted by those that do not understand and dies at their hands, only to rise again before ascending back into **Heaven**, leaving lives transformed.

The real alienation in the film comes in the relationship between children and adults: the children separated from an absent **father** down in Mexico and a barely coping working mother who must leave her apparently sick son at home and who dons a peculiar **cat** costume at **Halloween**. The doctors, scientists, and police are faceless for much of the film and nameless throughout; having spied and eavesdropped on this suburban neighborhood, they then take over Elliott's house via the doors and windows, inexplicable dressed in spacesuits. They show no concern for the feelings or safety of the children. Keys tells Elliott that he is jealous, having been seeking aliens all his life, but his reactions (albeit filtered through children's or alien's eyes) are more clinical than welcoming.

The film begins with a dysfunctional family and seems to end with the family reunited, presumably healed by their **sublime** encounter with the alien. This might represent a Spielbergean triumph of optimism over experience: the father is still absent, and the family must still struggle to stay together with Michael as uneasy substitute patriarch and with a sense of what they have lost. One might also wonder how the authorities would treat a family who have discovered that there are aliens.

The movie was a huge hit—redeeming Spielberg's career after the disappointing *1941* (1979)—and easily eclipsed the box office take of *Blade Runner*, *Videodrome* (1983), and *The Thing* (1982) (see *The Thing (from Another World)*), released in the same period and depicting a darker side of science fiction. A sequel was planned but never materialized, although William Kotzwinkle's novelization *E.T., The Extra-Terrestrial, in His Adventure on Earth* (1982) was followed by *E.T.: The Book of the Green Planet* (1985), which may have set up a sequel on an alien planet. In 2002 Spielberg released a twentieth anniversary version of the film, which cleaned up the soundtrack and enhanced some scenes with computer generated imagery. The Halloween scene was extended, and a sequence in the bathroom reinstated, but dialogue was softened and the guns of E.T.'s pursuers were transformed into radios, correcting a miscalculation that Spielberg felt he had made.

Bibliography

Ilsa J. Bick. "The Look Back in *E. T.*" *Cinema Journal*, 31 (Summer, 1992), 25–41.
James Clarke. *Steven Spielberg*. Harpenden, UK: Pocket Essentials, 2001.

Jeffrey L. Drezner. "*E.T.*: An Odyssey of Loss." *Psychoanalytic Review*, 70 (Summer, 1983), 269–275.

Andrew Gordon. "*E.T.* as Fairy Tale." *Science-Fiction Studies*, 10 (November, 1983), 298–305.

Maria Heung. "Why E.T. Must Go Home." *Journal of Popular Film and Television*, 11 (1983), 79–85.

Argiro L. Morgan. "The Child Alone." *Children's Literature in Education*, 16 (September, 1985), 131–142.

Terry Parker. "*E.T.*: Wonderful Movie Magic or Maudlin Melodrama?" *Fantastic Films*, 5 (February, 1983), 16–19.

Vivian Sobchack. "Child Alien Father Patriarchal Crisis and Generic Exchange, in Horror and Science-Fiction Films." *Camera Obscura*, (Fall, 1986), 7–34.

George E. Turner. "Steven Spielberg and E.T." *American Cinematographer*, 64 (January, 1983), 46–49, 80–85.

—Andrew M. Butler

THE EYE OF THE WORLD BY ROBERT JORDAN (1990)

Summary

Rand al'Thor, a farmer's son (see **Farms**), unknowingly possesses the ability to destroy the world. When soldiers of the Dark One assail his village looking for him, the bewildered **youth** flees with a group of friends (see **Friendship**), guided by a wandering sorceress and her bodyguard. Rand's flight through the land becomes a harrowing **Bildungsroman**. It emerges that he has an unmatched potential with the **magic** known as the One Power, and prophecies herald him as the Dragon Reborn, a **messiah** figure who will fight the Dark One in a battle leading to the **apocalypse**. Rand's friends also discover hidden **talents** that will affect the world's **destiny**. Perrin Aybara is revealed to be a **shapeshifter**; Mat Cauthon becomes the **reincarnation** of an **Arthur** persona known as Artur Hawkwing; and the innkeeper's daughter, Egwene, discovers her **psychic powers**.

Taken together, *The Eye of the World* and its sequels form a sprawling **heroic fantasy** series known as The Wheel of Time. The series comprises a single narrative spanning more than 11 novels and 6500 pages, and as a whole constitutes one of the longest fictional works ever written in English. Series installments repeatedly top the *New York Times* bestseller lists, with over 11 million copies in print and translations in 21 languages.

Discussion

The Eye of the World invites comparison with J.R.R. Tolkien's **The Lord of the Rings**. Rand's village in the **pastoral** Two Rivers area resembles the Shire, and the peaceful existence of the citizenry in both milieu is destroyed by intrusions of outside forces. Departures from **home** are predicated on a flight from danger, in which **heroes**, aided by **mentors**, outwit **supernatural creatures** as they traverse a quasi-medieval (see **Medievalism and the Middle Ages**) landscape sprinkled with **magical objects, castles,** and **taverns and inns.** At stake is the struggle against **personifications** of evil. In terms of thematic content, Jordan and Tolkien similarly concentrate on the exercise of power.

It is here, though, that the two works diverge. *The Lord of the Rings* is arguably about the renunciation of power, wherein Frodo must avoid the temptation to wear Sauron's mighty **ring** and destroy it in the **fires** of Mount Doom. His **quest** entails a straightforward goal. Rand, in contrast, faces no such clear denouement; he must learn to deploy power in a titanic **war** that will likely destroy the world. Rand's task is complicated by the fact that the One Power in The Wheel of Time universe is divided into male and female halves, and that the male half was corrupted during a bygone clash between armies of **light** and **darkness.** Any man who "channels" the male half consequently faces the almost certain prospect of insanity (see **Madness**).

As evidenced by the male/female dualism of the One Power, **gender** is a distinguishing theme of The Wheel of Time series. Jordan's female characters prove uniformly strong, capable, and central to the vast sweep of events. Heroines like Egwene, Nynaeve, and Faile are hot-headed and outspoken, quick to excoriate men and inevitably tenacious. However, since heterosexual **love** and **romance** color the lives of all the principal female characters, The Wheel of Time is by no means a radical feminist work (see **Feminism**). It does present societies ruled by women (see **Governance Systems**), though. The Atha'an Miere sea folk are governed by the Mistress of the Ships, Wavemistresses, and Sailmistresses, while the **barbarian** Aiel are directed by female Wise Ones. The Rose Crown presiding over the most influential kingdom in Jordan's panoply of realms, Andor, is by tradition a Queen, and the Aes Sedai sisterhood of sorceresses hatches schemes in every court, not unlike the Bene Gesserit of Frank Herbert's *Dune* novels. Given this context, Jordan's decision to cast the Dark One as a male is interesting, as is his choice to depict the male half of the One Power as tainted.

The Wheel of Time series weaves a tangled skein of subplots as it progresses, and characters and locations number in the hundreds. The hurtling pursuit of *The Eye of the World* generates myriad plot lines in the next four volumes, *The Great Hunt* (1990), *The Dragon Reborn* (1991), *The Shadow Rising* (1992), and *The Fires of Heaven* (1993). The series enters a new phase with publication of *Lord of Chaos* (1994), where narrative momentum slows to a languid pace as Jordan elaborates on the details of his world. In fact, in the following volumes—*A Crown of Swords* (1996), *The Path of Daggers* (1998), *Winter's Heart* (2000), *Crossroads of Twilight* (2002), *New Spring* (2004), and *Knife of Dreams* (2005)—details seem to have become the theme of The Wheel of Time. Entire chapters are devoted to political intrigue (see **Politics**), conversations, or descriptions of cavalry units mustering for war. The **architecture and interior design** of cities is elaborated upon at length, while the huge cast voyages between narrative venues via **horses, teleportation,** and **sea travel.** Character **psychology** is at the same time foregrounded against a multifarious backdrop of **invasions, seasons,** and sundry **cultures** constructed out of building blocks lifted from Celtic and Norse mythology, buttressed by recognizable elements of **Islam, Japan,** Native American societies (see **Native Americans**) and other sources. Any familiar signposts help the reader as The Wheel of Time rolls ever onward; for better and for worse, it is easy to become lost along the way.

Bibliography

Charlene Brusso. "Some Q & A with Robert Jordan." *Dark Regions & Horror Magazine*, No. 12 (Spring, 1999), 55–60.

Robert Jordan. "Robert Jordan: The Name Behind the Wheel." *Locus*, 44 (March, 2000), 6–7, 76.

Robert Jordan and Teresa Patterson. *The World of Robert Jordan's The Wheel of Time*. New York: Tor, 1997.

Edward Rothstein. "Flaming Swords and Wizards' Orbs." *New York Times Book Review* (December 8, 1996), 60–61.

Robert Silverberg. "Introduction." Silverberg, ed., *Legends*. New York: Tor Books, 1997.

Jesse Snedden. "A Robert Jordan Book Signing." Kurt Lancaster and Tom Mikotowicz, eds., *Performing the Force*. Jefferson, NC: McFarland, 2001, 68–70.

William B. Thompson. "Carving Stone Horses." *Starlog*, No. 162 (January, 1991), 16–18, 58.

Garry Wyatt. "Robert Jordan: The Old Ranger Speaks." *Sirius*, No. 2 (June, 1993), 4–6.

—Neal Baker

F

FAHRENHEIT 451 BY RAY BRADBURY (1953)

It was a pleasure to burn. It was a special pleasure to see things eaten, to see things blackened and changed. With the brass nozzle in his fists, with this great python spitting its venomous kerosene upon the world, the blood pounded in his head, and his hands were the hands of some amazing conductor playing all the symphonies of blazing and burning to bring down the tatters and charcoal ruins of history.

—Ray Bradbury
Fahrenheit 451 (1953)

Summary

In the twenty-first century, **books** and **reading** have been outlawed to keep the population complacent and docile, and firemen serve as an arm of law enforcement, burning forbidden books. Guy Montag, a fireman in an unnamed Midwestern **city**, has begun to have doubts about his job, and they are amplified the night he witnesses a woman willingly burn to **death** rather than part with her **library**. He has been secretly bringing **home** books to read, and under their influence he has grown increasingly enlightened and disdainful of the intellectually empty life his wife, Mildred, is content to live. With Faber, a former university professor, he schemes to fund an underground printing press. Before he can enact his plans, he badgers Mildred and guests she has invited to the house into discussing **poetry** that he reads to them from a stolen book. At work the next day, Montag discovers that Mildred has informed on him, and his next **fire** call is to his own house. At the site he kills Beatty, his supervisor, who has long been suspicious of him. Now a fugitive, Montag flees to the **forest** outside the city where exiled intellectuals and academics have set up their own society (see **Exile**). It is the task of each person in this **community** to memorize books and become repositories of the **knowledge** they contain, a service that becomes fundamental to preserving **civilization** when the city is destroyed by **war** at novel's end.

Discussion

Inspired by images of book burning by the Nazis and written at the height of Army–McCarthy "Red Scare" hearings in America, *Fahrenheit 451* (purportedly the temperature at which book paper burns) projects a future in which the government (see **Governance Systems**) forces obedience from its citizens through an insidious form of mind control: it denies them the right to think by denying them the right to read. Government justifies its anti-intellectual campaign as a means of protecting the populace: books have conflicting ideas that provoke disagreement and discord among readers. The government promotes the idea that a happy society is one where differences of opinion do not exist. The effectiveness of its tactics can be gauged by the fear that Montag inspires in others when he shows them an actual book: they recoil from it as though it is dangerous. Already, people have accepted the Orwellian rewriting of **history** that is possible in such an intellectually lazy climate: for example, it is common **wisdom** among the population that firemen have *always* been book burners, rather than firefighters (see **Role Reversals**). *Fahrenheit 451* can thus be read as a conventional **dystopia** exposing the dark side of a seemingly ideal world. The coddled people of this future **America** have purchased happiness at an exorbitant price: their right to think for themselves.

Bradbury presents books not just as springboards for intellectual discussion, but as emblems of a way of life modern society has given up. As Montag talks to others sympathetic to his feelings, he discovers that in the past the free exchange of ideas represented by books was a regular aspect of a world that was slower-paced, with fewer distractions, and a world where talk and discussion of substantive matters were not considered abnormal. (This sensibility is even more pronounced in "The Fireman," the novella published in 1950 that Bradbury expanded into this novel.) Bradbury juxtaposes this nostalgic evocation of the past with the present, where books have been supplanted by interactive television systems (see **Television and Radio**) that people build into the walls of their homes. The scripts of the government-approved entertainments that they feature continuously are vapid and vague enough that anyone can interact with them and feel a part of their story. In contrast to the stories people read in books, there is no imaginative or intellectual engagement with stories projected on television. Like other members of his society, Montag seemingly works mostly to earn **money** to buy bigger and more sophisticated television systems (see **Work and Leisure**). The stultifying impact of these entertainments is evident among Mildred's friends: they gather for television parties and seem oblivious to the escalating **suicide** rates among their peers and imminent threats of **nuclear war** against America.

Montag's conflict with his society is ultimately one between **individualism and conformity**. Once inspired by reading, he no longer feels a part of his **culture**. His growing **estrangement** from Mildred and her values is emblematic of his estrangement from his world. He experiences the **paranoia** that any outsider to a group would feel, and recognizes that paranoia and fear are tools the government uses to impose conformity by turning the group against the individual. Law enforcement is determined to suppress individuality at all costs, or at least to convey this to the public. Although Montag manages to **escape** pursuit, he discovers later that the government has faked his being tracked down and killed and broadcast it, to reassure society that the crime he represents will be punished (see **Crime and Punishment**).

Bibliography

Harold Bloom, ed. *Ray Bradbury's Fahrenheit 451*. Philadelphia: Chelsea House, 2001.

Ray Bradbury. "Burning Bright: A Foreword." Bradbury, *Fahrenheit 451: The 40th Anniversary Edition*. New York: Simon & Schuster, 1993, 11–21.

Katie De Koster, ed. *Readings on Fahrenheit 451*. San Diego: Greenhaven Press, Inc., 2000.

Rafeeq O. McGiveron. "Do You Know the Legend of Hercules and Antaeus?" *Extrapolation*, 38 (Summer, 1997), 102–109.

Rafeeq O. McGiveron. "What Carried the Trick?" *Extrapolation*, 37 (Fall, 1996), 245–256.

David Seed. "The Flight from the Good Life." *Journal of American Studies*, 28 (1994), 225–240.

Susan Spencer. "The Post-Apocalyptic Library." *Extrapolation*, 32 (Winter, 1991), 331–342.

William F. Touponce. *Ray Bradbury*. Mercer Island, WA: Starmont House, 1989.

Donald Watt. "Burning Bright: *Fahrenheit 451* as Symbolic Dystopia." Joseph D. Olander and Martin H. Greenberg, eds., *Ray Bradbury*. New York: Taplinger, 1980, 195–213.

—Stefan Dziemianowicz

FARSCAPE (1999–2003)

———————————————■———————————————

Summary

While testing an experimental space module, **scientist** and **astronaut** John Crichton accidentally flies through a wormhole to the far side of the galaxy. Taken aboard the living ship Moya, he joins its crew of former prisoners, who are escaping their jailers, the Peacekeepers, and who share Crichton's **dream** of returning to their **homes**. Moya and her passengers flee into the Uncharted Territories, hunted by vengeful Peacekeeper Captain Crais, whose brother was accidentally killed by Crichton. When an **elder race** gives Crichton a latent **knowledge** of wormhole **physics**, both Peacekeepers and their enemies, the Scarrans, begin a relentless pursuit to capture him and the advanced science that could give either side a huge military advantage.

This pursuit is the main engine of the plot for the series' remaining three seasons. However, many subsidiary and stand-alone stories occur along the way, as Crichton and his friends sort out their personal **destinies** and relationships. Along with science fiction themes like other **dimensions, time travel, psychic powers,** and **genetic engineering,** the series delves into dramatic themes such as **guilt and responsibility, romance, sexuality, betrayal,** and the consequences of **torture** and **violence**.

Discussion

Farscape's unexpected cancellation at the end of the fourth season left the story unresolved until the 2004 miniseries *Farscape: The Peacekeeper Wars*. The **space war** between the Scarrans and Peacekeepers has begun, and as Crichton and his lover Aeryn await the **birth** of their child, Moya is pursued by both sides. Aeryn gives birth in the midst of battle, while the warrior D'Argo dies defending his friends. Crichton, determined to protect his **family**, unleashes a wormhole weapon so terrifyingly destructive that the warring sides agree to a peace treaty, which enables Moya's crew to return to their homes while Crichton and Aeryn plan to raise their son in peace.

As usual with **exile** stories, themes of home and family are central to *Farscape*. As Crichton searches for a way back to **Earth**, his growing friendships with Moya's crew and **romance** with Aeryn force a constant evolution of his definitions of home and family. Former Peacekeeper Aeryn also seeks a new definition of **identity** throughout the series, in a **gender role reversal** of the clichéd tough-guy soldier who learns emotional openness through true **love**. Ultimately, what Crichton and Aeryn will do to protect their family becomes a linchpin of the story, in episodes like "Hot to Katratzi" (2003), in which Crichton goes into an enemy base with an armed nuclear warhead strapped to his body.

The **death** and **rebirth** of main characters, often a **cliché** in genre series, is raised to **tragedy** in *Farscape*. When Crichton causes Aeryn's death in "Die Me, Dichotomy" (2001), her revival is bought by the **sacrifice** of the priestess Zhaan, with heavy consequences of guilt and remorse for survivors. A **doppelgänger** scenario, in which Crichton is duplicated by an alien, provides the extraordinary opportunity to have the protagonist die permanently in mid-story. Rather than making the duplicate a copy or **evil** twin, both Crichtons are established as genuine over a thirteen-episode arc. The heroic death of one in "Icarus Abides" (2001) leaves the other grappling with Aeryn's bereavement and a romantic triangle in which he is his own rival.

A proliferation of dream and **imaginary worlds** where important slices of the story unfold constantly challenges **perceptions** of reality in *Farscape*. Most notable is the Looney Toons homage, "Revenging Angel" (2001), in which Crichton and others appear as cartoon characters. In another reality-bending story arc, a "neural clone" of Scorpius inhabits Crichton's mind for most of the series, becoming a perverse **mentor** to the hero and creating numerous surreal scenarios and confrontations in Crichton's imagination.

With the help of the Jim Henson Creature Shop, which created the Muppets, *Farscape* produced a remarkable variety of alien creatures from the almost familiar to the impossibly bizarre. Among the main characters are a tentacled warrior, a humanoid **plant**, biomechanical ships, and the cadaverous, **insect**-like **villain** Scorpius. Muppet and animatronic characters like the pint-sized despot Rygel and crustacean Pilot, though alien in appearance and **biology**, created strong audience identification by exploring the human condition through their actions and desires, and were as beloved as any character portrayed by a human actor.

In broad strokes *Farscape*'s premise, a human who becomes a pivotal figure in a **space war**, is a science fiction standard. The series quickly raised itself above the commonplace through sharply drawn and unusual characters, razor-sharp **humor** that draws heavily on contemporary cultural references, and a willingness to take dramatic risks. In portraying crew members who are as likely to pursue conflicting individual goals as to cooperate for their own **survival**, it is often regarded as the "anti-*Star Trek*." *Farscape* won wide critical acclaim and numerous awards and nominations. The outcry among both fans and critics following its abrupt and controversial cancellation was unprecedented even for a genre series, and was only mollified by subsequent production of the miniseries.

Bibliography

K. Stoddard Hayes. "The Importance of Being Evil." *Farscape*, No. 9 (October/November 2002), 42–47.

James Iaccino. "*Farscape*'s John Crichton and Buck Rogers in the 25th Century." *Popular Culture Review*, 12 (August, 2001), 101–110.

Joe Nazzaro. "Reflections on *Farscape*." *Farscape*, No. 12 (April/May 2003), 14–19.

Paul Simpson. *Farscape: The Illustrated Season 4 Companion*. London: Titan Books, 2003.

Paul Simpson and David Hughes. *Farscape: The Illustrated Companion*. London: Titan Books, 2000.

Paul Simpson and Ruth Thomas. *Farscape: The Illustrated Season 2 Companion*. London: Titan Books, 2002.

———. *Farscape: The Illustrated Season 3 Companion*. London: Titan Books, 2002.

———. "Rockne Rolls On." *Farscape*, No. 1 (June/July, 2001), 22–26.

Glenn Yeffeth, ed. *Farscape Forever*. Dallas: BenBella Books, 2005.

—*Karen Stoddard Hayes*

THE FEMALE MAN BY JOANNA RUSS (1975)

Summary

Joanna, Jeannine, Janet and Jael are the four protagonists of *The Female Man*. They meet and interact with each other in the novel, although each lives in a different probability/continuum. In fact, all J's are versions of the same person, but each is a product of life in widely diverging universes, each with its own economy, **history**, and **culture**. Janet, the main focus of the novel, is an envoy from Whileaway, a utopian world built by women after men are killed by a plague (see **Plagues and Diseases; Utopia**); Jael is an assassin from a future in which the battle of the sexes has degenerated into outright **war**; Jeannine is a meek librarian waiting for **marriage** in a world in which the Depression never stopped and the Civil Rights movements of the sixties never happened (see **Libraries**); and Joanna is a feminist academic struggling with life in **America** in the late 1960s (see **Feminism**). They are brought together by Jael in her **quest** for aid in the battle against the Manlanders, a patriarchal homosocial society, in which some men are forced by others to inhabit the social/sexual roles contemporarily assigned to women.

Discussion

The central theme of *The Female Man* is **gender**. In each world inhabited by a J, except for Whileaway, women's lives are deformed by gender expectations. The novel is explicit that these expectations are largely imposed by men, but also distort men's lives. The novel demonstrates its refusal of sexual dichotomy in part by its refusal of a linear, dichotomous structure. The "I" who speaks in the novel, which is largely written from the perspectives of the various J's, cannot clearly be identified as a particular J or the author. The narrative is experimental, has little plot, and works through a pastiche of dialogue, jokes, Whileawayan sayings, and fragments of news reports.

In *The Female Man*, Russ responds to and even anticipates a variety of feminist arguments about the relationship between biological sex, gender, **sexuality**, and the body. Materialist feminists, like Monique Wittig, argue that sex and gender do not exist, but are discursively products of heterosexuality, created by the "straight mind." Liberal feminists argue that liberation can best be achieved through equal access to work. Radical feminists believe that gender imprisons people and must be eliminated in the search for **freedom**. *The Female Man* plays with all these ideas. In one sense, it can be argued that Whileaway has no women, because "woman" exists only in relation to "man." Without men, "woman" disappears and what emerges is a pure **humanity** untainted by sex and gender. *The Female Man* is thus reminiscent of Ursula K. Le Guin's creation of a genderless alien race in *The Left Hand of Darkness*; both novels attempt to imagine a way in which it might be possible to live beyond gender (see **Androgyny**).

It is also possible to see Whileaway as a lesbian utopia because the lack of men means that female **homosexuality** is the only available option. In this respect *The Female Man* contrasts with Charlotte Perkins Gilman's *Herland*, wherein the all-female utopian society is celibate but reproduces without either sex or **technology**. Whileawayan women, living in a technologically sophisticated world, marry and create various kinds of **families**, but these institutions do not parallel those in the contemporary world. There is no insistence on monogamy, for example. *The Female Man*'s primary depiction of a lesbian relationship takes place between Janet and Laura, daughter of Janet's hosts in Joanna's universe. In Laura, Russ depicts the nearly impossible tension between wanting to refuse femininity yet not wanting to be seen as "abnormal." *The Female Man* uses this relationship to explore **taboos** (cross-age relationships are forbidden on Whileaway) and inquire about the ways in which gender **identity** relates to sexual identity.

Manlanders also engage in sex with people of the same sex, although their sexual objects are castrated men who are taught to act in ways that the "real-men" understand as feminine. Manlanders see themselves as heterosexual and Russ makes the astute comment that "real homosexuality would blow Manland to pieces." This statement anticipates the theoretical argument that contemporary male homosociality needs homophobia to enforce heterosexual behavior in men.

Critical reception of *The Female Man* has been mixed. Indeed, the deep division of opinion about the novel has replicated the "war of the sexes" that Russ discusses in one of her own articles on science fiction: women generally praise the novel, while men have mostly condemned it as shrill and angry. These are responses that Russ anticipates in the novel, printing snippets of fictitious reviews that accurately anticipate the major criticisms leveled against it. However, as Frances Bonner and others point out, feminist readings of *The Female Man* have not been consistent. Feminists in the 1970s focused on Janet and Whileaway, emphasizing the novel's utopian elements. **Cyberpunk** adapted Jael to its own purposes, while other feminist writers, like Marge Piercy, have concentrated on the figure of Davy, Jael's **cyborg** sex toy.

While some critics denounce *The Female Man* for what they see as its anger, it is also a funny book (see **Humor**), scathingly accurate in its portrayal of life for women academics in the 1960s and 1970s. It is also a political novel whose goal is presaged by Russ's final paragraph, looking forward to a world in which gender roles will have been so thoroughly undone as to make *The Female Man*'s subject matter incomprehensible.

Bibliography

Susan Ayres. "The 'Straight Mind' in Russ's *The Female Man.*" *Science-Fiction Studies*, 22 (March, 1995), 22–34.

Frances Bartkowski. *Feminist Utopias.* Lincoln: University of Nebraska Press, 1989.

Frances Bonner. "From 'The Female Man' to the 'Virtual Girl.'" *Hecate*, 22 (May, 1996), 104–120.

Heather J. Hicks. "Automating Feminism." *Postmodern Culture*, 9 (1999), 1–41.

Sarah Lefanu. *In the Chinks of the World Machine.* London: Women's Press, 1988.

Tom Moylan. *Demand the Impossible.* New York: Methuen, 1986.

Monique Witting. *The Straight Mind and Other Essays.* Boston: Beacon Press, 1992.

Jenny Wolmark. *Aliens and Others.* London: Harvester Wheatsheaf, 1993.

—Wendy Pearson

FIELD OF DREAMS (1989)

■

Summary

One night, Iowa farmer Ray Kinsella hears a mysterious voice whisper, "If you build it, he will come." In response, he builds a baseball field in his cornfield (see **Sports**), and soon, there appears the corporeal ghost of Shoeless Joe Jackson, expelled from baseball because of a scandal, followed by other famous players (see **Ghosts and Hauntings**). Ray again hears the whispering voice saying "Ease his pain," which he concludes refers to the **pain** of writer Terence Mann, now a recluse. Ray travels to Boston and persuades Mann to accompany him to a game, where they see the scoreboard refer a little-known former player, Archie "Moonlight" Graham, and issue the instruction: "Go the distance." They travel to Graham's hometown and find he has died after leaving baseball to became the local doctor. Preparing to abandon his **quest**, Ray **timeslips** to 1972, where he meets and invites Graham to pursue his dreams at the Iowa field—but Graham refuses. His wife phones to tell Ray bankruptcy looms; her brother Mark is about to foreclose their mortgage. Returning home, Ray and Mann pick up a hitchhiker, the youthful Graham, who joins the game but, when Ray's daughter requires medical attention, steps over the **threshold** of the baseball field's perimeter to become the aged Dr. Graham and tend to her. The players retreat to the **borderland**, as does Mann, at Shoeless Joe's invitation. Only Shoeless Joe and the catcher remain. Shoeless Joe repeats, "If you build it, he will come," and indicates the catcher, who Ray recognizes as his estranged dead **father**; the two are at last reconciled. As the film closes we see countless cars making the pilgrimage to Ray's field, presumably solving the Kinsellas' financial woes.

Discussion

Based on W.P. Kinsella's novel *Shoeless Joe* (1982), *Field of Dreams* is faithful to the spirit of the novel, though there are some significant differences between the book and the film. In the book's opening chapter, Ray at first builds only a representation of that part of the outfield where Shoeless Joe habitually played but is then urged by Shoeless Joe to expand it: if the places for other players are not created, those players cannot come. The film, in having Ray build the entire field at once, loses this important nuance. Also, in the novel the writer whom Ray recruits is not the fictional Terence Mann but a real writer famous for withdrawing from society, J.D. Salinger.

Most obviously, this is a film steeped in the mythos of baseball, a central theme in Kinsella's fiction. *Field of Dreams* foregrounds the **game** as a unifying force, an unchanging and innocent pastime that can bridge the gaps between the generations, bringing together fathers and sons, and Americans from the 1920s, the 1960s, and the 1980s, in common respect for and enjoyment of the game. The baseball diamond in the middle of a cornfield functions as a fairy circle, a timeless place where the dead and the living can escape from **time** in a game celebrated for its **pastoral** spirit and absence of time limitations. And, though Kinsella is a Canadian writer, the film enshrines baseball as a symbol of **America**—a nation that, though forever changing, can find a sense of permanence through constants like the game of baseball. In *Field of Dreams*, baseball is explicitly linked to the homespun American values of **family** and **community**, which, like the threatened family **farm** of the film, must be maintained and preserved, just as baseball itself has been maintained and preserved through the generations.

Also integral to the story is the matter of **perception**: the dead players and the game can be seen only by those with the imaginative power to believe in that mythos. The hard-headed Mark can see only an empty baseball field; but, on witnessing Graham step from the field and attend to Ray's daughter, Mark is finally capable of seeing the players. Similarly, the other fans at the Boston stadium see only a normal scoreboard, but Ray and Mann, keenly attuned to the **history** and traditions of baseball, can observe a reference to a forgotten player whose entire baseball career consisted of a single inning but who, nevertheless, is forever enshrined in the record books that are meticulously compiled and cherished by dedicated fans.

A further subtext relates to the notion of the afterlife, and in particular to differing ideas of **Heaven**. To the players the timeless baseball field on which they can eternally find **rebirth** is Heaven; to Mann, Heaven is the rediscovery of the yen to write; and Ray eventually discovers that Heaven is Iowa, his farm, his family, and their **love**. In passing there are implicit and explicit observations concerning the importance of **memory**: the magic of the film keeps working because Ray remembers Shoeless Joe, because he and his wife remember Terence Mann, and because Americans are presumably willing to drive long hours to again see the baseball players that they remember so well. A further mechanism of remembrance is the role played by **writing and authors**; just as Mann's novels keep his memory alive for young people who were inspired by his works in the 1960s, the film implies that Mann will eventually write the story of the film and thus help preserve the memory of Ray Kinsella and his remarkable baseball field.

Bibliography

Caroline M. Cooper. "*Field of Dreams*: A Favorite of President Clinton—but a Typical Reaganite Film?" *Literature/Film Quarterly*, 23 (1995), 163–169.

Kyle Counts. "Conjurer of Dreams." *Cinefantastique*, 20 (November, 1989), 4–5, 118.

Ann Knight. *W.P. Kinsella: A Partially-Annotated Bibliographical Checklist.* Iowa City: A-Cross Publications, 1983.

Mark R. Leeper. "*Field of Dreams.*" *Lan's Lantern*, 32 (March, 1990), 46–47.

Nick Lowe. "*Field of Dreams.*" *Interzone*, No. 33 (January/February, 1990), 33.

Don Murray. *The Fiction of W. P. Kinsella.* Fredericton, New Brunswick: York Press, 1987.

Daniel Schweiger. "*Field of Dreams.*" *Cinefantastique*, 20 (November, 1989), 7, 119.

James M. Wall. "A Playing Field for the Boys of Eternity." *Christian Century*, 106 (May 17, 1989), 515–516.

—*John Grant*

FLATLAND BY EDWIN A. ABBOTT (1884)

■

*Mark his perfect self-contentment, and
hence learn this lesson, that to be self-
contented is to be vile and ignorant, and
that to aspire is better than to be blindly
and impotently happy.*

—Edwin A. Abbott
Flatland (1884)

Summary

Flatland is narrated by A. Square, an inhabitant of the effectively two-**dimensional** world of Flatland (though it is explained that the world does possess an infinitesimal height). In Part I, A. Square describes the inhabitants and lifestyles of Flatland. The men are polygons—triangles, squares, pentagons, and other regular figures; women are line segments. Status and power in Flatland society are determined by how many sides a polygon has—the more the better—with hexagons and above considered royalty; each generation normally gives birth to offspring with one additional side, so **families** can gradually ascend to higher classes. Recognition is achieved by feeling (see **Touch**) or the diminishing visibility of sides. There is considerable discussion about the unrest that resulted from the introduction of **colors** to Flatland and their eventual removal.

In Part II, A. Square first encounters the King of Lineland, a one-dimensional world, and vainly endeavors to explain the existence of two dimensions. In a **role reversal**, he is then visited by a three-dimensional Sphere from Spaceland who attempts with little success to explain the existence of three dimensions. A. Square finally understands and accepts the third dimension when the Sphere takes him into Spaceland to see for himself. The two beings also speculate about the possibility of a four-dimensional world before A. Square returns to Flatland, to find of course that none of his fellow citizens believe his tales of a three-dimensional world. Soon, he is imprisoned for life as an unrepentant heretic.

Discussion

In 1880, the mathematician Charles Howard Hinton wrote a paper that may have suggested the concept of a two-dimensional world to Edwin Abbott, an important British educator who wrote voluminously on Biblical topics. Wherever the idea originated, however, Abbott undoubtedly had three purposes in mind when he wrote *Flatland*.

First, he wished to advance the cause of dimensional theory in **mathematics**. Although a few great mathematicians like Hinton had studied higher dimensions, the area was generally frowned on or even ridiculed. Abbott's answer was to have a Sphere visit Flatland and explain the third dimension, by implication defending the idea that a resident of a three-dimensional world might legitimately speculate about higher-dimensional worlds.

A second purpose was to carry out an elaborate exercise in logic, by developing and presenting an ethnographic account of life in a two-dimensional world. As such, *Flatland* is amusing, acute, and rigorous. Abbott thinks carefully about what polygons in a two-dimensional world would look like to each other, how they might deal with everyday problems like getting in and out of houses and recognizing individuals, and what sort of social structure might emerge in a world inhabited by various sorts of polygons. Abbott is especially ingenious in recognizing how the use of color might distort the polygons' **perceptions** of their peers, requiring their elimination. His briefer portrayal of Lineland is similarly derived from careful consideration of the extremely limited possibilities of a one-dimensional world.

Finally, Abbott wishes to present a **satire** on Victorian England, illustrating in the form of a **fable** or **allegory** various aspects of his society that were open to criticism: the low position of women, the rigid class distinctions sometimes bypassed by special interests, the brutal treatment of the lower classes (see **Class System**), the ruthlessness of a government that represses and slaughters dissidents (see **Governance Systems**), and the stifling of free thought by orthodoxy (see **Freedom**). The way that equilateral triangles look down upon isosceles triangles might further be taken as a commentary on **race relations**, though Abbott was probably not thinking in those terms. Unfortunately, Abbott's satire proved less successful than the other aspects of his work, since many misinterpreted his intentions. In particular, women of his day—like women of the present—might regard his portrayal of Flatland women as the height of **sexism**: since they are not polygons, women cannot attain power or social position, and since they are dangerous, needle-like creatures, they must perpetually issue warning cries so they do not accidentally puncture men. In his "Preface" to a hastily produced Second Edition, also published in 1884, Abbott found it necessary to address, among other issues, the charge that its author was a "woman-hater."

Abbott was not a gifted prose stylist, and many readers find it hard to get through *Flatland*'s dry and didactic Part I; however, the more narrative Part II is considerably livelier, allowing A. Square to come to life as a genuine character. Still, it is undoubtedly because of its strikingly elaborated conceit, not its literary quality, that Abbott's slender volume has had considerable influence on later writers. Hinton himself produced two responses to *Flatland*, "A Plane World" (1885) and *An Episode of Flatland* (1907). Other early **explorations** of Flatland were Alfred T. Schofield's *Another World* (1888) and Edwin Lassetter Bynner's "A Cruise in a Soap Bubble" (1891), while more recent homages to Abbott include Dionys Burger's *Sphereland* (1965), A.K. Dewdney's *The Planiverse* (1983), Rudy Rucker's

"Message Found in a Copy of *Flatland*" (1983), and Ian Stewart's *Flatterland* (2001). *Flatland* also inspired an episode of *The Outer Limits*, "Behold, Eck!" (1964), which describes the misadventures of a blob-like two-dimensional being who is temporarily trapped in our three-dimensional world.

Bibliography

Lawrence I. Berkove. "A Paradoxical American Appropriation of Flatland." *Extrapolation*, 41 (Fall, 2000), 266–271.

Martin Coonen. "Edwin Abbott Abbott: Primary and Secondary Checklists with Partial Annotations." *Bulletin of Bibliography*, 56 (December, 1999), 247–255.

Elliot L. Gilbert. "Upward, Not Northward." *English Literature in Transition*, 34 (1991), 391–404.

Banesh Hoffmann. "Introduction." 1952. Abbott, *Flatland*. New York: Dover, 1979, iii–iv.

Rosemary Jann. "Abbott's *Flatland*." *Victorian Studies*, 28 (Spring, 1985), 473–490.

Brian Stableford. "The Planiverse." Stableford, *The Dictionary of Science Fiction Places*. New York: Wonderland Press, 1999, 239–241.

Ian Stewart. *The Annotated Flatland*, by Edwin A. Abbott. Cambridge, MA: Perseus, 2002.

K.G. Valente. "Transgression and Transcendence." *Nineteenth-Century Contexts*, 26 (March, 2004), 61–77.

—*Gary Westfahl*

FLOWERS FOR ALGERNON BY DANIEL KEYES (1966)

Summary

Flowers for Algernon is narrated by Charlie Gordon, a 32-year-old man who, at the novel's beginning, has an IQ of 68. Unusually motivated to learn, Charlie is chosen to undergo an experimental surgical procedure that will raise his **intelligence**. The operation succeeds, and Charlie is overjoyed when he finally completes a maze faster than Algernon, a mouse who underwent the same surgical procedure (see **Rats and Mice**). Charlie's IQ almost triples, but his increased awareness of the world leads to alienation and disappointment. He realizes that people in his past who he thought were friends were really cruel and abusive and that the **scientists** behind the procedure are more interested in power and fame than in helping others. He also recovers **memories** of an abused childhood and falls in **love** with Alice Kinnian, his former night-school teacher. When Algernon shows signs of deterioration, Charlie plunges into his own research and discovers that the effects of the operation are not permanent. By the end of the novel, Algernon has died and Charlie has returned to his previous level of intelligence, though he carries with him the **knowledge** that other people are "not so smart like you once thot they were."

Discussion

Based on the author's Hugo Award-winning story of the same title (1958) and winner of the Nebula Award for Best Novel, *Flowers for Algernon* has enjoyed widespread critical and popular acclaim both inside and outside the science fiction field.

It has been adapted for radio, stage, film, and television (most famously as the 1968 feature film *Charly*, which earned Cliff Robertson an Academy Award for his portrayal of Charlie Gordon) and has been a staple of high-school reading lists for decades. Its fame derives in part from Keyes's tour-de-force use of first-person point of view, forcing readers to follow in Charlie's own words his rise from disability ("Dr Strauss says I should rite down what I think and remember and every thing that happins to me from now on") to genius ("they continually admonish me to speak and write simply so that people who read these reports will be able to understand me") and eventual decline ("Im glad I got a second chanse in life . . . please if you get a chanse put some flowrs on Algernons gave in the bak yard"). However, the novel also offers an unusually rich exploration of themes that science fiction and mainstream literature often approach from opposite directions.

In literary terms, the novel functions as both **Bildungsroman**, as Charlie grows from child-like naiveté to a sophisticated awareness of the world that surrounds him and the people who inhabit it, and **tragedy**, as Charlie's return to subnormal intelligence is presented as an inevitable "fall." However, the "tragic flaw" in the novel is not within Charlie but without him, in the **technology** that raises him to a great height and then allows him to fall back down, and, implicitly, in the arrogance of the scientists who tampered with Charlie's brain. The notion of Charlie's "fall" is reinforced by comments from two minor characters who compare his operation to the forbidden knowledge that led to **Adam and Eve**'s expulsion from Eden, while the novel's presentation of flawed technology and knowledge that causes more harm than good recalls the **Frankenstein monster**.

But Keyes does not deal with his material in a simplistic fashion. While traditional science fiction might argue that smarter is better, and classic Western literature might warn against **hubris** and tampering with nature, *Flowers for Algernon* suggests that things are more complicated than that. As Thomas D. Clareson points out, the novel combines the figures of **mad scientist** and **monster** in Charlie Gordon, who is both the creation of scientists and, in his genius phase, himself a scientist trying to unlock the secret of his rise and pending fall. Ultimately, the novel does not argue against the pursuit of knowledge but urges that knowledge be put in perspective, while realizing that intelligence alone is not enough. Charlie understands things much better after his IQ is raised, but his relationships with others are largely unimproved. Co-workers who tormented him are now afraid of him; scientists who ostensibly wanted to help him are now intimidated by him. Alice Killien, the night-school teacher who pitied him and the woman Charlie loves, is now as far below his intelligence as he used to be below hers. As the genius Charlie writes of his relationship with Alice, "all my intelligence doesn't help me solve a problem like this."

A notable amount of material in the novel added to the original story deals with Charlie's gradual recovery of childhood memory through **sleep**-learning and psychotherapy. In flashbacks, the reader learns that Charlie's emotionally unstable **mother** at first refused to admit Charlie was disabled and then, after his younger sister displayed normal intelligence, turned on her son, reacting violently to any evidence of Charlie's developing **sexuality** out of fear that he would molest his sister. Both Charlie's unusually strong motivation to learn and uncertain responses to women are rooted in his mother's abuse. The novel thus presents Charlie firmly in terms of orthodox Freudian **psychology**: it is only after recovering these memories and coming to term with them that Charlie can enjoy a complete emotional and sexual relationship with Alice.

Ultimately, *Flowers for Algernon* makes it clear that any single, narrowly focused approach to the world is simply not enough. Charlie's pursuit of his own **identity**, formed by both memory and intelligence, is inextricably bound up with his search for **community** among the people who surround him. While the novel's most famously poignant moments center on Charlie's loss of intelligence, it is worth noting that, while still a genius, he roams the streets of New York feeling an "unbearable hunger" for human contact. And while genius Charlie may be "living at a peak of clarity and beauty I never knew existed," he comes to realize that "intelligence and education isn't worth a damn . . . all too often a search for knowledge drives out the search for love."

Bibliography

Patrice Cassedy. *Understanding Flowers for Algernon.* San Diego, CA: Lucent Books, 2001.

Mark R. Hillegas. "Other Worlds to Conquer." *Saturday Review*, 49 (March 26, 1966), 33–34.

Daniel Keyes. *Algernon, Charlie, and I.* Boca Raton, FL: Challcrest Press, 1999.

Donald A. Palumbo. "The Monomyth in Daniel Keyes's *Flowers for Algernon.*" *Journal of the Fantastic in the Arts*, 14 (Winter, 2004), 427–446.

David Pringle. "*Flowers for Algernon* by Daniel Keyes." Pringle, *Science Fiction: The 100 Best Novels.* New York: Carroll and Graf, 1985, 121–122.

Robert Scholes. "Structural Fabulation." Scholes, *Structural Fabulation.* Notre Dame: University of Notre Dame Press, 1975, 45–76.

Robert Small, Jr. "*Flowers for Algernon* by Daniel Keyes." Nicholas J. Karolides, Lee Burress, and John M. Kean, eds., *Censored Books.* Metuchen, NJ: Scarecrow, 1993, 249–255.

Paul Williams. "More 'Flowers for Algernon.'" *New York Review of Science Fiction*, No. 8 (April, 1989), 5–6.

—*F. Brett Cox*

FORBIDDEN PLANET (1956)

■

[Ostrow:] But the Krell forgot one thing—
[Adams:] Yes, what?
[Ostrow:] Monsters, John. Monsters
from the id!

—Cyril Hume
Forbidden Planet (1956)

Summary

United Planets Cruiser C57D approaches the fourth planet (see **Alien Worlds**) of the Altair system, its mission to discover the fate of the *Bellerophon*, which landed there twenty years earlier. Despite warnings from Dr. Morbius, the *Bellerophon*'s sole survivor, Commander Adams lands and, with Lieutenants Farman and Ostrow, visits him. They learn that some mysterious **force** slaughtered the expedition members and destroyed their spaceship, leaving only Morbius and his wife alive; she died after giving **birth** to Altaira. A sexual innocent (see **Virginity**) whose only friends are wild animals (see **Lions and Tigers**), Altaira is perplexed by Farman's advances and labeled a **temptress** by Adams. An invisible creature (see **Invisibility**) sabotages C57D and Farman is killed in a later attack. Adams and Altaira kiss passionately, prompting her tiger to attack them. Morbius reveals the almost magical **technology** that the Krell, the original inhabitants of Altair-4, left behind when they were wiped out overnight. It transpires that the Krell technology creates a **monster** from Morbius's id, expressing his rage whenever he is defied, which wiped out the *Bellerophon* expedition and is now attacking Adams and Altaira. Morbius dies (see **Sacrifice**) so that they can **escape**, destroying the planet to prevent human access to **knowledge** they are not yet wise enough to utilize well.

Discussion

A loose adaptation of William **Shakespeare**'s *The Tempest* (c. 1611), *Forbidden Planet* tells a familiar story of **hubris** being clobbered. In seeking to become disembodied creatures of pure reason (see **Immortality and Longevity**), and leave interactions with gross materiality to their technology (see **Machines and Mechanization**), the Krell, whose superior intellects and greater rationality are evident from their larger heads, neglected their subconscious minds, their drives and desires. Consequently, like the suddenly deranged inhabitants of Lagash in Isaac Asimov's "Nightfall" (1941), they destroyed themselves and their **civilization** overnight (see **Madness**). Morbius, the *Bellerophon*'s philologist (see **Language and Linguistics**), uses Krell technology to boost his **intelligence**, becoming more rational and thus, in his eyes, the only person fit to oversee human access to this technology. But his excess rationality becomes irrational (see **Mad Scientists**), and his hubris unleashes destructive powers.

    Forbidden Planet—like *The Day the Earth Stood Still* and *Star Trek*, a series some consider it to have inspired—posits a human future dependent upon reason overcoming emotion and instinct, and, as is typical of much science fiction, conflates and confuses **evolution** and **progress**. However, like *Metropolis, Dr. Jekyll and Mr Hyde*, and *King Kong*, it is rather more concerned with displaying the spectacular destructive consequences of the failure of reason to repress psychosexual drives (see **Psychology**). While 1950s and 1960s technodramas like *Strategic Air Command* (1955) and *A Gathering of Eagles* (1963) problematically asserted the necessary subordination of desire to military-corporate structures, *Forbidden Planet* repeatedly foregrounds the potential, if clichéd, dangers of such surplus repression on male sexual drives (see **Clichés**). It is, however, unable to countenance **homosexuality** and seems uncertain as to whether Altaira should be blamed for arousing desire among C57D's all-male crew.

    Still, *Forbidden Planet* should really be considered alongside the 1950s melodramas of Douglas Sirk, Nicholas Ray, and Vincente Minnelli, as the remarkable **home** that Morbius has built on Altair-4 suggests. A hyperbolic version of the surburban ranch house (see **Architecture and Interior Design**), complete with labor-saving devices and even a servant in the form of Robby the Robot (see **Robots**), it is situated in beautiful **gardens** on the edge of the **frontier**, and is torn apart by an Oedipal conflict (see **Fathers**) as Morbius's refusal of his daughter's **sexuality** is manifested as an illicit and murderous desire. While such melodramas displace sexual **anxiety** onto their elaborate mise-en-scène, *Forbidden Planet* is able to use its fantastic prerogative to animate its mise-en-scène, to show the repressed returning in the form of a monster. Like Alfred Bester's ***The Stars My Destination*** and Stanislaw Lem's *Solaris*, it has, in this respect, more in common with Henry James's *The Turn of the Screw* (1898), Shirley Jackson's *The Haunting of Hill House* (1959), *The Haunting* (1963), and ***The Shining*** than its science fiction trappings, pseudo-scientific patter, and lengthy procedurals might suggest (see **Ghosts and Hauntings**).

However, considered alongside melodramas like *The Cobweb* (1955), *Picnic* (1955), *Rebel Without a Cause* (1955), *Imitation of Life* (1959) and *Splendor in the Grass* (1961), *Forbidden Planet* clearly squanders the opportunity to use the fantastic to say anything about teenage female sexuality. Adams patronizes Altaira's failure to understand why her "loss of innnocence" triggers the tiger's attack, but the scene ends clumsily without explanation; in the following scene when Adams talks to Ostrow, he nods in the direction of the garden and Altaira, but no reverse shot shows what they are looking at. Unable to speak or successfully visualize teenage female sexuality, *Forbidden Planet* is content to depict passion, desire, and burgeoning **romance** as the introduction of **sin** into paradise—as is signalled by one of the film's successful uses of melodramatic convention: Altaira's significant but not overplayed costume change from white full-length robe to overtly sexualized short black dress.

Novelized by W.J. Stuart in 1956, *Forbidden Planet* also inspired the stage musical *Return to the Forbidden Planet* (1983). Its striking character Robby the Robot went on to enjoy an independent career in other films and television programs.

Bibliography

F.S. Clarke and S. Rubin. "Making *Forbidden Planet*." *Cinefantastique*, 8 (Spring, 1979), 4–67.

John Jolly. "The Bellerophon Myth and *Forbidden Planet*." *Extrapolation*, 27 (Spring, 1986), 84–90.

Seth Lerer. "*Forbidden Planet* and the Terrors of Philology." *Raritan*, 19 (Winter, 2000), 73–86.

T.J. Matheson. "Marcuse, Ellul, and the Science-Fiction Film." *Science-Fiction Studies*, 19 (November, 1992), 326–339.

Bernard Shapiro. "Universal Truths." *Journal of Popular Film and Television*, 18 (1990), 103–111.

Margaret Tarrat. "Monsters from the Id." Barry Keith Grant, ed., *Film Genre Reader II*. Austin: University of Texas Press, 1995, 330–349.

J.P. Telotte. "Science Fiction in Double Focus: *Forbidden Planet*." *Film Criticism*, 13 (1989), 25–26.

John Trushell. "Return of *Forbidden Planet*?" *Foundation*, No. 64 (Summer, 1995), 82–89.

———. "A Postmodern (Re)Turn to *Forbidden Planet*." *Foundation*, No. 69 (Spring, 1997), 60–67.

—*Mark Bould*

THE FOREVER WAR BY JOE HALDEMAN (1975)

Summary

In 1997, William Mandella is one of a hundred elite male and female citizens drafted by the United Nations Exploratory Force (UNEF) to fight an alien **hive mind** embodied by the Taurans. Soldiers are trained to use the powered armor first envisaged by Robert A. Heinlein in *Starship Troopers*. Because both sides use collapsars (similar to **black holes**) to travel in **hyperspace**, their experience of **time** is relative: what may be a few months for combatants can be months or years for those at **home** (or on the opposing side). Back from the first **space war**, Mandella and his partner Marygay Potter find the Earth in 2023 badly overcrowded, dangerous, and populated largely by homosexuals (see **Homosexuality**). The violent deaths of Mandella and Potter's **families** cause the pair to rejoin the army. In 2458 A.D. the military separates Mandella and Potter, the only contact each has with the past. Surviving one last battle, the two are reunited after 1143 years of **war**. Humans have been replaced by a group mind known only as Man, which has negotiated peace with the Taurans. Mandella and Potter travel to one of the few planets inhabited by individual humans where Potter gives **birth** to their son.

Discussion

The Forever War has been adapted by artist Marvano (Mark van Oppen) as three graphic novels, and has been followed by three different kinds of sequels. *Forever Free* (1999) picks up twenty years after *The Forever War* to find Mandella, Potter, and their teenaged **children** about to explore the universe; it is a transcendental novel. The novella "A Separate War" (in Robert Silverberg's *Far Horizons* [1999]) recounts Marygay's final battle in the war. *Forever Peace* (1997) is a philosophical sequel to *The Forever War*, and considers the question of what might be necessary to stop war. Two editions of *The Forever War* have been published: the first (1975) has a relatively tame center section; the second (1997), the author's preferred edition, is bleaker, grittier, and truer to the original.

   The Forever War is considered by many to be a *roman á clef* about Haldeman's and **America**'s experiences in the Vietnam War ("Mandella" is a rough anagram of "Haldeman"). Although there are many compelling ties, the comparison obscures a novel that discusses the problems of military **governance systems**, **gender**, the **class system**, sexual **identity**, and the nature of **time** in war. *The Forever War* utterly rejects militarism, arguing that the military–industrial complex upon which many capitalist high-tech economies are based produces only endless (forever) war. In having their lives reduced to kilocalories on Earth, Mandella and Potter understand how little they are worth to the state unless they are energy producers rather than consumers. As soldiers they fuel the war; as civilians they eat up its profits. Concerned with **ecology** and **overpopulation**, *The Forever War* shows the military as careless about life, corrupt, and amoral. There is little combat in the novel, and what there is denies the myths of battlefield heroism seen in *Starship Troopers*. Things happen by mistake; people are killed by accident and for little or no reason.

Haldeman, like Orson Scott Card in **Ender's Game** and its sequels, concludes that the forces that make human life worthwhile are tied to **community, education, and art**. Mandella's long connection with Potter is not simply a **romance** but an inquiry into the power of **memory** and nostalgia. Because time is a character in the book, separating and uniting events and people, Mandella (trained as a physicist) considers how relativistic **space travel** alters his worldview. The book investigates the condition of people lost far from home, where all creatures and places have become alien. Neither Mandella nor Potter ever have a chance to work at peace, so tightly bound are they in military chains. When they are finally free the world they know has disappeared forever. The deep sadness each character feels becomes irony at the novel's apparent happy conclusion: Haldeman has warned repeatedly that a child born to the inmate of a human zoo guarantees no happy ending. War paves over the universe and makes all things miserably uniform.

Haldeman also condemns the science and **medicine** that agree to serve the military. Medicine's ability to recast bodies for combat by making them into **cyborgs** causes Mandella to wonder how much of him he will lose before his **humanity** goes too. Haldeman's description of powered battle armor quashes Heinlein's hymn to engineering: the armor brutally inserts itself into the soldiers' bodies, kills some, amputates others, and remakes humans in a machine image. Women prove to be as murderous and as innocent as their male counterparts (*Starship Troopers* romanticizes women's wartime intuition), and homosexuals prove to be people as fallible (and not) as the rest. Mandella is never at home with any of it—the armor, the military, the war, the future, the aliens, or finally, the peace. Ultimately all genders, like all individuals, are eradicated by the **clone** which, while it ends the "forever" war, also ends discussion, difference, and joy. Peace has come at a very high price.

Bibliography

Tim Blackmore. "Warring Stories." *Extrapolation*, 34 (Summer, 1993), 131–146.
Joan Gordon. *Joe Haldeman*. Mercer Island, WA: Starmont House, 1980.
———. "Joe Haldeman: Cyberpunk Before Cyberpunk Was Cool?" Donald E. Morse, ed., *The Celebration of the Fantastic*. Westport, CT: Greenwood, 1992, 251–257.
Joe Haldeman. *Vietnam and Other Alien Worlds*. Framingham, MA: NESFA Press, 1993.
Steffen Hantke. "Surgical Strikes and Prosthetic Warriors." *Science-Fiction Studies*, 25 (November, 1998), 495–509.
Stan Nicholls. "Joe Haldeman Frees Something Up." Nicholls, ed., *Wordsmiths of Wonder*. London: Orbit, 1993, 80–91.
Kathy Romer. "The Long Habit of Writing." *Extrapolation*, 30 (Summer, 1989), 166–175.
Alasdair Spark. "The Art of Future War." Tom Shippey, ed., *Fictional Space*. Atlantic Highlands, NJ: Humanities Press, 1991, 133–165.
Phillip E. Wegner. "Soldierboys for Peace." Amitava Kumar, ed., *World Bank Literature*. Minneapolis: University of Minnesota Press, 2003, 280–296.

—Tim Blackmore

FOUNDATION BY ISAAC ASIMOV (1951)

Summary

In the **far future**, Hari Seldon develops the predictive science of psychohistory and determines that the **galactic empire** will soon collapse, plunging the galaxy into ten thousand years of chaos. To reduce this interregnum to a thousand years, he establishes two secret Foundations to preserve human **knowledge** and prepare for the restoration of **civilization**. The nine stories from the 1940s assembled as the original Foundation trilogy—*Foundation, Foundation and Empire* (1952), and *Second Foundation* (1953)—follow the adventures of the First Foundation on the edge of the galaxy as it is assisted through various crises by precorded messages from Seldon, who had predicted each problem and its best resolution. However, since psychohistory only predicts the future of groups, Seldon fails to foresee the emergence of a single individual with **psychic powers**, the Mule, who briefly threatens all his plans. Meanwhile, the Second Foundation separately operates on Trantor, the urbanized planet that was the galactic empire's capital.

Later, Asimov extended his trilogy with four additional novels merging the Foundation series with his **robot** stories (see *I, Robot*). The final two novels, *Prelude to Foundation* (1988) and *Forward the Foundation* (1993), reveal that Seldon had been secretly assisted by robot R. Daneel Olivaw, who saw psychohistory as a new way to improve **humanity**. As another potential direction for humanity's future, Olivaw also arranged for the creation of a world of humans united as a **hive mind**, Gaia, introduced in *Foundation's Edge* (1982). In *Foundation and Earth* (1985), people searching for the lost planet **Earth** learn from Olivaw that the planet had deliberately been turned into a radioactive wasteland as another step in the robot's plan to enhance human development. Three Foundation novels by Gregory Benford, Greg Bear, and David Brin, commissioned by Asimov's estate after his death, add embellishments to this epic but fail to provide a grand conclusion.

Discussion

Isaac Asimov had the rationalist ability as a young fan and writer, nurtured by John W. Campbell, Jr., to conceive key general ideas and then extrapolate them widely (see **Hard Science Fiction**). This methodology is radical, imaginative, and genuinely literary in the same ways that Enlightenment thought shook up old thinking and the early church shook up the Roman Empire with something new. The ability is a key element in the emergence of science fiction, which is why Asimov credited Campbell with laying the "foundation" for the writing of superior science fiction—a revelatory choice of words indeed.

Asimov's central character Seldon, who figures as little more than an eminence in the first *Foundation* story, "The Psychohistorians" (1951), has the same abilities that Asimov so precociously demonstrated. He conceives a grand, general scheme of psychohistory, based on Asimov's **knowledge** of the Roman Empire and Enlightenment historian Edward Gibbon's critique of the Empire as destined to crumble under subversive pressure from the early church and reemerge with new imperial order as the Roman Church. Some criticize this use of **history** as unimaginative, but Asimov defended his scheme as a reasonable expectation that past historical **cycles** will keep repeating themselves in the future. The Seldon Plan proves so effective in its general conception that it is destined to live on after Seldon's **death**, just as Asimov's series endured after his death.

Asimov's other key general conception involves the relationship of a large and general empire to littler effects at the edges of the empire such as colonies, new **technologies**, and foundations. This word, again, carries great resonance and ambiguity. To lay the foundation for a new approach to literature, as Asimov claims for Campbell, is a subversive, even "sinister" move. In fact, the First Foundation, quietly established at the far edges of the galactic empire, is intended exactly to subvert empire values and influences. It accomplishes this, in part, by performing as most academic or philanthropic "foundations." Scholars working hard on the periphery produce the *Encyclopedia Galactica*, a compendium of information that will ultimately outweigh in importance the more visible knowledge systems generated by the sparkling Rome-like grandeur and technology of the empire's ruling planet. Asimov is fascinated by the symbiosis of big technology and little subversive ideas that emerge from creative thinking on the fringes. Hence, the concluding story in *Foundation* was originally entitled "The Big and the Little" (1944).

The way that this huge tale, which attained its own imperial force, could grow from a peripheral foundation of pulp stories—just as the powerful Roman Church grew to become a second Rome from its hidden beginnings, and just as the marginalized Foundations are destined to expand and replace the grand galactic empire— may be the key general irony of Asimov's achievement. The contradiction of Asimov is that he both deeply believed in, and could incredulously laugh at, his own grandiose ambitions of this nature, as demonstrated by the delightful combination of brash boastfulness and self-deprecating **humor** that characterized his writings about his own career. In similar fashion, the early Enlightenment poet Alexander Pope commissioned a marble bust of himself to resemble a Roman poet, H.P. Lovecraft venerated what he thought were his roots in ancient Rome, and both were conscious of the irony in such posturings.

The narration that Asimov wrote for his Foundation series is often stiff and general, as though it were Latin or some high language of authority. Some critics point to this style harshly. It is consistent, however, with a subversive and new literature of general and rationalist ideas, and Asimov mitigates its stiffness by presenting the style with some irony and comic effect. Thus, in a spirit of both somber seriousness and high humor, Asimov, inspired by his mentor Campbell, set out to changes things in science fiction, and he did.

Bibliography

Isaac Asimov. "Author's Note." Asimov, *Prelude to Foundation*. New York: Doubleday, 1988, ix–x.

David Brin. "The Robots and Foundation Universe," Brin, *Tomorrow Happens*. Framingham, MA: NESFA Press, 2003, 193–197.

James Gunn. *Isaac Asimov*. New York: Oxford University Press, 1982,

Donald M. Hassler. *Isaac Asimov*. Mercer Island, WA: Starmont House, 1991.

David LaBounty. "The Origins of Inspiration." *Extrapolation*, 39 (Winter, 1998), 364–372.

Joseph D. Olander and Martin Harry Greenberg, eds. *Isaac Asimov*. New York: Taplinger, 1977.

Donald E. Palumbo. *Chaos Theory, Asimov's Foundations and Robots, and Herbert's Dune.* Westport, CT: Greenwood Press, 2002.

Donald E. Palumbo. "Snatching Victory from the Jaws of Defeat." *Journal of the Fantastic in the Arts,* 12 (2002), 406–416.

Joseph F. Patrouch, Jr. *The Science Fiction of Isaac Asimov.* New York: Doubleday, 1974.

—Donald M. Hassler

FRANKENSTEIN (1931)

Summary

Obsessed with the desire to create a human being using the body parts of the recently deceased, Henry Frankenstein scours **cemeteries** and gallows with his assistant Fritz to realize his blasphemous aims. Fritz procures a brain for the creature, but it is an abnormal one, that of "the typical criminal." Frankenstein successfully creates a living being but, dismayed by its appearance and learning of its ancestry, decides to destroy it. However the creature **escapes** from his **castle** stronghold and terrorizes the local populace, killing a little girl and menacing Henry's fiancée Elizabeth on their wedding night. A mob of peasants hound the wretch to his apparent death in a flaming mill.

In the sequel *Bride of Frankenstein* (1935), however, it transpires that the creature miraculously survived. Invited into a blind man's house he learns the nature of **friendship** but is attacked once more by passing hunters and resumes his rampage. Encouraged by **mad scientist** Dr. Pretorius, the monster blackmails Henry into manufacturing a mate for him. Frankenstein succeeds but the outcome is not as anticipated: the resulting bride spurns the creature's advances. Realizing he is an abomination, the **monster** effects the destruction of his bride, Pretorius, and himself, allowing the repentant Frankenstein to escape.

Discussion

Although cinematic incarnations of *Frankenstein* had been produced since 1910, James Whale's 1931 version spawned the iconic representation of the **Frankenstein monster**. Universal Studios had acquired Peggy Webling's 1927 stage adaptation of *Frankenstein* as a potential successor to the successful *Dracula*. Whale's film effectively abandons all but the basic premise of the novel, but leaves enough material to allow for one sequel. The films approach their subjects' **Gothic** countenance in a visual sense: a domineering castle laboratory, desecrations of fog-strewn cemeteries, archaic **medicine**, and flaming (see **Fire**) mills. Emphasis is placed on dehumanizing the creature: stitched together piecemeal, with a flat squared head, bolts in his neck, and ill-fitting clothing, he is far more crude than Mary Shelley's articulate creation. Shunned by his creator and taunted by Fritz, he is angry and confused. The **horror** at the murder of little Maria while playing with **flowers** is countered with the **knowledge** that this act was a result of misunderstanding. His only friend is a blind man who judges him as a person rather than on his threatening cadaverous appearance. The **tragedy** lies in the fact that only those without a developed understanding of society's conventions can appreciate any **humanity** behind the grotesque physical features. An unusual aspect to these films is that they avoid any lasting repercussions (see **Crime and Punishment**) for Henry's **sin** against God and **nature**. Indeed in *Bride of Frankenstein* he is perceived as a victim, unwilling accomplice to mad scientist Pretorius.

Despite their reputations as part of Universal's horror cycle, Whale imbues his films with dark gallows **humor**. This is embraced in Mel Brooks's *Young Frankenstein* (1974), which manages to be both a pastiche of Whale's films and a homage. Its scatological slapstick **comedy** is balanced by loving recreations of the earlier films' aesthetics and black-and-white cinematography. Less respectful of Whale's vision were the later Universal films from other directors, which successively declined in quality: *Son of Frankenstein* (1939), *Ghost of Frankenstein* (1942), *House of Frankenstein* (1944), *House of Dracula* (1945), and *Abbott and Costello Meet Frankenstein* (1948).

Hammer's series of Frankenstein films, starting with *The Curse of Frankenstein* (1957) and culminating in *Frankenstein and the Monster From Hell* (1973), use color film stock and the controversial "X" rating to allow a level of sensational viscera and Grand Guignol theatrics. The focus shifts away from the creature and towards Frankenstein himself, following his many attempts to create a living being. Paul Morrissey's *Flesh For Frankenstein* (1973) uses 3-D effects to gross out and amuse the audience with body parts and entrails.

The TV movie *Frankenstein: The True Story* (1972) restores the Arctic (see **Polar Regions**) setting of the book's opening and explores the background to Frankenstein's obsession. The creature is handsome and intelligent and there is a particular emphasis on Frankenstein's attempt to introduce him into polite society, until he starts to decay into monstrosity. *Frankenstein: The True Story* explores the social horror as much as the spiritual or visceral horror that is normally highlighted. In contrast, actor-director Kenneth Branagh's *Mary Shelley's Frankenstein* (1994) is an operatic tragedy steeped in **blood** and punctuated by dizzying cinematography. Branagh's vision is an incestuous tale of vengeance (see **Revenge**), the creature demanding a bride from the corpse of Frankenstein's wife, whom he murdered before Victor had consummated their **marriage**. Frankenstein's motivation came from his **mother's** death—thus, the whole cycle of **birth** and tragedy endlessly repeats.

Frankenstein remains a popular subject for the cinema because of its morbid fascination with **death** and literal examination of the nature of humanity. The book's themes have evolved in the cinema to embrace contemporary scientific concerns, and constant reinterpretations have maintained the story's relevance. Like the **Golem** or the **androids** of *Blade Runner*, the Frankenstein monster allows audiences to examine human nature by focusing on something that is humanoid, but ultimately not human. The Cartesian mind–body problem is succinctly reflected in the monster's creation from other beings, while Frankenstein's unwillingness to accept natural order both shows his **hubris** and functions as a cautionary morality tale.

Bibliography

James Curtis. *James Whale*. Boston and London: Faber & Faber, 1998.
Denis Gifford. "Boris Karloff." *The House of Hammer*, No. 7 (January/February, 1977), 28–31.

Donald F. Glut. *The Frankenstein Legend*. Metuchen, NJ: Scarecrow Press, 1973.

Gregory W. Mank. *It's Alive*. San Diego: W. S. Barnes, 1981.

Martin F Norden. "Sexual References in James Whale's *Bride of Frankenstein*." Donald E. Palumbo, ed., *Eros in the Mind's Eye*. Westport, CT: Greenwood Press, 1986, 141–150.

Caroline Joan Picart, Frank Smoot, and Jayne Blodgett. *The Frankenstein Film Sourcebook*. Westport, CT: Greenwood Press, 2001.

Martin Tropp. *Mary Shelley's Monster*. Boston: Houghton Mifflin, 1976.

Janice R. Welsch and Syndy M. Conger. "Comic and the Grotesque in James Whale's Frankenstein Films." Barry K. Grant, ed., *Planks of Reason*. Metuchen, NJ: Scarecrow, 1984, 290–306.

—Michelle Le Blanc and Colin Odell

FRANKENSTEIN, OR THE MODERN PROMETHEUS BY MARY SHELLEY (1818)

It was on a dreary night of November, that I beheld the accomplishment of my toils. With an anxiety that almost amounted to agony, I collected the instruments of life around me, that I might infuse a spark of being into the lifeless thing that lay at my feet. It was already one in the morning; the rain pattered dismally against the panes, and my candle was nearly burnt out, when, by the glimmer of the half-extinguished light, I saw the dull yellow eye of the creature open; it breathed hard, and a convulsive motion agitated its limbs. How can I describe my emotions at this catastrophe, or how delineate the wretch whom with such infinite pains and care I had endeavoured to form?

—Mary Shelley
Frankenstein, or The Modern Prometheus
(1818)

Summary

One of the most famous works of fantastic literature, *Frankenstein* is better known to the public through its frequent and often wildly inaccurate screen adaptations. Thus many people who think they "know" the story do not. It has no accidental substitution of a "criminal brain" for the proper one by an inept hunchback, no tremendous "creation scene" with electricity crackling and thunderstorm raging, no ending in a burning windmill. The **Frankenstein monster** is actually quite articulate, even literate. The creature narrates a central portion of the story, and reads John Milton's *Paradise Lost* (1667), identifying itself with Milton's **Satan**.

The novel begins with an Arctic explorer (see **Polar Regions**) who encounters Victor Frankenstein wandering across the ice and hears his story. As a young Swiss medical student (see **Mad Scientists**), Frankenstein pursues forbidden research, creating a living being out of dead flesh. Upon beholding his creation, Victor is so repulsed by its ugliness that he flees. But the **monster** resents being rejected. It murders Victor's younger brother, though a servant girl is hanged for the crime (see **Crime and Punishment**). Meanwhile the monster becomes the unseen benefactor to a rustic **family**, and learns to speak and read because they, conveniently, are tutoring a foreign girl. When the monster demands that Victor make a bride for it, he begins, but destroys the female without animating it. In **revenge**, the monster murders Victor's own bride. Victor then pursues his creation to the Arctic, where he dies of exhaustion, the monster present at his **death**. The creature is last seen drifting away on an ice floe.

Discussion

Despite Mary Shelley's own testimony that the novel began as a **dream** of a student of the "unhallowed arts" with a monster stretched out before him, and that she was trying to discover an idea for a story that "would speak to the mysterious fears in our nature, and awaken thrilling **horror**," critics have had a field day discovering everything from political **allegory** to psychological symbolism in *Frankenstein* (see **Politics; Psychology**). Some of the interpretations stem from an awareness that the author was the daughter of Mary Wollstonecraft, a radical feminist (see **Feminism**) and the radical, atheist philosopher William Godwin. She was writing at a time of social ferment, when the Napoleonic Wars had just ended but England seemed on the verge of revolution. Her own life was anything but conventional. She was in Lord Byron's company in Switzerland because she had, while still a teenager, eloped with poet Percy Bysshe Shelley (whom she married after Shelley's wife committed **suicide**) and had to go abroad to escape the scandal. The small company had been reading a volume of ghost stories (see **Ghosts and Hauntings**). Byron proposed that everybody write one. The poets never got very far, but Mary, beginning with the core image from her dream, expanded what was first a short story into a novel over the next few months.

Brian W. Aldiss has made a convincing case that *Frankenstein*, even though it follows the conventions of **Gothic** novels (including an epistolary structure) and was intended as a "ghost story," is the first true science fiction novel. It is definitely a story of the consequences of science, rejecting the supernatural elements that figure in the related legends of Faust. Frankenstein's researches are "forbidden" by social and intellectual convention, not by God, despite all the rhetoric (particularly in film adaptations) of Frankenstein's **sin** being that of usurping the place of the Creator. But his transgressions are entirely of this world and his failure is one of responsibility (see **Guilt and Responsibility**). Aldiss's point is that this is the first novel of the consequences of new **knowledge** attained, not by a deal with Satan or other occult means, but from science. Frankenstein makes the crucial (and admittedly symbolic) decision to reject the accumulated **wisdom** he is taught at university and strike out into the unknown. This is a perfect example of Aldiss's description of science fiction as "hubris clobbered by nemesis." Frankenstein's problems are (literally) of his own making (see **Hubris; Tragedy**).

In *Frankenstein* we see the beginnings of all manner of **robot** and **android** stories. That the monster itself narrates about a third of the book is exceptionally important, as Shelley, without recourse to visitors from the spirit world, is able to imagine how **humanity** would look to a being that is other than human. The novel creates a **mythology** of origins in a post-theistic universe. She was writing at a time when electricity and magnetism were at the cutting edge of science, and the experiments of Erasmus Darwin relating to the nature of life aroused much attention. Here was the "blasphemous" suggestion that life is a chemical and electrical process, which may not only be understood but replicated. The author's attitude toward this is ambiguous. Her subtitle evokes the image of Prometheus, who took **fire** from the gods and gave it to humanity. But Prometheus, of course, was horribly punished for his infraction, as was Frankenstein. The difference is that Frankenstein is punished not by any outside agency, but by his own creation.

Bibliography

Brian W. Aldiss with David Wingrove. "On the Origin of Species." Aldiss with Wingrove, *Trillion Year Spree*. New York: Atheneum, 1986, 25–52.

Chris Baldick. *In Frankenstein's Shadow*. Oxford: Clarendon Press, 1990.

Radu Florescu. *In Search of Frankenstein*. Boston: The New York Graphic Society, 1975.

R. Glynn Grylls. *Mary Shelley: A Biography*. New York: Haskell House, 1969.

David Ketterer. *Frankenstein's Creation*. Victoria, British Columbia: University of Victoria Press, 1979.

George Levine and U. C. Knoepflmacher, eds. *The Endurance of Frankenstein*. Berkeley: University of California Press, 1979.

Anne K. Mellor. *Mary Shelley*. New York and London: Routledge, 1988.

Allene Stuart Phy. *Mary Shelley*. Mercer Island, WA: Starmont House, 1988.

Leonard Wolf, ed. *The Annotated Frankenstein*, by Mary Shelley. New York: Clarkson N. Potter, Inc. 1977.

—Darrell Schweitzer

FROM THE EARTH TO THE MOON BY JULES VERNE (1865)

■

If we are to believe certain narrow-minded people—and what else can we call them?—humanity is confined within a circle of Popilius from which there is no escape, condemned to vegetate on

> *this globe, never able to venture into interplanetary space! That's not so! We are going to the moon, we shall go to the planets, we shall travel to the stars just as today we go from Liverpool to New York, easily, rapidly, surely, and the oceans of space will be crossed like the seas of the moon!*
>
> —Jules Verne
> *From the Earth to the Moon* (1865),
> translated by Walter James Miller (1978)

Summary

From the Earth to the Moon is set in 1865, immediately after the end of the Civil War. Members of the Baltimore Gun Club, a group of artillery enthusiasts, are wondering what their next challenge might be now that the American **war** is winding down. They decide to build a giant gun to fire a projectile at the **Moon**. After some persuading by wandering French adventurer Michael Ardan, the Gun Club decides to turn the projectile into the world's first spacecraft. The gun is built (outside of Tampa) and, after some difficulties, is fired. The resulting explosion is the catalyst for a major storm that prevents the world's observatories from following the projectile for three days. When the clouds clear, however, these observatories report that the projectile is orbiting the Moon.

The sequel *Round the Moon* (1870) tells the story of the three **astronauts** in the projectile: Ardan, Gun Club president Impey Barbicane, and Barbicane's rival, Captain Nicholl. The astronauts circle the Moon, unable to escape the Moon's orbit. They do have **rockets**, which they intended to use to slow the fall of the craft to the Moon. They instead use the rockets to break free of the Moon's orbit and send the craft towards **Earth**. Three days later, the projectile falls into the Pacific.

Discussion

Jules Verne's popular reputation is as of a writer of adventurous **hard science fiction** novels. What is lost about Verne is that **knowledge** in his books is depicted as being playful and improvisational. *Round the Moon*, for example, is a novel where the world's first astronauts discover how cold space is by opening a window (which is then closed very quickly) and sticking a thermometer outside.

From the Earth to the Moon and its sequel are **satires**, and Verne's primary targets are **business** and **America**. The businessmen who comprise the Baltimore Gun Club love war, because it enables them to develop ever-stronger **weaponry**. They believe in scientific **progress**, but only as a tool that will enable them to produce more efficient and powerful guns that will provide fatter profits. Their rivals, the armorers, love the competition with the gunmakers, because larger guns are compensated by more orders for ever-thicker armor plate. The Gun Club is not really interested in space **exploration**; they just want to build the biggest gun of all. It's only when French adventurer Michel Ardan arrives that the Gun Club decides to replace a giant shell with a very roomy spacecraft (large enough for to carry three astronauts, two **dogs**, and several chickens).

The America Verne portrays is one where its people prefer practical skills to **culture**. "Nothing can astound an American," Verne writes. "In America, all is easy, all is simple, and for mechanical difficulties, they are overcome before they arise." Americans are a very sociable people, Verne further explains: "Now when an American has an idea, he directly seeks a second American to share it," Verne wrote. "If there be three, they elect a president and two secretaries. Given four, they name a keeper of records, and the office is ready for work; five, they constitute a general meeting."

America, according to Verne, is also a nation in love with weapons. The Baltimore Gun Club has over 30,000 members, each of whom is required to have designed a gun of some sort. And the Gun Club is able to raise five million dollars to build its giant cannon from donors who are equally divided between Europeans interested in advancing science and Americans in love with weapons. For all its satire, though, *From the Earth to the Moon* is a novel that is remarkably free of **politics**: no politician attempts to interrupt or alter the construction of the giant weapon in Florida; in fact, the invention of the gun is so important that politicians dare not object.

Considered as novels of **prediction**, *From the Earth to the Moon* and *Round the Moon* are only modestly successful. Verne did foresee that the first trip to the Moon would be undertaken by a crew of three and that the mission would be launched from Florida. Verne also uses a form of retro-rockets to slow the spacecraft's orbit around the moon to allow **gravity** to steer the craft back to Earth. But Verne does not foresee a way that a vehicle could land on the Moon and then head back to Earth. And while he realizes that astronauts would be under tremendous gravitational strain while leaving Earth, Verne did not realize that there is no gravity in outer space.

Although dated, Verne's novels of the Moon are important hard science fiction novels, as well as interesting satires. *From the Earth to the Moon* has been made into a film several times, including a farcical silent film directed by George Méliès, **A Trip to the Moon**, which also incorporated elements from H.G. Wells's *The First Men in the Moon* (1901), and a more straightforward adaptation in 1958.

Bibliography

William Butcher. *Verne's Journey to the Center of the Self*. New York: St. Martin's Press, 1991.

Arthur B. Evans. *Jules Verne Rediscovered*. Westport, CT: Greenwood Press, 1988.

I.O. Evans. *Jules Verne and His Work*. New York: Twayne, 1966.

Herbert R. Lottman. *Jules Verne*. New York: St. Martin's Press, 1998.

Andrew Martin. *The Mask of the People and the Extraordinary Fiction of Jules Verne*. New York: Oxford University Press, 1990.

Walter James Miller, ed. *The Annotated Jules Verne: From the Earth to the Moon*, by Jules Verne. New York: Thomas A. Crowell, 1978.

Edward J. Smyth. *Jules Verne*. Liverpool: Liverpool University Press, 2000.

Brian Taves and Stephen Michaluk, Jr. *The Jules Verne Encyclopedia*. Lanham, MD: Scarecrow Press, 1996.

—Martin Morse Wooster

FUTURAMA (1999–2003)

Summary

Futurama follows the comedic adventures of a twentieth-century delivery boy, Philip J. Fry, who is frozen during a cryonics facility mishap on New Year's Eve, 1999 (see **Suspended Animated and Cryonics**). Awoken a thousand years later, Fry navigates through New New York with the help of Bender, a hard-drinking, chain-smoking **robot** and thief (see **Theft**). Bender discovered that the girders he produced were being used to construct **suicide** booths and so he attempts to kill himself, but is stopped by the disturbed Fry (who had wrongly surmised that the device was a futuristic telephone booth). Pursued by a career assignment officer, a one-eyed mutant woman named Leela, Fry eventually locates his distant nephew, doddering inventor and **mad scientist** Professor Hubert J. Farnsworth, who hires the trio to be the new crew for his Planet Express delivery service. **Business** support staff includes Mars University intern and wealthy party girl Amy Wong, Jamaican bureaucrat Hermes Conrad, and incompetent staff doctor Dr. Zoidberg, who is a lobster-like **alien on Earth**. Recurring secondary characters include velour-loving Captain Zapp Brannigan and long-suffering Lieutenant Kif Kroker (parodying the Kirk/Spock dynamic), a **monster** newscaster inspired by *This Island Earth* (1955), thespian robot Calculon, Richard Nixon's head, sweetly **evil** entrepreneur Mom, and Lrrr, gruff alien ruler of Omicron Persei-8.

Discussion

The pilot episode, "Space Pilot 3000" (1999), introduces the initial premise for the show that was rounded out in the second episode, "The Series Has Landed" (1999); together, both set up major themes that would play out over the arc of the series like **space travel**, robots and their relation to **humanity**, **aliens in space**, technological advancements both plausible and fantastic (see **Technology**), **destiny** versus free will, and cultural **satire**.

A major plot thread involves Fry's **love** for Leela. Although Fry notices Leela in the pilot episode, his romantic feelings first surface in "My Three Suns" (1999), where a routine delivery to a **desert** planet inhabited by liquid aliens takes an unexpected turn after a thirsty Fry drinks their **king**. Their attraction would next grow during "A Flight to Remember" (1999), where their **romance** aboard the starship *Titanic* is thwarted by Brannigan's cruise by a **black hole**. While Fry and Leela are occasionally distracted by rival interests—including Zapp, Amy, a shape-shifting alien, a cryonic woman, a plastic surgeon, a **mermaid**, and a robotic Lucy Liu—Fry does manage to attract Leela's attention. In "Parasites Lost" (2001), Fry ingests a contaminated egg salad sandwich, and intelligent worm **parasites** (see **Snakes and Worms**) begin to rebuild Fry's body, reminiscent of Greg Bear's *Blood Music*; Leela falls for the newly intelligent, thoughtful, and muscular Fry. Fry realizes that Leela may not love his genuine self and battles the worms until they leave. Leela breaks off the relationship with the now normal Fry, who resolves to learn to play the holophoner (a flute-like device that projects holograms) and win her back.

Frustrated by his lack of musical skill (see **Music**), in "The Devil's Hands Are Idle Playthings" (2003) Fry wins the hands of the Robot Devil—first seen when Bender breaks the rules of the Church of Robotology in "Hell Is Other Robots" (1999)—and uses his new dexterity to impress Leela, only to regret his loss of human **touch**. Reverting to his normal self, Fry completes his concert for Leela, who is finally impressed with his genuine expression of emotion.

Although Fry was intended as the focal character, many notable episodes feature Bender, who would rival Fry in terms of screen time, complexity, and development. Bender's early exploits revolve around his predilection for drinking, smoking, stealing, gambling, and crooked schemes. Bender's vices are most humorously played out in "Anthology of Interest 2" (2002), where an alternate **dimension** machine has Bender become human, only to die of gluttony as he gorges his new senses. Bender's disdain of humanity is most evidenced in "Fear of a Bot Planet" (1999), where the members of Planetary Express must make a delivery to a group of "radical robot separatists" that left **Earth** to colonize their own planet, prompting Bender's comment, "just because a robot wants to kill humans, that makes him a 'radical.'" Although Bender remained mildly irritating and exploitative, he softens somewhat from his **dreams** of killing all humans. Beneath his irreverent exterior, in many ways Bender is an instructional foil for the show. In subsequent episodes, Bender engages in humorous existential **quests** to find his own meaning for existence. In "Godfellas" (2002), a nod to Theodore Sturgeon's "Microcosmic God" (1941), Bender becomes host to a small group of aliens that develop a **religion** around their new metal deity.

"Roswell That Ends Well" (2001) features the first instance of **time travel** in the series: a reaction between an exploding supernova and Fry's microwave popcorn propels the Planet Express ship back to 1947 and the infamous Area 51 of Roswell, New Mexico. While Leela and the Professor repair the ship, Dr. Zoidberg is captured by the U.S. Army and presumed to be the leader of an alien **invasion**, Bender's shattered body is mistaken for a **UFO**, and Fry accidentally kills, and in the process becomes, his own grandfather. During a final **escape**, Bender's head falls out of the ship and is subsequently recovered by Fry upon his return to the future, echoing a similar plot movement involving Data's head in "Time's Arrow" (1992) from *Star Trek: The Next Generation*.

Bibliography

Ethan Alter. "*Futurama*'s Final Frontier." *TV Guide*, 51 (August 2, 2003), 15.

Steve Bailey. "Virtuality and the Television Audience." *Communication Review*, 5 (July/ September, 2002), 239–257.

Kendall Hamilton. "Toon in Tomorrow." *Newsweek*, 133 (March 29, 1999), 70–71.

Bill Hunt and Todd Doogan. "*Futurama* on DVD." Hunt and Doogan, *The Digital Bits*. New York, NY: McGraw-Hill, 2004, 204–205.

Joe Rhodes. "Future Mock." *TV Guide*, 47 (April 3, 1999), 16–21.

Carol A. Stabile and Mark Harrison. *Prime Time Animation*. New York: Routledge, 2003.

Ken Tucker. "Goons And 'Toons.'" *Entertainment Weekly*, No. 479 (April, 1999), 73–74.

Frances Wood. "*Futurama*." *Sight and Sound*, 9 (June, 1999), 28.

—Stefan Hall

G

GALAPAGOS BY KURT VONNEGUT, JR. (1985)

> *The Captain looked up at the stars, and his big brain told him that his planet was an insignificant speck of dust in the cosmos, and that he was a germ on that speck, and that nothing could matter less than what became of him. That was what those big brains used to do with their excess capacity: blather on like that.*
>
> —Kurt Vonnegut, Jr.
> *Galapagos* (1985)

Summary

One million years in the **far future**, the ghost of Leon Trout (see **Ghosts and Hauntings**), son of hack writer Kilgore Trout, looks back at a key moment in human **history**: preparations in 1986 for the "nature cruise of the century" (see **Sea Travel**) from mainland **Latin America** to the Galápagos **islands**, a voyage coinciding with a worldwide **apocalypse** that will prevent **humanity** from reproducing. Amidst ever-increasing chaos in Ecuador, those planning to go on the cruise cope with calamities before finally managing to embark. With cruise participants representing humanity's final hope for **survival**, Mary Hepburn plays **Adam and Eve** by taking the Captain's sperm and inseminating other females on board. Over the next million years, humans on the Galapagos islands undergo **evolution**, growing furry skin and flippers to aid in fishing for food and gradually losing their **intelligence**. Finally Trout, absent without leave since the Vietnam War, decides to stop lingering on **Earth** and goes onto the next world, leaving humanity behind.

Discussion

This novel marked a return to science fiction for Vonnegut for the first time since *Slaughterhouse-5*, although a case could be made for *Slapstick, or Lonesome No More!* (1976) as possessing utopian elements (see **Utopia**) in suggesting state-sponsored middle names to signal a new system of clans. Vonnegut character-istically eschews a linear narrative and narrates a tale in which the telling itself is foregrounded (see **Writing and Authors**). Whereas *Slaughterhouse-5* had been focused through Billy Pilgrim's nonlinear view of **time** (and cameo appearances from Vonnegut himself), here we are distanced by Leon's omniscient **memories** of 1986 from the perspective of a million years hence. While a thousand millennia have passed, it would be a mistake to assume that **progress** had taken place in humanity; instead the forces of natural selection have led to a **metamorphosis** that has ensured the survival of the human species, but in radically different form. What Leon makes clear is that this does not result from divine intervention, but from inheritance of survival traits across many generations.

The location of the Galápagos islands for the million-year evolution references the major inspiration for Charles Darwin's theory of evolution, in particular the varieties of finch specific to each island. Versions of these finches, each with their own biological niche, make appearances in the novel (see **Biology**). The use of an island setting also allows for the separation of characters from the rest of humanity and the development of a localized utopia, albeit one that few readers would find attractive.

In Vonnegut's *Cat's Cradle* we witnessed the **disaster** first hand; here, the details of the collapse seem less important. Although big **business** is in trouble around the world and specific battles such as those between Peru and Ecuador have broken out, the sudden sterility of the human race remains unexplained. It seems simply to be a dead end of evolution. A recurrent complaint is the problem of humanity's intelli-gence or, rather, "big brains," from which particular ideas drive individuals to behave in foolish and often violent ways. These ideas can be summed up in the 20,000 quotations contained within a high-tech translation machine named Mandarax; with dry **humor** Vonnegut juxtaposes the collective **wisdom** of figures ranging from Plato and Socrates to Anne Frank and T.S. Eliot, but little is learned from them. These are not so much fragments shored against a ruin as irrelevant plat-itudes. The Mandarax is eventually hurled into the sea as useless; Mary, attempting to rescue it, is eaten by a shark.

Mary's demise is one of a series of meaningless **deaths** that punctuate the novel, Vonnegut forewarning us of the demises by placing an asterisk prior to the names of those who will die within the next day (compare the use of "So it goes" as epitaph in *Slaughterhouse-5*). It is difficult to care for many humans who die (or Kazakh, the **dog**), but we are surely meant to feel some compassion despite the senselessness of the deaths. Some deaths do benefit other characters, and in an ecological system (see **Ecology**) it may be necessary that some die so that others may live.

Paradoxically, Vonnegut ends the novel on an apparently optimistic note, echo-ing his epigraph from Anne Frank that people are basically decent. Things come out right through natural means or a series of accidents, which risks suggesting that humanity should continue unchecked because things are bound to come out right in the end. It is also curious that a novel so suspicious of intelligence should end with an endorsement of **education**—Leon will have to learn Swedish. Conversely, how-ever, these endorsements of optimism and education may be intended as bitter irony. As in his early **satires**, Vonnegut leaves us plenty to think about, but few solutions to our problems.

Bibliography

Charles Berryman. "Vonnegut and Evolution." Robert Merrill, ed., *Critical Essays on Kurt Vonnegut*. Boston: G. K. Hall, 1990, 188–200.

Kevin Alexander Boon, ed. *At Millennium's End*. New York: SUNY Press, 2001.

S.R. Clark. "Turtles, Blue-footed Boobies, and a Community of Readers." *Journal of Reading*, 34 (February, 1991), 380–383.

Oliver W. Ferguson. "History and Story." *Critique*, 40 (Spring, 1999), 230–236.

Peter Freese. "Surviving the End." *Critique*, 36 (Spring, 1995), 163–176.

Mary Lazar. "Sam Johnson On Grub Street, Early Science Fiction, Pulps, and Vonnegut." *Extrapolation*, 32 (Fall, 1991), 235–255.

Donald E. Morse. "Thinking Intelligently about Science and Art." *Extrapolation*, 38 (Winter, 1997), 292–303.

Leonard Mustazza. *Forever Pursuing Genesis*. Lewisburg: Bucknell University Press, 1990.

———. "A Darwinian Eden." *Journal of the Fantastic in the Arts*, 3 (1991), 55–65.

—Andrew M. Butler

THE GATE TO WOMEN'S COUNTRY
BY SHERI S. TEPPER (1988)

■

*You'll understand when you come there
at last, Achilles . . . .
Hades is Women's Country.*

—Sheri S. Tepper
The Gate to Women's Country (1988)

Summary

A **post-holocaust society** has an unusual social system: most men live as warriors in garrisons outside the **cities**, devoting themselves to practicing and waging **war**; women live in cities, along with a few men called servitors who reject military life. Men and women mingle and enjoy sexual relations only during periods of **carnival**; male sons are sent to their fathers when they are five and after ten years choose to either remain or return to the women. While an older woman, Stavia, rehearses her part in the annual play, *Iphigenia in Ilium*, flashbacks tell her story. As a young girl infatuated with an aspiring warrior, Chernon, she illegally gives him **books** before she departs for years of medical training. After returning, she and Chernon go exploring in the southern regions (see **Exploration**). They are captured by a **family** of religious fundamentalists who practice polygamy and treat women brutally; after she is severely injured, people from her city rescue her, but Chernon embraces this model of male domination and, returning to his garrison, encourages comrades to support a campaign to take direct control of the women's city. However, Stavia's **mother** kills the leaders of the planned **rebellion** and reveals the truth: servitors, not warriors, are the **fathers** of **children** claimed by warriors. Men who choose warfare

are not allowed to have offspring, so male aggressiveness can gradually be bred out of the human species.

Discussion

From one perspective, *The Gate to Women's Country* can be regarded as a feminist **utopia**, in the tradition of Charlotte Perkins Gilman's **Herland** and Marge Piercy's **Woman on the Edge of Time** (see **Feminism**). Its logic is explained by a passage in a book Chernon reads, describing how Laplanders killed reindeer who strayed too far from the herd and thus selectively bred reindeer who would not stray; Tepper proposes that a perfect society could be achieved by a similar program to eliminate male tendencies to wage war. Rejecting arguments that aggression is inextricably linked to the desires to innovate and **progress**, Tepper further portrays her women as intensely interested in preserving and improving human **knowledge**, including scientific **technology**, though much of it is suppressed or hidden to keep **weaponry** more advanced than **swords** and shields away from warriors. There is also the possibility that **psychic powers**, increasingly observed in servitors and their children, will emerge as a kinder, gentler alternative to the **machines and mechanization** that led to devastating **nuclear war**.

Tepper's anti-war message is reinforced by her story within a story, *Iphigenia in Ilium*, about the ghost of Iphigenia and other living and dead victims of the Trojan War lamenting their fates (see **Ghosts and Hauntings; Mythology**). Stavia fittingly portrays Iphigenia, who was cruelly sacrificed by a father determined to fight a war at all costs (see **Sacrifice**), because she has also been mistreated by men, raped by Chernon and struck with a shovel by a fundamentalist's son after trying to **escape**. Significantly, Stavia's profession is healing, the branch of science that women are most committed to mastering and practicing; for as long as warfare exists, people will suffer physical and psychic wounds requiring medical attention and loving care (see **Medicine**).

However, this apparent utopia is also disquieting. Though rarely noted, a central characteristic of most utopias is their transparency: everyone is completely open about their society's **philosophies** and policies, and indeed, much of the "action" in a utopia consists of residents patiently explaining how their system works to interested outsiders. In contrast, the governing Council of Women's Country depends upon and enforces secrecy, withholding key information both from warriors and their own citizens.

The Gate to Women's Country thus becomes a narrative about the importance of acting (see **Theatre**). Stavia plays a role not only in the play, but in everyday life, because in times of crisis she mentally separates herself into the actor Stavia and the observer Stavia, so that actor Stavia can calmly deal with the situation while observer Stavia helplessly watches. The women's scheme to improve **humanity** hinges upon the acting skills of their ruling Council, whose members must seem deferential to men while secretly wielding supreme authority and concealing their true intentions and abilities. One of Stavia's allies is a traveling stage magician who uses conjuring tricks to frighten the fundamentalists who are holding her captive. Every aspect of Tepper's program to eliminate war and purify the human species, then, requires artful pretenses; if key secrets are ever revealed, the entire society would immediately collapse. Therefore, although Tepper portrays a **culture** seemingly bound by firm traditions, her society, in actuality, is astoundingly fragile.

It must be remembered, finally, that this society was created as one woman's response to a global nuclear war, the sort of **disaster** that might naturally inspire extreme responses. Tepper's message may ultimately be this: humanity must find a way to eliminate war and **violence**; and if steps now being taken prove insufficient, then our descendents may in desperation turn to devious or draconian solutions. *The Gate to Women's Country*, then, does not ask readers to choose between the warrior's society and Women's Country; rather, it urges them to vigilantly strive to eliminate aggression with tools now in hand, so humanity will never have to make such a choice.

Bibliography

Norman Beswick. "Ideology and Dogma in the 'Ferocious' SF Novels of Sheri S. Tepper." *Foundation*, No. 71 (Autumn, 1997), 32–45.

William L. Clois and Catherine Mintz. "An Interview with Sheri S. Tepper." *Quantum*, Nos. 43/44 (Spring/Summer, 1993), 35–38.

Lorna Jowett. "The Female State." Karen Sayer and John Moore, ed., *Science Fiction, Critical Frontiers*. London: Macmillan, 2000, 169–192.

Sylvia Kelso. *A Glance From Nowhere*. New Lambton, Australia: Nimrod Publications, 1997.

Wendy Pearson. "After the (Homo)Sexual." *Science-Fiction Studies*, 23 (July, 1996), 199–226.

Beverly Price. "Sheri S. Tepper and Feminism's Future." *Mythlore*, 18 (Spring, 1992), 41–44.

Alice K. Turner. "The Triumph of Menopause." *New York Review of Science Fiction*, No. 95 (July, 1996), 1, 4–5.

Tamara Wilson. "Beyond Personal Introspection." Martha Bartter, ed., *The Utopian Fantastic*. Westport, CT: Praeger, 2004, 123–128.

—Lynne Lundquist

GATEWAY BY FREDERIK POHL (1977)

■

There is no greater dark than the dark between the stars.

—Frederik Pohl
Heechee Rendezvous (1984)

Summary

Robinette (usually Robin or Bob) Broadhead is a prospector on the Gateway asteroid (see **Comets and Asteroids**), an abandoned hangar for hundreds of spaceships made by the mysterious Heechee. No human prospectors understand how to pilot the Heechee ships, nor do they know the ships' destinations: they can only get in and begin their **explorations** through **hyperspace**. The Gateway corporation pays surviving prospectors science bonuses depending on what they find. Broadhead falls in **love** with prospector Gelle-Klara Moynlin and together they make a nerve-wracking, fruitless trip. Broadhead's terror at making each voyage is justified when his final destination turns out to be a **black hole.** To save himself Broadhead sacrifices Klara and other crew members. Now a wealthy, tormented man on **Earth,** he recounts his story to **computer** psychoanalyst "Sigfrid von Shrink" and perhaps achieves a measure of peace. The sequels continue Broadhead's story, his drive to find the Heechee and solve the world's continuing **ecology** problems. The Heechee appear in the third book where they join **humanity** in fighting a mysterious alien force intent upon destroying the universe. Klara is rescued from the black hole, Broadhead dies and experiences **rebirth** as a machine **intelligence,** and together they confront the alien "foe."

Discussion

Gateway, Beyond the Blue Event Horizon (1980), *Heechee Rendezvous* (1984), *Annals of the Heechee* (1987), and *The Boy Who Would Live Forever* (2004) consider what it is to be human in a universe of terror and marvels (the initial Heechee story "The Merchants of Venus" was reprinted with other vignettes about the Heechee in *The Gateway Trip* [1990]). The novels discuss a vast range of topics: ecological catastrophe, sociopolitical problems (as in John Brunner's **Stand on Zanzibar**), computers, artificial intelligence, future **medicine, aliens in space,** survivor guilt (see **Guilt and Responsibility; Survival**), **physics,** and astronomy. The idea of Gateway, Heechee **culture,** and its artifacts is as astounding as Frank Herbert's **Dune** series and Iain M. Banks's Culture novels (see **Consider Phlebas**). *Gateway* as a novel is part epistolary and part documentary: interviews, news articles, and mock computer code all lend it a sense of authenticity.

Pohl suggests various ways to be a worthwhile person. He proposes that sufficiently advanced computers like Robin's psychoanalyst (Freud) and science program (an affectionate incarnation of Albert Einstein) can understand, even without emotions, how to become people (compare Isaac Asimov's *I, Robot*). The argument is convincing partly because the Einstein program is full of **wisdom, humor,** and concern for humans. Robin's posthumous transformation to a machine intelligence alters his vision but does not lessen his desire to unravel the secrets of existence. Robin the machine knows **time** very differently than Robin the organic creature. The five books can be seen as meditations respectively on living, aging, **death, immortality and longevity,** and rebirth.

Gateway and *Beyond the Blue Event Horizon* concern themselves with Earth's ecology. Pohl predicts a grim **near future** for a society that has exhausted its fossil fuels and strip-mines the planet for oil shales. Food is grown from molds, and most people's health prospects are dark, as in Gregory Benford's **Timescape.** People sell their organs or whole bodies to those wealthy enough to afford "full medical" coverage. The divide between the haves and have-nots makes for a planet balanced on the edge of terrorism. Pohl's science characters point to a better future: reason (Sigfrid) and fearless inquiry (Einstein) reassure Robin that while the terror he feels is real, it can also be addressed. At the same time Robin resists Sigfrid's attempts to help him: at every chance he avoids telling his secret and hides the shame he feels for surviving the catastrophic event that made him who he is. Infantilizing him as "Robby" and "Bobby," Sigfrid slowly goads Robin into full revelation, allowing him to begin the process of growing up. Some Gateway prospectors, particularly Gelle-Klara and the legless Shikitei Bakin, have tried to teach Robinette about trust, generosity, and grace.

Discovery of all kinds drives the novel. The Gateway asteroid is a signpost to the Heechee who meddled in the formation of humanity, like the unseen aliens of Arthur C. Clarke's *2001: A Space Odyssey*. Prospectors are desperate scavengers hungry for interplanetary trash but face daily terror with grim resourcefulness. Their **sacrifices** pay off: Heechee technology allows humans to solve resource problems, travel in hyperspace, become immortal, and put **war** behind them. The Heechee seem our better, maturer selves, who have learned to live patiently and wisely.

Pohl's characters are painfully, beautifully drawn. Gelle-Klara's strength and fear are reflected in Robin, as panic-stricken and flawed a **hero** as there could be. Yet the two manage to love each other despite their claustrophobic relationship signified by tiny Heechee ships and cramped Gateway tunnels. Robin learns to continue in the face of panic, face the worst thing about himself (his survivor's guilt), and act as ethically as he can despite continuing tendencies to anger and fear. While the trip out from Gateway has been a terrifying one for human and Heechee prospectors alike, it has also been gloriously worthwhile.

Bibliography

K.V. Bailey. "Spindly Mazes, Dead Men and Doppels." *Foundation*, No. 63 (Spring, 1995), 40–55.

Martha Bartter. "Times and Spaces." *Extrapolation*, 23 (Summer, 1982), 189–200.

Harold Bloom. "Frederik Pohl." Harold Bloom, ed., *Science Fiction Writers of the Golden Age*. New York: Chelsea House, 1995, 157–172.

Thomas P. Dunn. "Theme and Narrative Structure in Ursula K. LeGuin's *The Dispossessed* and Frederik Pohl's *Gateway*." Michael Collings, ed., *Reflections on the Fantastic*. Westport, CT: Greenwood Press, 1986, 87–96.

Eric Heyne. "Gateway to an Erotics of Narrative." *Extrapolation*, 35 (Winter, 1994), 298–311.

Martin Jordin. "Contemporary Futures." Christopher Pawling, ed., *Popular Fiction and Social Change*. New York: St. Martin's, 1984, 50–75.

Terri Paul. "Sixty Billion Gigabits." Thomas P. Dunn, ed., *The Mechanical God*. Westport, CT: Greenwood Press, 1982, 53–62.

David N. Samuelson. "Critical Mass." *Science-Fiction Studies*, 7 (March, 1980), 80–95.

George Turner. "Frederik Pohl as a Creator of Future Societies." M. J. Tolley, ed., *The Stellar Gauge*. Carleton, Australia: Norstrilia, 1980, 109–134.

—*Tim Blackmore*

GODZILLA, KING OF THE MONSTERS (1954)

■

Summary

The story of Godzilla became a template for innumerable films along similar lines and is now embedded in the popular imagination: there are scarcely believable reports from sailors of a giant **monster**; the news is confirmed as a huge **dinosaur** moves onshore; the monster causes **deaths** and destruction upon reaching a major city; conventional **weaponry** is useless against the dinosaur; but a **scientist** finally devises a way to destroy it. *Godzilla, King of the Monsters* differs from its progeny in two interesting respects: extensive attention to the **pain** and suffering caused by the monster's rampage; and the unusual cause of its demise—a device that destroys oxygen in **water**, reluctantly deployed by a conscience-stricken scientist.

Discussion

Godzilla was inspired by the American film *The Beast from 20,000 Fathoms* (1953), wherein a dinosaur awakened by an Arctic nuclear test explosion (see **Nuclear Power**) destroys New York City, utilizing Ray Harryhausen's stop-motion animation. When producer Tomoyuki Tanaka saw the film, a recent **tragedy** in the ocean off **Japan** was on everyone's mind: a fishing trawler, ironically named "Lucky Dragon No. 5," ventured near an atomic test area and passed through residual radioactive ash. The crew succumbed to radiation sickness and tainted tuna reached Japanese markets, causing public outrage and anti-American sentiment. The incident terrified post-war Japan, leaving an indelible stamp on their public psyche—to some hitting even closer to home than the atomic bombs dropped on Hiroshima and Nakasaki (see **Nuclear War**). The incident personified the **horrors** of radiation exposure because it happened to a small group of everyday people.

On a Pacfiic flight, Tanaka claimed he had a vision of a large mutated creature rising from the ocean and wreaking havoc. Godzilla—in Japanese, "Gojira"—was born, launching the era of what the Japanese called "Kaiju-Eiga," "Kaiju" being the Japanese word for "Mythical Monster." "Gojira" combines the Japanese words for Gorilla ("Gorira") and Whale ("Kujira").

Tanaka wanted to make a film that depicted an atomic-mutated beast terrorizing Japan. Special-effects wizard Eiji Tsuburaya was chosen to create this monster, with Kurosawa-protégé Ishiro Honda directing. Time and money precluded use of stop-motion animation (though there are brief uses), so the technique of "Suitmation" was employed: an actor inside a rubber suit on a miniature cityscape. There was also some puppet work, using a variation of the creature's head designed to subtly suggest a mushroom cloud.

The film, released in Japan as *Gojira*, is quite an accomplishment in its original form. The message that nuclear weapons are a threat to not just Japan, but all **Earth**, resonates throughout the movie. More than that, it implies that any weapon that endangers **humanity**'s balance with **nature** will spell doom. Dr. Serizawa accidentally and secretly creates a weapon that eliminates oxygen in **water**—the "Oxygen Destroyer"—and kills everything living in it. Ultimately, the weapon is the only thing that can stop Godzilla, though Serizawa **sacrifices** himself in the process. A torn man, he fears being tortured to reveal the secret of his device, which he sees as far more devastating than nuclear weapons. Unlike J. Robert Oppenheimer, he does not want to contribute further to the arsenal of humanity's weapons of mass destruction.

Gojira was sold to American producer Joseph E. Levine, who toned down the film's antinuclear sentiments in English dubbing and had director Terry Morse awkwardly insert scenes of Raymond Burr as a visiting American reporter (see **Journalism**) to provide "star power." Thus, when the refurbished *Godzilla, King of* *the Monsters* was released in 1956, its message of nuclear warning was truncated for an American public then supportive of nuclear weapons. Another key aspect of the film received little attention: in American films, science usually solves the problem; in Japanese films like *Gojira*, science creates the problem, suggesting a sense of human helplessness in the face of nature.

The original film spawned not just a sequel but, to date, 28 Japanese-made motion pictures—the most ever for a pop culture icon, even beating out the James Bond series (see **Doctor No**). In the sequels, the issue of nuclear power was sidelined and Godzilla devolved into an unambiguously heroic figure loved by **children** who battles for humanity against various threats such as other monsters, gigantic **robots**, and **invasions** of **aliens on Earth**. After a decade-long "retirement" due to falling box office receipts, Toho and producer Tanaka saw renewed interest in Godzilla and, in 1984, made a sequel to the original film, released in America as *Godzilla 1985*, harkening back to the nuclear theme. This new film inspired a new string of movies, but Tanaka decided to kill him off in 1995. Ironically, Tanaka died the same year.

In 1998, Sony-Tristar made a much hyped and expensive American version of *Godzilla* that, to eliminate any aura of anti-Americanism, explained the monster's radioactive origins as resulting from *French* nuclear experiments in the 1960s. However, rather than a mystical "Kaiju" creation, this Godzilla was simply an oversized iguana, lacking the might and mystique of his Japanese predecessor. (Strangely, it turned out, the economical device of having Godzilla portrayed by a man in a suit seemed to enhance the monster's appeal.) Following this film's failure (which cancelled two planned sequels), Toho again restored Godzilla to life, producing six more films that jettisoned the previous mythos of Godzilla; they have also again announced plans to retire the character, though no one expects this new retirement to be any more permanent than previous absences.

Over the course of fifty years, Godzilla has moved being beyond a metaphor for the "nuclear threat" to a **personification** of the majesty and **mystery** of nature and humanity's limited power to master it. Thus, Godzilla both warns against western technological **hubris** and delights western audiences with images of extravagant **disaster**.

Bibliography

Nancy Anisfield. "Godzilla/Gojiro." *Journal of Popular Culture*, 29 (Winter, 1995), 53–62.

Stuart Galbraith IV. *The Monsters Are Attacking Tokyo*. Venice, CA: Feral House, 1998.

J.D. Lees and Marc Cerasini. *The Godzilla Compendium*. New York: Random House, 1998.

Susan J. Napier. "Panic Sites." *Journal of Japanese Studies*, 19 (Summer, 1992), 327–351.

Chon A. Noriega. "Godzilla and the Japanese Nightmare." *Cinema Journal*, 27 (Fall, 1987), 63–77.

Annette Roman, ed. *Japan Edge*. San Francisco: Cadence Books, 1999.

William Tsutsui. *Godzilla on My Mind*. New York: Palgrave Macmillan, 2004.

Lawrence Wharton. "Godzilla to Latitude Zero." *Journal of Popular Film and Television*, 3 (1974), 31–38.

—*Bob Eggleton*

GULLIVER'S TRAVELS BY JONATHAN SWIFT (1726)

Summary

In Jonathan Swift's *Travels Into Several Remote Nations of the World* (known almost from its publication as *Gulliver's Travels*), Lemuel Gulliver is a Cambridge-educated gentleman of small fortune who goes to sea in 1699 (see **Sea Travel**) after his medical practice fails. He makes four successive voyages to unknown lands (see **Exploration; Sea Travel**), which he recounts in the manner of the travel books then popular. Shipwrecked on the **island** of Lilliput, Gulliver discovers a kingdom of people only a twelfth the height of an adult human who initially imprison him, then involve him in their court intrigues, and finally seek to make him an instrument of imperial conquest. Fleeing the island, Gulliver returns to England and eventually travels to Brobdingnag, whose inhabitants are **giants**; to a series of countries, including the flying island of Laputa and **Japan**; and finally to the land of the Houyhnhnms, a race of intelligent **horses** whose just society (see **Utopia**) appears a profound rebuke to the affairs and accomplishments of humankind. Upon his return to England, Gulliver is so repelled by the "Vices and Follies" of **humanity** that he finds the very sight of people intolerable.

Discussion

Despite early recognition that *Gulliver's Travels* is a volume of entertaining adventures that also constitutes a **satire** of human behavior and institutions, almost everything concerning Swift's book has been called into question, and practically every aspect of it remains controversial. Swift did not intend his novel to be regarded as a **children**'s book, nor as an example of what has come to be called "fantasy." He would not have wished for Book I's conceit—which Samuel Johnson referred to when he claimed that "When once you have thought of the big men and little men, it is very easy to do all the rest" and which would today be called its "high concept"—to become the detachable source for numerous popular dramatizations. The volume that Swift called simply his "Travells" was intended, he said, "to vex the world rather than divert it," and its enduring appeal as a work of imaginative delights (the image of Gulliver awakening on the beach in Book I to find himself tied down by the thread-like cords of the Lilliputians is one of the most famous in Western literature) would not have pleased him. Yet both elements powerfully coexist for readers: the engaging tale of Gulliver's encounters with minute and then gigantic antagonists (offering perspectives on the themes of both **enlargement** and **miniaturization**); and the novel for adults that, notwithstanding its **humor**, emphatically scalds its readers.

Swift's volume, appearing at the dawn of the English novel, precedes the development of prose fantasy as a distinct form (the fact that many of the novel's events partake of the fantastic passed without comment by early readers); but its importance to fantasy (and later, science fiction) is enormous. Swift's carefully consistent dramatization of a radically different world was unprecedented in the genre of "imaginary voyages," and it presaged the rationalized future or extraterrestrial worlds (see **Alien Worlds**) of early science fiction. The Struldbruggs—perhaps the first depiction of immortality (see **Immortality and Longevity**) in prose fiction—explore the implications of an indefinitely prolonged lifespan with merciless verisimilitude. The debased Yahoos of Book IV (see **Barbarians**) offer literature's first portrayal of humans as they would appear beside a genuinely superior species, a little-remarked anticipation of one of modern science fiction's most unsettling themes (see Olaf Stapledon's *Last and First Men*). The detailed description of the Houyhnhnms' perfect society anticipates the leisurely tour of a rationalist social order that would later be popularized by Edward Bellamy's *Looking Backward, 2000–1887* and similar texts, while Swift's uses of **maps**, invented languages (see **Language and Linguistics**), and Japan as an exotic locale were taken up by genre writers more than 150 years later.

Daniel Defoe's *Robinson Crusoe* (1719)—the other great eighteenth-century novel of a contemporary Englishman cast ashore on a strange land—offers numerous similarities to Swift's novel, but the works are antithetical in almost every respect. While Crusoe (whose discovery of a footprint in the sand is the other indelible image that the early English novel bequeathed to western literature) attains mastery over his environment, Gulliver interacts more problematically with his and invariably comes off the worse, returning (like Crusoe) to his homeland but undone by what he has seen. If Crusoe represents the prototypical version of one of science fiction's most popular myths—the stalwart individualist who transforms the inhospitable world onto which he is cast into his own dominion—*Gulliver's Travels* offers a devastating rebuttal. Its relentless disabusing vision of a Fallen humanity (see **Sin**) rendered comically fatuous (see **Absurdity**) or pathetically inadequate when left to its own bare resources (see **Individualism and Conformity**) constitutes a massive dissent from the tenets of bourgeois individualism that began with Defoe, and that science fiction has historically celebrated.

Bibliography

Isaac Asimov, ed. *The Annotated Gulliver's Travels*, by Jonathan Swift. New York: Clarkson N. Potter, 1980.

R.S. Crane. "The Houyhnhnms, the Yahoos, and the History of Ideas." Denis Donaghue, ed., *Jonathan Swift: A Critical Anthology*. London: Penguin, 1971, 363–384.

Michael Foot. "Introduction." Peter Dixon and John Chalker, ed., *Gulliver's Travels*. London: Penguin Books, 1967, 7–29.

Christopher Fox, ed. *Jonathan Swift: Gulliver's Travels*. Boston: Bedford Books, 1995.

Dennis Nigel. "Swift and Defoe." Nigel, *Jonathan Swift: A Short Character*. New York: Macmillan, 1964, 122–133.

A.D. Nutall. "Gulliver Among the Horses." *Yearbook of English Studies*, 18 (1988), 51–67.

John D. Radner. "The Struldbruggs, the Houyhnhnms, and the Good Life." *Studies in English Literature*, 17 (1977), 419–433.

Edward J. Rielly. "Irony in *Gulliver's Travels* and *Utopia*." *Utopian Studies*, 3 (1992), 70–83.

Frederick N. Smith, ed. *The Genres of Gulliver's Travels*. Newark, Delaware: University of Delaware Press, 1990.

—*Gregory Feeley*

THE HANDMAID'S TALE
BY MARGARET ATWOOD (1986)

*There is more than one kind of freedom,
said Aunt Lydia. Freedom to and freedom
from. In the days of anarchy, it was freedom to. Now you are being given freedom from. Don't underrate it.*

—Margaret Atwood
The Handmaid's Tale (1986)

Summary

In the future, questionably authentic tapes and documents are discovered recording the **near future** experience, gradual self-awareness, and cultural challenges of Offred (June), a Handmaid, whose fertility is valued and controlled under an authoritarian regime, Gilead, established after an ecological **disaster** (see **Ecology**). Atwood's feminist **dystopia** operates in two time periods. Characters remember an era of second-wave **feminism,** when "take back the night" marches were set alongside women's relative equality of pay and equal rights, including women's "right to choose" an abortion, have bank balances, and enjoy egalitarian relationships. However, they now live in Gilead, where controlling Aunts brainwash fertile women as Handmaids to provide **children** for military controllers; free speech is denied; the rebellious are hanged, hooded, as warnings; and barren women are consigned to the toxic wastes of "the colonies." While Offred's Commander shares banned magazines and brothel parties with her, she mourns the loss of her husband and daughter and has a dangerous sexual relationship with the chauffeur, a member of an underground cell who eventually helps her to **escape.**

Discussion

Atwood's ironic science fiction novel contrasts a dystopian future dominated by reproductive **technologies** with the late twentieth century, when the narrator's mother campaigned against the ever-present danger of rape and burned pornography while women juggled conflicting multiple roles as **mothers**, lovers, mistresses, sisters, daughters, housewives, and workers. Gilead, informed by American Puritan **history** (see **America**) and Margaret Atwood's visit to Afghanistan, is a woman's world insofar as its ethos is domestic, focused on procreation and order. Here women's roles are separated, with each class clad in separate **colors** identifying their role: dull green for Marthas (houseworkers); blue for Wives; red, blue, and green stripes for Econowives (working class); brown for the thought-controlling/governess/matron Aunts; and red for Handmaids who bear children to household heads and whose long red gowns and white wimple headgear recall temple prostitutes. Handmaids are named after their employer, so that Offred means "Of" Fred.

In Gilead, a military regime keeps a tight rein on desires and behaviors. It is a theocratic tyranny, empowered and underpinned by the need for regulation, order, and fertility following the destruction of twentieth-century society. Social rules control **identity**, relationships, and sexual practices to ensure a steady state and continuation of the race. Since women are rarely fertile enough to produce healthy offspring, those with potential are siphoned off, indoctrinated by domineering Aunts who treat them as prisoners and train them to be silent, obedient, and procreative. The cowled, religiously garbed Handmaids then live in households with key military figures, their fertility substituting for that of barren Wives in strange triadic sexual relationships. Offred is a sacrificial victim (see **Sacrifice**) whose predecessor in the household broke down and committed **suicide**.

Offred, not an intellectual or imaginative person, finds herself unable to trust anyone. As with George Orwell's *Nineteen Eighty-Four* there are thought police and "newspeak," so Handmaids only communicate in order to praise or to remark on accepted topics. Initially numbed by being stolen from her partner and child in a terrible raid, she is gradually influenced by her friend Ofglen, a member of the revolutionary underground, and comes to question her position, wondering how and whether she can challenge anything and remain alive. Offred's alliance with the chauffeur is a dangerous moment of **freedom** that could also lead to treachery since we never really know which political cells are genuine underground movements determined to bring about more equality and which are in the service of the regime, so complex are the layers of deception and pretense. Women are divided against each other because of roles and the premium placed upon controlled fertility.

The 1990 film, directed by Volker Schlöndorff and written by playwright Harold Pinter, provides a persuasive visualization of Atwood's novel. Audiences see Kate captured by border guards in a terrifying snow-filled opening of barbed wire and shooting as her husband is killed and daughter lost. Everything to do with the state is black: storm-troopers in black uniforms, black helmets with black visors drive black vehicles and carry black guns. Schlöndorff focuses on the different emotional stresses the **war** places upon each character and effectively portrays the humiliating sexual ceremony. Based on the biblical story of Rachel, it requires Kate to lie between the Commander and his infertile wife, Serena Joy, to be impregnated—leaving Serena angry, the Commander unfulfilled, and Kate desperate for freedom. In tone and art direction the film is similar to a 1980s British miniseries, *The Knights of God* (1987), about a near future, civil war-torn totalitarian state.

Ironically, Atwood presents a bleak future in which some feminist wishes could be seen to have been fulfilled, with a society focused on female abilities and activities, though the values of **gender** equality and women's rights have been eroded beyond recognition. Atwood dedicates her novel to Harvard historian Perry Miller and to Mary Webster, Atwood's ancestor who was hanged as a **witch** in Connecticut but left alive because there was no "drop." Both dedications show how the story developed from Canadian and American Puritan history. Atwood points out that although it is a grim tale, nonetheless Offred does escape. Her story can act as a cautionary tale against both excessive feminist behaviors, leading to backlash, and excessive theocratic tyranny.

Bibliography

Pamela Cooper. "Sexual Surveillance and Medical Authority in Two Versions of *The Handmaid's Tale*." *Journal of Popular Culture*, 28 (1994/1995), 49–66.

Lois Feuer. "The Calculus of Love and Nightmare." *Critique*, 38 (1996/1997), 83–95.

Dorota Filipczak. "Is There No Balm in Gilead." *Literature and Theology*, 7 (1993), 171–185.

Dominick M. Grace. "*The Handmaid's Tale*." *Science-Fiction Studies*, 25 (November, 1998), 481–494.

Stephanie Barbé Hammer. "The World As It Will Be?" *Modern Language Studies*, 20 (1990). 39–49.

Mario Klarer. "Orality and Literacy as Gender-Supporting Structures in Margaret Atwood's *The Handmaid's Tale*." *Mosaic*, 28 (1995), 129–142.

Elisabeth Mahoney. "Writing So to Speak." Sarah Sceats and Gail Cunningham, eds., *Image and Power*. London and New York: Longman, 1996, 29–40.

Hilde Staels. "Margaret Atwood's *The Handmaid's Tale*." *English Studies*, 5 (1995), 455–467.

Karen F. Stein. "Margaret Atwood's *The Handmaid's Tale*." *University of Toronto Quarterly*, 61 (1991), 269–279.

—*Gina Wisker*

HARRY POTTER AND THE SORCERER'S STONE BY J.K. ROWLING (1997)

■

It is our choices, Harry, that show what we truly are, far more than our abilities.

—J.K. Rowling
Harry Potter and the Sorcerer's Stone (1997)

Summary

In *Harry Potter and the Sorcerer's Stone* (first published in Britain as *Harry Potter and the Philosopher's Stone*), Harry discovers many things on his eleventh birthday: he is a **wizard**; he has been invited to Hogwarts School of Witchcraft and Wizardry; his parents were murdered by Lord Voldemort (the most feared dark wizard in over a century) when Harry was a year old; the lightning-bolt scar on his forehead resulted from Voldemort's (failed) **death curse** against Harry; and Voldemort lost his powers and disappeared when the death curse failed. *Harry Potter and the Sorcerer's Stone* chronicles Harry's first year at Hogwarts as he, Ron Weasley, and Hermione Granger ascertain that the Philosopher's Stone is at Hogwarts and determine to keep it safe from Voldemort, culminating in Harry's saving the Stone and defeating Voldemort. Subsequent books in the series follow Harry as he progresses through the years at Hogwarts, thwarts Voldemort's attempts to regain power, and learns more about himself, his parents, and the reason why Voldemort is determined to kill him.

Discussion

With over 250 million Harry Potter books sold in less than ten years, J.K. Rowling is perhaps the world's most successful author. Rowling has said that the primary theme of the Harry Potter stories is the battle between good and **evil**, which is clearly a reason for the novels' enormous success. The Harry Potter stories, however, also tap into mythic aspects of heroic tales (see **Heroes; Mythology**), and as such they are Harry Potter's **Bildungsroman**. Throughout the six novels published thus far, Harry learns about himself and his heritage as he overcomes external and internal obstacles; he proves himself to himself and to the wizard community at large as he battles Lord Voldemort and his followers; and he acts selflessly and heroically in risking his life to save others.

In *Harry Potter and the Sorcerer's Stone*, Harry saves the Philosopher's Stone (see **Magical Objects**) from evil Lord Voldemort, who believes there is no such thing as good and evil, but only power "and those too weak to seek it." Voldemort wants to use the Stone to regain his previous powers and to gain **immortality and longevity**. During the Middle Ages and Renaissance, the Philosopher's Stone was sought by alchemists because of the belief that with it one could transmute base metals (such as lead) into gold and also create the elixir of life that would grant one immortality. Throughout *Harry Potter and the Sorcerer's Stone* and later books, Harry must overcome his own fears and doubts about himself and his abilities. In the first book, he wrestles with doubts about whether he can live up to his reputation as "the boy who lived," the boy who defeated Lord Voldemort.

In *Harry Potter and the Chamber of Secrets* (1999), Harry rejects the racist (see **Race Relations**) notion that only pureblood wizards ought to be taught at Hogwarts. He rescues Ginny Weasley in the Chamber of Secrets by defeating Tom Marvolo Riddle, the sixteen-year old Lord Voldemort and heir of Salazar Slytherin, a founder of Hogwarts who thought only pure-blood wizards should attend the school. Harry is able to kill the basilisk (see **Monsters**) and rescue Ginny because he shows great **courage** and loyalty to Albus Dumbledore. Harry learns that it is one's choices that show one's character, not one's **blood** or social standing.

In *Harry Potter and the Prisoner of Azkaban* (1999), Harry confronts two major obstacles: the first is Sirius Black, whom Harry wants to kill because he believes Sirius betrayed Harry's parents (see **Betrayal; Family**); the second is the presence of the Dementors, beings that feed on happy thoughts and **memories**, whose presence causes Harry to relive with increasing clarity and **pain** the screams and deaths of his parents. Learning that Sirius was framed and is Harry's godfather, Harry and Hermione stop Sirius and Professor Lupin from killing his parents' betrayer, Peter Pettigrew, and they save Sirius and Buckbeak the hippogriff from execution.

In *Harry Potter and Goblet of Fire* (2000) Harry competes against three other contestants in the Tri-Wizard tournament (see **Sports**). At the novel's climax Harry witnesses Lord Voldemort's **rebirth** and the return of his Death-Eaters. He also proves his character by altruistically risking his life: the first instance occurs in the second task when Harry refuses to leave the captives with the merpeople, thus showing moral courage the second is when Harry agrees to return Cedric Diggory's dead body to his parents after he escapes from Voldemort.

In *Harry Potter and the Order of the Phoenix* (2003), Harry discovers that few people believe his story that Lord Voldemort has returned because *The Daily Prophet* (see **Journalism**) has printed lies about him. Moreover, students face a new educational program and headmaster at Hogwarts when the Ministry of Magic (see **Education; Governance Systems**) removes Dumbledore and takes control. Throughout the year, Dumbledore (see **Mentor**) ignores Harry, which Harry does not understand, adding to Harry's anger and confusion. Harry also discovers that Voldemort sees into Harry's mind, just as Harry does Voldemort's (see **Psychic Powers**). Voldemort tricks Harry into attempting to save Sirius, thus causing Harry to suffer his greatest loss. Dumbledore tells Harry of the prophecy that says he must kill, or killed by, Lord Voldemort, which is why Voldemort attempted to kill him when he was a baby (see **Destiny**).

Bibliography

Giselle Liza Anatol, ed. *Reading Harry Potter*. Westport, CT: Praeger, 2003.

Francis Bridger. *A Charmed Life*. New York: Doubleday-Image, 2002.

John Granger. *Looking for God in Harry Potter*. Carol Stream, IL: Tyndale-SaltRiver, 2004.

Emily Griesinger. "Harry Potter and the 'Deeper Magic.'" *Christianity and Literature*, 51 (Spring, 2002), 455–480.

Elizabeth E. Heilman, ed. *Harry Potter's World*. New York: Routledge, 2003.

Kerrie Anne Le Lievre. "Wizards and Wainscots." *Mythlore*, 24 (Summer, 2003), 25–36.

Farah Mendlesohn. "Crowning the King." *Journal of the Fantastic in the Arts*, 12 (2001), 287–308.

John Pennington. "From Elfland to Hogwarts, or the Aesthetic Trouble with Harry Potter." *Lion and the Unicorn*, 26 (January, 2002), 78–97.

Galadriel Waters and Astre Mithandir. *The Ultimate Unofficial Guide to the Mysteries of Harry Potter*. Niles, IL: Wizard World Press, 2002.

—*Theodore James Sherman*

HEAVEN CAN WAIT (1978)

Summary

Heaven Can Wait tells the story of Joe Pendleton, a saxophone-playing quarterback for the Los Angeles Rams (see **Sports**). An instant before what appears to be his inevitable **death** in a traffic accident, a guardian **angel** plucks Pendleton's soul from his body, only to learn that the athletic football star would actually have avoided the accident. In fact, it is Pendleton's **destiny** to take his team to the Super Bowl. A new body must be found: that of recently murdered industrialist Leo Farnsworth, whose unfaithful wife and former accountant are shocked to be confronted by the newly reanimated body of the man they just killed. Their confusion increases when Farnsworth buys the Rams and begins training to play as the team's new quarterback. Pendleton tries to recruit his former trainer, Max, to help him, but his old friend refuses until Pendleton convinces him of his true **identity**. Meanwhile, Pendleton falls in **love** with Betty, an environmental activist intent on reforming Farnsworth's ecologically destructive **business** practices (see **Ecology**). The would-be murderers finally succeed in killing Farnsworth, and Pendleton must fulfill his destiny—and continue his pursuit of Betty—by assuming the identity of a former teammate killed during the course of the climactic game.

Discussion

It is rare for a romantic **comedy** to receive critical recognition and awards; it is even rarer for a romantic comedy with a fantasy theme to do so. Yet *Heaven Can Wait* was nominated for nine Academy awards, including Best Actor, Best Screenplay Adaptation, Best Directing, and Best Picture. An important storytelling decision to be made in any film about **reincarnation** or body-switching is whether to show each character's outer form or represent the inner person with the same actor in each of his character's incarnations. An example of the first option is *All of Me* (1984), in which Steve Martin was wildly successful at embodying his co-star Lily Tomlin's character. In *Heaven Can Wait* director Warren Beatty chooses the second option: even though the rest of the characters in the film see Farnsworth, the audience sees Pendleton. This technique, routinely used in the television show *Quantum Leap* (1989–1993), allows the audience to identify with the main character from one incarnation to the next.

Although *Heaven Can Wait* is about a football quarterback who leads his football team to victory in the most important football game of the year, the film is not really a "football" movie. This is evidenced by the fact that in *Here Comes Mr. Jordan*, the 1941 film on which it was based, the protagonist is a boxer, while in *Down to Earth*, the 2001 remake starring comedian Chris Rock, he is a stand-up comic. While football plays a significant part in the film, what makes the movie work is the sincerity with which the fantasy elements are presented. One of the most important of these elements is the film's depiction of angels. The angelic realm described in *Heaven Can Wait* mirrors the corporate world in which Farnsworth himself operates. Heavenly functionaries wear business suits and work within a strictly bureaucratic hierarchy. If **Heaven** itself operates like a business, the movie seems to say, then why can't earthly businesses, in turn, behave morally?

One theme of the film seems to be that the human spirit is capable of overcoming the physical limitations and circumstances in which it finds itself. Yet the film also acknowledges that one's capabilities are largely determined by one's character. As Farnsworth, Pendleton can persuade fellow industrialists to adopt policies that are good for the environment, something that Betty has been unable to do; but despite Max's assistance, it becomes clear that Farnsworth will never succeed as a professional quarterback.

Another important theme in the film is destiny. The angels who help Pendleton cannot put him back in his original body after it has been cremated. They are limited by the restrictions of what has already been and what must be. In fact, it is only because they discover that Pendleton is destined to play in the Super Bowl that they decide to offer their assistance in the first place.

Heaven Can Wait successfully blends a world of angels and a heavenly afterlife with a story about earthly reincarnation. It does this by presenting reincarnation not as the ordinary course of events, but as an exception that arises due to the inadvertent disruption of Joe Pendleton's life. This is an exceptional case, so the rules are being bent. As a result, the audience is unable to predict the outcome. When Pendleton temporarily resides in Farnsworth's body he retains his **memory**, but when he assumes his new **identity** at the film's conclusion he forgets the experiences of his former life. This allows him to live out a normal life, but it also raises an additional challenge for the audience's hope of seeing Joe and Betty get together. Their love must transcend not only death, but a complete loss of identity.

Bibliography

Ellis Amburn. *The Sexiest Man Alive*. New York: Harper Entertainment, 2002.

Alan Cartnal. *Warren Beatty*. New York: Scribner, 1985.

Katherine A. Fowkes. *Giving Up the Ghost*. Detroit, MI: Wayne State University Press, 1998.

John Kercher. *Warren Beatty*. New York: Proteus Press, 1985.

Suzanne Munshower. *Warren Beatty*. New York: St. Martin's Press, 1983.

Lawrence J. Quirk. *The Films of Warren Beatty*. New York: Citadel Trade, 1979.

James Spada. *Shirley and Warren*. New York: Macmillan, 1985.

David Thomson. *Warren Beatty and Desert Eyes*. New York: Doubleday, 1987.

—*Ed McKnight*

HELLICONIA SPRING BY BRIAN W. ALDISS (1982)

Summary

Helliconia is a planet in a binary **star** system, whose complex motion gives it a double **cycle** of **seasons**. The familiar yearly sequence is overwhelmed by that of the "Great Year" orbit (2,592 Earth years) around the second, hotter sun. *Helliconia Spring* sees the world emerging from a 500-year Great Winter into 900 years of spring. Mellowing climate shifts the balance between Helliconia's two races: the horned, Minotaur-like phagors who rule the winter and near-humans now approaching dominance. **Civilization** blooms, evoked with poetic joy in language and seen through closely observed individual lives. **Cities, politics**, primitive **technology**, and **money** are rediscovered. Each **rebirth** is a reminder of the **tragedy** of what was lost in the long **disaster** of winter.

Helliconia imposes extraordinary constraints on its people: "First, fate moulds our character; then character moulds our fate." Above the action, **Earth** watches via interstellar **communications** relayed by its orbiting **habitat** Avernus. Though there is **time** enough ahead, many centuries of it, the question already looms: can "**humanity**" rise far enough to preserve its **memory, culture** and **history** unbroken through the *next* Great Winter? Aldiss's grandiose scope pays deliberate homage to Olaf Stapledon's *Last and First Men.*

Discussion

The ambitious trilogy is completed with stories, or sheaves of stories, set in later periods of the Great Year: *Helliconia Summer* (1983) and *Helliconia Winter* (1985). The lush summer volume uses cadences intentionally echoing William **Shakespeare**'s *A Midsummer Night's Dream* (c. 1594). **Kings, queens** and **marriages** dominate the realm of politics, while a renaissance is in full swing for **art** and **scientists**. At the height of summer, though, the equatorial regions spontaneously catch **fire**. Many lifetimes later, the inevitable winter begins to close in, affecting both the mental as well as the physical climate.

Helliconia is a world imagined in enormous detail. Animals are given reminiscent names: horse-like "hoxneys" (recalling "hack" and "hackney"), and easily imagined "yelk." The humanoids' **evolution** has reached an uneasy balance with the helico virus (see **Plagues and Diseases**), whose name suggests the DNA double helix (see **Biology**) and which brings both **death** and adaptation to the changing **ecology**: as "bone fever" it strips away body fat reserves for spring, while as "fat death" it prepares survivors for winter.

Thus the cycle of enantiodromia, of qualities turning into their opposites (see **Yin and Yang**), which pervades Helliconia. As Aldiss himself remarks in "Helliconia: How and Why," "knowledge becomes by turns a blessing and a curse, as does religion." Subjection and **freedom** swap roles. Humanoids and the phagors who regard them as food undergo cyclic **role reversal**, alternating between dominance and **slavery**. In part the phagors represent the animal flipside of human nature, the bestiality that seems to recur no matter how often repressed by civilization.

Epigraphs from the rational scientist-poet Lucretius's *De Rerum Naturae* (c. 55 BCE) contrast with sympathetically handled mysticism. **Perception** of the ley-like "land-octaves" and "air-octaves" that are significant to phagor migrations may involve subtle **psychic powers**. Humans sense a literal afterlife of angry ghosts far underground, spirits whose apparent rage becomes empty benevolence as the world warms (see **Ghosts and Hauntings**). The **mythology** naturally includes **gods and goddesses** like Wutra, who brings the winter. Less metaphorical are the "tutelary biospheric spirits," which Aldiss imagines as aspects of Helliconia's overall planetary balance or consciousness—James Lovelock's Gaia hypothesis exported to another world. Indeed, Gaia and the Helliconia-soul achieve empathic communication.

Certain scenes are knowingly adapted from older science fiction. *Helliconia Spring* echoes a passage of Jules Verne's *Hector Servadac* (1877)—quoted approvingly in Aldiss's *Billion Year Spree* (1973)—in which an ice fragment thrown into a supercooled sea converts it rapidly to a sheet of ice (see **Physics; Water**). In the Helliconian version, the quick-freezing lake becomes a trap for pursuing phagors, a first hint that these **monsters** can be defeated. *Helliconia Winter* features the Great

Wheel that revolves horizontally inside a **mountain**, hauled by entrapped volunteers whose efforts—in a metaphor suggesting ancient **Egypt**—supposedly pull Helliconia through the long winter. This architecture-cum-machine pays homage to the revolving temple/**prison** of Edgar Rice Burroughs's *The Gods of Mars* (1918) (see *A Princess of Mars*).

Ultimately Aldiss shows a triple choice for humanity and near-humanity. The voyeuristic scientists of the artificial satellite Avernus (a name which, like Helliconia itself, suggests a classical **Hell**) lapse into **decadence**, **barbarian** strife, and eventual death. Earth, recovering from an **apocalypse** brought on by **nuclear war** in the **far future**, develops into a contented, harmonious **utopia**. And Helliconia struggles onward, locked in the Great Year's endless cycle of planetary **metamorphosis**, a punishing cycle that is also the vital rhythm of life.

Aldiss is careful to avoid the easy **puzzle**-solving of pulp science fiction, whose conventions would demand both a "magic bullet" of advanced **medicine** to break the hold of the virus and sustainable high technology for comfortable winter survival. As Helliconia has been conceived, though, this solution is no solution but rather a disaster, a poisoning of the biosphere's delicate self-regulation. The actual ending, or lack of ending, is more grimly resonant. Despite many fine inventions, however, the second and third volumes do not equal the magical, **color**-splashed unfurling of *Helliconia Spring*.

Bibliography

Brian W. Aldiss. "Helliconia: How and Why." Aldiss, *The Pale Shadow of Science*. Seattle, WA: Serconia, 1985, 121–128.

Peter Caracciolo. "*Helliconia Summer* and *Helliconia Winter*." *Foundation*, No. 35 (Winter 1985/1986), 70–73.

Mary Gentle. "The Three Ages of Man." *Vector*, No. 109 (August, 1982), 42–45.

Brian Griffin and David Wingrove. *Apertures*. Westport, CT: Greenwood Press, 1984.

Roz Kaveney. "In Celebration of Brian Aldiss." *Interzone*, No. 38 (August, 1990), 25–28.

David Langford. "On the Bestseller Trail." *Extro*, 1 (July/August, 1982), 23.

R.G. Meadley. "Half an Eye and Tono-Bungay." *Foundation*, No. 27 (February, 1983), 71–78.

Denise Terrel. "Is Brian Aldiss's Helliconia a Metaphorical Earth?" *Metaphores*, 12/13 (March, 1986), 217–226.

—*David Langford*

HERCULES: THE LEGENDARY JOURNEYS (1994–2000)

■

Summary

The series *Hercules: The Legendary Journey* began with five two-hour telemovies (all in 1994) which reinterpreted mythical **quests**, including several Labors of Hercules. *Hercules and the Amazon Women* gives a feminist version of Hercules' romance with **Amazon** Queen Hippolyta, as the chauvinistic **hero** learns to respect the Amazons (see **Feminism**). *Hercules and the Circle of Fire* and *Hercules and the Lost Kingdom* revisit the rescues of Prometheus and a Trojan princess but primarily serve to establish Hera as Hercules's chief adversary, who sends **evil** minions to oppress **humanity**. *Hercules in the Underworld* updates the Labor of Cerberus, while *Hercules in the Maze of the Minotaur* places the hero in the role taken by Theseus in myth.

The films' success led to the series, which begins with Hera's murder of Hercules's wife and **children**, thus launching Hercules on his journeys. The typical episode begins with the hero learning of some wrong that he must right or some danger to the innocent that he must thwart. Adversaries are often traditional fantasy characters such as **gods and goddesses, kings, queens,** or **monsters,** and Hercules must call on not only his strength and **courage,** but also his **wisdom** and compassion to resolve the problem. A few loose dramatic arcs are provided by Hercules's relationships with his loving **mother** Alcmene, his charming but self-centered **father** Zeus, and especially his friend Iolaus, who becomes more central as the series progresses, even playing the lead in some episodes. The final episode, "Full Circle" (1999), sees Hercules reconciled with Zeus and Hera and continuing on his adventures with Iolaus. Hercules makes a final appearance in the *Xena: Warrior Princess* episode "God Fearing Child" (2000) in which he is forced to kill Zeus to protect Xena and her newborn.

Discussion

The mythical strongman Hercules has been portrayed on screen many times, including a few animated incarnations. The most famous big screen Hercules was bodybuilder and former Mr. Universe Steve Reeves, star of the Italian feature films *Hercules* (1957) and *Hercules Unchained* (1958). Exciting action and Reeves's imposing screen presence made these films huge international successes and gave birth to the "sword and sandal" genre. Though many others followed in Reeves's sandals, the genre was generally panned by critics for wooden performances and poor scripts, and petered out within a few years.

Sword and sandal films were long out of date by 1993, when American producers Robert Tapert and Sam Raimi were commissioned to update the myth for a series of Hercules telefilms. Known for their tongue-in-cheek horror film *The Evil Dead* (1983), Raimi and Tapert brought the same serio-comic spirit to Greek **mythology,** emphasizing Hercules's **humor** and humanity over god-like feats of strength and epic solemnity.

As portrayed by handsome, likable Kevin Sorbo, the new Hercules is as far from the stoic strongmen of the 1950s as he is from the slow-witted hero of myth. Instead he reflects a post-feminist ideal of a hero who combines **intelligence** and courage with emotional accessibility and a wry sense of humor. Togas are replaced by open shirts and woven leather trousers, and Hercules rarely uses a **sword**; instead, he kicks and punches through stunt fights that are as visually entertaining as they are cartoonish in their lack of realistic damage.

Filmed in New Zealand, *Hercules* is set in a **sword and sorcery** version of the ancient world, populated with characters not only from Greek myth, such as centaurs (see **Horses**) and **giants**, but from other traditions such as Celtic, Norse, and Near Eastern mythology. While adventure and drama provide exciting moments and over-the-top special effects, **comedy** is a staple of *Hercules,* which tried virtually every comic form from **romance** to slapstick to farce. Contemporary cultural references abound, ranging from Aphrodite's "valley girl" dialogue and glib toga salesman Salmoneus, to entire episodes that parody genres such as **westerns**, musicals, and drag shows. Like sword and sandal films, these new adventures generally omit the bloody and tragic elements of the myths in favor of happy endings more palatable to American television audiences, though **tragedy** is occasionally permitted in the series.

Even in comic episodes, heroism always remains the central theme. In *Hercules,* a hero must have not only strength and courage, but compassion. Heroism is not just Hercules's dedication to helping others: it is the dashing thief Autolycus giving up his booty to help the poor, or the timid Salmoneus braving a **villain**'s wrath. While Greek myths often made their heroes the helpless pawns of the Fates, in *Hercules,* individuals are always masters of their own **destiny,** so long as they have the courage to stand up for themselves and their **dreams.**

A closely related theme, and perhaps the most important, is being true to oneself. It is explored most effectively when Hercules, grieving for Iolaus's heroic death, forsakes the way of the hero and flees to Ireland. There he is defeated by another demigod, the Irish warrior Morrigan, because he no longer has the heart to stand against evil. A druid's teaching helps him rediscover his heroic calling, enabling him to defeat Morrigan in battle and later win her heart ("Resurrection" [1998]).

Hercules generated two syndicated spin-off series, *Young Hercules* (1998–1999), and *Xena: Warrior Princess,* as well as an animated feature film, *Hercules and Xena—The Animated Movie: The Battle for Mount Olympus* (1998). By updating classic myths with humor and a contemporary outlook, *Hercules: The Legendary Journeys* helped to create a new genre of television fantasy.

Bibliography

Kate Barker. "The Last Labour of Hercules." *Xena: Warrior Princess,* 1 (March, 2000), 16–20.

Arthur Chappell. "Xena and Hercules." *Matrix,* No. 134 (November/December, 1998), 18–20.

K. Stoddard Hayes. "Bad to the Bone." *Xena: Warrior Princess,* 1 (December, 2000), 38–42.

Patrick Luciano. *With Fire and Sword.* Metuchen, NJ: Scarecrow Press, 1994.

Joe Nazzaro. "Robert Tapert." Nazzaro, *Writing Science Fiction and Fantasy Television.* London: Titan Books, 2002, 196–210.

Marc Shapiro. "The Labors of Hercules." *Starlog,* No. 211 (February, 1995), 55–58.

Jim Smith. "The Long Path." *Xena: Warrior Princess,* 1 (March, 2000), 22–26.

Robert Weisbrot, *Hercules: The Legendary Journeys: The Official Companion.* New York: Doubleday, 1998.

———. *Hercules: The Legendary Journeys: An Insider's Guide to the Continuing Adventures.* Boulder, CO: Taylor Trade Publishing, 2004.

—Karen Stoddard Hayes

HERLAND BY CHARLOTTE PERKINS GILMAN (1915)

∎

> *Here was evidently a people highly skilled, efficient, caring for their country as a florist cares for his costliest orchids.*
>
> —Charlotte Perkins Gilman
> *Herland* (1915)

Summary

Herland is a **utopia** set in an isolated country, reached by plane by three young American men during a scientific expedition. Herland is inhabited only by women who reproduce through parthenogenesis. They are a peaceful, highly specialized, technologically advanced, and ecological society (see **Ecology**). After initially being imprisoned, Terry, the expedition leader, Jeff, and Van, the narrator, are hosted by the Herlanders, who want information about the outside world and are interested in eventually becoming a two-sexual society again. Motivated initially by curiosity and titillated by the prospect of sexual encounters, the men react differently to the customs of Herland. Each is assigned a tutor and undergoes a process of **education** before being released to socialize with Herlanders. They are encouraged to teach their tutors about U.S. society. It is through these parallels, and through comparing the men's reactions, that Gilman criticizes **gender** stereotypes, sexual discrimination, and the economic and social realities of western **culture**. The three explorers eventually marry three Herlanders. At the end of the novel, Jeff, who idealizes and romanticizes women, declines to return **home**; Terry, unable to respect the customs and feelings of the Herlanders with respect to **marriage**, is expelled from Herland for attempted rape. Van, changed and enriched by the experience, travels to the U.S. with his wife, with whom he has an egalitarian relationship. This journey is the subject of the sequel *With Her in Ourland* (1916).

Discussion

Rather than focusing on the future, *Herland* exploits traditional elements of utopian narrative to reflect on the shortcomings of contemporary society. The conflicting world views of the Herlanders and explorers also provide a critique of the myths of conquest, the **frontier**, and **exploration** of **lost worlds**, which are here exposed as narratives of patriarchal imperialism.

In *Herland* women possess **knowledge** and power, whereas the male explorers must adjust to the expectations and values of a society from which they are estranged. In a monosexual, classless, egalitarian society without **family** structures, **children** are raised by professional educators and loved by the whole **community**. No emotional claims or official ties bind people. In contrast to the restrictive gender roles in contemporary western society, Herlanders enjoy independent living space and are free from financial necessity and household chores. This critique stems from Gilman's contact with and response to utopian socialism and material **feminism** of the second half of the nineteenth century.

Herland is a community that works for its own preservation in the future. Instead of valuing the past and **history,** the Herlanders honor motherhood and children above all else. But motherhood is not seen as natural for women. Those who desire it, but are not deemed to possess the required physical and psychical characteristics to be good **mothers,** are dissuaded from motherhood. The number of children that may be born each year without overstraining the limited resources is established by a council. Since reproduction does not require sexual intercourse, the Herlanders do not have any interest in **sexuality.** Their androgynous clothes and appearance (see **Androgyny**), as well as their social structure, suggest that gender roles and stereotypes are socially constructed. Terry is only interested in women as sexual objects, but in Herland there is no room for this predatory view of women (see **Sexism**).

Some critics argue that Gilman's social critique still posits the home as women's sphere of activity and motherhood as their main interest. Here, however, the home is expanded to constitute the entire community, thus undermining the differentiation of public and private spheres on which numerous stereotypical gender roles rely. Herland is a purely democratic, classless, decentralized, and unchanging society (see **Governance Systems**). **Politics** and hierarchy are replaced with relations of sisterhood and motherhood. The explorers are attracted to Herland after finding a piece of finely woven material in the jungle: by using this product of a typically female activity to define the advancement of civilization in Herland, Gilman applies alternative criteria to patriarchal concepts of **civilization.**

All inhabitants work and constantly move around the country. Except for electric cars, Gilman does not describe any other technological item. Herlanders are economically self-sufficient, producing everything they need without impoverishing the soil and polluting the environment. Herland is covered by **forests,** but there are no wild areas (see **Wilderness**). All forests are giant orchards, providing the main nourishment for the population. The extremely efficient husbandry is run on an ecological basis, and all waste products are recycled and turned into feed for the soil. The link between women and **nature** is a tenet of ecofeminism, and the novel has therefore been hailed by scholars as a precursor of feminist ecotopias. Herlanders have eliminated cattle, considered a wasteful source of nourishment, and have bred **cats** that do not hunt.

However, this aspect and the authoritarian eugenics of Herland give rise to uneasiness about the racist undertones characterizing the novel. Herlanders are indeed described as being of "Aryan" stock and their qualities are compared to the negatively characterized neighboring tribes encountered by the explorers just before entering the country (see **Race Relations**). Moreover, it has been observed that the novel displays a rather naïve faith in the moral qualities and material benefits of scientific **progress,** which somewhat maims the strength of its social critique.

Bibliography

Frances Bartkowski. *Feminist Utopias.* Lincoln: University of Nebraska Press, 1989.

Laura Donaldson. "The Eve of De-Struction." *Women's Studies,* 16 (1989), 373–387.

Val Gough. "Lesbians and Virgins." David Seed, ed., *Anticipations.* Syracuse, NY: Syracuse University Press, 1995, 195–215.

Val Gough and Jill Rudd, eds. *A Very Different Story.* Liverpool: Liverpool University Press, 1998.

Susan Gubar. "*She* in *Herland.*" Sheryl L. Meyering, ed., *Charlotte Perkins Gilman.* Ann
    Arbor: University of Michigan Research Press, 1989, 139–149.
Joanne Karpinski. *Critical Essays on Charlotte Perkins Gilman.* New York: G.K. Hall, 1992.
Ann J. Lane. *To Herland and Beyond.* New York: Pantheon, 1990.
Sarah Lefanu. *In the Chinks of the World Machine.* London: The Women's Press, 1988.
Margaret Miller. "The Ideal Woman in Two Feminist Science-Fiction Utopias." *Science-
    Fiction Studies,* 10 (July, 1983), 191–198.

—Laura Scuriatti

THE HITCHHIKER'S GUIDE
TO THE GALAXY BY DOUGLAS ADAMS (1979)

■

*Don't you understand, this is the first
time I've actually stood on the surface of
another planet . . . a whole alien world
. . . ! Pity it's such a dump though.*

—Douglas Adams
The Hitchhiker's Guide to the Galaxy (1979)

Summary

Arthur Dent, a thoroughly average human, is surprised to find that his friend Ford
Prefect is an alien researcher for an intergalactic travel guide, and furthermore that
a race of bureaucratic aliens called Vogons plan to demolish the **Earth** in accordance
with planning regulations. Arthur and Ford "hitch a lift" on a Vogon spacecraft but
are quickly thrown into space. Fortunately, they are accidentally rescued by a starship powered by improbability that has been stolen by two-headed Galactic President (and Ford's cousin) Zaphod Beeblebrox. Also aboard are Zaphod's human
girlfriend Trillian and a manically depressed **robot**, Marvin. Beeblebrox is searching
for—and finds—the mythical planet-building world Magrathea where Arthur meets
coastline designer Slartibartfast and discovers that the Earth was not a real planet
but merely a giant **computer**. It transpires that pan-dimensional beings, who exist in
our dimension as mice (see **Rats and Mice**), paid Magratheans to build the Earth to
discover the ultimate question of "life, the universe and everything," having already
built a computer called Deep Thought to calculate the answer—which turned out to
be "42." Galactic police arrive to arrest Beeblebrox, but Marvin rescues his comrades by persuading the police spaceship's computer to commit **suicide**.

Discussion

The Hitchhiker's Guide began life as a six-part radio serial, Douglas Adams's background being in **comedy** sketch-writing, although he was also a writer and script
editor for *Doctor Who*. The novel covers only the first four radio episodes because

Adams fell out with John Lloyd, co-writer of parts five and six—hence the sudden, somewhat **deus ex machina** ending—although elements from those episodes were used in the sequel, *The Restaurant at the End of the Universe* (1980). Largely ignorant of earlier works in the field of science fiction **humor**, Adams's primary stylistic influences were the comic novels of P.G. Wodehouse and the surreal television series *Monty Python's Flying Circus* (1970–1974). In this story he creates a **satire** on human existence, openly acknowledging the influence of Jonathan Swift's *Gulliver's Travels*. Swift's work also informs the picaresque nature of the story, although the primary reason for this was Adams's episodic writing of the original scripts without a predetermined story line.

The Hitchhiker's Guide to the Galaxy is the title of not only the radio serial, the first novel, and the book series *in toto* but also of the electronic travel guide (see **Books**) for which Ford Prefect works (see **Journalism**). Adams uses this as a narrative device, literally, to explain aspects of his fictional universe to both his everyman protagonist (Arthur) and his audience. The destruction of Earth at the story's outset exemplifies a recurring theme of planetary **disaster** in Adams's surprisingly nihilistic fiction, contrasting ironically with a gradually developing amateur interest in **ecology** and **evolution** (stimulated by a close friendship with Professor Richard Dawkins), which is evident here but really shines through his later works. The arts-trained author's cynical attitude to **technology** (at this stage in his career) is evident in the book's most popular character, Marvin the Paranoid Android (see **Paranoia**), whose depression stems from his having been fitted with a "Genuine People Personality" and in his rather simplistic and traditional view of computers as talking boxes.

The story of *Hitchhiker's Guide* does not parody specific works of science fiction but instead lampoons general science fiction tropes. For example, the problem of interspecies **communication** is solved by the existence of the babel fish, a naturally occurring universal translator (see **Language And Linguistics**). The vast **galactic empire** over which the vastly unsuitable Beeblebrox recently ruled is our own world writ large, where alien races construct "hyperspace bypasses" (see **Transportation**) and a world of expensive planet-builders goes to sleep (see **Suspended Animation and Cryonics**) during a period of fiscal depression. It is an epic, comic **space opera** that uses the freedom of science fiction to highlight by exaggeration the **absurdity** of human existence. **Philosophy** and **religion** are both dealt with somewhat facetiously in the book; Adams was an outspoken atheist in later life but when writing *Hitchhiker's Guide* he was merely an agnostic humorist.

A third novel, *Life, the Universe and Everything* (1982), adapted from an unproduced *Doctor Who* script, posited that cricket (see **Sports**) is a race memory of an ancient interplanetary **war**. Two further novels, *So Long, and Thanks for All the Fish* (1984) and *Mostly Harmless* (1992), followed Arthur Dent's return to a version of Earth that has been rescued from another dimension by dolphins (see **Fish and Sea Creatures**). A six-part television series (1981), also written by Adams, approximately followed the plot of the radio series and an "interactive fiction" computer game (1984), co-written with Steve Meretzky, added a great deal of peripheral information to the setting while taking the plot in new directions. The story has also been adapted numerous times for the **theatre**. A feature film version of *The Hitchhiker's Guide to the Galaxy* released in 2005 after 25 years in development, departed radically from earlier versions. The screenplay by Karey Kirkpatrick, adapted from an earlier draft by Adams, introduced new ideas and characters, to debatable effect.

Bibliography

John Fleming. "Don't Panic: An Interview with Douglas Adams." *Starburst*, No. 31 (March, 1981), 28–33, and No. 32 (April, 1981), 38–42.

Neil Gaiman. *Don't Panic*. Third Edition. London: Titan Books, 2002.

Carl R. Kropf. "Douglas Adams's *Hitchhiker* Novels as Mock Science Fiction." *Science-Fiction Studies*, 15 (March, 1988), 61–70.

Stan Nicholls. "Douglas Adams: Will Never Say Never Again, Probably." Nicholls, *Wordsmiths of Wonder*. London: Orbit, 1993, 169–181.

Dee Pilgrim. "Douglas Adams Explains Why You Shouldn't Panic!" *Ad Astra*, No. 16 (1981), 10–11.

M.J. Simpson. *Hitchhiker: A Biography of Douglas Adams*. London: Hodder & Stoughton, 2003.

———. *The Pocket Essential Hitchhiker's Guide*. London: Pocket Essentials, 2001.

Nick Webb. *Wish You Were Here*. London: Headline, 2003.

Nicholas Wroe. "Prologue." Douglas Adams, *The Salmon of Doubt*. New York: Harmony, 2002, xv–xxix.

—*M.J. Simpson*

THE HOBBIT BY J.R.R. TOLKIEN (1937)

■

> *In a hole in the ground there lived a hobbit.*
>
> —J.R.R. Tolkien
> *The Hobbit* (1937)

Summary

Originally presented as an independent work, *The Hobbit* is now regarded as the precursor to J.R.R. Tolkien's ***The Lord of the Rings***, sharing two of its characters and the setting of Middle-earth. Bilbo Baggins, a respectable hobbit, travels with the **wizard** Gandalf, Thorin Oakenshield, and other **dwarfs** to the Lonely Mountain to reclaim the dwarfs' **treasure** from the **dragon** Smaug. Thorin and company hire Bilbo to be their "burglar" and their lucky number (the fourteenth member). During his adventures, Bilbo is captured by trolls (see **Supernatural Creatures**); befriended by Elrond and the Rivendell **elves**; helped by Beorn, a shapeshifting man (see **Shapeshifters**); captured by **goblins**; and lost in **caverns** under the Misty Mountains, where he discovers a magical **ring** that makes the wearer invisible, (see **Invisibility; Magical Objects**); and engages in a **riddle** contest with a creature named Gollum. Bilbo is also stalked by giant spiders in Mirkwood Forest (see **Insects**), nearly captured by Wood-Elves, almost drowned in a **river**, and nearly burned alive by Smaug. Only his ring enables him to **escape** Gollum, defeat the spiders, elude capture by the Wood-elves, steal from Smaug's hoard, and take the Arkenstone (the dwarfs' most priceless treasure) to the Bard of Laketown as a bargaining chip to try to prevent full-scale **war** between Laketown men and the dwarfs, who finally join in a common battle against the goblins. His **quest** completed, Bilbo contentedly returns to his **home** in the Shire.

Discussion

Bilbo Baggins is an unlikely **hero**, though a hero nonetheless. A result of his adventures with Gandalf and the dwarfs is that Bilbo's narrow, provincial view of the world and its inhabitants is greatly enlarged. He discovers that there is much more to the world than the Shire, that his stereotypes of other races and lands are misguided, and that appearances are often misleading; he recognizes, moreover, that he is not such a timid little hobbit, but is rather resourceful, courageous, and heroic. He finally learns that, although he is only a very small person in a very wide world, he has nevertheless played a role in the fulfillment of old prophecies (see **Destiny**).

Bilbo agrees to go with the dwarfs because, as Gandalf says, all the warriors are off fighting each other in faraway places and there are no heroes in the area. Bilbo is not hired for his martial prowess, but as a burglar to sneak into the Lonely Mountain (see **Mountains**) and return with some treasure. The fact that Gandalf recommends Bilbo as a substitute for a hero suggests that the dwarfs are not heroes themselves, which is proven later when the dwarfs discuss leaving him in the goblins' caverns. In his first attempt at burglary, early in the story, Bilbo is caught trying to pick the pocket of William the Troll (see **Theft**). Much later, in his second attempt, he successfully steals a large two-handled cup from Smaug's hoard in the Lonely Mountain (the image and episode are from the Old English poem *Beowulf* [c. 800 CE]). In between these events, Bilbo proves his heroic nature by rescuing and freeing the dwarfs from giant spiders and the Wood-elves of Mirkwood Forest.

After getting knocked unconscious, lost, and separated from the dwarfs in the caverns, Bilbo discovers a golden, magic ring. Later, he meets Gollum, a shriveled hobbit-like creature with whom he engages in a riddle contest; if he wins the contest, then Gollum must show him the way out. Bilbo realizes just before Gollum prepares to kill him that the ring makes him invisible, so he uses it to escape Gollum and the goblins. The ring of invisibility subsequently proves extremely useful to Bilbo, who employs its powers repeatedly and without displaying any ill effects. It is only in *The Lord of the Rings* that this same ring is revealed to be an **evil** and dangerous object, the One Ring of Power, whose use should be avoided at all costs.

The Laketown men and the dwarfs prepare for war because neither side trusts the other and both act according to their greed and their stereotyped beliefs about other races (see **Race Relations**). The dwarfs claim Smaug's treasure and refuse to give some of it to the men, who argue that a portion of the treasure should be theirs because the treasure of their ancestors was mixed with the dwarfs' treasure in Smaug's hoard and the dwarfs would have no treasure at all if Bard had not killed Smaug. Into this situation come the Wood-elves of Mirkwood, who offer aid and comfort to the men of Laketown. The dwarfs and elves here and in *The Lord of the*

Rings are habitually wary and untrusting of each other because of events related in Tolkien's *The Silmarillion* (1977).

When war finally erupts, the dwarfs, men, elves, and eagles unite against a common enemy, the goblins and wargs (or wolves). They realize that what they have in common is more important than what separates them, and that only by uniting can they defeat a fearsome, merciless enemy. After the battle, in which they receive assistance from the eagles (see **Birds**), the dying Thorin forgives Bilbo for giving the Arkenstone to Bard, saying that in Bilbo **wisdom** and **courage** are equally mixed. He even says that the world would be better if more people valued food (see **Food and Drink**), song, and cheer above hoarded gold (see **Gold and Silver**). Thus, Thorin praises Bilbo, suggesting that his outlook on life is superior to that of dwarfs and human heroes, who may seek only treasure and fame.

Bibliography

Douglas Anderson, ed. *The Annotated Hobbit*, by J.R.R. Tolkien. Revised Ed. Boston: Houghton Mifflin, 2002.

Janet B. Croft. "The Great War and Tolkien's Memory." *Mythlore*, 23 (Fall/Winter, 2002), 4–21.

Jared Curtis. "On Re-Reading *The Hobbit*, Fifteen Years Later." *Children's Literature in Education*, 15 (1984), 113–120.

William H. Green. "King Thorin's Mines." *Extrapolation*, 42 (Spring, 2001), 53–64.

James L. Hodge. "Tolkien's Mythological Calendar in *The Hobbit*." William Coyle, ed., *Aspects of Fantasy*. Westport, CT: Greenwood Press, 1986, 141–148.

Christina Scull. "*The Hobbit* Considered in Relation to Children's Literature Contemporary With Its Writing and Publication." *Mythlore*, 14 (Winter, 1987), 49–56.

Tom Shippey. *J.R.R. Tolkien: Author of the Century*. London: HarperCollins, 2000.

———. *The Road to Middle-earth*. London: HarperCollins-Grafton, 1992.

J.R. Wytenbroek. "Rites of Passage in *The Hobbit*." *Mythlore*, 13 (Summer, 1987), 5–8, 40.

—*Theodore James Sherman*

HOSPITAL STATION BY JAMES WHITE (1962)

Summary

This collection of linked stories opened James White's popular Sector General science fiction series, in which problems of **medicine**, surgery, **psychology** and **first contact** are tackled by dedicated medical workers. Sector Twelve General Hospital is a vast **space habitat** constructed and staffed by many species, including **humanity** and various exotic **aliens in space** (referred to as "e-ts," or extraterrestrials). The 384 levels of Sector General are equipped to house patients from numerous environments: water-, oxygen- and chlorine-breathers, high- and low-**gravity** species, and a temperature range from cryogenic chill to superheated steam. In this near-**utopia**, healing resources are considerable, enthusiasm is boundless, and the worst social crime is **xenophobia**.

In the first six books, the initially naive Dr. Conway is the problem-solving protagonist; O'Mara, the tetchy, sarcastic Chief Psychologist, is Conway's foil, goad, and authority figure; Nurse (later Pathologist) Murchison provides his **love** interest; and Dr. Prilicla, the dragonfly-like alien empath (see **Insects; Psychic Powers**), is his best friend. The complete sequence of books is *Hospital Station*, *Star Surgeon* (1963), *Major Operation* (1971), *Ambulance Ship* (1979), *Sector General* (1983), *Star Healer* (1985), *Code Blue—Emergency* (1987), *The Genocidal Healer* (1992), *The Galactic Gourmet* (1996), *Final Diagnosis* (1997), *Mind Changer* (1998), and *Double Contact* (1999).

Discussion

The stories offer a series of ingenious and entertaining **puzzles** of alien **biology** and other e-t quirks. Early cases include a damaged **hive mind** of **insect**-like creatures who live on hard radiation; the need to teach an alien **dinosaur** the psychic powers its species requires to avoid extinction; a **shapeshifter** running amok in Sector General, too immature to be responsible for its actions; a seeming case of terminal illness coupled with **madness** that is in fact the symptoms and defensive reflexes of a larva undergoing natural **metamorphosis**; and difficulties with an unseen physician that lives in **symbiosis** with its patient and resists Conway's ministrations.

Underlying these **detective** plots is a compassion and reverence for life that Conway—as a new and idealistic Sector General doctor—cannot reconcile with the presence of the military Monitor Corps. This force exists mainly to stop planetary **wars** with stun guns and sleepy gas (see **Weaponry**), but in *Star Surgeon* is required to defend Sector General itself when **space war** is initiated by a small, unpleasant, would-be **galactic empire** that objects to outside interference with the **plagues and diseases** it inflicts on one of its own **planetary colonies**. White's loathing of armed conflict, reflecting personal experience in the Troubles of his native **city** Belfast, does not blind him to its occasional inevitability.

Two science fiction gimmicks recur throughout the series. The physiological classification system used to encode basic information about bodily types is based on E.E. "Doc" Smith's (see *Triplanetary*) but without his anthropocentrism. Earth-humans, for example, are type DBDG, to the four places usually quoted: they are barely distinguishable from alien DBDGs resembling **toy** teddy-bears, and not significantly different from other warm-blooded oxygen-breathers like DBLFs, who are shaped like huge furry caterpillars.

White's other trademark device is the Educator (see **Education**) that tapes eminent doctors' medical skills for playback into other minds as required. Unfortunately this expertise is tinged with personality, producing a mild case of **possession**. At one point the tape-ridden Conway is almost fatally distracted from surgery by a lovely nurse who is a giant crab. At another, when Sector General's vital Translation **computer** (see **Language and Linguistics**) is damaged by attack, he accepts multiple e-t tapes and acts as interpreter.

Sector General frequently spearheads first contact as aliens in space are discovered in damaged or dangerously primitive spacecraft. Among the oddest is a giant, lifeless **bird** encrusted with barnacles; the bird proves a mere carrier for "barnacle" space explorers who propel their bizarre vehicle by explosive ejection, like bombardier beetles. The Monitor Corps fleet is routinely called in for larger medical emergencies: surgery on the continent-spanning alien of *Major Operation* requires heavy weaponry, and the huge mass of a Corps flagship is called into play for the equivalent of applying a tourniquet. Another distressed spacefarer is a kind of Midgard Serpent (see **Snakes and Worms**) shipped in dismantled form as nearly 1,000 segments in suspended animation (see **Suspended Animation and Cryonics**), needing not only complex space-rescue operations but reassembly.

With Conway promoted to the top medical rank of Diagnostician and burdened with responsibility, later books introduce new protagonists, three being aliens who explore the non-medical byways of Sector General. *Code Blue—Emergency* shows the complex infrastructure of hospital maintenance and supply. The title character of *The Genocidal Healer* ceases to practice medicine after a terrible misjudgment, and develops a kind of secular **religion** of confession and atonement that comforts not only himself but others. *The Galactic Gourmet* has the amusing premise of an egotistic alien chef tackling the oxymoronic task of making institutional **food and drink** taste good; his triumph is to persuade a dying but obdurate species to make necessary changes in its diet, a unique case of "culinary first contact."

James White's gentle **humor** and charm permeate the entire sequence. He satisfyingly pictures an ultimately reasonable universe where xenophobia is curable and, almost always, to understand all is to forgive all.

Bibliography

Graham Andrews. "Stars and Scalpels." *Foundation*, No. 52 (Summer 1991), 20–30.
John Clute. "Introduction." James White, *General Practice*. New York: Orb, 2003, 7–12.
Edward James. "Life in Sector General." *Zenith Science Fiction*, 5 (June/July, 1964), 9–13.
David Langford. "Introduction." James White, *Alien Emergencies*. New York: Orb, 2002, 7–14.
———. "James White and Sector General." Langford, *Up Through an Empty House of Stars*. Holicong, PA: Cosmos Books, 2003, 185–188.
Brian Stableford. "Introduction." James White, *Beginning Operations*. New York: Orb, 2001, 7–12.
Phil Stephensen-Payne and Gordon Benson Jr. *James White: Doctor to Aliens*. Second Ed. Leeds, UK: Galactic Central, 1989.
Gary Westfahl. "Doctors' Ordeals." Westfahl and George Slusser, eds., *No Cure for the Future*. Westport, CT: Greenwood Press, 2002, 111–118.
James White. *The White Papers*. Framingham, MA: NESFA Press, 1996.

—*David Langford*

HYPERION BY DAN SIMMONS (1989)

Summary

At the edge of the Hegira, a diasporic movement into space after the destruction of Old **Earth**, the planet Hyperion (see **Alien Worlds; Borderlands; Frontier; Planetary Colonies**) is contested ground between a human **galactic empire** and their post-human rivals, the Ousters. Hyperion is of interest to both groups because it hosts the Time Tombs, a group of buildings that move backwards in **time** (see **Time Travel**), apparently sent by the future remnants of **humanity** (see **Far Future**) to aid in bringing about a utopian future. These tombs are guarded by the enigmatic Shrike, a machine-like **monster**, made of metal and decorated with various blades and spikes, who can also move through time. The Shrike plays an important role in the lives of the so-called "pilgrims," a group of humans sent to the Time Tombs at the approximate time of their opening in an effort to have their wishes granted, which the Shrike also has the power to do. What is concealed until only late in the two-novel sequence that make up the first half of the series, *Hyperion* and *The Fall of Hyperion* (1990), is the role that the AIs, sentient computer **intelligences** (see **Computers**), play in the manipulation of events, disguising their own antihuman efforts behind what they construct to appear as an Ouster attack (see **War**) against human planets. By the close of *Fall of Hyperion*, the AIs are seemingly defeated, an amiable truce is declared between humanity and the Ousters, and the seven pilgrims' journey draws to a close. But the pilgrims' **quest** makes up the majority of the first novel and informs the action of the second.

Discussion

Each of the seven pilgrims has had some **tragedy** visited upon them or a loved one (see **Family; Love**) at the hands of the Shrike, and they are chosen for this final pilgrimage to the Time Tombs due to their apparent closeness to the tombs' guardian. Some tragedies are time-related, such as one character who ages backwards, which invokes themes of classic **Judaism** and Abraham's **sacrifice** of Isaac; another is doomed to outlive everyone he knows (see **Immortality and Longevity**); and a third is cursed with a "cruciform," a symbiote (see **Parasites; Symbiosis**) that resurrects him upon each **death** and which, in the third novel in the series, *Endymion* (1995), takes on explicitly Catholic themes. The other pilgrims play essential roles in the future of humanity, being picked for their ability to mediate between humanity and the Ousters, achieve military victory, and give birth to the reincarnated empathic aspect of a future godhead. Each of the personal tragedies is related via stories, *Hyperion* reading much like a postmodern version of Geoffrey Chaucer's *The Canterbury Tales* (1386).

John Keats, the poet (see **Poetry; Writing and Authors**), plays a central role in both *Hyperion* and *The Fall of Hyperion*, resurrected through advanced AI **technology** in a genetically engineered body (see **Rebirth**). This "cybrid" has all the memories of Keats and often regales readers with snippets of Keats' poetry; Keats' innocence and sensitivity is mirrored in the figure of Martin Silenus, an aged poet (see **Old Age**), whose coarse mannerism obscures his great poetic mind.

Throughout the novels, Simmons makes ongoing critiques of capitalism (see **Economics**), colonialism, and imperialism (see **Postcolonialism**), discussing the ways in which advanced capitalism sustained itself through mining the resources of **alien worlds**, and when confronted with what might be or might become a sentient species, resorted to **violence** to achieve dominance. This stands in contrast to the Ousters, who developed both machines and biological enhancements that allowed them to inhabit the space between planets (see **Space Habitats**), therein creating mobile ecosystems with no negative impacts on the closed **ecology** of alien worlds.

One pilgrim, the Consul, hails from Maui Covenant, an ocean world that has been ravaged by the demands of capitalism; it is this ecological **disaster** that motivates his eventual aid of the Ousters in their efforts against humanity.

These diverse colonies, spread throughout the galaxy, are traversed through a complex **technology** referred to as "farcasters" (see **Teleportation**) that had been constructed by the AIs. Unknown to the humans that used farcasters to transport themselves, the AIs were able to weave together an interstitial realm within the far-caster network from which they could direct humanity while remaining protected. When this is revealed, the humans strike out against their technological masters and render themselves backwards on the technological scale, making much of their high technology obsolete, and making travel between planets much more difficult (ships that can traverse **hyperspace** are non-existent).

At the heart of *Hyperion* and its sequels are questions of the body, of what it means to be human, and the **politics** that become justified to achieve certain types of bodily purity. The challenges to humanity, as seen in the repeated destruction of native forms of sentient life, are always dealt with harshly, and the Ousters are no exception: they are subject to diverse discourses within the Hegira regarding their otherness, and citizens of the Hegira are staunchly opposed to Ouster cooperation. Moreover, the fear of cybrids and AIs is pervasive, although the latter are often taken for granted, leading to their subtle manipulation of humanity, which, eventually, is squashed through the efforts of the Hegira leadership, aided by the pilgrims.

The final books in the sequence, *Endymion* and *The Rise of Endymion* (1997), center around many of the legacies of the last pilgrims to the Time Tombs, showing how their influence spread deep into the future, and often re-imagining the roles that particular items and individuals played in the first two novels in inventive and surprising ways. Although these novels are more traditionally adventure novels, they develop much of the work that Simmons accomplishes in the first two novels in the sequence, continuing his critiques of capitalism, colonialism, and **religion**.

Bibliography

John Clute. "On the Cusp of Far." Damien Broderick, ed., *Earth Is But a Star*. Crawley, W.A.: University of Western Australia Press, 2001, 151–163.

Michael Levy. "Interview with Dan Simmons." *SFRA Review*, No. 263/264 (March/June, 2003), 10–11.

Michael J. Mitchell. "*Hyperion*: Some Notes on Structure and Literary Antecedents." *Science Fiction: A Review of Speculative Literature*, 13 (1996), 15–19.

Christopher Palmer. "Galactic Empires and the Contemporary Extravaganza." *Science Fiction Studies*, 26 (March, 1999), 73–90.

Dan Simmons. "Dan Simmons: Hyperion Revealed." *Locus*, 38 (May, 1997), 4–5, 72.

Altara Stein. "Fictionalized Romantics." *Journal of the Fantastic in the Arts*, 13 (2003), 379–88.

Janeen Webb. "The Hunting of the Shrike." *Foundation*, No. 51 (Spring, 1991), 78–89.

Gary Westfahl. "Introduction." *Hyperion*, by Dan Simmons. Norwalk, CT: Easton Press, 1993, v–x.

—Matthew Wolf-Meyer

J

I, Robot by Isaac Asimov (1950)

Summary

Robots, human-like machines created to perform tasks that humans cannot perform or cannot perform as economically or find too monotonous (machine-like), have been part of imaginative literature almost from its beginnings, but Isaac Asimov helped to bring them into modern science fiction with a series of nine stories, all but one published in John W. Campbell, Jr.'s *Astounding Science-Fiction*, which were later assembled as *I, Robot*. In the introduction to his second collection of robot stories, *The Rest of the Robots* (1964), he explained the thought processes that originally inspired these works. Reacting against the concept of robotic **Frankenstein monsters** without souls or emotions who inevitably rebel against their creators, Asimov imagined that robots would be built with safeguards, like hilts on knives, banisters on stairs, insulation on wires, or safety valves on pressure cookers. Accordingly, he envisioned future robots being governed by the built-in Three Laws of Robotics—which Asimov attributed to Campbell, though the editor said that they were already implicit in Asimov's stories. They were first articulated in Asimov's third robot story, "Liar!" (1941): "1. A robot may not injure a human being or, through inaction, allow a human being to come to harm; 2. A robot must obey the orders given it by human beings except when such orders would conflict with the First Law; 3. A robot must protect its own existence as long as such protection does not conflict with the First or Second Law." In "Liar!" and later robot stories, these laws became the basis for **puzzle** stories involving malfunctioning robots that were usually resolved either by spacefaring adventurers Gregory Powell and Michael Donovan or by robot psychologist Dr. Susan Calvin (see **Psychology**).

Discussion

In 1950 Gnome Press first published *I, Robot*, as publisher Marty Greenberg overrode Asimov's compunctions about re-using the title of Eando Binder's 1939 story. Some stories had little substance, serving merely as frameworks for presenting an intriguing puzzle—fitting the pattern of what Sam Moskowitz has termed the "scientific problem" stories common in the 1930s. For example, in "Runaround" (1942), a robot on **Mercury** especially designed with a strengthened Third Law is stuck in a pattern of running in a circle around a hazardous site he was ordered to visit, the Second Law of following human orders precisely balancing his intensified Third Law of self-preservation; the pattern is broken when one man deliberately endangers himself, forcing the robot to break the pattern and respond to the over-riding First Law of protecting humans. Other stories delve into deeper issues, as a humanoid robot secretly becomes a political leader (see **Politics**) and begins to develop what Asimov would later term the Zeroth Law of Robotics, allowing robots to act to benefit all of **humanity** even though it might conflict with other laws.

The remainder of Asimov's robot stories were scattered through seven later collections, or gathered into his final collections: *Robot Dreams* (1986), *Robot Visions* (1990), and *The Complete Robot* (1992). The most noteworthy of these was the award-winning "The Bicentennial Man" (1976), the story of a robot who successfully sought to become human, which was filmed in 1999. Asimov also wrote two robot novels in the 1950s, followed by two more in the 1980s that wove together his robot series and *Foundation* series into one consistent future **history**.

The Caves of Steel (1954), perhaps Asimov's finest novel, was set in a future when Spacers lived long lives on spacious other-world estates served by hundreds of robots, and Earthers lived short, crowded lives huddled together under huge, roofed-over **cities** and feared robot competition. **Detective** Elijah Bailey, assigned to solve the murder of a spacer, is forced to accept the aid of a robot named R. Daneel Olivaw. He solves the murder only by overcoming his distrust of Daneel and diagnosing the agoraphobia that afflicts all Earthers. In the sequel, *The Naked Sun* (1957), Elijah has to solve another locked-door **mystery** on a Spacer planet by conquering his own agoraphobia and diagnosing the Spacers' claustrophobia. Asimov's later robot novels, *The Robots of Dawn* (1983) and *Robots and Empire* (1985), officially revealed the Zeroth Law and explained why robots arranged to make Earth a radioactive wasteland, as in Asimov's first novel, *Pebble in the Sky* (1950), to send humanity off to colonize the **stars**, as in the *Foundation* series. Later *Foundation* novels also include the virtually immortal R. Daneel Olivaw (see **Immortality and Longevity**), who altruistically lingers on in various guises to help shape humanity's **destiny** during and after the fall of the **galactic empire**.

Overall, Asimov's influence has not entirely eliminated the older tradition of the rebellious robot, now often observed in the form of **computers** or artificial intelligences gone awry, like HAL in *2001: A Space Odyssey* and, ironically, the out-of-control computer in the film *I, Robot* (2004), which bore little relationship to Asimov's original stories. Yet there have also been innumerable tales inspired by Asimov that feature benign and benevolent robots, one example being Webster of Clifford D. Simak's **City**. The robotic Data of *Star Trek: The Next Generation*—who is said to possess a "positronic brain" like Asimov's robots—is one of the many figures who pay explicit tribute to Asimov's works.

Bibliography

Isaac Asimov. "Introduction." Asimov, *The Rest of the Robots*. New York: Doubleday, 1964, ix–xiii.

Jean Fielder and Jim Mele. *Isaac Asimov*. New York: Ungar, 1982.

James Gunn. *Isaac Asimov*. New York: Oxford University Press. 1982.

Neil Goble. *Asimov Analyzed*. Baltimore: Mirage Press, 1972.

Donald M. Hassler. *Reader's Guide to Isaac Asimov*. Mercer Island, WA: Starmont House, 1991.

Joseph F. Patrouch, Jr. *The Science Fiction of Isaac Asimov*. Garden City, NY: Doubleday, 1974.

Joseph D. Olander and Martin H. Greenberg, eds. *Isaac Asimov*. New York: Taplinger, 1977.

George E. Slusser. *Asimov: The Foundations of His Science Fiction*. San Bernardino, CA: Borgo Press, 1980.

Gary Westfahl. "Rules for Robots, v. 1.0." *Interzone*, No. 185 (January, 2003), 53–55.

—*James Gunn*

THE INCREDIBLE SHRINKING MAN (1957)

I felt my body dwindling, melting, becoming nothing. My fears melted away. And in their place came acceptance. All this vast majesty of creation, it had to mean something. And then I meant something, too. Yes, smaller than the smallest, I meant something, too. To God, there is no zero. I still exist!

—Richard Matheson
The Incredible Shrinking Man (1957)

Summary

Scott Carey and wife Lou are enjoying a boating holiday at sea when Scott is exposed to a mysterious cloud that leaves his skin glittering. Lou, below decks, is unaffected. Back home, his clothes no longer fit him and a visit to his doctor reveals that he has shrunk by several inches. As the shrinking continues, the relationship between Scott and Lou changes; Scott compensates for his newfound physical inferiority by becoming tyrannical and domineering to his wife. Forced to leave his job, he can only earn an income by selling his story to the press. Medical tests conclude that radiation from atomic fallout (see **Nuclear Power**) combined with an insecticide to cause Scott's unique condition. At barely three feet tall he meets, and briefly finds solace with, a **carnival** midget named Clarice, but his shrinking continues till she too towers over him. Reduced to living in a doll's house, Scott survives an attack by the family **cat** only to tumble into the cellar; Lou cannot hear his cries for help and assumes the worst from bloodied dolls' clothes. Now isolated from all **humanity**, Scott battles and defeats a large spider (see **Insects**). Eventually he becomes so small that he seemingly begins to enter another realm of existence, concluding that "To God, there is no zero."

Discussion

Richard Matheson wrote the screenplay for the film, based on his 1956 novel *The Shrinking Man*. Although nominally part of a subgenre dealing with **enlargement** and **miniaturization** extending back as far as *Gulliver's Travels* and including films like *Attack of the 50 Foot Woman* (1958) and television series like *Land of the Giants* (1968–1970), *The Incredible Shrinking Man* stands alone in its intelligent, thoughtful exploration of not just the physical effects of such situations but also their psychological ramifications (see **Psychology**). The film, which follows the novel's plot closely but not slavishly, is very much about the title character and his loss of **identity**, whereas in its most obvious counterpart, the more exploitative *The Amazing Colossal Man* (1957), the title character is merely a threat to which other characters react (see **Giants**).

Another topical theme explored in a unique fashion is the use of radiation from an A-bomb test as a trigger, creating not, as one might expect, a **monster** (like *Godzilla, King of the Monsters*) but the reverse situation wherein everything around the affected party becomes monstrous. Normally unfrightening aspects of everyday life—cats, spiders, and even a small splash of **water** (see **Flood**)—threaten the **hero** as he continues to shrink ever smaller. His only relief might lie in the arms of Clarice, the carnival midget (see **Dwarfs**) but her resemblance to him is superficial and, he knows, temporary. He is a freak who cannot even find empathy among other freaks.

The film also represents postwar **anxiety** that the constantly accelerating progress of **civilization** is somehow "softening" modern humans, leaving them devoid of the basic life skills that were extant in their ancestors. In that respect, the film has often been read as an early treatment on **feminism**. Lou Carey is an archetypal media portrayal of a 1950s housewife: well-presented and happily subservient (see **Gender**). But her husband's unstoppable shrinking—literally making him "less of a man"—reverses the roles in their **marriage**, reducing him to an ersatz child and eventually to little more than a plaything. His residency in a doll's house (see **Dolls and Puppets**) is so demeaning as to almost nullify its practicality. Matheson's novel dwells at considerable length on the sexual—and psychosexual—aspects of the situation (see **Sexuality**), although this is unsurprisingly not explored to any great degree in the film.

In its relentless, progressive development of a single idea, the story stands comparison with the works of J.G. Ballard (see *The Drowned World*) and explores themes of isolation and **survival** that Matheson also examined in his twice-filmed 1954 novel *I Am Legend* (see **Last Man**). Rather than providing a pat resolution to Scott's plight or a finale of **horror** akin to the tiny hero's demise in the near contemporary *The Fly* (1958), the film concludes with an extraordinarily deep philosophical idea such as would not be attempted again in science fiction cinema until *2001: A Space Odyssey* more than a decade later. Below the level of reality that science can measure, it transpires, may lie a whole other **microcosm** in which the hero may survive, free from the mundane threats of cats and spiders.

The story was filmed again in 1981 as an obscure, utterly forgettable "comedy" with gender roles reversed, retitled *The Incredible Shrinking Woman*.

Bibliography

Rosi Brandotti. "Meta(l)morphoses." *Theory, Culture and Society*, 14 (May, 1997), 67–80.

Douglas Brode. *"The Incredible Shrinking Man."* Brode, *The Films of the Fifties.* Secaucus, NJ: Citadel Press, 1976, 205–206.

John Hartl. "Retrospect: *The Incredible Shrinking Man.*" *Cinefantastique,* 4 (Summer, 1975), 26–29.

Cyndy Hendershot. "Darwin and the Atom." *Science-Fiction Studies,* 25 (July, 1998), 319–335.

Shawn Rosenheim: "Extraterrestrial: Science Fictions in *A Brief History of Time* and *The Incredible Shrinking Man.*" *Film Quarterly,* 48 (Summer, 1995), 15–21.

W.M.S. Russell. "They Who Shrank." *Foundation,* No. 82 (Summer, 2001), 74–83.

George Slusser. "Pocket Apocalypse." David Seed, ed., *Imagining Apocalypse.* New York: St Martin's, 2000, 118–135.

Paul Wells. "The Invisible Man." Pat Kirkham and Janet Thumin, eds., *You Tarzan.* New York: St Martin's, 1993, 181–199.

David Zinman. *"The Incredible Shrinking Man."* Zinman, *Fifty from the '50s.* New Rochelle, NY: Arlington House, 1979, 133–140.

—M.J. Simpson

INTERVIEW WITH THE VAMPIRE BY ANNE RICE (1976)

∎

Summary

Journalist Daniel records the first-person narrative of Louis, initially a reluctant **vampire**, who was a bored, decadent, nineteenth-century plantation owner before being rescued from despair over his brother's **death** when the vampire Lestat made him a vampire in a homoerotic exchange (see **Homosexuality**). This experience leads to riot, partying, conflagration, and feasting, mostly on local women such as Louis's mulatto servant. Lestat and Louis travel from New Orleans to London and Paris, searching for other vampires and a sense of **history** and **community**. They also adopt Claudia, an eternal child orphan Louis saves from the plague. Claudia's anger leads to revolt and to Lestat's burning, but her **escape** with Madeline, the woman who became her vampire companion, is short-lived: the women are left, embracing, to die in the **Sun** by vengeful members of the Paris Theatre de Vampires, and Louis seems again alone.

Discussion

Anne Rice has acknowledged that she developed *Interview with the Vampire* as a response to the death of her daughter from leukemia before she was six. The book's international success began years after its publication when readers turned to the vampire as an icon of the paradoxes and potential of what it means to be human. Rice's novel and its sequels have spawned a cult following, which Rice caters to by wearing **Gothic** outfits, appearing on television at a **cemetery** and on websites discussing death, and giving explanatory interviews about her novels and their film adaptations.

Rice's novel mixes **family** sagas and historical, supernatural **horror**, encouraging moral and philosophical speculation. Her vampires are glamorous, amoral aesthetes lacking a social conscience. The world is their spectacle, but mortals ultimately dull. They mostly desire and admire each other. However, Rice's vampires are also thoughtful, questioning their need to kill and drink **blood**, and keenly interested in their origins, **mythology**, and other vampires. American vampires are disappointed to discover that Eastern European vampires, descendants of Vlad Dracul (who inspired Bram Stoker's *Dracula*), lack their **sexuality** and energies and instead resemble **zombies**, dead inside and emptied out.

Homosexuality is a key element in Rice's work. Relationships between male vampires are largely homoerotic, producing alternative family groupings rife with jealousy, **ritual**, pretenses, closeness, and companionship. Her novels engage with decadence, problematizing traditional boundaries and simplistic characteristics of **gender**, instead offering androgyny, bisexuality and incest. Like Poppy Z. Brite, Rice has become a gay icon because of her sympathetic and provocative treatment of homoeroticism.

Interview with the Vampire additionally foregrounds the thinking, performative vampire, exploring the potential for a feminization of **culture** by refusing the binary divisions—good and **evil**, angelic and demonic, alive and dead, female and male—enabling readers to understand both the terror and disgust, and the endlessly beautiful possibilities, that the vampire represents. The staged performances in Theatre de Vampires (see **Theatre**), where the ostensible **illusion** of vampiric feeding attracts audiences tricked into observing the real devouring of mortals, align vampires with the complexities of the postmodern world (see **Postmodernism**), blurring the lines between pretending to be a vampire and actually being one. Thus, Rice's vampires open up liberating space for rereadings of relationships of power, eroticism, and questions of personal **identity**. Additionally, Rice offers a paradoxical and stimulating juxtaposition of the traditions of Catholicism, inspiring linguistic lushness, images of blood and crucifixes, and an engagement with contemporary critical issues aligning Rice with radical writers and filmmakers who highlight gender as performance and with postmodernists who question notions of shared reality.

Interview with the Vampire launched a series of novels, the Vampire Chronicles, which generally adopt the voice and stance of a gay male vampire. *The Vampire Lestat* (1985) develops Lestat as an evil, comic rock star who survives **fire** and dismemberment and introduces the Egyptian vampire **queen** Akasha (see **Egypt**). Louis and Daniel reappear in *The Queen of the Damned* (1988), Rice's most philosophical novel, wherein Akasha awakens after 6000 years determined to destroy both vampires and humanity. Other novels in the sequence are *The Tale of the Body Thief* (1992), *Memnoch the Devil* (1995), *The Vampire Armand* (1998), *Blood and Gold* (2001), and *Blood Canticle* (2003), which Rice announced as the final book in the series.

The film adaptation of *Interview with the Vampire* (1994) initially attracted attention because of the casting of handsome Tom Cruise as Lestat and Rice's initial displeasure at the decision. Still, Rice later enthusiastically endorsed the film, which offered striking visualizations of her story. Lestat's transformation of Louis is a homoerotic rape or embrace in which they fly heavenward as **angels**. Louis's melancholic, wooden distaste for human blood (he generally prefers to drain rats) gives way in a blackly comic scene at a plantation ball, where he flatters a grotesque old woman, feeding first on her poodle and her fop. Lestat, depicted as a bored, glittering, Satanic figure, outrageously overplays his vampiric drainings of partying mortals, with prostitutes flung about a grand apartment, one popping in and out of her coffin like a puppet. Blood drinking as metaphor is for some too realistic in the film. Claudia's desire to grow into a woman is depicted compellingly as personal hell, leading to immature tantrums and morally vacuous evils as she takes a petrified corpse to bed like a doll. The burning of Claudia and her chosen **mother** figure is a stark scene emphasizing their isolation and powerlessness as they are trapped in the Sun, turning to ashes like the corpses in Pompeii. The lesser film adaptation of *Queen of the Damned* (2001), starring the singer Aaliyah, offered no such memorable moments.

Bibliography

Linda Badley. *Writing Horror and the Body*. Westport, CT: Greenwood Press, 1996.

George Beahm, ed. *The Unauthorized Anne Rice Companion*. Kansas City: Andrews and McMeel, 1996.

Gary Hoppenstand and Ray B. Browne, eds. *The Gothic World of Anne Rice*. Bowling Green, OH: Bowling Green State University Popular Press, 1996.

Jana Marcus. *In the Shadow of the Vampire*. New York: Thunder's Mouth Press, 1997.

Paulina Palmer. *Lesbian Gothic Fiction*. London: Cassell, 1998.

Katherine Ramsland, ed. *The Anne Rice Reader*. New York: Ballantine, 1997.

Katherine Ramsland. *The Vampire Companion*. New York: Ballantine, 1993.

Michael Riley. *Interview with Anne Rice*. London: Chatto and Windus, 1996.

Jennifer Smith. *Anne Rice*. Westport, CT: Greenwood Press, 1996.

—Gina Wisker

INVADERS FROM MARS (1953)

Summary

One night, amateur astronomer and science fiction fan David Maclean witnesses a flying saucer (see **UFOs**) landing in the sandpit behind his house. He is sent back to bed, but his **father** George investigates. When George returns, he is being controlled by aliens via an implant in his neck that makes him cold and brutal (see **Possession**). Cathy Wilson, a neighbor's child, is swallowed by the mysterious hole that opens in the sandpit and, once "possessed," she torches her parents' house. Whether "possessed" or not, the town's adults try to return David to his parents. Dr. Pat Blake, realizing that he is genuinely scared, refuses to let his parents—his **mother**, Mary, is now "possessed"—take him away. At the local observatory, Dr. Stuart Kelston (see **Mentors**) lectures David and Pat about the possibility of extraterrestrial life, postulating Martian invaders (see **Aliens on Earth; Invasion; Mars**) concerned by experiments in nuclear rocketry (see **Nuclear Power; Nuclear War**) at a nearby base. Through his telescope, they see George lure General Mayberry to the sandpit. Kelston notifies Colonel Fielding, who mobilizes the army. David and Pat are captured by

Martians but Fielding and Stuart lead a successful rescue mission to their underground lair (see **Caverns**). The flying saucer is blown up. David wakes up—it has all been a **dream**—but then he sees a flying saucer landing in the sandpit.

Discussion

Invaders from Mars is one of a handful of **children**'s fantasy and science fiction movies made in **America** in the 1950s, such as *The Invisible Boy* (1957), a spin-off from *Forbidden Planet*, and *The 5,000 Fingers of Dr. T* (1953). The latter, a disturbing fantasy by Dr. Seuss in which a young boy is trapped in a nightmare land ruled by a sadistic piano teacher who forces abducted children to practice the piano, follows the perverse kinds of dream logic pervading Lewis Carroll's *Alice's Adventures in Wonderland* and the film *The Wizard of Oz*. In contrast, *Invaders from Mars*'s retrospective revelation that it was all a dream seems like a device deployed to make the destruction of the Martians more acceptable while also excusing its various solutions to obvious budgetary constraints, which include extensive and repetitive use of stock footage of the army, repeated use of the same footage of Martian "mutants" running through subterranenean tunnels, and the mirror-reversed car chase footage.

However, one solution suggests that the movie's dream-like narrative was planned from the beginning. Whereas films noirs typically dealt with such restrictions through lighting that produced dark, heavy shadows capable of obscuring deficiencies, *Invaders from Mars* makes a virtue of vast barren sets. The police station, the observatory, and Dr. Wilson's laboratory are simplified almost to abstraction, thus resembling a child's imagination of unseen spaces; similarly, the flying saucer's interior is stripped down to an evocative bare minimum, as if such spaces are beyond imagination.

Although often spoken of as being like *Invasion of the Body Snatchers* and other 1950s possession movies that capture the decade's **paranoia** about either Communist infiltration or, more convincingly, subordination to the greyness of corporate–suburban existence (see **Individualism and Conformity**), the film's focus on the **family** suggests a different set of concerns. In some senses it has more in common with the family melodrama, from *Meet Me in St. Louis* (1944) to *The Texas Chain Saw Massacre* (1974), and the **horror** about generational differences and sexuality that underpins them. Indeed, the whole movie can be seen as a primal scene fantasy: woken in the middle of the night by strange noises, David bursts into his parents' bedroom, and from that moment on they begin to behave very differently around him; David replaces his parents with purer versions (Pat, dressed in white, refuses to return him to Mary, dressed in black), but this does not prevent his descent into a **labyrinth** of gynecological tunnels; and the whole U.S. army, it seems, must be brought in to save Pat from being penetrated by a sleek and monstrous phallic machine.

Invaders from Mars was re-edited for its European release a year later. Five minutes longer, it contains a lengthier observatory sequence, in which Stuart explains all about flying saucers, but more significantly this version discarded the "it was a dream" ending. Instead, Stuart and Pat reassure David that his parents will recover and put him to bed. (There is a third version, edited together a couple of decades later, which attempts to combine these two.)

Invaders from Mars was remade by Tobe Hooper in 1986. A workman-like affair, it is undone by aiming for the wrong audience. If it had aimed at younger viewers, it could have allowed the **monsters** to be as comic as their design while developing its nostalgic intertextuality sufficiently to please accompanying parents, as in the best of Joe Dante's films. If it had aimed for an older teen audience, the horror of parental weirdness could have been better developed, as in *Parents* (1989) and *Society* (1989), and it could have achieved the effective combination of school, horror, action, and **comedy** found in *Hiruko the Goblin* (1990), ***Buffy the Vampire Slayer***, and *The Faculty* (1998). However, caught between these various audiences, it failed to please anyone, despite its occasional successful evocation of unease. Although its pronounced **xenophobia** is discomfiting in a children's film, the primal scene fantasy suggested by the final shot neatly encapsulates the Oedipal basis of the narrative.

Bibliography

Vincent di Fate. " 'This Means Something!' " Gregg Rickman, ed., *The Science Fiction Film Reader*. New York: Limelight, 2004, 60–67.

Dennis Fischer. "William Cameron Menzies." Fischer, *Science Fiction Film Directors, 1895–1998*. Jefferson: McFarland, 2000, 432–445.

Barry K. Grant. "*Invaders from Mars* and the Science Fiction Film in the Age of Reagan." *Cineaction!*, 8 (Spring, 1987), 77–83.

Cyndy Hendershot. "The Invaded Body." *Extrapolation*, 39 (Spring, 1998), 26–39.

Mark Jancovich. *Rational Fears*. Manchester: Manchester University Press, 1996.

Rob Latham. "Subterranean Suburbia." *Science-Fiction Studies*, 66 (July, 1995), 198–208.

Patrick J. Lucanio. *Them or Us*. Bloomington: Indiana University Press, 1987.

Robert Skotak and Scot Holton. "William Cameron Menzies' *Invaders From Mars*." *Cinefantastique*, 16 (July, 1986), 27–31, 55–56.

Errol Vieth. *Screening Science*. Lanham, Maryland: Scarecrow, 2001.

—*Mark Bould*

INVASION OF THE BODY SNATCHERS (1956)

Quite simply, the great pods were leaving a fierce and inhospitable planet . . . . I understood that nothing in the whole vast universe could ever defeat us. Did this incredible alien life form "think" this or "know" it? Probably not, I thought, or anything our minds could conceive. But it had sensed it; it could tell with certainty that this planet, this little race, would never receive them, and would

*never yield. And Becky and I, in refusing
to surrender, but instead fighting their
invasion to the end, giving up any hope
of escape in order to destroy even a few
of them, had provided the final and con-
clusive demonstration of that unchange-
able fact. And so now, to survive—their
one purpose and function C the great
pods lifted and rose, climbing up
through the faint mist, and out toward
the space they had come from, leaving a
fiercely inhospitable planet behind.*

—Jack Finney
The Body Snatchers (1955)

Summary

Dr. Miles Bennell, a rational man, is not prone to hysteria or flights of fancy. As such, he is initially skeptical about reports by some acquaintances that their relatives have changed, replaced by someone, or something, that appears to be them but is devoid of emotion or individualism. Bennell's views change when his friends Jack and Teddy call him away from a date with his old flame Becky and ask him to examine a strange corpse that bears a curious resemblance to Jack. It becomes apparent that when the townsfolk succumb to **sleep** they are replaced by alien vegetable pods that replicate their features perfectly. Miles races to Becky and finds a duplicate growing in her cellar, but he manages to wake her before she is assimilated. Before long Santa Mira has been overtaken by extraterrestrials, all working to propagate their race, manufacturing pods to populate **city** after city. The only thing Bennell can do is join with Becky and the last few survivors to **escape** and warn the rest of **America** of the imminent **invasion**. The problem is that he needs to stay awake, and who is going to believe his sleep-deprived tales of **paranoia**?

Discussion

Don Siegel's film originally ended with Bennell screaming "You're next!" at passing traffic on the highway, his warnings seemingly destined to be unheard and unheeded; however, the studios felt that this was too depressing. Hence, a conclud-ing scene was added in which Bennell manages to escape and, after corroborating evidence emerges, successfully persuades the authorities to take action against the invasion.

Invasion of the Body Snatchers was released at the height of cold war paranoia and was widely interpreted as providing a hysterical metaphor for the threat of Communism taking over the American way of life. A normal middle-class **commu-nity** is assimilated by **aliens on Earth** because it does not understand the threat it faces from those "outside" (see **Xenophobia**) who wish to impose conformity on the individualism that represents American **identity** (see **Individualism and Conformity**). The **hive minds** of the aliens are contradictory to personal **freedom**, but the film's

horror lies with the ideological takeover of a person and their personality. The townspeople's appearance and behaviors are the same, but they have been possessed by an alien **parasite** that grows from a **plant** pod (see **Possession**). The surviving humans feel an inherent sense of **betrayal** and denial of trust because their visual judgment tells them their relatives are unchanged, but their instinct tells them otherwise. The paranoia lies in the fact that, unless unbroken contact is maintained with a victim, it is impossible to tell whether that person has been turned, a fate exacerbated by the need to stay awake. When Becky finally succumbs to sleep Miles only realizes that she has been possessed when her attempts at **romance** lack emotion. There is a sense of nihilistic inevitability of this takeover; after all Miles himself must sleep eventually.

This general fear can also be seen as indicative of the dehumanizing aspects of paranoia, people literally turned into vegetables, reborn into an untroubled world where everyone is the same. The situation is given an added air of plausibility through naturalistic black-and-white cinematography (which becomes more expressionist after the discovery of the pods in order to emphasise the distortion of society) and because the audience trusts the central character, who is a respected man of **medicine**.

In Philip Kaufman's remake *Invasion of the Body Snatchers* (1978), the noirish chiaroscuro lighting of the original has been replaced by naturalistic Seventies color stock. Intrinsically the story has remained unchanged, but events have been scaled up, being set in San Francisco rather than a small town, thus emphasizing the invasion's magnitude but also indicating the shift towards urban city living. There is a sense in which the city itself has a dehumanizing influence, so public paranoia about people changing is initially less credible. It features Kevin McCarthy (Bennell from the original film) in a cameo, still on the run, but the political dimensions (see **Politics**) have been dropped in favor of an emphasis on the nature of trust and the survivors' **estrangement** from the new society.

Abel Ferrera's *Body Snatchers* (1993) subverts the anti-communist message of the original by placing its emphasis on the flaws of the government-run military. By retaining the claustrophobic single community setting for most of its running time (here even more explicit in that it is fenced from the outside world), Ferrera's left-field credentials provide the necessary twist to detach it from the realm of the pointless remake. Where better to start an invasion than from within the core of the organization meant to protect you from it?

The continued influence of *Invasion of the Body Snatchers* can be seen in a multitude of films including *The Stepford Wives* (1975, remade 2004), *Village of the Damned* (1960, remade 1995) and *The Faculty* (1998).

Bibliography

Craig W. Anderson. "*Invasion of the Body Snatchers.*" Anderson, *Science Fiction Films of the Seventies*. Jefferson, NC: McFarland, 2001, 203–207.

Michael J. Collins. "Version/Inversion." Michael A. Morrison, ed., *Trajectories of the Fantastic*. Westport, CT: Greenwood Press, 1997, 195–202.

Cyndy Hendershot. "The Invaded Body." *Extrapolation*, 39 (Spring, 1998), 26–39.

Al LaValley, ed. *Invasion of the Body Snatchers*. New Brunswick: Rutgers University Press, 1989.

Arthur Le Gacy. "*The Invasion of the Body Snatchers.*" *Literature/Film Quarterly*, 6 (Summer, 1978), 285–292.

David Seed. "Alien Invasions by Body Snatchers and Related Creatures." Victor Sage and Allen L. Smith, eds., *Modern Gothic*. Manchester: Manchester University Press, 1996, 152–170.

Nancy Steffen-Fluhr. "Women and the Inner Game of Don Siegel's *Invasion of the Body Snatchers*." *Science-Fiction Studies*, 11 (July, 1984), 139–153.

George Turner. "A Case for Insomnia." *American Cinematographer*, 78 (March 1997), 77–81.

—Michelle Le Blanc and Colin Odell

THE INVISIBLE MAN (1933)

Summary

Chemist Jack Griffin discovers the secret of **invisibility** in a cocktail of **drugs**; one active constituent is a **plant** derivative called monocaine, which not only has powerful bleaching properties but is also known, though not to Griffin, to cause **madness**. Turning himself invisible, he finds the condition irreversible and seeks refuge in the guest room of what Britishers would regard as a most unusual English village pub: available from the barrel are rye and, complete with an "e," whiskey; a darts game in progress has half a dozen darts sticking from the board (see **Taverns and Inns**). He attempts to pursue his research, but locals will not leave him alone, and in fury he reveals his secret by way of physical assault and vindictive poltergeist-like pranks, exulting in his role as all-powerful **trickster**.

As the hunt for him continues, he visits colleague Dr. Kemp, spells out his plans for terrorizing the world into "submission," and intimidates—or so he believes—Kemp into being his partner in these schemes. While returning to the pub to collect his notebooks, Griffin brains a policeman. Back home, Kemp phones their boss Dr. Cranley and then the police. Cranley arrives with daughter Flora, Griffin's sweetheart, who pleads unsuccessfully with him. When the police arrive, Griffin **escapes**, promising he will kill Kemp at the stroke of ten the following night. Despite police protection, Griffin succeeds, then conducts a brief reign of terror, murdering searchers and causing a dreadful train **disaster**. At last, with snow falling, he is located sleeping in a barn. The police set the barn on **fire**, Griffin's footprints in the snow betray his presence, and he is fatally shot. It is only as he dies in hospital, Flora at his bedside, that he again becomes visible.

Discussion

This film's director, James Whale, was riding high at the time, notably for his recent film *Frankenstein*. In *The Invisible Man* he attempts to repeat the elements which made that film a success, mixing **humor**, mob panic, the central figure of a **mad scientist**, a **villain** who is both monstrous and very human, and a lot of screaming. In short, out of H.G. Wells's thoughtful 1897 novel he created a genre **horror** movie, perhaps abetted more by the film's uncredited co-scriptwriter, Philip Wylie, than by its stated one, English playwright R.C. Sherriff. There are sequences, indeed, during which one can sense an undeclared war between Sherriff's (and Wells's) sensibilities, on one hand, and Whale's sensationalism, on the other.

Whale also portrays a bizarre **perception** of England. In addition to the noted idiosyncrasies of the pub, the local police station has a sign that reads "Police Dept." and the Chief Constable is a "Chief of Police." More seriously, he labors to render crowds of English villagers as their Middle European counterparts, supposedly from a century earlier, in *Frankenstein*; one expects the blazing brands to appear any moment.

The film's moral, stated near the start and more definitively at the end, is "I meddled in things that man was meant to leave alone"—as in *Frankenstein*. Of course, it is only a plot coincidence (the side-effect of monocaine) that Griffin's invisibility comes complete with homicidal megalomania, so the moral is undercut. Other works, including Wells's novel, have suggested more meaningfully that invisibility would confer such a colossal advantage on the individual as to make megalomania near-inescapable; this is the thesis of the film *Hollow Man* (2000), in which an invisible scientist becomes a psychopathic stalker. The same point is made about a **superman** in general, more seriously, in Olaf Stapledon's novel *Odd John* (1935).

Largely because of its impressive special effects, *The Invisible Man* was a successful movie—it made Rains a bankable star, although he appears for just seconds, as a corpse—and spawned sequels and imitations, among them *The Invisible Man Returns* (1940), *The Invisible Man's Revenge* (1944), *The Invisible Monster* (1950), and, inevitably, *Abbott and Costello Meet the Invisible Man* (1951); much later came such films as *The Invisible Kid* (1988). Two films entitled *The Invisible Woman* (1940, 1983) are both comedies; *Terror of the Invisible Man* (2001) has much the same basis as *Hollow Man* but is also played more for laughs. The three Topper movies—*Topper*, *Topper Takes a Trip* (1939), and to a lesser extent *Topper Returns* (1941)—were clearly inspired by these films, although their characters can become invisible not due to misused science but because they are ghosts (see **Ghosts and Hauntings**). There have additionally been at least four television series based on the central trope, all called *The Invisible Man*, in 1958–1959, 1975, 1984 and 2000; the third of these was a six-part dramatization of Wells's novel. H.F. Saint's novel *Memoirs of an Invisible Man* (1987), a social **satire**—the protagonist is essentially invisible even before becoming physically so—was filmed as a **comedy** under the same title in 1992, with much of the satire removed.

Although most of these works endeavor to explain invisibility in scientific terms, they ignore the fact that an invisible man would be blind (see **Vision and Blindness**), since light would pass unimpeded through his invisible retina. Wells, at least, understood and attempted to deal with the problem, albeit unpersuasively.

Bibliography

James Curtis. *A New World of Gods and Monsters*. London: Faber & Faber, 1998.

Ray Edwards. "Movie Gothick: A Tribute to James Whale." *Sight and Sound*, 27 (Autumn, 1957), 95–98.

Mark Gattis. *James Whale*. London: Cassell, 1995.

G. Wesley Holt. "*The Invisible Man* (1933)." *Filmfax*, 37 (February/March, 1993), 24, 26.

E.A. Martinelli. "Photographing *The Invisible Man*." *American Cinematographer*, 56 (July, 1975), 774–777.

Ellis Reed. *A Journey into Darkness*. North Stratford, NH: Ayer Publishing, 1980.

Dan Scapperotti. "*The Invisible Man.*" *Cinefantastique*, 33 (October/November, 2001), 52–53.

John T. Soister, with JoAnna Wioskowski. *Claude Rains*. Jefferson, NC: McFarland, 1999.

—*John Grant*

THE ISLAND OF DOCTOR MOREAU BY H.G. WELLS (1896)

They say that terror is a disease, and anyhow, I can witness that, for several years now, a restless fear has dwelt in my mind, such a restless fear as a half-tamed lion cub may feel. My trouble took the strangest form. I could not persuade myself that the men and women I met were not also another, still passably human, Beast People, animals half-wrought into the outward image of human souls, and that they would presently begin to revert, to show first this bestial mark and then that.

—H.G. Wells
The Island of Doctor Moreau (1896)

Summary

Edward Prendick is rescued from a shipwreck (see **Sea Travel**) by the captain of the *Ipecacuana* before being unwillingly disembarked at Noble's Isle (see **Islands**). There, Prendick meets Dr. Moreau, a research biologist, and his assistant, Montgomery (see **Biology**). Prendick initially believes Moreau to be performing vivisection on humans but later learns that Moreau is attempting to humanize animals (see **Mad Scientists; Uplift**). Prendick is repulsed by Moreau's work and afraid of his victims, though he realizes, due to the isolation of the island, that he must come to terms with its inhabitants. Moreau keeps order on the island through the beastfolk's fear of the House of **Pain** (Moreau's laboratory) and inculcates a sort of **religion** that deifies Moreau as the creator and the one who punishes. During vivisection on a puma (see **Cats**), however, Moreau is killed. His **death** leads to general unrest among the Beastfolk and provokes Montgomery to lose his composure and ply the beastfolk and himself with alcohol, resulting in his death as well. Alone with the now reverting beastfolk, Prendick gradually assumes beastfolk manners and apparently goes insane (see **Madness**). When he is finally picked up by a passing ship and returned to England, he lives as a recluse, suspecting that his fellow humans will soon revert to their bestial origins.

Discussion

The Island of Doctor Moreau readily falls into the tradition of island narrative as demonstrated by stories of **survival** like William Golding's *Lord of the Flies* as well as **utopias** like Thomas More's *Utopia*. Wells's debt to these traditions in the story, however, is perhaps slighter than his debt to more contemporary issues like nineteenth-century advances in biological science and related discussions concerning **ethics**, **civilization**, and the role of religion in society.

Bernard Bergonzi has noted the importance of **evolution** in *The Island of Doctor Moreau*, claiming that Moreau stands for both the power of directed science and the **violence** and arbitrariness of evolutionary **nature**. Frank McConnell was the first critic to focus on Moreau's mental manipulation of the beastfolk, seeing his experiments as attempts to create a race of perfectly conditioned human beings (see **Frankenstein Monsters**). He relates the story to **dystopia**, concluding that Noble's Isle is the first totalitarian regime depicted in western literature. According to Thomas C. Renzi, the fact that nature undoes naturally what Moreau has done artificially demonstrates that the **scientist**'s efforts crossed into the realm of **taboo**. Robert M. Philmus acknowledges the biological debate encapsulated within *The Island of Doctor Moreau* and relates it to an older literary tradition, describing Wells's emphasis on human beings as superficially civilized animals as Swiftian and arguing that Wells effectively "Darwinizes" the Yahoos and Houyhnhnms of *Gulliver's Travels*.

Leon Stover credits Wells with initiating the literary tradition of **genetic engineering**, which led to numerous stories about **mutations** in which, by artificial or natural means, new forms of life often result in **monsters** to be combated. Charles De Paolo, in studying **prehistoric fiction**, emphasizes Moreau's surgical skills, seeing the beastfolk's abilities to read, write, compute, think abstractly, devise **technology**, and participate in **rituals** as clearly human traits, while noting that Moreau's incapacity to recognize the **humanity** he has fashioned ironically places his own lack of humanity into sharp relief.

Patrick Parrinder points out how thin a veneer **civilization** proves to be in the novel as, by its end, not only have the beastfolk lost nearly all traces of the civilized imprint including speech (see **Talking Animals**), but Montgomery has succumbed to a form of bestiality and Prendick is compelled to live as an animal among the animals. Far from this degeneration being a result of life on Noble's Isle, however, John Hammond observes that the humans Prendick encounters both before and after his experiences on the island are selfish and violent and imbued with the animal traits of greed and cruelty. To prevent such animality occurring on the island, Hammond identifies the use of religion, such as the **satire** on the Ten Commandments (the Litany of the Law), the priesthood (the Sayer of the Law), theological speculation (Big Thinks), and punishment in **Hell** (the House of Pain). The use made of religion to control the beastfolk and to channel their hate against miscreants foreshadows such ceremonies, according to Mark R. Hillegas, as the Day of Unanimity in Yevgeny Zamiatin's *We*, the Soma Solidarity Service in Aldous Huxley's *Brave New World*, and the Two-Minutes Hate in George Orwell's *Nineteen Eighty-Four*.

Bibliography

Bernard Bergonzi. *The Early H.G. Wells.* Manchester: Manchester University Press, 1961.

Charles De Paolo. *Human Prehistory in Fiction.* Jefferson, NC: McFarland, 2003.

John Hammond. "*The Island of Doctor Moreau*: A Swiftian Parable." John S. Partington, ed., *The Wellsian: Selected Essays on H.G. Wells.* [Oss]: Equilibris, 2003, 45–54.

Mark R. Hillegas. *The Future as Nightmare.* 1967. Carbondale: Southern Illinois University Press, 1974.

Frank McConnell. *The Science Fiction of H.G. Wells.* Oxford: Oxford University Press, 1981.

Patrick Parrinder. *Shadows of the Future.* Liverpool: Liverpool University Press, 1995.

Robert M. Philmus. "Introducing *Moreau*." Philmus, ed., *The Island of Doctor Moreau*, by H.G. Wells. Athens: University of Georgia Press, 1993, xi–xlviii.

Thomas C. Renzi. *H.G. Wells: Six Scientific Romances Adapted for Film.* Second Ed. Lanham, MD: Scarecrow, 2004.

Leon Stover. *Science Fiction from Wells to Heinlein.* Jefferson, NC: McFarland, 2002.

—John S. Partington

ISLAND OF LOST SOULS (1933)

■

Summary

Edward Parker, adrift after a shipwreck, is rescued by the SS *Covena* (see **Sea Travel**). He is nursed by Montgomery and sends a radio message to Apia, where his fiancée, Ruth Thomas, is waiting for him. However Parker fights with the drunken captain and is thrown overboard when the ship meets Dr. Moreau's schooner. Along with Montgomery, a cargo of caged animals, and mysteriously bestial natives, Parker is taken to Moreau's island (see **Islands; Jungles**). Moreau, who has been experimenting on animals to make them into men (see **Hubris; Uplift**), leaves Parker with the exotic Lota, curious to see whether she will fall in **love**. Parker discovers a village of beastmen. Governed by the Sayer of the Law (see **Rituals**), they live in terror of Moreau and his House of **Pain** (see **Religion; Torture**). Moreau destroys the schooner to prevent Parker's escape. Parker almost succumbs to Lota's charms (see **Temptress**), but her claw-like nails betray her animal nature: Moreau created her from a panther. Ruth and Captain Donahue come to rescue Parker; Montgomery agrees to help them **escape**. Moreau orders the beastman Ouran to kill Donahue, and Moreau's transgression of the Law with which he has ruled the beastmen (see **Sin**) triggers a revolution among them (see **Rebellion**). Parker, Ruth, and Montgomery flee, Lota dies while killing Ouran, and Moreau is killed by his creations (see **Frankenstein Monsters; Revenge**).

Discussion

Erle C. Kenton's adaptation of H.G. Wells's *The Island of Doctor Moreau*, co-written by occasional science fiction author Philip Wylie, is one of the best movies in the 1930s and 1940s **horror** cycle, although being made by Paramount rather than Universal has resulted in its relative neglect when compared to *Dracula*, *Frankenstein*, *The Mummy* (1932), *The Invisible Man*, and *The Wolf Man* (1941).

Although they also produced **Dr. Jekyll and Mr. Hyde** and *Murders in the Zoo* (1933), horror was not a Paramount staple; noted for their **comedies**, they ended the decade with Bob Hope's spooky comedy-thrillers *The Cat and the Canary* (1939) and *The Ghost Breakers* (1940). *Island of Lost Souls* can also be regarded as part of a jungle/tropical adventure cycle, along with *Tarzan, the Ape Man* (1932) (see **Tarzan of the Apes**), *The Most Dangerous Game* (1932), and **King Kong**.

Island of Lost Souls retains elements of Wells's **satire** on the **class system** and ambivalent critique of colonialism (see **Postcolonialism**), with the beastmen cast as house and field slaves (see **Slavery**). However, there is an ambiguity at the heart of the movie. It typically depicts the beastmen in terms of racial stereotypes as being lazy and clumsy, with Ouran as a violent rapist (see **Race Relations**). That these stereotypes are accepted by white outsiders without question—for example, no one on the *Covena* questions that they are natives of the **South Pacific**, albeit extremely ugly ones—seems to reinforce the equation between nonwhites and bestial primitivism that the film simultaneously renders uncomfortable. This tension is evident both visually and narratively. Karl Struss's cinematography repeatedly isolates the white characters, their color emphasized by lighting and costume so that they almost glow, in pools of **light** surrounded by **darkness** made more ominous by the use of offscreen sound; but Moreau, the most monstrous and the most whitened character, is in the circle, too. When the beastmen assault Moreau's compound, itself an ambiguous fortress or **prison**, dark inhuman figures come directly at the camera—our viewpoint coincides with Moreau's, confronting us with a terrifying threat with which we nonetheless sympathize.

Island of Lost Souls is also remarkable for the extent to which it succeeds in bringing out the homosexual subtext of Wells's novel, itself reputedly inspired in part by the persecution of Oscar Wilde. Laughton performs Moreau not only as an outrageously sadistic **mad scientist** but also one who flirts with both Parker and Montgomery. Although his **homosexuality** is the locus of a range of negative connotations—centrally, his fascination with bestialism in the form of mating Parker with Lota (see **Adam and Eve**)—the movie as a whole draws a connection between the repression of desire and brutal scientific and imperialist ventures. Variants of this idea also surface in films like **Metropolis**, *Dr. Jekyll and Mr. Hyde, White Zombie* (1932), *Cat People* (1942), *I Walked with a Zombie* (1943), **Forbidden Planet, Alien**, and *Jurassic Park*.

Two later adaptations, both called *The Island of Dr. Moreau*, retain the character of the Panther Woman. The major innovation of the first, directed by Don Taylor in 1977—shared by Ann Halam's *Dr. Franklin's Island* (2001)—is Moreau's attempt to return the protagonist to an animal state, a reversion more effectively captured by his struggle to retain his **memories** than by the hairs he sprouts. The 1996 version directed by John Frankenheimer, despite its updated setting, is more overtly concerned with religious parallels. Ultimately, it is undone by its descent into mediocre action sequences and Marlon Brando's ill-judged performance as Moreau. Although it reinstates the bleak Wellsian conclusion derived from **Gulliver's Travels**, nonwhite faces predominate in the footage accompanying the protagonist's account of **humanity**'s resurgent bestial nature.

In addition to the silent *L'Ile d'Épouvante* (1913), there have been at least two other adaptations of Wells's novel, the U.S./Phillipines co-productions *Terror Is a Man* (1959) and *The Twilight People* (1972), neither of which acknowledges its source.

Bibliography

Harry M. Benshoff. *Monsters in the Closet*. Manchester: Manchester University Press, 1997.

Rhona J. Berenstein. *Attack of the Leading Ladies*. New York: Columbia University Press, 1996.

Judith Buchanan. "*Forbidden Planet* and the Retrospective Attribution of Intentions." Deborah Cartmell, I.Q. Hunter, and Imelda Whelehan, eds., *Retrovision*. London: Pluto Press, 2001, 148–162.

Thomas C. Renzi. *H.G. Wells: Six Scientific Romances Adapted for Film*. Metuchen, NJ: Scarecrow, 1992.

Bryan Senn. "*Island of Lost Souls*." Senn, *Golden Horrors*. Jefferson, NC: McFarland, 1996, 144–153.

Michael Sevastakis. *Songs of Love and Death*. Westport, CT: Greenwood Press, 1993.

Don G. Smith. *H.G. Wells on Film*. Jefferson, NC: McFarland, 2002.

Alan Wykes. *H.G. Wells in the Cinema*. London: Jupiter, 1977.

—*Mark Bould*

ISLANDIA BY AUSTIN TAPPAN WRIGHT (1942)

Summary

John Lang, a young American, is appointed American consul to Islandia in 1907, with the intent of opening the country to world **trade**. Islandia, an agrarian nation, has for centuries limited its contact with foreigners to preserve its traditional way of life, but in response to pressures from the West it is considering a change of policy. Lang travels through Islandia, coming to love its geography, **culture**, and people. The Islandians are self-sufficient, both economically and spiritually: their individualistic way of life is rooted in traditions emphasizing the intertwined significance of **family** and land. Lang contrasts Islandia unfavorably with the West and develops his own sense of individuality through relationships with two strong Islandian women, Dorna and Nattana. He celebrates the Islandians' ultimate decision to remain isolationist, despite the fact that it will mean his own **exile**. He foils a plot by foreigners to invade the country, however, and in gratitude the Islandian government permits him to stay. Lang, indecisive, returns to **America** to see where his interests truly lie; a year spent working in commerce convinces him that he prefers Islandia. He returns with his fiancée, Gladys Hunter. She too must adjust to the more individualistic culture of Islandia, which clashes with her socialization as a woman dependent on men. Together she and John make Islandia their **home** by establishing a **farm**, family, and commitment to mutual equality.

Discussion

Austin Tappan Wright's *Islandia* is often described as a **utopia**, but it is primarily notable as one of the most detailed and internally consistent **imaginary worlds** ever created, on a par with that of J.R.R. Tolkien's *The Lord of the Rings*. Wright was a Professor of Law, first at the University of California, and then at the University of

Pennsylvania until 1931, when he was killed in a car crash. Upon his death his family discovered the vast manuscript of the novel together with a four-hundred-page **history** detailing every facet of the world that Wright had been developing in private since childhood. His surviving manuscripts included the detailed geography and geology of Islandia's **landscape**; the complexities of its **seasons, governance system, ecology**, and **language and linguistics** (including a brief grammar and glossary, as well as translations from Islandian **fables**); and its agrarian way of life, in which both **nature** and the family are central. Wright also prepared several **maps**, tables of population, notes on **weather**, and even a detailed bibliography of "secondary works" devoted to his invented world. Wright's daughter Sylvia cut about a third of the novel so it could be published in 1942.

The numerous "reality effects" of Wright's novel are not merely the results of an academic penchant for detail. They are critical to the central theme of the novel, which has to do with the necessity—and the difficulty—of creating an independent "world view" while still being able to relate to the external reality of others. The country of Islandia is thus metonymic for the existence of an internal foundation (see **Knowledge**) that Wright believes each individual must develop on his or her own, and which can be almost impossible to attain in early twentieth-century America. The novel is a **Bildungsroman** in which a young man establishes his own **identity** by leaving his native culture, with its emphasis on **progress** and materialism, and determining his own attitudes toward **individualism and conformity, sexuality, sexism, machines and mechanization, work and leisure**, and much else by immersing himself in a culture very different from western nations. Lang finds the Islandians to be independent, relatively free from the opinions of others or materialist desires, unlike the culture he knows in America, which is dominated by Victorian pieties, rigid social conventions, and a consumerist mentality. Islandians achieved this autonomy partly because their society is relatively homogeneous (there is a conventional attitude of the time towards **race relations** in Wright's novel), and partly because of their emphasis on the security that comes from family and ties to the land. He finds these conservative qualities can have progressive results: Islandians may be "naturally aristocratic" in their emphasis on honor and maintenance of a symbolic monarchy akin to that of modern Britain (see **Politics**), but they are also egalitarians, perhaps most notably in **gender** relations. The women in *Islandia* are frequently as independent as the men, and Lang learns to develop his own self-sufficiency through romantic relationships with two Islandian women (see **Love; Romance**).

Islandia, like other utopian novels, is a critique by its author of aspects of his own society that he disliked—which, ironically, includes utopians, or at least reformers who insist that others live as they do. Living in an age in which Atlantic nations dominated the world (see **Globalization**), Wright's novel is an indictment of western imperialism as well as the mindless worship of **business** and **technology** as ends in themselves. Islandia's plight is at times compared to the forced opening of **Japan** by western powers in the nineteenth century. Wright continues the comparison by contrasting the values of a traditional society that respects nature, craftsmanship, and a nondoctrinaire form of worship with the hypocrisies attendant on western **advertising**, capitalist **economics**, and **Christianity**.

However, what sets *Islandia* apart from conventional utopias is its wealth of detail as an imaginary world, and the way that Wright uses this concept as an analogue for the creation of subjective habitations, "sources of the self" in an age when selfhood is seen as protean, that is, made rather than given. Lang often finds himself questioning the divide between "reality" and "imagination." Certainly Wright himself may have turned to the creation of Islandia as a way to **escape** from elements of modernity he disliked, but one senses that he, no less than Lang (or Tolkien), was also able to establish a degree of psychic autonomy through being rooted in geographies both imaginary and real.

Bibliography

Leonard Bacon. "Introduction." Austin Tappan Wright, *Islandia*. New York: Farrar & Rinehart, 1941, v–viii.

Basil Davenport. "Islandia." Austin Tappen Wright, *An Introduction to Islandia*. New York: Farrar & Rinehart, 1941, 1–32.

Verlyn Flieger. "Wright's Utopia." Marleen Barr, ed., *Women and Utopia*. New York: Lanham, 1983, 96–107.

Naomi Jacobs. "*Islandia*: Plotting Utopian Desire." *Utopian Studies*, 6 (1995), 75–89.

Kenneth Oliver. "The Spectator's Appraisal: *Islandia* Revisited." *The Pacific Spectator*, 9 (1955), 178–182.

Lawrence C. Powell. "All That Is Poetic in Life." *Wilson Library Quarterly*, 31 (1957), 701–705.

John Silbersack. "Introduction." Austin Tappan Wright, *Islandia*. New York: Overlook Press, 2001, v–x.

Sylvia Wright. "Introduction." Austin Tappan Wright, *Islandia*. New York: Signet Books, 1975, v–xii.

—*Michael Saler*

IT'S A WONDERFUL LIFE (1946)

■

Remember, George, no man is a failure who has friends.

—Frances Goodrich, Albert Hackett,
Frank Capra, and Jo Swerling
It's a Wonderful Life (1946)

Summary

On a winter night in Bedford Falls voices are heard praying, for a man named George Bailey. In the heavens, an **angel** is summoned to intervene on his behalf, but first he is given details about Bailey's life: the boyhood incident in which he saved his brother from drowning and lost hearing in one ear; his **romance** and **marriage**; his difficult decision to postpone college to save the family **business** after his father's **death**; his hostile encounters with the **evil** banker Potter, who continually seeks to take over George's Building and Loan company; and the apparently accidental loss (actually, Potter's expedient **theft**) of eight thousand dollars in company funds, which threatens Bailey with scandal and financial ruin. Frantic and demoralized, George looks down at a turbulent **river**, contemplating **suicide**. Instead of killing himself, however, he saves the life of a drowning man whom he discovers is the angel, Clarence. When George wishes he had never been born, Clarence grants his wish: Bedford Falls is replaced by Pottersville (after the now-triumphant banker), its streets lined with seedy nightclubs. Neighbors whose homes George once helped buy are destitute; his wife is a lonely librarian (see **Libraries**); and his brother's gravestone lies forgotten in the local cemetery. George begs to live again, and returns to find Bedford Falls restored, and the missing funds replaced by friends and neighbors grateful for all the help that George has given them over the years.

Discussion

After failing to capture the public imagination when first released after World War II, *It's a Wonderful Life* became a **Christmas** television favorite when its copyright was allowed to lapse in the 1970s. It fell into the public domain, and any television station with a copy of the film could show it as often as it liked at no charge. The emergence of cable television stations in the 1980s created a need for high quality, inexpensive programming, and *It's a Wonderful Life* met the need perfectly. It wasn't long before this postwar **fable** became an obligatory part of the traditional American holiday season. Like Charles Dickens's *A Christmas Carol*, which it structurally resembles, it is both a tale of human redemption on Christmas Eve by means of divine intervention and a vision of dark alternatives, transplanted from Victorian Britain to an American small town and given a more likable protagonist.

Another aspect of the film's appeal is its lighthearted depiction of the angelic afterlife through the inept but loveable Clarence. The reverential depiction of angels typical of more traditional religious epics would have been out of place in this film, but Clarence, with his bumbling ways and his omnipresent copy of Mark Twain's *Tom Sawyer* (1876), was an endearing addition to the picture. More importantly, his successful **quest** to earn his wings by saving George's life further illustrates Frank Capra's theme that the possibility for human redemption extends even into the afterlife. The belief in social mobility embodied on **Earth** by George and his Building and Loan company is paralleled by Clarence's ascension within the heavenly hierarchy.

The primary reason why the film has become so popular, however, is the inspiring message of individualism conveyed by its compelling "what if" premise. How might the world be affected by the life of one man? *It's a Wonderful Life* does not simply describe the positive influence of one man's life, but it also vividly depicts the negative consequences of his absence. It is a **time travel** story about the alarming consequences of changing the past, yet without the distraction of actually going into the past to change it. Clarence's angelic intervention allows the film to focus exclusively on the consequences of George Bailey's nonexistence without the bother of explaining how he came not to be. In this regard *It's a Wonderful Life* resembles the science fiction subgenre of **alternate history**, which came to prominence in the decades following the film's release. While an alternate history usually describes sweeping historical changes that affect the entire world, however, *It's a Wonderful Life* restricts its changes to the fictional town of Bedford Falls. No Nazi storm troopers march through the streets of Pottersville as a result of George's retroactive erasure from history. Only the fictional universe of the film is changed by Clarence's alteration of the past.

This is due, in part, to the importance of the small town setting to the overall theme of the film. George always dreamed of traveling beyond the limits of his **home** town, but those **dreams** have been thwarted by personal responsibility and external circumstance. Clarence's dystopian nightmare allows Bailey to see that, despite the fact that he has accomplished little in the world at large, his life has had a profound effect on his own **community**. Had the impact of George Bailey's life spilled out of the fictional town of Bedford Falls to change the actual **history** of the world (as it would in an alternate history story), it would have undermined the central message of the film. The value of a person's life is measured not by its impact on the entire world, but by its influence on the local community.

Bibliography

Jeanine Basinger and Frances Goodrich. *The "It's a Wonderful Life" Book.* New York: Knopf, 1986.

Mark Connelly. *Christmas at the Movies.* London: I.B. Tauris Publishers, 2000.

Matthew Costello. "The Pilgrimage and Progress of George Bailey." *American Studies*, 40 (1999), 31–52.

Randall Fallows. "George Bailey in the Vital Center." *Journal of Popular Film and Television*, 25 (1997), 50–56.

Christopher Garbowski. "*It's a Wonderful Life* as Faerian Drama." *Mythlore*, 23 (Fall/Winter, 2002), 38–49.

Robert E. Lauder. "*It's a Wonderful Life.*" John R. May, ed., *Image and Likeness*. New York: Paulist, 1992, 135–144.

Charles J. Maland. *Frank Capra.* New York: Twayne Publishers, 1995.

Gary Westfahl. "A Christmas Cavil, or, It's a Plunderful Life." *Interzone*, No. 151 (January, 2000), 40–41.

—Ed McKnight

J

JASON AND THE ARGONAUTS (1962)

Summary

The **hero** Jason, on a **quest** to reclaim his throne from usurper King Pelias, sets his eye on a fabled **treasure**: the Golden Fleece, located in Colchis, at the far side of the world. He has a ship built, the *Argo* (named after its builder), and holds a series of **games** to determine who will sail with him for glory and riches. Various heroes from all over the country arrive, including the mighty Hercules, whose place is reserved for him on the ship. The Argonauts' journey is long and hard (see **Sea Travel**), made more difficult by the strange beings they encounter. Even with help from the goddess Hera, Jason's crew run afoul of the bronze **giant** Talos on the Isle of Bronze. Seeking advice from the blind Phineas, the Argonauts must first dispatch the harpies that torment him and eat his food (see *Food and Drink*). Phineas tells Jason of the Clashing Rocks and gives him an amulet of Triton as a gesture of thanks. When Jason throws the amulet into the **water**, Triton rises up from the depths and holds the rocks apart for the *Argo* to sail safely through. On the other side, they rescue Medea, priestess of Hecate, who guides them to Colchis. At the palace of King Aeetes, Jason is betrayed by Acastus, the son of Pelias and traitor to the Argonauts, and is imprisoned. Medea is revealed to be the daughter of Aeetes, and she confesses her **love** for Jason (see **Romance**) and helps him **escape** her father's dungeons. Jason heads for the Fleece and is confronted by the Hydra, a multi-headed **dragon** and guardian of the **magical object**. He dispatches the beast and flees with Medea, heading back to the *Argo*. Aeetes calls upon Hecate to avenge him for Jason's **betrayal** and the **theft** of the Fleece, and from the Hydra's teeth, he grows a **skeleton** army to send after Jason and his men. They battle in the ruins until Jason lures them off a cliff. The movie ends with Medea in Jason's arms, presumably about to sail back to Pelias and reclaim his throne.

Discussion

The eighth collaboration between producer Charles Schneer and special effects wizard Ray Harryhausen, *Jason and the Argonauts* plays fast and loose with Greek **mythology**, truncating relationships and rearranging events to better serve the film. While details are scrambled, the overall plot is remarkably faithful to the original story of the Argonauts and true to the spirit of Greek mythology. Many heroic deeds originally given to various crewmen of the *Argo* were reassigned to Jason or his benefactor, Hera, for the film. In fact, the concept of the Argonauts in Greek mythology (where every crew member has a special talent or ability that is utilized during the voyage) as the first team of **superheroes** is largely ignored, with the exception of the inclusion of Hercules. It is Hercules's **hubris** that brings the vengeance of the giant Talos upon the Argonauts, and he leaves the crew one third of the way through the movie. Medea, too, is softened considerably and made more noble and less mercenary. The largest deviation from Greek myth is the film's restructuring of events; all the obstacles occur on the way to Colchis, rather than on the return voyage. Absent altogether is Jason's ultimate fate as a former **king**, now a wandering vagabond, who comes upon the wreck of the *Argo* and is killed by its falling debris.

What the movie does very well is showcase the relationship between **humanity** and the **gods and goddesses**. Pelias attempts to cheat his fate by disposing of the heirs to the kingdom of Iolcus, but in doing so, he creates the "one-sandaled man" that will be his undoing when Jason is spirited away by a sympathetic soldier. Jason is himself agnostic and doesn't want to believe in the gods until taken to Mount Olympus and shown around by Hermes. Even after seeing proof of Hera's power, he **curses** the gods for their vagaries and **riddles** during his encounter with the Clashing Rocks. Despite his insolence, he is saved again by divine intervention (see **Deus ex Machina**). In completing his self-imposed quest, Jason is fulfilling his **destiny**. The gods themselves are portrayed as bored, squabbling royalty, cheating at the games they play with one another and not concerned with the humans they govern in the outcome of the games.

The real star of the film is Ray Harryhausen, the stop-motion animator who co-produced, co-wrote, and co-edited the movie, in addition to creating all the miniatures, stop-motion models, and technical effects. There are several memorable sequences in the film, such as the three-hundred-foot-tall animated **statue** of Talos menacing the crew of the *Argo*, but none is as visually arresting or as influential on future moviemakers as the climactic skeleton fight. Harryhausen animated seven skeletons by hand and had them interacting with the front-screen projected actors, whom he had coached in the **sword** fighting months before. Certain shots were so complicated that Harryhausen shot as little as three frames of film a day. The special effects, however, are still impressive in the age of CGI, and animation aficionados rank the ending sequence of *Jason and the Argonauts* as the pinnacle of Harryhausen's career. Many current special effects artists today cite Harryhausen as a critical influence, and *Jason and the Argonauts* as the impetus to their wanting to create cinematic illusions.

Bibliography

Ray Harryhausen. *Film Fantasy Scrapbook*. Third Ed. San Diego: Barnes, 1981.

Ray Harryhausen and Tony Dalton. *Ray Harryhausen*. London: Aurum, 2003.

Paul M. Jensen. *The Men Who Made The Monsters*. New York: Twayne, 1996.

Jeff Rovin. *From the Land Beyond Beyond*. New York: Berkley, 1977.

E. Stein. "Thirteen Voyages of Ray Harryhausen." *Film Comment*, 13 (November/December, 1977), 24–28.

Steve Swires. "*Starlog* Interview: Ray Harryhausen." *Starlog*, No. 100 (November, 1985), 34–37.

Tom Weaver. "Lady and the Argonauts." *Starlog*, No. 151 (February, 1990), 51–53.
Gary Westfahl. "Extracts from *The Biographical Encyclopedia of Science Fiction Film*."
    Foundation, No. 64 (Summer, 1995), 45–69.

—*Mark Finn*

LA JETÉE (1962)

Summary

A boy stands atop the jetty at Orly, the Paris airport, sometime before World War III. He is captivated by the expression on a woman's face. There is a loud noise and the woman registers astonishment; a nearby man falls to the ground and the boy realizes that he has seen a murder. This **memory** obsesses him as an adult, even after **civilization** collapses and survivors scavenge in ruined **cities**. Now a prisoner in a subterranean camp, the man's obsession is put to use. **Scientists** identify him as someone who can picture another **time**. They administer **drugs** to transport him back into the past as a prelude to a voyage into the future so that he can summon aid for the present (see **Time Travel**). In the past, the man encounters the woman whose expression mesmerized him on the airport jetty. They fall in **love** before the man is sent to the future. The inhabitants of the future not only give him **technology** to aid the present but offer to help him **escape** into the future. Instead, he requests refuge in the past. He arrives on the airport jetty, runs toward the woman, and is shot by an agent from the **prison** camp, thus becoming the man whose murder he witnessed.

Discussion

La Jetée is one of the many films directed and written by Chris Marker, an experimental French director known for documentaries. In works like *Letter from Siberia* (1958) and *Sunless* (1982), Marker turned the documentary form into a kind of personal essay, characterized by philosophical inquiry and striking visuals. He frequently examines aspects of **cultures** undergoing rapid transitions—Chile, Cuba, **Russia**, and particularly **Japan**—which in Marker's hands seem more like alternate worlds (see **Parallel Worlds**). Only twenty-eight minutes in length, *La Jetée* is more intellectually challenging than dozens of mainstream feature films taken together.

   La Jetée is first of all an exercise in **metafiction and recursiveness**; its subject is cinema itself. The "film" is comprised of individual photographs projected in sequence so as to resemble what are usually thought of as motion pictures. There is no movement, nor any acting, because characters in the photographs never speak. Musical accompaniment links the images together along with the plot, and inasmuch as the photographs are arranged, *La Jetée* exhibits editing of a sort. The time travel narrative is perfectly suited for Marker's project, since it enables him to move between past, present, and future and in so doing, foreground how films always arrange time via the editing process.

La Jetée is also an exercise in **perception**, the cognitive precondition of cinema. Marker's film questions point-of-view throughout. Paradoxically, the film is about a boy who witnesses his own murder as a man. This intellectual conundrum is further complicated by the voice-over narration, in which a narrator from what is presumably a different place and different time relates events that the boy/man sees (has seen? will see?). The narrator is the controlling viewpoint for a narrative that calls into question the perceptions of its main character, and moreover, the very incident on which the plot hinges. "Had he really seen it?" wonders the narrator at the outset.

Regardless of the viability of the main character's perception, *La Jetée* offers complex meditations on **death** and **destiny**. The film begins and ends with a death, depicts the death of civilization as we know it, and ultimately reveals that the protagonist is obsessed by the moment of his own death. He seems to be at once a literal prisoner in the subterranean camp of a **post-holocaust society** and also prisoner of his own destiny. It is precisely his obsession with his own death that ensures such a denouement in the future (or past?). When he arrives in the far future and solicits aid for the present, it is granted on the grounds that because **humanity** had survived, it could not refuse its own past the means of its **survival**. The narrator relates that "this sophism was taken for destiny in disguise."

Given such complexity, it is surprising that *La Jetée* was remade as a mainstream film entitled *12 Monkeys* (1995). Whereas Marker's experimental short was fashioned out of still photographs, Terry Gilliam's feature-length film is a conventional motion picture, in which the director of *Brazil* shows his gifts for convoluted narrative and his interest in **madness** to good effect. *12 Monkeys* follows the efforts of a convict from 2035 as he attempts to uncover information about a virus that killed 5,000,000 people in 1996. He is erroneously sent back in time to 1990, though, where he becomes romantically entangled with a psychiatrist. Gilliam focuses on the perplexed mental state of his protagonist and eschews the omniscient narrator of *La Jetée*. As a result, viewers must fend for themselves in untangling the temporal skeins of the narrative. While the plot is consequently more demanding than Marker's, Gilliam's audience is at least sure of the fact that they are indeed watching a film. However, *La Jetée* and *12 Monkeys* each in their own ways challenge spectators to an extent rarely encountered in science fiction cinema.

Bibliography

Réda Bensmaïa. "From the Photogram to the Pictogram." *Camera Obscura*, 24 (September, 1990), 139–161.

Paul Coates. "Chris Marker and the Cinema as Time Machine." *Science-Fiction Studies*, 14 (November, 1987), 307–315.

Elena Del Rio. "The Remaking of *La Jetée's* Time-Travel Narrative." *Science Fiction Studies*, 28 (November, 2001), 393–398.

Samuel Douhaire and Annick Rivoire. "Marker Direct." *Film Comment*, 39 (May/June, 2003), 38–41.

Eli Friedlander. "*La Jetée*: Regarding the Gaze." *Boundary 2*, 28 (Spring, 2001), 75–90.

Howard Hampton. "Remembering of Revolutions Past." *Film Comment*, 39 (May/June, 2003), 33–35.

Lee Hilliker. "The History of the Future in Paris." *Film Criticism*, 24 (Spring, 2000), 1–22.

Chris Marker. *La Jetée*: *Cine-Roman*. New York: Zone Books, 1992.
Paul Sandro. "Singled Out by History." *French Cultural Studies*, 10 (February, 1999), 107–127.

—*Neal Baker*

JURASSIC PARK BY MICHAEL CRICHTON (1990)

What makes you think human beings are sentient and aware? There's no evidence for it. Human beings never think for themselves, they find it too uncomfortable. For the most part, members of our species simply repeat what they are told—and become upset if they are exposed to any different view. The characteristic human trait is not awareness but conformity, and the characteristic result is religious warfare. Other animals fight for territory or food; but, uniquely in the animal kingdom, human beings fight for their "beliefs." The reason is that beliefs guide behavior, which has evolutionary importance among human beings. But at a time when our behavior may well lead us to extinction, I see no reason to assume we have any awareness at all. We are stubborn, self-destructive conformists. Any other view of our species is just a self-congratulatory delusion.

—Michael Crichton
The Lost World (1995)

Summary

A group of people, including paleontologists Alan Grant and Ellie Sattler, chaos theorist Ian Malcolm, and lawyer Donald Gennero, are invited on an all-expenses-paid pre-opening visit to Jurassic Park, a zoo-like (see **Animals and Zoos**) amusement park that features bioengineered (see **Genetic Engineering**) **dinosaurs** set up on the **island** of Isla Nublar near Costa Rica. The visitors are joined by the island's owner, John Hammond, his grandchildren Tim and Alexis, and InGen employees. The

violence begins with the **theft** of dinosaur embryos by Dennis Nedry, chief programmer of the software that controls Jurassic Park (see **Betrayal**), for a deal with
one of Hammond's competitors (see **Espionage**). To steal and get away, he must turn
off the electricity to the park's security fences, and a number of dinosaurs—
including a Tyrannosaurus Rex—**escape** from their enclosures. To ensure their own
survival, the island's human occupants pit their wits and **weaponry** against the prehistoric **monsters**.

For the sequel to *Jurassic Park*, Crichton paid homage to the **prehistoric fiction**
classic, Arthur Conan Doyle's *The Lost World*. Crichton's *The Lost World* (1995)
is set six years after the destruction of the Isla Nubla facility. Mathematician Ian
Malcolm travels to a nearby island, where Hammond had created his genetically
bred dinosaurs. Malcolm and his companions find themselves lost in the **jungles**,
running for their lives from more killer dinosaurs, and dodging murderous rival **scientists** who want to steal the dinosaur eggs for their own nefarious plans.

Discussion

Both books were adapted to films with the same names. *Jurassic Park* (1993),
directed by Steven Spielberg, was immensely popular with critics and movie-goers
alike due to its remarkable special effects. It spawned two sequels, *The Lost World:
Jurassic Park* (1997)—notable for the sequence where InGen brings a baby T. Rex
to **America** and **disaster** soon follows—and *Jurassic Park III* (2001).

Crichton's *Jurassic Park* is a cautionary tale on the risks of biological tinkering,
a theme dating back to Mary Shelley's **Frankenstein**. It explores the consequences
of an attempt to make **clones** of dinosaurs to serve as amusement park attractions.
As with all great **technothrillers**, Crichton unites timely scientific **knowledge** with
suspenseful narrative to make *Jurassic Park* an unforgettable story of an extraordinarily good idea gone extraordinarily bad. The apparent realism of the science
instills *Jurassic Park* with a grounding that makes this dinosaur **fable** acceptable to
readers living in a world of high **technology**.

In 1977, science fiction writer Charles Pellegrino suggested that well-preserved
dinosaur cells could be found in amber because the fossilized tree resin sometimes
contains **insects** in a state of near-perfect preservation. This idea inspired Crichton
to posit that extinction may not be forever. In *Jurassic Park*, **blood** extracted from
prehistoric mosquitoes preserved in amber enables InGen's scientists to manufacture
the **rebirth** of the dinosaur species. Real-life scientists, however, were quick to con-
demn *Jurassic Park* as unrealistic fiction. Crichton admitted in interviews that he
had intended to put across a clear anti-science message when he wrote the book;
still, the public was reassured by respectable biologists that the **rebirth** of dinosaurs
was not even remotely feasible. Of course, that was before the 1996 birth of Dolly
the sheep, the first large animal to be cloned using the genes of an adult cell—a scientific breakthrough that brings the recreation of dinosaurs a small step closer to
reality.

Jurassic Park also popularized the relatively new mathematical field of chaos
theory (see **Mathematics**). For centuries, the known laws of **physics** implied an
absolute connection between cause and effect. People accepted that it is always possible to make accurate **predictions** of physical systems, as long as one knows the
starting conditions. The discovery of chaotic systems in **nature** around the turn of

the twentieth century challenged that notion. In the novel, Malcolm's interpretation of chaos theory asserts that the park, as a complex physical system based on a synthetic Jurassic **ecology** placed on present-day soil, will progress in a drastically unpredictable manner inevitably resulting in catastrophe. A prime example of this is the fact that even though InGen's scientists only clone females to eliminate mating, the dinosaurs somehow adapt (see **Evolution**) and find a way to reproduce.

The overarching themes of this technothriller are the risks associated with genetic engineering and the recklessness of relying on **computers** that may fail at crucial moments. A revolution in genetics is negatively depicted as a merging of scientific advancement and commercial interests with the aim of using biotech developments to make **money**. Crichton points out that this is the opposite of the traditional way of practicing science, in which scientists were employed by universities and not linked to **business** interests. Now the best opportunities are given those who are affiliated with corporations, since that is where the profit lies. The entire book illustrates this critique of the practice of molecular **biology** in the modern world. Thus, underlying the fast-paced action in *Jurassic Park* is a dire warning about the disastrous effects of combining human ingenuity with greed and indifference and without concern for **ethics** or any supervision by responsible **governance systems**.

Bibliography

Rob DeSalle and David Lindley. *The Science of Jurassic Park and The Lost World*. New York: Basic Books, 1997.

Jody Duncan. *The Making of The Lost World: Jurassic Park*. London: Boxtree, 1997.

Stephen Jay Gould. "Dinomania." *The New York Review of Books* (August 12, 1993), 51–56.

Dave Hinton. "*Jurassic Park* and the Generic Paradox in Science Fiction." Derk Littlewood and Peter Stockwell, eds., *Impossibility Fiction*. Amsterdam: Rodopi, 1996, 177–190.

James J. Miracky. "Replicating a Dinosaur." *Critique*, 45 (Winter, 2004), 153–171.

Mary Schweitzer and Tracy Staedter. "The Real Jurassic Park." *Earth*, 6 (June, 1997), 54–57.

Don Shay. *The Making of Jurassic Park*. New York: Ballantine, 1993.

Elizabeth A. Trembley. "*Jurassic Park*." Trembley, *Michael Crichton*. Westport, CT: Greenwood Press, 1996, 119–134.

—*Nick Aires*

Jurgen: A Comedy of Justice by James Branch Cabell (1919)

■

Summary

Jurgen, a middle-aged pawnbroker of medieval Poictesme (an imaginary province of France, scene of many of Cabell's fantasy novels and subject of an elaborate, invented **mythology**) thinks himself "a monstrous clever fellow," speaks a good word for the Devil (see **Satan**), and is granted a wish. Although he asks to be rid of his nagging wife, Lisa, social and mythic expectations require that he embark on a **quest** to recover her, in the course of which he has many allegorical adventures (see **Allegory**). He regains his **youth** and tries to find the ideal woman and true happiness, dallying with Guenevere (see **Arthur**), sex goddess Anaitis, and Helen of Troy. None prove satisfactory. He also visits **Heaven** and **Hell** and ultimately learns that the cosmos as a whole (see **Cosmology**) is not what it seems. Heaven is an **illusion** created by Koshchei the Deathless (a Slavic **demon**, not very bright, but apparently in charge of the universe). Hell exists to flatter those who think themselves capable of committing a **sin** worthy of damnation. Disillusioned, Jurgen, can only return to Lisa, with whom (it turns out) he is not all that unhappy after all.

Discussion

A controversial and widely influential **comedy**, *Jurgen* defined high-end literary fantasy for the middle of the twentieth century, so that "Cabellesque" became a standard critical adjective, used as late as 1961 to describe Robert A. Heinlein's Cabell-influenced *Stranger in A Strange Land*. It is a philosophical **romance**, harkening back to the romances of Voltaire like *Candide* (1759), or even *The Golden Ass* of Apuleius (c. 158 CE), in which the naive **hero** undergoes a series of enlightening encounters driven more by thematic concerns than plot. Meaning is all, and in Cabell, meaning is something to be delved into endlessly, as all his books are rich with **satire**, subtle allusions, and verbal trickery like anagrams. For instance, the three judges of the Philistines, who send Jurgen to Hell, are named Ageus (usage), Vel-Tyno (novelty), and Sesphra (phrases). At one point he meets the Master Philologist who tells him that concepts like **love** and **beauty** are just words (see **Language and Linguistics**).

Thus, *Jurgen* may arguably be cast as an early postmodernist fantasy novel about the meaning of meaning (see **Postmodernism**). It also maintains much of its comic tension through the conflict between a modernist deflation of ancient myths (which give life a meaning beyond the squalid deeds of an individual) and Jurgen's (and, one senses, the author's) desire for such things to be true and his regret that they are not. Beautiful illusions may come crashing down, but they are nonetheless beautiful. As such, the novel (and much of Cabell's work) is out of step with most post-Tolkien fantasy, which either takes its mythology straight or else descends into slapstick in the manner of Piers Anthony or, on a more sophisticated level, Terry Pratchett. If any contemporary fantasist has approximated the effect of Cabell, it is perhaps Salman Rushdie in *The Satanic Verses* (1988), which is also a riot of allegory and shifting meanings. Elements of Cabell's technique are evident in the works of Fritz Leiber and are overtly evoked in John Brunner's *The Traveler in Black* (1971) and Heinlein's *Job: A Comedy of Justice* (1984), which also borrows Cabell's subtitle.

The controversy around Cabell's work stemmed from its alleged raciness. When John Sumner of the New York Society for the Suppression of Vice managed to get the book banned, Cabell, before then only a modestly successful author, became a bestseller and *cause celebre*. The result was the most celebrated literary court case prior to that of James Joyce's *Ulysses* (1922), in which Cabell was completely exonerated. In a short satirical volume, *Taboo* (1922), Cabell effusively thanked Sumner. In later works, particularly *Something About Eve* (1927), Cabell playfully inserted all sorts of "naughty" and frequently Freudian symbolism for the likes of Mr. Sumner to discover. But one has to work hard to discover the indecency. While much of Cabell's fiction is about desire and its consequences, and his heroes are always seeking ideal, if illusory women who personify perfect beauty, real eroticism in Cabell is very sublimated or even (as the Master Philologist would tell us) just a word.

Cabell's reputation for being "dirty" was ultimately distracting. It made him a bestseller for the wrong reasons and doubtless contributed to the shift in literary fashion away from Cabell by the mid-1930s. When his work was revived in Lin Carter's Ballantine Adult Fantasy Series in the early 1970s, the first book sold very well, the rest far less well, apparently because readers discovered that Cabell was making fun, albeit regretfully, of the very elements that made William Morris or J.R.R. Tolkien so popular. Cabell is unlikely to be a bestseller ever again, but he remains a unique voice and a continuing presence because his themes ultimately are valid. He appeals to the sort of person who cannot resist, however much he may regret it, pulling back the curtain to discover that the **wizard** is a humbug.

Bibliography

Don Bregenzer and Samuel Loveman, eds. *A Round-Table in Poictesme*. Cleveland: Colophon Club, 1924.

Joe Lee Davis. *James Branch Cabell*. New York: Twayne, 1962.

Thomas Inge and Edgar MacDonald, eds. *James Branch Cabell: Contennial Essays*. Baton Rouge: Louisiana State University Press, 1983.

Edgar MacDonald. *James Branch Cabell and Richmond-in-Virginia*. Jackson: University Press of Mississippi, 1993.

Warren A. McNeill. *Cabellian Harmonics*. New York: Random House, 1928.

James D. Riemer. *From Satire to Subversion*. Westport, CT: Greenwood Press, 1989.

Desmond Tarrant. *James Branch Cabell*. Norman: University of Oklahoma Press, 1967.

Carl Van Doren. *James Branch Cabell*. New York: McBride, 1925.

—Darrell Schweitzer

Ҝ

KINDRED BY OCTAVIA E. BUTLER (1979)

Summary

Dana Franklin, a modern African-American novelist, finds herself repeatedly being transported back in time to nineteenth-century Maryland, where she experiences the life of a plantation slave (see **Time Travel**). She learns that the son of the plantation's owner, Rufus, will someday mate with a slave named Alice and have a child, Hagar, who will be Dana's ancestor. By unexplained means, Rufus can summon his descendant whenever he is in danger; Dana remains in the past until she feels threatened, which returns her to the present. Though she grows to dislike Rufus as he matures into a cruel slaveowner, Dana must keep him alive until Hagar is born so as to guarantee her own existence, even when he beats her and misleads her. Dana's white husband, Kevin, accompanies her on one trip and is stranded in the past for five years until she retrieves him. After Hagar is born, Rufus's mean-spirited deception drives Alice to **suicide**; he then attempts to rape Dana, but she fatally stabs him instead. Dana's abrupt return to the present slices off her left arm, leaving her permanently wounded but freed from Rufus's power.

Discussion

Octavia E. Butler says that she wrote *Kindred* primarily to inform younger African-Americans about the grim realities of **slavery** in **America**. The novel is particularly successful in describing slavery's corrosive effects on both slaves and slaveowners, as the friendly Rufus is molded into a tyrannical sadist. Alice is the novel's tragic figure (see **Tragedy**), said to resemble Dana and presented as her **doppelgänger**; however, while the modern Dana enjoys a fulfilling writing career (see **Writing and Authors**), the nineteenth-century Alice is forced into physical and sexual servitude, leading to despair and suicide. Dana's loss of her left arm might symbolize the lingering effects of slavery on contemporary African-Americans, able to function in society but handicapped in crucial respects.

Those who characterize *Kindred* principally as a commentary on **race relations** downplay the novel's science-fictional elements, regarding its time travel only as a device to describe a repugnant period in American **history** from a contemporary perspective. Yet Butler's background as a science fiction writer serves to explain Dana's excessive caution, or even apparent complicity, in supporting the institution of slavery. Dana not only must insure that her ancestor is born, but also must worry about changing the past in other ways, leading to unpalatable results. Previous science fiction stories illustrate the problem: in Ray Bradbury's "A Sound of Thunder" (1952), trampling a butterfly during a visit to the Mesozoic Era alters the outcome of a future election. More relevant to *Kindred* is Ward Moore's **alternate history** *Bring the Jubilee*, where a historian from a contemporary America in which the South won the Civil War journeys back to the Battle of Gettysburg, inadvertently alters its outcome, and creates a new history—our own—in which the South was defeated. If Dana attempts to improve the lives of Rufus's slaves or hasten the end of slavery, there might be unforeseen consequences; thus, she reveals little about the future and limits her activism to surreptitiously teaching slave **children** how to read.

Still, Dana's actions are disquieting, especially when she persuades Alice to become Rufus's mistress. One might view Dana as someone exclusively concerned with her own **survival**; she helps Rufus as she must until Hagar is born, then murders him to liberate herself. *Kindred* therefore conveys a characteristic theme in Butler's fiction, including *Dawn* and its sequels—that individuals must do what they need to do to survive, even if their decisions upset liberal sensibilities.

Dana's role in Alice's oppression also raises questions about her relationship with Kevin. As Dana resembles Alice, Kevin is Rufus's doppelgänger, since Kevin once reminds Dana of Rufus. Her partnership with the likable, supportive Kevin seems utterly unlike Alice's subjugation to Rufus. Still, there are hints of a dominating streak in Kevin—he pressures Dana to type his manuscripts, though she dislikes doing so—and the novel begins with the couple moving from a Los Angeles apartment to an upscale suburban house. Arguably Kevin is, like Rufus, controlling Dana and uprooting her to serve his needs. Perhaps the legacy of slavery imposes undercurrents of dominance and submission even on apparently egalitarian mixed **marriages**.

The novel's title announces **family** ties as a central theme: all major characters—Dana and Kevin, Rufus and his family, Alice and her children—are related to each other; more broadly, the novel argues that all Americans, black and white, are part of one family. Paradoxically, Dana and Kevin are cut off from their own families, who have rejected them for marrying outside their races. Dana begins to regard Rufus's plantation (see **Farms**) as her **home**, and despite its unpleasantness she seemingly becomes reconciled with it, suggesting that Americans must learn about and embrace their own, sometimes unpleasant histories in order to understand themselves better and compensate for the absence of other family relationships. Dana and Kevin's final visit to Maryland, to research the fate of her nineteenth-century relatives, could represent the important undertaking Butler recommends for all Americans.

Bibliography

Dorothy Allison. "The Future of Female." Henry Louis Gates, Jr., ed., *Reading Black, Reading Feminist*. New York: Meridian, 1990, 471–378.

Pamela Bedore. "Slavery and Symbiosis in Octavia Butler's *Kindred*." *Foundation*, No. 84 (Spring, 2002), 73–81.

Janet Giannotti. *A Companion Text for Kindred*. Ann Arbor: University of Michigan Press, 1999.

Sandra Y. Govan. "Homage to Tradition." *Melus*, 13 (Spring/Summer, 1986), 79–96.

Nancy Jesser. "Blood, Genes and Gender in Octavia Butler's *Kindred* and *Dawn*." *Extrapolation*, 43 (Spring, 2002), 36–61.

Christine Livecq. "Power and Repetition." *Contemporary Literature*, 41 (Fall, 2000), 525–553.

Lisa A. Long. "A Relative Pain." *College English*, 64 (March, 2002), 459–483.

Angelyn Mitchell. "Not Enough of the Past." *Melus*, 26 (Fall, 2001), 51–70.

Ashraf H.A. Rusdy. "Families of Orphans." *College English*, 55 (February, 1993), 135–157.

—*Gary Westfahl*

KING KONG (1933)

It wasn't the airplanes. It was beauty killed the beast.

—James Ashmore Creelman and Ruth Rose
King Kong (1933)

Summary

Famed for outlandish stunts and crazy schemes, filmmaker Carl Denham brings his crew—including young starlet Ann Darrow—to an uncharted **island** in the Indian Ocean, using a **map** of dubious origin, to make a film about the legendary god Kong. They discover a lost race in the midst of a **ritual** for the mysterious Kong. The natives offer to **trade** for the blonde Darrow. When Denham and crew refuse, the islanders kidnap Darrow to employ as a human **sacrifice**. Denham's men, led by first mate Driscoll, give chase through the **jungle**, confront **dinosaurs**, and eventually encounter the **giant** ape Kong, who kills all the pursuers except Denham and Driscoll. The first mate ultimately rescues Darrow; Kong chases them; and the **ape** is eventually captured. He is then brought to New York City in chains to be displayed to crowds. The gorilla, billed as King Kong, Eighth Wonder of the World, **escapes** when he is startled by photographers' flash bulbs while appearing on stage. His rampage causes a panic in the **city**. Kong grabs Darrow and ascends the Empire State Building, where he is gunned down by airplanes and falls to his **death**. Denham stands over the dead gorilla and proclaims, "It wasn't the airplanes. It was beauty killed the beast" (see **Beauty**).

Discussion

The first giant ape movie, *King Kong* remains one of the greatest giant **monster** movies film ever made. Derived from an idea by crime writer Edgar Wallace and producer/co-director Merian C. Cooper, *King Kong* is first of all impressive in depicting the **horror** of a huge creature rampaging through a contemporary city, endangering terrified residents, in scenes that would be replicated in scores of films in the 1950s and thereafter, including *The Beast from 20,000 Fathoms* (1953), also set in New York City, and **Godzilla, King of the Monsters**. *King Kong*'s superior, ground-breaking special effects were developed by Willis O'Brien, who improved upon the existing technology of stop-motion animation technology; his work remained the industry standard until the 1980s with the emergence of computer-generated effects.

Even though *King Kong*'s scenes of destructive mayhem have since been replicated and even surpassed, no other film of its subgenre has succeeded so well as a **love** story. As suggested by its famous closing line, *King Kong* invites consideration as a retelling of Marie Laprince de Beaumont's "Beauty and the Beast" (1756) (see **Beauty and the Beast**). For all his immense size and ferocity, Kong is like the Beast in that he also reveals himself to be a kindly soul at heart, inviting sympathy because of his genuine affection for Darrow and his gentle treatment of her. Unfortunately, this **fairy tale** has an unhappy ending, as Darrow spurns her gigantic suitor and her cruel society, blind to his finer qualities, mercilessly guns him down. Later efforts to humanize large monsters like Godzilla and Gamera have focused on making them seem like overgrown pets with a special affinity for **children**, making them likable after a fashion, but without the dignity and **sexuality** that is unique to Kong.

King Kong in fact displays a rich variety of symbolic roles. Coming from a jungle island where he is worshipped by primitive natives, Kong represents **nature** in conflict with **civilization**. As a human-like creature humiliatingly displayed in chains before crowds of onlookers, Kong also recalls images of African-American slaves in chains, taken from their **homes** by profit-hungry white men; it is not surprising to learn that *King Kong* in the 1930s and 1940s was especially popular with African-American audiences, who undoubtedly enjoyed watching Kong tear off his chains and inflict violent **revenge** on the whites who had mistreated him. And, since he is seized by an exploitative filmmaker, Kong's story arguably is even a **fable** about the dangers of succumbing to the lures of a show business career, with Kong as a contented country boy who finds only **pain** and misery amidst the bright lights of Broadway.

To follow up on the tremendous success of *King Kong*, his creators endeavored to shrink the character down to more humanlike dimensions to make him even more sympathetic. In the immediate sequel, the hastily-produced *Son of Kong* (1933), the bankrupt and disgraced Denham returns to the uncharted island, where he encounters Kong's friendly, albino offspring, a somewhat smaller giant ape who eventually sacrifices his own life to save his human friends. Years later, the makers of *King Kong* teamed up again to make another movie about an ape only twelve feet high, *Mighty Joe Young* (1949), who also demonstrates his virtues by saving lives, rescuing some children from a burning building (see **Fire**). After the original Kong was brought back in two minor Japanese features—*King Kong vs. Godzilla* (1963) and *King Kong Escapes* (1967)—Dino di Laurentiis produced a disastrously updated and farcical remake, *King Kong* (1976), which even replaced O'Brien's meticulous stop-motion animation with a man in a monkey suit. The film eventually generated the limp sequel *King Kong Lives* (1986). In the early twenty-first century, however, fans of King Kong were happy to hear that director Peter Jackson, fresh from the success of **The Lord of the Rings: The Fellowship of the Ring** and its sequels, had agreed to produce a more respectful remake, which was released in 2005.

Bibliography

David Annan. *Ape.* New York: Bounty Books, 1975.

Bruce Bahrenburg. *The Creation of Dino De Laurentiis' King Kong.* New York: Pocket Books, 1976.

Bob Burns, with John Michlig. "Kong and Kin." Burns with Michlig, *It Came From Bob's Basement!* San Francisco: Chronicle Books, 2000, 122–138.

Edward Edelson. "The Big Beasts." Edelson, *Great Monsters of the Movies.* 1973. New York: Pocket Books, 1974, 69–86.

Cynthia M. Erb. *Tracking King Kong.* Detroit: Wayne State University Press, 1998.

Orville Goldner and George E. Turner. *The Making of King Kong.* New York: Ballantine, 1975.

Paul M. Jensen. "Willis O'Brien." Jensen, *The Men Who Made The Monsters.* New York: Twayne, 1996, 59–97.

Jerry Pascall. *The King Kong Story.* New Jersey: Chartwell Books, 1977.

—*Rick Klaw*

THE KING OF ELFLAND'S DAUGHTER BY LORD DUNSANY (1924)

Summary

When the people of Erl come before their lord and ask for more **magic** in their humdrum lives, the ruler sends his son, Alveric, "beyond the fields we know," into the realm of Elfland (see **Elves; Fairies**) to wed the King of Elfland's daughter, Lirazel. Equipped with a magic **sword** provided by a **witch**, he brings Lirazel back into the mortal world with him. But they do not live happily ever after. The Elf King (see **Kings**) writes a mighty rune that summons Lirazel home, reminding her of immortal things (see **Immortality and Longevity**). Alveric then embarks on a hopeless **quest** to recover her, but Elfland is not a physical place, but a different realm of existence, which he cannot now recover. Meanwhile Orion, son of Alveric and Lirazel, becomes a hunter, killing **unicorns,** which graze near the borders of Elfland. Eventually the lovers are reunited because of Lirazel's longing. The Elf King expends his final and most powerful rune, and Elfland flows over and absorbs Erl.

Discussion

Edward Plunkett, the eighteenth Baron Dunsany, wrote magical, mythic, intensely poetic shorter works, beginning with *The Gods of Pegana* (1905) which earned him a very high place in the pantheon of imaginative literature. Of his novels, *The King of Elfland's Daughter* is of foremost importance, the one genuine classic that may be ranked with J.R.R. Tolkien's ***The Lord of the Rings***, Hope Mirrlees's *Lud-in-the-Mist* (1926) or E.R. Eddison's ***The Worm Ouroboros*** in the forefront of the field. Its virtues are considerable, although some later readers may find its long unicorn-hunting scenes difficult to bear.

The King of Elfland's Daughter contains some of the finest descriptive passages in the entire literature. Dunsany's Elfland, like the mystical Faerie of Celtic lore, is a timeless realm where nothing ages, where different and strange **flowers** bloom in endless twilight, where the years that pass in the lands of men seem as fleeting moments. It is glimpsed far across earthly fields at sunset, although when the Elf King withdraws his **frontiers**, he leaves a wasteland that to cross, "would weary the comet." Yet when Alveric is far away, "Elfland came racing back, as the tide over flat sand." Such metaphors are extremely apt for, as Dunsany once wrote, the basis of his fantasy was in the observation and appreciation of **nature**. His magical fields have their basis in real fields and real evenings. A keen outdoorsman and hunter, Dunsany also felt the curious contradiction that he both admired the **beauty** of nature and sought to destroy it. (Indeed, he even wrote a poem about how the **birds** will celebrate when he is dead, and the hunter with his gun is no more.) But the hunting scenes go on and on with loving relish. The paradox was never quite worked out.

Dunsany's Elfland though immune to **death**, also lacks life. It is a place of ice, mist, and stasis. There the princess Lirazel exists more like a beautiful figurine than as a living person. She elopes with Alveric because he promises her an intensity of experience she has never known before. Such motifs are common in folklore and **fairy tales**, as in such stories as Baron del la Motte Fouque's *Undine* (1811), which is about a magical maiden who must give up immortality to gain a human soul and experience **love**. Lirazel, too, moves into full **humanity** at the evident cost of her immortality, even as an adolescent ultimately accepts the inevitability of death as the price of an adult life. Only in a fairy tale (which is how Dunsany described *The King of Elfland's Daughter*) can Lirazel both have her cake and eat it too. She floats back to Elfland, but, when Elfland overwhelms Erl, is reunited with Alveric. Presumably everyone becomes immortal, except for the Christian friar, who disapproves of such things. For him is preserved a small patch of "earthly" field.

How "serious" was Dunsany about any of this? His aesthetics were Romantic (see **Romance**) in the late nineteenth-century sense. He would have agreed with Oscar Wilde's dictum that "The artist is the creator of beautiful things." *The King of Elfland's Daughter*, one might argue, is a beautiful **dream**, a wish expressed with a sigh of "if only things were that way." Dunsany, a veteran of the Boer War and World War I who had been wounded in the Easter Rebellion in Dublin in 1916, knew how the world actually worked. A political and social conservative, a typical member of the aristocratic class, he must have realized at some level that the day of the aristocrat was over, so he had reasons to express impossible dreams with a full awareness of their fragility. His philosophical outlook, as S.T. Joshi demonstrates, was actually quite modern, derived more from Friedrich Nietzsche than **religion**. (Dunsany was apparently an atheist.) This was the key to his appeal to H.P. Lovecraft (whose praise helped significantly in keeping Dunsany's name alive), who shared similar views.

Thus Dunsany, in exquisite prose, was creating a **mythology** for a universe that had none. His **gods and goddesses** are more likely to provide cosmic laughter than comfort. *The King of Elfland's Daughter* is in a gentler mode, a dream that the reader is not really expected to "believe."

Bibliography

Mark Amory. *Lord Dunsany*. London: Collins, 1972.

Martin Gardner. "The Fantasies of Lord Dunsany." Gardner, *Gardner's Whys & Wherefores*. Chicago: University of Chicago Press, 1989, 138–150.

S.T. Joshi. "Lord Dunsany: The Career of a *Fantaisiste*." Joshi, *The Weird Tale*. Austin: University of Texas Press, 1990, 42–86.

————. *Lord Dunsany*. Westport, CT: Greenwood Press, 1995.

Hazel Littlefield. *Lord Dunsany*. New York: Exposition Press, 1959.

Linda Pashka. "'Hunting for Allegories' in the Prose Fantasy of Lord Dunsany." *Studies in Weird Fiction*, No. 12 (Spring, 1993). 19–24.

Andy Sawyer. "The Horns of Elfland, Faintly Winding." *Crystal Ship*, No. 14 (1988), 10–20.

Darrell Schweitzer. *Pathways to Elfland*. Philadelphia: Owlswick, 1989.

—Darrell Schweitzer

L

LAST AND FIRST MEN BY OLAF STAPLEDON (1930)

*Man himself, at the very least, is music, a
brave theme that makes music also of its
vast accompaniment, its matrix of storms
and stars. Man himself in his degree is
eternally a beauty in the eternal form of
things. It is very good to have been man.
And so we may go forward together with
laughter in our hearts, and peace, thank-
ful for the past, and for our own courage.
For we shall make after all a fair conclusion to this brief music that is man.*

—Olaf Stapledon
Last and First Men (1930)

Summary

Published in 1930 by a philosopher and social reformer who knew virtually nothing about the relatively new genre of "science fiction," *Last and First Men* is an
ambitious future **history** of the human race, which it charts through eighteen separate species and three planets. It was strongly influenced by H.G. Wells's concern
with **evolution** and **progress**, and the speculations of the biologist J.B.S. Haldane—
whose visions of a future **humanity** colonizing **Venus** was, like Wells's invaders from
Mars, adopted and expanded into Stapledon's visionary plan.

Written as if a record composed by a member of the eighteenth (and final?) species
of humanity and imprinted upon the mind of an obscure English academic in the early
twentieth century, *Last and First Men* explores **destiny** and **eschatology** as they are
worked out in the tension between the spiritual and pragmatic poles of human
thought. Stapledon takes us through a historical and evolutionary epic marked by
carefully scaled time-charts (see **Time**). The sojourn of the Fifth Men and their successors on Venus, Stapledon remarks, lasts longer than humanity's entire career on
Earth. By the fourth chart, First Men—we—have been squeezed out between the Rise

of the Mammals and the Second Men. By the final chart the entire span of human existence is squeezed between two lines in a scale from ten million million years ago to five million million years hence: "Planets Formed" and "End of Man."

Discussion

Whereas Stapledon's "contemporary" record proved significantly unprophetic (famously, his vision of **Europe** immediately following the First World War was hardly one of science fiction's most effective **predictions**, being rapidly overtaken by the rise of Fascism), his vision of a twentieth century dominated by **globalization** and rivalry between **America** and **China** seems more prescient. The First Men, after an initial collapse into **decadence** succeeded by a temporary flowering in **Latin America**, are brought to an end by **nuclear war**. The Second Men are weakened by an **invasion** by the semi-gaseous, telepathic Martians, and the moral dilemma expressed by the invasion—Stapledon spends much time suggesting that the Martians, however alien, have a right to **survival**—is revisited in reverse. The Fifth Men, in their turn escaping to Venus to avoid the fall of the **Moon**, discover and conquer a native species in the planet's oceans and begin a project of **terraforming** the new world. Planetary transformation is not the only exercise. Several species of humanity, including the Third but also the Eighth Men, **escape** to Neptune (see **Jupiter and the Outer Planets**) from the expansion of the **Sun,** and their successor species on Neptune themselves create their own successors (see **Superman**) by means of **genetic engineering.** Finally, the Eighteenth or "Last" men are engaged in a project of reclaiming the past through telepathic contact with previous **civilizations,** but this becomes endangered by Neptune's own imminent destruction. All that can be done is to disseminate human spores throughout space in the hope that some will find a home.

In *Last Men in London* (1932), Stapledon attempted to attach this vision to a narrower compass, by means of combining his "Eighteenth Man" narrator and the consciousness of his "host" Paul, a man growing up in the early years of the twentieth century through World War I and its aftermath. In this sequel, Stapledon's Wellsian concern with political and sexual reform comes to the fore and the novel is of great interest for its autobiographical aspects; but its fusion of cosmic and individual perspectives makes it one of the more difficult of his novels. The unalloyed cosmic perspective of *Last and First Men* was returned to in *Star Maker*, while more successful exercises in smaller-scale **estrangement** were *Odd John* (1935) and *Sirius* (1944).

Stapledon's vision can be seen as bleak: a tour through a history of **future wars** and **disasters** and a search for **wisdom** that time after time ends in **tragedy**. But he called *Last and First Men* an exercise in "myth creation," not a novel. His concerns were to consider the fate of the human race as a whole through ethical **philosophy** and the conflict between materialist science and transcendent **religion** rather than to create a story of individual character. There are, therefore, few incidences of dialogue in the story, and fewer named individuals. Instead, the human species and the cosmos are the main "characters." The rise and fall of humanity allows for much speculation about **biology**, and Stapledon ingeniously and imaginatively describes possible variations of the human form, especially as he refocuses his gaze on the Last Men, with their extra eyes and multiple tones of skin **color** and texture, but also as he describes the **flying** men of Venus.

In this epic, Stapledon creates one of science fiction's most effective examples of the **sublime**, greatly influencing subsequent writers like Arthur C. Clarke (see

Childhood's End) and Brian W. Aldiss (see *Helliconia Spring*). It may also have influenced another major future history, Wells's *The Shape of Things to Come* (1933). Although it was not until some years after the publication of *Last and First Men* that Stapledon was introduced to genre science fiction, his vision can be seen as the quintessence of that **sense of wonder** which lies at its heart.

Bibliography

K.V. Bailey. "Time Scales and Culture Cycles in Olaf Stapledon." *Foundation*, No. 46 (Winter, 1989), 27–39.

Robert Branham. "Stapledon's 'Agnostic Mysticism.'" *Science-Fiction Studies*, 28 (November, 1982), 249–256.

Robert Crossley. *Olaf Stapledon: Speaking for the Future*. Liverpool: Liverpool University Press, 1994.

Leslie A. Fiedler. *Olaf Stapledon: A Man Divided*. Oxford: Oxford University Press, 1983.

John Huntington. "Remembrance of Things to Come." *Science-Fiction Studies*, 28 (November, 1982), 257–264.

Stanislaw Lem. "On Stapledon's *Last and First Men*." *Science-Fiction Studies*, 13 (November, 1986), 272–291.

Patrick A. McCarthy, "*Last and First Men* as Miltonic Epic." *Science-Fiction Studies*, 34 (November, 1984), 244–252.

Patrick A. McCarthy, Charles Elkins, and Martin Harry Greenberg, eds. *The Legacy of Olaf Stapledon*. Westport, CT: Greenwood Press, 1989.

Curtis C. Smith. "William Olaf Stapledon." *Extrapolation*, 13 (December, 1971), 5–15.

—Andy Sawyer

THE LAST MAN BY MARY SHELLEY (1826)

> Earth is to me a tomb, the firmament a vault, shrouding mere corruption. Time is no more, for I have stepped within the threshold of eternity; each man I meet appears a corpse, which will soon be deserted of its animating spark, on the eve of decay and corruption.
>
> —Mary Shelley
> *The Last Man* (1826)

Summary

In *The Last Man* two unnamed people find a series of written fragments in the cave of the Cumaean Sibyl, which they translate and arrange in a coherent narrative. In this, Lionel Verney recounts the events that have caused him to be the **last man** left alive on Earth, after the rest of its population is wiped out by an unidentified plague (see **Apocalypse; Plagues and Diseases**). Set at the end of the twenty-first century, the novel first describes the fall from grace of the noble Verney family and Lionel Verney's restoration by Adrian, Earl of Windsor, son of the former King of England, a friend of Verney's father. Verney eventually marries Adrian's sister, Idris. Verney's sister, Perdita, marries Lord Raymond. England has become a republic and all three men are active in national **politics**. Raymond is Lord Protector of the country, before dying in battle in Greece. Later, when plague strikes the country, Adrian in turn becomes Lord Protector. When he realizes it is no longer possible to stop the onset of the plague, he and his companions flee to the Continent, where many die from plague, but Adrian and Verney's adopted daughter both drown, leaving Verney to live on alone, to write his account of events.

Discussion

The Last Man can be defined as a work of proto-science fiction, containing a number of science-fictional tropes familiar to modern readers. Although the novel is set in what Shelley would regard as the far future, the end of the twenty-first century. Shelley does not attempt to construct a world that is overtly different from her own. Apart from a brief mention of steerable balloons, prefiguring the later development of airships (see **Air Travel**), there are no distinctive technological differences—ships are still wind-powered (see **Sea Travel**), **horses** and carriages are used for land travel, and there are no signs of automation.

Drawing on her own family background—her parents, William Godwin and Mary Wollstonecraft, both argued in favor of republicanism—Shelley portrays England's transformation into a republic as a bloodless revolution, the **king** abdicating at the behest of his subjects and the heir presumptive being himself a republican (see **Governance Systems**). Republican England appears idyllic, but Shelley's narrative implies that this transformation is superficial, as the same hierarchical and paternalistic **class system** persists into the republic. Shelley herself seems ambivalent as to the value of the republic over the monarchy. The anti-monarchist Lord Protector is found wanting as a leader when plague strikes, whereupon Adrian is required to assume his place, the suggestion being that he, as heir presumptive, is in some way better fitted to lead the country. And yet, in the face of natural **disaster**, he is equally unable to stem the tide of **deaths**.

England's insularity in relation to **Europe** is illustrated in the way that an awareness of the plague barely impinges on the country until halfway through the novel, despite various reports from abroad, the arrival of a ship in Portsmouth, a flood of refugees from Europe, and most pertinently, the collapse of **trade** with other countries. The struggle to support the increased population is once again portrayed in idealistic terms, as the nobles gladly surrender their land and houses to feed and accommodate the influx. At the same time, Shelley also understands, and conveys, that the failure of trade is as debilitating to England as the plague itself, although this is something that the English themselves fail to perceive. But even at the end, when the final few characters recognize the inevitability of their death, the journey they undertake reflects the educational Grand Tours of former times. Europe remains a playground until the end, not a social and economic force.

In Shelley's hands, the plague is an elegant killer; the upper classes and deserving poor die onstage in an appropriately pathetic and decorous manner, while the bulk of humanity dies offstage. We rarely see people suffering in the throes of the plague, except when Verney is attacked by a man crazed with illness and himself becomes infected. However, we do see people who are infected by the terror of death (see **Anxiety**) and use various methods to keep it at bay. Most notably, Shelley is critical of those who turn to **religion** and provides a harsh portrait of a group of people exploited by a religious leader. There are frequent touches of **Gothic** sensibility in Shelley's descriptions of the plague, but it is as if Shelley herself cannot quite comprehend the enormity of the apocalypse she is proposing. Rather than portraying dead bodies, she describes empty **landscapes**, turning again to Romantic notions of the **sublime**. The most elegiac passages in the latter part of the book describe a landscape reverting to **nature**, prefiguring such post-apocalyptic stories as Richard Jefferies's *After London* (1885), George R. Stewart's *Earth Abides*, and John Wyndham's *The Day of the Triffids*.

This further emphasises Verney's position as the last man, whose isolation is both physical and spiritual. Portrayed in the early part of the novel as a Wordsworthian force of nature, a solitary man educated as much by the **mountains** as by Adrian Windsor, Verney's life comes full circle in the end as he travels through the mountains of Europe to find a final resting place in Rome, where he takes solace in his studies and in writing the account he leaves for posterity.

Bibliography

Michael Bradshaw. "Mary Shelley's *The Last Man*." Derek Littlewood and Peter Stockwell, eds., *Impossibility Fiction*. Amsterdam: Rodopi, 1996, 163–176.

Ryszard Dubanski "The Last Man Theme in Modern Fantasy and SF." *Foundation*, No. 16 (May, 1979), 26–31.

R.J. Frost. "Mary Shelley and the Plague." *Vector*, No. 196 (November/December, 1997), 10–11.

William Lomax. "Epic Reversal in Mary Shelley's *The Last Man*." Michele K. Langford, ed., *Contours of the Fantastic*. Westport, CT: Greenwood Press, 1990, 7–17.

Anne McWhir. "Mary Shelley's Anti-Contagionism." *Mosaic*, 35 (June, 2002), 23–38.

Anne K. Mellor. "Introduction." *The Last Man*, by Mary Shelley. Lincoln: University of Nebraska Press, 1993, vii–xxvi.

Victoria Middleton. "Strategies of a Survivor." Mary Lowe-Evans, ed., *Critical Essays on Mary Wollstonecraft Shelley*. New York: G. K. Hall, 1998, 166–182.

Samantha Webb. "Reading the End of the World." Betty T. Bennett and Stuart Curran, eds., *Mary Shelley in Her Times*. Baltimore, MD: Johns Hopkins University Press, 2000, 119–133.

—Maureen Kincaid Speller

THE LAST UNICORN BY PETER S. BEAGLE (1968)

Summary

One day the **unicorn** living in a lilac forest learns she is the only unicorn left in the world and thus sets out to find the rest of her kind. Her journey leads her and her two helpmates, the incompetent magician Schmendrick and robber's bride Molly

Grue, to the wasteland of King Haggard, whose Red Bull has captured all unicorns for the **king**. When the bull appears to catch the only unicorn left, Schmendrick's **magic** intervenes and transforms the unicorn into a young girl, the ethereal Lady Amalthea. All three then can enter Haggard's castle unhindered. While they search for the unicorns, Amalthea becomes more and more human and starts to forget her true self. When it is almost too late, Haggard's secret is revealed: the bull holds the unicorns captured in the sea, where the king can watch and delight in them. In a climactic last confrontation on the beach below the **castle**, the unicorn, back in her true form, defeats the bull and drives it into the sea. The unicorns are set free, and Haggard dies within the crumbling walls of his castle. Irrevocably altered by the human emotions she has learned, the unicorn returns to her **forest**.

Discussion

As the basis for his novel, Beagle took the classic **fairy tale** structure: the story of a **quest** with the typical helpmates and **talking animals**. Yet it soon becomes clear that the act of story-telling itself is a major issue of the novel (see **Metafiction and Recursiveness**): hunters enter the unicorn's forest and discuss whether unicorns are real or not, thereby referring to Pliny's description of unicorns. Beagle based his unicorn on that fairy-tale creature—solitary, immortal, the most beautiful of creatures (see **Beauty; Immortality and Longevity**)—and has several characters allude to or reenact the story of the virgin maiden who lures the unicorn to **sleep** in her lap (see **Virginity**). The most obvious sign of metafiction, however, is the awareness of the characters themselves that they are part of a story and their attempt to behave accordingly. Thus, Haggard's adopted son Lír tries to embody the ideal of a **hero** and slays ogres and **dragons** to win the **love** of the Lady Amalthea. He finally becomes a true hero when he rejects a happy ending for him and his lady and insists on telling this story properly by ending the quest and freeing the unicorns.

Despite the pseudo-medieval setting of the novel (see **Medievalism and the Middle Ages**), Beagle frequently alludes to later **history** and our own everyday reality. Thus, the robbers mistake Schmendrick for the ballad researcher Francis Child, and the butterfly the unicorn meets early on in her journey strings together snatches from classic literature like William **Shakespeare** quotations, pop songs, and even commercials (see **Advertising**).

By slipping back and forth between fantasy and reality, Beagle calls the fictitious **time** of his story into question. And indeed, time in *The Last Unicorn* proves to be unstable. In the Edenic **garden** of the unicorn's forest, time is suspended in an eternal spring. Yet once she starts out on her journey, the unicorn's progress is described by travelling through the **seasons**, through time, until she reaches Haggard's castle, where time is disturbed and distorted, reflecting the distortedness of the king. The land suffers under unnatural seasons, an almost perpetual winter (in contrast to the spring in the unicorn's forest), and in the castle itself the clock (see **Clocks and Timepieces**), hiding the entrance to the lair of the Red Bull, is broken and never strikes the right hour. Yet time is not only disturbed on the outside, but also on the inside of the clock, where time itself becomes the path to the bull's **caverns** under the castle.

There the unicorn reaches the extent of her travels, which span the symbolic **landscape** from her forest to Haggard's caves. The unicorn's forest resembles paradise; it is a **pastoral** world of peaceful and uncorrupted existence, an **Arcadia** where life passes by unhindered by humans. When she leaves her forest, she enters a decadent world, where people no longer believe in magic and unicorns are no longer recognized. Humankind is described as corrupted and greedy in their ambitions for profit. Haggard's land symbolizes the utmost extent of this corruption, embodied in the people of the cursed village Hagsgate who prefer their wealth to **children**, and thus, to hope. Just as Haggard is the most corrupted character in the novel, his castle harbors the most **evil** place, the bull's caves, this world's version of **Hell**. Yet hope returns to the world with the unicorns, as reflected by the healing of Haggard's wasteland after his **death** and the passing of the unicorns.

Beagle also wrote the screenplay for the animated film version of *The Last Unicorn* (1982), thereby transforming his novel into a story for children. The darker side of the novel, human corruption, is generally downplayed and most intertextual references are removed. Nevertheless, the film contains poignant and beautiful images like the appearance of the Red Bull from a circle of **fire**, so that it might serve as a good introduction to the more complex world of the novel.

Bibliography

George Aichele. "Two Forms of Metafantasy." *Journal of the Fantastic in the Arts*, 1 (1988), 55–68.

R.E. Foust. "Fabulous Paradigm." *Extrapolation*, 21 (Spring, 1980), 5–20.

David M. Miller. "Mommy Fortuna's Ontological Plenum." Michele K. Langford, ed., *Contours of the Fantastic*. Westport, CT: Greenwood Press, 1990, 207–216.

D.P. Norford. "Reality and Illusion in Peter Beagle's *The Last Unicorn*." *Critique*, 19 (1977), 93–104.

A.H. Olsen. "Anti-Consolation." *Mosaic*, 13 (1980), 133–144.

John Pennington. "Innocence and Experience and the Imagination in the World of Peter Beagle." *Mythlore*, 15 (Summer, 1989), 10–16.

David Stevens. "Incongruity in a World of Illusion." *Extrapolation*, 20 (Summer, 1979), 230–237.

David van Becker. "Time, Space and Consciousness in the Fantasy of Peter S. Beagle." *San José Studies*, 1 (1975), 52–61.

—*Sandra Martina Schwab*

THE LEFT HAND OF DARKNESS BY URSULA K. LE GUIN (1969)

∎

Light is the left hand of darkness
and darkness the right hand of light.
Two are one, life and death, lying
together like lovers in kemmer,
like hands joined together,
like the end and the way.

—Ursula K. Le Guin
The Left Hand of Darkness (1969)

Summary

When the planet Gethen (Winter) is discovered by members of the interstellar alliance known as the Ekumen, a Terran male, Genly Ai, is sent to observe the Gethenians and tell them that they are not alone in the universe. The Gethenians are hermaphrodites (see **Androgyny**), with both male and female sexual characteristics, and see the single-sexed Genly Ai as a pervert. Both the Terran and Gethenians have trouble adjusting to the idea that there are other ways of experiencing biological sex. However, as Genly becomes embroiled in the political struggles between two states (see **Politics**), Karhide and Orgoreyn, he is befriended and rescued by Estraven, the one Gethenian he mistrusts. To **escape** Orgoreyn, Genly and Estraven journey across the Ice of Gethen's northern **polar regions**. Learning to know each other through hardship, each character sheds existing prejudices while coming to **love** the other. Genly's escape is completed with his return to Karhide, but Estraven, branded a traitor by Karhide's **king** for supporting the alien, is shot. Genly's return is both triumphal and tragic, as he completes his mission and summons other members of the Ekumenical mission to Gethen from their orbiting ship.

Discussion

The Left Hand of Darkness is the best-known and most controversial of Le Guin's Hainish series of novels and stories. These tales share a common **history** in which the Hainish long ago seeded intelligent life on planets throughout the galaxy. Other novels in the series, notably *The Dispossessed* (1974), focus on different themes, although sex, **gender** and **sexuality** are consistent areas of concern in all Hainish novels. *The Left Hand of Darkness* is narrated primarily by Genly, but also by Estraven, foregrounding their different perspectives.

While *The Dispossessed* is utopian in tone, Le Guin describes *The Left Hand of Darkness* as a "thought experiment," the object being to examine what life might be like in a world without gender. Le Guin asks whether a genderless society would develop harmful practices and institutions like hierarchy, rape, and **war**. Behind such questions lurks the assumption in certain kinds of **feminism** that gender roles deform humanity. Notably, the Hainish series assumes that **humanity** is a quality shared among sentient species, not only inhabitants of **Earth**.

The Left Hand of Darkness has received critical acclaim and is the most taught and researched science fiction novel. Despite feminist underpinnings, *Left Hand* has been attacked by some feminist critics for its use of language and lack of women. Sarah Lefanu maintains that because Le Guin chose to use the pronoun "he" for genderless Gethenians, *The Left Hand of Darkness* becomes a novel about men. Patricia Frazer Lamb and Diana Veith further argue that the heart of the novel is a homosexual affair between Genly, a man, and Estraven, whom readers inescapably regard as male. Le Guin responds to such criticisms primarily by agreeing with them, noting that women have the right to expect more from her and she should have been more courageous in both tackling the language issue and making it obvious that Gethenians could practice **homosexuality** as well as heterosexuality when in kemmer (heat). Le Guin addresses these issues in "Coming of Age in Karhide" (1995), which revisits Gethen to tell a story of sexual maturation from the perspective of a Gethenian for whom the neuter state is normal and both maleness and femaleness are transitory states experienced only through sexual desire.

Since the 1990s, scholars have attempted to balance idolization and criticism, suggesting that readers are capable of imaginative acts and anti-stereotypical **reading** practices allowing them to understand Gethenians as androgynous despite the male pronouns. Christine Cornell points out that Genly, who is not entirely sympathetic, actually "reads" Gethenian society badly, missing clues that would identify Estraven as his only real friend. Such a reading focuses on the process by which Genly—and readers along with him—learns to "read" Gethenians properly.

The Left Hand of Darkness is a novel that draws on Le Guin's background in **anthropology**: her father was a noted anthropologist and her mother wrote about anthropological topics. *The Left Hand of Darkness* portrays a fully realized world in which characters' lives are both similar and dissimilar to those of readers. **Cultural** differences result from both **biology** and environment; the Gethenians are different not just because they are hermaphrodites, but because they live in a world of nearly perpetual winter. Le Guin also portrays them as capable of change; while Karhide continues to be ruled by **kings**, Orgoreyn is developing a different form of social organization. Both peoples, however, share a **mythology** based on their unified biology and opposed to dualism. The quasi-**religion** of the Foretellers, like the mythological tales Le Guin creates for the Gethenians, reflects her interest in Taoism (see **Yin and Yang**).

A powerful, subtle novel, *The Left Hand of Darkness* remains a prime example of how science fiction can capture the imagination of readers and reflect on social and political realities, serving as a model for thinking through issues of gender, biology, and society. Feminist novels written in response to *The Left Hand of Darkness* include Nicola Griffith's *Ammonite* (1993) and Gwyneth Jones's Aleutian trilogy, beginning with *White Queen* (1991). Undoubtedly, *The Left Hand of Darkness* will continue to inspire a variety of responses from new generations of writers and readers.

Bibliography

Craig Barrow and Diana Barrow. "*The Left Hand of Darkness*." *Mosaic*, 20 (Winter, 1987), 83–96.

Christine Cornell. "The Interpretive Journey in Ursula K. Le Guin's *The Left Hand of Darkness*." *Extrapolation*, 42 (Winter, 2001), 317–327.

Mona Fayad. "Aliens, Androgynes and Anthropology." *Mosaic*, 30 (September, 1997), 59–73.

Patricia Frazer Lamb and Diana Veith. "Again, *Left Hand of Darkness*." Donald E. Palumbo, ed., *Erotic Universe*. Westport, CT: Greenwood Press, 1986, 221–231.

Sarah Lefanu. *In the Chinks of the World Machine*. London: Women's Press, 1988.

Ursula K. Le Guin. "Is Gender Necessary?" Le Guin, *Dancing at the Edge of the World*. New York: Harper & Row, 1989, 7–16.

Wendy Pearson. "Sex/uality and the Figure of the Hermaphrodite in Science Fiction." Veronica Hollinger and Joan Gordon, eds., *Edging into the Future*. Philadelphia: University of Pennsylvania Press, 2002, 108–123.

John Pennington. "Exorcising Gender." *Extrapolation*, 41 (Winter, 2000), 351–358.

Warren Rochelle. "The Story, Plato, and Ursula K. Le Guin." *Extrapolation*, 37 (Winter, 1996), 316–329.

—Wendy Pearson

LILITH BY GEORGE MACDONALD (1895)

∎

Summary

Lilith is a **bildungsroman** about **death**—not death in the ordinary sense, but death as an almost sacramental mode of thought (see **Religion**). Most of the novel is set in a **parallel world** that George MacDonald describes as having seven **dimensions**; its physical laws differ from ours, but its moral laws are the same. This realm can be entered through a **mirror**.

The protagonist of the novel is Vane, and the overarching motive of the narrative is his stubborn unwillingness to accept death. His mentor and critic is our ancestor Adam (see **Adam and Eve**), not a savage but (as in Talmudic and Gnostic understanding) a supernatural being still bearing the power of God. Adam has repented and has been entrusted with the **sword** with which the **angel** drove him out of Eden; he appears too as a raven (Noah's messenger of salvation) (see **Birds**) or a librarian, Mr. Raven (see **Libraries**). His wife Eve is maternal **love**; their daughter Mara (sorrow) is the **pain** necessary for eradicating inborn **evil** and is Lilith's counterbalance. Lilith is a vampiric being; the first wife of Adam (in Talmudic folklore), she refused submission, chose individuality, and has become a demonic creature, possessed by **evil**. The ruler of the horrible **city** of Bulika, she is also the Victorian femme fatale.

In the course of the novel, Vane makes four trips to the parallel world and grows spiritually. He sees the **hells** intended for the unredeemed and a dry and wounded land inhabited by **children** who have been frozen by Lilith. He meets and frees Lilith, who attacks our world (see **Vampires**) before being overcome and redeemed by Mara. Vane ultimately cures the land by bringing **water** to it, and he ends in Adam's **dream** state.

Discussion

Certain aspects of *Lilith* seemingly demand that it be regarded as an **allegory**: the name of the protagonist, Vane, suggests that he symbolizes both a thoughtless vanity and an unrepentant worldliness (recalling William Makepeace Thackery's *Vanity Fair* [1848]). The name of the city that Lilith governs, Bulika, is possibly derived from the Hebrew root b-l-k, to destroy, indicating that she is represents an ancient destructive **force**. The restorative water employed in the novel's conclusion simultaneously references human tears, repentance, and the power of growth. Nevertheless, because the novel's narrative incidents are complex, *Lilith* as a whole cannot be neatly analyzed in the manner of John Bunyan's *Pilgrim's Progress* (1678, 1684).

Some of the symbols in *Lilith* can be properly interpreted because they had previously appeared in MacDonald's **fairy tales** for children, albeit in a rather sugar-coated fashion. It is also evident that the novel as a whole is spiritually indebted to the work of the Romantic German poet Novalis (i.e., Friederich Leopold, Freiherr von Hardenberg), whose best works attempted to unite poetry, **philosophy**, and science into an allegory of human existence in the world. For all its abstruseness, *Lilith* conveys one clear message that is common to Christian mysticism (see **Christianity**): the self, the carnal envelope, must die to bring the spiritual Self to life. This sentiment is usually taken figuratively, but in *Lilith* MacDonald seems to have meant it quite literally, making this a singular book, which Elizabeth Saintsbury has described as "a sermon on the resurrection of the dead."

Still, the redemption that MacDonald provides in *Lilith* is decidedly heterodox. The words *Jesus, Christ*, and *God* are not mentioned, and the key concept of theandric redemption by Jesus is lacking, even if one considers Adam an anticipatory type of Christ. Instead, MacDonald outlines a curious process of psychic **evolution**: some individuals, refusing to "die," remain in hells until they have evolved enough to accept death, at which time they enter a purgative **sleep** where dreams seem to purify them. At the next stage they come alive, but MacDonald is silent about what happens to them when they awake: life in a Christian paradise? Mystical union with the Godhead? MacDonald was a Scottish Congregational minister who left his calling because of his unorthodox beliefs, but those beliefs in themselves do not provide answers to the questions he is posing, especially since *Lilith* was his final work, left unfinished and unpublished at the time of his death.

Critical opinion has differed widely on *Lilith*: many are fascinated by its unique atmosphere, but most readers find its gloomy religiosity repellant. According to biography William Raeper, MacDonald himself "was excruciatingly aware of its shortcomings and inadequacies." MacDonald's wife even wanted the story suppressed as inferior work, although his son Greville considered it beautiful and insisted on editing the manuscript for posthumous publication. Later, the renowned poet W.H. Auden praised MacDonald's ability to dredge up unconscious symbolism, while critic Rolland Hein considers it "an uneven performance . . . inferior to *Phantastes*." One regrets that MacDonald did not approach and complete *Lilith* when he was younger and more certain of his material, for in the final analysis, the assessment of another critic, Robert Lee Wolff, seems the strongest and most likely to endure: "one might forgive its cruelty, its ugliness . . . [but] it is feeble, ambiguous, full of senile hatreds."

Bibliography

W.H. Auden. "Introduction." George MacDonald, *The Visionary Novels of George MacDonald*. New York: Noonday Press, 1954, v–x.

Rolland Hein. *The Harmony Within*. Grand Rapids: Christian University Press, 1982.

Janet McCann. "George MacDonald's Romantic Christianity in *Lilith*." *Renascence*, 54 (Winter, 2002), 109–118.

William Raeper. *George MacDonald*. Tring, UK: Lion, 1987.

William Raeper, ed., *The Gold Thread*. Edinburgh: Edinburgh University Press, 1990.

Richard H. Reis. *George MacDonald*. Boston: Twayne, 1972.

Elizabeth Saintsbury. *George MacDonald*. Edinburgh: Canongate, 1987.

J.M. Walker. "The Demoness and the Grail." Robert A. Collins, ed., *Scope of the Fantastic*. Westport, CT: Greenwood Press, 1985, 179–190.

Robert Lee Wolff. *The Golden Key*. New Haven: Yale University Press, 1961.

—Richard Bleiler

THE LION, THE WITCH AND THE WARDROBE BY C.S. LEWIS (1950)

■

Summary

The Lion, the Witch and the Wardrobe recounts the adventures of four young children—Peter, Susan, Edmund, and Lucy Pevensey—in Narnia (see **Parallel Worlds**). When hiding in an old wardrobe in a country house, Lucy enters Narnia, where she meets Tumnus the Faun who tells her about the White **Witch**, so-called **Queen** of Narnia, and says that any human found in Narnia must be brought to her. Edmund also finds his way into Narnia; tricked by the White Witch into thinking she is the true Queen, he promises to bring her his siblings. After hearing about the great lion, Aslan (see **Lions and Tigers**), the others go to the Stone Table to meet him, while Edmund goes to the White Witch. Though Narnians rescue Edmund from the Witch, she goes to Aslan and claims the boy traitor's **blood** by ancient right. But Aslan offers himself in Edmund's place, and that night the Witch slays him on the Stone Table. At sunrise, Aslan is resurrected and helps the children and good Narnians defeat her. The children become **kings** and queens of Narnia. While hunting the White Stag, the now-adult kings and queens see a lamppost in the **forest** and head towards it; they eventually come back through the wardrobe and discover that no time has passed in the real world (see **Timeslips**). The next four books in the series—*Prince Caspian* (1951), *The Voyage of the Dawn Treader* (1952), *The Silver Chair* (1953), and *The Horse and His Boy* (1954)—trace the adventures of the Pevenseys and other children in Narnia; *The Magician's Nephew* (1955) is a prequel about the creation of Narnia; and *The Last Battle* (1956) concludes the series with the destruction of Narnia and transition (for those accepting Aslan) to the idealized Narnia of **Heaven**.

Discussion

The Lion, the Witch and the Wardrobe, the first novel in the Chronicles of Narnia, begins *in medias res* of Narnian **history**; *The Magician's Nephew* explains Aslan's creation of Narnia and the coming of Jadis of Charn (the White Witch of *The Lion, the Witch and the Wardrobe*) into Narnia. She tempts (see **Temptress**) young Diggory Kirke to take an apple from a forbidden tree in an enclosed **garden** to his **mother**, who is sick, but Diggory refuses. Because of his obedience to Aslan, the great lion and the Son of the Emperor-over-the-Sea, Diggory is given the apple to take to his mother for her healing. Later, Diggory plants the appleseeds and grows a tree, from whose wood the wardrobe is made that Lucy and the other Pevensey children use to enter Narnia the first time. Many commentators have written about the correct order for reading the Chronicles, with some suggesting reading them by publication date, beginning with *The Lion, the Witch and the Wardrobe*, and others by internal chronological order, beginning with *The Magician's Nephew*.

Though often read allegorically, C.S. Lewis denied that the Chronicles of Narnia were on **Allegory**. Rather, he called them "supposals," by which he meant that he imagined what the Christian story (see **Christianity; Religion**) would be like if it occurred in a land of **talking animals** and **magic** in everyday life. The character of Aslan is usually read as an image of Christ because he is the Son of the Emperor-over-the-Sea, he **sacrifices** himself to redeem Edmund Pevensey, he rises from the dead (see **Rebirth**), and he has a name in the real world that the children must know him by. Cementing the linkage is the fact that the children, at the end of *The Voyage of the Dawn Treader*, see him as a lamb beside a **fire** with fish on it, specifically referencing John 1.29 and John 21. And at the end of *The Last Battle* (see **Apocalypse**), he ushers in the New Narnia and welcomes all those who have been faithful to him.

On another level, *The Lion, the Witch and the Wardrobe* and its sequels are widely considered to be modern **fairy tale** classics. Narnia is populated with talking animals and a wide variety of **supernatural creatures**: centaurs, dryads, fauns, flying **horses**, minotaurs, naiads, satyrs, **dwarfs**, **giants**, hags, ogres, and **werewolves**. Narnia is a medieval world (see **Medievalism and the Middle Ages**) wherein the code of **chivalry** and virtues such as **courage**, **freedom**, **love**, loyalty, honesty, **reading**, and trust are celebrated while the vices of greed, **divination**, **slavery**, and **torture** are condemned. Another fairy tale element is the battle between good and **evil** that figures prominently in each book. Sometimes the battle is literal, as when Peter kills the wolf Maugrim/Fenris Ulf in *The Lion, the Witch and the Wardrobe* with the **sword** given him by Aslan. At other times the battle is more symbolic, as when Puddleglum, Eustace, and Jill combat the lies of the Queen of Underland in *The Silver Chair* regarding the reality of Narnia, alluding to Plato's famous Allegory of the Cave.

Several commentators note that the Chronicles of Narnia (re)awaken or initiate a **sense of wonder** in the reader. Lewis accomplishes this chiefly by making Aslan a mysterious, enigmatic character. In Narnia, moreover, actions seem to have more significant consequences than in the real world, thus emphasizing the importance of the individual and one's decisions and actions.

Bibliography

Kirk H. Beetz. *Exploring C.S. Lewis' The Chronicles of Narnia.* Osprey, FL: Beacham Publishing Co., 2001.

Paul Ford. *Companion to Narnia.* New York: HarperSanFrancisco, 1994.

Thomas Howard. *The Achievement of C.S. Lewis.* Wheaton, IL: Harold Shaw, 1980.

William G. Johnson and Marcia K. Houtman. "Platonic Shadows in C.S. Lewis's Narnia Chronicles." *Modern Fiction Studies*, 32 (Spring, 1986), 75–87.

Paul A. Karkainen. *Narnia Explored.* Old Tappan, NJ: Fleming H. Revell, 1979.

Colin Manlove. *The Chronicles of Narnia.* New York: Twayne, 1993.

Jay Ruud. "Aslan's Sacrifice and the Doctrine of Atonement in *The Lion, the Witch and the Wardrobe.*" *Mythlore*, 23 (Spring, 2001), 15–21.

M.C. Sammons. *Guide Through Narnia.* Wheaton, IL: Shaw, 1979.

Peter J. Schakel. *Imagination and the Arts in C.S. Lewis.* Columbia: University of Missouri Press, 2002.

—*Theodore James Sherman*

LITTLE, BIG BY JOHN CROWLEY (1981)

∎

Summary

Little, Big, or, The Fairies' Parliament is perhaps the finest standalone fantasy of the 1980s, receiving the 1982 World Fantasy Award. It combines a warm-hearted, multi-generational **family** saga—extending from Victorian England to a decayed **near future** United States—with delicate evocations of **fairies** and other **supernatural creatures**, worlds within worlds (see **Microcosm**), and a high density of allusions to Lewis Carroll's *Alice's Adventures in Wonderland* and its sequel.

Despite past and future ramifications, the main story is contained within the life of Smoky Barnable, an outsider who marries a daughter of the Drinkwater family and is absorbed into their dreamy existence in the remarkable country house Edgewood— built by an eccentric architect as an anthology of **architecture and interior design**, with every facade different. Like other aspects of *Little, Big*, Edgewood may be larger inside than out. A repeated phrase is "The further in you go, the bigger it gets."

Smoky never understands the **secret history** surrounding him, his wife Alice, and others living around Edgewood, who only dimly remember that they inhabit a Story (see **Metafiction and Recursiveness**) and have a **destiny**. Ultimately, the surviving characters—ironically excluding Smoky, who dies on the **threshold**—do not so much attain as become (possibly with some twisting of **time**) the **lost world** of Faerie.

Discussion

The earliest roots of *Little, Big*'s family and narrative lie in the nineteenth-century England of maverick **religions** like theosophy and spiritualism. A vein of **divination** about collective destiny begins here, with a seeress who senses (see **Perception**) but cannot communicate the truth of gateways and **borderlands** with Faerie. In later generations, divination through cards ("The Least Trumps") provides ambiguous guidance. Even the telephone directories that Smoky proofreads contain unrecognized **omens and signs**.

Another Victorian echo is the family member who, like Carroll, is obsessed with both **children** and the **technology** of photography. Reflecting Arthur Conan Doyle's hapless involvement with the "Cottingley Fairies" hoax, he wastes his life taking countless photographs of presumed brownies, **elves**, and fairies, "genuine" yet useless as proof since the underlying reality is incommunicable.

Instead, supernatural presences at Edgewood are taken for granted, to the extent of becoming invisible through familiarity. Smoky's father-in-law writes children's books about **talking animals**, with dialogue cribbed from actual animal conversation. The oracular fish "Grandfather Trout" (see **Fish and Sea Creatures**) is a human victim of **metamorphosis**; later another character becomes a tree (see **Plants**) and a third unwillingly achieves **reincarnation** in **bird** form. **Personifications** like Father **Christmas** and Father Time appear in brief, matter-of-fact glimpses. The household includes a changeling and, for Smoky's son Auberon, a not wholly imaginary companion. There is an orrery (see **Clocks and Timepieces**), which in a magical **role reversal** does not merely reflect the heavens but is driven by them, a working perpetual motion machine. Edgewood life has the quality of a delicious and comforting though intermittently disturbing **dream**.

Contrasting **darkness** and danger inhabit the **city**, a decayed New York that is specifically equated with the Wild Wood of Kenneth Grahame's *The Wind in the Willows* (1908). Abandoned city blocks have become **farms**, walled by buildings against **evil** on the streets. The grown Auberon seeks his fortune there, not with great success, but he does finds **love** with the Puerto Rican Sylvie—who in another Carrollian echo has a brother called Bruno. Sylvie has a personal destiny, prophesied by a **witch**, and a secret family nickname mentioned just once in the text: Titania, also one name of the fairy **queen**.

Also city-based is the **politics** of power; the U.S. inner circle called the Noisy Bridge Rod and Gun Club is troubled by the rise of a charismatic leader who proves the returned or reincarnated Holy Roman Emperor Frederick Barbarossa. This is discovered by the mage Ariel Hawksquill, another Edgewood family connection, whose **magic** includes a grisly means of **invisibility** but is principally based on Giordano Bruno's Art of **Memory**, adapted as a means of divination. Crowley returns to Bruno and the Art in his novel sequence beginning with *Aegypt* (1987).

A central image of *Little, Big* is the **garden** of Carroll's *Through the Looking Glass* (1871), an elusive **labyrinth** where desired goals can be reached only by walking in the opposite direction. This is represented overtly by a city-square garden and metaphorically by the indicated futility of all direct assault on the **mysteries** of Edgewood and its Story. Those who have given up seeking, have forgotten to seek, or no longer believe the old **fairy tale** of a family Story are unknowingly closest to the final revelation and transition.

The transition itself is not **death**—as some fear—but an equally irrevocable metamorphosis. Auberon and Sophie-Titania take on new roles as **king** and queen of a realm infinitely smaller or larger than ours, with the extended family as their court (the Fairies' Parliament), and Smoky's Alice becomes a kind of goddess.

Little, Big is a hauntingly memorable fantasy, lush with nostalgia for times and places that never quite existed, and departed glories "as once upon a time they were" (the book's final words). Crowley's sometimes indirect, sometimes elliptical, sometimes audacious handling of fantastic tropes carries conviction through delicacy of touch and sensual prose.

Bibliography

Michael Bishop. "*Little, Big*." *Foundation*, No. 27 (February, 1983), 80–82.

John Clute. "*Little, Big*." *Interzone*, No. 2 (Summer, 1982), 31.

Paul Kincaid. "*Little, Big*." *Vector*, No. 106 (February, 1982), 33–35.

David Pringle. "*Little, Big* by John Crowley (1981)." Pringle, *Modern Fantasy: The Hundred Best Novels*. London: Grafton, 1988, 211–213.

Thelma J. Shinn. "Fable of Reality: Mythoptics in John Crowley's *Little, Big*." *Extrapolation*, 31 (Spring, 1990), 5–14.

Jennifer Stevenson. "Memory and the World of John Crowley." *New York Review of Science Fiction*, No. 119 (July, 1998), 1, 8–11.

Sue Thomason. "*Little, Big*." *Paperback Inferno*, 47 (April, 1984), 12–13.

Alice K. Turner. "Daily Alice's Childhood" and "Thornton W. Burgess and *Little, Big*." *The New York Review of Science Fiction*, No. 137 (January, 2000), 9–10.

Alice K. Turner and Michael Andre-Driussi, eds. *Snake's-Hands: The Fiction of John Crowley*. Holicong, PA: Cosmos Books, 2003.

—*David Langford*

LOOKING BACKWARD, 2000–1887 BY EDWARD BELLAMY (1887)

■

> *As men grow more civilized, and the subdivision of occupations and services is carried out, a complex mutual dependence becomes the universal rule. Every man, however solitary may seem his occupation, is a member of a vast industrial partnership, as large as the nation, as large as humanity. The necessity of mutual dependence should imply the duty and guarantee of mutual support; and that it did not in your day constituted the essential cruelty and unreason of your system.*
>
> —Edward Bellamy
> *Looking Backward, 2000–1887* (1887)

Summary

In 1886 Julian West, a severe insomniac, builds underground sleeping quarters, where a hypnotist sends him into **sleep** (see **Hypnotism**). Through some unexplained accident, Julian does not awaken until the year 2000. Joining the **family** of Dr. Leete, an official in New Boston, he learns through conversations and guided tours that New Boston is a syndicalist, socialist **utopia**. People are organized into guilds, including the professions of **medicine, education, art,** literature, and **journalism.** Guilds are combined into a single organization known as the work or industrial army, which is central to the new culture; rank and job specialization are assigned according to elaborate qualification mechanisms. Men and women remain in the educational system until they are twenty-one years old, then they serve in the work army for twenty-four years. People are first assigned rough work, but gradually are sorted into specialties. Women follow the same life pattern as men, but are allowed maternity leave. Everyone works for the state and receives the same wage, paid by a yearly credit card, against which the worker buys price-controlled items; the state guarantees everyone **food and drink** from communal dining halls, housing, and jobs.

There are no **money**, no **crime and punishment**, no lawyers, no **war**, no army, and no navy. Dissidents are assumed to be suffering from **madness** and placed in mental institutions. While absorbing and responding positively to this information, Julian falls in **love** with Leete's daughter, and after a brief nightmare about returning to his former time, he prepares for a long, happy life in New Boston.

Discussion

The last quarter of the nineteenth century saw great social and political turmoil in the United States, when several idea-movements attained power: socialism (state control of utilities), communism (restriction of personal property), land ownership reform (Henry George's land tax), syndicalism (guild-structured government), free silver (abandonment of the gold standard), and universal suffrage (women permitted to vote), to say nothing of more eccentric systems. The result was many literary works describing various kinds of ideal societies. Among these panaceas, the one that aroused the most enthusiasm was Bellamism, a form of regimented socialism created by Edward Bellamy, a well-known mainstream writer who propounded it novelistically in two books, *Looking Backward, 2000–1887* and its sequel *Equality* (1897).

Although Bellamy sets his ideal society in the future, he is not greatly interested in technological or scientific advances, which receive little attention. His interest focuses on the state, with a few simple ideas: a utopia can be attained without violent class struggle (see **Class System**); political and economic change is an evolutionary process; regimentation assures efficiency and felicity; and **humanity** is more or less perfectible in the context of the proper environment.

As the summary suggests, most of the novel consists of long conversations, usually involving Dr. Leete explaining and praising his new society to an attentive Julian—the typical format of utopias. But Bellamy was also a skillful writer of fiction who could sporadically make characters seem persuasively real, and not just authorial mouthpieces, and the novel to this date makes for reasonably entertaining reading. Demanding special attention is the conclusion of the novel, clearly indebted to the final passages of Jonathan Swift's *Gulliver's Travels*, in which traveler Julian returns **home** and, transformed by his experiences in a better society, now regards everything he had previously accepted as normal as a miasma of unspeakable **horrors**. The novel might have ended more effectively if it had left Julian in the Boston of 1886, inspired by a new resolve to improve his world to achieve the ideal conditions he had observed. However, motivated by a passionate belief in his own ideas, and well aware that crusading reformers are often denigrated as "dreamers," Bellamy did not want to authorially invalidate his carefully constructed alternative to contemporary **America** by having it ultimately revealed as "only a dream." Thus, by returning Julian to the utopia of New Utopia, his new reality, Bellamy reaffirms that it is not simply a fantasy, but a **governance system** that might actually be constructed within the next hundred years.

In *Equality* (and two minor papers) Bellamy answers questions readers had raised about *Looking Backward* and attempts to refute criticisms. *Equality* describes the total emancipation of women, state ownership of land, the reduction of **religion** to the social gospel, the absence of economic corruption, and cancellation of the boom-and-bust production cycle. Dr. Leete describes in more detail the non-violent class struggle that produced the new **culture**. During **air travel** over New

Boston Dr. Leete reveals that electricity is now the main source of power. Bellamistic states cover the world and a universal language is in use.

Bellamy's novel inspired numerous responses, some of them sympathetic to his ideas: Edward Berwick's "Farming in the Year 2000 A.D." (1890) and Ludwig A. Geissler's *Looking Beyond* (1891) extend Bellamy's system to **farms** and rural life, while Solomon Schindler's *Young West* (1894) fleshes out details of life in a Bellamistic world while wondering whether Bellamistic economic security is too high a price for loss of individual **freedom**. Others harshly attacked Bellamy, often characterizing his work army as a euphemism for **slavery**: Richard Michaelis's *Looking Further Forward* (1890) criticizes Bellamy's suppression of dissent, impossible economic controls, and government from above; Pauline Carsten Curtis's "In the Year '26" (1890) suggests that rapacious individuals in New Boston still could evade laws and inspectors to gain power and wealth; and Conrad Wilbrandt's *Mr. East's Experiences in Mr. Bellamy's World* (1891) uses classical economic theory to demonstrated that Bellamy's system is flawed. Bellamy's influence is felt less strongly today, although he did inspire one modern rewriting of *Looking Backward*, Mack Reynolds's *Looking Backward, From the Year 2000* (1973), followed by *Equality in the Year 2000* (1977).

Bibliography

Merritt Abrash. "*Looking Backward*: Marxism Americanized." *Extrapolation*, 30 (Fall, 1989), 237–242.

Sylvia E. Bowman. *Edward Bellamy Abroad*. Boston: Twayne, 1962.

———. *Edward Bellamy*. Boston: Twayne, 1986.

Martin Gardner. "Looking Backward at Edward Bellamy's Utopia." *The New Criterion*, 19 (September, 2000), 19–25.

Wilfred M. McClay. "Reappraisal: Edward Bellamy and the Politics of Meaning." *American Scholar*, 64 (Spring, 1995), 264–271.

Daphne Patai, ed. *Looking Backward, 1988–1888*. Amherst: University of Massachusetts Press, 1988.

Harold V. Rhodes. *Utopia in American Political Thought*. Tucson: University of Arizona Press, 1967.

Phillip E. Wegner. *Imaginary Communities*. Berkeley: University of California Press, 2002.

Toby Widdicombe and Herman S. Preiser. *Revisiting the Legacy of Edward Bellamy*. Lewiston, PA: Edwin Mellen, 2002.

—*Gary Westfahl*

Lord Foul's Bane
by Stephen R. Donaldson (1977)

Summary

An author named Thomas Covenant (see **Writing and Authors**) has lost everything due to a sudden onset of leprosy (see **Plagues and Diseases**). He is mysteriously transported to The Land, a **parallel world** infused with a **beauty** and inherent health that is tangible—an Eden inhabited by people dedicated to its preservation and

natural well-being who regard Covenant as a reincarnated **hero** (see **Reincarnation**). Counterpoised against this **Arcadia** is an ancient enemy, Lord Foul the Despiser, who seeks to use Covenant as a catalyst to destroy the Land and free himself of its power, by which he is imprisoned. Believing his experiences are all a **dream**, however, Covenant becomes an anti-hero, at odds with what he perceives as an **imaginary world**, continuing the **estrangement** he experienced in his own life. This premise allows Donaldson to explore the meaning of good and **evil**, despair and hope (see **Optimism and Pessimism**), **guilt and responsibility**, **crime and punishment**, beauty and corruption, **love** and hatred, **courage** and cowardice, honor and **betrayal**, **hubris** and acceptance, **individualism and conformity**, and the self versus **sacrifice**, all within the context of an existential odyssey of the soul.

Discussion

Donaldson's initial Chronicles of Thomas Covenant—*Lord Foul's Bane*, *The Illearth War* (1977), and *The Power That Preserves* (1977)—attracted some readers because Donaldson was drawing upon many of the conventions established by J.R.R. Tolkien's *The Lord of the Rings* and similar works. However, he uses these themes for ends more attuned to contemporary issues of relative existence and our place within the world—the very nature of choice and responsibility. This is unlike most **heroic fantasy**, which assumes a world in which right and wrong, acceptance and rejection—indeed **perception**—are clearly identified matters. Donaldson further sought to repudiate the Christian values and romantic elements (see **Christianity**) underlying Tolkien's writing by employing a central character who actively undermines the traditional ideals of heroism.

Time, in its more modern sense, also plays a significant role because it both is measured differently in Donaldson's two worlds and also serves as a **prison** and fundamental mortise for The Land's **cosmology**. The appearances of the **Sun** and **Moon** are barometers of health and corruption, the former eventually becoming a metaphor for environmental pollution (see **Ecology**). Many of the story's players are restricted by systems of **taboos**, and **blood** becomes an informing theme, both in terms of **identity** as well as **ritual** and **magic**. Further, not only do **suicide** and **death** haunt many characters, but Donaldson's fantasy is far more grim and graphic in its use of **torture** and **violence**, including a rape that later leads to implications of incest (see **Sexuality**), which are elements that connect the series to **horror** and **dark fantasy**. Finally, in continually shifting between the contemporary world and an imaginary realm—even if eventually devolving into contrivance—the narrative attempts to bridge the gulf between realism and fantastic fiction, in this respect anticipating the themes and tone of **urban fantasy**.

Unlike Tolkien and other fantasists, Donaldson also eschews clear redemptive conclusions, and what triumphs or successes his heroes have in battling Lord Foul and his minions are equally accompanied by **tragedy** and unanticipated consequences which lead to further struggles in the books that follow. The first trilogy ends with a triumph that, it eventually transpires, will be undone in a few millennia, and Covenant returns to his own world with imminent threats of eviction and death thwarted but no lasting improvements in his circumstances, except what he has learned about himself, the nature of despair, and his will to confront it.

The Second Chronicles of Thomas Covenant—*The Wounded Land* (1980), *The One Tree* (1982), and *White Gold Wielder* (1983)—return Covenant to The Land several thousand years later, now under even greater threat larger due to his own choices and actions in previous novels. This trilogy follows the more conventional format of a **quest** to replace The Staff of Law lost in the first trilogy, which is needed to restore the natural order and defeat a reinvigorated Lord Foul. Though Donaldson further explores earlier themes, he does little to expand upon them, beyond differences in the surface narrative and the introduction of Linden Avery, a conflicted **love** interest who shares many of Covenant's own doubts and despairs and serves as an alternate **mirror** for his own role. However, its conclusion offers more finality, as Covenant comes to terms with himself and his relationship to The Land as well as Lord Foul. Through the **sacrifice** of his death—foreshadowed in the real world by the opening of The Second Chronicles—Covenant destroys Lord Foul, a nemesis who personified not only The Land's corruption but Covenant's as well. Linden Avery is left to restore The Land and return to her own world, where Covenant is already dead.

Donaldson's two Chronicles—especially the first—remain one of the most important, thematically complex, and individual works of epic fantasy written by an American writer. After a hiatus of two decades, Donaldson decided to begin a third and concluding series with *The Runes of the Earth* (2004); readers hope that its projected four books will both significantly expand upon the motifs of the earlier books and move in stimulating new directions.

Bibliography

Christine Barkley. "Donaldson as Heir to Tolkien." *Mythlore*, 10 (Spring, 1984), 50–57.
Malcolm Edwards and Robert Holdstock. *Realms of Fantasy*. Garden City, NY: Doubleday, 1983.
Matthew A. Fike. "The Hero's Education in Sacrificial Love." *Mythlore*, 14 (Summer, 1988), 34–38.
Matthew A. Fike. "Nature as Supernature." *Mythlore*, 18 (Spring, 1992), 17–20, 22.
Margaret Hammit-McDonald. "Textual Surveillance of Masculinity." Susanne Fendler and Ulrike Horstmann, eds., *Images of Masculinity in Fantasy Fiction*. Lewiston, ME: Edwin Mellen Press, 2003, 165–182.
Pythia Peay. "Magic and the Imagination." *Bloomsbury Review*, 3 (April/May, 1983), 15–19.
W.A. Senior. *Stephen R. Donaldson's Chronicles of Thomas Covenant*. Kent, OH: Kent State University Press, 1995.
Gordon E. Slethaug. "The Discourse of Arrogance, Popular Power, and Anarchy." *Extrapolation*, 34 (Spring, 1993), 48–63.
Cynthia L. Walker. "They're Fusing Just the Way They Should." Michelle K. Langford, ed., *Contours of the Fantastic*. Westport, CT: Greenwood Press, 1990, 141–147.

—*William Thompson*

LORD OF LIGHT BY ROGER ZELAZNY (1967)

■

Summary

Long ago, the starship *The Star of India* colonized an **alien world**. Its crew controlled and misused the **technology**, becoming effectively immortal (see **Immortality and Longevity**) because they could transfer their consciousnesses into new bodies.

Their long-lived minds ultimately developed **psychic powers**, and the crew became identified with Hindu deities (see **Gods and Goddesses**). As such, they shaped and warped the technological and social **evolution** of the masses on the planet for their own ends. Divine dissension arises when one of the original crew believes that his fellow gods have become corrupt; he wants to let the masses develop technology freely and to permit the dispersal of ideas recalling Buddhism (see **Religion**). This colonist, Mahasamatman, prefers to be called Sam (see **Messiahs**). His psychic power is the control of electromagnetic forces; he is the Lord of Light whose powers enabled him to bind the original inhabitants of the planet, the Rakasha. Sam leads a revolution that fails (see **Rebellion; War**) and as punishment is sentenced to nirvana: his **identity** is broadcast into the planet's magnetic field (see **Crime and Punishment**). However, the Rakasha have given him the capacity to maintain a discorporate identity, and Sam's followers reincarnate him to lead another, more successful revolution, though his victory is not without personal cost.

Discussion

Lord of Light owes much to the ideas endemic during the 1960s, particularly the belief in the adage that "the truth will set you free." In Sam's valiant struggle against a corrupt establishment, he epitomizes the counterculture **hero** or the **freedom** marcher of the 1960s, a person who is at **home** in established "society" yet who has rejected most of its values in recognizing that power should lie with the people.

There is presently a tendency, particularly by English and European critics, to denigrate many of Roger Zelazny's writings, and *Lord of Light* is not immune from their criticism. Two of its more notable flaws involve plotting and structure. Each chapter has in effect two prefaces, one in deliberately archaic and highly "romantic" language that tells the **history** of Sam and his fellow deities, the other from a Vedic treatise (among them the *Dhammapada* [c. 250 BCE], the *Anguttara-nikaya* [c. 250 BCE], and the *Chandogya Upanishad* [c. 550 BCE]) that recounts the same events; the rest of the chapter generally consists of a parallel exegesis that moves the character to the next heroic or dramatic event. Needless to say, the value of all this redundancy can be questioned. Furthermore, and unnecessarily, the novel starts *in media res*, with Sam's reincarnation, followed by an extended flashback that brings Sam (and the reader) up to the present.

A third problem, though, may be most damning for contemporary readers. While the novel's premises are rooted in the values of the 1960s, its dialogue tends to reveal auctorial attitudes and mores from the 1950s, as when Sam baits Brahma into revealing that he was a woman by stating, "what's it feel like, madam, to be a real stud after having been a gal to start out with? Bet every Lizzie in the world would envy you if she knew." Indeed, and embarrassingly enough, *Lord of Light* might be regarded as the last major work of science fiction that evidences a significant degree of old-fashioned **sexism**.

Nevertheless, even if it does not qualify as a work for all times and all seasons, there remains much to commend about *Lord of Light*. In its idiosyncratic attempts to justify the ways of gods to men, the novel no more patronizes its subject matter than does John Milton's *Paradise Lost* (1667). And in depictions of **cultures** and portrayal of religions, as well as in the questions it raises about messiahs and divinities, it is successful and thought-provoking.

Further, while it is not the first fantastic work to make use of non-Christian beliefs—since Greek and Roman classics have been euhemerised by any number of writers—it is one of the first to make a sustained use of Buddhist lore as its narrative device, particularly those writings that seek to present aspects of Hindu **mythology** in an irreverent, anti-brahminical light. In this respect, the novel is again a perfect reflection of its era, since it was precisely at the time of its publication that the Beatles were helping to popularize Indian **music** and **philosophy**; yet Zelazny made a serious effort to capture both the colorful surface features and underlying depths of the Hindu religion.

Lord of Light is finally an exemplary work for studying the rise of the American New Wave of science fiction writers during the 1960s, illuminating both the worthwhile innovations and troubling excesses of that movement—although, of course, all writers now considered key figures in that movement deny that they were part of any movement at all. Still, whatever conclusions one might draw, *Lord of Light* remains an ambitious effort that reveals a talented writer approaching the height of his considerable powers. It is likely to endure when the majority of Zelazny's later work has faded from view.

Bibliography

Joseph V. Francavilla. "Promethean Bound." Robert Reilly, ed., *The Transcendent Adventure*. Westport: Greenwood, 1984, 207–222.
Joseph V. Francavilla. "These Immortals." *Extrapolation*, 25 (Spring, 1984), 20–33.
S.C. Fredericks. "Roger Zelazny and the Trickster Myth." *Journal of American Culture*, 2 (Summer, 1979), 271–278.
Theodore Krulik. *Roger Zelazny*. New York: Ungar, 1986.
Jane Lindskold. *Roger Zelazny*. New York: Twayne, 1993.
Michael Moorcock. *Wizardry and Wild Romance*. London: Victor Gollancz, 1987.
Joe Sanders. "Dancing on the Tightrope." Carl B. Yoke and Donald M. Hassler, eds., *Death and the Serpent*. Westport, CT: Greenwood Press, 1985, 135–144.
Joe Sanders. "Zelazny: Unfinished Business." Thomas D. Clareson, ed., *Voices for the Future, Volume 2*. Bowling Green, OH: Bowling Green State University Popular Press, 1979, 180–196.

—*Richard Bleiler*

LORD OF THE FLIES BY WILLIAM GOLDING (1954)

■

> *With filthy body, matted hair, and unwiped nose, Ralph wept for the end of innocence, the darkness of man's heart, and the fall through the air of the true, wise friend called Piggy.*
>
> —William Golding
> *Lord of the Flies* (1954)

Summary

A party of English public schoolboys is shipwrecked on a remote **island** while being evacuated from some unspecified **disaster**. The first thing they realize is that there are no adults around: to survive, they must call upon their own resources. Fair-haired Ralph tries to mimic adult order, calling all the boys together in a council and using a conch shell as a symbol of authority. He is assisted by Piggy—overweight, short-sighted, and suffering from asthma—who is the inevitable butt of schoolboy jokes. An older boy, Jack, first seen leading a group of choirboys as though they were soldiers on parade, is the focus of opposition to Ralph, at first through his authoritarianism and later through his embrace of wildness. The discovery of a dead parachutist dangling from trees in the heart of the island is like an irruption of the irrational. The **children** do not understand what they see, so he becomes a **monster**, a **demon**, the Lord of the Flies, both representing and sanctioning the boys' increasing primitivism (see **Barbarians**). Under Jack's lead the children revert to savagery, painting their faces and responding to ever darker superstitions, until eventually they turn completely against the civilized order represented by Ralph. Piggy is murdered, and Ralph himself survives only by the fortuitous arrival of a Royal Navy rescue ship. The impeccably clad officer does not understand the fall from grace that occurred on the island, imagining that the boys have simply been playing **games**.

Discussion

William Golding was a teacher at an English public school when he wrote this, his first novel. He has said that he wrote it to counter the image of boys preserving English **civilization** presented in R.M. Ballantyne's *The Coral Island* (1857), and the names Jack and Ralph deliberately echo the names of characters in that popular children's book. But he also used the novel to express his religious beliefs about the fallibility of man, beliefs that would surface again and again in later books, notably *Free Fall* (1959) and *Pincher Martin* (1956). The boys on this island are not just reverting to savagery; they are falling from grace, which is made explicit at the end of the novel when Ralph "wept for the end of innocence, the darkness of man's heart, and the fall through the air of the true, wise friend called Piggy."

Like any novel about islands, *Lord of the Flies* is concerned with **survival**, but not simply physical survival. The children seem to have enough food: true, the officer at the end, our only adult perspective on what has happened, notices that some boys have "distended bellies," but there is no real sense of hunger; it is their spiritual survival that is at stake. In that respect, Piggy's death might be seen as a **sacrifice** that redeems Ralph, though the **rituals** invented by Jack and the increasingly savage children and the **taboos** they break—particularly that of murder—show that they can never again achieve innocence.

Nor is it just the innocence of childhood that lies at the heart of this novel. On this island the **post-holocaust society** that the boys create is a **microcosm** of our wider modern world. Ballantyne suggested that, when all else was lost, **education** was all that was needed to preserve a decent, successful society, that civilization is inherent in us and needs only our best wishes to survive. Golding conveys quite the opposite—that what is inherent in **humanity** is savagery, and civilization is something that might be lost all too easily without a struggle. Nor is this savagery confined to schoolboys. Although we never witness the **future war** that brought the boys to this island in the first place, its existence is tangible throughout the novel, and as the boys grow more wild we see by reflection the **war** degenerating similarly. One must remember that *Lord of the Flies* was written at roughly the same time as, and out of the same consciousness that generated, the despairing vision of **apocalypse** we find in Nevil Shute's *On The Beach* (1960) and Peter George's *Red Alert* (1958).

Lord of the Flies has twice been filmed. The first version, in 1963, stayed remarkably true to the novel, inasmuch it was still a time when it was shocking to realize that well-brought-up English boys might revert to savagery and murder. However, the remake, in 1990, translated the English schoolboys into older American teenagers so that the fall from grace loses its resonance and the story becomes one of straightforward survival, macho posturing, and sexual awakening far removed from the emotional and spiritual impact of Golding's novel.

Bibliography

Jeanne Delbaere-Garant. "Rhythm and Expansion in *Lord of the Flies*." Jack I. Biles and Robert O. Evans, eds., *William Golding*. Lexington, KY: University Press of Kentucky, 1978, 72–86.

John F. Fitzgerald and John R. Kayser. "Pride as Original Sin." *Studies in the Novel*, 24 (Spring, 1992), 78–88.

William Golding. "Utopias and Antiutopias." Golding, *A Moving Target*, London: Faber and Faber, 1982, 171–184.

Suzanne Gulbin. "Parallels and Contrasts in *Lord of the Flies* and *Animal Farm*." *English Journal*, 55 (January, 1966), 86–88.

Peter Hollindale. "*Lord of the Flies* in the Twenty-First Century." *Use of English*, 53 (Autumn, 2001), 1–12.

Maurice L. McCullen. "*Lord of the Flies*: The Critical Quest." Jack I. Biles and Robert O. Evans, eds., *William Golding*. Lexington: University Press of Kentucky, 1978, 203–236.

George Purvin. "Golding's *Lord of the Flies*: An Alternate Interpretation." *Media and Methods*, 17 (September, 1980), 53–54.

Kathleen Woodward. "On Aggression." Eric S. Rabkin, Martin H. Greenberg, and Joseph D. Olander, eds., *No Place Else*. Carbondale: Southern Illinois University Press, 1983, 199–224.

—Paul Kincaid

THE LORD OF THE RINGS
BY J.R.R. TOLKIEN (1954–1955)

Three Rings for the Elven-kings under the sky,
*   Seven for the Dwarf-lords in their halls of stone,*
Nine for Mortal Men doomed to die,
*   One for the Dark Lord on his dark throne*

In the Land of Mordor where the Shad-
ows lie.
    One Ring to rule them all, One Ring
to find them,
        One Ring to bring them all and in the
darkness bind them
In the Land of Mordor where the Shad-
ows lie.

—J.R.R. Tolkien
The Fellowship of the Ring (1954)

Summary

When Bilbo Baggins, a hobbit of the Shire—hobbits being a short, human-like race, fond of beer, good food, and staying at home (see *The Hobbit*)—vanishes with the aid of his **magic** ring, it is the beginning of the end of his nephew Frodo's hopes for a contented life. Frodo inherits the **Ring**, which attracts the attention, first, of the benevolent **wizard** Gandalf, and then of several menacing black riders, before whom Frodo must flee, into the larger, unknown world in the company of Sam Gamgee and two other friends. The jolly tone of the story's opening quickly darkens, as the hobbits' journey becomes a nightmare punctuated by brief moments of wonder. The One Ring of Power, which Frodo bears, was forged by Sauron, a monstrous embodiment of **evil**, in the remote past. It now seeks to be reunited with its master.

Frodo's **quest**, unlike that of most heroes in the look-alike fantasies that followed in the wake of Tolkien's success, is strikingly not to *obtain* a **magical object** but to get rid of one—for Frodo must carry the Ring into Sauron's domain and cast it into the **fires** from which it was forged. As the Ring corrodes all who bear it, if Frodo dallies, he will lose the moral strength to complete his mission. Initially accompanied by Gandalf, two men, a **dwarf**, an **elf**, and the other hobbits, Frodo and Sam are later assisted only by Gollum, a debased hobbit who once owned, and desperately hopes to regain, the Ring. Epic struggles ensue, against the backdrop of the War of the Ring, as Sauron strives to conquer Middle-earth. The Ring is finally destroyed, but at great cost. A shattered Frodo has no place left in the world and passes on an elven ship into the West, out of the mortal lands (see **Immortality and Longevity**).

Discussion

Tolkien himself denied that *The Lord of the Rings* should be read as **allegory**, for the World Wars, the atomic bomb, or anything else, and was offended by suggestions that in Sauron's bestial orcs he had demonized the German soldiers of World War I. One must take him at his word, but certainly much of the intensity of writing, with its depictions of struggle and **sacrifice**, stemmed from Tolkien's own experiences in the Battle of the Somme, arguably the most horrific military encounter in **history**, from which Tolkien only **escaped** by a fortuitous bout of trench fever. Everyone else he knew in the army was killed.

But of course *The Lord of the Rings* is more than fantasized autobiography. Out of the carnage of the Somme came an epic myth, which, Tolkien would doubtless argue, was just as valid a response to the experience as Erich Maria Remarque's *All Quiet on the Western Front* (1929). Tolkien drew on his own reading in ancient and medieval literature (he was a leading Anglo-Saxon scholar) to celebrate heroism in a manner (see **Heroes**) quite out of step with the twentieth century. While Tolkien can write funny verse or delightful **children**'s stories, he is, in *The Lord of the Rings*, completely serious, without the postmodern irony one finds in other fantasies. There is no parody, no sly winks that, hey, it is just make-believe. This is Tolkien's greatest strength; it astonishes and refreshes jaded, modern readers. Its spirit may be found in Anglo-Saxon heroic poetry, particularly in the doomed characters of *The Battle of Maldon* (c. 950), one of whom remarks, toward the end, "Thought shall be the harder, heart the keener, courage the greater, as our might lessens." So too must the defenders of Tolkien's Gondor have felt at the darkest hour.

The Lord of the Rings is carved out of a much larger mass of mythic writings, on which Tolkien labored most of his adult life. Numerous volumes of alternate drafts and miscellaneous material appeared after his death, the most anticipated of which was *The Silmarillion* (1977), a mythic history (or Elvish Bible) going back to the very creation of the author's **imaginary world**, on such a time-scale that the events of the famous trilogy are related in less than a page. Lacking the humanizing viewpoint of the hobbits, it never proved as popular as the original trilogy. But ultimately the source for all of Tolkien's imaginings is his fascination with **language and linguistics**. He created the peoples of Middle-earth as speakers for invented Elvish languages, and then told the story to bring them to life.

Michael Swanwick has commented that when one reads *The Lord of the Rings* in adolescence, it is the most exciting adventure story (see **Heroic Fantasy**) in the world. In middle age, it seems infinitely sad, because it is about good people struggling with all their strength against evil, but nevertheless losing everything they have ever valued. Sauron may be defeated, but the elves are leaving Middle-earth. The magic fades. Again, avoiding allegorical interpretations, we cannot escape an association with the loss of childhood and inevitable confrontation with **death**. If any work resonates on many levels, it is *The Lord of the Rings*, which goes far toward explaining its position as one of the major literary works of the twentieth century, and certainly the most popular.

Bibliography

Humphrey Carpenter. *Tolkien*. Boston: Houghton Mifflin, 1977.

George Clark and Daniel Thomas, eds. *J.R.R. Tolkien and His Literary Resonances*. Westport, CT: Greenwood Press, 2000.

L. Sprague de Camp. "Merlin in Tweeds: J.R.R. Tolkien." De Camp, *Literary Swordsmen and Sorcerers*. Sauk City, WI: Arkham House, 1976, 215–251.

Verlyn Flieger and Carl F. Hostetter, eds. *Tolkien's Legendarium*. Westport CT: Greenwood Press, 2000.

John Garth. *Tolkien and the Great War*. Boston: Houghton Mifflin, 2003.

Karen Haber, ed. *Meditations on Middle Earth*. New York: St. Martin's Press, 2001.

Paul H. Kocher. *Master of Middle-earth*. Boston: Houghton Mifflin, 1972.

Tom Shippey. *J.R.R. Tolkien: Author of the Century*. London: HarperCollins, 2002.

—*Darrell Schweitzer*

THE LORD OF THE RINGS: THE FELLOWSHIP OF THE RING (2001)

Summary

Director Peter Jackson's *The Lord of the Rings: The Fellowship of the Ring*, *The Lord of the Rings: The Two Towers* (2002), and *The Lord of the Rings: The Return of the King* (2003) were filmed simultaneously, though additional footage was shot while preparing the second and third films. With omissions and minor changes that only purists could object to (and they did), the films accurately retell the story of J.R.R. Tolkien's *The Lord of the Rings*. Frodo Baggins, member of a diminutive race known as hobbits, obtains a **magic** ring from his uncle Bilbo (whose story is told in Tolkien's *The Hobbit*). The **wizard** Gandalf has learned that this ancient **ring** is desperately sought by the **evil** Sauron, who can successfully reconquer Middle-earth if he obtains its powers. A fellowship of hobbits, humans, a **dwarf**, an **elf**, and Gandalf forms to accompany Frodo to fiery Mount Doom, the only place the Ring can be destroyed, but ultimately only Frodo and fellow hobbit Sam Gamgee are left to accomplish the task, while others—prominently including exiled **King** Aragorn—are separated from Frodo and become involved in epic battles against Sauron's armies of vile orcs (see **Goblins**). With assistance from their unreliable ally Gollum—a former hobbit, turned into a **monster** by long possession of the Ring, which he desperately wants back—Frodo and Sam eventually destroy the Ring, dooming Sauron, as Aragorn attains his throne and marries the elf woman Arwen. Later, while Sam settles into contented domesticity, the still troubled Frodo accompanies Bilbo and the elves on a westward voyage symbolic of **death**.

Discussion

In most respects, these films are magnificent achievements that fully do justice to Tolkien's classic. Effective use of the natural **landscapes** of New Zealand, and evocative renderings of the sentient trees known as ents (see **Forests**), convey that this is a conflict between the beautiful **nature** of Middle-earth and the demonic **technology** of Sauron's ally Saruman, who constructs a dismal factory to construct orc-warriors. Although the producers' requirement that Jackson tell the entire story within a three-hours-per-film limitation left little time for singing Tolkien's songs, the film's lush, omnipresent score appropriately adds the **music** that Tolkien would have wanted for his fantasy world, and a haunting song by Annie Lennox nicely concludes the final film. While the computer-generated orcs and Gollum attracted more attention, the understated makeup employed for the ethereal elves, the dignified **elder race** of Middle-earth, was just as striking. The language of the scripts is either directly derived from Tolkien or reminiscent of his style, including passing use of his invented languages (see **Language and Linguistics**). And, unlike many films involving numerous scenes shot before a blue screen, with effects added later, performers uniformly communicate an absolute sense of conviction in responding to unfolding events, with Ian McKellen as Gandalf and Viggo Mortenson as Aragorn garnering the most acclaim.

Still, in one crucial respect, these films tell a story that is different from Tolkien's. *The Lord of the Rings* is unquestionably the story of Frodo, with the adventures of other characters functioning as subplots, their battles and activities clearly labeled as diversions of only secondary importance. *The Lord of the Rings: The Fellowship of the Ring* and its sequels, as others note, seem more the story of Aragorn and other human and elf characters, with Frodo shifted to a subordinate role. Language from Tolkien is retained emphasizing that Frodo's mission is ultimately the only important one, but the appearance and construction of the films conflictingly contrive to emphasize Aragorn instead. Thus, while Tolkien primarily describes a **quest**, Jackson is primarily describing a **war**. The reasons for this may in part be unintentional and inevitable: in a culture that esteems height, tall characters may naturally command more attention than short characters; for audiences that crave spectacle, battle scenes involving thousands of warriors may naturally command more attention than scenes of three characters climbing a rocky **mountain**; for filmmakers influenced by cinematic stereotypes, the conventionally and ruggedly handsome Mortenson may naturally command more attention than the fragile-looking, almost effeminate Elijah Wood as Frodo.

Nevertheless, Jackson—and perhaps circumstances beyond Jackson's control—contribute to the discrepancy. All the battles seem unnecessarily larger and grander than the ones Tolkien wrote about; where hundreds of orcs and human opponents would have more than sufficed, Jackson feels compelled to provide thousands and thousands of them, as if determined to show off the powers of computer-generated imagery. The visualizations of Tolkien's "oliphaunts," though derived from his descriptions, are unpleasantly reminiscent of the Imperial Walkers in George Lucas's *The Empire Strikes Back* (1980) (see *Star Wars*), functioning to heighten the impressiveness of the success of Aragorn and his comrades in opposing them. Arwen, barely visible in Tolkien's trilogy, is strangely elevated to the status of a major character, apparently because a prominent actress, Liv Tyler, was cast in the role and needed to receive an ample amount of screen time. The Steward of Gondor, merely a weak man in Tolkien's books, is transformed into a conniving **villain** to make the story of Aragorn's ascension to the throne more involving and to justify devoting more time to this minor aspect of the plot.

However, in comparison to what might have been, or to the only other attempt to film the trilogy—Ralph Bakshi's incomplete and unsatisfying animated film *The Lord of the Rings* (1978)—Jackson's films richly deserve the nearly universal praise they have received. And, as expanded and fuller DVD versions, including many deleted scenes, become the standard way to view them, their reputation may be even further enhanced.

Bibliography

Sean Astin with Joe Layden. *There and Back Again*. New York: St. Martin's, 2004.

Jody Duncan. "Ring Masters." *Cinefex*, No. 89 (April, 2002), 64–131.

Joe Fordham. "Q & A: Peter Jackson." *Cinefex*, No. 96 (January, 2004), 55–61.

Ross Plesset. "*The Lord of the Rings: The Fellowship of the Ring*." *Cinefantastique*, 33 (October/November, 2001), 6–7.

Ross Plesset. "*The Lord of the Rings: The Fellowship of the Ring*: Peter Jackson." *Cinefantastique*, 33 (December/January, 2001/2002), 42–43.

Ian Pryor. *Peter Jackson*. New York: St. Martin's, 2003.

Brian Sibley. *The Lord of the Rings: The Making of the Movie Trilogy*. New York: Houghton Mifflin, 2002.
Brian Sibley. *The Lord of the Rings Official Movie Guide*. Boston: Houghton Mifflin, 2001.

—*Gary Westfahl*

LOST HORIZON BY JAMES HILTON (1933)

∎

We believe that to govern perfectly it is necessary to avoid governing too much.

—James Hilton
Lost Horizon (1933)

Summary

Englishman Hugh Conway, his young colleague Mallinson, and two other castaways are taken to the mystical, **dream**-like lamasery of Shangri-La after their plane is hijacked. Conway finds himself at **home** and enjoys the company of Chang, the lama with whom the castaways have the most contact. Touring the lamasery's expansive **library**, Conway discovers that great works of **art** and literature in many languages are collected here; he also falls in **love** with the beautiful Lo-Tsen for her intellectual prowess. Eventually, Conway meets with High Lama Father Perrault, a Capuchin friar who became exiled in Shangri-La during a failed expedition in 1719. Knowing his **death** is imminent, Perrault chooses Conway as his successor (see **Destiny**), warns him of a time when humanity's murderous passions will all but destroy **civilization**, and prophesies that after this destruction, the humility and peace of Shangri-La will overtake the world. Conway understands Perrault's vision, but he is torn between leaving and staying when Mallinson reveals his deep love for Lo-Tsen and their desire to **escape**. Conway decides to help them cross the perilous terrain of the Himalayas (see **Mountains**), but Mallinson dies, and Conway finds himself with amnesia aboard a ship. When **memory** suddenly returns, he sets out to find Shangri-La, but it is uncertain whether he is successful.

Discussion

James Hilton wrote *Lost Horizon* as a response to the devastation of World War I. Differences in **religion** and worldviews and fights for cultural superiority cause **wars**. Hilton establishes the mystical people (see **Elder Races**) and **communities** of Shangri-La as a **utopia** where all worldviews, religions, **cultures**, and their arts are valued and studied, and other senses, like telepathy, are cultivated (see **Psychic Powers**). Shangri-La is a kingdom of **knowledge** hidden from the world that maintains its own **secret history**. For this reason, it is unspoiled by other civilizations' power struggles. Since Shangri-La is an **Arcadia** where the aging process slows considerably (see **Immortality and Longevity**) and speeds up rapidly if individuals leave, Hilton suggests that the longevity of the human race depends upon harmonious living.

Possessing qualities Perrault finds necessary to preserve Shangri-La, Conway is an ideal candidate for High Lama because he is a marriage of East and West. A diplomat from the west, Conway is well-versed in Chinese culture, is drawn to learning, and respects eastern culture. This contrasts with other castaways, representing negative western traits like religious superiority, when seeking to Christianize the natives (see **Christianity**) and greed, when coveting gold (see **Gold and Silver**). However, a part of Conway doubts the realities of Shangri-La. Mallinson and Chang function as Conway's **doppelgängers**: one part of Conway is educated and reserved like Chang and wishes to stay in Shangri-La; the other is passionate and irrational like young Mallinson, and this side wins out when he discovers how much Mallinson and Lo-Tsen are in love, implying that this kind of passion leads to conflict and destruction. Still, Conway's departure is an unselfish act to aid those he loves.

All can strive for lamahood and educate themselves as they please; there are no **gender** or racial biases, and Lo-Tsen is free to have **romances** with Conway and Mallinson. These presentations of racial and gender equality were radical in 1933 and further Hilton's point that to have a society free of war and strife, everyone must have the same opportunities and be treated equally; it becomes more difficult to murder lives if they are valued. However, Hilton's western bias is apparent. Conway and Mallinson are attracted to Lo-Tsen's stereotypical exotic **beauty**; she appears as a passionless china doll. The stately and reserved Chang is almost a caricature of the wise Chinese servant (see **Clichés**). A European, not an Asian, founds Shangri-La, makes himself theocrat, and teaches residents the way they should follow. This suggests colonialism (see **Postcolonialism**), a cause of war and unrest, and the antithesis of Hilton's message. Perrault mentions that his best subjects are the "Nordic and Latin races of Europe," which explains why Perrault chooses Conway as his successor instead of Chang, a resident for decades. Perrault becomes optimistic (see **Optimism and Pessimism**) when the castaways arrive because there have been so few white people at the lamasery. Perhaps Hilton felt that this emphasis on western characters was necessary to convey a message of eastern **philosophy** to western readers.

Frank Capra's 1937 film adaptation is similar to the novel, but several characters have been changed—most noticeably George Conway, Robert's brother, replaces Mallinson, and Maria and Sondra, white women, replace Lo-Tsen, who has been removed to eliminate an interracial relationship (see **Race Relations**). George falls in love with the disgruntled Maria, and they prepare to leave Shangri-La. Sondra, Robert's intellectual equal and love interest, is responsible for his kidnapping after reading his **books** and realizing that, despite his success, he is unhappy in life. George and Maria seem childish and petulant in convincing Robert that Chang and Father Perrault have lied about Shangri-La's secrets and treated Maria badly. The fact that George and Maria cannot appreciate the peace and **freedom** of Shangri-La leads to their deaths and makes their manipulation of Robert all the more tragic. The film ends on a happier note than the book, with Robert returning to Shangri-La. A 1973 musical version, with additional character changes, was widely viewed as a disastrous failure.

In all three versions, the castaways' plane is hijacked by someone involved with Shangri-La. The lamasery promises freedom, but the castaways have been kidnapped.

Perhaps Hilton's ultimate message is that individuals will never choose to leave their destructive lifestyle unless they are forced to experience the alternative.

Bibliography

Allienne R. Becker. *The Lost Worlds Romance*. Westport, CT: Greenwood Press, 1992.

Felicia F. Campbell. "Shangri-La." Michael S. Cummings and Nicholas D. Smith, eds., *Utopian Studies III*. Lanham, NY: Univ. Press of America, 1991, 86–91.

J.W. Crawford. "Utopian Eden of *Lost Horizon*." *Extrapolation*, 22 (Summer, 1981), 186–190.

James Hilton. "Introduction." Hilton, *Lost Horizon: Author's Edition*. New York: W. Morrow, 1936, 1-3.

Nadia Khouri. "Lost Worlds and the Revenge of Realism." *Science-Fiction Studies*, 10 (July, 1983), 170–190.

Roger J. King. "Utopian Fiction as Moral Philosophy." Michael S. Cummings and Nicholas D. Smith, eds., *Utopian Studies III*. Lanham, NY: University Press of America, 1991, 72–78.

Paul B. Sears. "Utopia and the Living Landscape." Frank E. Manuel, ed., *Utopias and Utopian Thought*. Boston: Houghton Mifflin, 1966, 137–149.

Samuel H. Vasbinder. "Aspects of Fantasy in Literary Myths About Lost Civilizations." R.C. Schlobin, ed., *The Aesthetics of Fantasy Literature and Art*. Notre Dame: University of Notre Dame Press, 1982, 192–210.

Thomas Reed Whissen. "*Lost Horizon*." Whissen, *Classic Cult Fiction*. Westport, CT: Greenwood Press, 1992, 153–158.

—Toiya Kristen Finley

The Lost World
by Arthur Conan Doyle (1912)

Summary

Professor Challenger, a violent-tempered, egotistical (see **Hubris**), brilliant explorer leads an expedition into the wilds of South America, to prove his claims of an inaccessible plateau (see **Lost Worlds**) inhabited by **dinosaurs** and ape-men. Perilous adventure ensues, in which the professor discovers that the dinosaurs are all too real and his companions side with an Indian tribe in a virtually genocidal **war** against the ape-men. Returning to **civilization**, Challenger confronts his critics. His proof is a live pterodactyl, which escapes during a scientific meeting, vindicating him in the most dramatic manner possible.

Discussion

The first thing a modern reader will notice about *The Lost World* is that it remains an enormously exciting story, but some of its features make one distinctly uncomfortable. There is considerable casual racism (see **Race Relations**), as in the description of the faithful Negro servant, Zambo, as, "a black Hercules, as willing as any horse, and about as intelligent." Actually, Zambo proves competent, fearless, and reliable. He is one of those ever-faithful, socially inferior companions so common in Victorian fiction, akin to J.R.R. Tolkien's Samwise (see *The Lord of the Rings*), but one wonders if perhaps Zambo's loyalty has been misplaced.

All of Doyle's characters, furthermore, seem to be caricatures or stereotypes. Challenger is an impossible person (see **Mad Scientists**), even by the standards of his time. Of Herculean strength himself, he lifts his wife onto a pedestal until she will behave. At least Doyle has a little fun at his expense: Challenger is also a short, broad-chested, extremely hairy man, and the ape-men accept him as one of their own, although the narrator, the reporter Malone, remarks that their sloping brows are no match for Challenger's magnificent European forehead. Malone is a young man in **love**, determined to be a **hero** to impress a sweetheart. The other two members of the party are Professor Summerlee, one of Challenger's harshest critics who comes along to argue, and Lord John Roxton, a manly outdoorsman and hunter.

All four display a certain self-righteousness. Roxton had once decided to break up the Amazonian slave trade, recruiting followers and exterminating slavers (see **Slavery**). But when the Indians of the plateau, whose "superior" physical qualities are remarked upon repeatedly (see **Anthropology**), enslave the remnants of the ape-folk, the whites approve. It is **survival** of the fittest (see **Social Darwinism**). This victory of human over sub-human, Malone rhapsodizes, is one of the few in **history** that really matters.

To modern readers, other aspects of *The Lost World* will seem not so much offensive as quaint. Doyle's allosaurs hop like kangaroos. From the perspective of modern **ecology**, it seems unlikely that a plateau that contained dinosaurs would also support proto-humans and Irish elk; further, if a tribe of no more than a thousand Indians has been living there all this time, handsome or not, why hasn't genetic stagnation set in? However, written as it was at the high tide of European imperialism (see **Postcolonialism**), the book does give a clear sense of the adventurous expectation of an era in which pith-helmeted white adventurers really were uncovering wonders in the world's last unexplored places. The order of things seemed clear; disillusionment was still in the future.

The Lost World should be regarded, therefore, as the product of a more innocent era, before World War I, when prowess with a gun and "love of danger" might still be seen as heroic ideals. It is also a fantasy of **evolution**, as the concept was popularly understood in 1912. Challenger speculates that only because of the plateau's isolation (see **Wilderness**), resulting from a vast volcanic upheaval that raised it above the surrounding countryside, have such inferior creatures as dinosaurs or submen been able to survive. Otherwise, the forces of evolution would have eliminated them. For its time, this qualifies as reasonably intelligent evolutionary thought.

The influence of *The Lost World* was vast. The story was first filmed as *The Lost World* in 1925, with the pterodactyl upgraded to a brontosaurus, the first of countless cinematic dinosaurs to rampage through a major **city**. The film *King Kong* also owes a great deal to its plot and structure, the major difference being that, for all his egotism, Challenger treats the natives better and that, rather than showing off a mere pterodactyl at the end, the hero of the film produces Kong, the 100-foot gorilla. Edgar Rice Burroughs's *The Land That Time Forgot* (1924) takes place on an **island** plateau in the Pacific, complete with cave-men and dinosaurs and a similar concern with evolution. Even when the lost world story itself evolved into the inter-planetary story (see **Space Opera**), Terran heroes tended to intervene in a local **war**, deciding with finality issues of good and evil (see E.E. "Doc" Smith's *The Skylark of Space* [1928]). In *The Lost World*, too, we observe the origin of numerous pulp stories about heroic Cro-Magnons defeating bestial Neanderthals, one example being Manly Wade Wellman's "Hok Goes to Atlantis" (1939) and its sequels.

Professor Challenger reappeared in four other stories. *The Poison Belt* (1913) tells how the Earth is imperilled by passage through a toxic "ether"; "When the World Screamed" (1928) turns on the much-imitated concept of the **Earth** as a living organism; "The Disintegration Machine" (1929) is about a machine that dis-solves matter; and *The Land of Mist* (1926), disappointingly, converts Challenger to spiritualism.

Bibliography

Allienne R. Becker. *The Lost Worlds Romance*. Westport, CT: Greenwood Press, 1992.

Everett Bleiler. "Lost Worlds and Lost Opportunities." *Science-Fiction Studies*, 23 (November, 1996), 355–362.

Thomas D. Clareson. "Lost Lands, Lost Races." Clareson, ed., *Many Futures, Many Worlds*. Kent, OH: Kent State University Press, 1977, 714–723.

Rosamund Dalziell. "The Curious Case of Sir Everard im Thurn and Sir Arthur Conan Doyle." *English Literature in Transition*, 45 (2002), 131–157.

Andrew Darlington. "Our Eyes Have Seen Great Wonders." *Fantasy Commentator*, 7 (Spring, 1992), 181–188.

Tobias Doring. "Scales and Ladders." Elmar Schenkel and Stefan Welz, eds., *Lost Worlds and Mad Elephants*. Glienicke: Galda + Wilch Verlag, 1999, 243–258.

Robert Silverberg. "Introduction." Arthur Conan Doyle, *The Lost World*. Norwalk, CT: Easton Press, 1995, vii–xvi.

Robin H. Smiley. "Books into Film: *The Lost World*." *Firsts: The Book Collector's Magazine*, 12 (October, 2002), 53–55.

Daniel Stashower. *Teller of Tales*. New York: Henry Holt, 1999.

—Darrell Schweitzer

MAD MAX (1979)

They say people don't believe in heroes anymore. Well, damn them. You and me, Max, we're gonna give them back their heroes.

—James McCausland and George Miller
Mad Max (1979)

Summary

Set in a near-future **Australia** in which the social order is breaking down, *Mad Max* depicts a **war** on the country roads between outlaw gangs and beleaguered police. The society we are shown is a chaotic **dystopia**, marked by almost uncontrollable **violence**. Max Rockatansky is a police officer whose best friend, wife, and child have been killed by a sadistic biker gang led by the Toecutter. At the movie's climax, Max and the Toecutter hunt each other, both motivated by vengeance (see **Revenge**). Max prevails in a running battle involving guns, explosives, motorbikes, trucks, and modified **automobiles**.

In *Mad Max 2* (1981), retitled *The Road Warrior* for release in the United States, Max is caught up in warfare between a **community** of settlers, deep in the Australian outback, and a motorized horde of **barbarians** who want the settlers' gasoline. The barbarians are led by a physically awesome man, the Humungus, and their vehicles are even more baroque than those in *Mad Max*. Thanks to Max's reluctant intervention, most settlers **escape** from their compound and commence a long journey to the coast.

Mad Max Beyond Thunderdome (1985) shows two communities that have survived (see **Survival**), and even prospered, in the red Australian **desert**. Bartertown is a **frontier** society whose economy depends on slave labor (see **Slavery**), led by the formidable Aunty Entity. Not far away, a hidden oasis has been settled by **children** who await their **messiah**, Captain Walker, to lead them to a better land. Thanks to Max's intervention, once again, some of Bartertown's slaves and the children **escape** to the ruins of Sydney, where they build a new society.

Discussion

It is difficult to reconcile the realities depicted in the three movies or to establish exactly what events have taken place in Australia and beyond. The first movie implies that western society, or the world order as a whole, is already in a state of decay that can be extrapolated into the future (see **Decadence**). *Mad Max 2* opens with an expository narrative, which describes a global **disaster** involving conflict over oil, including the destruction of entire **cities**, though we are given no unequivocal indication of a full-scale **nuclear war**. *Beyond Thunderdome* suggests more strongly that a nuclear holocaust has taken place, with only a few survivors, firmly categorizing Max's world as a **post-holocaust society**.

Still, it does not seem possible to establish definitively when these events happen, relative to the events shown in the three films, or how much time has passed between the movies themselves. Max clearly ages from movie to movie, especially by the time of *Beyond Thunderdome*, but we are offered only a sketchy impression of how he has lived in his desolate world, or for how long. Some hoped that there would be a fourth *Mad Max* film to resolve some of these questions, but such a project now seems unlikely.

To date, Mad Max has remained a lonely, alienated figure throughout the series, feeling a sense of **estrangement** from his society, and he is always a force of vengeance against evil-doers. All three movies emphasize the institution of law, especially the concepts of **crime and punishment**. But the law is shown as unjust, corrupt, or simply ineffectual. In this reprimitivized future, we are almost back to a Hobbesian state of nature—a war of all against all—so Max is repeatedly forced to take the law into his own hands.

However, he does become more than a vigilante or malcontent avenger. While he struggles against formidable adults such as the Toecutter, the Humungus, and Aunty Entity, he also forges important relationships with children. In *Mad Max*, he is pychologically traumatized by the **deaths** of those closest to him, including his baby, the Sprog. In *Mad Max 2*, he is shown as almost a surrogate **father** to the Feral Kid, who later becomes leader of the settler "tribe" following its escape to the coast. In *Beyond Thunderdome*, he helps an entire community of children, led by Savannah Nix. Having been deprived of his original **family** in the first film, Max seems impelled to constantly seek out surrogate families, even while carrying on the lifestyle of a lonely nomad.

Max may remain a **mystery** because his adventures, it seems, are always been told from the perspective of other people in some future time. In voiceovers at the end of both *Mad Max 2* and *Beyond Thunderdome*, children speak of Max as a **hero** whose battles enabled their new societies to be built on the ruins of the old **civilization**. This can be interpreted as either a resonant piece of mythmaking or an unpleasant survivalist fantasy. *Mad Max 2* is narrated by the Feral Kid. As he speaks, he is now old, but he recalls Max as the warrior who helped his people to escape. Similarly, *Beyond Thunderdome* is narrated by Savannah, who tells the story many years after the events that we are shown.

Still, each movie concludes with Max alone in the vast **landscape**, a dangerous man whose talents are mostly for destruction. The old civilization has gone, and there seems no place for such men in any new one that he helps to bring about.

Bibliography

Mick Broderick. "Heroic Apocalypse." Christopher Sharrett, ed., *Crisis Cinema*. Washington, DC: Maissoneuve Press, 1993, 250–272.

Delia Falconer. "We Don't Need to Know the Way Home." Steven Cohen and Ina Rae Hark, eds., *The Road Movie Book*. London: Routledge, 1997, 249–270.

Peter Fitting. "Count Me Out/In." *cineACTION*, 11 (December, 1987), 42–51.

Peter C. Hall and Richard Erlich. "Beyond Topeka and Thunderdome." *Science-Fiction Studies*, 14 (November, 1987), 316–325.

Adrian Martin. *The Mad Max Movies*. Sydney and Canberra: Currency Press and Screenbound Australia, 2003.

Meaghan Morris. "White Panic or Mad Max and the Sublime." Kuan-Hsing Chen, ed., - *Trajectories*. London and New York: Routledge, 1998, 239–262.

Jerome F. Shapiro. *Atomic Bomb Cinema*. New York: Routledge, 2002.

Christopher Sharrett. "The Hero as Pastiche." *Journal of Popular Film and Television*, 13 (Summer 1985), 80–91.

John Stratton. "What Made *Mad Max* Popular?" *Art & Text*, No. 9 (Autumn 1983), 37–56.

—*Russell Blackford*

THE MAN IN THE HIGH CASTLE
BY PHILIP K. DICK (1962)

■

> Sometimes one must try anything, he decided. It is no disgrace. On the contrary, it is a sign of wisdom, of recognizing the situation.
>
> —Philip K. Dick
> *The Man in the High Castle* (1962)

Summary

In an **alternate history**, **America** lost World War II and is now partitioned between Germany and **Japan**. Robert Childan sells Americana from his shop in San Francisco, part of the Japanese zone. Meanwhile Frank Frink, a Jew (see **Judaism**) who is hiding his **identity**, has been fired from his job faking American artifacts and goes into **business** with a friend, Ed, manufacturing original jewelry, which Childan agrees to sell. A local Japanese official, Tagomi, learns that the Germans have now decided to liquidate the Japanese. A group of Germans attack his building, but Tagomi defends himself with a faked Colt .45. Troubled by his killing, he tries to sell the gun back to Childan but ends up buying a triangular **art** pendant, the contemplation of which sends him through to a **parallel world** where the Axis powers lost the war. Back in the real world, Tagomi refuses to allow Frank to be extradited to Germany, thus saving his life. Meanwhile, in Denver, Frank's ex-wife Juliana visits Hawthorne Abendsen, author of *The Grasshopper Lies Heavy*, a book that is an alternate history of the Allies winning the war. Juliana learns that Abendsen has written his novel with the aid of the *I Ching*, which notes the novel has "Inner Truth." She considers going back to Frank.

Discussion

This novel was nearly Philip K. Dick's last, as he had failed to sell his non-science fiction novels and had a young **family** to support. His third wife, Anne Rubenstein, suggested he have one more try and as a result won the only Hugo Award of his career. Like his alter ego Abendsen (partially also inspired by A.E. van Vogt and Robert A. Heinlein), Dick plotted the novel using the **books** of the *I Ching*, casting the coins for **yin and yang** when his characters did so. The significance of this **divination** has been disputed by various critics.

One interpretation is that *The Grasshopper Lies Heavy* is true, which is to say the Allies did indeed win the Second World War and that the **dystopia** of a German/Japanese run world is an **illusion**. This might be more convincing if it were not so clear that Abendsen's world is not our world. Perhaps, in this novel of **metafiction and recursiveness**, the *I Ching* is arguing that we are as fictional as the characters in *The Man in the High Castle*. Alternately, it might be that *Grasshopper*, despite being a work of fiction, has an Inner Truth of authenticity, and by extension science fiction has value despite being a derided genre. As elsewhere in Dick's work, God may be found in the trash.

Also as elsewhere in Dick's oeuvre, characters have a duty of **humanity** or empathy (see **Guilt and Responsibility**) toward others irrespective of the closeness of their relationship. To save one life, Tagomi has taken two. He redresses the imbalance by saving Frank's life, a man he has never met although he is connected via the triangular pendant he bought and Frank made. This ethical commitment (see **Ethics**) holds regardless of whether the world is real or not; indeed, the novel is filled with example of functional fakes (such as the Colt .45 that can still shoot people dead) and false **identities**: Juliana's Italian lover, with whom she travels to see Abendsen, is really an assassin; Tagomi learns of the German plans via Baynes (the name of the translator of the *I Ching*) who is really Rudolf Wegener; Tagomi feels he is concealing his real identity; and Frank has hidden his Jewish origins. Even the high **castle** of the title turns out to be an ordinary **home**. What matters is how people behave. The ethical commitment between people is continuous; it does not depend on the reality that they may (or may not) inhabit.

The Man in the High Castle is a novel of rich detail, creating **estrangement** via an array of subtle differences between our world and the fictional world. It might be argued that Dick's **politics** are a little naïve, in suggesting that the Japanese-dominated area of the United States would be infinitely preferable to the Nazi-run section, but we do only see a small slice of the world. Despite this criticism, the novel stands with *Do Androids Dream of Electric Sheep?* as some of the best literature that science fiction has produced and was a worthy winner of the genre's highest award.

Bibliography

Laura E. Campbell. "Dickian Time in *The Man in the High Castle*." *Extrapolation*, 33 (Fall, 1992), 190–201.

Howard Canaan. "Metafiction and the Gnostic Quest in *The Man in the High Castle*." *Journal of the Fantastic in the Arts*, 12 (2002), 382–405.

Cassie Carter. "The Metacolonization of Dick's *The Man in the High Castle*." *Science-Fiction Studies*, 22 (November, 1995), 333–342.

Lorenzo Di Tommaso. "Redemption in Philip K. Dick's *The Man in the High Castle*." *Science Fiction Studies*, 26 (March, 1999), 91–119.

John Rieder. "The Metafictive World of *The Man in the High Castle*: Hermeneutics, Ethics, and Political Ideology." *Science-Fiction Studies*, 15 (July, 1988), 214–225.

John L. Simons. "The Power of Small Things in Philip K. Dick's *The Man in the High Castle*." *Rocky Mountain Review of Language and Literature*, 39 (Winter, 1985), 261–275.

Patricia Warrick. "The Encounter of Taoism and Fascism in Philip K. Dick's *The Man in the High Castle*." *Science-Fiction Studies*, 7 (July, 1980), 174–190.

Paul Williams. "The Author and the Oracle." *PKDS Newsletter*, No. 25 (1990), 1–10.

Jianjiong Zhu. "Reality, Fiction, and Wu in *The Man in the High Castle*." *Journal of the Fantastic in the Arts*, 5 (1993), 36–45.

—Andrew M. Butler

THE MAN WHO FELL TO EARTH (1976)

Summary

A **UFO** lands on **Earth**. A pale, thin, androgynous man, Thomas Jerome Newton, wanders into a remote town to sell his wedding **ring**. Time passes and several wedding rings later he approaches patent lawyer Oliver Farnsworth with a large amount of cash and a number of **inventions**. They form a company, World Enterprises, which becomes enormously successful; but despite his multimillionaire status, Newton shuns all publicity and allows Farnsworth to act on his behalf. He leaves the **city** and develops a relationship with Mary Lou, eventually revealing to her that he is an **alien on Earth**. Meanwhile seedy college professor Nathan Bryce joins the company and discovers Newton's secret. Newton plans to build a device that will transport **water** back to his drought-stricken home planet but on the eve of the launch he is betrayed and handed over to the authorities (see **Betrayal**). Farnsworth is murdered. Locked in an opulent mansion, Newton is ruthlessly experimented upon. A staged reunion with Mary Lou fails. Eventually the alien **escapes** from his captors but remains trapped on Earth in human form. Newton starts a new career and when an aging Bryce spots a recording of The Visitor in a local record store, he tracks down the alien for a final meeting.

Discussion

Nicolas Roeg's use of nonlinear structure, relational editing, and overlapping sounds across cuts were characteristic of most of his films up until the late 1980s. These techniques enable him to juxtapose images and ideas conceptually, forcing audiences to construct the narrative from spatially and temporally distanced scenes. Despite the antirealist style, however, the outcome of *The Man Who Fell to Earth* is rational. Based on the 1963 novel by Walter Tevis it tells the story of an alien on Earth seeking to return to his home planet; he has not come as part of an **invasion** or as ambassador, but simply to find water for his dying race.

Although the premise is essentially the same, screenwriter Paul Mayersberg removed political elements from the book to produce a film that is a **tragedy**, full of genuine yearning and knowing futility, focusing on the alien's personal needs in human terms. When Newton arrives he already has an understanding of **economics** and quickly builds a corporate empire, bringing **knowledge** through his inventions. These inventions do not further human development but provide consumers with entertainment products, such as self-developing photographic film. Newton seeks to understand Earth **culture** by fixing up banks of machinery and delves into a world of **television and radio**. However, the multiple perspectives of the televisions, their scores of channels flicking by, begin to reflect not his assimilation into Earth's **civilization** but his increasing **estrangement** from it. He is uncomfortable around humans, suffers from motion sickness, and is cautious and considered in his actions, aware of the potential consequences of being detected. Although he wants to remain reclusive, his commercial success means that he cannot avoid being in the public eye. Attention is focused on him, and as a result his grandiose plans are wrecked, rendering the mission to ensure the **survival** of his **family** futile. He is incarcerated and experimented upon. His appeals to his captors reflect his fear and distress, and in the moment the fake "human" eyes are fused to his own, his fate on Earth is sealed.

The fragile nonlinear structure of the film is also reflected in his state of mind as **anxiety** takes hold and spirals into **madness** and **paranoia**. His **memories** become fragmented as the years pass so the audience, like the alien, sees half-delirious glimpses of a distant **desert** planet (see **Alien Worlds**) and a family on the brink of **death**. As an **exile**, the creeping knowledge emerges that there is no hope of return: Newton's insurmountable riches that allowed him to wallow in a decadent lifestyle of hedonism, **drugs**, and loveless sex (see **Decadence; Sexuality**) are no substitute for reunion with his dying family.

Tevis's novel opens with the chapter "Icarus Descending," a metaphor that runs through both the film and book, as Newton's plans to escape from Earth and ascend to the heavens are dashed. Despite his failure, Roeg's film gives him a philosophical outlook, the final scene having a tone of resignation about it rather than bitterness and resentment. As he meets with Bryce he confesses that "we'd have probably treated you the same if you'd come over to our place," echoing the universality of distrust between species.

The casting of David Bowie in the key role is not only a furtherance of Roeg's use of pop icons (Mick Jagger in *Performance* [1970], Art Garfunkel in *Bad Timing* [1980]) but also a reflection of Bowie's perceived **androgyny** within the prevalent popular culture of the time. Indeed for all the film's sizeable amounts of **nudity**, there is an emotionally detached quality to the carnally driven sex without **love** that reflects his alienness, estrangement, and increasingly desperate plight. That Newton breaks into the recording industry and has a hit record, hoping that the radio broadcasts will eventually reach his family, further reflects this casting choice.

Bibliography

Craig W. Anderson. "*The Man Who Fell to Earth*." Anderson, *Science Fiction Films of the Seventies*. McFarland, 2001, 119–122.

Earl G. Ingersoll. "A Conversation with Walter Tevis." *Extrapolation*, 26 (Winter, 1985), 300–308.

James Leach. "*The Man Who Fell to Earth*." *Literature/Film Quarterly*, 6 (Fall, 1978), 371–379.

Gerard Loughlin. *Alien Sex*. Malden, MA: Blackwell, 2004.

Paul Mayersberg. "Story So Far: *The Man Who Fell to Earth*." *Sight & Sound*, 44 (Autumn, 1975), 225–231.

David P. Pettus. "Interview: Walter Tevis." *Parsec*, 1 (June, 1982), 11–18.

Neil Sinyard. *The Films of Nicolas Roeg*. London: Letts. 1991.

Bhob Stewart. "*The Man Who Fell to Earth*." *Cinefantastique* 5 (Fall, 1976), 28–29, 31.

W.F. Van Wert. "Film as Science Fiction." *Western Humanities Review*, 33 (Autumn, 1979), 141–148.

—*Michelle Le Blanc and Colin Odell*

THE MARTIAN CHRONICLES
BY RAY BRADBURY (1950)

∎

*"I've always wanted to see a Martian,"
said Michael, stiltedly. "Where are they,
Dad? You promised."*

*"There they are," said Dad, and he
shifted Michael on his shoulder and
pointed straight down.*

*The Martians were there, all right. It
sent a thrill chasing through Timothy.*

*The Martians were there—in the
canal—reflected in the water. Timothy and
Michael and Robert and Mom and Dad.*

*The Martians stared back up at them
for a long, long silent time from the
rippling water . . . .*

—Ray Bradbury
"The Million-Year Picnic" (1946)

Summary

Human exploration of **Mars** begins in 1999, and the first three expeditions to the planet end in the **deaths** of all on board at the hands of Martians, who regard humans with suspicion and hostility. By the turn of the twenty-first century, Martian **civilization** is dead and indigenous Martians have vanished, but for occasional ghostly sightings. Human colonization of the planet begins in earnest, and Earth people begin setting up towns amidst the ruins of Martian **cities**, highlighting contrasts between the two **cultures** that persist as an underlying tension in the colonists' new **homes**. In the span of a few years, **humanity** dominates the planet, stamping it with the imprint of **Earth** and superimposing its culture so firmly that there is little difference superficially between Mars and Earth. With the influx of human settlers on Mars come many of the same social problems that colonists fled: racial prejudice, censorship, class warfare, and **violence**. Indeed, problems are so rampant on Earth that **nuclear war** breaks out in 2005, devastating the mother planet. Just as quickly as they settled Mars, the majority of colonists return to Earth to pick up the pieces of their shattered planet. The few settlers who choose to stay on Mars acknowledge that they have become the new Martian race.

Discussion

Although sometimes treated as a novel, *The Martian Chronicles* is a "fix-up" collection of stories with Mars settings that Bradbury published independent of one another in the 1940s, then revised slightly and bridged with connecting pieces into an informal history of the first ten years of humanity's **exploration** and colonization (see **Planetary Colonies**) of the planet. The narrative structure of the book is loose enough that Bradbury was able to exchange one story not incorporated into the American edition, "The Fire Balloons" (1951), for the episode "Usher II" (1950) in the British edition, published as *The Silver Locusts*. Nevertheless, the stories are organized to fit a clearly determined arc and evoke an elegiac tone. Bradbury left out several key Martian stories that did not fit the book's final scheme, notably "Dark They Were, and Golden Eyed" (1949), in which a prolonged stay on Mars effects an insidious physical transformation of humans into Martians. A 1980 television miniseries adaptation of the book was largely regarded as stilted and unsuccessful.

Bradbury has cited Edgar Rice Burroughs's Mars novels as an influence (see *A Princess of Mars*), but while his Mars differs markedly from Burroughs's depiction of the planet as a setting for swashbuckling costume drama, it is similarly unscientific in its rendering. Bradbury's Mars has a breathable atmosphere, and its Martian civilization is more recognizably human than alien. In part, this is because Bradbury's Mars serves a purpose more poetic than science-fictional: Mars is the **mirror** in which human civilization inspects its highlights and flaws.

The Martian Chronicles is Bradbury's science fiction **allegory** of the settling of the American **frontier** (see **America**). His spacefaring humans are the equivalent of Wild West (see **Westerns**) homesteaders, who travel in **rockets** rather than covered wagons to their new land. Bradbury's Martians are stand-ins for **Native Americans**, a once-glorious race now in its twilight that died out before it could be displaced. This analogy is seen most clearly in the story "And the Moon Be Still as Bright" (1948), in which a member of a rocket crew sympathetic to the Martian culture sees his crewmates as invaders and defilers who will never understand the civilization they have come to replace. Although this relationship evokes the tradition of **space opera**, which depicts human–alien contact as jingoistic cowboys-versus-Indians adventures transplanted to outer space, Bradbury's concerns are different. His tales focus on the frustrating fallibility of his humans and the paradoxically humanistic aspects of the Martian culture.

By presenting the colonization of the planet in terms of America's frontier mythology, Bradbury also evokes the **pastoral** tradition, in which characters leave the world that defines them for a simpler, natural world (see **Nature**) that gives them a new perspective and allows them chances for transformation and self-improvement. But Bradbury's humans, for the most part, forsake the opportunity to start anew and repeat many of the their race's past mistakes. The story "Way in the Middle of the Air" (1950) suggests that ignorant human misunderstanding of Martians has its parallel in long-standing troubled **race relations** between white and blacks on Earth. "Usher II" shows **book**-burning guardians of the public interest trying to impose their censorship laws on Mars. The more sympathetic "The Fire Balloons" (in *The Silver Locusts*) shows a similar lack of imagination on the part of a human cleric who struggles to accept that Martians are born without original **sin**. The threat of nuclear war that compels many on Earth to flee to Mars is ultimately the same event that draws them back home, effectively shutting down colonization of the planet.

There is a tragic dimension to the novel's events, which suggest that humankind's fate is inescapable (see **Destiny**), and that the destruction of Earth civilization is perhaps as inevitable as the destruction of Martian civilization. At the same time, the **role reversal** that marks the end of the novel—in which the few humans who choose to stay on their adopted planet now think of themselves as Martians—suggests a continuity with the past and bittersweet optimism about **survival**.

Bibliography

Kent Forrester. "The Dangers of Being Earnest." *Journal of General Education*, 28 (1976), 50–54.

Kevin Hoskinson. "*The Martian Chronicles* and *Fahrenheit 451*." *Extrapolation*, 36 (Winter, 1995), 345–359.

Walter J. Miller. *Ray Bradbury's The Martian Chronicles*. New York: Monarch Press, 1987.

David Mogen. *Ray Bradbury*. Boston: Twayne, 1986.

Walter J. Mucher. "Being Martian." *Extrapolation*, 43 (Summer, 2002), 171–187.

Joseph D. Olander and Martin H. Greenberg, eds. *Ray Bradbury*. New York: Taplinger, 1988, 55–82.

Robert Plank. "Expedition to the Planet of Paranoia." *Extrapolation*, 22 (Summer, 1981), 171–185.

H.L. Prosser. "Teaching Sociology with *The Martian Chronicles*." *Social Education*, 47 (March, 1983), 212–215.

N.M. Valis. "*The Martian Chronicles* and Jorge Luis Borges." *Extrapolation*, 20 (Spring, 1979), 50–59.

—*Stefan Dziemianowicz*

MARY POPPINS BY P.L. TRAVERS (1934)

Summary

Mary Poppins is the story of a magical nanny (see **Magic**) who transforms the lives of four London **children** by taking them on fantastic outings and introducing them to strange and wonderful people. Outwardly, Mary Poppins is the epitome of correctness; firm, polite, distant but kind, always properly dressed. She does the kinds of things Jane, Michael, and the twins would expect of her: requiring them to take medicine and be kind to the elderly, and taking them on improving and educational outings. However, beneath the surface, the propriety becomes flawed or twisted, resulting in a carnivalesque situation, where breaking rules leads to amusement and power structures break down. The chore of visiting the elderly leads to tea on the ceiling; being horribly wicked results in the reward of a trip around the world for the children. Even Mary Poppins herself is flawed, and the children learn to play on her vanity to increase the length or quality of the adventure. Like all **carnivals**, however, the Banks children find theirs must come to an end. At the conclusion of each book, Mary Poppins leaves the household to return to the sky, and normal order returns.

Discussion

P.L. Travers created her magical nanny, Mary Poppins, in 1930s England, a time when many institutions—including education, the **family**, and the **class system**—were facing transformation, and the series reflects these changes. The character of Mary Poppins challenges the pre-World War I notion of what constituted proper upbringing for middle-class British children. While the Banks family is in chaos without Mary Poppins, the implication is not that they need a nanny so much as they need to rethink child-rearing practices. Mr. and Mrs. Banks **love** their children but do not know what to do with them; Mr. Banks threatens to leave **home** when Mary Poppins is absent. Mrs. Banks, unlike **mothers** in Victorian and Edwardian fiction, is incapable of providing the cement that holds the household together and is often in tears or at very least puzzled without the magical nanny. Mary provides a model they both feel comfortable with—a no-nonsense tough love veneer combined with a willingness to allow children to enjoy learning through adventure—that will also shore up the institution of the family and provide children with a moral **education**.

Mary Poppins also opens up the world for the middle-class Banks family; the adventures she directs and **fairy tales** she tells encourage the children to be aware of and appreciate other classes and other **cultures**, mirroring and commenting on the situation in postwar Britain. The 1964 film of the novel, while in many ways exemplary, erases much of this commentary by setting the action in Edwardian England instead.

Despite the emphasis on teaching both the child characters and readers, the *Mary Poppins* books are far from didactic. Instead, the combination of **comedy** and magic mask any serious moral purpose. Mary Poppins's superior ability to manage Jane, Michael, and the twins is balanced by the **absurdity** of her inflated ego. The emphasis on learning proper manners is softened by the **surrealism** of learning them in a tea party on the ceiling or sharing a comic book and ices with a marble **statue** of a naked boy. Many adventures in the *Mary Poppins* books begin and end in real places familiar to the children—parlors, parks, and shops—but Mary Poppins makes the ordinary magical. Partly because of the very ordinary nature of much of the surroundings, the Banks children are frequently left wondering whether the magic is real. Mary Poppins herself denies many events, but the children and even some adults often have **memories** and even souvenirs of their adventures.

The series never comes to any firm conclusions about the type of magical person that Mary Poppins is; however there are several suggestive remarks. At several points it is mentioned that Mary Poppins was around when animals were created;

she can communicate with them all but is especially familiar with **birds** and **fish and sea creatures**. She also spends evenings with the **stars**, and they and the animals all at one time or another bow down before her. Thus, it seems unlikely that she is a mere **witch** or even a **fairy**, but perhaps she is an **angel**. This notion is reinforced by the film version, where Mary Poppins is seen during the opening credits, properly attired for a nanny, but sitting in the clouds.

The initial novel was followed by seven others—*Mary Poppins Comes Back* (1935), *Mary Poppins Opens the Door* (1943), *Mary Poppins in the Park* (1952), *Mary Poppins from A to Z* (1962), *Mary Poppins in the Kitchen* (with Maurice Moore-Betty) (1975), *Mary Poppins in Cherry Tree Lane* (1982), and *Mary Poppins and the House Next Door* (1989)—along with two related chapbooks, *Mr. Wiggs' Birthday Party* (1952) and *The Magic Compass* (1953). Most adhere to the pattern of pre-Poppins chaos followed by adventures with and stories told by Mary Poppins, which continue until her sudden and magical departure. The ellipsis that concludes each novel, however, suggests that Mary Poppins, and her adventures, will continue ad infinitum.

Bibliography

Staffan Bergsten. *Mary Poppins and Myth*. Stockholm: Almquist and Wiksell, 1978.

Jonathan Cott. "The Wisdom of Mary Poppins." Cott, *Pipers at the Gates of Dawn*. New York: Random House, 1983, 195–240.

Patricia Demers. *P.L. Travers*. Boston: Twayne, 1991.

Ellen Dooling Draper and Jenny Koralek, eds. *A Lively Oracle*. New York: Larson, 1999.

Valerie Lawson. *Out of the Sky She Came*. Sydney, Australia: Hodder Headline, 1999.

Albert V. Schwartz. "*Mary Poppins* Revised." *Interracial Books for Children Bulletin*, 5 (1974), 1–5.

Brian Szumsky. "All That Is Solid Melts into the Air." *Lion and the Unicorn* 24 (2000), 97–109.

P.L. Travers. *What the Bee Knows*. London: Aquarian Press, 1989.

—*Karen Sands-O'Connor*

THE MATRIX (1999)

◼

Welcome to the desert of the real.

—Andy Wachowski and Larry Wachowski
The Matrix (1999)

Summary

Thomas A. Anderson lives two lives: one as a respectable software programmer, the other as the hacker Neo. But Neo is plagued by the notion that there must be something more, later identified and drawn from Aristotle as "the question that drives us." In pursuit of this, Anderson discovers that the world he has taken for granted is only an **illusion**, the Matrix, a **virtual reality** generated by **computers** to harvest

humanity's cerebral electromagnetic energy. His actual existence is as a dreaming body in a vat (see **Suspended Animation and Cryonics**). Freed from his illusion, he joins his rescuers in a **rebellion** against the machine world, led by a prophetic figure called Morpheus who believes that Neo is The One, a **messiah** who will liberate humanity from enslavement to the machine world. But to do this, Neo first must free himself from the **prison** of his mind as well as come to know and understand the Matrix itself (see **Knowledge**). Having eluded efforts by the computer masters of the Matrix to eliminate him, Neo vows to continue his struggle against them.

Discussion

Due to the overwhelming success of *The Matrix*, Neo had the chance to continue his struggle in two sequels, *The Matrix Reloaded* (2003) and *The Matrix Revolutions* (2003). The prevailing consensus, measured by the responses of critics and audiences, is that the first film was the most successful, while the other two represented a steady decline in cinematic presentation. This is not, however, the view of some philosophers and theologians, including Cornell West and Ken Wilber, who view the later films as a continuation and necessary expansion upon the religious and philosophical themes presented in *The Matrix* (see **Philosophy; Religion**).

Even to casual viewers, the films' use of religion is apparent. Neo's early conflation with Christ (see **Christianity**) is reinforced throughout the films through **names** and anagrams, associated symbols, **allegory**, and the reiterative use of triune numerology (not the only instance where numbers play an informing role). One obvious example is the Mary figure of Trinity, who is triunal as well as representative of **mythology**'s triple goddess, just as Neo's actions throughout the films can be viewed as analogous to the mythic sun-king, of which Christ is but one incarnation. However, Neo's messianic identification shares more in common with Gnostic gospels, and in later films elements of Buddhism and Hinduism are introduced as well as other mythological referents, along with increasing suggestions that Neo is reenacting the heroic pattern of Joseph Campbell's *The Hero of a Thousand Faces* (1949).

But philosophy is important as well. Neo's process of enlightenment mirrors that of the prisoners in the cave of Plato's *Republic* (c. 380 BCE). The metaphysical and perceptual issues raised by Plato and later philosophers are revisited throughout all three films, including allusions to Cartesian skepticism, Pedro Calderón de la Barca's dictum that "life is a dream," the screening or distortion of reality that occupied Jacques Lacan, Immanuel Kant, and Georg Hegel, and by direct reference, Friedrich Nietzsche and Jean Baudrillard. The films explore the meaning of free will and choice, versus the universal interrelatedness and absence of chance posited by Morpheus, the **destiny** that is implied by the programs of The Oracle (here again, appearances can be deceptive), the mathematical determinism of The Architect, the causality of The Merovingian, or the rationalism expressed as purpose by Agent Smith, all of which can also be viewed as alternative beliefs by which Neo as Christ is tempted. Aristotelian materialism is questioned, and the Cartesian conflict between body and mind—the mechanistic nature of the physical world as opposed to the ghost in the machine represented by the mind—is explored and mirrored, sometimes explicitly. And the moral dimensions of choice, the one versus the many, become symbolized by the opposite poles of Neo's individual actions for Kant's highest good and Agent Smith's replication of himself (another figure whose role must be viewed through triunal **metamorphosis**).

The science behind *The Matrix* is more problematic and speculative. Internal contradictions exist regarding the virtual reality of its **cyberspace:** at one point Neo fails in his attempt to "leap between tall buildings in a single bound," but the street he lands on responds as a cushion. However, when Trinity falls in the second film, it is determined that she will die, both in the virtual and real world, just as others in the Matrix can be killed by virtual bullets. As the physical laws that govern the real world are the same as those in *The Matrix*, the idea that these laws can be bent or broken by someone such as Neo, who knows its true nature, raises questions of **physics** as well as narrative credibility and convenience.

Overall, the first movie emphasizes questions of the mind and **perception**; the second materiality and the body; and the last concentrates upon emergence of the spirit, reinforced at the end by Neo's physical blindness (see **Vision and Blindness**), which forces him to abandon what he can see and touch—normal modes of human perception—and look beyond the intellectual and material constructs of the mind and body as well as the dualities posed during earlier films. This passage to a perception of a higher reality allows Neo, by seeing outside the perceptual reality of body and mind, to defeat the determinism and limitations of self represented by nemesis Smith, as well as bring about peace between the machine world and humanity. Neo's epiphany becomes an act of will and creation that changes and transforms the reality of the films' end, denying the inevitable conclusions posed by various characters and actions throughout the narrative and offering Neo's world, as well as the audience, an alternative possibility transcending the limitations of materialism and reason.

Bibliography

Stephen Faller. *Beyond The Matrix*. St. Louis: Chalice Press, date.

Karen Haber, ed. *Exploring The Matrix*. New York: St. Martin's Press, 2003.

Jake Horsley. *Matrix Warrior*. New York: St. Martin's Press, 2003.

William Irwin, ed. *The Matrix and Philosophy*. Chicago: Open Court, 2002.

Matthew Kapell and William G. Doty. *Jacking Into The Matrix Franchise*. New York: Continuum International Publishing Group, 2004.

Michael Marriot. *The Matrix Cultural Revolution*. New York: Thunder's Mouth Press, 2003.

Chris Seay and Greg Garrett. *The Gospel Reloaded*. Colorado Springs: Piñon Press, 2003.

Glenn Yeffeth, ed. *Taking the Red Pill*. Dallas: Benbella Books, 2003.

—*William Thompson*

METROPOLIS (1926)

■

Summary

A future **city** is divided into two parts: the wealthy live glorious lives of **decadence** above ground whereas the workers work underground as slaves (see **Slavery; Work and Leisure**) at various machines which power the rulers' lifestyle (see **Machines and Mechanization**). Freder, son of Fredersen—leader of the society—has fallen in **love** with the beautiful, rebellious Maria from the workers' **habitat** and descends into it to look for her. There he takes the place of an exploited worker, learning first-hand about the **horrors** of their everyday lives. In the meantime, Fredersen has learned of Maria's developing **rebellion**, and with the aid of **mad scientist** Rotwang, he plans to discredit her by replacing her with a **robot doppelgänger**. The false Maria inspires workers to bring about a disastrous **flood** in the lower levels; in the ensuing chaos, Freder is feared lost. However, he survives to reunite with Maria and see harmony brought to the society, as workers and rulers reach an agreement to work together in the future.

Discussion

Despite being the first undisputed classic of science fiction cinema—although numerous genre films were made in the previous thirty years—its disastrous **economics**, combined with the later box office failures *Just Imagine* (1930) and *Things to Come*, meant that little science fiction was filmed outside of horror hybrids for many years, and the epic scale was avoided until the eras of *2001: A Space Odyssey*, George Lucas, and Steven Spielberg. The original version of *Metropolis*, between three and four hours long, was almost immediately cut to a more manageable duration for the German market and reduced to even shorter lengths for the British (around two hours) and American (less than two hours) markets. From the late 1960s there have been various attempts to locate lost footage or alternate takes, to return the running time to something like Lang's original vision, with some versions using stills or intertitles to cover lost sequences. Some of these versions are: the 150-minute Munich Film Museum version; the 87-minute Georgio Moroder version (1984) with a rock soundtrack and some coloration of footage; the Jef Films so-called director's cut of 139 minutes (1992); a 147-minute version shown at the Berlin Film Festival; and a 123-minute version by the F.W. Murnau Foundation (2002). To some extent the timings are misleading because, until the introduction of synchronized sound in the late 1920s, there was no standard projection speed; some restorations are designed to run at 18 frames per second, some at 20, and some at 25. The basic story remains the same in all versions, although the absence of footage can cause confusion about character motivation.

This **dystopia** is a perhaps too-literal **allegory** of the horrors of the **class system**, which exploits workers en masse (see **Individualism and Conformity**), such workers being indistinguishable. In some ways the division echoes the Eloi and Morlock split of H.G. Wells's *The Time Machine*. The kinder side of **business** and economics, nevertheless, is suggested at the end of the film with the naïve suggestion that love in the form of the heart can mediate between the head (the wealthy) and the hand (the workers). This denouément, which left the director Fritz Lang uncomfortable, was introduced by scriptwriter Thea von Harbou, also his wife.

But it is the visuals—partially inspired by Lang's vision of New York City—that make the film truly memorable. We are given a view of future cities not matched until *Blade Runner* and anime such as *Akira* (1988) as well as a range of rather brutalist **architecture and interior design**. This modernist futurism is juxtaposed with elements of the **Gothic**, most notably the **fairy tale** cottage where Rotwang lives and the **labyrinth** of underground **caverns**. Lang and director of photography Karl Freund (who later directed *The Mummy* [1932] in Hollywood and worked with James Whale) drew on the lighting design and odd camera angles of German

Expressionist cinema to offer many striking scenes. The bringing to life of the robot Maria, amidst machinery and sparks of electricity, surely influenced Whale's depictions of **Frankenstein monsters** being animated in *Frankenstein* and *Bride of Frankenstein* (1935); and one machine is filmed as if it is a site of **sacrifice** to the Biblical **demon** Moloch.

Such allusions to **religion** are taken up elsewhere; Freder is a **messiah** figure who suffers when he substitutes himself for a worker, presumably trying to complete circuits by moving his hands on the clock-like faces of the machinery (see **Clocks and Timepieces**). (As one telling detail in the film, rational **progress** has led to a day based on ten-hour cycles, showing the alienation of working-class **humanity** from its "natural," or at least traditional, rhythms.) Maria acts as a forerunner of Freder's savior and is filmed surrounded by crosses. Her robot double, meanwhile, is hunted down like many other artificial **monsters**, a blasphemous affront to genuine life.

Lang made one more science fiction film, *The Girl in the Moon* (1929), again from von Harbou's script, before leaving Germany for Hollywood in 1933—prompted by Hermann Goebbels's offer to make him part of the Nazi propaganda machine because of Adolf Hitler's appreciation of *Metropolis*. Later, long after World War II, he would return to Germany to make one more film of genre interest, the **technothriller** *The Thousand Eyes of Dr. Mabuse* (1960).

Bibliography

Thomas B. Byers. "Kissing Becky." *Arizona Quarterly*, 45 (Autumn, 1989), 77–95.
David Desser. "Race, Space and Class." Judith B. Kerman, ed., *Retrofitting Blade Runner*. Bowling Green, OH: Bowling Green State University Popular Press, 1991, 110–123.
Thomas Elsaesser. *Metropolis*. London: BFI, 2000.
Regien-Mihal Friedman. "Capitals of Sorrow." *Utopian Studies*, 4 (1993), 35–43.
Michael Minden and Holger Bachman. *Fritz Lang's Metropolis*. Rochester, NY: Camden House, 2000.
Nigel Morris. "*Metropolis* and the Modernist Gothic." Jeff Wallace, ed., *Gothic Modernisms*. Houndmills: Palgrave, 2001, 188–206.
Constance Penley, Elisabeth Lyon, Lynn Spigel and Janet Bergstrom, eds., *Close Encounters*. Minneapolis: University of Minnesota Press, 1991, 161–168.
Lane Roth. "*Metropolis*, The Lights Fantastic." *Literature/Film Quarterly*, 6 (Fall, 1978), 342–346.
Andy Sawyer. "More Than Metaphor." *Foundation*, No. 64 (Summer, 1995), 70–81.

—Andrew M. Butler

THE MISTS OF AVALON
BY MARION ZIMMER BRADLEY (1982)

Summary

As **Christianity** sweeps across Britain, threatening the great Mother Goddess, High Priestess Viviane of Avalon schemes to insure her **religion's survival**. Viviane arranges the **marriages** of her younger sisters (see **Family**), Morgause and Igraine, to powerful Christian lords, hoping to influence matters outside of Avalon. Igraine bears her husband Gorlois a daughter, Morgaine, and later marries Uther and gives birth to **Arthur**. Viviane arranges for Morgaine and Arthur to sleep together without recognizing each other. Arthur is proclaimed High King and, vowing to remain true to the Goddess, he receives the **sword** Excalibur from Viviane as confirmation of his royal status. Learning that she is pregnant by her half-brother, Morgaine flees to Morgause and bears Mordred in secret. Morgause, fearing that the child's claim on the throne could supplant her own son Gawain, convinces Morgaine to leave him in her care.

Courting Christian support, Arthur decides to marry convent-raised Gwenhwyfar, who secretly **loves** his best friend Lancelot; he then gathers a circle of knights, including Lancelot, at his **castle** in Camelot. Queen Gwenhwyfar convinces Arthur to renounce the Goddess, resulting in the loss of Excalibur. As his kingship then begins to falter, Arthur and his knights embark upon a **quest** for the Holy Grail, but to no avail. Mordred betrays Arthur and delivers his **death** wound (see **Betrayal**), but Arthur manages to kill him in the same encounter. Morgaine then takes Arthur back to Avalon.

Discussion

Although Marion Zimmer Bradley spent a long and prolific career writing science fiction and fantasy novels about strong female characters, none captured readers' imaginations more than this refreshing antidote to the **heroic fantasy,** which had come before, the book that brought Bradley to the best-seller lists. Mainstream readers were less interested in its magical aspects and instead focused on its feminist message of independence (see **Feminism**) and **rebellion** against male authority. Bradley's priestesses, fighting against a brutal Christianity, have also influenced neo-pagans in real life, and many of them have incorporated the symbols and mysticism of Avalon into their **rituals**.

Bradley always insisted that her only purpose in writing *The Mists of Avalon* was to retell the story of Arthur from the losing side. She cites scholar Geoffery Ashe's examination of the Arthur legend created by Geoffery of Monmouth in the twelfth century as the springboard for generating the novel. As analyzed by Ashe, Monmouth had patched together meager historic details and hearsay into a heroic **cycle** of **chivalry** and **romance** (see **Medievalism and the Middle Ages**). Historical fact and Arthurian legend may never agree, but it is precisely this absence of concrete fact that makes the story so appealingly malleable to contemporary authors like Bradley. As one result of her study of Ashe, Bradley strikingly decided to return to an older spelling of the character generally known as Guinevere. On the one hand, this may have been her way of signalling that her version of the Arthur saga, unlike others, was actually derived from research; on the other hand, it may have represented her desire to de-familiarize Arthur's wife and allow readers to ignore past perceptions in evaluating Bradley's version of the character.

By its nature, a retelling of the Arthurian legend cannot generate sequels, so Bradley instead responded to the popularity of *The Mists of Avalon* by writing three prequels. In *The Forest House* (1995), Druid-girl Eilan and Briton Gaius are yet another pair of star-crossed lovers whose offspring Gawen will serve Avalon. In *Lady of Avalon* (1998), Bradley explores **reincarnation**, as Gawen, his lover Sianna, and his foster **mother** Caillean serve the Goddess in three successive lives. Finally,

Priestess of Avalon (2002), written with Diana Paxson, follows the life of Helena, the priestess exiled from Avalon and the mother of Emperor Constantine. Her pilgrimage to the Holy Land yields the insight needed to bring about the union between the Goddess and Christ.

A television miniseries based on *The Mists of Avalon* (2001) was also produced, with mixed results. Of necessity, some plot lines were merged or discarded to fit the story into a four-hour time frame. Of greater interest are the changes to key characters. The miniseries portrays Viviane as more concerned with her own earthly powers and influence than with the Goddess's survival. Lady Gwenhwyfar is dealt with more gently. While Bradley depicted her as a pious tool of the Church, completely in thrall to the dogma taught by its priests, the miniseries creates a more balanced character, torn between her loyalty to her husband and her love for Lancelot. The greatest change, however, comes with its portrayal of Morgaine, its narrator. Perhaps to insure the sympathies of mainstream viewers, Morgaine becomes a powerless victim of Viviane's plotting, with no responsibility for her own actions. This change strips her of the resonant dual nature Bradley so carefully constructed in the novel, that of a woman trapped between two demanding worlds—the physical and the spiritual, the real world and the mystical Avalon.

Bibliography

Geoffrey Ashe. *The Discovery of King Arthur*. London: Guild, 1985.

Carrol L. Fry. "The Goddess Ascending." *Journal of Popular Culture*, 27 (Summer, 1993), 67–80.

Melinda Hughes. "Dark Sisters and Light Sisters." *Mythlore*, 19 (Winter, 1993), 24–28.

Caitlin Matthews. *Arthur and the Sovereignty of Britain*. London: Arkana, 1989.

Diana L. Paxson. "Marion Zimmer Bradley and *The Mists of Avalon*." *Arthuriana*, 9 (Spring, 1999), 110–126.

Rosalyn Rossignol. "The Holiest Vessel." *Arthuriana*, 5 (Spring, 1995), 52–61.

S.M. Schwartz. "Marion Zimmer Bradley's Ethic of Freedom." Tom Staicar, ed., *The Feminine Eye*. New York: Ungar, 1982, 73–88.

Charlotte Spivack. "Morgan le Fey." Sally K. Slocum, ed. *Popular Arthurian Traditions*. Bowling Green, OH: Bowling Green State University Popular Press, 1992, 18–23.

Lee A. Tobin. "Why Change the Arthur Story?" *Extrapolation*, 34 (Summer, 1993), 147–157.

—*Charlene Brusso*

MORE THAN HUMAN
BY THEODORE STURGEON (1953)

■

The idiot lived in a black and gray world, punctuated by the white lightning of hunger and the flickering of fear. His clothes were old and many-windowed.

> *Here peeped a shinbone, sharp as a cold chisel, and there in the torn coat were ribs like the fingers of a fist. He was tall and flat. His eyes were calm and his face was dead.*
>
> —Theodore Sturgeon
> *More Than Human* (1953)

Summary

More Than Human consists of three linked novellas, one previously published. In "The Fabulous Idiot," an apparent fool is taken in by the Prodd family and, after trying and failing to say he was "all alone," is called Lone. Lone discovers that he is in among **children** with amazing powers: twins Beanie and Bonnie can teleport (see **Teleportation**); Little Janie practices telekinetics; and Baby is a "brilliant but faultless computer." Working together, the five people are a group mind, with powers far stronger than any individual.

"Baby is Three" (1952) is narrated by Gerry, a child genius adopted by the group mind. When Lone dies, the group seeks help from his old acquaintance Alicia Kew, a prissy spinster who, unlike Lone, attempts to wield parental authority. When she tries to send Baby away, the children rebel, and Gerry eventually feels compelled to kill Kew—but not before he enters her mind and learns about the conversations she had with Lone about the nature of *Homo gestalt*—a **hive mind**. Then Gerry assumes Lone's place as the group's leader.

"Morality" takes place ten years later. Hip Barrows, former Air Force engineer, is released from **prison** having lost most of his **memory**. He falls in **love** with Janie, who while nursing him back to health helps him recall how he found the anti-**gravity** generator Lone built for the Prodds' **farm**; Gerry then tampered with his mind—first with delusions, later inspiring amnesia and self-destructive psychosis—to preserve the group's secret. Now understanding the gestalt and what it lacks, he immobilizes Gerry in a fight and has him read a credo of morality from Hip's mind. Now at last the gestalt is complete, incorporating Hip as the formerly missing conscience. Earth's other gestalts reveal themselves and welcome the new member, hitherto quarantined for its immaturity.

Discussion

More Than Human touches on some of the perennial themes of 1950s science fiction, including the conflict between man and **superman** and the nature and limitations of **psychic powers**. But instead of using his advanced humans as the basis for a power fantasy (like A.E. van Vogt's *Slan* [1940]), or a gloomy post-apocalyptic tale (like John Wyndham's *Re-Birth* [1955]), Sturgeon characteristically tackles more difficult issues. If *homo gestalt* is in some ways superior to *homo sapiens*, but is unable to advance, what does this say about **evolution**? If the hive mind cannot be educated by traditional means (since Kew's attempt to be their teacher ends with her demise), how can the hive mind learn and change?

Another problematic question is the relationship between the group mind and the rest of **humanity**. Traditionally, *homo superior* is viewed as the race destined to supplant ordinary humans, with advanced **intelligence** and powers that make them the natural rulers, or natural exterminators, of their lesser predecessors. This is why so many stories depict bitter conflicts between the two species; and in *More Than Human*, Barrows's justifiable antagonism to the group mind demonstrates that members must anticipate widespread hostility from the ordinary people around them. Yet Sturgeon's supermen are in a paradoxical position: while they can link together to form a collective intelligence with vast powers, all members of the group, as Janie repeatedly tells Hip, retain their own **identities** and spend much of their time as separate individuals. Sturgeon's *homo gestalt* thus seems destined to be both in opposition to humanity, and an integral part of humanity.

Ultimately, as is not surprising, Sturgeon concludes essentially that the answer is love. To avoid conflict with other humans, members of *homo gestalt* must learn to realize that their goal is not to suppress or supplant humanity, but rather to help humanity **progress** through suggestions instead of commands. Through mental contact with the other group minds at the end of the novel, Gerry sees them inspiring geniuses to use their intelligence: one whistles themes to Joseph Haydn, while another gives a young Henry Ford a vision of an assembly line. Thus, both *homo sapiens* and *homo superior* can harmoniously co-exist, each race evolving and improving in its own way.

More Than Human can also be viewed as a metaphorical depiction of how people need to form and become a part of **families**. All members of *homo gestalt* were separated or alienated from their birth families, but they are driven to find each other and come together to establish a support system and achieve much more than they could have achieved as individuals. Sturgeon therefore affirms everyone's natural impulse to connect with other humans through love and build a **home** as protection from the stresses and strains of the world. Because Sturgeon can limn these and other evocative themes in a clean, spare, and forceful style, *More Than Human* is generally regarded as Sturgeon's best novel, and as one of science fiction's greatest novels.

Bibliography

Michael Bishop. "More Than a Masterpiece?" *Quantum*, No. 36 (Spring, 1990), 5–6.

Lahna F. Diskin. *Theodore Sturgeon*. San Bernardino, CA: Borgo Press, 1982.

David G. Hartwell, "Interview With Theodore Sturgeon." *New York Review of Science Fiction*, No. 7 (March, 1989), 8–11; No. 8 (April, 1989), 12–15.

N.B. Hayles. "Imperfect Art." *Extrapolation*, 22 (Spring, 1981), 13–24.

Paul Q. Kucera. "Intimate Isolation." *Extrapolation*, 44 (Winter, 2003), 437–445.

Lucy Menger. *Theodore Sturgeon*. New York: Ungar, 1981.

Sam Moskowitz. "Theodore Sturgeon." Moskowitz, *Seekers of Tomorrow*. Cleveland and New York: Crown, 1963, 229–248.

Brian Stableford. "The Creators of Science Fiction, 2: Theodore Sturgeon." *Interzone*, No. 93 (March, 1995), 43–45, 55.

Paul Williams. "Story Notes: 'Baby is Three.'" Theodore Sturgeon, *Baby is Three*, ed. Williams. Berkeley, CA: North Atlantic Books, 1999, 401–415.

—*Martin Morse Wooster*

ℜ

The Narrative of Arthur Gordon Pym
by Edgar Allan Poe (1838)

*And now we rushed into the embraces
of the cataract, where a chasm threw
itself open to receive us. But there arose
in our pathway a shrouded human figure, very far larger in its proportions
than any dweller among men. And the
hue of the skin of the figure was of the
perfect whiteness of the snow.*

—Edgar Allan Poe
The Narrative of Arthur Gordon Pym (1838)

Summary

Arthur Gordon Pym, a **youth** with more daring than sense, decides with the con-
nivance of a friend to stow away on the whaler *Grampus*. A previous close call in a
sailing accident, instead of frightening him, has awakened in Pym an overpowering
thirst for more thrills. He gets his wish. Almost as soon as the *Grampus* leaves
Nantucket, things go wrong, spectacularly. Pym, stowed away amid barrels and
crates in the hold, suffers from perpetual **darkness** with suggestions of being buried
alive. Mutiny, murder, storms, dereliction, shipwreck, near-starvation, cannibalism, a
plague ship, and the gangrenous death of a friend all add to Pym's woes until he and
Dirk Peters, a friendly sailor, are rescued by the whaler *Jane Guy*, which heads south,
finding a warm polar sea and the unknown archipelago of Tsalal, where there are
strange animals and ground **water** is a multicolored viscous fluid (see **Polar Regions**).
The word *"Tekeli-li!"* is numinous to the natives, who at first seem friendly but
finally slaughter all the *Jane Guy* crew except Pym and Peters, who **escape** in a canoe.
Carried south by currents, Pym and Peters encounter an enormous cataract of mist,
and "there arose in our pathway a shrouded human figure, very far larger in its proportions than any dweller among men. And the hue of the skin of the figure was of
the purest whiteness of the snow." That is the end of the story. In a dissociative disclaimer, Poe states that the remainder of Pym's story has been lost.

Discussion

The Narrative of Arthur Gordon Pym of Nantucket (its original full title) was commissioned by publishers to capitalize on the popularity of sea stories like the novels of Frederick Marryat and the then-current interest in Antarctic **exploration**, particularly the voyages of Benjamin Morrell and Jeremiah Reynolds. In form, Poe's only novel is an uneasy chimera. Its first half seems like one of Poe's **horror** stories, with typical tropes like the fear of premature burial; the ship becomes more like a **prison** to Pym than a liberating pathway to adventure. However, the second half opens up to become the sort of fantastic travelogue that his publishers wanted and is rather uncharacteristic of Poe's other works. Reflecting its dual nature, critical assessments of *The Narrative of Arthur Gordon Pym* are sharply divided: some admire its first half but feel that Poe stumbles and drifts in its second half; others are bored by the early horrors and believe that Poe's narrative only later becomes more innovative and interesting.

The novel is filled with inconsistencies suggesting that Poe was not comfortable in writing a story of this length. Peters, in appearance likened to "negroes" and a "demon," is introduced as the son of a **Native American** woman and a white trader, one of the many nonwhite companions of white **heroes** in nineteenth century narratives analyzed in Leslie Fiedler's *Love and Death in the American Novel* (1960). But later, amidst the natives of Antarctica, Pym says that he and Peters are "the only living white men upon the island." Pym, like Jonathan Swift's Gulliver (see *Gulliver's Travels*), does not have a consistent personality, responding differently to each different situation. At one point the story is told through Pym's dated journal entries and references to certain numbers of days having passed; but careful study reveals that Poe has inadvertently added an extra month to the year.

Most critical attention, naturally enough, has focused on efforts to interpret the novel's ambiguous conclusion. Descriptions of the Antarctic natives include intriguing biblical references: the word *"Tekeli-li!"* suggests "mene tekel," the words written on Nebuchnezzar's wall; the **king's** name Tsalemon or Psalemoun suggests Solomon; and fissures in the **landscape**, according to Poe, form Semitic letters (actually, as an authorial in-joke, one reads "Ed. Allan Poe" in fractured letters). In such a context, the figure in white might have been intended to suggest an outpost of the Lost Tribes of Israel. Another common theory is that Poe originally planned to write a story about a **hollow Earth**, building upon the then-popular theory of John Cleve Symmes that **Earth**'s hollow interior might be accessed by means of openings at the poles. Another possibility is that Poe intended his Antarctic current to enter the Abyss of Waters, based on an early belief that the Earth was riddled with water-filled chambers, replenished by maelstroms, which in turn emitted surface water. It is not clear why Poe chose to end his novel as he did: perhaps he had simply tired of the story and resolved to conclude it as quickly as possible; or he may have preferred to end on a note of **mystery**, allowing readers to ponder where Pym might have gone—or to wonder, like the author of the postscript, if the story was simply an elaborate hoax (see **Metafiction and Recursiveness**).

Another idea that might occur to modern readers—that Poe was hoping to stimulate interest in a possible sequel—is certainly not the case, given the publishing climate of Poe's day. However, other authors have taken up the challenge of completing his story. In Charles Romyn Dake's *A Strange Discovery* (1899), Pym finds a lost race at the South Pole, and in Jules Verne's *The Sphinx of the Ice* (1897), a second expedition visits the area of Tsalal and finds an enormous natural magnet. In a less direct reference, the Antarctic explorers of H.P. Lovecraft's "At the Mountains of Madness" (1936) hear the cry "*Tekeli-li!*," linking Poe and Lovecraft's **elder races**. Also worth mentioning is Rudy Rucker's pastiche *The Hollow Earth* (1990), in which Poe himself and some colleagues enter the hollow Earth through an Antarctic opening.

Bibliography

R.L. Carringer. "Circumscription of Space and the Form of Poe's *Arthur Gordon Pym*." *PMLA*, 89 (1974), 506–516.

F.S. Frank. "The Gothic at Absolute Zero." *Extrapolation*, 21 (Spring, 1980), 21–30.

David Halliburton. *Edgar Allan Poe*. Princeton: Princeton University Press, 1973.

Kevin J. Hayes, ed. *The Cambridge Companion to Edgar Allan Poe*. Cambridge; Cambridge University Press, 2002.

A. Robert Lee. *Edgar Allan Poe*. New York: Barnes and Noble, 1987.

G.F. Lee. "The Quest of Arthur Gordon Pym." *Southern Literary Journal*, 4 (1972), 22–33.

Burton R. Pollin. *The Imaginary Voyages of Edgar Allan Poe*. Boston: Twayne, 1981.

J.H. Stroupe. "Poe's Imaginary Voyage." *Studies in Short Fiction*, 4 (1967), 315–321.

Terence Whalen. *Edgar Allan Poe and the Masses*. Princeton: Princeton University Press, 1995.

—Gary Westfahl

NEUROMANCER BY WILLIAM GIBSON (1984)

—————————————■—————————————

The sky above the port was the color of television, tuned to a dead channel.

—William Gibson
Neuromancer (1984)

Summary

Case, a **computer** hacker—now small-time because former employers he tried to defraud cut off his ability to access **cyberspace**—is recruited by the mercenary Molly into a sophisticated technological heist of the corporate databanks of media conglomerate Sense/Net and globalized industrial company of Tessier-Ashpool (see **Globalization**). The power behind the scheme is Wintermute, an Artificial Intelligence wishing to unite with its alter ego Neuromancer. Molly's employer Armitage restores Case's abilities and assembles a gang of thieves, stealing the recorded personality of McCoy Pauley ("The Dixie Flatline") from Sense/Net and kidnapping Peter Riviera, a decadent cabaret artist (see **Decadence**) with implanted holographic projectors. Leaving **Japan** for **space station** Freeside, the crew penetrates Tessier-Ashpool's corporate headquarters in a **family** mansion within Freeside. Riviera ingratiates himself to 3Jane, daughter of the Tessier-Ashpool clan, gaining access that Molly acquires by stealth; with assistance from Maelcum and his ship *Marcus Garvey*, Case and the Flatline deploy a software virus to crack Tessier-Ashpool's security. Riviera proves traitorous, Molly stumbles upon Ashpool's **suicide**, and Armitage crumbles into an earlier **paranoia**, so Case and Maelcum must physically enter Straylight, where they extract from 3Jane the secret code to release the cybernetic locks preventing AI **evolution**. The metamorphosed AI contacts similar intelligences in the Centauri system, and Case returns to his petty, self-destructive life.

Discussion

Usually regarded as *the* paradigm of **cyberpunk**, *Neuromancer* opens a series called the Sprawl Trilogy—with *Count Zero* (1986) and *Mona Lisa Overdrive* (1988). More a triptych than a trilogy, these high-tech **near future** fictions share a postcolonial **landscape** (see **Postcolonialism**)—debris-strewn **cities** and **virtual reality** havens, urban undergrounds and bourgeois playgrounds—dominated by supranational corporations, not nation-states. Though involving similar characters, themes, and situations, the triptych does not tell a single, continuous story.

Neuromancer remains the most discussed science fiction novel since 1984, especially in mainstream literary scholarship. The first novel to sweep all the major science fiction awards in a single year, it alternately energized and enraged the entire field, exerting tremendous influence on young writers and filmmakers—as seen in Dan Simmons's **Hyperion, The Matrix**, Neal Stephenson's **Snow Crash**, and many more. Similarly, the novel draws on earlier works by Alfred Bester (see **The Stars My Destination**), Philip K. Dick, and Samuel R. Delany (*Babel-17* [1966] or *Nova* [1968] more than *Triton*). Portions of *Neuromancer* poach from the visual saturation of **Blade Runner**, the pastiche techniques of William S. Burroughs, the cybernetic **inventions** in Vernor Vinge's *True Names* (1981), and the counter-hegemonic sensibilities of the American avant-garde and pop **culture**, notably rock **music** and **youth** culture.

Any adequate account of the novel's intertexts would invoke several other sources, including hard-boiled **detective** novels and film noir of the 1930s and 1940s. The novel's appealing, diverse intertextual density aligns it with **postmodernism**; this density is especially evident in *Neuromancer*'s remarkable style—sometimes wildly flamboyant, sometimes coldly understated, by dazzling turns technically formal and colloquially vulgar, but always fast, visual, and oxymoronic. In its corrosive lyricism, pixilated iconography, and paratactical accretions, the prose occasionally approaches **poetry**. Though many readers initially suffer information overload, this obsessive, anxious texture remains one of the novel's most compelling and influential qualities.

As befits the cyberpunk anti-**hero**, each displaced, wounded character is estranged from both their society and each other (families do not exist in *Neuromancer*); all are low-life but street-wise, trolling the criminal underworld (see **Crime and Punishment; Estrangement**) for "biz" (see **Business**), alternately practicing **betrayal** or betraying psychological paralysis. Gibson frequently remarks that these flat, shallow figures result not from any specific intellectual agenda but his "limited capacity to do complex characterization." Other signs mark the book as "adolescent," like the novel's disturbingly aestheticized **violence**, romanticized **drug** addiction, and commodity fetishism—a manic concern with **fashion**, best seen in compulsive use of hip brand **names** (see **Advertising**).

Those weaknesses intermingle with and oddly support the complex network of thematic antinomies and involutions, especially the way the novel conflates categories of the natural and artificial. Even the human body is *mediated*, changed by invasive **technologies**, primarily prostheses (both physical and cognitive) but also sophisticated medical techniques. Now "hard wired," even individual volition seems merely a program, effectively subverting conventional concepts of personal **identity**. Most criticism focuses on these structural ambivalences and resulting ethical imperatives (see **Ethics**). Ironically, although the novel rethinks conventions, it also reinforces a traditional psychophysical dualism, where the body ("the meat") prevents and so compels the mind toward cybernetic ecstasy (see **Sublime**) within the matrix. Case desires absolute **escape** from the physical, the motif that concludes *Mona Lisa Overdrive*.

Some devices, characters, and buzzwords—mirrorshades, *shuriken*, cyberspace—appeared in Gibson's earlier stories, collected as *Burning Chrome* (1986). Clever parts of a triptych and filling out much of the landscape's detail, *Count Zero* and *Mona Lisa Overdrive* present warmer people who have families. More about **art** and life than interpenetrating technologies, their plots become less the formal pattern of *noir* **technothriller** and more about human relationships. Yet these books are distinctly more sentimental, melodramatic, and clichéd—their prose increasingly clipped, becalmed, and simple. They are also more mystical and diffuse: apparently the fused AI's encounter with its Centauri kindred causes a personality fragmentation (akin to Armitage's), and these ghostly remnants manifest themselves as **gods and goddesses, voodoo** *loa*. In the Bridge Trilogy—*Virtual Light* (1993), *Idoru* (1996), and *All Tomorrow's Parties* (1999)—and *Pattern Recognition* (2003), Gibson's skill as a writer has kept growing, his characters have become more complex, and the themes and prose are more subtle. However, none of this more mature work has had the power or impact of *Neuromancer*.

Bibliography

Scott Bukatman. *Terminal Identity*. Durham: Duke University Press, 1993.

Istvan Csicsery-Ronay, Jr. "Antimancer: Cybernetics and Art in Gibson's *Count Zero*." *Science-Fiction Studies*, 22 (March, 1995): 63–86.

———. "The Sentimental Futurist." *Critique*, 33 (Spring, 1992), 221–240.

Cynthia Davidson. "Riviera's Golem, Haraway's Cyborg." *Science-Fiction Studies*, 23 (July, 1996), 188–198.

Neil Easterbrook. "The Arc of Our Destruction." *Science-Fiction Studies*, 19 (November, 1992), 378–394.

Larry McCaffery, ed. *Storming the Reality Studio*. Durham: Duke University Press, 1991.

Tony Myers. "The Postmodern Imaginary in William Gibson's *Neuromancer*." *Modern Fiction Studies*, 47 (Winter, 2001), 887–909.

George E. Slusser and Tom Shippey, eds. *Fiction 2000*. Athens: University of Georgia Press, 1992.

—Neil Easterbrook

NINETEEN EIGHTY-FOUR
BY GEORGE ORWELL (1949)

War is peace
Freedom is slavery
Ignorance is strength

—George Orwell
Nineteen Eighty-Four (1949)

Summary

Winston Smith rewrites old newspaper articles at London's Ministry of Truth to suit the shifting propaganda of the Ingsoc Party. Due to falsification of **history**, he struggles to recall (see **Memory**) England before the Revolution of the fifties or if Oceania has always been at war with Eurasia, and not with East Asia (see **Future War**). English is being emended into "Newspeak" (see **Language and Linguistics**) to make "thoughtcrime" impossible. Outer Party members are subjected to surveillance by intrusive telescreens and spying by their **children** (see **Espionage**). Distortion of production statistics and retrospective correction of Big Brother's predictions conceal the decline of their economy. Party members are required to participate in indoctrination activities, including expressions of hate against the archenemy Goldstein. All social intercourse is controlled, upon penalty of **torture**, execution, and removal from records as an "unperson." The Inner Party, on the other hand, enjoys both control and privileges. The Proles, the unindoctrinated majority of the populace, are largely ignored.

Winston purchases a blank book and keeps a journal (see **Writing and Authors**) to develop his increasingly dissident thoughts. He is seduced (see **Love**) by Julia, outwardly an enthusiastic Anti-Sex League participant, but actually a sexual rebel. They rent a private room in the Prole district and approach O'Brien, a member of the Inner Party, hoping to help the Brotherhood overthrow the regime. Unfortunately, O'Brien is a double agent, their tryst-nest is discovered and the lovers are tortured to the point that they betray one another (see **Betrayal**).

Discussion

Influenced by Yevgeny Zamiatin's *We*, and in all likelihood, Aldous Huxley's *Brave New World*, *Nineteen Eighty-Four* is the most prominent dystopian fiction (see **Dystopia**). Although the repressive regime in the novel is technologically backward, "Big Brother" has entered modern English misused as denoting the constraint of personal expression by **governance systems** utilizing new technical means of surveillance.

The novel conveys Orwell's second thoughts as a former Socialist sympathizer regarding the U.S.S.R. under Stalinist repression. Government-channeled cults of the supreme leader, the practice of intentional censorship of history, denunciation by **family** members, show trials, and the disappearance of "unpersons" reflect the

Soviet purges. Given his Jewish surname, Emmanuel Goldstein probably refers to Stalin's arch-enemy Leon Trotsky, whose natal surname was Bronstein. The sheer racism regarding Asians resembles Nazi attitudes in Adolf Hitler's Germany (see **Race Relations**). Other readers discern attacks on Western **culture** (the state's provision of cheap entertainment to Proles), Britain and the BBC (wartime news censorship), and references to Orwell's conflicted **youth**, especially regarding Winston's sexual attitudes and aversion to rats (see **Rats and Mice**).

This is a truly masochistic novel. Every aspect of Winston's realm is significantly degraded. **Technology** is largely old-fashioned and unreliable, that is, when it is available. Furnishings are tawdry; dress is uniform and drab. Much of the **food and drink** is poor artificial imitations and the rest often resembles vomit. Every social interaction is subject to surveillance. No natural human relationships remain, which further disorients party members. The Anti-Sex League works to subvert the marital bond; even the orgasm is to be eliminated. No aspect of truth is invulnerable from Party distortion; O'Brien flatly states that the planets and stars revolve around the **Earth**. Outer Party members are scrutinized for nonverbalized facial gestures; the loyal Parsons incriminates himself in his **sleep**. Indeed Orwell bestows the regime with prescient powers inasmuch as it is able to anticipate Winston's actions and set traps (see **Paranoia**). O'Brien says the Party will last a thousand years with no nobler aim than that of maintaining power and being cruel: the image of the future is "a boot stamping on a human face—for ever" (see **Optimism and Pessimism**). A quintessential case of internalized repression, Winston's guilt feelings toward the regime help expose him (see **Guilt and Responsibility**). Whether keeping a diary, having sex with Julia, renting the Prole room, or applying to O'Brien to join the Brotherhood, they know they are acting in a suicidal manner. Near the end of the novel Winston and the reader learn what is in Room 101: nothing less than their greatest fear.

Of special interest in the novel are inserted texts by Goldstein and speeches by O'Brien regarding the management of power for power's sake, if not sheer sadism, amounting to the most chilling political vision since Nicolai Machiavelli's *The Prince* (1532). Orwell's "doublethink" has entered our idiom in the form of highly ironic Ingsoc slogans such as "Freedom Is Slavery" and "He who controls the present, controls the past." The **torture** and interrogation of Winston, naturally, is essential reading in the art of brain washing.

Nineteen Eighty-Four was adapted for television (1954) and film (1955); in the 1984 version, Richard Burton was brilliant in his last role as O'Brien.

Bibliography

Elaine Hoffman Baruch. "Love and the Sexual Object in Zamyatin's *We* and Orwell's *1984*." Baruch, *Women, Love and Power*. New York: New York University Press, 1991, 207–229.

James Connors. "Zamyatin's *We* and the Genesis of *1984*." *Modern Fiction Studies*, 21 (Spring, 1975), 107–124.

Brett Cooke. "Utopia and the Art of the Visceral Response." Gary Westfahl, George Slusser, and Eric S. Rabkin, eds., *Foods of the Gods*. Athens, Georgia: University of Georgia Press, 1996, 188–199.

Isaac Deutscher. "1984: The Mysticism of Cruelty." Deutscher, *Heretics and Renegades and Other Essays*. London: Hamish Hamilton, 1955, 35–50.

Irving Howe, ed. *Orwell's Nineteen Eighty-Four*. New York: Harcourt, Brace & World, 1963.

Earl G. Ingersoll. "The Decentering of Tragic Narrative in George Orwell's *Nineteen Eighty-Four*." *Studies in the Humanities*, 16 (December, 1989), 69–83.

Elizabeth Maslen, "One Man's Tomorrow Is Another's Today." George Slusser, Colin Greenland, and Eric S. Rabkin, eds., *Storm Warnings*. Carbondale: Southern Illinois University Press, 1987, 146–158.

Malcolm Pittock. "The Hell of *Nineteen Eighty-Four*." *Essays in Criticism*, 47 (April, 1997), 143–164.

William Steinhoff. *George Orwell and the Origins of 1984*. Ann Arbor: University of Michigan Press, 1975.

—*Brett Cooke*

NORSTRILIA BY CORDWAINER SMITH (1975)

Summary

The planet Norstrilia was settled many generations ago by farmers from Old North **Australia**. Their descendants maintain a harsh lifestyle despite immense wealth, derived from sales of stroon, a near-immortality-inducing **drug** harvested from giant sick sheep (see **Farms; Immortality and Longevity**). Young Rod McBan is about to be executed because he cannot clearly spiek or hier (words for telepathic communication) like other Norstrilians (see **Psychic Powers**). But with the help of an ancient family **computer**, McBan manipulates the stroon market until he becomes the wealthiest man in the universe. He buys Old **Earth**, to which he **escapes**, and there falls in love with the **cat**-woman C'mell. She recruits him into a Holy Insurgency in which the Underpeople, genetically manipulated **talking animals** who serve as slave labor, rebel against their human masters (see **Uplift**). The Catmaster, Earth's last clinical psychologist, gives Rod intensive psychotherapy, helping him to resolve his anger against his dead parents, to forgive his enemies back on Norstrilia, and to spiek and hier normally. The charismatic leader of the Underpeople, a **bird**-man called the E'telekeli, then enables Rod and C'mell to experience "whole centuries of real bliss" together in an intense shared **dream**, which lasts half an hour in real time. Rod donates most of his fortune to the Holy Insurgency and returns to Norstrilia to settle down and marry his longtime human sweetheart.

Discussion

Norstrilia is a **Bildungsroman** inspired in various ways by the remarkable life of Cordwainer Smith, whose real name was Paul Linebarger. Linebarger lived in many countries and among varied **cultures** throughout his life. He often felt psychologically isolated from his peers, just as Rod McBan does through his inability to spiek and hier telepathically. Linebarger's early years in **China**, as well as his father's role as Sun Yat-sen's legal advisor and propagandist, led him to become an expert on China and on psychological warfare. A major theme in his science fiction, found in

Norstrilia as well as in many of his short stories, is the value of each sentient individual regardless of that individual's place in the **class system**. This theme has often been interpreted as reflecting Linebarger's concern about **race relations** in the United States. But in fact the Underpeople were inspired primarily by the common Chinese masses, for whose **freedom** both Linebarger and his **father** worked throughout their lives. In his later years Linebarger found personal comfort in **Christianity**. The Underpeople's Holy Insurgency (based on the "Old Strong Religion") emerged during his writing of *Norstrilia* as his own religious faith became stronger (see **Religion**).

Linebarger's immersion in the literary classics of China is reflected in the loose overall structure of *Norstrilia* as well as in its cast of characters, both based on a Chinese epic, Wu Cheng-en's *Journey to the West* (c. 1550). The dry Norstrilian **landscape**, its huge sheep, and its flinty survivalist culture, were inspired by two lengthy visits to Australia late in Linebarger's life. ("Norstrilia" should be pronounced as Australians typically pronounce the name of their country: Nor-STRILE-ya.)

Norstrilia is a central part of Cordwainer Smith's future history, depicting a **galactic empire** in the **far future**. The other stories in this future history are available in the 1993 NESFA Press edition of *The Rediscovery of Man* (not to be confused with at least two much briefer collections published under the same title). Norstrilia and its inhabitants appear in several of these stories, especially "Mother Hitton's Littul Kittons" (1961) and "The Dead Lady of Clown Town" (1964). C'mell reappears as well, most prominently in "Alpha Ralpha Boulevard" (1961) and "The Ballad of Lost C'mell" (1962). Inspired by Linebarger's favorite cat, C'mell represents both personal freedom and **romance** in her relationship with Rod McBan. In "The Ballad of Lost C'mell," she and her soulmate Lord Jestocost represent mature and self-sacrificing love.

Norstrilia's publication history was unusually irregular. Linebarger finished it in 1963; several long excerpts soon appeared in science fiction magazines. A publisher bought the manuscript but felt it was too long for mass-market paperback publication. Roughly the first half of the novel was published in late 1964 under the title *The Planet Buyer*. Linebarger wrote a two-page conclusion to that half, as well as a new introductory section for the remaining half, so each could be read separately. He died before the second half was published in 1968 as *The Underpeople*. A nearly complete version of the entire novel (with many typos) was published as *Norstrilia* in 1975. That version has subsequently been reprinted by several publishers. The complete manuscript, with most typos corrected, was finally published by NESFA Press in 1994.

Bibliography

Alan C. Elms. "Introduction." *Norstrilia*, by Cordwainer Smith. Framingham, MA: NESFA Press, 1994.

———. "From Canberra to Norstrilia." *Foundation*, No. 78 (Spring, 2000), 44–58.

Johan Heje. "On the Genesis of *Norstrilia*." *Extrapolation*, 30 (Summer, 1989), 146–155.

Karen L. Hellekson. *The Science Fiction of Cordwainer Smith*. Jefferson, NC: McFarland, 2001.

Ursula K. Le Guin. "Thinking about Cordwainer Smith." Le Guin, *The Wave in the Mind*. Boston: Shambhala, 2004, 57–69.

Carol McGuirk, "The Rediscovery of Cordwainer Smith." *Science Fiction Studies*, 28 (July, 2001), 161–200.

John J. Pierce. "Introduction." Cordwainer Smith, *The Rediscovery of Man*, ed. James A. Mann. Framingham, MA: NESFA Press, 1993.

Gary K. Wolfe and Carol T. Williams. "The Majesty of Kindness: The Dialectic of Cordwainer Smith." Thomas D. Clareson and T.L. Wymer, eds., *Voices for the Future, Volume 3*. Bowling Green, OH: Bowling Green State University Popular Press, 1984, 52–74.

—*Alan C. Elms*

O

OUT OF THE SILENT PLANET
BY C.S. LEWIS (1938)
∎

Summary

Elwin Ransom, an English philologist (see **Language and Linguistics**), is drugged and taken to Malacandra (see **Mars**) by two men, Weston (see **Scientists**) and Devine. There, Ransom **escapes** and is befriended by Hyoi, a hross, a large seal-like, rational creature. While living among the hrossa, Ransom learns the Malacandrian language, Old Solar. When Hyoi is killed by Weston and Devine, an eldil (see **Angel**) orders Ransom to go to Oyarsa at Meldilorn. While traveling, Ransom meets Augray, a sorn, who teaches Ransom why **Earth** is called Thulcandra, the silent planet: the Oyarsa of Earth (see **Satan**) was banished from the heavens because he rebelled against Maleldil. Ransom learns that what is **mythology** and story on Earth may be fact and truth on other worlds. Ransom meets Oyarsa of Malacandra, the angelic being ruling the planet, who explains that each planet has an Oyarsa and then sends Ransom, Weston, and Devine back to Earth, forbidding them to return to Malacandra.

Out of the Silent Planet and its two sequels are often described as C.S. Lewis's Space Trilogy. In *Perelandra* (1942), Ransom is sent by eldils to Perelandra (see **Venus**) to prevent Tinidril, the Perelandrian **Queen**, from suffering her own fall from grace (see **Christianity**). In *That Hideous Strength* (1945), Ransom and his followers call upon eldils and the **wizard** Merlin (see **Arthur**) to help defeat Lord Feverstone (Devine), N.I.C.E. (National Institute for Co-ordinated Experiments), and their **demonic** masters.

Discussion

C.S. Lewis wrote *Out of the Silent Planet* as a result of a challenge with J.R.R. Tolkien, upon whom the character of Ransom is somewhat based, in which Tolkien would write a **time travel** story and Lewis a **space travel** story. Although a work of science fiction, *Out of the Silent Planet* does not emphasize science or **technology** as a means of better understanding or controlling reality. Rather, Ransom's **perception** and understanding of the world around him grow clearer and keener largely through language and story. During his first days on Malacandra, Ransom comes to trust alien creatures and disregard the **illusions** regarding aliens instilled in him by works like H.G. Wells's *The War of the Worlds*. He learns new truths about himself, **humanity**, and Earth that are not easy to accept because they challenge his previous beliefs. Ultimately, he must accept as truths the myths that gods or intelligences rule the planets and that Mars is somehow masculine and martial while Venus is feminine and sensual.

In *Perelandra*, Oyarsa of Malacandra sends Ransom to Perelandra to intervene in its **Adam and Eve** story. Arriving on a watery planet with floating **islands**, he discovers that he and the Green Lady (Queen Tinidril) are the only people in the area and that she is completely innocent. Into this paradise comes Weston, who announces that his previous goal of preserving and spreading human **biology** was misguided. Now, he seeks to spread Spirit, the Life-Force, Creative Evolution; Ransom, trying to get Weston to see that Christians do not worship Spirit just because it is spirit, responds that there are good and **evil** spirits. Weston will hear none of it, saying the Life-Force is both God and Satan and calling that **force** into himself completely to become the Un-man—something with a human body but inhabited by a **demon**. The spirit then uses the reason in Weston's mind to tempt Tinidril to disobey Maleldil's prohibition, suggesting that Maleldil really wants Tinidril to show her maturity by disobeying Maleldil.

Ransom now realizes that his purpose on Perelandra is to thwart Weston, using physical force. When shying away from this realization, he hears Maleldil say that he is also named Ransom. Slowly, Ransom comprehends that if he does not stop the temptation, Maleldil will have to do something greater than he did when he became a man on Earth. Convinced of the necessity to act, Ransom kills Weston/Un-man, throws him off a cliff, and witnesses the Great Dance, wherein Perelandra takes its rightful place in the universe as the first inhabited world to enter into perfection.

In *That Hideous Strength*, Ransom and colleagues convince Jane Studdock, a seer (see **Psychic Powers**), to help them find Merlin and oppose N.I.C.E., a quasi-scientific institute that hired Jane's sociologist husband Mark to write journalistic propaganda to provide it with the **freedom** to pursue its programs and experimentation on people (see **Ethics**). Mark discovers that N.I.C.E. is controlled by demonic powers who want to destroy all life on Earth. Ransom invokes the Oyereseu (plural of Oyarsa) of the planets for help; they use Merlin to bring chaos and destruction to N.I.C.E., allowing Mark to escape and reunite with Jane. The novel's end shows Mark and Jane entering a cottage full of images of fertility and love, showing that what is most important is for them to **love** one another.

Bibliography

David C. Downing. *Planets in Peril*. Amherst: University of Massachusetts Press, 1992.

Cath Filmer-Davies. "A Place in Deep Heaven." Gisbert Kranz, ed., *Inklings*. 3. Band. Lüdenscheid, Germany: Stier, 1985, 187–196.

Verlyn Flieger. "The Sound of Silence." Peter J. Schakel and Charles Huttar, eds., *Word and Story in C.S. Lewis*. Columbia: University of Missouri Press, 1991, 42–57.

Thomas Howard. *The Achievement of C.S. Lewis*. Wheaton, IL: Harold Shaw, 1980.

C.S. Lewis, Kingsley Amis, and Brian W. Aldiss. "Unreal Estates." Lewis, *Of Other Worlds*, ed. Walter Hooper. New York: Harcourt Brace Jovanovich, 1966, 86–96.

Douglas Loney. "Humpty Dumpty in the Heavens." *Mythlore*, 16 (Winter, 1989), 14–20.

Peter J. Schakel. *Imagination and the Arts in C.S. Lewis*. Columbia: University of Missouri Press, 2002.

Sanford Schwartz. "Cosmic Anthropology." *Christianity and Literature*, 52 (Summer, 2003), 523–556.

—*Theodore James Sherman*

The Outer Limits (1963–1965)

There is nothing wrong with your television set. Do not attempt to adjust the picture. We are controlling transmission. We will control the horizontal, we will control the vertical. We can change the focus to a soft blur, or sharpen it to crystal clarity. For the next hour, sit quietly and we will control all that you see and hear. You are about to participate in a great adventure. You are about to experience the awe and mystery which reaches from the inner mind to . . . The Outer Limits.

—Leslie Stevens
The Outer Limits (1963)

Summary

The Outer Limits debuted on ABC television in September 1963, and in its initial incarnation ran for only forty-nine episodes before mid-season cancellation in January, 1965. An anthology program with a different story, cast, and production crew for each episode, the show was created by Leslie Stevens as an alternative to the juvenile **space opera**-oriented programs that had defined television science fiction since the early 1950s. Stevens sought to employ science fiction's **sense of wonder** to bring adult television drama to a higher level and appeal to viewers who were not science fiction fans. Though some episodes were adapted from published stories, most were original, and their overall quality attests to the sympathy of the show's writers and directors for science fiction as a storytelling form rich with ideas and the metaphors for conveying them. In 1995, *The Outer Limits* was revived as a cable television series (1995–2000) that soon superseded the original in longevity if not originality.

Discussion

The Outer Limits had the misfortune to debut in the wake of almost a decade of B-movies in which the look of science fiction was synonymous with bug-eyed alien **monsters** and alien **invasions**. As a result, there was constant tension between the show's creators aiming to deliver provocative drama, and a network expecting monster-driven thrillers. Producers ultimately turned this tension to their advantage, using monsters as **mirrors** for **humanity**, and the sense of **horror** they evoked as a lens for examining the dark side of many science fiction themes.

The first episode, "The Galaxy Being" (1963), provided a template for the show's approach. It tells of an amateur inventor (see **Inventions**) whose irresponsible experiments with television effect **communication** with a being from an alternate **dimension**. After the creature's accidental **teleportation** into our world, its efforts to return **home** prompt hysteria and **violence** from misunderstanding humans. After warning about dangerous powers in the universe beyond human comprehension, the being destroys itself, knowing that it would be eliminated by its own peaceful race for contact with destructive humanity.

Subsequent episodes similarly explored the dangerous potential of **technology** in the hands of fallible humans. "The Man with the Power" (1963) features a **scientist** who amplifies his innate **psychic powers** only to see them turn into a **force** of uncontrollable destruction driven by subconscious feelings of anger and hostility. In "The Sixth Finger" (1963), a scientist accelerates the **evolution** of a test subject, unexpectedly turning him into a **superman** who is both alienated from the life he knew and ultimately hostile to his "inferiors." In these and other episodes, science is a neutral tool whose rationality highlights the often irrational behavior of humans who employ it.

Aliens on Earth were another means by which *The Outer Limits* used a science fiction theme to dramatize issues fundamental to the human condition. **First contact** stories like "The Bellero Shield" (1964) and "Counterweight" (1964) juxtaposed nonviolent representatives of morally superior aliens to scheming, self-centered humans. In its most complex treatment of this theme, "The Inheritors" (1964), benevolent extraterrestrials with no ability to procreate send genetic material to **Earth** in a meteor to infect human emissaries who will bring them crippled and unwanted human **children** to repopulate their dying planet.

Invasion stories often featured manipulative aliens who exploit the worst aspects of human nature. One of the show's best-known episodes, "The Zanti Misfits" (1963), is a powerful critique of capital punishment (see **Crime and Punishment**). The planet Zanti coerces Earth into serving as a **prison** for its most intractable criminals. When the creatures **escape** and are annihilated in a cataclysmic battle with the army, Zanti informs Earth that this was the intention all along: although they as a race are incapable of murder, they knew that human beings were not. Alien encounters served as touchstones for exploring many ideas on the program, ranging from **xenophobia** in "The Architects of Fear" (1963), in which government executives conspire to create an illusory alien menace to unite warring nations against a common enemy, to the Cold War **paranoia** of "O.B.I.T." (1963) and "The Invisibles" (1964), which propose a fifth column of aliens on Earth masquerading as normal human beings whose plans for domination are keyed to common human selfishness and mendacity. Humanity was not always presented in a bad light, though: in "Fun and Games" (1964) and "Keeper of the Purple Twilight" (1964), humanity triumphs over intellectually and physically superior aliens through powers of **love** and compassion which the aliens lack.

The Outer Limits brought a humanist slant to other science fiction themes. **Space travel** provides a hothouse environment in which human flaws and vulnerabilities flourish in "Second Chance" (1964), "The Mutant" (1964), and other episodes set on **alien worlds**. **Time travel**, another popular theme, inspired depictions of futures despoiled by **war** and devastation in "Soldier" (1964), which projects a future world of endless combat fought by a genetically bred soldier class, and "Demon with a Glass Hand" (1964), in which a self-sacrificing humanoid **robot** carrying the entire human race electronically translated into its circuitry fights a lone battle lasting 1200 years against alien invaders.

Like *The Twilight Zone*, whose last two years it overlapped, *The Outer Limits* showed that science fiction could provide a powerful vehicle for thoughtful dramas indistinguishable in their concerns from other television dramas save by their employment of genre motifs. The producers turned handicaps of low budgets and skimpy production values to their advantage, eschewing science fiction's gaudier set pieces to focus on fundamental human issues. Arguably, the program laid a foundation for *Star Trek* and other "high-concept" science fiction series that followed. Its successor series, while more lavishly budgeted and initially distinguished by efforts to employ experienced science fiction writers and adapt classic stories like George R.R. Martin's "Sandkings" (1995) and Larry Niven's "Inconstant Moon" (1996), rarely matched the quality of the original series.

Bibliography

J.G. Ballard. "*Outer Limits.*" *American Film*, 23 (October, 1987), 57–62.

David Bischoff. "The New *Outer Limits.*" *Omni*, 17 (April, 1995), 34–43.

Mike Clark and Mark Phillips. "Voice of Control." *Starlog*, No. 154 (May, 1990), 41–44, 58.

Kyle Counts. "Please Stand By." *Starlog*, No. 152 (March, 1990), 23–27, 34.

Frank Garcia. "*Outer Limits.*" *Cinefantastique*, 30 (September, 1998), 24–103.

John Javna. "*The Outer Limits.*" Javna, *The Best of Science Fiction TV*. New York: Harmony Books, 1987, 20–23.

Mark Phillips and Frank Garcia. "Outer Limits (1963–1965)." Phillips and Garcia, *Science Fiction and Television Series*. Jefferson, NC: McFarland, 1996, 231–243.

David J. Schow and Jeffrey Frentzen. *The Outer Limits: The Official Companion*. New York: Ace Books, 1986.

Rick Worland. "Signposts Up Ahead." *Science-Fiction Studies*, 23 (March, 1996), 103–122.

—*Stefan Dziemianowicz*

THE OWL SERVICE BY ALAN GARNER (1967)

Summary

In *The Owl Service*, contemporary Welsh and English **children** and adults find themselves living in a **cyclical** pattern dating back hundreds of years. Roger and Alison, step-brother and sister, are vacationing in Wales with their newly married parents in a house left them by Alison's uncle; Nancy, a local woman, keeps house, assisted by her son Gwyn and an odd handyman, Huw Halfbacon. Gwyn and Roger become rivals for Alison's attention, and the tension that develops spreads to include the adults. As events unfold, it becomes obvious that Gwyn, Alison, and Roger are experiencing a **love** triangle that Huw, Nancy, and Bertram (Alison's uncle) experienced before them and that can be traced to a similar pattern in the Fourth Branch of the medieval Welsh document known as the *Mabinogion* (compiled 1838–1849). The power behind this **cycle** is released through Alison, who can be either "owls" (see **Birds**) or "flowers," the former denoting fierceness (and possibly hatred and **death**) and the latter gentleness (and possibly love). In the end, Roger can put aside his bitterness toward Gwyn and refocus Alison on the **flower** aspect of her being, bringing the novel to a peaceful if not wholly happy ending.

Discussion

The Owl Service, named for the set of dishes that Alison and Gwyn find in the attic of the house, is a novel operating on many levels. The Gwyn-Alison-Roger love triangle is one level, the tension between teenagers and their parents is another, the conflict between the lower class Welsh and upper-middle class English is still a third (see **Class System**), and the almost tribal friction between the local Welsh **family** and vacationing English family is a fourth. Garner might have used these themes to write a realistic problem novel; however, the power of an ancient myth is still alive in this Welsh valley near Aberystwyth (see **Mythology**), and its presence not only makes *The Owl Service* a fantasy novel but deepens the conflicts among characters and adds another significant level to the novel.

The major conflicts on the realistic level reflect actual cultural and economic situations. The Welsh–English friction is a centuries-old animosity—the English are the conquerors and the Welsh are the conquered. The English, as conquerors, look down upon the Welsh, and the Welsh still resent the English and wish to be politically free of them. In addition, property in Wales in the latter part of the twentieth century has been foreclosed upon and sold for back taxes; many buyers have been from England and have turned property into vacation **homes**. This has created an animosity between the local Welsh and new English property owners. Thus, in addition to being rivals for Alison's attention, Gwyn, as a Welshman, and Roger, as an Englishman, inherit an age-old cultural rivalry as well.

In the final section of the Fourth Branch of the *Mabinogion*, Lleu's wife, Blodeuedd, has an affair with a neighboring noble, Gronw Bebyr, and they plot Lleu's **death**. They think themselves successful when Lleu flies off, wounded, in the shape of an eagle; but Gwydion, the magician, finds him, restores him to health, and aids him in taking revenge (see **Magic**). Lleu slays Gronw with a spear as Gronw had tried to slay Lleu, and Gwydion, who with his uncle Math's help had made Blodeuedd out of flowers to be Lleu's wife, turns Blodeuedd into an owl. Lleu then rules successfully but alone.

The ancient powers of these characters are still in this valley, cycling down through the generations; Gwyn is Lleu, Alison is Blodeuedd, and Roger is Gronw. In the previous generation, Huw, who has now become Gwydion for the three teenagers, was Lleu, Nancy was Blodeuedd, and Bertram was Gronw. Bertram died when Huw removed the brake blocks from his motorcycle. The power that destroyed Lleu, Blodeuedd, and Gronw will manifest itself through Alison; and while there is a possibility that the power could arise as a productive, gentle **force** (symbolized by the flowers from which Blodeuedd was created), it seems, once again, to be manifesting itself as a destructive, predatory force (symbolized by the owl into which Blodeuedd was transformed).

The ending of *The Owl Service* is controversial. The sympathetic figure, Gwyn, is unable to save Alison, and the unsympathetic figure, Roger, is. Moreover, critics disagree on whether or not Roger's refocusing Alison from owls to flowers means the cycle is ended. At various points in the novel, it is made clear that Alison could be either owls or flowers, and so the more logical conclusion is that Roger has ended this episode and that when the conditions are right again the cycle will continue.

Garner's use of Welsh Celtic mythology in *The Owl Service* does more than make what could have been a realistic novel into a fantasy novel. In fact, Garner includes very little of the original story though he makes allusions to it. What Garner is really addressing is how we are shaped by the past; in the case of characters in *The Owl Service*, they are shaped not just by the **history** of England and Wales but also by the accumulated cultural history, including a mythology, which they share and by which they are still affected.

Bibliography

Sarah Beach. "Breaking the Pattern." *Mythlore*, 20 (Winter, 1994), 10–14.

Eleanor Cameron. "*The Owl Service*." *Wilson Library Bulletin*, 44 (December, 1969), 425–433.

Emrys Evans. "Children's Novels and Welsh Mythology." Charlotte F. Otten, ed., *The Voice of the Narrator in Children's Literature*. Westport, CT: Greenwood Press, 1989, 92–100.

Paul Hardwick. "Not in the Middle Ages?" *Children's Literature in Education*, 31 (March, 2000), 23–30.

Kathleen Herbert. "*The Owl Service* and the Fourth Branch of the Mabinogi." *Labrys*, No. 7 (November, 1981), 115–122.

Michael Lockwood. "A Sense of the Spoken." *Children's Literature in Education*, 23 (1992), 83–92.

Neil Philip. *A Fine Anger*. New York: Philomel, 1981.

C.W. Sullivan III. "One More Time." *Journal of the Fantastic in the Arts*, 9 (1998), 46–54.

Andrew Taylor. "Polishing Up the Pattern." *Children's Literature in Education*, 23 (1992), 93–100.

—*C.W. Sullivan III*

P

THE PAST THROUGH TOMORROW BY ROBERT A. HEINLEIN (1967)

There ought not to be anything in the whole universe that man can't poke his nose into—that's the way we're built and I assume that there's some reason for it.

—Robert A. Heinlein
Methuselah's Children (1958)

Summary

In 1941, Robert A. Heinlein realized that several of his published stories could be fitted together to conform to a unified future **history**; he devised a chart, chronologically listing both published and planned stories alongside major events in this future, which appeared in the May, 1941 issue of *Astounding Science-Fiction*. During the 1940s and 1950s, Heinlein continued writing Future History stories, which appeared in five volumes collectively presenting stories by internal chronological order: *The Man Who Sold the Moon* (1950), *The Green Hills of Earth* (1951), *Revolt in 2100* (1963), the novel *Methuselah's Children* (1958), and *Orphans of the Sky* (1963). *The Past Through Tomorrow* reprints all the stories in one volume, omitting "'Let There Be Light'" (1940), "Universe" (1941), and "Common Sense" (1941) and adding "The Menace from Earth" (1957) and "Searchlight" (1962).

Heinlein's Future History envisions vigorous technological **progress** in the **near future**, including large moving roadways ("The Roads Must Roll" [1940]) and **space travel** ("The Man Who Sold the Moon" [1950], "Requiem" [1940], *The Green Hills of Earth*) until establishment of a religious dictatorship (see **Religion**) in the United States of the early twenty-first century brings progress to a halt. Later in the century, the dictatorship is overthrown ("'If This Goes On—'" [1940]), and **humanity** achieves a more enlightened **civilization**. In the twenty-second century, it is discovered that a secret group of "Howard Families" achieved great longevity through selective breeding (see **Immortality and Longevity**); to escape persecution, they embark on a journey outside the solar system, though upon returning they learn that humanity has independently found another way to indefinitely extend human lifespans (*Methuselah's Children*).

Discussion

Heinlein tells his Future History from two different perspectives. Some stories focus on the movers and shakers of the future, **scientists** and entrepreneurs responsible for major achievements. Memorable characters of this type include Larry Gaines, the brilliant administrator who crushes a threatening strike in "The Roads Must Roll"; D.D. Harriman, the millionaire who single-handedly effects space flight in "The Man Who Sold the Moon" and later achieves his dying wish by flying to the **Moon** in "Requiem"; and Andrew Jackson Libby, the misunderstood boy genius of "Misfit" (1939) who later assists the Howard Families in *Methuselah's Children*. These stories appear to support the "Great Man" theory of history, celebrating the extraordinary people who benefit humanity by means of their extraordinary talents.

Yet other stories, mostly written for mass-market magazines in the late 1940s, focus on ordinary people who are just trying to make a living in the future, though they are capable of heroic actions in an emergency (see **Heroes**). These include Rhysling, the "Blind Singer of the Spaceways" who **sacrifices** his life to save crewmates in "The Green Hills of Earth" (1947); Jake Pemberton, the talented space pilot who considers quitting but decides to stay on the job in "Space Jockey" (1947); William Saunders, a space pilot grounded by a fear of heights that he ultimately overcomes to rescue a **cat** on a ledge in "Ordeal in Space" (1948); and Gloria McNye, the female space engineer who proves her capabilities to skeptical male colleagues in "Delilah and the Space Rigger" (1949). These stories suggest instead that it is thousands of anonymous, everyday individuals, all making their own small contributions, that propel humanity forward. The point is driven home most sharply in "Coventry" (1940), in which a man who believes he can make it on his own receives his comeuppance and realizes that he is necessarily dependent upon fellow citizens, with whom he must learn to cooperate.

Heinlein extended his Future History in the 1970s and 1980s with four novels focusing on Lazarus Long, the only truly immortal member of the Howard Families who first appeared as the somewhat passive hero of *Methuselah's Children*. He came to the forefront in *Time Enough for Love* (1973), in which he is saved from attempted **suicide** by a future society determined to preserve this unique source of **knowledge** and **wisdom**. Garrulously expressing his opinions on a wide variety of subjects, many taking the form of proverbs later published separately as *The Notebooks of Lazarus Long* (1978), he presents the characteristic **philosophy** of the mature Heinlein: common people, and the **governance systems** that cater to them, primarily function to unreasonably restrict the **freedom** of highly intelligent and multitalented people like Lazarus Long, who must withdraw from society and settle in new **frontiers** whenever their governments begin to become too large and too powerful.

Lazarus Long appeared as a minor character in two later novels, *The Number of the Beast* (1980) and *The Cat Who Walks Through Walls* (1985), now engaged in a massive struggle against mysterious beings, called "Black Hats" in the first novel, who oppose humanity as it expands through multiple **dimensions** of time and space containing innumerable **parallel worlds** and well-known fictional universes, including L. Frank Baum's Oz (see *The Wonderful Wizard of Oz*) and E.E. "Doc" Smith's Lensman universe (see *Triplanetary*). However, this grand cosmic battle between good and **evil** never fully engages Heinlein's attention, and the Future History concludes weakly with *To Sail Beyond the Sunset* (1987), the meandering, sometimes salacious story of Lazarus Long's mother, Maureen Smith.

Bibliography

John W. Campbell, Jr. "History to Come." *Astounding Science-Fiction*, 27 (May, 1941), 5–6.
———. "Introduction." Robert A. Heinlein, *The Man Who Sold the Moon*. Chicago: Shasta Publishers, 1950, 11–15.
H. Bruce Franklin. *Robert A. Heinlein*. Oxford: Oxford University Press, 1980.
Robert A. Heinlein. "Concerning Stories Never Written." Heinlein, *Revolt in 2100*. 1953. New York: Signet Books, 1955, 189–192.
Damon Knight. "Introduction." Robert A. Heinlein, *The Past Through Tomorrow*. New York: Putnam, 1967, 9–12.
Farah Mendlesohn. "Corporatism and the Corporate Ethos in Robert Heinlein's 'The Roads Must Roll.'" Andy Sawyer and David Seed, eds., *Speaking Science Fiction*. Liverpool: Liverpool University Press, 2000, 144–157.
Joseph D. Olander and Martin Harry Greenberg, eds. *Robert A. Heinlein*. New York: Taplinger, 1978.
Alexei Panshin. *Heinlein in Dimension*. Chicago: Advent, 1968.
George Slusser. *The Classic Years of Robert A. Heinlein*. San Bernardino, CA: Borgo Press, 1977.

—*Gary Westfahl*

PAWN OF PROPHECY
BY DAVID EDDINGS (1982)

Summary

Garion, an orphaned **farm** boy, learns of the ancient struggle between the Alorn kingdoms of the West and Angarak kingdoms of the East. Long ago, Torak, one of the seven gods, stole an orb made from a stone that glows blue, possesses powerful properties, and was created by the god Aldur. The orb can only be held by one with pure intentions, and it resists Torak and causes a rift in the world in addition to horribly disfiguring him. Ever since, Torak and the Angaraks have sought a way to recover the orb and use it against the West, and, by finding a mysterious child who is capable of holding the orb without harm, they set off a chain of events that are recounted in the plot. Garion learns that he is a sorcerer descended from a line of disciples of Aldur who can hold the orb, scion of the last Rivan King, and hence Overlord of the West. He is prophesied to face Torak in a final battle to decide the fate of the world. Garion and his companions—who are also named in the prophecy and have their own roles to play—travel through many lands and experience adventures in their **quest** to recover the orb and fulfill the prophecy.

Discussion

Pawn of Prophecy is the first of five books that comprise The Belgariad sequence, the others being *Queen of Sorcery* (1982), *Magician's Gambit* (1983), *Enchanter's End Game* (1984), and *Castle of Wizardry* (1984). The story functions as a **Bildungsroman** in that it follows the development of Garion from childhood until his maturity as an adult. It also relies on many conventions and **clichés** found in the **heroic fantasy** or **sword and sorcery** subgenres of fantasy.

Garion is typical of **heroes** in these subgenres, as evinced by his humble origins and **destiny** as a force for good struggling against **evil**. The prophecy recounted in the book is the **divination** that ultimately serves to drive the plot forward. As in other books in these subgenres, heroes must engage in perilous quests, like the recovery of the orb of Aldur, a typical **magical object**. As in J.R.R. Tolkien's *The Lord of the Rings*, control of this object determines the fate of good versus evil. Garion is tutored by the **wizard** Belgarath to become a sorcerer and so learns **magic**, which Eddings describes as the concept of "The Will and the Word."

Ostensibly a high epic tale depicting the cosmic struggle between good and evil, Eddings's work is punctuated by a flair for **comedy**. This **humor**, which is laced throughout, serves to reduce some of the seriousness of the circumstances that characters face, and is perhaps best exemplified by Garion's companion the wily thief Silk, although it is also present in the banter between Polgara, Garion's aunt, and her **father** Belgarath. Belgarath has been given the gift of **eternity**, as disciples of Aldur must deal with the two-edged sword of **immortality and longevity**. They are the constant reference points in an elaborate backdrop of **history** of an **imaginary world** that Eddings constructs and that includes a pantheon of all too human **gods and goddesses**. This imaginary world is detailed by accompanying **maps**, and to a certain extent the plot is driven by the map, as no region is left unexplored.

In travels through the many lands, Garion encounters different proto-medieval **cultures**. For example, Mandorallen is a knight who practices the art of **chivalry**. Another character, Hettar, is from a culture centered around **horses** not unlike Rohan in Tolkien's *The Lord of the Rings*. Barak is from a country of Viking-like warriors. The country of Tolnedra is a thinly disguised Rome. Other characters also embody stock characterizations. Further genre conventions abound as they must battle various **supernatural creatures** including **demons**, go on an **underground adventure**, and make frequent use of **taverns and inns**. Ultimately, Garion fulfills his destiny and returns as heir to a lost line of kings, which is highly reminiscent of Aragorn in *The Lord of the Rings*.

The Belgariad sequence is followed by The Malloreon, consisting of *Guardians of the West* (1987), *King of the Murgos* (1988), *Demon Lord of Karanda* (1988), *Sorceress of Darshiva* (1989), and *The Seeress of Kell* (1991), wherein largely the same cast of characters representing good square off against the forces of evil over control of the orb, prophecy, and the fate of the universe. Some later books acknowledge Eddings's wife, Leigh Eddings, as co-author, including the prequels *Belgarath the Sorcerer* (1995) and *Polgara the Sorceress* (1997), recounting the events preceding The Belgariad, and *The Rivan Codex* (1998), a compilation of background material. Eddings's other works—including The Tamuli (*Domes of Fire* [1992], *The Shining Ones* [1993], and *The Hidden City* [1994]), The Elenium (*The Diamond Throne* [1989], *The Ruby Knight* [1990], and *The Sapphire Rose* [1991]), and The Dreamers sequences with Leigh Eddings (*The Elder Gods* [2003], *The Treasured One* [2004], and *The Crystal Gorge* [2005]), as well as the Eddings's standalone novel *The Redemption of Althalus* (2001)—are largely derivative of these earlier efforts insofar as they variously feature the same stock characters, pet phrases, humor, bickering, infantile sleeping gods, mysterious **children**, prophecies, and quests for omnipotent blue stones.

Bibliography

Mark Bould. "The Dreadful Credibility of Absurd Things." *Historical Materialism*, 10 (December 5, 2002), 51–88.

David Eddings and Leigh Eddings. *The Rivan Codex*. New York: Ballantine/Del Rey, 1998.

Robbie B.H. Goh. "Consuming Spaces." *Social Semiotics*, 10 (April 1, 2000), 21–39.

Joseph Grixti. "Consumed Identities." *Journal of Popular Culture*, 28 (1994), 207–228.

Stan Nicholls. "Prime U.S. Beef: David Eddings Interviewed." *Interzone*, No. 85 (July, 1994), 25–30.

Stan Nicholls. "Ring Bearer." *Starlog*, No. 210 (January, 1995), 76–81.

Catherine Raymer. "David Eddings." *Sirius*, No. 1 (March, 1993), 16–18.

Madawc Williams. "Surface and Substance in 'The Belgariad.'" *Overspace*, No. 14 (December, 1991), 8–11.

—*Glenn R. Gray*

PERDIDO STREET STATION BY CHINA MIÉVILLE (2000)

■

Summary

The protagonist of *Perdido Street Station* is the **scientist** Isaac Dan der Grimnebulin, and nearly all the action takes place in New Crobuzon, a meticulously detailed city-state that almost counts as the main "character" of the novel (see **Cities**). It is partly a fantastic version of Victorian London (see **Urban Fantasy**), with a substantial dose of old New Orleans thrown in. Isaac stands at the center of several distinct but interlocking plots. These include (but are not limited to) his search to rescue his beloved girlfriend Lin, member of a species of **insect**-headed women and an artist who has been kidnapped by the hideous crime boss Motley; his comradeship with the left-wing journalist Derkhan, a friend of Lin's, who is involved in a revolutionary movement against the despotic capitalist authorities of New Crobuzon; his attempts to restore the power of flight to Yagharek, a bird-like creature (see **Birds**) whose wings have been amputated as punishment for a crime (see **Crime and Punishment**) committed in a faraway land about which Isaac knows little; and, above all, his efforts to defeat the monstrously inhuman slake-moths (see **Monsters**), who literally suck the consciousness out of sentient beings of all species. Some story lines are resolved in ways more satisfactory to the characters than others, but none has a true "happy ending" of the Dickensian sort.

Discussion

China Miéville's second novel and the first set in the **imaginary world** of Bas-Lag—the setting, too, of *The Scar* (2002) and *Iron Council* (2004), which form the subsequent volumes of a loose trilogy—*Perdido Street Station* is a book of vast scope and almost endlessly imaginative detail, but also one with an intricate, rigorous organization. As such, it is as difficult to summarize as the major London novels of Charles Dickens, who is one of the many important influences on Miéville. The novel won the Arthur C. Clarke Award (for science fiction) and the British Fantasy Award, was short-listed for the World Fantasy Award, and was long-listed for the Bram Stoker Award (for horror fiction). As these varied accolades suggest, it is a book of extraordinarily complex generic heterogeneity. It can, however, be argued that science fiction is dominant among the different genres at work in the novel. Though no overt or implied story connects Bas-Lag to our own empirical environment, the imaginary planet is perhaps best understood as the equivalent of **Earth** in an alternate historical line (see **Alternate History**). Furthermore, the epistemology of *Perdido Street Station* is unswervingly materialist. Although **magic** is fairly common in the book, and the ambassador from **Hell** is a minor character, such narrative elements bear no taint of the supernatural; thaumaturgy, for instance, is presented as a straightforward, even scientific, technique, learnable and teachable like any other. Still, the book is undeniably a generic hybrid. It is even arguable that no major work of science fiction before *Perdido Street Station* had ever featured the presence of other genres (fantasy, **horror**, urban **magic realism**) so consequentially.

The heterogeneity of the novel's composition is matched by the prominence of heterogeneity and hybridity on the level of content; they are themes of Miéville's work that nearly every critic has pointed out. For instance, the **love** story of the human Isaac and the khepri Lin produces an exquisite image of species and cultural difference (see **Cultures**) that is not just tolerated but joyously affirmed; and the way the reader is made to feel the love between the two as intensely sexual, while never forgetting Lin's insect-like appearance, constitutes one of the most brilliant effects of Miéville's writing (see **Sexuality**). At the same time, *Perdido Street Station* is an intensely political novel (see **Politics**). Though never didactic, it clearly comes from not only an author of "weird fiction" (Miéville's preferred metageneric term) but also a Marxist scholar and a militant of revolutionary socialism. The novel, accordingly, does not celebrate hybridity and difference for their own sake, in the manner of much **postmodernism** (a category toward which Miéville has expressed antipathy). It rather shows how, under certain circumstances (like those of Isaac and Lin), difference can function as resistance to the oppression and bigotry that would forbid relationships like theirs. In other words, oppression and resistance to it, rather than **identity** and difference, constitute the main axiological standard of the book. It is thus no accident that, for all its concern with and sometime endorsement of hybridity, *Perdido Street Station* also takes care to show that, for instance, Motley—one of the most thoroughly **evil** and capitalistic characters (see **Villains**)—is also (as his name implies) one of the most extravagantly hybrid.

Perdido Street Station is such an exciting and (despite its considerable bulk) constantly readable novel that readers will likely be entirely caught up in its narratives, characters, and setting before noticing that it is also one of the most powerful contemporary statements against the oppressions of class society (see **Class System**).

Bibliography

Mark Bould. "What Kind of Monster Are You?" *Science Fiction Studies*, 30 (November, 2003), 394–416.

Iain Emsley. "Crunch Fantasy: China Miéville Interviewed." *Interzone*, No. 180 (June/July, 2002), 27–32.

Joan Gordon. "Hybridity, Heterotopia, and Mateship in China Miéville's *Perdido Street Station*." *Science Fiction Studies*, 30 (November, 2003), 456–476.

Joan Gordon. "Reveling in Genre: An Interview with China Miéville." *Science Fiction Studies*, 30 (November, 2003), 355–373.

Scott Maisano. "Reading Underwater; or, Fantasies of Fluency from Shakespeare to Miéville and Emshwiller." *Extrapolation*, 45 (Spring, 2004), 76–88.

Farah Mendlesohn. "*Perdido Street Station* and the Edge of the Fantastic." *SFRA Review*, No. 262 (January/February, 2003), 9–13.

China Miéville. "The Conspiracy of Architecture: Notes on a Modern Anxiety." *Historical Materialism*, No. 2 (Summer, 1998), 1–32.

China Miéville. "Editorial Introduction." *Historical Materialism*. 10 (December 5, 2002), 39–49.

Steve Shaviro. "Capitalist Monsters." *Historical Materialism*, 10 (December 5, 2002), 281–290.

—Carl Freedman

PETER AND WENDY
BY J.M. BARRIE (1911)

> *I want always to be a little boy and to have fun; so I ran away to Kensington Gardens and lived a long time among the fairies.*
>
> —J.M. Barrie
> *Peter Pan* (1904)

Summary

Peter and Wendy (usually republished as *Peter Pan*) retells in prose the story that had enthralled London audiences as J.M. Barrie's play *Peter Pan*, which premiered in 1904 (though not published until 1929). The magically ageless boy Peter

Pan pays a nocturnal visit to the Darling **children**—Wendy, Michael, and John—searching for his lost shadow, which Wendy retrieves and reattaches. With pixie dust from his **fairy** companion Tinker Bell, he teaches them to fly and they travel to his **home** in the sky, called Neverland, where they join the underground household of Peter and his companions the Lost Boys, with Wendy assuming the role of **mother**. They also engage in adventures with Indians (see **Native Americans**) led by Tiger Lily and **pirates** led by Captain Hook. When Hook kidnaps the children and tries to poison Peter, Tinker Bell saves him by drinking the poison and Peter flies to their rescue, defeating Hook in a climactic swordfight (see **Swords**). The Darling children fly back to London with the Lost Boys, who are adopted by their parents, but Peter remains in Neverland. When he finally returns to visit Wendy, she is a grown woman with a child of her own, Jane, who takes Wendy's place in traveling to Neverland. The book adds that the pattern carried on with Jane's daughter Margaret and will continue "as long as children are gay and innocent and heartless."

Discussion

Peter Pan first appeared in four chapters of Barrie's *The Little White Bird, or Adventures in Kensington Gardens* (1902) as a naked little boy living with fairies in a London park; the chapters were later rearranged and published separately as *Peter Pan in Kensington Gardens*. In creating a marvelous new setting and story for the character, Barrie both drew upon and modified various traditions. His fairy had a conventional appearance and attributes, but in contrast to more sentimentalized portrayals, Barrie made Tinker Bell stupid, petulant, and cruel, happy to kill Wendy as a rival for Peter's affections, though she also proves willing to altruistically **sacrifice** her own life to save him. His Indians were derived from images in dime novels (see **Westerns**), not actual Native Americans, but Barrie uncharacteristically made Tiger Lily a dominant figure, a strong-willed, resourceful woman who seems the true leader of her tribe, not her **father** the chief. His pirates adhere to convention in flying the Jolly Roger and making victims walk the plank, but they seem more mischievous than menacing, as gullible and ineffectual as the Lost Boys.

Peter Pan is centrally a commentary on children, and it is important to note that Barrie's portrayal is not entirely positive. While Peter is friendly and energetic, he can also be thoughtless, careless, and obtuse; in particular, he is utterly blind to the embryonic **sexuality** in his attractiveness to Wendy, Tinker Bell, and Tiger Lily. His endless life of playful adventures in Neverland, while briefly attractive to the Darling children, is obviously unfulfilling, since he and the Lost Boys are eager for Wendy to tell them stories about other people and places. Peter's final refusal to abandon Neverland to have a normal childhood only isolates him and makes his life even emptier, periodically enlivened only by visits from Wendy's progeny. Manifestly, Barrie states, it is not a good thing to never grow up.

The stage version communicates this point with two effective devices. First is Barrie's use of **flying**, achieved by putting performers in harnesses attached to wires above the stage. In the opening scenes in London, the flying symbolizes the exhilarating **freedom** apparently offered by Peter's child-like world, as the Darling children soar above the stage, thrilled and delighted by their newfound abilities. Once they are in Neverland, however, the flying stops, demonstrating that a life of endless play, while briefly appealing, is ultimately mundane and unrewarding. There is also the menacing crocodile who chewed off Hook's hand and wants more, his looming presence indicated by the loud ticking of the clock he swallowed (see **Clocks and Timepieces**). The sound conveys that **time** marches on, even in Neverland, and that childhood revelries must eventually and naturally end, as children mature into adulthood.

However, Barrie criticizes parents as well as children, especially the style of parenting then common in upper-class British households. As a father, Mr. Darling is a cold tyrant, barking out irrational orders to hapless **family** members; his cruel nature is communicated in stage productions by the convention of having the same actor play Mr. Darling and Hook. As a mother, Mrs. Darling tries to be kinder and gentler but invariably defers to her harsher husband. Ironically, the best parenting in the Darling household is provided by their **dog** and nanny, Nana, who unlike Mrs. Darling is willing to defy Mr. Darling to protect the interests of her charges. When the children go off to Neverland, the repentant Mr. Darling significantly punishes himself by moving into Nana's doghouse, signalling his determination to become a more sensitive and caring parent in the future.

Arguably, *Peter and Wendy* is the best version of the story, since it incorporates both the action and dialogue of the play and the language and spirit of Barrie's charming stage directions, unavailable to audiences; but stage and film adaptations are undoubtedly more familiar, particularly the Broadway musical version originally starring Mary Martin (1958) and the Walt Disney animated film (1954), both of which soften Barrie's stern message about the mixed blessings of childhood. The stage convention of casting a young woman as Peter, inevitably giving the character an aura of **androgyny**, was abandoned by Disney and by later adaptations like Steven Spielberg's disastrously revisionist *Hook* (1991), which recast Peter as an adult businessman called back to Neverland, and the better-received *Peter Pan* (2003).

Bibliography

Andrew Birkin. *J.M. Barrie and the Lost Boys*. London: Constable, 1979.

Maureen Duffy. "Do You Believe in Fairies?" Duffy, *The Erotic World of Faery*. 1972. New York: Avon Books, 1980, 331–347.

Bruce K. Hanson. *The Peter Pan Chronicles*. New York: Carol Publishing/Birch Lane, 1993.

R.D.S. Jack. *The Road to the Never Land*. Aberdeen: Aberdeen University Press, 1991.

Lynne Lundquist. "Living Dolls." George Slusser, Gary Westfahl, and Eric S. Rabkin, eds., *Immortal Engines*. Athens: University of Georgia Press, 1996, 201–210.

Leonée Ormond. *J.M. Barrie*. Edinburgh: Scottish Academic Press, 1987.

Jacqueline Rose. *The Case of Peter Pan, or, The Impossibility of Children's Fiction*. Philadelphia: University of Pennsylvania Press, 1993.

Allen Wright. *J.M. Barrie*. Edinburgh: Ramsay Head Press, 1976.

Jackie Wullschläger. *Inventing Wonderland*. New York: Free Press, 1995.

—Lynne Lundquist

THE PICTURE OF DORIAN GRAY BY OSCAR WILDE (1891)

There is no such thing as a moral or an immoral book. Books are well written, or badly written. That is all.

—Oscar Wilde
The Picture of Dorian Gray (1891)

Summary

Lord Henry Wotton admires the portrait that a painter is finishing and asks to meet the subject, a **youth** called Dorian Gray. Concerned that the innocent Dorian might be tainted by the **decadence** of Wotton's debauched lifestyle, the painter refuses, but the two meet anyway. While discussing the misfortune whereby youth's **beauty** inevitably turns into age's ugliness, Dorian wishes that, rather having the portrait preserve his youthful appearance while he ages, it would be the other way round. Wotton gives Dorian a **book** describing a young man's **sins** (inferrably Joris-Karl Huysmans' *À Rebours* [1884]), which becomes Dorian's guidebook.

Dorian falls in **love** with beautiful actress Sibyl Vane, and his love is returned. However, he loves the actress, not the woman; when her love undermines her acting prowess, he spurns her (see **Theatre**). He then notices a cruel cast to the face in the portrait. Resolving to reform, he writes her a passionate **marriage** proposal but discovers before sending it that she has committed **suicide**. This turns Dorian toward **evil** and a licentious life, reveling in the contrast between his ever-youthful features and the increasing hideousness of his portrait. The wish has become a **curse**; effectively he has sold his soul to **Satan**.

When the painter visits, Dorian shows him the portrait. Aghast, he urges repentance; instead, Dorian murders him, then blackmails Alan Campbell into disposing of the body. Soon Campbell too is dead. Sibyl's brother James begins stalking Dorian, seeking **revenge** for Sibyl's death, but he accidentally dies. These **deaths** terrify Dorian, who remorsefully attacks his portrait with a knife. In so doing, he kills himself; the body found stabbed is a hideous old man—"withered, wrinkled, and loathsome of visage."

Discussion

Part **horror** novel, part **Gothic** fantasy, part **fin de siècle comedy** of manners, *The Picture of Dorian Gray* is not altogether a coherent work, although its imagery of what is effectively a created **doppelgänger** suffering for the sins of its original, only for the original to encounter a final, cataclysmic comeuppance, has resonated throughout horror literature and cinema ever since. It was originally published in *Lippincott's Monthly Magazine* in the summer of 1890, and revised and expanded the following year for book publication.

The Picture of Dorian Gray caused outrage at the time, since the conventional morality of its ending could scarcely conceal the fact that the novel was, in many ways, an extended celebration of decadence. Feelings of outrage may have been exacerbated by the "Preface" that Wilde added to the book, expressing, through a series of proverbs, his belief in the complete disconnect between **art** and morality or **ethics**—famously concluding that "All art is quite useless."

The novel gained further associative notoriety after its publication when Wilde's own practicing **homosexuality** became widely known. Indeed, one might argue that the novel had autobiographical overtones, representing Wilde's gloomy prediction that his own debauchery would probably lead to his early demise (though Wilde did not anticipate that a **prison** sentence for homosexual behavior including hard labor would contribute to his death at the age of forty-six). The relationship between Dorian's portrait and the effects of his lifestyle also seemed a metaphor for another important aspect of Wilde's expressed **philosophy**—namely, that people should strive to live in a way that would make their own lives into works of art. The irony in the novel, of course, is that the artwork Dorian creates through his activities is the antithesis of artistry.

While strikingly original in several respects, *The Picture of Dorian Gray* was not without precursors, notably Robert Louis Stevenson's ***Strange Case of Dr. Jekyll and Mr. Hyde***—in which the good and evil in a single man express themselves separately—and, in a sense, Wilde's own "Lord Arthur Savile's Crime" (1887), whose protagonist becomes obsessed by a palmist's prediction that he will commit murder and tries to manipulate fate (see **Destiny**) so that the victim will not be his innocent fiancée (another Sibyl, Sibyl Merton); here, the dichotomy is between the evil of the intended crime and the virtue of the motive. Also of minor relevance is Wilde's story "The Portrait of Mr. W.H." (1889), where a portrait is the key to literary detection concerning William **Shakespeare**'s dedicatee.

The Picture of Dorian Gray has been filmed several times, including a sanitized 1970 miniseries, better than one might expect; the French *Le portrait de Dorian Gray* (1977); and a television movie, *The Sins of Dorian Gray* (1982), which features a female Dorian. The best known version, however, remains the 1945 film starring Hurd Hatfield as Dorian and directed by Albert Lewin. This version is fairly faithful—perhaps too faithful—to the book, although Sybil's fall from Dorian's favor occurs in consequence of her yielding to his Wotton-engineered seduction (see **Sexism**). A **statue** of an Egyptian **cat** serves as seeming arbiter of Dorian's trade of his soul for youth. Although often regarded as a minor classic, especially for its noir-influenced cinematography, the film has had detractors as well.

Bibliography

Karl Beckson, ed. *I Can Resist Anything Except Temptation*. New York: Columbia University Press, 1997.

Richard Ellmann, ed. *Oscar Wilde*. Upper Saddle River, NJ: Prentice Hall, 1969.

Michael Patrick Gillespie. *The Picture of Dorian Gray*. New York: Twayne Publishers, 1995.

Donald L. Lawler. *An Inquiry into Oscar Wilde's Revisions of The Picture of Dorian Gray*. New York: Garland, 1988.

Donald L. Lawler, ed. *The Picture of Dorian Gray*. New York: Norton, 1988.

Jerusha Hull McCormack. *The Man Who Was Dorian Gray*. New York: St Martin's Press, 2000.

Mark Nicholls. *The Importance of Being Oscar*. New York: St Martin's Press, 1980.

John P. Riquelme. "Oscar Wilde's Aesthetic Gothic." *Modern Fiction Studies*, 46 (Fall, 2000), 609–631.

Kenneth Womack. "Withered, Wrinkled, and Loathsome of Visage." Ruth Robbins and Julian Wolfreys, eds., *Victorian Gothic*. New York: Palgrave, 2000, 168–181.

—*John Grant*

PLANET OF THE APES (1968)

■

Summary

After their spaceship crashes, three **astronauts** find themselves on a planet where intelligent **apes** rule over primitive, mute humans. One astronaut, Taylor, is shot in the throat and captured; his two companions are likewise injured. Taylor, along with other human prisoners, is brought to an ape **city** where they are penned in and caged like animals. Still unable to speak due to his injury, Taylor attempts to communicate with Dr. Zira, the chimpanzee **scientist** in charge of his care. Zira, who believes that humans are capable of speech, becomes intrigued with Taylor and focuses her research and experimentation on him. Zira's theories about the evolutionary possibilities (see **Evolution**) of humans are unpopular with peers, including Dr. Zaius, an orangutan who vehemently dislikes and distrusts Taylor. Taylor **escapes** from his cage and tries to make it out of the city. He is recaptured by a mob of angry apes, but before he is dragged back to his cage, Taylor angrily curses the crowd, stunning them with his ability to speak. Taylor is then put on trial and Zira and her husband, Cornelius, are accused of scientific heresy. The court charges that Taylor's speech is nothing more than mimicry and Zira somehow operated on his brain. Zira and Cornelius help Taylor and Nova, a female primitive, escape. They journey into the Forbidden Zone and hide out at an excavation site where Cornelius once found evidence of a long-extinct human **culture**. Zaius, along with gorilla soldiers, arrives to take Taylor back into custody. Taylor and Nova flee farther into the wasteland, where the sight of a half-buried Statue of Liberty reveals the horrible truth—that Taylor has traveled into his own future, and his people destroyed their **civilization** in a **nuclear war**.

Discussion

Based on Pierre Boulle's absurdist science fiction novel *Planet of the Apes* (1963) (see **Absurdity**), the film adaptation aggressively handles the story's ironic and satirical (see **Satire**) notes but adds thrilling action and a visual flair that the more Swiftian novel only hinted at. Although the film's flaws are obvious—for instance, why is Taylor so surprised to discover that he has been on **Earth** all along when the apes (see **Talking Animals**) have been speaking perfect English?—the screenplay by Michael Wilson and Rod Serling deftly emphasizes the thought-provoking themes of **race relations** and class (see **Class System**) without abandoning its entertainment value. Intended as a film for the whole family, not a political polemic (see **Politics**), its relative sophistication, complexity, and **humor** always manage to keep more inflammatory subtexts balanced and in check.

Race and class were not the only controversial issues explored, since the film also addressed the subject of vivisection (see **Animals and Zoos**), as the other astronauts captured with Taylor are experimented on by the apes and lobotomized (see **Ethics**). And though later installments in the film series would deal with the antiwar movement more overtly, one cannot ignore the political underpinnings of the first film's final apocalyptic image. Coming at the height of the Vietnam War, the somber yet exhilarating conclusion remains one of the most potent and iconic cinematic images ever (see **Dystopia; Post-Holocaust Societies**).

Planet of the Apes was a major hit for 20th Century Fox and four theatrical sequels were made, along with a short-lived television series (1974) and animated series (1975–1976). The first sequel, *Beneath the Planet of the Apes* (1970), was a more streamlined and action-oriented film than its predecessor, involving another astronaut seeking to determine the fate of Taylor who reaches the same planet and finds Taylor, who then confronts underground mutants and ultimately triggers a nuclear explosion that destroys Earth. The film was another hit, although its nihilistic ending generated criticism from audiences and critics alike. But like the first film, *Beneath*'s lack of hope seemed to **mirror** the societal **anxieties** at large. *Escape from the Planet of the Apes* (1971) found the characters of Zira, Cornelius, and Milo rocketing from their doomed planet and winding up in contemporary **America** in the early 1970s (see **Time Travel**). Unlike the palpable atmosphere of **violence** and destruction of *Beneath*, this entry lightened things up considerably and focused more on satire and light **comedy**, although a strain of danger, especially in the latter part of the film, was never far off. For the fourth entry, *Conquest of the Planet of the Apes* (1972), the themes of class warfare and racism were no longer subtexts. Cornelius and Zira's offspring, Caesar, becomes an ape **messiah** in the **near future**, leading a **rebellion** against humans who employed apes as slaves. Despite the film's faults and lower budget, it is the most intriguing, angriest, and exciting of the sequels. But when the last film came around, *Battle for the Planet of the Apes* (1973), the series was obviously running out of ideas and steam, and the film wisely sought to bring the saga full circle, seemingly describing events leading up to the scenario of the first film.

In 2001, director Tim Burton resurrected the series for a big-budget, special-effects-driven remake, significantly changing its story but striving for a similarly evocative surprise ending (here, the ape takeover of Earth is signalled by discoving a **statue** of a seated ape, instead of a seated Abraham Lincoln, in the Lincoln Monument). The film's mixed critical and audience reaction eliminated provisional plans for an immediate sequel, but the durable ape franchise still seems destined to live on.

Bibliography

Michael Atkinson. *Ghosts in the Machine*. New York: Limelight Editions, 1999.

Eric Greene. *Planet of the Apes as American Myth*. Jefferson, NC: McFarland, 1996.

David Hofstede. *Planet of the Apes: An Unofficial Companion*. Toronto: ECW Press, 2001.

Jonathan Kirshner. "Subverting the Cold War in the 1960s." *Film and History*, 31 (2001), 40–44.

Diana Landau, ed. *Planet of the Apes Re-imagined by Tim Burton*. New York: Newmarket Press, 2001.

Herb Lightman. "Filming *Planet of the Apes*." *American Cinematographer*, 49 (April, 1968), 256–259, 278.

Joe Russo, Larry Landsman, and Edward Gross. *Planet of the Apes Revisited*. New York: Thomas Dunne Books, 2001.

Dale Winogura. "Dialogues on Apes, Apes and More Apes." *Cinefantastique*, 2 (Summer, 1972), 16–37.

Paul A. Woods, ed. *The Planet of the Apes Chronicles*. London: Plexus, 2001.

—Derek Hill

A PRINCESS OF MARS
BY EDGAR RICE BURROUGHS (1917)

■

There are many things on Mars incredible to the narrow, earthbound men of our little speck of dust.

—Edgar Rice Burroughs
Llana of Gathol (1941)

Summary

John Carter is a mysterious American who remembers no childhood and never ages beyond thirty. In Arizona after the Civil War, Carter is paralyzed by gas. He escapes his seemingly lifeless body by an act of will and finds himself standing naked and alive beside it. Raising his hands to **Mars**, he is drawn instantly to the red planet. There, Carter is captured by the Tharks, a tribe of war-like, six-limbed green men of Mars, called Barsoom by its inhabitants, but his fighting ability earns him respect, particularly from a great warrior named Tars Tarkas. The Tharks shoot down the airship of Dejah Thoris, princess of Helium, a city of copper-skinned humanoids. Carter falls in **love** with Dejah and helps her **escape** but is captured by other green men for their arena. He fakes **death** and escapes again, hiding temporarily at an atmosphere factory, which maintains Mars's thinning air. Carter finds that Dejah is captive in Zodanga where she must marry that city's prince to stop a **war** against Helium. Carter persuades the Tharks to help attack Zodanga. Helium is saved; Dejah and Carter wed (see **Marriage**). The two are expecting a child when the atmosphere factory breaks down. Carter unlocks the factory but collapses from oxygen starvation. He awakens in his original body on **Earth** and longs for Mars.

Discussion

A Princess of Mars is a stand-alone novel but can be considered with two subsequent works as a trilogy. In *The Gods of Mars* (1918), John Carter again seemingly dies on Earth and returns to Barsoom. He arrives in the Valley Dor, a pilgrimage place for many Martians, who believe it is **Heaven**. The Martian faith is a hoax, however, reflecting Burroughs's negative views on organized **religion**. The pilgrims are murdered. With the help of Tars Tarkas, a slave girl named Thuvia, and his son, Carthoris (see **Family; Fathers**) whom he has never seen, Carter overthrows the corrupt religion. Dejah Thoris and Thuvia are captured, however, and the book ends with them imprisoned and threatened with death. In *The Warlord of Mars* (1919), Carter breaks into the **prison** but discovers that Dejah and Thuvia have been spirited away by religious fanatics. Carter follows, overturning other decadent regimes (see **Decadence**) before reuniting with Dejah and being named "Warlord of Barsoom."

Overall, Burroughs wrote seven Martian books in addition to the trilogy: *Thuvia, Maid of Mars* (1920), *The Chessmen of Mars* (1922), *The Master Mind of Mars* (1928), *A Fighting Man of Mars* (1931), *Swords of Mars* (1936), *Synthetic Men of Mars* (1940), and *Llana of Gathol* (1948); there was also a posthumous compilation of two Mars stories, *John Carter of Mars* (1964). A possible influence on Burroughs was Edwin L. Arnold's *Lieut. Gullivar Jones: His Vacation* (1905), wherein Gullivar Jones reaches Mars with a **flying** carpet and has adventures similar to John Carter's.

Later novels sometimes involve protagonists other than John Carter. Carthoris is the **hero** of *Thuvia, Maid of Mars*. *The Chessmen of Mars* features a Martian and is noted for introducing Jetan, Martian **chess**. Battles with living pieces are fought in Jetan arenas marked off in one hundred squares, and the book even includes the rules of play. *The Master Mind of Mars* features earthman Ulysses Paxton, who became fascinated with tales of John Carter and is transported to Mars in similar fashion after being fatally wounded in World War I. Paxton encounters Ras Thavas, a brilliant surgeon who creates **monsters** and transfers the brains of the old and powerful into the youthful, beautiful bodies of slaves. Thavas trains Paxton to transfer the surgeon's brain into a younger body, but then betrays his apprentice by trying to destroy the woman Paxton loves (see **Betrayal**). Desperate adventures follow before Paxton wins his own Martian princess.

The Martian books are often called juvenile fiction but many fans are in their thirties, forties, or older. Most *are* men, though some prominent women writers, like Leigh Brackett, admired and emulated the books. Planetary **romance** along the lines of Burroughs's Barsoom books is no longer written and published in the mainstream press, but the Mars books themselves remain in print and continue to attract new readers.

The Barsoom series is popular, in part, because it provides a fantasy version of the rags-to-riches tale. Carter and Paxton, and other series heroes, are capable and talented men but their personal situations have not allowed them to reach their full potential. Only in the midst of "grand adventure" can the inner character of such men be revealed, and only there will they find great love and achieve the **freedom**, **friendship**, and success that is their **destiny**. These men are heroes in the classic sense: action-oriented, courageous, intensely ethical, and eternally optimistic (see **Courage; Ethics; Optimism and Pessimism**). They treat women with **chivalry**, and although they are not skilled at flattery and seductive words, beautiful women recognize their basic goodness as well as their strength and are attracted to them. Such stories resonate with readers who, in their own lives, may feel underappreciated and overlooked for their talents.

The Barsoom books are also read simply because they are great stories—inventive, fast-paced, and full of daring deeds. They stir readers' imaginations, allowing them to escape from mundane realities or day-to-day stress by taking them to a world where desperate battles rage and brave warriors face glory and death with **blood**-stained **swords** in their fists.

Bibliography

Clark Brady. *The Burroughs Cyclopedia*. Jefferson, NC: McFarland, 1996.

Erling B. Holtsmark. *Edgar Rice Burroughs*. Boston: Twayne, 1986.

Richard Lupoff. "For the Love of Mars!" *Outré*, 33, (2003), 42–49.

Richard Lupoff. *Edgar Rice Burroughs: Master of Adventure*. New York: Ace, 1974.

John Flint Roy. *A Guide to Barsoom*. New York: Ballantine, 1976.

John Taliaferro. *Tarzan Forever*. New York: Scribner, 1999.

James Van Hise, ed. *Edgar Rice Burroughs' Fantastic Worlds*. Yucca Valley, CA: Van Hise, 1996.

Robert Zeuschner. "John Carter, Warlord of Mars." Zeuschner, ed., *Edgar Rice Burroughs*. Jefferson, NC: McFarland, 1996, 16–32.

—Charles Gramlich

THE PRISONER (1967–1968)

I will not make any deals with you. I've resigned. I will not be pushed, filed, stamped, indexed, briefed, debriefed, or numbered. My life is my own.

—George Markstein and David Tomblin
"Arrival," episode of *The Prisoner* (1968)

Summary

Spy fiction frequently deals with issues of **paranoia** and **identity**, with alienated agents who are at **home** neither in their own country nor in those they infiltrate. The cult series *The Prisoner* traps a former Western **espionage** agent in an eccentric locale called The Village, whose bright **colors** and holiday atmosphere disguise a miniature **dystopia** of total surveillance. Both jailers and inmates—the distinction is often unclear—are allotted numbers in place of names, and there is heavy pressure to conform (see **Individualism and Conformity**). The "crime" of the protagonist, Number Six (played by series creator Patrick McGoohan), was to resign from his employment; he has apparently been imprisoned by his own distrustful masters (see **Prison**). Again and again the current Number Two—executive chief of The Village, regularly replaced—attempts to break the hero's stubborn silence by psychological attack frequently involving science-fictional devices. Embodying the spirit of **rebellion**, Number Six fights back in resourceful ways, sometimes attempting **escape**, sometimes content simply to thwart The Village. In the deliriously surreal final episode, "Fall Out" (1968), Number Six at last confronts the previously unseen Number One, assumed to be ultimately responsible for all his travails. The glimpse is momentary, almost subliminal. The face is his own.

Discussion

"Who are you?" "The new Number Two." "Who is Number One?" "You are Number Six." "What do you want?" "Information . . . ." This regular introductory dialogue concludes with Six's catchphrase, "I am not a number, I am a free man!"— and mocking laughter from Number Two.

The Prisoner presents a seemingly unequal struggle, of one free-spirited man against the full force of a microcosmic state that treats individuals as disposable pawns (**chess** is central to the episode "Checkmate" [1967]) and operates by inscrutable rules that might have been designed by Franz Kafka. Number Six may be physically trapped within The Village, but each time he preserves his mental integrity he scores another moral victory.

The Village itself is the "Italianate village" of Portmeirion in North Wales, designed as an architectural whimsy by Sir Clough Williams-Ellis. This setting adds an unusual, exotic flavor. So does another inanimate character, the **robot** Village guard "Rover," which kills by suffocation and is played by a **weather** balloon.

Brainwashing and **drugs** are routine Village tools, although a supposed lobotomy inflicted on Number Six proves to be a bluff. One episode ("Free for All" [1967]) sees him dazed by brainwashing and caught up in a mock election, which offers him the position, though not the real power, of Number Two; there is much **satire** of **politics**. Another features a perversion of behavioral **psychology** as— subdued with drugs—he is conditioned to be left-handed rather than right-handed. The assault on his personal identity is augmented by cosmetic changes to his appearance and by confrontation with a double who looks and acts more like Number Six than the real one ("The Schizoid Man" [1967]).

This attack through existential **anxiety** is later escalated into outright science fiction with a mind-transfer device that swaps the hero into an entirely different body (see **Possession**) ("Do Not Forsake Me Oh My Darling" [1967]). A further remarkable gadget displays the sleeping Number Six's **dreams** on a wall screen for Number Two to study—also allowing the introduction of taped scenarios and characters to assess the Prisoner's reactions in the unguarded playground of dream ("A, B and C" [1967]). Yet another dream-like attack, mediated by hallucinogenic drugs, inserts Number Six into a **western** horse opera as the reluctant sheriff expected to deal with a rogue gunman in this **virtual reality** ("Living in Harmony" [1968]). A "speed learn" program tested on all villagers uses **hypnotism** via television to instil rapid, involuntary **education**, innocuous in the tests but with obvious darker possibilities. Number Six discovers that this system depends on an allegedly omniscient **computer** which—in a traditional, risible science fiction trope—he destroys by entering the question "Why?" ("The General" [1967]).

The final onslaught by a desperate Village authority is the "Degree Absolute" procedure of "Once Upon a Time" (1968), a one-to-one psychological contest for mastery that begins with Number Six hypnotically regressed to infancy (see

Children). He and the final Number Two are sealed in a room that neither can leave until one of them yields. Number Six's indomitable will-power makes him a formidable opponent even in a succession of subordinate roles as a child, a schoolboy, and so on. Ultimately his driving will forces **role reversal** with the interrogator, exerting such total authority that Number Two collapses into literal **death** at his command.

In the icon-rich chaos that follows, including a travesty of legal procedure and partly symbolic rocket launch (see **Space Travel**), the notion of complicity and shared responsibility (see **Guilt and Responsibility**) is underlined. The obsessed dialogue of the Degree Absolute psychodrama included many repetitions of the phrase "Six of one"—Number Six and Number One—"Six of one and half a dozen of the other," assigning blame to both sides of a dispute. To what extent was the Prisoner his own jailer, as suggested by that lightning glimpse of Number One? Even the reality of his final escape is called into question when he returns to his London **city** home and the front door opens unaided, exactly like the eerie (for the 1960s) automatic doors of The Village. It is a powerful, haunting **fable**.

Bibliography

Brian Aldiss. "Kissingers Have Long Ears." Aldiss, *This World and Nearer Ones*. London: Weidenfeld & Nicolson, 1979, 170–172.

Mark Askwith and Dean Motter. *The Prisoner: Shattered Visage*. New York: Warner, 1990.

M. Keith Booker. *Strange TV*. Westport, CT: Greenwood Press, 2002.

Mike Gold. "*The Prisoner*." *Fantastic Films*, 3 (July 1980), 66–71.

Max Hora. *The Prisoner of Portmeirion*. Ipswich, UK: Six of One, 1985.

Mark Phillips and Frank Garcia. "*The Prisoner*." Phillips and Garcia, *Science Fiction Television Series*. Jefferson, NC: McFarland, 1996, 263–270.

Tom Soter. "Uncaging The Prisoner." *Starlog*, No. 135 (October, 1988), 37–43, 59.

Matthew White and Jaffer Ali. *The Official Prisoner Companion*. New York: Warner, 1988.

—David Langford

THE PURPLE CLOUD BY M.P. SHIEL (1901)

Summary

The Purple Cloud describes the strange experiences and psychic regeneration of a madman after a global **apocalypse**. Adam Jeffson, a physician who always felt torn between good and **evil** psychic forces, joins an expedition to the North Pole (see **Polar Regions**). However, only Jeffson survives to reach the North Pole, where there is a small lake of open **water** with a central pillar, around which he fantasizes strange letters. Returning south, Jeffson gradually discovers that surface life is extinct; he scours the English countryside, looking for survivors but finding none. From newspaper reports he learns that an eruption of hydrocyanic acid gas, probably from an Indonesian volcano, has wiped out life, leaving him as the **last man** on **Earth**. Apparently a trick of convection currents prevented the deadly gas from reaching the North Pole.

For the next two decades Jeffson lives a life of mad grandeur, building a palace of gold bricks on Imbros, covering it with gems, filling it with loot from the world's great museums, and placing a lake of wine beside it. He sails around the world like a new Nero, clearly insane, setting **fire** to the great cities. The crisis comes when Adam sees human footprints in Istanbul; following them, he meets a young woman who survived, mute, in a sealed cellar of the imperial palace. Though Jeffson originally determined to kill other survivors, he instead accepts the woman, calls her Eve, and educates her (see **Education**), though refusing to mate with her and reestablish **humanity**. As the situation becomes unbearable, he decides that one of them must commit **suicide**. On drawing lots, Eve loses, but when her suicide attempt fails, Jeffson discovers that he **loves** her and resolves to continue the human race.

Discussion

There had been a few earlier novels about worldwide catastrophes leading to a last man, including Jean Cousins de Grainville's *The Last Man* (1805), Mary Shelley's *The Last Man*, and Camille Flammarion's *Omega* (1894), and the theme has remained common during the last century. Still, Matthew Phipps Shiel's *The Purple Cloud* remains an important text in the history of science fiction and is generally accepted as Shiel's most important work, in both its vision and accomplishment. One thing that distinguishes Shiel's story is its graphic account of the sole survivor descending into destructive **madness** before achieving redemption.

Modern readers may not grasp the significance of the North Pole in Shiel's novel, since it means little today. However, in the nineteenth century, reaching the North Pole represented the ultimate human achievement, equivalent to climbing Mount Everest in the middle of the twentieth century or reaching the **Moon** two decades later. However, Shiel transforms this geographical goal into a **taboo**: in some mysterious way, the North Pole is sacred, and it is the height of human **hubris** to trespass on it. When Jeffson does so, it triggers a cosmic **disaster** for humanity, though he is paradoxically spared from its effects. Shiel thus anticipates later novels and films featuring global catastrophes attributed to human overreaching, usually in the form of a scientific experiment gone awry, but here the connection between fatal misstep and horrific consequences is not direct, but rather symbolic and mystical.

Another aspect of *The Purple Cloud* that may be overlooked is the way that Jeffson's **philosophy** mirrors the Persian **religion** of Zoroastrianism. To Jeffson the Earth, and indeed the universe, is a battleground between two hostile powers, one good, the other evil. As in Zoroastrian thought, the powers are about equal in strength, though one may attain temporary local dominance. As Jeffson perceives the situation, the **tragedy** of *The Purple Cloud* is that the evil became dominant on Earth and was able to almost wipe out animate life; the good, however, by concentrating its strength on small areas, was able to prevent total extinction. Thus, the good force manipulates events to ensure Jeffson's safety and preserve Eve in Istanbul. While the good cannot control Jeffson's mind or diminish his madness, it can restrain his physical acts—preventing him, for example, from carrying out his plan to kill and eat Eve. The final issue becomes whether the good can overcome Jeffson's madness and have him effect a restoration of humanity.

At the novel's conclusion, another religious influence emerges, the biblical Book of Job. Jeffson, like Job, is being tested as part of a contest between opposing forces of good and evil; despite **pain** and suffering, Jeffson must recover his faith and realign himself with the good. As the novel ends with Jeffson making the proper choice, he significantly quotes Job: "Though he slay me, yet will I trust in him."

Such interpretations might be challenged because the story is, after all, being told by Jeffson, whose fits of madness render him an unreliable narrator. All the incidents, feelings, and cosmic processes he describes might exist only in his mind. Still, Shiel is not known as a subtle author, so it seems safe to conclude that Jeffson's sentiments, by and large, are also Shiel's.

The great strength of *The Purple Cloud*, however, lies not in its ideas, but in its surface texture and ambience. While in 1901 Shiel was no longer writing in the ornamented style of his youthful works, *The Purple Cloud* remains: remarkable for inventive details and brilliant language.

Bibliography

Harold Bloom. "M.P. Shiel." Bloom, ed., *Modern Fantasy Writers*. New York: Chelsea House, 1995, 137–150.

David G. Hartwell. "Introduction." *The Purple Cloud*, by M.P. Shiel. Boston: Gregg, 1977, v–xviii.

A. Reynolds Morse, ed. *Shiel in Diverse Hands*. Cleveland: Reynolds Morse Foundation, 1983.

A. Reynolds Morse. *Works of M.P. Shiel: A Study in Bibliography*. Los Angeles: Fantasy Publishing Company, 1948.

Sam Moskowitz. "The World, the Devil, and M.P. Shiel." Moskowitz, *Explorers of the Infinite*. Cleveland: World Publishing, 1963, 142–156.

John D. Squires. "Rediscovering M.P. Shiel (1865–1947)." *New York Review of Science Fiction*, No. 153 (May, 2001), 12–16.

Brian Stableford. "The Politics of Evolution." *Foundation*, No. 27 (February, 1983), 35–60.

William L. Svitavsky. "From Decadence to Racial Antagonism." *Science Fiction Studies*, 31 (March, 2004), 1–24.

—*Gary Westfahl*

THE QUATERMASS EXPERIMENT (1953)

What can there be concerning outer space but ignorance?

—Nigel Kneale
The Quatermass Experiment (1953)
[script] [4114]

Summary

Professor Bernard Quatermass is a pioneering rocket **scientist**, based in Britain (the character is variously played as British or American). His British Rocket Group sends the first manned vehicle into space with three crewmen aboard, but when it crash-lands it contains only one traumatized **astronaut**, Victor Caroon. Quatermass discovers that an alien substance infiltrated the **rocket** in space, which is capable of absorbing any life-form. Caroon escapes from the hospital, growing and mutating, before being cornered and destroyed in London's Westminster Abbey.

In *Quatermass II* (1955), Quatermass is working on his second rocket when he is brought an unusual meteorite; investigating its origin he discovers a top-secret synthetic food factory that is bizarrely similar to his own (unbuilt) Moonbase designs. Inside the factory's domes, an alien **intelligence** is growing, using controlled humans as its workforce, but Quatermass destroys it by exposing it to oxygen, which it finds lethal (see **Aliens on Earth; Invasion**).

In *Quatermass and the Pit* (1958–1959), workmen in London unearth a mysterious metal cylinder that turns out to be a five-million-year-old spaceship containing the remains of ancient Martians (see **Mars**). A quasi-supernatural **force** is unleashed and threatens **civilization** as Quatermass discovers that early humans were genetically altered by war-like Martians for use as biological **weaponry**, creating racial **memories** of devils and **demons**. The Martian energy is defeated using iron, a traditional means of defeating **Satan**.

Discussion

Of the original three television serials featuring the Quatermass character, all written by Nigel Kneale, only *Quatermass and the Pit* has long been available on home video, so audiences are generally more familiar with the feature film remakes, respectively entitled for American release *The Creeping Unknown* (1955), *Enemy from Space* (1957), and *Five Million Years to Earth* (1967). (Recently, however, the second series, and two surviving episodes of the first, have been released on home video, and in 2005 BBC broadcast an exact recreation of the first series.) The films are generally faithful to the television stories (Kneale himself worked on the scripts of the second and third), with some necessary abridgement; generally the first two films are praised by critics, although they tend to prefer the third television serial to its film adaptation.

The Quatermass trilogy explores three types of alien invasion, all markedly different from the traditional military conquest attempted in H.G. Wells's **The War of the Worlds** and innumerable B-movies. Quatermass himself is a curiously mutable character, played very differently by several actors, but the stories are less about him than they are about the potential dangers of **first contact**, played out against a contemporary background of primitive rockets and early attempts at **space travel**. The success of the series lies in the realism of Kneale's writing, in terms of both characters and settings, their very lack of memorability reinforcing their believability. Although Quatermass and his colleagues must, in each story, battle against alien invaders, to do so they must first defeat the bureaucracy of the state—government, military and church—in post-war Britain (see **Politics**).

All three tales feature a clear struggle between **individualism and conformity**. This can be seen in Caroon's absorption of his colleagues, made more obvious in the original teleplay when he speaks with their voices. It is reflected in the worker **zombies** operating the "food plant" in the first sequel and the **hive mind** of the gelatinous alien beings that control them. And it is evident in the militaristic Martians of the third film (glimpsed through a technological visualization of racial memory) and the riots that their re-emergence creates as the human race finally acts on its five-million-year-old programming. Kneale also has a recurring interest in providing scientific rationales for **supernatural creatures** and religious manifestations—including **goblins, ghosts and hauntings** and even Satan himself—which he explored further in later television productions like *The Stone Tape* (1972). Very much of their time and place, the Quatermass serials (which all exist in published script form) reflect the cautious hopes and fears of 1950s Britain (see **Optimism and Pessimism**), a country still rebuilding itself after six years of devastating **war**.

The Quatermass saga broke considerable new ground in science fiction, especially in dramatized science fiction, which was very much in its infancy in the mid-1950s. For example, the Martian **genetic engineering** of prehistoric humans in the third serial and film is an early example of **uplift**, while portrayals of women in the stories are unusually strong and well-drawn for the era. In addition, the film versions, made by the British company Hammer, proved historically important as direct precursors of the **horror** boom that blossomed towards the end of the decade. Although not planned as a trilogy, a certain development can be seen across the three stories: *Experiment* involves a newly created threat, centered on one person; the threat in the second tale is firmly (albeit secretly) established and involves a whole **community**; *Pit*'s threat is as ancient as **time** and lies within every one of us (see **Humanity**).

Professor Quatermass returned in 1979 in a four-part television serial simply titled *Quatermass* (also distributed as an ersatz feature film, *The Quatermass Conclusion*). This again mixed scientific ideas with **religion** and the supernatural as the **youth** of the world flock to a "new age" cult, which is a cover for wholesale alien abduction. As another pendant to the series, a retired Quatermass reflected on his career in a five-part radio serial, *The Quatermass Memoirs*, in 1996.

Bibliography

Stephen R. Bissette. "The Quatermass Conception." *Video Watchdog*, No. 12 (July/August, 1992), 32–47.

Marcus Hearn. "Rocket Man." *Hammer Horror*, No. 7 (September, 1995), 16–20.

Lelia Loban. "We are the Martians Now." *Scarlet Street*, No. 15 (Summer, 1994), 34–44.

Denis Meikle and Jonathan Rigby. "*The Quatermass Xperiment*." *Hammer Horror*, No. 7 (September, 1995), 21–32.

Randy Palmer. "The Quatermass Experience." *Filmfax*, No. 37 (February/March, 1993), 68–75.

Dave Rolinson and Nick Cooper. "Bring Something Back." *Journal of Popular Film and Television*, No. 30 (Fall, 2002), 158–165.

M.J. Simpson. "The *SFX* Interview: Nigel Kneale." *SFX*, No. 14 (July, 1996), 34–39.

Bill Warren. "Nigel Kneale." *Starlog* No. 139 (February, 1989) 32–36, 57; No. 140 (March, 1989), 52–56, 62; No. 141 (April, 1989) 48–52, 70.

—*M.J. Simpson*

Ʀ

Red Dwarf (1988-1999)

Summary

"This is an SOS distress call from the mining ship *Red Dwarf*. The crew are dead, killed by a radiation leak. The only survivors are Dave Lister, who was in suspended animation during the disaster, and his pregnant cat, who was safely sealed in the hold. Revived three million years later, Lister's only companions are a life form who evolved from his cat, and Arnold Rimmer, a hologram simulation of one of the dead crew."

The introduction to the first episode of *Red Dwarf* succinctly summarizes the plot of this British science fiction situation **comedy**. The first series of 1988 revolves around the antagonism between two main characters, space-bum Dave Lister and neurotic, dead superior Arnold Rimmer, in classic sit-com fashion. Adding light relief to adversarial plots are the deadpan one-liners of the ship's senile **computer**, Holly, and the physical comedy of the Cat.

As the show developed, its focus and genre shifted considerably. The second series has the crew venturing outside the claustrophobic confines of *Red Dwarf* for the first time, to planets, other ships and parallel universes. This expanded universe allowed the show to develop a more traditional science fiction format for the third series, in which the repressed **robot** Kryten becomes part of the crew and Holly inexplicably becomes a woman. The first five series depict the *Red Dwarf* crew's attempts to return **home** to **Earth** (see **Space Travel**). The seventh Series marks the addition of Lister's lost-**love** Kristine Kochanski to the crew and the search for the missing mothership, *Red Dwarf*, which is recovered in the eighth series with its dead crew reanimated by overzealous nano-robots.

Discussion

Red Dwarf signals its concern with **religion** from the beginning when in the first episode Lister discovers that he is God to the cat-species. Due to Lister's refusal to hand his **cat** over to the Ship's captain for dissection—the reason why Lister is put into suspended animation as punishment and escapes the fatal radiation leak—he appears in the Cat holy-book as "Cloister the Stupid," the father of catkind. This story line is expanded upon in the significantly titled fourth episode "Waiting for God" (1988). Although initially pleased with his newfound status as a deity, Lister discovers that the Cat species drove themselves to the point of extinction in absurd religious **wars** over what **color** hats they should wear. The allusion to Samuel Beckett's play *Waiting for Godot* (1952) in this episode's title hints at the influence of existentialism on *Red Dwarf*'s engagement with what it is to be human. The post-apocalyptic scenario (see **Apocalypse**) of characters being trapped together in a confined space (see **Prisons**) recalls Samuel Beckett's *Endgame* (1957) and Jean Paul Sartre's famous assertion that "hell is other people." Other episodes addressing this issue include "The Last Day" (1989), where Kryten is forced to confront the possibility that Silicon Heaven (android afterlife) may not exist, and "The Inquisitor" (1992), where an atheistic robot decides to erase from **time** those it judges unworthy to have existed. The existentialist concern over being and nothingness (see **Death**) is also signalled by one of *Red Dwarf*'s biggest contributions to the science fiction genre: the idea of a hologram being a crew member.

Intimately connected with the theme of religion is *Red Dwarf*'s preoccupation with the question of free will. Lister's attempts to "break" Kryten of his programming is a traditional use of the robot to raise questions about the nature of **humanity**: the programming that makes Kryten a slave takes the form of a religion and sense of guilt. Kryten is not an emotionless robot, like *Star Trek: The Next Generation*'s Data, but one who is *burdened* by emotion to repress him.

Questions of free will are also raised by techniques of **time travel** and parallel universes (see **Parallel Worlds**). The brilliant time travel sequences in "Future Echoes" (1988) suggest that our lives are predetermined, as does the revelation in "Ouroboros" (1997) that Lister is his own **father**. However, an alternate view of free will is highlighted by the existence of an infinite number of parallel universes, each arising when a different choice is made. After early use of this theory in "Parallel Universe" (1988), a satirical episode (see **Satire**) that defamiliarizes concepts of **gender** by having the crew end up in a universe where women are the dominant sex, the idea of seemingly minute differences in choice having massive effects is highlighted when we meet an alternate universe's Arnold Rimmer in "Dimension Jump" (1991). This heroic, successful officer, test-pilot, and adventurer (see **Heroes**) is the polar opposite of the neurotic, cowardly Rimmer due to one minor childhood event.

The series has spawned four novels—*Infinity Welcomes Careful Drivers* (1989) and *Better than Life* (1990), jointly written by series creators Robert Grant and Doug Naylor as "Grant Naylor"; *Last Human* (1995) by Naylor alone; and *Backwards* (1996), by Grant alone—which merit consideration in their own right as accomplished science fiction works.

Bibliography

Bruce Dessau. *The Official Red Dwarf Companion.* London: Titan, 1992.

Dennis Fischer. "*Red Dwarf* IV." *Cinefantastique,* 29 (October, 1997), 114.

Elyce Rae Helford. "Reading Masculinities in the 'Post-Patriarchal' Space of *Red Dwarf.*" *Foundation,* No. 64 (Summer, 1995), 20–31.

Chris Howarth and Steve Lyons. *The Red Dwarf Programme Guide.* London: Virgin, 1995.

Robert Llewellyn. *The Man in the Rubber Mask.* London: Penguin, 1994.

Joe Nazzaro. *The Making of Red Dwarf.* London: Penguin, 1994.

————. "*Red Dwarf.*" *Starlog*, No. 186 (January, 1993), 75–80.
Patrick Parrinder. "Back to the Far Future? Futures of Destiny and Desire in British Science Fiction." *Foundation*, No. 85 (Summer, 2002), 79–88.

—Kevin P. Smith

RED MARS BY KIM STANLEY ROBINSON (1992)

We all want different things from Mars.

—Kim Stanley Robinson
Red Mars (1992)

Summary

It is many years after 2027, when the first one hundred **scientists** landed on **Mars**. Two erstwhile leaders have differing intentions: Frank Chalmers is a conciliator, and John Boone is an idealist. After Frank engineers the murder of John, the story shifts back in **time** to the voyage from **Earth** to Mars and the many approaches that these first colonists want to take to ensure **survival** on this initially hostile planet. They also face a hostile atmosphere of contending intentions for human life on Mars and its relationship to Earth's ecological and economic dilemmas. *Red Mars* ends with a failed revolution, in 2061, which causes the **death** of many of the first settlers and firms up several underground movements of survivors, each of which interprets the means, needs, and **ethics** of human life on Mars differently.

Discussion

Red Mars is the first book in a trilogy about settling and **terraforming** Mars (the others being *Green Mars* [1994] and *Blue Mars* [1996]) that has set a new fictional standard for imagining human settlement of our legendary planetary neighbor and modeling ecological systems (see **Ecology**). In *Green Mars*, the sequel, rampant terraforming ends in **disaster** for many colonists but humans have achieved some of their goals in making the planet habitable and circumventing the intentions of Earth's unrestrained capitalism, successfully achieving Martian independence. In *Blue Mars*, some differences between what is described as the Red **philosophy** (preserve as much of the original Martian **landscape** as possible) and the Green philosophy (terraform the planet as rapidly as possible into an earth-like ecosystem) have resolved into what Eric Otto calls an ecopoesis or land-human symbiosis. There was also a collection of related stories, *The Martians* (1999).

As the story progresses, Mars emerges as a thought-experiment through the arguments of characters like Ann Clayborne, quintessential Red supporter, and Sax Russell, who begins as a Green and, due to the availability of longevity **drugs** that allow them to survive over 200 years (see **Immortality and Longevity**), helps to form the Blue approach, a synthesis of human needs and respect for Mars's innate nature. While the novels are philosophically and ethically interesting, they also fascinate through many speculations on state-of-the-art science and **technology**, a testament to the author's extensive absorption of material like NASA Viking Mission reports and treatises on ecology, chemistry, engineering, and architecture.

At the beginning of *Red Mars*, the planet is a huge **desert** with a small variety of landforms and an inhospitable climate and atmosphere. When the first 100, all of them scientists with one major specialty and at least one secondary one, land on Mars after a long voyage from Earth, they face life similar to that in Antarctica (see **Polar Regions**), where they trained for the voyage. The expedition, funded by the UN and other Earth entities, is multiracial and multicultural and has been sent in the expectation that they will be governed by Earth's intentions. However, while they are still traveling to Mars, one scientist starts to argue for severing that link and creating an egalitarian **utopia**; this signals that they will succeed in surviving their first decades but will split apart into separate groups, each contending for its own economic, ecological, and social agenda. They will be forced to accept colonists from the Arab world and **Japan**, further complicating the utopian intent of egalitarianism and reintroducing the tensions of class, race, and postcolonial **cultures** (see **Class System; Postcolonialism; Race Relations**).

This novel and its sequels have been discussed in various contexts: utopia; appropriate uses of science and technology; ethics; parallels with American and other colonial economies (see **America**); the interrelationship of humans and landscape; and the "areoforming" of humans (Mars changing humans as they change Mars). There are intentional parallels with the colonization of North America, but under more controlled conditions. Some characters see themselves as exploring a fascinating **frontier** with its own inherent **beauty** while others see a blank slate on which humans can write a new story. The Martians' successful revolution in 2127 paves the way for a uniquely Martian constitution and **governance system** that emphasizes egalitarianism, sustainable development, and independence.

The position of science and technology in human culture is explored in relation to human survival. The biologists, ecologists, geologists, physicists, botanists, and psychologists, far from sharing a dream of a collective Martian future, fragment into groups around their own disciplines which, in "The Crucible" of this new and hostile land, become competing ideas about humanity's ideal relationship to Mars. They cooperate to create a series of **habitats**: first, primitive, windowless dwellings; then, an underground colony; and then a domed **city**, with the understanding that terraforming is just an extension of their humanized habitats. Yet each stage of development is also viewed by some as a hideous incursion on the land. To mine minerals and produce needed materials, they create huge holes, slag heaps, smokestacks, and nuclear waste, and they begin reducing frozen stores of **water** at the planet's poles. These activities lead to guerrilla warfare, with Reds sabotaging the work of the Greens and both opposing large corporations on Earth who circumvent their own conservation laws to exploit Mars's natural resources. Yet this novel and its sequels also celebrate science and technology in many detailed descriptions of its workings.

Bibliography

K.V. Bailey. "Mars is a District of Sheffield." *Foundation*, No. 68 (Autumn, 1996), 81–86.

William Dynes. "Multiple Perspectives in Kim Stanley Robinson's Mars Series." *Extrapolation*, 42 (Summer, 2001), 150–164.

Bud Foote. "Assuming the Present." Joe Sanders, ed., *Functions of the Fantastic*. Westport, CT: Greenwood Press, 1995, 161–167.

Carol Franko. "Working the 'In Between.'" *Science-Fiction Studies*, 21 (July, 1994), 191–211.

Shaun Huston. "Murray Bookchin on Mars!" Rob Kitchin and James Kneale, eds., *Lost in Space*. London: Continuum, 2002, 167–179.

Fredric Jameson. "If I Find One Good City, I will Spare the Man." Patrick Parrinder, ed., *Learning From Other Worlds*. Liverpool, UK: Liverpool University Press, 2000, 208–233.

Robert Markley. "Falling Into Theory." *Modern Fiction Studies*, 43 (1997), 773–799.

Eric Otto. "Kim Stanley Robinson's Mars Trilogy and the Leopoldian Land Ethic." *Utopian Studies*, 14 (2003), 118–135.

Ernest J. Yarnarella. "Terra/Terror-Forming and Death Denial in Kim Stanley Robinson's Martian Stories and Mars Trilogy." *Foundation*, No. 89 (Autumn, 2003), 13–26.

—*Janice M. Bogstad*

RENDEZVOUS WITH RAMA
BY ARTHUR C. CLARKE (1973)

Summary

In 2130, there are several colonized worlds in our solar system: the **Moon, Mars, Mercury** (whose inhabitants are called "Hermians"), Ganymede, Titan, and Triton (see **Planetary Colonies**). When a huge alien artifact, given the name "Rama" by astronomers, enters the solar system, the spaceship *Endeavour* is sent to study it. Leaders on **Earth** and the colonized worlds are sensitive to the possibility of **disaster** from space, since much of northern Italy, including Venice, Padua, and Verona, was destroyed in 2077 by a huge meteor. Throughout *Rendezvous with Rama*, some voices advocate destruction of Rama as a potential threat.

Even before the *Endeavour* commences its mission, an unmanned probe demonstrates that Rama is an artificial object—a hollow cylinder fifty kilometers long and twenty in diameter, large enough to have its own internal **landscape, ecology,** and **weather.** Commander William Norton and his crew of **astronauts** have only a limited time in which to establish whether it is dangerous.

The novel's main events involve **exploration** of Rama's interior. Norton and his crew are dwarfed by this world, which has hurricanes, electrical storms, sea, cliffs, and giant waves. There are also bizarre semi-robotic or biological creatures (see **Aliens in Space**). Rama's environment continually tests the astronauts' ingenuity (see **Puzzles**), and Rama itself defies human **knowledge** and understanding to the very end. A crisis occurs when Hermians attempt to take matters into their own hands by positioning a nuclear missile and threatening to destroy Rama. This, however, is foiled by Norton and his crew. Rama ultimately taps matter from the **Sun** to refuel, then heads in the direction of the Greater Magellanic Cloud, leaving no real clues about its purpose.

Discussion

Rendezvous with Rama won the Hugo, Nebula, and John W. Campbell Awards. It is a classic example of **hard science fiction**, with an emphasis on scientific accuracy and logic. Perhaps its greatest strength lies in its concern for plausible detail, whether in descriptions of the artificial landscape inside of Rama (see **Architecture and Interior Design**), the **technology** required for **space travel,** or procedures for defusing a nuclear weapon in space.

Clarke also uses this form of science fiction to suggest the narrowness of many of our current social assumptions. Though *Rendezvous with Rama* may be said to satirize our confidence in the possibility of explaining and understanding the universe, the novel is by no means a *social* satire. On the contrary, Clarke paints an attractive picture of how a reasonable space-going society might operate in the future. Despite diplomatic squabbles and Hermian machinations, the solar-system-spanning society of 2130 is close to being a **utopia**. Yet its mores are also dramatically different from those of our own society (see **Ethics**).

For example, Norton has two wives on two different planets (see **Marriage**) and a total of three **children**. His **families** are described as being on excellent terms, so sexual jealousy does not play the same role that it does in our own society. Similarly, two other male characters on the *Endeavour* share a wife back on Earth. We also learn that some people are still working, though over a century old; one character is aged 115 but belongs to the Rama Committee of the United Planets Science Organization (see **Immortality and Longevity**). The *Endeavour*'s crew comprises both men and women, which is hardly surprising in itself, but they are also joined by "simps": genetically engineered **apes** or monkeys with prehensile tails and high **intelligence,** trained to do menial work (see **Genetic Engineering**). All these developments are presented as logical, given the technology and social organization portrayed.

After *Rendezvous with Rama*, Clarke wrote three sequels in collaboration with Gentry Lee (actually authored mainly or entirely by Lee, with input from Clarke): *Rama II* (1989), *The Garden of Rama* (1991), and *Rama Revealed* (1993). These are set further in the future and form a trilogy with different characters from those of the original novel. It transpires that the alien intelligences behind the Rama artifacts are involved in classifying and studying lifeforms, particularly space-faring ones, in our part of the galaxy. Ultimately a religious explanation is given for the aliens' activities (see **Religion**).

These novels reveal that the future society of *Rendezvous with Rama* has since been destroyed by economic collapse. The social arrangements depicted are closer to our own: it no longer seems common for people to live extended lives, and developments in sexual and familial arrangements shown in Clarke's original novel have apparently been forgotten. This allows the authors to present far more conventional characters and motivations. Though successful in their own terms, *Rama II* and its sequels rely on formulaic best-seller elements like passionate confrontations, forbidden secrets, scheming women, and sexual intrigue.

Bibliography

Peter Brigg. "Three Styles of Arthur C. Clarke." Joseph D. Olander and Martin Harry Greenberg, eds., *Arthur C. Clarke*. New York: Taplinger, 1977, 15–51.

Gregory Feeley. "Partners in Plunder or, Rendezvous with Manna." *Foundation*, No. 49 (Summer 1990), 58–63.

Betsy Harftst. "Of Myths and Polyominoes." Joseph D. Olander and Martin Harry Greenberg, eds., *Arthur C. Clarke*. New York: Taplinger, 1977, 87–120.

John Hollow. *Against the Night the Stars*. New York: Harcourt Brace Jovanovich, 1983.

Christopher Priest. "Metaphorical Egyptian Tomb." *Foundation*, No. 5 (January, 1974), 91–94.

Eric S. Rabkin. *Arthur C. Clarke*. West Linn, OR: Starmont House, 1979.

Robin Reid. *Arthur C. Clarke*. Westport, CT: Greenwood Press, 1997.

George Edgar Slusser. *The Space Odysseys of Arthur C. Clarke*. San Bernardino, CA: Borgo Press, 1978.

E. Michael Thron. "The Outsider from Inside." Joseph D. Olander and Martin Harry Greenberg, eds., *Arthur C. Clarke*. New York: Taplinger, 1977, 72–86.

—Russell Blackford

S

SHE BY H. RIDER HAGGARD (1887)

A story that began more than two thou-
sand years ago may stretch a long way
into the dim and distant future.

—H. Rider Haggard
She (1887)

Summary

Leo Vincey is a modern man whose **family** has a secret, passed down since ancient times, in the form of a potsherd telling a strange story. Around 400 BCE, Kallikrates, priest of Isis, and Amenartas, princess of **Egypt**, fell into forbidden **love** and fled into the interior of **Africa**, where they discovered the lost city of Kor, ruled by Ayesha, an immortal white "goddess" (see **Immortality and Longevity**) who promptly fell in love with Kallikrates as well. When he refused her, she killed him in a fit of rage, but Amenartas was allowed to **escape**. To her son by Kallikrates, Amenartes assigned the task of **revenge**, but all descendents up to modern times have failed to find Kor. Vincey, accompanied by his friend Holly, succeeds. Ayesha, who has spent all this **time** brooding over her loss, realizes that Vincey is the **reincarnation** of Kallikrates. This ancient **temptress** again displays all her seductive, supernatural charms, but the ancient love triangle replays itself, with Amenartas reincarnated in a native girl, Ustane. Matters are resolved when Ayesha tries to make Vincey/Kallikrates immortal like herself. To show him how the Flame of Immortality will not burn him, she steps into it for a second time, withering away into a dead husk.

Discussion

Even after more than a century (during which the novel has never been out of print), H. Rider Haggard's *She: A History of Adventure* (its original title) remains a masterpiece of thrilling adventure, filled with vivid descriptions, first of the **quest** for Kor, then of the haunted, charnel-house atmosphere of the **city** itself (see **Lost Worlds**). There are nasty moments, as when the **heroes** are captured by cannibals who place red-hot pots over the heads of live victims, and quite a bit of barely sublimated eroticism (see **Sexuality**), which not only superheats the narrative but provides odd moments. Ancient mummies are used as torches in Kor, but bodies are so perfectly preserved that, amid the ashes of one, the hero finds a beautiful female foot, which he keeps as a kind of fetish.

The character of Ayesha herself is one of the great creations of popular fiction, on par with Bram Stoker's **Dracula** or Sax Rohmer's Fu Manchu. As She-Who-Must-Be-Obeyed, she has passed into the English language itself. The story is utterly archetypal; psychologists have had a field day with it. Indeed, the great Carl Jung was fascinated by *She* and cited Ayesha as an example of the Anima Archetype, as she certainly is, showing the Victorian preoccupation with the sexual woman as temptress and destroyer.

As a publishing phenomenon, *She* was as important as Horace Walpole's *The Castle of Otranto* (1765) or J.R.R. Tolkien's **The Lord of the Rings**. This and Haggard's *King Solomon's Mines* (1885), the two greatest lost world adventures, spawned a whole category of publishing, just as *The Castle of Otranto* created the **Gothic** and *The Lord of the Rings* created modern fantasy. There were literally hundreds of imitations, including the major novels by A. Merritt and Edgar Rice Burroughs. Merritt's various seductresses and Burroughs's La of Opar, encountered by **Tarzan of the Apes**, are among Ayesha's many literary descendants.

Through Hollywood, the elements of the Haggardian tale are now familiar to all: pith-helmeted explorers pressing through the Africa **jungle** or other remote regions; encounters with savages (see **Barbarians**); white men venturing into "forbidden" realms shunned (for good reason) by native "superstition"; and discovery of awesome secrets amid ruins of immemorial antiquity. The character of Ayesha is, along with Cleopatra, perhaps the best "vamp" role ever conceived. In three film versions of *She*, Ayesha has been played by Helen Gahagan (1935), Ursula Andress (1965), and Sandahl Bergman (1985). Indiana Jones would be right at home in the Caves of Kor, though he would more likely be battling **villains** (cannibals and acolytes) than wooing Ayesha.

Lost race novels are products of the high tide of European imperialism, when white explorers really were pushing into all the world's previously inaccessible realms. As ruined cities such as Zimbabwe or Machu Picchu were brought to light, writers like Haggard upped the ante by describing similar cities as still inhabited by mysterious and timeless **cultures** possessing occult **wisdom** unknown to the outside world. In Kor, characters venture into a kind of dreamland, beyond the restrictions of Victorian morality, a place of forbidden sensuality carefully balanced with menace. Remember that Ayesha lives in **caverns** illuminated by burning corpses.

She is also the product of a time when Europeans saw themselves as the Earth's most enlightened people, on a benevolent mission to tame and uplift barbarous parts of the world. Haggard, who had been to Africa and written a book about it, *Cetywayo and His White Neighbors* (1882), may have held political opinions typical of his time (see **Politics**) regarding imperialism as basically benign, but he also developed respect for the natives and his works are, for their time, remarkably free of racism (see **Race Relations**). While the politically correct may object to Haggard's cannibals who grovel before their immortal White Queen, one can counter that she is, after all, a supernatural being who also awes white characters, and Kor is outside of the bounds of mundane reality. Elsewhere, as in *Nada the Lily* (1892), Haggard showed that he could also write persuasively about actual African cultures.

Although Ayesha was destroyed at the end of *She*, the public demanded to see her again. *Ayesha: The Return of She* (1905) is a direct sequel, in which Vincey and Holly seek the reincarnated Ayesha in central Asia. *She and Allan* (1920) tells how the hero of *King Solomon's Mines*, Allan Quatermain, visited Kor shortly before the events of *She*. And *Wisdom's Daughter* (1923) is the story of Ayesha in ancient Egypt, where she incurred the wrath of the goddess Aphrodite.

Bibliography

Harold Bloom. "H. Rider Haggard." Bloom, ed., *Classic Fantasy Writers*. New York: Chelsea House, 1994, 82–95.

Morton Cohen. *Rider Haggard*. London: Hutchison, 1960.

Norman Etherington. *The Annotated She*, by H. Rider Haggard. Bloomington: Indiana University Press, 1991.

Barri J. Gold. "Embracing the Corpse." *English Literature in Transition*, 38 (1995), 305–327.

D.S. Higgins. *Rider Haggard*. London: Cassell, 1981.

Wendy J. Katz. *Rider Haggard and the Fiction of Empire*. Cambridge: Cambridge University Press, 1987.

Bette Roberts. "The Mother Goddess in H. Rider Haggard's *She* and Anne Rice's *The Queen of the Damned*." James C. Holte, ed., *The Fantastic Vampire*. Westport, CT: Greenwood Press, 1997, 103–110.

Lindy Stiebel. *Imagining Africa*. Westport, CT: Greenwood Press, 2001.

Catherine Storr. "H. Rider Haggard's *She*." *Children's Literature In Education*, 22 (September, 1991), 161–168.

—*Darrell Schweitzer*

The Shining by Stephen King (1977)

Summary

Fired from a teaching position for hitting a student (see **Education**), Jack Torrance, recovering alcoholic and blocked writer, hopes to redeem himself as winter care-taker of Overlook, a luxury hotel in the Colorado **mountains**. With him are his wife Wendy and five-year-old Danny, a telepath who can predict the future (see **Psychic Powers**). Tony, a spirit only Danny can see, warns Danny that the Overlook is dangerous. Hallorann, the hotel's African-American cook and also a psychic, tells Danny to summon him telepathically if Danny is ever in danger. Isolated at the Overlook, Jack descends into **madness**. Initially, Jack's monstrous behavior might plausibly be explained as the psychological legacy of an abusive **father**. Toward the end, however, hotel ghosts become unequivocally tangible and supply Jack with real alcohol. When Jack attempts to kill his **family**, Danny summons Hallorann. The cook makes his way through heavy snow to rescue Wendy and Danny just before the hotel's boiler explodes, destroying Jack and the hotel.

Discussion

The Shining was adapted twice as a film. Stanley Kubrick's film (1980) follows the novel's plot but focuses on Jack rather than Danny. Not the loving husband and father of the novel, Jack embraces madness as a welcome moral holiday. The ABC television miniseries (1997) was scripted by King as an alternative to what he considered Kubrick's misinterpretation of the novel.

In this **horror** novel, the Overlook resembles a **Gothic** castle. Its **ghosts and hauntings** are manifestations of the violent and corrupt guests and employees who, throughout the hotel's history, partied and died there. Jack becomes fatally obsessed with the Overlook through the Gothic device of the "found manuscript," a scrapbook whose newspaper clippings and photographs prompt his obsessive research into the hotel's unsavory past. Like H.P. Lovecraft's *Necronomicon*, the scrapbook is a preternaturally **evil** book, dooming anyone unfortunate enough to open it.

As the scrapbook device suggests, **books**, as well as **writing and authors**, are major themes. *The Shining*'s metaphors often invoke the written word: Danny's memory of Tony's warning "was all gone, dissolved into a sticky mess like a wet bundle of paper." *The Shining* is full of allusions, most importantly to Edgar Allan Poe's "Masque of the Red Death" (1842) (masked ball and sinister clock), Charles Perrault's "Bluebeard" (1697) (a forbidden chamber), and Lewis Carroll's *Alice's Adventures in Wonderland* (Jack's choice of a croquet mallet as a murder weapon).

The Torrances are bookish. At the job interview, Jack says that solitude will not be a problem because "my wife and I both like to read." Regaining a place in society, Jack believes, depends on succeeding as a writer. Disastrously, Jack changes his writing project from a play to a **history** of the Overlook. Like King's other author protagonists, Jack's destructive energy is unleashed through writing (as in *The Dark Half* [1990], "Secret Window, Secret Garden" [1990]) and obsessive research ("Apt Pupil" [1982]).

Because his psychic **talents** (telepathy and precognition) take a peculiarly verbal form, Danny concentrates on learning to read. Tony's **omens and signs** are usually words a five year-old can neither read nor understand, the most significant being the puzzling REDRUM, a reversal of the word "murder." Danny's perceptions of the thoughts of adults (DIVORCE, LOOSING YOUR MARBLES) expose him to adult motives he is too young to understand. Joseph Reino suggests that Danny's "shining" is a metaphor for television (see **Television and Radio**), which delivers age-inappropriate information to **children**.

Telepathic Danny is burdened by his parents' economic insecurity; and, indeed, **business** and **economics** are important themes in *The Shining*. Overwhelmed by the prospect of supporting a small child without marketable skills, Wendy does not **escape** the Overlook when it is still possible. Grady, ghost of the former caretaker, tempts Jack with corporate advancement. If he murders his wife and son, Jack may rise, Grady suggests, "all the way to the position of manager." Horace Derwent, who embodies greedy, unscrupulous American capitalism, purchased the Overlook in 1945 and became a millionaire through bootlegging, smuggling, and gambling enterprises; he made the Overlook a playground for the badly behaving rich.

More important than its critique of American capitalism is *The Shining*'s concern with family. At the Overlook, Jack becomes his father, an alcoholic who brutally abused his sons and nearly killed his wife. Jack voices his father's patriarchal rationalizations: beatings are "medicine," a "fatherly duty." Disappointingly, the novel permits Jack to evade full moral responsibility for his violent abuse of wife and child by attributing them to **possession** by the Hotel. "You're not my daddy," Danny tells the being about to murder him.

With Hallorann as **mentor**, Danny will succeed in breaking the **cycle** of alcoholism and rage that doomed his father. As adoptive father, Hallorann provides a model of a male whose feminine side is well developed. He encourages Danny to cry and helps him manage his psychic talents. Though Danny is still a child at the end, Tony provides a glimpse of the responsible young man he will become.

Bibliography

John Brown. "The Impossible Object." John Orr and Colin Nicholson, eds., *Cinema and Fiction*. Edinburgh: Edinburgh University Press, 1992, 104–121.

Steven Bruhm. "On Stephen King's Phallus." *Narrative*, 4 (January, 1996), 55–73.

Ronald T. Curran. "Complex, Archetype, and Primal Fear." Tony Magistrale, ed., *The Dark Descent*. Westport, CT: Greenwood, 1992, 33–46.

Bud Foote. "Getting Things in the Right Order." Gary Westfahl and George Slusser, eds., *Nursery Realms*. Athens: University of Georgia Press, 1999, 200–209.

Stephen King. "Before the Play." *Whispers*, Nos. 17/18 (August, 1982), 19–47.

———. "On Becoming a Brand Name." King, *Secret Windows*. New York: Book-of-the-Month Club, 2000, 39–69.

Tony Magistrale, ed. *Discovering Stephen King's The Shining*. San Bernardino, CA: Borgo Press, 1998.

Joseph Reino. "Strange Powers of Dangerous Potential." Reino, *Stephen King*. Boston: Twayne, 1988, 34–42.

Douglas E. Winter. "*The Shining*." Winter, *Stephen King*. San Bernardino, CA: Borgo Press, 1982, 46–54.

—*Wendy Bousfield*

THE SIMPSONS (1989–)

Summary

Since its inception, *The Simpsons* has been heavily influenced by, and has repeatedly paid homage to, the great (and not-so-great) stories and characters of science fiction and fantasy history. Though the show focuses on the humorous exploits of a middle-class **family** (parents Homer and Marge, and **children** Bart, Lisa, and Maggie), its vast cast of characters extends well beyond the Simpson family itself: several recurring characters and settings, as well as an annual "Treehouse of Horror" episode in the style of *The Twilight Zone* provide constant reminder that the show relies heavily on science fiction and fantasy as fodder for its imagination. *The Simpsons* is also well known for its lovingly satirical portrayal of science fiction fan **culture** (see **Satire**), including the worlds of collectors, in-store comic book signings, science fiction conventions, and Internet **communities**. The show's writers are well aware that their fanbase significantly overlaps with those of science fiction and fantasy shows, and this has afforded them ample opportunity to both honor and mock their fans on a regular basis.

Discussion

The Simpsons' metafictional aspect (see **Metafiction and Recursiveness**), its clear awareness of its own status as an iconic program and object of adoration and obsession, is most clearly represented in the character known only as Comic Book Guy, portly proprietor of Springfield's comic book and collectibles store, The Android's Dungeon. Comic Book Guy embodies sci-fi fandom; his store is the center of many a science-fiction-related plot and subplot, and he functions as both a curmudgeonly critic (he has a Master's degree in folklore and **mythology**) and repository of all kinds of arcane **knowledge** on the subject of science fiction and fantasy. He affects a smug, superior attitude whenever discussing the merits of television shows, comic books, or movies, and thus functions as a perpetual parody of the most avid contributors to *The Simpsons*' own websites and message boards.

Another recurring, science-fiction-inspired character is Professor John Frink, a **scientist** modeled on Jerry Lewis's character in *The Nutty Professor* (1963), who uses his considerable intellect primarily to invent zany, futuristic contraptions of dubious social value, like a **flying** motorcycle and **computer** that predicts the outcome of football games, the Gamble-Tron 2000 (see **Inventions**). *The Simpsons* also features two sets of fictional characters, a **superhero** comic book duo—Radioactive Man and Fallout Boy—and cartoon **cat** and mouse team—Itchy and Scratchy (see **Rats and Mice**)—both of which rely on comics and cartoon conventions of fantastical exaggeration and hyper-reality, thereby conferring an ironic verisimilitude on the world of Springfield.

The **nuclear power** plant where Homer Simpson works provides many occasions for imagining the fantastical effects that radiation might have on both Homer and the Springfield community. Nuclear waste has caused sensational **mutations** in the local wildlife, giving Springfield squirrels that shoot laser beams out of their eyes and a resident three-eyed fish nicknamed "Blinky" (see **Fish and Sea Creatures**). One episode suggests that to sneak out of the plant undetected, Homer must defeat a gigantic (presumably radioactively enhanced) spider (see **Insects**). Borrowing the concept of fantastical mutation from science fiction, *The Simpsons* manages to portray nuclear power as simultaneously **evil** and comical.

Though the show's references to classic works of science fiction, fantasy, and horror are too numerous to catalogue, a few works have become important touchstones. *Batman*, particularly the 1960s television series, has profoundly influenced the show's look and sensibility, from the design of Bart's short-lived alter ego "Bartman" to frequent parodies of the show's theme song, catchphrases, and spinning-image scene changes. *The Simpsons* also nods frequently to *Star Wars* (which Bart lists, along with the Revolutionary War and World War II, as one of only three "good" **wars**) and *Star Trek*. Occasionally, *The Simpsons* moves beyond simple reference or allusion and engages fantastical material on a more substantive level, as in episode-long parodies of *The X-Files* and *The Prisoner*.

While the scope of reference to fantastical fiction in *The Simpsons* is vast, there are two masters of the genre whose impact on *The Simpsons* supersedes that of all others: Stanley Kubrick and Edgar Allan Poe. In addition to being the sources for many segments in the "Treehouse of Horror" episodes (including parodies of Kubrick's *The Shining* [see Stephen King's **The Shining**] and Poe's "The Raven" [1845]), the work of these two artists has frequently been woven thematically into a variety of *Simpsons* plotlines. Kubrick's **2001: A Space Odyssey** has been mined repeatedly for images of primitive humans (used at least once to suggest a certain un-evolved quality in Homer), its vision of life in space, and its stirring, classical score (used to convey transcendence). *The Simpsons* has also drawn repeatedly on Kubrick's **Dr. Strangelove** for its satirical portrayal of the military. Poe exerts an equally powerful influence: not only has he been featured in many throwaway references (his gravestone being cleaned on an infomercial, his family **home** bursting into flames when the home-mover loses control of his truck, etc.), but his story "The Tell-Tale Heart" (1843) has been the basis for two different episodes on the maddening power of guilt ("The Telltale Head" [1990] and "Lisa's Rival" [1994]). Though *The Simpsons* functions primarily as parody, its thoughtful engagement with Kubrick and Poe, among many others, demonstrates a deep respect for the genres of science fiction and fantasy.

Bibliography

John Alberti, ed. *Leaving Springfield*. Detroit: Wayne State University Press, 2003.

Kurt Borchard. "Simpsons as Subculture." Will Wright and Steven Kaplan, eds., *The Image of Technology in Literature, the Media, and Society*. Pueblo, CO: University of Southern Colorado, 1994, 329–336.

David Dark. *Everyday Apocalypse*. Grand Rapids, MI: Brazos Press, 2002.

Scott M. Gimple, ed. *The Simpsons Forever!* New York: HarperCollins, 1999.

Steven Keslowitz. *The Simpsons and Society*. Tucson, AZ: Hats Off Books, 2004.

Jesse L. McCann, ed. *The Simpsons Beyond Forever!* New York: HarperCollins, 2002.

Jason Mittell. "Cartoon Realism." *Velvet Light Trap*, No. 47 (Spring, 2001), 15–28.

Allan Neuwirth. *Makin' Toons*. New York: Allworth Press, 2003.

Rich Raymond and Antonia Coffman, eds. *The Simpsons*. New York: HarperCollins, 1997.

—*Michael Sharp*

SLAUGHTERHOUSE-FIVE
BY KURT VONNEGUT, JR. (1969)

◾

I am a Tralfamadorian, seeing all time as you might see a stretch of the Rocky Mountains. All time is all time. It does not change. It does not lend itself to warnings or explanations. It simply is.

> *Take it moment by moment, and you will*
> *find that we are all, as I've said before,*
> *bugs in amber.*
>
> —Kurt Vonnegut, Jr.
> *Slaughterhouse-Five* (1969)

Summary

Billy Pilgrim is a World War II chaplain's assistant taken prisoner during the Battle of the Bulge. Shipped to Dresden, supposedly not a military target, Billy survives the 1945 Allied firebombing of that **city**. Back in **America** and experiencing schizophrenic episodes, Billy spends time in mental hospitals where he begins to read science fiction and engage in **time travel**. He becomes a successful optometrist in Ilium, is abducted by aliens called Tralfamadorians, is taken to Tralfamadore, and is put into a human zoo with actress Montana Wildhack. Billy's time traveling takes him randomly across his life, into **death** and back again. His interactions with the Tralfamadorians teach him about the nature of **time**, which they understand as a collection of discrete moments rather than a chain of events. Billy's wife dies in an accident, his daughter is convinced he is insane (see **Madness**), his son becomes a Green Beret and goes to Vietnam, and, finally, Billy and Montana have a **baby** in the Tralfamadorian zoo. In the novel as in Billy's life, these events occur out of sequence. Because of his helplessness during the **war** and in the face of his time traveling, Billy becomes largely passive about life's joys and **tragedies**.

Discussion

At the center of *Slaughterhouse-Five, or The Children's Crusade: A Duty-Dance with Death* (its lengthy subtitle usually ignored) is the Dresden firestorm, a military and scientific success but a human catastrophe. The image of an **apocalypse** appears in other Vonnegut texts like ***Cat's Cradle***, *God Bless You, Mr. Rosewater* (1965), and *Galápagos*. "Apocalypse" takes on at least two meanings in *Slaughterhouse-Five*: it signifies the end of the world as the characters know it, and the revelation of truths. Vonnegut, too, was a prisoner of war in Dresden when it was firebombed and inserts himself into the novel in a number of ways: these inclusions, stylistic devices, overriding irony, and acceptance of chaos have caused the novel to be flagged as a postmodern text (see **Postmodernism**). Like many of Vonnegut's other works, *Slaughterhouse-Five* satirizes science, war, **America**, human miscommunication, and belief. The book questions the idea of human agency, suggesting that we exist at the whim of enormous corporate forces about which we can do little.

That Billy is an optometrist suggests the importance Vonnegut puts on seeing the world clearly (see **Perception; Vision and Blindness**). Billy sees himself as prescribing "corrective lenses for Earthling souls." Once he visits Tralfamadore, Billy is increasingly uncertain about right and wrong. His experiences in war taught him that tragedies befall the innocent and guilty without any logic. He finds in science fiction's alternate realities ways of understanding his life's surreal pilgrimage, as his name—perhaps a reference to John Bunyan's *The Pilgrim's Progress* (1678)—suggests. But *Slaughterhouse-Five* is a **satire** that is closer to Jonathan Swift's

Gulliver's Travels and Mark Twain's *A Connecticut Yankee in King Arthur's Court* than Bunyan's text: in leaving behind **Earth** and traveling to other times, planets, or places, Vonnegut can look back and regret the ways of human foolishness at **home**.

Sanity is another problem in the text. Given the strange humans he meets, it seems possible that Billy is the only sane person on Earth, and the other characters are keepers of the asylum, the insane. Because Vonnegut is sympathetic to Billy as Swift is to Gulliver, Billy's vision of the world seems justified. As with a similar traveler, Gulliver Foyle in Alfred Bester's *The Stars My Destination*, the clown's mask covers the face of truth. Billy understands life as a series of unconnected events that must be prized one by one: nothing is more important than anything else, not even the end of life, rendered meaningless by Vonnegut's hammering repetition of "So it goes" after each death. Michael Sacks perfectly captures the essence of the child-man Billy in George Roy Hill's astute 1972 film adaptation.

Slaughterhouse-Five is a forceful antiwar text, suggesting that the firebombing of Dresden, largely an unknown Allied atrocity until Vonnegut publicized it, was created by insane men of military science; Nobel Laureate Freeman Dyson concurs, discussing Vonnegut's novel and recounting events at Bomber Command in his 1979 memoir *Disturbing the Universe. Slaughterhouse-Five* attacks the militarist culture that Vonnegut feels is responsible not only for America's then-current presence in Vietnam, but also for the assassination of peacemakers like Martin Luther King, Jr. and Bobby Kennedy. In making Billy a hero who has no control over his life, Vonnegut goes against the myth that combat makes men: in Billy's sharpest moments he sees humans as machines who can only execute the programs they have inside them. The novel takes its place with other darkly funny satires like Joseph Heller's *Catch-22* (1961), **Dr. Strangelove**, and Thomas Pynchon's *Gravity's Rainbow* (1973). Despite what seems a bleak picture of the world, Vonnegut's cheerful rage about free will and **destiny** is certain to upset and involve readers in ways playwright Bertolt Brecht would recognize: this is not simply a book of despair. Instead it becomes a series of Zen utterances, little **puzzles** about human existence. Vonnegut concludes that even if we cannot do much to control our lives, we must work harder to treat each other better than we do, here, now.

Bibliography

Harold Bloom, ed. *Kurt Vonnegut's Slaughterhouse-Five*. Philadelphia: Chelsea House, 2001.

Kevin A. Boon, ed. *At Millennium's End*. Albany: State University of New York Press, 2001.

Lawrence Broer. *Sanity Plea*. Alabama: University of Alabama Press, 1994.

Morris Dickstein. "Black Humor and History." *Partisan Review*, 43 (1976), 185–211.

Julie A. Hibbard. "In Search of *Slaughterhouse-Five*." Marc Leeds and Peter J. Reed, eds., *Kurt Vonnegut*. Westport, CT: Greenwood, 2000, 135–146.

Jerome Klinkowitz. *Slaughterhouse-Five*. Boston: Twayne, 1990.

Thomas F. Marvin. *Kurt Vonnegut*. Westport, CT: Greenwood Press, 2002.

Walter J. Miller and Bonnie E. Nelson. *Kurt Vonnegut's Slaughterhouse-Five*. New York: Monarch Press, 1973.

Robert Scholes. "History as Fabulation." Robert Merrill, ed., *Critical Essays on Kurt Vonnegut*. Boston: G. K. Hall, 1990, 37–39.

—Tim Blackmore

SNOW CRASH BY NEAL STEPHENSON (1992)

■

*All information looks like noise until you
break the code.*

—Neal Stephenson
Snow Crash (1992)

Summary

In a **near future** America dominated by multinational corporations, samurai **sword**-wielding Hiro Protagonist and skateboard messenger Y.T. form a partnership to share information. Despite being one creator of the Metaverse, a form of **cyberspace** where users log onto **computers** and represent themselves as avatars, Hiro holds several marginal jobs: pizza deliverer for the Mafia, manager of a heavy metal rock band (see **Music**), and freelance contributor to the **Library** of the Central Intelligence Corporation (CIC). Y.T. is a precocious fifteen-year-old who keeps her career as Kourier for the RadiKS delivery service a secret from her **mother**. Hiro and Y.T. become ensnared in a plot for global domination by Christian evangelist and fiberoptic media monopolist L. Bob Rife (see **Christianity**). Rife funds a worldwide cult to take over people's minds with Snow Crash, a Sumerian brain virus that disrupts cognition, turning victims into nonsense-babbling followers or, for computer programmers, causing brain death. The CIC Librarian tells Hiro the **history** of the virus and its potential to cause an Infocalypse, where all **knowledge** will be subsumed to Rife's will. Rife employs Raven, a seemingly invincible foe with a nuclear bomb wired to his skull. Y.T. is seduced by Raven but **escapes,** only to be captured by Rife. Hiro rescues his former lover Juanita from Rife's Raft, a floating congregation of Asian refugees who, in exchange for the **promise** of landing in California, have succumbed to Snow Crash. He broadcasts a countervirus to the Raft refugees, decapitates Raven's avatar in the Metaverse, and writes SnowScan as an antidote to the cyberspace version of Snow Crash. An electronic watchdog implanted with the **memory** of Y.T.'s lost **dog** runs to her aid and crashes into Rife's jet, destroying Rife and the virus.

Discussion

In *Snow Crash*, Neal Stephenson weaves a complex tale that takes the **cyberpunk** subgenre beyond the **clichés** that became prominent in 1980s science fiction after the success of William Gibson's *Neuromancer*. Stephenson has stated that *Snow Crash* was originally intended to be a graphic novel. The plot maintains a frenetic comic book pace, slowed only by lectures from the CIC's Librarian. *Snow Crash* is predominantly a **satire,** as even the two main characters' names suggest. Stephenson uses **humor** constantly, directing barbs at numerous social institutions, including the government (see **Governance Systems**), the police, **business**, **religion**, street gangs, and the Mafia. His character Rife parodies the supposedly self-made entrepreneur who nonetheless depends on government computer programmers to write the code to spread Snow Crash. Stephenson's **America** is fractured into city-states called

Burbclaves, exclusive gated **communities** protected by private security forces. Burb-clave residents drive minivans (derisively nicknamed bimbo boxes) on roads and highways owned by corporations and only patronize stores with familiar franchise logos. Cyberpunk clichés of humans merging with **technology** are skewered by means of the Gargoyles, people covered in multimedia gear constantly connected to the Metaverse, and Y.T.'s dentata device, which renders a would-be lover uncon-scious. The concept of **cyborgs**, humans integrated with machinery, is shown to be an **absurdity** through the tough but ridiculous Raven linked to his own nuclear weapon. "Wireheads" is Stephenson's unflattering word for those implanted with antennae tuned to Rife's messages.

However, beyond the over-the-top details of Stephenson's future, his satire also comments on **race relations**. Many Burbclaves are based on racial segregation, and Stephenson's descriptions of the beliefs of particular race-based enclaves can be blunt. Criticism has been directed at Stephenson's depiction of the Raft as insensi-tive fear-mongering about Asian refugees arriving en masse to California, and Y.T.'s initials do sound like the word whitey. But Stephenson arguably rises above racial stereotypes through Hiro, who has an African-American father and Korean mother. A subplot of *Snow Crash* suggests that political decisions (see **Politics**) based on feel-ings of racial superiority have lingering consequences. Hiro's father won the samurai swords Hiro uses in a fight with Raven's father during World War II. The Aleutian Raven seeks revenge on America for attacking his father twice with nuclear weapons, once in Nagasaki, and the second time when the Aleutian homeland **island** Amchitka was deemed expendable for weapons testing.

Another prominent theme in *Snow Crash* concerns **language and linguistics**. To Stephenson, words are code, and just as the proper codes make computer programs run, the right words control human behavior. Ancient Sumerian priests ruled their society through *me*, neurolinguistic commands that kept the population docile. A Rife-funded excavation of Eridu finds the *me* preserved in a clay envelope. The virus causes believers to speak in tongues, lose their ability to reason, and become obedi-ent wireheads who can only comprehend Rife's instructions.

Ultimately, *Snow Crash* is a dense but entertaining tract about how boundaries on information and knowledge have always been created by those seeking to main-tain power. Through the extensive interpretations that Stephenson provides of ancient **cultures**, **mythology**, **Judaism**, and **Christianity**, he argues that viruses, reli-gions, and **drugs** are indistinguishable in terms of their effect on human reason. Despite Hiro's fondness for cyberspace, the ending reaffirms life in the flesh. Hiro rekindles his **romance** with Juanita, and Y.T. returns home with her mother to the Blooming Greens Burbclave. *Snow Crash* succeeds as an ambitious, thought-provoking novel seeking to prove that throughout history people have always lived in an Information Age one misstep away from an Infocalypse.

Bibliography

David V. Barrett. "Cyber Noir? Neal Stephenson Interviewed." *Interzone*, No. 109 (July, 1996), 18–21.

Andrew M. Butler. *Cyberpunk*. Harpenden, UK: Pocket Essentials, 2000.

Talia Eilon. "Hacking the Spew." *Science Fiction*, No. 44 (2002), 28–57.

Daniel Grassian. "Discovering the Machine in You." *Journal of the Fantastic in the Arts*, 12 (2001), 250–267.

N. Katherine Hayles. *How We Became Posthuman*. Chicago: University of Chicago Press, 1999.

Sabine Heuser. *Virtual Geographies*. Amsterdam: Rodopi, 2003.

Michelle Kendrick. "Space, Technology and Neal Stephenson's Science Fiction." Rob Kitchin and James Kneale, ed., *Lost in Space*. New York: Continuum, 2002, 57–73.

David Porush. "Hacking the Brainstem." Robert Markley, ed., *Virtual Realities and Their Discontents*. Baltimore: Johns Hopkins University Press, 1996, 107–142.

—*Jeff D'Anastasio*

SNOW WHITE AND THE SEVEN DWARFS (1937)

Summary

The first animated feature film ever made, widely described in the industry beforehand as "Disney's Folly," *Snow White and the Seven Dwarfs* premiered December 21, 1937. Based on the **fairy tale** recounted by the Brothers Grimm, the film tells of beautiful young princess Snow White, loathed for her **beauty** and **youth** by her wicked Stepmother, who is both **queen** and **witch**. When a handsome Prince falls in **love** with the girl, the Stepmother becomes insane with jealousy. She sends her huntsman to murder Snow White, but he relents and instead tells her to flee into the **forest**. Lost, Snow White comes across a little cottage that is **home** to seven **dwarfs**—Bashful, Doc, Dopey, Grumpy, Happy, Sleepy and Sneezy—who work in a diamond mine. The dwarfs take Snow White into their home; in return, she becomes their housekeeper and surrogate **mother**.

Time passes. The Stepmother has a magic **mirror**, through which she can scry. One day she discovers that her huntsman lied about killing Snow White. A **shapeshifter**, she transforms herself into an old crone and sets off for the dwarfs' cottage bearing a poisoned apple. While she talks the girl into eating the apple, the dwarfs, working in the mine, are warned by forest animals that Snow White is in danger. They rush home but are too late: Snow White has bitten the apple and seems dead. The dwarfs and animals chase the Stepmother to her **death**, but still all seems lost. However, there is a caveat to Snow White's apparent death: "True Love's First Kiss" can restore her to life. By chance, the Prince happens by and kisses the lips of the "dead" girl, and she awakens.

Discussion

This movie was by no means the Disney studio's introduction to animating classic fairy tales: of the hundreds of shorts the studio had made to date, a high proportion had been similarly inspired. In this Disney was not alone; rival animation studios were likewise plowing the rich soil of traditional tales. However, most of these short movies, no matter which studio produced them, used the device of stereotyped animal characters in lieu of human ones; the convincing animation of human figures was regarded at Disney even as late as 1933 as being far in the future. However, when Walt Disney became obsessed with the idea of making a feature-length animation, and equally determined that it should be based on this particular tale, the studio packed a great deal of technical development into a very few years. At the same time, his love of the **pastoral** was not abandoned; the film is packed with representations of forest animals.

The astonishing box office success of *Snow White and the Seven Dwarfs* impelled Walt Disney and his studio to create a string of further feature animations based on classic fairy tales; they include *Pinocchio* (1940), *Cinderella* (1950), and *Sleeping Beauty* (1959). Years after Walt Disney's death, the studio continued this sequence with such films as *The Little Mermaid* (1989), *Beauty and the Beast* (1991), and *Aladdin* (1992). Most of these have been among the studio's most commercially successful animated releases. The template employed for nearly all of them—as for most other Disney animated features—included strong elements of **humor** and **romance** (with obvious exceptions like *Pinocchio*, Disneyfied fairy tales end in **marriage** or the imminence thereof); colorfully zany, wisecracking, sympathetic, small-animal secondary characters; emotional and moral simplification (with few gray areas in the portrayal of good and **evil**); much use of **music** and song; and a setting that is usually ill-definedly medieval (see **Medievalism and the Middle Ages**). It is an approach that has been imitated by other studios, notably by Don Bluth in films like *Thumbelina* (1994).

Defenders of this form of adaptation point out, reasonably, that the original versions of classic fairy tales, if translated directly to film, would not make palatable **family** fare. A further truth is that sanitization of fairy tales did not begin with Disney, but rather started in the nineteenth century. Detractors observe, with justification, that the Disneyfication process has destroyed the power and meaning of the originals and has also largely driven the originals from the popular consciousness—a process enhanced by the merchandizing blitz produced by Disney in support of its feature releases. It is common to find U.S. children and indeed adults believing that the stories like *Snow White and the Seven Dwarfs* originated with Disney. Richard Schickel's important book *The Disney Version* (1968; third edition 1997) embodies such concerns, expressed by many others. From a different perspective, many claim that Disney's determination to tailor these adaptations to **children** has done a disservice to commercial animation in general, so that the medium is commonly regarded as being only for juveniles.

Earlier film adaptations include *Snow White* (1916), based on a 1912 Broadway play, and the 1933 Betty Boop animated short *Snow-White*. There have been many other animated versions since Disney's, but none are memorable. Two contrasting adaptations of note, both live action, are the traditional *Snow White: The Fairest of Them All* (2002) and the impressively mature *Snow White in the Black Forest* (1997).

Bibliography

John Grant. "*Snow White and the Seven Dwarfs.*" Grant, *Encyclopedia of Walt Disney's Animated Characters.* New York: Harper & Row, 1987, 136–145.

Richard Holliss and Brian Sibley. *The Disney Studio Story.* London: Octopus, 1988.

———. *Walt Disney's Snow White and the Seven Dwarfs and the Making of a Classic Film.* New York: Simon & Schuster, 1987.

Leonard Maltin. *The Disney Films*, Fourth Ed. New York: Disney Editions, 2000.

Richard Schickel. *The Disney Version*. Third ed. Chicago: Ivan R. Dee, 1997.
Frank Thomas and Ollie Johnston. *Disney Animation*. New York: Abbeville, 1981.
———. *The Disney Villain*. New York: Disney Editions, 1993.
Linda Witowski and Martin Krause. *Walt Disney's Snow White and the Seven Dwarfs*. New York: Disney Editions, 1995.
Jessica Yates. "The Other 50th Anniversary." *Mythlore*, 16 (Spring, 1990), 47–50.

—*John Grant*

SOLARIS (1972)

Summary

Men stationed on a **space station** orbiting the planet Solaris have been going mad (see **Madness**). When **astronaut** Kris Kelvin is sent to investigate, he discovers that the ocean world is mysteriously alive and attempting to communicate with humans via "phantoms" (see **Ghosts and Hauntings**), which are recreations of people from each individual's past. Kelvin rapidly loses his objectivity when confronted with the phantom of his wife, who committed **suicide**. Although aware that this is not really her, he sees this as a second chance to work out their difficulties (see **Marriage**). Ultimately he chooses emotion over reason and is swallowed up in the **illusions** of Solaris, but he may be happier that way.

Discussion

Imperfectly adapted from Stanislaw Lem's classic *Solaris*, the Russian version (1972), directed by Andrei Tarkovsky, is considered by some the finest science fiction film ever made, and by others a bore. A more balanced view is that it looks like a rough cut of a brilliant film, technically crude and (to western eyes at least) in desperate need of editing. It should be seen in the shortest version possible. When the hero is taken to the spaceport to begin his trip to Solaris, for example, we are given nearly five minutes of footage of twentieth-century freeway traffic. One waggish critic suggests that this is the safe time to adjourn to the restroom.

However, **beauties** and subtleties emerge. The film is best when concentrating on the space station interior, becoming claustrophobic as Kelvin is trapped in an intimate relationship with his phantom wife. After his first encounter, he tries to get rid of her by shutting her out the airlock. Her nonhuman nature shows startlingly as she nearly claws through the metal. She returns and all is forgiven. The planet has reconstituted the phantom and left that part out of her **memory**. There are other eerie moments reminding us of her alien nature. When Kelvin tries to help her out of her dress, he discovers that the buttons on her clothing do not work. The planetary mind has copied the image but does not know what buttons are for.

The essential problem here is the nature of **identity**. If the phantom is not really the dead wife, is it a sentient being in its own right? When it/she suffers grief from realization of its own predicament and attempts suicide, it would seem so, but when the planet merely produces another copy (see **Rebirth**), is it still the same being? The result is one of the great science fiction **love** stories (see **Romance**), which captures the core of Lem's novel, although narrowing its focus.

Solaris was remade by 20th Century Fox in 2002, directed by Steven Soderbergh, as if in a deliberate attempt to address problems in the Tarkovsky film. This version is visually beautiful and tightly edited, although there are even more departures from Lem's story than before. The result was not a critical or commercial success, although it may be seriously underrated. It, too, is an obsessive, bleak love story (the background of the hero and his late wife is made clearer; **Earth** seems like a dreary place where it is always raining) as if Soderbergh is copying and adapting Tarkovsky without really understanding him. There was, admittedly, a promotional problem in selling the public on a serious science fiction art film starring George Clooney, not known for such roles, at a time when audiences expect spaceships to whiz, whir, and explode. But certainly the Soderbergh version is an honest effort, pointing the way for a possible third rendition that might combine the best features of the first two.

Both versions pay little attention to the planet Solaris itself, which is a major character in the book. Tarkovsky presumably did not have the resources to deal with the planet's propensity for creating strange structures. Producer James Cameron and Soderbergh could have but were seemingly more interested in remaking Tarkovsky than filming Lem. It would be possible for uninitiated audiences to come away with no idea of what is going on at all.

Both versions end at the same point, with Kelvin seemingly at home on Earth, but actually living an illusion (see **Perception**) in a reconstructed country house on the surface of Solaris. For once, the Russian version trumps the American visually. Tarkovsky shows us Kelvin puttering about the kitchen. He seems old, tired. Then we gradually realize that it is raining *indoors*. The camera then pulls back, out the window, showing the entire house, then back again, showing that it exists on a tiny **island** on the surface of the planet, then back again and again until it vanishes into Solaris as seen from space. It is a stunning image, as fine as any in science fiction cinema.

Solaris remains one of the most challenging films in the science fiction repertoire. It will never be popular but will continue to be admired, as the novel is, for attempting to probe matters that ultimately are beyond the comprehension of either the human mind or human heart. The central **mystery** of the story is both the universe itself and our place in it as thinking, feeling beings.

Bibliography

Daniel J. Goulding. *Five Filmmakers*. Bloomington: Indiana University Press, 1994.

Vida T. Johnson. *Tarkovsky: A Visual Fugue*. Bloomington: University of Indiana Press, 1994.

Elga Lyndina. "In the Orbits of the Future." *Soviet Literature*, No. 12 (1988), 148–154.

Gerald Peary. "Found in Space: *Solaris* (1972)." *Technology Review*, 94 (July, 1991), 69–70.

J.M. Purcell. "Tarkovsky's Film *Solaris* (1972)." *Extrapolation*, 19 (May, 1978), 126–131.

Jonathan Rosenbaum. "Inner Space." *Film Comment*, 26 (July/August, 1990), 57–62.

Andrei Tarkovsky. *Sculpting in Time*. Trans. Kitty Hunter-Blair. Austin: University of Texas Press, 1986.

———. *Time Within Time*. Trans. Kitty Hunter-Blair. London: Faber & Faber, 1994.

Michael Wilmington. "Andrei Tarkovsky." Danny Perry, ed., *Omni's Screen Flights and Screen Fantasies*. New York: Doubleday, 1984, 287–292.

—*Darrell Schweitzer*

SOLARIS BY STANISLAW LEM (1961)

We take off into the cosmos, ready for anything: for solitude, for hardship, for exhaustion, death. Modesty forbids us to say so, but there are times when we think pretty well of ourselves. And yet, if we examine it more closely, our enthusiasm turns out to be all sham. We don't want to conquer the cosmos, we simply want to extend the boundaries of Earth to the frontiers of the cosmos . . . . We have no need of other worlds. We need mirrors.

—Stanislaw Lem
Solaris (1961), trans. Joanna Kilmartin
and Steve Cox (1970)

Summary

In the **far future**, the planet Solaris holds a vast **puzzle** of quasi-**biology**: a probably sentient ocean (see **Fish and Sea Creatures**) that defies known **physics** in its apparent manipulation of **gravity** and **time** to maintain the world's impossibly stable orbit in a double-**star** system. This sea seems unresponsive to, or aloof from, the prolonged study by **humanity**, which has spawned entire **libraries** of fruitless theory. The **hero** Kelvin is the latest investigator to arrive (after long **space travel**) at the airborne **habitat**, which is the center of "Solarist" field research. He finds squalor and apparent **madness**. The resident **scientists** are troubled with disturbing "visitors." Kelvin's scientific **mentor**, dogged by a **giant** black woman, has committed **suicide**.

Soon Kelvin has his own inseparable companion, Rheya, a recreation (see **Identity**) of a dead woman from his past, evoking both **love** and guilt at past **betrayal** (see **Guilt and Responsibility**). The ocean is producing these living probes—based on human **memories**—to investigate humanity (see **Role Reversal**). However, no real **communication** ensues.

Discussion

Solaris, the first novel by this talented, intellectual Polish author to reach English translation, was later filmed as *Solaris*. Characteristically for Stanislaw Lem, it addresses problems of **first contact** and flawed communication on an **alien world**.

Solaris includes extensive, exhausting descriptions of the enigmatic activity of the ocean, whose **blood**-colored foam and mists suggest life at a primal, organic level. There are elaborate cod-scientific taxonomies of the structures it repeatedly forms and destroys, with names like symmetriads and asymmetriads: complex biological machines depicted in terms of architecture rather than **technology**, the **violence** of whose internal operations seems scientifically impossible. Some apparently correspond to **computers** or, perhaps, simply thoughts. Some—"mimoids"—shape increasingly fantastic parodies of nearby inanimate objects, though *not* of humans— which is perhaps an accidental side-effect of their operation.

It is made clear that the scientists' countless **books** describing these phenomena contain no real particle of understanding. One precursor of the story's **doppelgängers**— an eyewitness report of a man's memories being actualized in giant, solid form by the ocean after his accidental **death**—is dismissed as a hallucination (see **Illusion**) and preserved only in a collection of pseudoscience, *The Little Apocrypha*. In these ways Lem explicitly compares science, and its intolerance of unorthodoxy, with **religion**.

Humanity is frustrated by the sea's indifference and cannot find an appropriate channel for much-desired first contact. Earlier deaths of many researchers in the "natural" dissolution of an ocean structure almost ignited a **nuclear war**, both as **revenge** and a desperate bid for the sea's attention. One scientist hopes to use **antimatter** in an attack, and the "visitors" may represent Solaris's reaction to recent, unauthorized x-ray bombardment of the ocean.

The dangerous inappropriateness of these human approaches is more subtly mirrored by the sea's doppelgänger probes, which, shaped from traumatic memory, principally evoke **horror**. Apart from a compulsion to stay near their **Earth**-born counterparts, these constructs are mentally quite human and thus presumably as enigmatic as any other human to their creator—a typical Lem Catch-22 situation of blocked information flow. Nor do the doppelgängers possess any conscious information about their maker. As one character says, "We're unlikely to learn anything about *it*, but about ourselves . . . ."

Learning that Rheya is physically indestructible (see **Immortality and Longevity**), the panicky Kelvin fires her into space; she is soon replaced. With longer acquaintance, though, their attitudes change. Kelvin begins to enjoy the restoration of the woman whose original killed herself when he walked out. Pseudo-Rheya learns that she is not a natural creature but (below the cellular level) a neutrino structure powered and continually regenerated by proximity to the ocean. She therefore attempts another suicide, without success, and later submits willingly to **weaponry** devised by other scientists to disperse neutrino creations. The irony here is that after well over a century of failed contact attempts, the peak achievement of human ingenuity on Solaris is to destroy the ocean's reciprocal probes.

Ultimately the indecipherable ocean of Solaris is a **microcosm** of the universe, an enigma too vast for human **intelligence** to fathom. Kelvin, bereft of Rheya, is left only with "faith that the time of cruel miracles was not past"—the novel's closing line.

Although he has also written much in the way of quirkily intellectual **humor**, Lem's theme of the extreme difficulty or impossibility of communication with genuine **aliens in space** features in several of his other novels. The early *Eden* (1959) explores a less unusual but still highly enigmatic alien world whose inhabitants are undergoing deviant **evolution**. In *The Invincible* (1964), a cybernetic **ecology** lacks intelligence yet reactively counters the most potent human weaponry. *His Master's Voice* (1968) weaves a **labyrinth** of speculation about a mysterious broadcast that humanity deciphers in various ways (probably wrongly, as though **music** were read as a computer program) as conveying extraordinary information on biology and physics. The transmission, however, may actually be of natural origin. Aliens in *Fiasco* (1986), with a vast **war**-driven technology, are not even correctly identified until a final, irrevocable **disaster**. Lem takes a consistently bleak view of the limitations of human cognition.

Bibliography

Edward Balcerzan. "Seeking Only Man." *Science-Fiction Studies*, 2 (July, 1975), 152–156.

Algis Budrys. "*Solaris.*" Budrys, *Benchmarks*. Carbondale and Edwardsville, IL: Southern Illinois University Press, 1985, 306–312.

Istvan Csicsery-Ronay, Jr. "The Book Is the Alien." *Science-Fiction Studies*, 12 (March, 1985), 6–21.

Neil Easterbrook. "The Sublime Simulacra." *Critique*, 36 (Spring, 1995), 177–194.

Manfred Geier. "Stanislaw Lem's Fantastic Ocean." *Science-Fiction Studies*, 19 (July, 1992), 192–218.

Peter Nicholls. "*Solaris.*" *Foundation*, No. 1 (March, 1972), 60–65.

Darko Suvin. "The Open-ended Parables of Stanislaw Lem and *Solaris.*" *Solaris*, by Stanislaw Lem. London: Faber, 1971, 205–216.

Abraham Yossef. "Understanding Lem." *Foundation*, No. 46 (Autumn, 1989), 51–58.

—*David Langford*

THE SPACE MERCHANTS
BY FREDERIK POHL AND C.M. KORNBLUTH (1953)

■

> *An ancient, basic tenet of justice is: "Better that one thousand innocents suffer unjustly than one guilty person be permitted to escape."*
>
> —Frederik Pohl and C.M. Kornbluth
> *The Space Merchants* (1953)

Summary

In a future New York City, Mitchell Courtney is an executive in Fowler Schocken's **advertising** agency, employing various techniques to encourage consumers to buy worthless products like the addictive beverage Coffiest. Taking over the Venus Project, Courtney must persuade thousands of people to voluntarily immigrate to a planet with scorchingly hot **weather** and poisonous air; he also learns that someone is trying to kill him. After meeting a negligent colleague, Courtney awakens with the new **identity** of George Groby, forced to endure the harsh existence of a "scum-skimmer," harvesting algae from hydroponic tanks. Contacted by Consies (conservationists), an underground movement advocating radical changes to reduce pollution and restore **Earth**'s depleted resources, Courtney demonstrates his ability to generate effective propaganda and is dispatched to New York, where he confronts Schocken's rival B.J. Taunton, the man who tried to kill him, and is framed for murder. He then resumes life as Courtney and takes over Schocken's agency after his **death**. Working with his wife, a Consie who arranged his abduction to educate him about his world's harsh realities, Courtney secretly ensures that all participants in the Venus Project are Consies, eager for the challenge of colonizing and transforming **Venus** as an alternative to life on an overpopulated, polluted Earth; when Taunton exposes Courtney's dubious past as Gorby, Courtney and his wife join the other Consies in immigrating to Venus.

Discussion

The Space Merchants is the preeminent expression in science fiction of widespread concerns in the 1950s over the damaging effects of advertising, as also observed in mainstream novels like Sloan Wilson's *The Man in the Grey Flannel Suit* (1956) and nonfictional exposés like Vance Packard's *The Hidden Persuaders* (1957). Employing **satire**, Pohl and Kornbluth attack the tunnel vision of the typical "adman," obsessively focused on increasing sales at all costs even if consumers' best interests are not being served. In the case of the Venus Project, Courtney perceives no ethical problems (see **Ethics**) in deftly employing an array of techniques like carefully worded slogans, jingles, flashy advertisements, and false rumors to swindle people into a life of hellish conditions on Venus; it only represents another job that he must successfully complete. Advertising has become so effective in the future, in fact, that *The Space Merchants* envisions advertising agencies becoming more powerful than governments, so the President of the United States briefly functions only as Courtney's ineffectual ally.

To contemporary readers, however, *The Space Merchants* may command attention more because it deals with **humanity**'s negative impact on the environment (see **Ecology**). There is an awareness of the looming problem of **overpopulation**, as described by Jack O'Shea, the midget **astronaut** who first traveled to Venus—"Too damn many people, Mitch. Too damn much crowding." But this is also a world where people calmly accept the necessity of wearing air filters to minimize the effects of a polluted atmosphere, and where people must tolerate a steady diet of tasteless, processed food made from algae and sources of artificial protein like Chicken Little, the overgrown chicken heart that Courtney observes when living as Gorby; naturally grown **plants** and meat are rare luxuries for the upper class (see **Enlargement; Food and Drink**). In their propaganda, the Consies also complain about deforestation and depletion of Earth's mineral resources, issues that would not be widely aired until the 1960s. Significantly, these are the issues that ultimately drive Courtney away from Earth, not its pervasive advertising, something that he never explicitly rejects.

Pohl and Kornbluth also attack the future's **class system**: while a few people like Courtney live comfortably, corporations force the majority of citizens into manipulative contracts that keep them perpetually in debt to the company and trapped in a life of drudgery and virtual **slavery**, relieved only by hypnotic entertainment and

drugs. At novel's end, Courtney accepts the fact that on Venus, he will have to learn to live in a new classless society, no longer enjoying special privileges.

Although a focus on such matters is not common in science fiction of the 1950s, *The Space Merchants* is conventional in one respect: while initially characterizing the Venus Project as an outrageous racket, the novel ultimately validates the colonization of Venus as worthwhile, supporting **space travel** for standard reasons: to provide people with new environments to inhabit and new resources to exploit.

Years after Kornbluth's death, Pohl wrote a sequel, *The Merchant's War* (1984), which takes place a few generations after the Consies' colonization of Venus but tells a similar story: another dedicated advertising executive, Tarrison Tarb, has horrific experiences amidst the suffering lower classes and awakens to the need for social reform. Leaders of Earth and Venus each take novel, nonmilitary approaches to **war**: Venusians seek to destroy Earth's economy so it can no longer threaten their existence, while advertising agencies are preparing to employ techniques of mind control to turn Venusians into compulsive consumers. Uneasy with both sides' plans, Tarb hopes that telling citizens the truth about their society will inspire significant changes. Although *The Merchant's War* has moments of inspired satire, its renewed focus on the menace of advertising, so pertinent in the 1950s, seemed dated to many readers in the 1980s, who had long accepted advertising as relatively benign and probably felt that there were now more significant dangers for science fiction writers to fret about.

Bibliography

J.P. Brennan. "Mechanical Chicken." *Extrapolation*, 25 (Summer, 1984), 101–114.

Richard D. Erlich. "Odysseus in Grey Flannel." *Par Rapport*, 1 (Summer, 1978), 126–131.

Donald M. Hassler. "Swift, Pohl, and Kornbluth." *Extrapolation*, 34 (Fall, 1993), 245–250.

Martin Jordin. "Contemporary Futures." Christopher Pawling, ed., *Popular Fiction and Social Change*. New York: St. Martins, 1984, 50–75.

Charles Platt. "C.M. Kornbluth." *Foundation*, No. 17 (September, 1979), 57–63.

Frederik Pohl. "Pohlemic: Cyril Redivivous." *Science Fiction Chronicle*, 17 (February, 1996), 35–36.

———. "Reminiscence: Cyril M. Kornbluth." *Extrapolation*, 17 (May, 1976), 102–109.

David Pringle. "*The Space Merchants* by Frederik Pohl and C. M. Kornbluth (1953)." Pringle, *Science Fiction: The 100 Best Novels*. New York: Carroll and Graf, 1985, 43–44.

David Seed. "Take-over Bids." *Foundation*, No. 59 (Autumn, 1993), 42–58.

—*Gary Westfahl*

A SPELL FOR CHAMELEON BY PIERS ANTHONY (1977)

Summary

This inventive **comedy-cum-heroic fantasy** opens Piers Anthony's long series set in the **magic** kingdom Xanth, whose shifting **borderlands** adjoin "Mundania" or **Earth**. Magical **talents** are many and diverse; all citizens must demonstrate talent.

The seemingly magicless young **hero** Bink begins a **quest** of self-discovery by consulting "Good Magician" Humfrey (see **Wizards**), who specializes in **divination**. To enter Humfrey's **castle**, **puzzles** must be solved and guardians circumvented—a repeated series feature. Despite wizardly assurance of hidden talent, Bink is condemned to **exile** in Mundania.

He is captured by the exiled **Evil** Magician Trent, who can transform others (see **Metamorphosis**) and plans a **war** to regain power in Xanth. Bink and female fellow-captive Chameleon—an involuntary **shapeshifter** whose **curse** is an endless **cycle** between **beauty** and ugliness—oppose Trent but must make a truce during **sword and sorcery** adventures in a **monster**-infested **wilderness**. Threats include **dragons**, beasts from **mythology**, magical **mutations** and crossbreeds, and an invisible **giant** (see **Invisibility**).

Ultimately Bink's "Magician-class" talent is revealed: immunity from magical harm, enabling him to block Trent—whose **courage** and honesty, however, he now admires. Ultimately Trent is acclaimed as a worthy **king** of Xanth; for Bink there is **marriage**.

Discussion

Early Xanth novels have a fresh charm thanks to Anthony's knack of inventing off-beat talents, creatures, and **magical objects**, and of exploring the logical consequences of magic in fields like **ecology** and **evolution**. Love potions facilitate interspecies crosses like harpies and centaurs; **goblins** prove to be humans debased by a kind of anti-evolution spell. **Plants** use magic to compete—for example, tentacled, carnivorous "tangle trees." Thirsty **insects** cast sweat spells on travellers. Even a **river** adapts magic to restock itself: those who drink its **water** become fish (see **Fish and Sea Creatures**).

Another vein of invention is the punning **humor,** which supposedly underlies Xanthean magic, with shoes growing on shoe trees and feared nickelpedes being five times larger than centipedes. Later excesses sometimes disrupt the story logic, as when great danger is arbitrarily associated with a wall-mounted trophy consisting of the rear end of a **cat**; that is, a catastrophe. Even the **map** of Xanth is a geographical pun, showing it to have the shape of Florida, where this British-born author has long resided.

The second of these slick commercial fantasies is *The Source of Magic* (1979), in which Bink and companions—including a miniature **golem**—seek magic's wellspring. This quest is driven by **scientist**-like curiosity rather than heroic fantasy aims, but meets strong opposition from something that fears the consequences. An **underground adventure** reveals that all magic is incidental leakage from an immensely powerful but bound **demon** whose true **name** is Xanth. Driven by **ethics** though aware that **disaster** may follow, Bink gives Xanth **freedom** from his **prison**. (Such unexpectedly tough moral choices are characteristic of this author.) The resulting **apocalypse** strips the land of magic but normality is restored by Xanth's whimsical **deus ex machina** return.

In *Castle Roogna* (1979), Bink's magician son (see **Family**) Dor uses mental **time travel** to participate in the centuries-past building of the eponymous castle (long disused and **zombie**-infested in book one), and its defense during a war of harpies and goblins. Magical **weaponry** abounds, including a potent amnesia spell that causes part of the **landscape** to remain "forgotten" centuries later (see **Memory**). While he is in the past, Dor occupies the body of a **barbarian** warrior through **possession**, leading to some coyly handled conflict between adolescent ignorance and adult **sexuality**.

The first Xanth novel contained a measure of heroic fantasy's default **sexism**, which Anthony reconsidered in later books. When successive male kings of Xanth are put out of action in *Night Mare* (1982), it is recognized that women can also rule (see **Feminism**), even nonhuman females like the title's **dream**-bearing, intelligent **horse**. Such rejection of "speciesism" had already emerged in *Ogre, Ogre* (1982), whose title character transcends his innate nature as a brutishly destructive, language-impaired giant. It continues in *Dragon on a Pedestal* (1983), where even a zombie is shown as something other than repulsive and pitiable.

Many adults are irritated by Anthony's slow-witted young protagonists, to whom morality and the nature of this **imaginary world** are explained at didactic length. (Five pages into a **history** lesson in book one, a centaur commends Bink "because you pay such good, responsive attention.") Xanth found its best-selling audience among younger readers who can sympathize with the later running joke about sexual knowledge being an inscrutable "adult conspiracy," productive of endless giggles and blushes. The general tone is summed up in the title of book fourteen, *The Color of Her Panties* (1992).

This audience dotes on Anthony's puns and eccentric magic talents, and bombards him with suggestions for both. Many of these are duly incorporated. The twenty-eighth Xanth novel, *Currant Events* (2004), contains an Author's Note—another regular feature—crediting about 150 such collaborators for droll notions like "Centaur of attention" or "Steel toad boots."

Despite these later puerilities, Anthony's fluency of invention and intermittent thoughtfulness make the first few books enjoyable as light, undemanding fantasy. *A Spell for Chameleon* was honored with the 1978 British Fantasy Award.

Bibliography

Piers Anthony. *Bio of an Ogre*. New York: Ace, 1988.

Piers Anthony. "The Pun-derful Wizard of Xanth Takes a More Serious Look at Life." *Science Fiction Age*, 2 (May, 1994), 30–32.

Piers Anthony and Jody Lynn Nye. *Piers Anthony's Visual Guide to Xanth*. New York: Avon, 1989.

Michael R. Collings. "Words and Worlds." R.A. Collins, ed., *Scope of the Fantastic*. Westport, CT: Greenwood Press, 1985, 173–182.

David Langford. "*Dragon on a Pedestal*" and "*Golem in the Gears*." Langford, *The Complete Critical Assembly*. Holicong, PA: Cosmos Books, 2001, 50, 156.

———. "Xanthopsia." Langford, *He Do the Time Police in Different Voices*. Holicong, PA: Cosmos Books, 2003, 22–23.

Phil Stephensen-Payne. "*A Spell for Chameleon*." *Paperback Parlour*, 12 (December, 1978), 6.

———. *Piers Anthony: Biblio of an Ogre*. Albuquerque, NM: Galactic Central, 1990.

—David Langford

STAND ON ZANZIBAR BY JOHN BRUNNER (1968)

—■—

> *Some troubledome just figured out that*
> *if you allow for every codder and shiggy*
> *and appleofmyeye a space one foot by*
> *two you could stand us all on the six*
> *hundred forty square mile surface of the*
> *island of Zanzibar.*

—John Brunner
Stand on Zanzibar (1968)

Summary

In the early years of the twenty-first century the problems of **overpopulation** have brought the world to a crisis point. We are told that the entire population of the world could now stand shoulder-to-shoulder on the **island** of Zanzibar. In **America**, most states have legislated to limit breeding by those with genetic defects, and social pressures frequently result in people running amok, randomly killing and maiming. Manhattan Island is domed. The Philippines are now a state (Isola) of the United States, while the new Eastern Power of Yatakang (approximately Indonesia) is becoming a threat to rival Red **China**. Many decisions are made through the advice of a powerful heuristic **computer**, Shalmaneser, which may be becoming self-aware. Norman House, an "Afram" or African-American, is an executive with the giant General Technics Corporation. He is sent to revive a project in the tiny African state of Beninia (see **Africa**), which has oddly stayed peaceful (if impoverished) through the surrounding imperialistic chaos. Donald Hogan is a government researcher activated by shadowy superiors to investigate claims made about the Yatakangese molecular biologist, Sugaiguntang. Chad Mulligan, a sociologist who identified many world problems in a series of books that made him a millionaire but have not changed society at all, returns from alcoholism to investigate both Beninia's peacefulness, which might offer a slim chance of world **survival**, and Shalmaneser.

Discussion

One of an otherwise unconnected series of books that deal with issues being identified in the late 1960s and early 1970s as major global problems (another work, *The Sheep Look Up* [1972] is a frightening extrapolation of pollution), *Stand on Zanzibar* is a **dystopia** no less alarming for its roots in the everyday. Brunner builds up his picture of a **near future** world by a series of mosaic effects: snippets from the media of his world ("The Happening World": a TV-script like series of chapters), snapshots from the consciousness of a series of minor characters, quotations from contemporary newspaper articles he has drawn upon as foundations for trends in the early twenty-first century, and advertisements (see **Advertising**) from his future media, all woven into counterpoint with his main plot in the fashion of John Dos Passos's U.S.A. trilogy beginning with *The 42nd Parallel* (1930). One of the most chilling scenes involves a "forfeit party" thrown by the sadistic head of General

Technics, Georgette Tallon Buckfast, whose array of transplants and prosthetics make her virtually a **cyborg**. The theme—the Twentieth Century—allows Brunner to satirize **fashion** and other aspects of consumerism (see **Satire**), but also gives him scope to build a long view in his vision of how this future developed. Unlike many science fiction futures, this is not imagined in exotic isolation but is firmly rooted in its own past.

As would be expected in such a vast and at times bitter novel, a range of social **anxiety** is covered. Much of the plot involves the maneuvers of the military and capitalist corporations, and Hogan's mission to Yatakang is concerned with Dr. Sugaiguntang's expertise in **genetic engineering**. House's experiences as a GT executive, and his brittle relationship with Hogan, with whom he shares an apartment, show us **race relations** reaching a cusp point. Young women ("shiggies") virtually prostitute themselves to gain room space, suggesting a society built upon **sexism**. There is little room in Brunner's future for **feminism**. But Brunner has cleverly described a society in which sex has become divorced from reproduction. The possession of "prodgies" (progeny, or **children**) is both a hope of people forbidden by eugenic legislation to reproduce and source of anxiety for those who clash with social and legal pressures to limit family size. Brunner's mosaic picture of his world shows a number of human **tragedies** caused by this contradiction. His depiction of pathological **sexuality**, although somewhat dated, resonates. Although it would be a mistake to consider this novel purely a matter of **predictions**, it was written as an angry warning of the world likely to result if contemporary trends continued. It is unsurprising that, despite the lack of a domed Manhattan, permanent Moonbase, or genuinely aware computers, the tensions and pressures of Brunner's world are recognizable.

Also illuminating and guiding the reader is the running commentary extracted from the works of Chad Mulligan who, like similar characters in novels by Robert A. Heinlein (see *Stranger in a Strange Land*), knows and explains the world. It is Mulligan who discovers the anomaly of Benina, which seems to affect Shalmaneser's inability to analyze General Technics's project. While the reason for the world's problems not affecting Benina is something of a science fiction **cliché**, Brunner's choice not to foreground this **mutation** is in keeping with his desire to make the novel one that dramatizes issues rather than creating easy generic solutions. By the end of the book, although some minor characters have received positive solutions, we are told that the human race would now be, by tens of thousands, knee-deep in the waters around Zanzibar. The future is bleak.

Bibliography

John Brunner. "The Genesis of *Stand on Zanzibar*." *Extrapolation*, 11 (May, 1970), 34–43.

Neal Bukeavich. "Are We Adopting the Right Measures to Cope?" *Science Fiction Studies*, 86 (March, 2002), 53–70.

Joe de Bolt. *The Happening Worlds of John Brunner*. Port Washington, NY: Kennikat, 1975.

Stephen H. Goldman. "John Brunner's Dystopia." *Science-Fiction Studies*, 5 (November, 1978), 260–270.

Stephen H. Goldman. "The Polymorphic Worlds of John Brunner." *Science-Fiction Studies*, 9 (July, 1976), 103–211.

Patrick Murphy. "Dialogics and Didacticism." *Science-Fiction Studies*, 14 (March, 1987), 21–33.

David N. Samuelson. "New Wave, Old Ocean." *Extrapolation*, 15 (December, 1973), 75–96.

Norman Spinrad. "*Stand on Zanzibar*." Thomas D. Clareson, ed., *Science Fiction: The Other Side of Realism*. Bowling Green, Ohio: Bowling Green State University Popular Press, 1971, 181–185.

Michael Stern. "From Technique to Knowledge." *Science-Fiction Studies*, 5 (July, 1978), 112–129.

—Andy Sawyer

STAR MAKER BY OLAF STAPLEDON (1937)

> *Two lights for guidance. The first, our little glowing atom of community, with all that it signifies. The second, the cold light of the stars, symbol of the hypercosmical reality, with its crystal ecstacy. Strange that in this light, in which even the dearest love is frostily assessed, and even the possible defeat of our half-waking world is contemplated without remission of praise, the human crisis does not lose but gains significance. Strange, that it seems more, not less, urgent to play some part in this struggle, this brief effort of animalcules striving to win for their race some increase of lucidity before the ultimate darkness.*

> —Olaf Stapledon
> *Star Maker* (1937)

Summary

The narrator mentally projects himself, as a bodiless viewpoint, on a journey throughout the universe, during which he visits thousands of other planets inhabited by sentient creatures (see **Aliens in Space**). On the first planet to which he travels, he makes mental contact with the native Bvalltu (see **First Contact**). They learn how to meld their minds and continue the journey together (see **Space Travel**), frequently making mental union with other **intelligences**.

As an increasingly composite and wise spirit, these intellects become incipiently god-like, with **psychic powers** not to create or punish but rather to communicate telepathically with members of evolving alien races and encourage them to join a galactic **community**. They watch the rise, imperialistic conquests (see **Galactic Empire**), and fall of many species, including **humanity**. Stapledon often, if subtly, alludes to his earlier *Last and First Men* (see **Far Future**).

The narrator, using both the singular and plural first person, explains how they apprehend the creator of the cosmos, or Star Maker, and, by developing the power to visit the earliest years of the universe and grasp a vision of its end, how they finally gain an appreciation of the nature and purposes of the Star Maker (see **Cosmology; Destiny**). Clearly Stapledon uses this novel to come to grips with the human impulses for **religion** and theodicy, for the narrator repeatedly praises the Star Maker, even as he cries out against many **tragedies** he witnesses. He concludes that the creative spirit of the Star Maker is neither one of sympathy nor of **love** for its creatures, but rather one of contemplation and striving for grander creations (see **Eschatology**).

Discussion

Stapledon scholars generally agree that he chose for political and moral purposes, rather than religious inspiration, to write this documentary-style biography of this and other universes. His diction often mimics, or mocks, that of the Bible, but he makes it clear throughout that he has no indoctrination in, nor patience for, the scriptures of either Old or New Testament, even though theodicy is a major theme.

Star Maker opens with a preface that almost begs forgiveness for choosing to write about **politics** rather than entering an activist cause, and acknowledges that both Leftists and Rightists are likely to misconstrue and resent his "imaginative sketch of the dread but vital whole of things," by which he means, particularly, German and Italian imperialistic tendencies during the 1930s, but also, generally, the **history** of humanity's atrocities unto itself. (He does not, interestingly, apologize for writing science fiction.) On the first page, the narrator explains that it is **horror** at the "world's delirium" that drives him out of his house one night to gaze at the **stars** and yearn to know its cause.

As the narrator and his fellow pilgrims observe a multitude of **civilizations**, they see the same sorts of struggles enacted over and over throughout the galaxy: between **individualism and conformity**, pacifism and belligerence, striving for true community based on love and **xenophobia** born of fascism and Nazism. Stapledon expresses these struggles as the political crisis Europe faced at the time of writing, but also as a spiritual crisis, seeking what he terms the right attitude toward the universe. The narrator watches races, too often, destroy themselves, so he increasingly senses the Star Maker to be indifferent or even cruel, in view of such futility and waste.

Stapledon describes a wondrous variety of aliens, some more and some less humanoid, though all faced with problems similar to those of humanity. The reader meets marine creatures, symbiotic intelligences (see **Symbiosis**), composite beings (see **Hive Minds**), **plant** men, and others. Those who survive and achieve **wisdom** also develop telepathy on a planetary, then interspecies scale, evolving into what Stapledon calls minded worlds, who then seek others. Pacifist minded worlds throw themselves into the joys of **work and leisure**, while others pursue interplanetary **war**.

Stapledon's narrative is almost entirely free of dialogue or character development; it is, instead, a series of **sublime** visions of world organisms, which may use their powers to leave their solar systems and tour the galaxy. The vast panorama of **time** and space he depicts, despite the wearisome **cycles** of races making **progress** toward enormous mental and technological powers only to collapse again (see **Apocalypse**), conveys a true **sense of wonder**. The narrator discovers intelligence in the universe's first nebulae and in its latest stars, and himself achieves something like omniscience (see **Immortality and Longevity**), though not omnipotence. This is reserved for the Star Maker, whom the narrator adores; he describes it as a spirit— not a God or Holy Ghost, but an animating principle of creativity. The narrator finally apprehends the Star Maker but finds no love there, only dispassionate attention, and understands that the Star Maker is disappointed with the universe it has created and intends to create others, while this one decays and dies. He envisions an infinity of other universes, many richer and more complex than our own, all striving for perfection. Stapledon explains that tragedy and **death** are essential parts of this perfection, and must be accounted as such (see **Philosophy**), in order to face the limitations of human life with equanimity.

Bibliography

Robert Crossley. *Olaf Stapledon*. Syracuse, NY: Syracuse University Press, 1994.

John Huntington. "Olaf Stapledon and the Novel About the Future." *Contemporary Literature*, 22 (Summer, 1981), 349–365.

John Kinnaird. *Olaf Stapledon*. Mercer Island, Wash.: Starmont House, 1986.

Stanislaw Lem. "On Stapledon's *Star Maker*." *Science-Fiction Studies*, 14 (March, 1987), 1–8.

Douglas A. Mackey. "Science Fiction and Gnosticism." *Missouri Review*, 7 (1984), 112–120.

Patrick McCarthy. *Olaf Stapledon*. Boston: Twayne, 1982.

Patrick A. McCarthy, Charles Elkins, and Martin Harry Greenberg, eds. *The Legacy of Olaf Stapledon*. New York: Greenwood Press, 1989.

A.A. Rutledge. "*Star Maker*." *Science-Fiction Studies*, 9 (November, 1982), 274–283.

Robert H. Waugh. "Spirals and Metaphors." *Extrapolation*, 38, (Fall 1997), 207–221.

—Fiona Kelleghan

STAR TREK (1966–1969)

Space . . . the final frontier. These are the voyages of the starship Enterprise. Its five-year mission: to explore strange, new worlds; to seek out new life, and new civilizations; to boldly go where no man has gone before.

—Gene Roddenberry
Star Trek (1966)

Summary

In 1964, veteran television writer Gene Roddenberry decided to write and pitch a science fiction series that would allow him to explore issues like **race relations, war,** and **religion** without complaints from censors—because it would be set in the future. He characterized the proposed series as a sort of **western**, a "Wagon Train to the

Stars": a **space opera** charting a starship's adventures on the **frontiers** of space. Hoping the series would last five years, Roddenberry established the premise that the starship *Enterprise* had been sent by the benevolent Federation of Planets on a five-year mission to explore unknown realms of the galaxy. After a rejected first pilot and cast adjustments during the first year, the regular crew of the *Enterprise* was established, featuring brave, impetuous Captain James T. Kirk; brilliant, enigmatic half-human, half-Vulcan First Officer Spock; and irascible, homespun Doctor Leonard McCoy. Along with Engineer Scott, Helmsman Sulu, Communications Officer Uhura, Ensign Chekov, and Nurse Chapel, they battle evil aliens like the Klingons and Romulans (see **Space War**), interact with newly discovered races, and confront strange phenomena in outer space.

Discussion

Several well-known episodes of *Star Trek* illustrate its central themes and concerns. "Arena" (1967) argues against **violence** as a way to solve problems: commanded by a race of god-like beings to engage in a duel to the **death** with a reptilian alien, Kirk instead defeats but refuses to kill the alien, proving humans have transcended their violent **history** on **Earth** and are committed to the peaceful **exploration** of space. The same message figures in "Spectre of the Gun" (1968), "Day of the Dove" (1968), and "The Savage Curtain" (1969). The introduction of the Prime Directive in "Bread and Circuses" (1968), forbidding interference with developing alien **civilizations**, signalled *Star Trek*'s concerns for tolerance of diverse **cultures**, and "Let This Be Your Last Battlefield" (1969) attacks the folly of racism by depicting the mutual hostility of two-toned alien races virtually identical except that one is black on the left side and the other black on the right. Roddenberry opposes religion in "Who Mourns for Adonais?" (1967) and "The Apple" (1967), both episodes suggesting that belief in **gods and goddesses** is a child-like delusion that intelligent beings inevitably abandon as they mature. Similarly, "The Return of the Archons" (1967), "A Taste of Armageddon" (1967), and "The Ultimate Computer" (1968) warn against allowing all-powerful **computers** to dominate people. At times, *Star Trek* critically examines current events: "A Private Little War" (1968) allegorizes the Vietnam War (see **Allegory**), "The *Enterprise* Incident" (1968) retells the seizure of the American boat *Pueblo* by North Korea in 1968, and "The Way to Eden" (1969) examines the hippie phenomenon.

Like other episodes involving **time travel**, "The City on the Edge of Forever" (1967) is a parable of **destiny**: stranded in the 1930s, Kirk falls in **love** with social reformer Edith Keller but must let her die to avoid catastrophically changing the future and allowing Nazi Germany to win World War II. This is one of several episodes focused on the theme of thwarted love, as crew members enamored of beautiful alien women must abandon them to carry on with their duties, and a recurring subplot involves Chapel's unrequited love for Spock.

A favorite concern of this and later *Star Trek* series, as noted by Michéle Barrett and Duncan Barrett, is probing into the nature of **humanity**. In "The Enemy Within" (1966), a **teleportation** accident splits Kirk into two people, each with half of his personality: good and **evil**. The evil **doppelgänger** is devoid of **ethics** and creates havoc aboard the ship; his other half is weak and unable to take command. Recognizing that Kirk needs both the benign and malevolent aspects of his personality to function, Spock and McCoy use advanced **technology** to reunite his two halves. "Mirror, Mirror" (1967) provides other crew members with evil twins in a **mirror** universe where humans have created a **galactic empire** based only on conquest and fear; here, Kirk's message to the mirror Spock is that a such a brutal system must be reformed, because it is inherently unstable and will lead to **rebellion** and barbarism. Several episodes, including "The Galileo Seven" (1967) and "Journey to Babel" (1967), criticize Spock's rejection of emotion in favor of logic, but an excess of emotionalism is also revealed as a danger in "The Naked Time" (1966). Still, to balance its usual air of moral earnestness, *Star Trek* would occasionally relax and have fun in humorous episodes (see **Humor**) like "Shore Leave" (1966), "The Trouble with Tribbles" (1967), and "A Piece of the Action" (1968).

Throughout its three seasons, *Star Trek* consistently distinguished itself with intelligent and thought-provoking storylines. Even after cancellation, the series remained alive with episodes endlessly rerun in syndication; a short-lived animated series, also called *Star Trek* (1973–1975), which reunited the show's cast and several of its original writers; comic books; various items of merchandise; and large quantities of original fan fiction. Eventually, the series' continuing popularity inspired a series of films beginning with ***Star Trek: The Motion Picture***, to be followed by four successor series.

Bibliography

Michéle Barrett and Duncan Barrett. *Star Trek: The Human Frontier*. New York: Routledge, 2001.
Karin Blair. *Meaning in Star Trek*. Chambersberg, PA: Anima Books, 1977.
H. Bruce Franklin. "*Star Trek* in the Vietnam Era." *Film & History*, 24 (1994), 36–46.
David Gerrold. *The World of Star Trek*. Third Edition. London: Virgin Books, 1996.
Taylor Harrison, Sarah Projansky, Kent A. Ono, and Elyce Rae Helford, eds. *Enterprise Zones*. Boulder, CO: Westview Press, 1996.
Mike Hertenstein. *The Double Vision of Star Trek*. Chicago, IL: Cornerstone Press, 1998.
Jennifer E. Porter and Darcee L. McLaren, eds. *Star Trek and Sacred Ground*. Albany, NY: State University of New York Press, 1999.
Herbert F. Solow and Robert H. Justman. *Inside Star Trek*. New York, NY: Pocket Books, 1996.
Bjo Trimble. *The Star Trek Concordance*. New York: Ballantine Books, 1976.

—*Lincoln Geraghty*

STAR TREK: DEEP SPACE NINE (1993–1999)

Summary

Star Trek: Deep Space Nine is set on the eponymous **space station**, a crossroads between the Bajorans and their former conquerors, the imperialistic Cardassians. The station also guards a wormhole, which leads to the far side of the galaxy. In the premiere, Starfleet Commander Benjamin Sisko (*Star Trek*'s first African-American leading man, Avery Brooks) arrives with his son Jake to take command.

He accidentally discovers the wormhole and makes **first contact** with the Prophets, powerful, noncorporeal **aliens in space** whom the Bajorans worship as benevolent gods. Supported by a diverse crew of officers, Sisko must keep the peace between Cardassians and Bajorans and maintain the security of the wormhole. He is also regarded by the Bajorans as the Prophets' Emissary, a mystical role that the agnostic Sisko finds troubling.

The first few seasons relate mainly episodic stories of adventure, **exploration** and alien encounter, addressing familiar science fiction themes like **time travel**, **genetic engineering**, and **parallel worlds**. However, by the third season the series began a major story arc involving conflict with the Dominion, an empire beyond the wormhole, ruled by a xenophobic race of **shapeshifters**. Alarmed by Starfleet incursions through the wormhole, the Dominion allies with the Cardassians and invades Starfleet space. The resulting **space war** lasts nearly three television seasons. In the final episode, the Dominion is vanquished and peace restored, at considerable cost in lives; Sisko **sacrifices** himself to save Bajor from demonic beings and is taken by the Prophets into their own plane of existence.

Discussion

The third *Star Trek* television series, and the first developed after the death of *Star Trek* creator Gene Roddenberry, *Deep Space Nine* departs from previously established *Star Trek* formats in several important aspects. In contrast to the "road show" format of previous series, where a starship's crew encounters new aliens and situations every week, the fixed setting of a space station demanded a more serial narrative following the evolving relationships between the station and its neighbors. Especially important are the two nearest, the Cardassians and Bajorans. Their **history** of brutal conquest generated many stories exploring **race relations** and reconciliation, in episodes like "Wrongs Darker Than Death or Night" (1998), in which the station's Bajoran First Officer, Kira, discovers that her **mother** was mistress of the hated commander of the Cardassian occupation. This historical approach also contributed to the development of nearly thirty recurring guest characters with major roles in extended story arcs.

In a second departure, not all the main characters are Starfleet officers, and the venal Ferengi Quark is not even, by *Star Trek* standards, a good guy. And these characters are often in conflict with each other, in contrast to Roddenberry's idealized future where all races get along in a harmonious Federation. Every *Star Trek* series has had an outsider character, who provides an alien perspective on human ways. While previous outsiders, Spock (in *Star Trek*) and Data (in *Star Trek: The Next Generation*) portray a simple polarity of logic versus emotion, the alienation of *Deep Space Nine*'s shapeshifter Odo arises from his different physical nature. As a shapeshifter, he must maintain a false human form just to win acceptance from those around him, and as a member of the Dominion's master race, he struggles also with divided loyalty between his human friends and his own people, who are at war with each other.

While **war** is occasionally addressed in earlier series, *Deep Space Nine* makes war its central theme—again, a far cry from Roddenberry's vision. The second half of the series explores many aspects of war, including biological warfare, genocide, dehumanization, and the tortuous **politics** of alliance. Among many episodes worth mentioning are "In the Pale Moonlight" (1998), in which Sisko sacrifices his integrity by condoning an assassination to enlist a new ally in the war, and "The Siege of AR-558" (1998), a gritty study of the daily stresses of battle.

The most surprising departure from *Star Trek* tradition is the exploration of religious themes, which Roddenberry, an atheist, had forbidden (see **Religion**). His death allowed *Deep Space Nine*'s writers to examine religious belief through the deeply spiritual Bajorans and to show Sisko's agnosticism gradually turning to faith in the Prophets. Unlike previous *Star Trek* series, in which religious belief is often dismissed as superstition, *Deep Space Nine* portrays faith positively. When Sisko defies the Prophets in "Tears of the Prophets" (1998), **disaster** follows. When he bargains with them, he saves the Federation from **invasion** ("Sacrifice of Angels" [1997]). And when he obeys them, he completes a **quest** that affects the outcome of the war ("Shadows and Symbols" [1998]).

Deep Space Nine's breaks with *Star Trek* tradition were controversial both during and after its run. While many critics and fans hailed it as the best *Star Trek* series for its complex, realistic stories and characters, others felt it departed too far from what *Star Trek* should be, especially in focusing on such dark themes as war. The new ground broken by the series proved largely a one-time creative detour for the franchise, as two subsequent series, *Star Trek: Voyager* and *Star Trek: Enterprise*, returned to the starship setting, harmonious crew, and episodic format.

Bibliography

Billie Aul and Brian Frank. "Prisoners of Dogma and Prejudice." *Foundation*, No. 85 (Autumn, 2002), 51–64.

Terry J. Erdmann, with Paula M. Block. *Star Trek: Deep Space Nine Companion*. New York: Pocket Books, 2000.

Kathy E. Ferguson. "This Species Which Is Not One." *Strategies*, 15 (November, 2002), 181–195.

Lincoln Geraghty, "Homosocial Desire on the Final Frontier." *Journal of Popular Culture*, 36 (Winter, 2003), 441–465.

Hanley E. Kanar. "No Ramps in Space." Elyce R. Helford, ed., *Fantasy Girls*. Lanham: Rowman&Littlefield, 2000, 245–264.

Matthew Kappell. "Speakers for the Dead." *Extrapolation*, 41 (Summer, 2000), 104–114.

Peter Linford. "Deeds of Power." Jennifer E. Porter and Darcee L. McLaren, eds., *Star Trek and Sacred Ground*. Albany: State University of New York Press, 1999, 77–100.

Joe Nazzaro. "Michael Piller." Nazzaro, *Writing Science Fiction and Fantasy Television*. London: Titan Books, 2002, 167–170.

—*Karen Stoddard Hayes*

STAR TREK: ENTERPRISE (2001–2005)

Summary

Star Trek: Enterprise (originally entitled *Enterprise*) is the fifth television series in the *Star Trek* universe. **Star Trek** and its spin-offs remain the most culturally influential science fiction shows to ever grace the airwaves. Along with the four sequel series, countless toys, books, and other products have been released. With *Star Trek: Enterprise*, the producers' intent was to honor and preserve *Star Trek* creator Gene Roddenberry's original vision while at the same time moving the thirty-five-year-old franchise into the twenty-first century. The only direction that made sense to *Enterprise*'s creators was backward—a decision that, in retrospect, may have been a mistake. They took Roddenberry's idea to an earlier time when humans were not accustomed to **space travel**, equipment and **technology** were still rough around the edges, and the crew could wear baseball caps and be seen in their underwear—in other words, people more like modern humans. To capture the **space opera** spirit of the original series, the first two seasons of *Star Trek: Enterprise* focused on **humanity's exploration** of space, the final **frontier**, where familiar races like the Klingons are encountered. Die-hard fans and neophytes to the *Star Trek* universe could witness the galactic upheaval that led to the **birth** of the Federation. However, in response to disappointing ratings, the third season brought a radical departure, instead emphasizing a unified story arc involving a menacing alien race, the Suliban, who wish to erase humans from existence. The fourth and final season again changed its focus to connect story ideas to the original series.

Discussion

Star Trek: Enterprise initially attempted to answer questions on many fans' minds: How did humanity go from the bottom to the top in the galactic pecking order? Why did it take about 100 years for the first starship *Enterprise* to be built and launched after **first contact** with the Vulcans? What happened between the era of *Enterprise* in the twenty-second century, and the time of the original *Star Trek* series, some 115 years later?

In its answers, *Star Trek: Enterprise* endeavored to follow the best *Star Trek* traditions by making the era seem brand new and full of surprises, even though the viewers knew how things would ultimately turn out. Still, only the big picture of the future was known, allowing viewers to form attachments to the characters. The uncertainty of the **survival** of the brave, enthusiastic characters matched the uncertainty of our times here on twenty-first century **Earth**. And everyday life on *Enterprise* was easier for viewers to relate to than in previous series because things do not always work right and the crew is wary of new technology like the transporter (see **Teleportation**). Unlike the other *Star Trek* shows, where Starfleet personnel were well-trained and nonplussed by **aliens in space**, the crew of the *Enterprise* set off into space a little rough around the edges. Despite the humans' supposed **friendship** with the Vulcans, their **mentors** shared little **knowledge** of other **alien worlds** and alien **cultures**. The only seasoned pros who join Captain Archer on the *Enterprise*'s maiden voyage are a Vulcan science officer (see **Scientists**), T'Pol, and alien chief medical officer (see **Medicine**), Dr. Phlox.

The show chronicled the adventures of the first human interstellar ship, which can achieve warp speed (see **Hyperspace**), a form of faster-than-light propulsion. Warp drive is first mentioned in the *Star Trek* pilot episode "The Cage" (1966), under the name "timewarp," and some Trek fans complain that *Star Trek: Enterprise* should have used this earlier label. Fans were also bothered by other elements of the show that violated the canon, like using "phase pistols" when phasers should not yet exist, or having Romulan ships with cloaking devices when in *Star Trek*'s

"Balance of Terror" (1967) cloaking technology is presented as a new invention (see **Inventions**). However, the producers of *Star Trek: Enterprise* claimed that they were not strictly bound to preserve continuity from previous series. On the other hand, *Star Trek: Enterprise* took pains to depict the genesis of some things taken for granted in previous series. Two notable examples are Reed's invention of force fields, and an episode where Archer's musings pose questions that are later answered by the Prime Directive, Starfleet's most prominent guiding principle of noninterference with the natural **progress** of underdeveloped societies.

Some saw *Star Trek: Enterprise* as an attempt to move *Star Trek* away from the political correctness of recent series toward more traditional action adventure. The casting of a white male as captain, his preference for unilateral action, his often-expressed hatred for Vulcans, the introduction of the Suliban as one-dimensional **villains**, and even the initial dropping of the words "*Star Trek*" from the title were seen as distancing the new series from those that came before. In many ways, the first two seasons gave the impression that the crew thought they were on a wild "road trip" rather than an important, and immensely expensive, mission for Earth's government. This perhaps contributed to the less than stellar ratings that inspired the new direction of the third season, including the restoration of the words "*Star Trek*" in the title and introduction of a complex new enemy, the Xindi. Some critics suggest that the Xindi were actually too complex, because of the high suspension of disbelief needed to accept that insectoid (see **Insects**), reptilian, arboreal sloth, aquatic (see **Fish and Sea Creatures**), avian (see **Birds**), and simian (see **Apes**) species were all the same race. In the belief that humans will one day eradicate them (see **Race Relations**), Xindis built a weapon (see **Weaponry**) capable of destroying Earth. But the Xindi were mere pawns, deceived by the time traveling Suliban, who wished to avoid **future wars** with the Federation (see **Time Travel**). The entire third season then focused on the *Enterprise*'s mission to stop the Xindi and guarantee the **survival** of humanity.

Many fans thought that the fourth season, which emphasized connections to the original series, was the series' best year, but the ratings did not improve and *Star Trek: Enterprise* was cancelled, making it the first *Star Trek* series after the original that did not achieve the desired seven-season run. The much-disparaged, anticlimactic final episode capped off four uneven seasons by relegating the cast to mere characters in a holographic reenactment (see **Virtual Reality**). Perhaps, the series' creators were consciously or subconsciously suggesting, *Star Trek: Enterprise* had never managed to rise above the status of a pale replication of its genuinely successful predecessors.

Bibliography

Jeff Bond. "*Enterprise*." *Cinefantastique*, 35 (June/July, 2003), 63.

John Hodgson. "A Quick Sketch of the *Enterprise*." Russell, ed., *Digging Holes in Popular Culture*. Oxford, UK: Oxbow Books, 2002, 97–103.

Anna L. Kaplan. "*Enterprise*." *Cinefantastique*, 33 (October/November, 2001), 18–19.

Kylie Lee. "Confronting *Enterprise* Slash Fan Fiction." *Extrapolation*, 44 (Spring, 2003), 69–82.

Evelyn Lewes. "Roddenberry's Children." *Interzone*, No. 179 (May, 2002), 55–58.

Gregory L. Norris and Laura A. Van Fleet. "*Enterprise*: Scott Bakula." *Cinefantastique*, 33 (October/November, 2001), 20–21.

Kay Reindl. "*Enterprise.*" *Cinefantastique*, 35 (June/July, 2003), 62.
Tim Robins. "Report from Farpoint." *Interzone*, No. 176 (February, 2002), 60–63.

—Nick Aires

STAR TREK: GENERATIONS (1994)

■

[Picard:] Someone once told me that time was a predator that stalked us all our lives. I rather believe that time is a companion who goes with us on the journey and reminds us to cherish every moment, because it will never come again. What we leave behind is not as important as how we've lived. After all Number One, we're only mortal.
[Riker:] Speak for yourself, sir. I plan to live forever.

—Ronald D. Moore and Brannon Braga
Star Trek: Generations (1994)

Summary

Star Trek: The Next Generation finished its seventh and final season in 1994, but by the start of March that year filming had already started on *Star Trek: Generations*, the first movie to star the crew of the second *Enterprise*. The success of the series had guaranteed that these movies would have a loyal and eager audience. Picard, Riker, Data, and the others who had taken over the mantle from the original **Star Trek** series were now the focus of a new cycle of feature films: along with *Generations*, these were *Star Trek: First Contact* (1996), *Star Trek: Insurrection* (1998), and *Star Trek: Nemesis* (2002).

Although *Generations* proved popular with fans and the box office, it was *First Contact* that received the most plaudits and earned Paramount the most money—the main reason perhaps being the return and big screen debut of the villainous **cyborgs**, the Borg. Like the original six movies, starting with **Star Trek: The Motion Picture**, these movies have a recognizable story arc. In *Generations* the torch is officially passed to the new crew as, after a prologue featuring Kirk, Scott, and Chekov, the new *Enterprise* crew takes center stage and Picard witnesses Kirk's death. In *First Contact*, Picard learns to deal with the emotional trauma caused by his assimilation by the Borg in "The Best of Both Worlds" (1990). During *Insurrection*, Picard and the crew begins to cope with their approaching **old age** and retirement. And in *Nemesis*, Picard must come to terms with his lack of a real **family**. In fact,

Nemesis is the concluding episode in a story line that tackles issues raised by Picard's feelings toward life and death, **family** and individuality (see **Individualism and Conformity**), **sacrifice**, and greed.

Discussion

Both *Generations* and *First Contact* deal with **time travel** stories, where the crew must go back in **time** to save **Earth**. In the former, Picard enlists the help of Kirk to defeat Dr. Soran who plans to destroy an entire planet to change the course of an energy ribbon (see **Threshold**), which leads to a temporal realm called the Nexus. Within the Nexus people can live for **eternity**, and Soran is willing to kills millions to secure this **utopia**. The latter story sees the Borg travel back in time to assimilate **humanity** before it can make **first contact** with the Vulcans. By eliminating humans, the Borg can prevent formation of the Federation and eradicate the one force able to stop them from assimilating the galaxy.

One striking aspect of *First Contact* is that we are introduced to the Borg Queen (see **Queens**) who controls the **hive mind** of the Borg collective. Although the Borg appear to show no emotion, the Borg Queen has her own unique **identity** and can communicate with Picard as an individual. Using powers of **communication** and insidious **sexuality**, the Queen tries to convince Data to give her control of the ship's **computers** in return for the human emotions he long sought to attain. To accomplish her goals, she grafts skin to Data's **android** body allowing him to feel **pain** as well as pleasure. Meanwhile, on Earth, other members of the *Enterprise* crew are trying to reverse the damage of the Borg attack (see **Weaponry**) by helping Dr. Zefram Cochrane rebuild and launch his pioneering warp ship, which, the crew knows, will inspire the Vulcans to initiate first contact with Earth. However, the unconventional Cochrane, who drinks heavily and listens to early rock'n'roll **music**, proves a difficult ally, as this natural-born rebel is uncomfortable with the notion that he will someday be regarded as a great historical figure. At one point he runs away, attempting to **escape** from his **destiny**; but he finally agrees to return and make the flight that will positively change the course of human history.

In *Insurrection* the crew of the *Enterprise* must stop the enforced relocation of the inhabitants of Ba'ku, a planet that holds secret properties for eternal **youth**. These people renounced **technology** to lead a simpler life, leaving them vulnerable to attack. This is an **allegory** of events in nineteenth-century **America** where **Native Americans** were forcibly removed from their land and pushed onto reservations, viewed as people of the past, not the future.

In *Nemesis*, Picard first learns of the imminent **marriage** of Ryker and Troi; then he must confront and defeat his youthful **clone**, secretly created by Picard's old enemies and sent on a mission to destroy Earth. Picard succeeds, but not without mixed feelings, realizing that he is in a sense fighting both against himself and the son that he never had.

While the failure of *Nemesis* at the box office, and the aging of cast members, probably means that there will be no more films in this cycle, these four films remain impressive achievements, depicting in **microcosm** the concerns for family and **community** that exemplify both the series and desires of two of its major characters: Picard and Data. Through these protagonists we obtain a new sense of the process of human **progress**.

Bibliography

Michèle Barrett, and Duncan Barrett. "Part III: The Post-Modern Tack." Barrett and Barrett, *Star Trek: The Human Frontier*. Cambridge: Polity Press, 2001, 137–197.

Ilsa J. Bick. "*Star Trek: Generations*." *The Psychoanalytic Review*, 82 (1995), 458–462.

Anne Cranny-Francis. "The Erotics of the (cy)Borg." Marleen S. Barr, ed., *Future Females: The Next Generation*. Lanham, MD: Rowman and Littlefield Publishers, 2000, 145–163.

Chris Gregory. "Diplomacy, Family, Destiny: *The Next Generation*." Gregory, *Star Trek: Parallel Narratives*. London: Macmillan Press, 2000, 43–67.

Máire Messenger Davies and Roberta Pearson. "Patrick Stewart as an Agent of Cultural Mobility." Thomas Austin and Martin Barker, eds., *Contemporary Hollywood Stardom*. London: Arnold, 2003, 167–186.

Larry Nemecek. *Star Trek: The Next Generation Companion*. New York, NY: Pocket Books, 2002.

Roberta Pearson and Máire Messenger Davies. "You're Not Going to See That on TV." Mark Jancovich and James Lyons, eds., *Quality Popular Television*. London: BFI, 2003, 103–117.

Christine Wertheim. "*Star Trek: First Contact*." Ziauddin Sardar and Sean Cubitt, eds., *Aliens R Us*. London: Pluto Press, 2002, 74–93.

—Lincoln Geraghty

STAR TREK: THE MOTION PICTURE (1979)

> *[Dr. McCoy:] Why is any object we don't understand always called a thing?*
>
> —Harold Livingston
> *Star Trek: The Motion Picture* (1979)

Summary

Initially **Star Trek** was to be reborn as a second television series, but the success of **Star Wars** prompted Paramount to instead plan *Star Trek*'s return as a film. The premise for *Star Trek: The Motion Picture* was a story from the scrapped second series, with the *Enterprise* facing an alien threat to **Earth** that transpires to be the interstellar space probe *Voyager VI*, returning after an alien encounter with augmented powers and a desire to seek its human creator. Although the story failed to ignite critics' imaginations, audiences were pleased by the return of *Star Trek* and the movie's improved special effects. For the sequel, Harve Bennett was brought in as Executive Producer to provide more action. As a result, *Star Trek II: The Wrath of Khan* (1982) shifts attention from **exploration** of the unknown, the central theme of the series and first film, and instead focuses on darker themes like **revenge**, obsession, and **death**.

The second film also concludes with the biggest change to the series to date, the death of Spock. The other films in the cycle would be shaped by this event: his complex resurrection would be observed in *Star Trek III: The Search for Spock* (1984), with loose ends tied up in *Star Trek IV: The Voyage Home* (1986), while in *Star Trek V: The Final Frontier* (1989) and *Star Trek VI: The Undiscovered Country* (1991) Spock's more human attitudes to life, **religion**, and his **friendship** with Kirk reflect his experiences of death and **rebirth**.

Discussion

In *The Wrath of Khan*, Kirk's nemesis Khan Noonien Singh, last seen in the *Star Trek* episode "Space Seed" (1967), seeks revenge for the death of his wife and his **exile** to a barren planet. Khan had been a key figure in the Eugenics Wars (see **War**), which ravaged Earth in the late 1990s, by leading a group of superhumans (see **Superman**) created by selective breeding and **genetic engineering**. In trying to kill Kirk and seize the life-creating Genesis **technology** developed by Kirk's ex-wife and his son, Khan almost destroys the *Enterprise*, but Spock **sacrifices** his life to save his crewmates and ensure Khan's defeat. *The Search for Spock* reveals that, before dying, Spock had transferred his *Katra*, or Vulcan "soul," to McCoy, and the discovery of his rejuvenated body on the Genesis planet inspires Kirk to defy Starfleet orders and embark upon a **quest** to reunite Spock's mind and body and restore his friend to life, though this in turn requires sacrifices from Kirk—the loss of the *Enterprise* and his son's life.

Together the first three films represent a **cycle** of rebirth, death, and resurrection, with stories reminiscent of the original series adapted to the big screen but overlaid with references to **old age**, regret, loss, and death. In large part these were screenwriters' necessary responses to the use of visibly aging actors from the original series as **heroes**; maintaining their centrality also foregrounded the issue of conflicts between generations and demanded a pattern of **role reversals** in which older people would prevail over younger people, instead of the usual outcome of triumphant **youth**. Thus, in *The Motion Picture*, Kirk demonstrates that he is a more capable commander than the younger captain he replaced; *The Wrath of Khan* introduces Kirk to a previously unknown adult son, who proves an impotent rival and is killed off in *The Search for Spock*; and the second film features a young and capable Vulcan officer, Saavik, who is mentored by Spock, but when the actress playing her role demanded a salary equivalent to the series regulars for *The Search for Spock*, she was replaced by a conspicuously less talented performer, effectively eliminating a potential replacement for Spock.

The next three films shift to different themes. In *The Voyage Home*, the reunited crew takes a Klingon ship on a **time travel** mission to retrieve two humpback whales (see **Fish and Sea Creatures**) from the twentieth century to communicate with a mysterious alien presence approaching the Earth; many fans especially appreciated this film because the cast's adventures in twentieth-century San Francisco brought back the **humor** of the original series, which previous films had lacked. The film, however, also had a serious ecological message about preserving endangered species and protecting the environment (see **Ecology**). *The Final Frontier*, the weakest film in the series, features Spock's half-brother as a would-be **messiah** leading Kirk and the *Enterprise* to an encounter with a purported alien god (see **Gods and Goddesses**), a tired redaction of the original series' jeremiads about the dangers of false **religions**. *The Undiscovered Country* forces Kirk to overcome his prejudice against Klingons (see **Race Relations**) and negotiate a peace treaty between the Federation and the Klingons, thus explaining the detente observed in the now-launched successor series *Star Trek: The Next Generation*. It is also noteworthy for making frequent references to William **Shakespeare** and offering the first criticism of Kirk's proclivity for sexual encounters with young females (see **Sexism; Sexuality**).

Overall, the six films featuring the original *Star Trek* cast proved worthy continuations of the original series, maintaining a focus on characteristic themes like peaceful **first contact** with **aliens in space** while making essential adjustments to the demands of big-screen storytelling and older performers. But after *The Undiscovered Country*, it was time to turn the film franchise over to the younger cast of *Star Trek: The Next Generation*, and the changing of the guard duly occurred in the next film, *Star Trek: Generations*.

Bibliography

Ilsa J. Bick. "Boys in Space." *Cinema Journal*, 35 (1996), 43–60.

Lincoln Geraghty. "The American Jeremiad and *Star Trek*'s Puritan Legacy." *Journal of the Fantastic in the Arts*, 14 (2003), 228–245.

Ina Rae Hark. "The Wrath of the Original Cast." Deborah Cartmell and Imelda Whelehan, eds., *Adaptations*. London: Routledge, 1999, 172–184.

Elizabeth Jane Wall Hinds. "*The Wrath of Ahab*; or, Herman Melville Meets Gene Roddenberry." *Journal of American Culture*, 20 (1997), 43–46.

Larry Kreitzer. "The Cultural Veneer of *Star Trek*." *Journal of Popular Culture*, 30 (1996), 1–28.

Ian Maher. "The Outward Voyage and the Inward Search." Jennifer E. Porter and Darcee L. McLaren, eds., *Star Trek and Sacred Ground*. Albany, NY: State University of New York Press, 1999, 165–191.

Ace G. Pilkington. "*Star Trek V*: The Search for God." *Literature/Film Quarterly*, 24 (1996), 169–176.

April Selley. "I Have Been, and Ever Shall Be, Your Friend." *Journal of Popular Culture*, 20 (1986), 89–104.

William Shatner and Chris Kreski. *Star Trek Movie Memories*. London: Voyager Books, 1996.

—Lincoln Geraghty

STAR TREK: THE NEXT GENERATION (1987–1994)

Space . . . the final frontier. These are the voyages of the starship Enterprise. *Its continuing mission: to explore strange, new worlds; to seek out new life, and new civilizations; to boldly go where no one has gone before.*

—Gene Roddenberry
Star Trek: The Next Generation (1987)

Summary

After the success of the *Star Trek* movies, starting with *Star Trek: The Motion Picture*, Paramount decided that another television series would have an audience eager for more episodic space-based adventures. Gene Roddenberry was asked to develop another series, but not one that would rehash the original. *Star Trek: The Next Generation* would be a new departure: a new ship, new crew, and new time frame would make the series unique and attractive for a different generation. The series would still be identifiable as *Star Trek*—an epic **space opera** set in a future where **exploration** and optimism (see **Optimism and Pessimism**) still defined the human experience—but this time the captain would be less the aggressive cowboy and more the intellectual diplomat. The new captain, Jean-Luc Picard, was French and enjoyed **reading**, classical **music**, William **Shakespeare**, archaeology (see **Anthropology**), and theatre. His crew also differed from the original, including a blind engineer (see **Vision and Blindness**); a Klingon officer; females as the doctor, security chief, and counselor; and an **android** called Data. This new series would stress **family** and **community** over individuality (see **Individualism and Conformity**) and conflict.

Discussion

The pilot episode, "Encounter at Farpoint" (1987), set the premise for the following seven seasons. Picard and his crew, on mission to Farpoint Station, encounter an omnipotent alien being called Q (see **Gods and Goddesses**) who detains them in a dystopian recreation of post-World War III **Earth** where humans are recovering from nuclear war (see **Post-Holocaust Societies**). He sees humans as savage **barbarians** and **humanity** as a disease that must not be allowed to leave Earth and travel through space (see **Space Travel**). Q puts humanity on trial (see **Crime and Punishment**) and shows Picard that humans have had a **history** of **violence** and **war**; therefore they could not possibly be ready to explore space. As a member of the Q Continuum, he is but one of a number of omnipotent **aliens in space** that meet humans (the captains on *Star Trek: Deep Space Nine* and *Star Trek: Voyager* are also visited by Q). However the Q that torments Picard is more juvenile than his colleagues and delights in teasing and testing humans for his own sadistic pleasure. He is one of the few members of the continuum who uses physical and **psychic powers** to dabble in the affairs and **politics** of humans.

After proving their worthiness to Q, Picard and his crew continue on their mission as galactic peacekeepers. Throughout the series the core group of characters went through many changes; young Wesley Crusher originally served as Picard's **apprentice**, but the character left the series and Data took over that role as he began learning how to be more human and as their **friendship** became stronger. In one noteworthy episode, "The Measure of a Man" (1989), Data is placed on trial and forced to prove that he merits the same legal status as humans. The **death** of Tasha Yar at the end of the first season in the episode "Skin of Evil" (1988) served to gel cast members as a family, while Majel Barrett's guest performances as Counselor Troi's eccentric **mother** brought occasional **humor** to the series.

In "Q Who" (1989), Q introduces Picard to the Borg, an **evil** race of cybernetic **cyborgs**. The Borg would become the main **villains** in the series, partly due to their advanced **technology** but more because their **civilization** is a threatening **hive mind**. The antithesis of human society, lacking individual **identity** and **freedom**, they assimilate all who stand in their way of galactic conquest. In the memorable two-part episode that provided a "cliffhanger" ending to the third season, "The Best of Both Worlds" (1990), Picard himself is assimilated by the Borg and instructed to attack the Earth, a traumatizing experience that was revisited in the film *Star Trek: First Contact* (1996) (see ***Star Trek: Generations***). Another race of aliens, the Ferengi, introduced in "The Last Outpost" (1987), prove more annoying than threatening, with their obsession for gaining wealth through **business** and **trade**.

The final episode, "All Good Things . . ." (1994) brought closure to the series' voyage of astronomical and personal discovery. Q returned to serve judgment on Picard, stating that he had given humanity seven years to prove its potential but it had failed; as punishment he would wipe humans from the fabric of **time**. In a story involving **time travel** Picard attempts to stop the paradox created by his own future self when he destroyed Earth in the past before life could begin (see **Evolution**). Recognizing the paradox and fixing its effects was the evidence Q wanted of humanity's worthiness to exist, so he leaves the crew to continue their mission. Humanity's **progress** is marked not by the amount of space explored or the number of **alien worlds** visited but by its capacity to understand its position in relation to the universe. The overall philosophical message arising from Q's meddling, and the series, is that human **destiny** is not fixed and that everyone has a part to play in the success of humanity's continuing mission of exploration. The **frontier** is not a place for personal heroism, but rather a site for communal self-improvement.

Bibliography

Daniel L. Bernardi. *Star Trek and History*. New Brunswick, NJ: Rutgers University Press, 1998.

Lincoln Geraghty. "Carved from the Rock Experiences of Our Daily Lives." *European Journal of American Culture*, 21 (2002), 160–176.

Lee E. Heller. "The Persistence of Difference." *Science-Fiction Studies*, 24 (July, 1997), 226–244.

Paul Joseph and Sharon Carton. "The Law of the Federation." *University of Toledo Law Review*, 24 (1992), 43–85.

Lynne Joyrich. "Feminist Enterprise." *Cinema Journal*, 35 (1996), 61–84.

Larry Nemecek. *The Star Trek: The Next Generation Companion*. New York, NY: Pocket Books, 2002.

Robin Roberts. *Sexual Generations*. Urbana, IL: University of Illinois Press, 1999.

Sue Short. "The Measure of a Man?" *Extrapolation*, 44 (Summer, 2003), 209–223.

Rhonda V. Wilcox. "Shifting Roles and Synthetic Women in *Star Trek: The Next Generation*." *Studies in Popular Culture*, 13 (1991), 53–65.

—*Lincoln Geraghty*

STAR TREK: VOYAGER (1995–2001)

Summary

During *Star Trek: The Next Generation*'s final season, and just as *Star Trek: Deep Space Nine* started its first season, Paramount executives decided to launch a third "new" *Star Trek* series. Not only would *Star Trek: Voyager* be set in the same **time** as the previous two series, but it would be the first to feature a woman as captain, breaking one of the last **taboos** in science fiction television. The series' premise was presented in the first episode, "Caretaker" (1995): starship *Voyager*, seeking to apprehend a group of terrorists called the Maquis, gets transported by an **alien in space** called The Caretaker to a distant and unexplored region of the galaxy, the Delta Quadrant, which is so far from **Earth** that it would take seventy years traveling at top warp **speed** to get **home**. *Voyager*'s Captain Janeway invites the renegade members of the Maquis to join her crew so they can work together to find a way home. The rebel leader, the Native American Chakotay, becomes her first officer (see **Native Americans**), and the first season displays antagonism between two crews learning to work alongside each other. As the series progresses, however, the crews become a genuine **community**, as, for example, B'Elanna Torres—a half-human, half-Klingon Maquis—becomes *Voyager*'s chief engineer.

Discussion

The Delta Quadrant is a violent part of the galaxy: alien species fight **space wars** and contest the **borderlands** of their **galactic empires**, often seeing *Voyager* as a threat to their unstable positions. As was not true in the more settled **frontier** of previous *Star Trek* series, Federation ships are perceived as invaders, requiring Janeway to navigate both through uncharted territory and tense diplomatic situations to find a safe path home. She often seeks to gain information and **technology** to effect a speedy return through **trade**, as in the episode "Prime Factors" (1995), but is necessarily unsuccessful, given the series' premise; indeed, many aliens refuse to help or even attempt to steal *Voyager*'s own technology for themselves.

In many early episodes, the crew is given false hope of getting home. In "Eye of the Needle" (1995) *Voyager* encounters a cosmic wormhole, which the crew believes will lead back to Earth. However, after sending messages to a ship on the other side of the wormhole the crew realizes that it opens on to the past and going through it would be a form of **time travel**. In "Threshold" (1996) Paris builds a shuttle that can travel at warp ten, a feat never before achieved. Crossing the **threshold** into **hyperspace**, however, causes Paris and Janeway to mutate into another stage of **evolution**. Some later episodes, however, revert to the old *Star Trek* pattern of pure **exploration** leading to interesting discoveries on **alien worlds**, like "Blink of an Eye" (2000), wherein the *Voyager* memorably visits a planet of accelerated **time** that lives through several generations during the few weeks that *Voyager* lingers in its vicinity.

In the numerous encounters the ship has with the Borg (see **Cyborgs**), Janeway endeavors to barter and steal valuable technology that will facilitate their quick return. The most valuable asset she gains is the Borg crewmember Seven of Nine, who became a member of the crew in the third season cliff-hanger "Scorpion" (1997); Janeway immediately takes her under her wing as an **apprentice**, teaching her how to be human. Notions of individuality (see **Individualism and Conformity**), ethics, humanity, love, and identity are alien to Seven since she has been connected to the **hive mind** for so long. Yet Janeway and the holographic Doctor act as **mentors** to Seven and through their guidance she becomes a loyal and important part of the *Voyager* **family**.

Another series regular who goes through a striking process of development is the ship's holographic doctor, known only as the Doctor (see **Medicine**; **Virtual**

Reality); initially only a **computer** program discomfited by the transition from being an emergency backup to the regular ship's physician, he evolves into having a genuine personality. With an irregular crew and no support from the Federation, Janeway regularly has to discipline misbehaving crew members like Paris, Torres, and Seven of Nine, at times making her seem like a domineering **mother**, in contrast to the gentler **father** figures of Picard and Sisko. In the final episode "Endgame" (2001), the ship does reach Earth, but only after a future version of Janeway helps the crew defeat the Borg threat.

Overall, the benefit of crewmembers being lost in space was to stimulatingly test the optimistic ethos of *Star Trek* as it had never been tested before (see **Optimism and Pessimism**): with no help from an omniscient, omnipresent Federation, the *Voyager* crew had to struggle on their own to solve complex moral and ethical issues, often achieving resolutions that neither they nor audiences regarded as entirely satisfactory. Yet, unlike the equally weighty *Star Trek: Deep Space Nine*, *Voyager* also paid tribute to the original series in episodes filled with colorful conflict and **violence** on the final frontier, where **first contact** with aliens often ended in **tragedy** and bloodshed. This appealing combination of seriousness and **space opera** made *Star Trek: Voyager* a consistently popular series during its seven seasons.

Bibliography

Neal Baker. "Creole Identity Politics, Race, and *Star Trek: Voyager*." Elisabeth Anne Leonard, ed., *Into Darkness Peering*. Westport, CT: Greenwood Press, 1997, 119–130.

Karin Blair. "*Star Trek* Old and New." George McKay, ed., *Yankee Go Home (And Take Me With You)*. Sheffield: Sheffield Academic Press, 1997, 78–88.

Susan De Gaia. "Intergalactic Heroines." *International Studies in Philosophy*, 30 (1998), 19–32.

Darcee L. McLaren and Jennifer E. Porter. "(Re)Covering Sacred Ground." Porter and McLaren, eds., *Star Trek and Sacred Ground*. Albany: State University of New York Press, 1999, 101–115.

Robin Roberts. "The Woman Scientist in *Star Trek: Voyager*." Marleen S. Barr, ed., *Future Females: The Next Generation*. Lanham, MD: Rowman and Littlefield Publishers, 2000, 277–290.

Robin Roberts. "Science, Race, and Gender in *Star Trek: Voyager*." Elyce Rae Helford, ed., *Fantasy Girls*. Lanham, MD: Rowman and Littlefield Publishers, 2000, 203–221.

Jon Wagner and Jan Lundeen. *Deep Space and Sacred Time*. Westport, CT: Praeger, 1998.

Gary Westfahl. "Janeways and Thaneways." *Interzone*, No. 140 (February, 1999), 31–33.

—*Lincoln Geraghty*

STAR WARS (1977)

May the Force be with you.

—George Lucas
Star Wars (1977)

Summary

Luke Skywalker learns that his new "droid" R2D2, a **robot**, once belonged to Obi-Wan Kenobi; Luke finds Obi-Wan, discovers that Princess Leia placed plans for the Empire's most destructive battleship, the Death Star, into R2D2, and learns that Darth Vader, Obi-Wan's former **apprentice**, killed his **father** (see **Family**). Obi-Wan teaches Luke about the **Force**, a mystical energy field, and gives him his father's light saber (see **Swords**), the **weaponry** of a Jedi Knight. After Luke's aunt and uncle are killed by imperial stormtroopers, Luke and Obi-Wan hire smugglers Han Solo and Chewbacca to take them to Alderaan to deliver the plans to the Rebel Alliance. Although their ship, the *Millennium Falcon*, is caught by the Death Star's tractor beam, they elude capture; as Obi-Wan disables the tractor beam, Luke and Han rescue Princess Leia. Later, Luke sees Darth Vader kill Obi-Wan. The rebels **escape**, bringing the Death Star plans to the Rebel Alliance (see **Rebellion**). Prior to the attack against the Death Star, Han Solo leaves to pay off his debts, but as Luke makes his final run against the Death Star, Han returns to knock Darth Vader off his tail, and Luke uses the Force to fire the shot that destroys the Death Star.

Discussion

Star Wars opened in 1977 to near universal acclaim by critics and record box office success. Coming shortly after the Watergate scandal and the Vietnam War, *Star Wars* offered a welcome bit of escape from real life and a clear battle of good versus **evil**. The opening words of the film—"A long time ago in a galaxy far, far away"—echo the traditional **fairy tale** beginning, "once upon a time." Indeed, *Star Wars* has all the elements of traditional fairy tales: a young **hero**, a **quest**, a **mentor**, a beautiful princess and an evil enemy. The plot pits Luke Skywalker and his friends in the Rebel Alliance against the Empire (see **Galactic Empire**), a totalitarian regime that rules by fear and force, led by the Emperor and his disciple, Darth Vader.

Luke's quest takes him on a journey not only across the galaxy but also ultimately into his own past and future. On the way to Alderaan, Obi-Wan Kenobi explains that the Force—energy produced by all living things flowing into, through, and around everything in the universe—can be controlled by freeing one's conscious mind and feeling the Force flowing through. Han Solo, on the other hand, places no faith in "ancient weapons and hokey religions" and says there is no all-powerful Force guiding his actions. Rather, he trusts in blasters, advanced **technology**, and individual **freedom**. In the end, it is a mixture of individual freedom (Han's decision to return), technology (Luke's X-wing fighter), and faith in the Force (Luke's turning off the targeting computer and trusting the Force) that enables Luke to destroy the Death Star.

Destiny is significant in the *Star Wars* films. In *The Empire Strikes Back* (1980), Darth Vader (whose name can be read as Darth=dearth, Vader=Dutch for **father**) provides Luke with significant new information: the Force is strong within Luke; Darth Vader is actually Luke's father; it is Luke's destiny to destroy the Emperor; the Emperor, foreseeing this, wishes to kill Luke, though Darth Vader instead wishes to recruit him to the Dark Side. Rather than joining Darth Vader, however, Luke flees. In *Return of the Jedi* (1983), after Luke returns to his mentor Yoda and becomes a full-fledged Jedi Knight, he surrenders to Vader and the Emperor to keep his friends out of jeopardy. Luke, using the Force, senses Darth Vader's feelings and tells him that he (Luke) can feel that there is still good in him. Vader's reply, that it is too late for him, implies that, though he might wish to return to the good side of the Force, he is beyond redemption. Later, when Luke is being tortured by the Emperor (see **Torture**), he calls out to Vader for help. As the camera focuses on Vader turning from the Emperor to Luke, the audience senses that Vader is consumed by an inner struggle, so it comes as no surprise when he destroys the Emperor. Luke's appeal to the good buried within him enables Vader to overcome the Dark Side and again become Anakin Skywalker in his dying moments. Thus, Vader's comment and the Emperor's foreknowledge about Luke's destiny are both correct, though not in the way they meant.

Years after completing the third *Star Wars* film, George Lucas returned to the series to launch a three-film prequel to explain the events leading up to the original *Star Wars* film, now frequently described as *Episode Four: A New Hope*. *The Phantom Menace* (1999) tells the story of young Anakin Skywalker, who was born without a father and who, at the age of ten, is so strong with the Force that Qui-Gon Jinn, Obi-Wan's mentor, believes he may be the one prophesied to bring balance to the Force. After Qui-Gon's death, Obi-Wan takes Anakin as his **apprentice**, training him to be a Jedi Knight. In *Attack of the Clones* (2002), Anakin secretly falls in **love** with and weds Padmé Amidala and begins his transformation into Darth Vader by killing the Sand People who captured and killed his **mother**. A final film, *Revenge of the Sith* (2005), completes the story of Annakin's descent into the Dark Side and leads up to the scenario of the first film.

Bibliography

Laurent Bouzereau. *Star Wars: The Annotated Screenplays*. New York: Ballantine, 1997.

Ted Edwards. *The Unauthorized Star Wars Compendium*. Boston: Little, Brown, 1999.

Steven A. Galipeau. *The Journey of Luke Skywalker*. Chicago: Open Court Press, 2001.

Andrew Gordon. "*Star Wars*: Myth for Our Time." *Literature and Film*, 6 (Fall, 1978), 314–326.

Koenraad Kuiper. "*Star Wars*: An Imperial Myth." *Journal of Popular Culture*, 21 (Spring, 1988), 77–86.

Daniel Mackay. "*Star Wars*: The Magic of the Anti-Myth." *Foundation*, No. 76 (Summer, 1999), 63–75.

Doris Robin, Lee Vibber, and G.F. Elwood. *In a Faraway Galaxy*. Pasadena, CA: Extequer Press, 1984.

J.P. Telotte. "The Dark Side of the Force." *Extrapolation*, 24 (Fall, 1983), 216–226.

R.L. Velasco. *Guide to the Star Wars Universe*. New York: Ballantine, 1984.

—*Theodore James Sherman*

STARGATE (1994)

Summary

Archaeologists digging on the Giza Plateau in 1928 discover a **ring**-shaped device made of a metal not found on **Earth**, inscribed with strange symbols. Several decades later, Egyptologist Daniel Jackson, a genius ostracized because he believes that the pyramids predate Egyptian **civilization** (see **Egypt**), is hired by the Air Force to translate the symbols, which prove to be the coordinates of a distant world. Jackson travels through the "stargate" along with a military team led by suicidal Special Forces Colonel Jack O'Neill. They make contact with humans descended from ancient Egyptians transported to the planet by an alien posing as the god Ra. O'Neill and Jackson help the natives gain their **freedom** and destroy the alien; while O'Neill returns to Earth, Jackson stays behind to marry a native woman and teach people about their **history**.

In 1997, the film was adapted as a television series, *Stargate SG-1* (1997–), by Brad Wright and Jonathan Glassner, who had worked on the new *The Outer Limits*. In the series, O'Neill and Jackson are joined by Captain Samantha Carter, a brilliant astrophysicist, and alien defector Teal'c, in ongoing efforts to free humans across the galaxy from oppression by a parasitical race.

Discussion

Many films by Dean Devlin and Roland Emmerich explore the tension between science and the military, represented in *Stargate* by the characters of Jackson and O'Neill. The first half of the film centers on research into the stargate by **scientists**, who learn the device can transport people across the galaxy, forming wormholes that allow for almost instantaneous **teleportation**. However, they cannot use the stargate until Jackson's expertise in **languages and linguistics** enables him to decipher the symbols that form the address of another world.

A military reconnaissance team is sent to the alien **desert** world, evocative of Egypt, complete with a pyramid. They make **first contact** with the natives, whose leader sees the medallion that Jackson wears, found with the stargate, and believes it to be an **omen and sign** that he is sent by the god Ra (see **Gods and Goddesses**). At first, **communication** is difficult, until Jackson realizes that the natives are speaking a dead language; they are descendants of ancient Egyptians but unaware of their own history, as **reading** has been forbidden. Jackson teaches the leader's daughter about the **rebellion** of her ancestors; she shares this **knowledge** with young men of the village. As is common in narratives of **race relations**, natives receive the power of knowledge from white representatives of **civilization**, in this case soldiers and scientists of **America**.

Ra's arrival in a spaceship transforms the **heroes** into underdogs. O'Neill and his soldiers are captured, and Jackson is killed, although he is revived in a sarcophagus (see **Rebirth**). He speaks with Ra, an **alien in space** who has possessed the body of a young Egyptian man for nearly 10,000 years (see **Immortality and Longevity**). The depiction of Ra's court draws on familiar cinematic imagery of Egypt as a land of cruel oppression and **decadence**; Ra maintains a **class system**, using superior **technology** for his pleasure while forcing natives to use primitive tools. With the help of newly empowered young men, O'Neill and Jackson **escape**, leading the natives in their bid for freedom from **slavery** and killing Ra with **nuclear power**. The combination of western science and American military destroys the threat posed by the alien and frees the racialized Other from oppression and superstition.

In the television series (1997–), Jackson discovers a **map** of a stargate network, enabling the newly formed Stargate Command to send teams throughout the galaxy to find advanced **weaponry** to aid in the **war** against the Goa'uld, intelligent **parasites** who use humans as hosts (see **Snakes and Worms**). During their **exploration**, they encounter technologically superior races who see twentieth-century humans as primitive but full of potential, as in "The Fifth Race" (1999) or "The Nox" (1997). Unlike the Federation in *Star Trek*, Stargate Command does not follow a Prime Directive, and contact with less advanced cultures sometimes leads to **disaster**, as in "One False Step" (1999) and "Red Sky" (2001). In both types of encounter, unearned technological advancement poses a threat.

Aside from references to world **mythology**, the series makes use of established science fiction themes. The team discovers that the stargate can be used for **time travel** in "1969" (1999) and "2010" (2001), an homage to Arthur C. Clarke's novels (see *2001: A Space Odyssey*). In "A Matter of Time" (1999) the stargate connects to a planet caught in a **black hole**, while **parallel worlds** are explored in "There But for the Grace of God" (1998) and "Point of View" (1999). In the seventh season finale, "The Lost City" (2004) of **Atlantis** becomes the basis for a spin-off series, *Stargate: Atlantis* (2004–); the team's relationships and adventures have also been continued by fans writing fan fiction. That characters maintain strong bonds of **friendship** despite being on opposing sides in ongoing debates between the military and scientists explains why *Stargate* has such a devoted fan following.

Bibliography

Gary L. Bennett. "Stargate: Fact or Fiction?" *Ad Astra*, 7 (July-August, 1995), 44–48.

John C. Eisele. "The Wild East." *Cinema Journal*, 41 (2002), 68–94.

P.N. Elrod and Roxanne Conrad, eds. *Stepping Through the Stargate*. Dallas, TX: BenBella Books, 2004.

Dennis Fischer. "*Lawrence of Arabia* Meets *Star Wars* in *Stargate*." *Science Fiction Age*, 2 (September, 1994), 18–24.

Margaret Malamud. "Pyramids in Las Vegas and in Outer Space." *Journal of Popular Culture*, 34 (Summer, 2001), 31–47.

Christine Scodari. "Resistance Re-Examined." *Popular Communication*, 1 (2003), 111–130.

Keith Topping. *Beyond the Gate*. Tolworth, UK: Telos, 2002.

Mark C. Vaz. "Through the Stargate." *Cinefex*, No. 61 (March, 1995), 82–97.

Hernan Vera and Andrew Gordon. *Screen Saviors*. Lanham, MD: Rowman & Littlefield, 2003.

—Christine Mains

THE STARS MY DESTINATION
BY ALFRED BESTER (1956)

This was a Golden Age, a time of high adventure, rich living, and hard dying . . . but nobody thought so. This was a future of fortune and theft, pillage and

> *rapine, culture and vice . . . but nobody admitted it.*
>
> —Alfred Bester
> *The Stars My Destination* (1956)

Summary

This seminal novel tells of the **revenge** of Gully Foyle, the three women who change his life, and his spectacular transformation of **humanity**. Gully is a brutish crewman whose spaceship is wrecked (see **Space Travel**). Another **rocket**, the *Vorga*, approaches but abandons him. Driven by rage to discover his hitherto latent ambitions and **intelligence**, Gully reaches an asteroid (see **Comets and Asteroids**) where atavistic colonists tattoo his face with a *moko* tiger mask. Eventually, he returns to Earth a wealthy man, determined to destroy the *Vorga*'s crew for leaving him to die. In doing so, he will take advantage of his **psychic power** of **teleportation**, here called "jaunting," which allows residents of the twenty-fifth century to instantly travel up to 1000 miles away.

Foyle meets beautiful, black Robin Wednesbury, whom he blackmails into helping him against billionaire Presteign, owner of the *Vorga*. Imprisoned (after attacking Presteign's estate) in the nightmarish Gouffre Martel (see **Prisons**), Foyle meets beautiful redhead Jisbella McQueen, with whom he **escapes**. Jisbella and Robin socialize Foyle, teaching him to read, manage his fortune, and speak with sophistication; but they hate Foyle for his obsessive, vengeful **quest**. Jisbella arranges for his facial tattoo to be removed, but its outline manifests whenever he grows angry, making him look like a "tiger-man." Gully falls in **love** with a third woman, beautiful albino **temptress** Olivia Presteign, although her father is his prey.

Discussion

The Stars My Destination is distinguished, among other features, by Bester's authorial energy, flashy style, knowledge of **psychology**, thoughtful **ethics**, transcendent ending, and unforgettable antihero, all creating an enduring **sense of wonder**. *Stars* is also literarily allusive, primarily to Alexandre Dumas's classic story of revenge and **secret identity**, *Le Comte de Monte-Cristo* (1844), but also to William Blake, whose "The Tyger" (1794) gave the novel its original British title, *Tiger! Tiger!*, which some argue better describes the metaphysics at work in the novel than the recasting of Stephen Dedalus's chant from James Joyce's *Portrait of the Artist as a Young Man* (1916), its better-known American title.

The novel is almost a **Bildungsroman**; Gully matures from the mechanic's mate who famously growls, "*Vorga*, I kill you filthy." Although he rapes, murders, and tortures (after being himself subjected to **torture**), his **courage** and **wisdom** grow as he seeks to avenge his **betrayal**, and he exhorts several crowds to **rebellion** against supercilious corporations. *Stars* is populated by hyperreal **heroes** and **villains** (Bester previously wrote for comic books, and the influence is evident), like lawyer Saul Dagenham, who is radioactively toxic to all he touches. Jaunting in particular makes characters seem like **superheroes**.

The **civilization** that Gully traverses, in **disguise** as parvenu Geoffrey Fourmyle, is bizarre and colorful. Megalomaniacs oppress the masses (**governance systems** are based on **social Darwinism**). The corporate heirs ruling the world gallivant about like Renaissance princes. The poor resort to "jack-jaunting" (see **Theft**) and **violence** to survive. As a **satire** against authoritarianism, the novel succeeds brilliantly. Gully travels with the Fourmyle Circus, a troupe of entertainers (see **Clowns and Fools**) invited to perform for the pretentious. It is amid such elegant **decadence** that Gully engineers Presteign's downfall.

The rapid, exciting pace of the novel is partly due to Bester's inventiveness in regards to social change, gadgetry, and expansion of the mental **frontier**, all of which accredit him as the primary progenitor of **cyberpunk**. For example, Gully cyborgizes himself with technological enhancements that accelerate his movements by a factor of five (see **Cyborgs**), enabling him to become a killing machine when necessary—as when **Jupiter and the Outer Planets** launch a **space war** against **Earth**. Foyle is also distinguished by his unwitting possession of the superweapon called PyrE and another singular talent, the ability to jaunt across interplanetary and even interstellar space.

Stars is innovative in other ways. It features a black woman and Chinese man as major characters; **race relations** are healthy in Bester's future. An intriguing element is the mysterious "Burning Man," Foyle's time travelling future self, who appears at critical moments (see **Time Travel**). The novel also contains a welter of typographical experimentation at the climax, when Gully endures an assault of synaesthesia (see **Perception**).

Gully is nefarious, but in Bester's capable hands he becomes a delightful force for advancement in human **knowledge**. He suffers as much as the characters whom he abuses—more so, because ultimately he loathes himself and seeks redemption (see **Guilt and Responsibility**). Bester's jocularity and fondness for wordplay redeem the grim incidents he describes. The pyrotechnic finale is unequalled in science fiction for sheer ebullience.

Bester, like Gully a delighter in **fire**, fights, and rebellion, hurled himself into the unknown like a burning spear. Due to his ambition, skill, and wild talent, science fiction was thrust boldly forward through an innovative, enduring work of the imagination.

Bibliography

Alfred Bester. "My Affair with Science Fiction." Brian W. Aldiss and Harry Harrison, eds., *Hell's Cartographers*. London: Weidenfeld and Nicholson, 1975, 46–75.

William Godshalk. "Alfred Bester." *Extrapolation*, 16 (May, 1975), 149–155.

Fiona Kelleghan. "Hell's My Destination." *Science-Fiction Studies*, 21 (November, 1994), 351–364.

Patrick McCarthy. "Science Fiction as Creative Revisionism." *Science-Fiction Studies*, 10 (1983), 58–69.

Charles Platt. "Alfred Bester." Platt, ed., *Dream Makers*. New York: Berkley, 1980, 93–102.

Charles Platt. "Attack-Escape." Michael Moorcock, ed., *New Worlds Quarterly, Volume 4*. London: Sphere, 1972, 210–220.

Darrell Schweitzer. "Alfred Bester." Schweitzer, ed., *Science Fiction Voices*. San Bernardino, Calif.: Borgo, 1979, 18–25.

Paul Walker. "Alfred Bester." Paul Walker, ed., *Speaking of Science Fiction*. Oradell, NJ: Luna, 1978, 302–314.

Carolyn Wendell. *Alfred Bester*. San Bernardino, CA: Borgo Press, 1982.

—Fiona Kelleghan

STARSHIP TROOPERS
BY ROBERT A. HEINLEIN (1959)

———————————————■———————————————

Anyone who clings to the historically untrue—and thoroughly immoral—doctrine that "violence never settles anything" I would advise to conjure up the ghosts of Napoleon Bonaparte and of the Duke of Wellington and let them debate it. The ghost of Hitler could referee, and the jury might well be the Dodo, the Great Auk, and the Passenger Pigeon. Violence, naked force, has settled more issues in history than has any other factor, and the contrary opinion is wishful thinking at its worst. Breeds that forget this basic truth have always paid for it with their lives and freedoms.

—Robert A. Heinlein
Starship Troopers (1959)

Summary

As Johnnie Rico, son of wealthy parents, graduates from high school, his friend Carl joins the armed forces, inspiring Johnnie to follow suit. Johnnie becomes a member of the Mobile Infantry (space marines) as humanity begins a **space war** against an **insect** alien **hive mind** known simply as "the Bugs." Members of the Mobile Infantry are known both for their toughness and the armored suits that enclose their bodies, which allow them to fight in almost all conditions (vacuum, hostile atmospheres), magnify physical strength (wearers can almost fly), and protect them from their own nuclear weapons. Johnnie comes to believe that military honor is the most important thing one can earn, and his **culture**, which allows only veterans of government service to vote, agrees. In his high school "History and Moral Philosophy" classes and during training, Johnnie and his fellow troopers have extended discussions about the individual's personal and public responsibilities. As a successful junior officer, Johnnie believes that only free-willed human individuals can defeat the Bugs' "ant-like communism." Johnnie's example causes his **father** to reject his complacent life and join the Mobile Infantry. Now a commander, Johnnie and his father fight together in the apparently endless Bug war.

Discussion

Starship Troopers has been and continues to be both immensely popular and problematic. Its filming by Paul Verhoeven in 1997, the 2004 sequel *Starship Troopers 2: Hero of the Federation*, and the 35-episode animated television series *Roughnecks:*

The Starship Trooper Chronicles (1999) have widened its audience. The book is a **Bildungsroman** similar to Heinlein's other "juvenile" novels (like *Have Space Suit—Will Travel* [1958]), but its overt **politics** and military theme were considered by the regular publisher of his juveniles, Scribner's, to be too mature for **children**. *Starship Troopers* launches a debate about the military and **war** in the future that continues in Joe Haldeman's *The Forever War*, Jerry Pournelle's *The Mercenary* (1977), John Steakley's *Armor* (1984), Orson Scott Card's *Ender's Game*, and Sheri S. Tepper's *The Gate to Women's Country*. Although the novel features contact with **aliens in space**, the aliens (both "Skinnies" and the "Bugs") are never developed into more than military targets.

At the novel's forefront is the discussion of the citizen's duties. Heinlein uses Socratic dialogues between **youth** (Johnnie and friends) and two Mobile Infantry father figures to outline a society dedicated to individual rights and **community** loyalty. In science fiction the hive mind often acts as a cold war sign for Communism, as in Heinlein's *The Puppet Masters* (1951), *Invasion of the Body Snatchers*, and *Aliens* (1986) (see *Alien*): Heinlein's Bugs care nothing for individual purpose, emotion, or life. Because of the book's attack on Communism and romanticization of the military, it has been seized on by various political groups. It has been interpreted as a libertarian manifesto enshrining above all the individual's rights; a fascist document valorizing the *übermensch*; and an explanation for **America**'s colonial wars. *Starship Trooper's* proponents see in it a chance for universal citizenship: the present **class system** can be destroyed if the key to **politics** and power is that one volunteers one's life.

Another key issue is the use of military force. Heinlein's troopers argue consistently that a **civilization** can and will survive only when it is vigilant about its rights and prepared to go to war and die for them. Johnnie is portrayed as an Everyman who, like the reader (presumably), must be shown the truth about **governance systems** and civil society. A series of historical military examples is given to prove points about civilization, culminating with America's then-recent participation in the undeclared Korean War. Johnnie accepts that culture and war are co-created, and neither can exist without the other. Military force is embodied in the Mobile Infantry's powered armor, which reappears in Haldeman's *The Forever War*. The armored shell, representing the hostility of the universe against which humans must protect themselves, is testament to human ingenuity and the miracle of the apes-turned-tool-users who successfully climbed the family tree to prosper and spread. The suits argue for **social Darwinism**.

Finally, Heinlein deals with the interconnected issues of **gender** and **family**. While women are combatants in the Bug war because of their apparently intuitive ability to fly spacecraft (Heinlein's prediction of female air force pilots predated American women climbing into cockpits), they are also treated with a sort of nineteenth-century romantic idealism that sees them as finer and better creatures than the "apes" (as the sergeants call the troops) staffing the Mobile Infantry. Because he will not initially take up arms and earn the rights of a true citizen, Johnnie's father is depicted as henpecked and effeminate, worse off than Johnnie's neurotic society **mother**. The novel is a hymn of praise to fathers, sons, and the pure souls who are good women. *Starship Troopers* is militarist and intolerant, and while it appears to be a discussion, it really has only one conclusion: that war provides the best and only way to live, and to die.

Bibliography

Everett C. Dolman. "Military, Democracy, and the State in Robert A. Heinlein's *Starship Troopers.*" Donald M. Hassler and Clyde Wilcox, eds., *Political Science Fiction.* Columbia: University of South Carolina Press, 1997, 196–213.

H. Bruce Franklin. *Robert A. Heinlein.* New York: Oxford, 1980.

A.C. Garr. "The Human as Machine Analog." Joseph D. Olander and Martin H. Greenberg, eds., *Robert A. Heinlein.* New York: Taplinger, 1978, 64–82.

Steffen Hantke. "Surgical Strikes and Prosthetic Warriors." *Science-Fiction Studies,* 25 (November, 1998), 495–509.

Robert James. "The Age of Reasoning." *Heinlein Journal,* No. 8 (January, 2001), 38–42.

K.A. MacDermott. "Ideology and Narrative." *Extrapolation,* 23 (Fall, 1982), 254–269.

Alexei Panshin. *Heinlein in Dimension.* Chicago: Advent, 1968.

D.E. Showalter. "Heinlein's *Starship Troopers.*" *Extrapolation,* 16 (May, 1975), 113–124.

Alasdair Spark. "The Art of Future War." Tom Shippey, ed., *Fictional Space.* Atlantic Highlands, NJ: Humanities Press, 1991, 133–165.

—*Tim Blackmore*

STARTIDE RISING BY DAVID BRIN (1983)

Summary

In **humanity's far future,** the spacecraft *Streaker* is crewed almost entirely by uplifted dolphins (see **Fish and Sea Creatures; Uplift**), though humans and an uplifted **ape** are also on board. The story concerns their harrowing **escape** from the starships of the Five Galaxies races as they try to protect a startling discovery: the hulks of ships hidden away for millennia, which are probably evidence of the earliest race, the Progenitors. The sequel *The Uplift War* (1987) continues the story of humans attempting to escape aliens' battles for ascendancy over one another on a broader scale. The books of the New Uplift trilogy—*Brightness Reef* (1995), *Infinity's Shore* (1996) and *Heavens Reach* (1998)—are set on one planet, Jijo, and bring together myriad races, including some of the earliest in the Uplift universe, detailing strategies for **survival** adopted by races uplifted over the eons and putting humans in contact with even more ancient intergalactic **civilizations.**

Discussion

Brin's Uplift series actually began with the little-noted *Sundiver* (1980), a **space opera** about humans' early interactions with **aliens in space** taking place over two hundred years before the other Uplift novels. At this point, humans are new to interstellar society, with alien visitors sequestered in protective reservations on **Earth,** and they are only beginning to understand **intelligence** as they struggle to uplift dolphins and chimpanzees and fit into and protect themselves from a federation of aliens (see **Galactic Empire**) eons older than humans, with vast experience in uplifting other races. In *Sundiver,* humans foil the attempt of one alien race to embarrass their uplifters and force humans into a client status. However, *Startide Rising* brought the series wide popularity and was hailed as a masterpiece.

A dominant theme is Brin's concept of uplift, the notion that one race of sentient beings has the right and responsibility to select other races and make them intelligent according to their standards. Unfortunately, this is often done more for the convenience of the uplifters than the benefit of the uplifted. In these novels, there were originally five alien races that uplifted other races, which in turn uplifted other races. However, instead of invariably progressing to independence, second-level races may remain clients for as long as their uplifters require, in some cases probably forever. What seems like a benign and beneficial idea—raising animals to the status of civilized, sentient beings—can become an endless **Hell** for those animals, in obvious parallels to shameful historical treatments of colonized or aboriginal peoples (see **Race Relations**).

Several Uplift stories are set on **water** worlds or feature sea creatures, demonstrating Brin's extensive interest in and knowledge of experiments involving the intelligence of dolphins and whales; for example, *Startide Rising* involves a water-dominated planet where humans, uplifted dolphins, and orcas struggle for survival against older alien races trying to find the abandoned ships. Since characters in this space adventure are mostly dolphins, and humans have adapted to living with dolphins in ships, the evolution of these **cultures** recall evolutionary theories about human origins in Earth's oceans (see **Evolution**).

First contact with aliens is also complicated by uplift. Aliens who contact humanity are of three types: members of the Five Galaxies (and eight others who hid themselves away in the distant past); members of races they have uplifted to sentience, usually in an "indentured" status to pay off the debt incurred by uplift; and a few immensely old alien races of which little is revealed. It cannot be said that human contact with aliens is always improving, but that contact puts in stark relief historical **tragedies** of racism, **sexism**, ethnocentrism, and appalling treatment of animals. In *Sundiver*, for instance, human fears of alien client status are mirrored by questions about the **ethics** of transforming dolphins and whales so they are more intelligent. In its sequels, the potential for mistreating uplifted species is explored in detail. While a Galactic Council is supposed to protect client races, enforcement is inadequate, as humans in *Startide Rising* and the New Uplift Trilogy woefully discover.

The dark side of uplift destroys rosy **illusions** about benign galactic empires. In Brin's series, the Five Galaxies Civilizations constantly **war** with each other and with client races. They may have evolved methods of traveling through interstellar space and preserving life, but they have also killed off entire client races, held others in **slavery**, and worked to confuse their own origins. Uplift stories allude to this violent past. The planet Kithrup in *Startide Rising* is inhabited by a client race so abused by its uplifters that the Galactic Council gave them an embargoed planet to themselves. The planet JiJo in the New Uplift Trilogy is a hideout for six client races trying to escape servitude that have evolved a complicated religious and social structure to hide their settlements while having a minimum impact on the planet's environment. Their **religion** is built around fears of a "judgment day" when they will be discovered by their galactic masters.

Yet each novel is also an adventure story full of space opera conventions. There are easily identifiable **heroes** and **villains** as well as unexpected discoveries hinging upon both powers of reasoning and the **courage** and adaptability especially attributed to humans. Brin's voyages of research, experimentation, and **exploration** are also opportunities for speculations in **hard science fiction**. **Physics**, astronomy, chemistry, genetics, **biology**, and **ecology** are subjects in numerous lectures, reports, and conversations. Brin conveys a **sense of wonder** in depicting exotic **alien worlds**, races, and **governance systems**. Readers can further appreciate references to authors like Aldous Huxley, Jules Verne, Mark Twain, and other science fiction writers and traditions that Brin self-consciously draws upon in crafting these future worlds.

Bibliography

Greg Bear, Gregory Benford, and David Brin. "Building on Isaac Asimov's Foundation." *Science Fiction Studies*, 24 (March, 1997), 17–32.

David Brin. "The Profession of Science Fiction." *Foundation*, No. 39 (Spring, 1987), 21–26.

David Brin and Kevin Lenagh. *Contacting Aliens*. New York: Bantam, 2002.

L.W. Currey. "Work in Progress: David Brin." *New York Review of Science Fiction*, No. 9 (May, 1989), 22.

Oscar De Los Santos. "Of Dystopias and Icons." Martha Barter, ed., *The Utopian Fantastic*. Westport, CT: Praeger, 2004, 109–122.

Thomas R. McDonough and David Brin. "The Bubbling Universe." *Omni*, 15 (October, 1992), 84–90.

Sandy Moltz. "Forging Futures with Teens and Science Fiction." *Voice of Youth Advocates*, 26 (April, 2003), 15–18.

Stan Nicholls. "David Brin Won't Cop the Rap." Nicholls, *Worldsmiths of Wonder*. London: Orbit, 1993, 33–42.

—Janice M. Bogstad

THE STORY OF DOCTOR DOLITTLE BY HUGH LOFTING (1920)

Summary

John Dolittle, a doctor in a small British town, begins running out of human patients as his house becomes increasingly populated with animals (see **Animals and Zoos**). His parrot (see **Birds**), Polynesia, convinces him to learn the language of animals and become an animal doctor instead (see **Language and Linguistics**). Although well-liked (if not well-paid) by animals in Puddleby-on-the-Marsh, he leaves Britain to find a cure for an epidemic that is killing off monkeys in **Africa**. He is welcomed by the monkeys (see **Apes**), but Dolittle and his animal companions are forbidden passage to the monkey country by the tribal leader of the fictional country of Jolliginki. Polynesia helps them **escape** from **prison**, and Dolittle is able to save the monkeys. However, they face further trials returning **home**, as they must once again cross Jolliginki and battle **pirates** near the Canary Islands. Due to his unique ability to communicate with animals, Dolittle surmounts all difficulties and returns to his practice in

Puddleby-on-the-Marsh. The series continues with more adventures, where Dolittle is again joined by Polynesia, Dab-Dab the duck, Gub-Gub the pig, and Jip the **dog**, as well as—starting in *The Voyages of Doctor Dolittle* (1922)—his young human companion, Tommy Stubbins. Other volumes are *Dr. Dolittle's Post Office* (1923), *Dr. Dolittle's Circus* (1924), *Dr. Dolittle's Zoo* (1925), *Dr. Dolittle's Caravan* (1926), *Dr. Dolittle's Garden* (1927), *Dr. Dolittle in the Moon* (1928), *Dr. Dolittle's Return* (1933), *Dr. Dolittle and the Secret Lake* (1948), *Dr. Dolittle and the Green Canary* (1950), and *Dr. Dolittle's Puddleby Adventures* (1952).

Discussion

Doctor Dolittle is perhaps the most famous human ever to take care of sick animals, yet he disdains veterinarian **medicine**. His ability comes, not from observing animals, but through **communication** with them. All animals, Polynesia tells him, are **talking animals**, but humans are too stupid to bother to learn their languages. Because Dolittle makes the effort, not only does he become the best animal doctor in the world, but he also gains their trust and help throughout his adventures. Animals, in the Doctor Dolittle series, are constantly placed in a privileged position over humans. Dolittle gives up human medicine for animals without a second thought; his sister leaves because he will not give up a crocodile when she asks him to; and human communication is not seen as an interesting challenge compared to languages of shellfish or **Moon** vegetation. When Dolittle faces conflict with other humans, he often resorts to trickery, not negotiation, to resolve it.

This disinterest in humans suggests the perceived failure of **civilization** in general—Dolittle and his animal friends find the economic system of exchanging goods for **money** unreasonable. The educational system is also mocked. Tommy has no formal schooling, Dolittle is trained for the wrong career, and Prince Bumpo learns the art of malapropism at Oxford. Real **education**, the books suggest, is achieved through discovery and **exploration**, not sitting in a classroom. Dolittle's travels begin as **games**—Tommy picks a random spot in the atlas to travel to—but proceed and conclude with increased **knowledge** that benefits all humankind.

Many books focus on Dolittle's **sea travel** to Africa and various **islands** to examine the flora and fauna abroad. While some critics argue this is an imperialist attitude of treating colonized areas as vast storehouses for the benefit of the colonizers, akin to Joseph Conrad's "Heart of Darkness" (1899) (see **Postcolonialism**), Lofting actually displays a positive image of uncivilized areas, giving the books a **pastoral** quality. Although representations of people of color are far from unproblematic (see **Race Relations**), it is important to note that it is only when people in these countries have had contact with Britain that they become corrupt and dissatisfied with themselves and their lot. Again, the Doctor Dolittle books argue that human—particularly British—civilization has made things worse rather than better, and that to redeem ourselves we must look to other (particularly animal) societies.

If the Doctor Dolittle books indicated that the doctor was the only human who could understand animal language, the books might suggest a feeling of hopelessness with and for **humanity**. However, hope can be found in **children**. Tommy, the boy that Dolittle **mentors**, also learns to talk to animals and is useful in communicating Dolittle's pro-animal, environmentally sound manifestos, suggesting that there is hope in future generations. Dolittle looks on Tommy as part of his **family**, a term that is broadly defined in the series. Dolittle is the head of his family, but all other members contribute to its welfare according to their abilities, whether animal or human. Thus, when he is briefly elected **king** of the Popsipetel tribe, Dolittle considers all its members as part of his family for whom he is responsible. While this again can be seen as an imperialist, patriarchal version of the family, not to mention the British Empire, Lofting clearly conveys that *all* members of a family contribute to all others, and Dolittle accepts new knowledge from his "children" as easily as he imparts it. Lofting's Doctor Dolittle series imparts an understanding of interconnectedness through its fantastic journeys, and this remains its lasting legacy.

Lofting's hero has occasionally appeared on screen: a German silent cartoon, *Doctor Dolittle und Seine Tiere* (1928); a lavish but unsuccessful musical adaptation starring Rex Harrison, *Doctor Dolittle* (1967); two animated television series (*Doctor Dolittle* [1970–1972] and *The Voyages of Doctor Dolittle* [1984]); and two films starring Eddie Murphy (*Doctor Dolittle* [1998] and *Doctor Dolittle 2* [2001]) that had little to do with the original series except a doctor (now in contemporary **America**) who talks to animals.

Bibliography

Edward Blishen. *Hugh Lofting*. London: Bodley Head, 1968.

Margaret Blount. "If Only They Could Speak." Blount, *Animal Land*. New York: Avon, 1977, 191–207.

Anne Collett. "Sharing a Common Destiny." *New Literatures Review*, 33 (Summer, 1997), 81–93.

Helen Dean Fish. "Doctor Dolittle." Fish, *Horn Book Reflections: On Children's Books and Reading*. Boston: Horn Book, 1969, 218–224.

M. Daphne Kutzer. "Imperial Fantasies: Lofting and Milne." Kutzer, *Empire's Children*. New York: Garland, 2000, 79–106.

Mike Lyons. "*Doctor Dolittle*." *Cinefantastique*, 30 (July, 1998), 14–50.

Gary D. Schmidt. *Hugh Lofting*. New York: Twayne, 1992.

Estelle Shay. "*Dr. Dolittle*: Animals with Attitude." *Cinefex*, No. 75 (October, 1998), 35–48, 142.

—*Karen Sands-O'Connor*

STRANGE CASE OF DR. JEKYLL AND MR. HYDE BY ROBERT LOUIS STEVENSON (1886)

All human beings are commingled out of good and evil.

—Robert Louis Stevenson
Strange Case of Dr. Jekyll and Mr. Hyde
(1886)

Summary

Well-respected doctor Henry Jekyll has left a strange will with his friend, lawyer Utterson, a will which leaves everything to the mysterious Edward Hyde should Jekyll disappear. When Utterson hears of Hyde behaving abominably, trampling over a young girl, he decides to find out more. Jekyll is large, handsome, and fifty; Hyde is small and young, and everyone describes him as having an indefinable deformity, though we eventually realize this is a physical manifestation of a moral deformity. Then Hyde is witnessed beating a man to **death**; Utterson rushes to Jekyll, who seems ill and promises to have nothing further to do with Hyde. But Jekyll grows more solitary and curious in his habits, and eventually Utterson is called upon to break into Jekyll's laboratory when servants have not seen the doctor for some days. There Utterson finds the newly dead body of Hyde and two manuscripts. One, by mutual friend Dr. Lanyon, recounts Jekyll's use of **drugs**; the second is Jekyll's own confession, which finally describes his periodic transformations from Jekyll into Hyde.

Discussion

The double or **doppelgänger** is something of a feature of Calvinist fiction. It was there, significantly, in James Hogg's *Confessions of a Justified Sinner* (1824), and Stevenson was also familiar with the real case of Deacon Brodie, a respectable cabinet maker by day and notorious criminal by night. From Hogg and Brodie, Stevenson picked up on the idea that the double allowed him to illuminate the conflict between outward respectability and inner lusts and perversions (see **Sexuality**). The story started as a nightmare, what Stevenson called "a fine bogey tale," and he wrote a first draft immediately afterwards, but his wife Fanny felt it was a mere **horror** story and he could use the idea to say more about human nature. The way Stevenson expanded the original story to follow his wife's suggestions produced a tale so effectively highlighting the fallibility of human nature that it was by far his most successful work to date and was soon being mentioned in pulpits.

Most commentaries on the novel, and practically all dramatizations (see *Dr. Jekyll and Mr. Hyde*), have picked up on the transformation of Jekyll into Hyde, but few have paid attention to the fact that Jekyll was not changing but simply releasing something already inside him. We hear that he had a somewhat wild **youth**, and in the drugs he uses to liberate Hyde he finds a way to return to the guilt-less **freedom** of being young (see **Guilt and Responsibility**). This is not, as in Mary Shelley's *Frankenstein*, the creation of a **monster**, but the release of the **darkness** contained in everyone. Stevenson is careful to point out both the seductive pleasure represented by Hyde (Jekyll is an addict foreswearing Hyde again and again but helplessly called back), and also the fact that Jekyll feels imprisoned by his addiction.

There is clearly a **decadence** about Jekyll that suits the novel's **fin de siècle** mood, and Stevenson extends what is in Jekyll's soul to the whole of his society. A maid witnesses the murder, and a loyal butler summons Utterson to break into Jekyll's laboratory and find the body, but all other characters in this novella are educated middle-aged men of the same social class. They strive for respectability in all things (see **Class System**), so much so that when Hyde is seen to trample the girl the greatest sanction that can be levelled against him is that his name will be dragged through the mud. This is a threat that clearly cows Hyde. Though a **detective** is brought into the case briefly after the murder, there is never a suggestion that this might be a conventional story of **crime and punishment** with a judicial outcome. These are upright men, presented in all things as severe, unbending, and alone—no wives come into the story—and the release of Jekyll's inhibitions in the persona of Hyde is not to be seen as criminality but as social upheaval, a threat to the rigidity of their place in society, to their notions of **civilization**. Hyde's mental and moral darkness upsets the proper order of things as **barbarians** do, or more as **werewolves** do, rather than as a simple murderer does.

Two characters, Jekyll and Lanyon, are doctors, though they are presented more as **scientists** than as men of **medicine**. By tampering with drugs that effect his change, Jekyll is seen as a **mad scientist**, as Lanyon certainly argues, and the end of their **friendship** comes about because Jekyll espouses radical ideas. So Jekyll's fall from grace in the persona of Hyde represents an **allegory** of not just social disorder but intellectual disorder. Jekyll's disorder leads inevitably to his death because he has dared to question his **identity** as a member of his society, and the intellectual elite, and that questioning is more deadly than murder.

Bibliography

Jenni Calder. "Introduction." Robert Louis Stevenson, *Dr. Jekyll and Mr. Hyde and Other Stories*. Harmondsworth, Penguin, 1979, 7–23.

H.M. Geduld. *The Definitive Dr. Jekyll and Mr. Hyde Companion*, New York: Garland, 1983.

Mark Jancovich. "Identity and Repression in *Dr. Jekyll and Mr. Hyde*." Michael Stuprich, ed., *Horror*. San Diego, CA: Greenhaven Press, 2001, 143–147.

Donald L. Lawler. "Reframing Jekyll and Hyde." W. Veeder, ed., *Dr. Jekyll and Mr. Hyde After One Hundred Years*. Chicago: University of Chicago Press, 1988, 247–261.

Colin N. Manlove. "Closer Than the Eye." C.W. Sullivan, III, ed., *The Dark Fantastic*. Westport, CT: Greenwood Press, 1997, 3–14.

Lawrence McCallum. "The Many Faces of Evil." *Eldritch Tales*, 7 (1990), 31–36.

Raymond T. McNally and Radu Florescu. *In Search of Dr. Jekyll and Mr. Hyde*. Los Angeles: Renaissance Books, 2000.

John Pennington. "Textual Doubling and Divided Selves." *Journal of the Fantastic in the Arts*, 6 (1994), 203–216.

Susan J. Wolfson and Barry V. Qualls. "Tensions and Anxieties in *Dr. Jekyll and Mr. Hyde*." Michael Stuprich, ed., *Horror*. San Diego, CA: Greenhaven Press, 2001, 148–156.

—Paul Kincaid

STRANGER IN A STRANGE LAND BY ROBERT A. HEINLEIN (1961)

Once upon a time there was a Martian named Valentine Michael Smith.

—Robert A. Heinlein
Stranger in a Strange Land (1961)

Summary

Michael Valentine Smith is born to two members of the first expedition to **Mars** and raised by Martians after the expedition's demise. Discovered by the second expedition, Smith is returned to **Earth** in his mid-twenties. As a human raised by aliens, Smith has no **knowledge** of Earth or human customs; as sole survivor of the first expedition, he is heir to the space drive invented by his **mother** and, potentially, to Mars itself. The world government of Earth holds Smith in captivity, but he is freed by sympathetic nurse Jill Boardman and investigative reporter Ben Caxton (see **Journalism**), who hide him at the estate of Jubal Harshaw, a wealthy eccentric who is also a physician, attorney, and author. As Harshaw sorts out Smith's legal difficulties, he tutors the young man in the ways of **humanity**, and Smith, accompanied by Jill, eventually makes his way into the world, where he founds the Church of All Worlds, a **religion** based on Martian **philosophy** whose adherents practice **nudity** and group **marriage**. The Church inspires considerable opposition, and Smith is eventually killed by a mob. However, Smith has made an impact on society, and his Church, whose fundamental precept is "Thou art God," will clearly continue.

Discussion

Stranger in a Strange Land is one of a handful of novels, science fiction or otherwise, whose influence has been felt not just in fiction but society at large. Beyond winning the Hugo Award, it became the first science fiction novel to make the *New York Times* best-seller list; during the 1960s and 1970s, it gained cult status among members of the **youth** counterculture who appreciated its critique of western values, interrogation of religion, celebration of **sexuality**, and championing of "free love" and open marriage. The novel gained unwelcome notoriety when reports surfaced that it had influenced mass murderer Charles Manson—reports, which were later discredited; it also added a word to the language of 1960s youth **culture**—"grok," a Martian term meaning to understand fully.

 Stranger in a Strange Land attempts to knock over any number of sacred cows. As Plato to Harshaw's Socrates, Heinlein fills the novel with extended dialogues in which Harshaw puts to the test many of the other characters' basic assumptions concerning life, **love**, and proper conduct. Why is one religion preferable to another? Why should I care if you sleep with my spouse? Why should we feel compelled to wear clothes? What the novel's countercultural audience arguably failed to realize was the degree to which Heinlein's visions of guilt-free sex and non-hierarchical religion were based on the elite libertarianism that informs his later works. Anyone can join the Church of All Worlds, but to be admitted to the Inner Nest, one must learn the Martian language (see **Language and Linguistics**) and understand Martian philosophy. When fully in command of the powers taught him by Martian "Old Ones," Smith can perform miracles, including making things (and people) disappear; when he opens up jails, he does not hesitate to "discorporate" criminals whom he judges a clear danger to society. Group sex is cool, but only if you are Martian.

 Less commented upon is the degree to which Heinlein's novel offers not only a critique of western values but also an extended satirical commentary on American **politics** and society (see **America; Satire**). If the near-omniscient Harshaw can defend Mike against those who want to control him, it is thanks to his knowledge of politicians as individuals of varying degrees of **intelligence** and sincerity beholden to both their own self-interest and an elaborate code of manners—a code Harshaw understands flawlessly and manipulates at will. Equally important is Harshaw's canny sense of media; his use of a "panic button" that triggers television coverage of government officials invading his **home** is a striking forecast of the 24-hour cable news cycle of today (see **Television and Radio**). The summaries of news events that begin several chapters show a world where happenings of grave import vie for attention with preposterous outbursts of popular culture. Little wonder that Smith's martyrdom is broadcast live and frequently interrupted by **advertising**.

Despite its wide popularity and cultural impact, *Stranger in a Strange Land* has never enjoyed universal praise. Some view the novel's celebration of cheerful promiscuity as naïve at best and pernicious at worst, while others grow impatient with the novel's lack of formal rigor and Harshaw's ongoing lectures (a complaint intensified by 1991 publication of the "uncut" version of the novel, wherein his ramblings were even longer). Readers considering the book from a feminist perspective find it especially wanting (see **Feminism**). Although the book's female characters are resourceful, intelligent, and, eventually, sexually "liberated," they are also all, in the end, subservient to the **wisdom** of Harshaw and charismatic sexuality of Smith—as are, indeed, most male characters.

The novel is most affecting as an account of the **education** of Smith, an innocent whose factual knowledge does not yield true understanding until, witnessing a group of **apes** fighting in a zoo, he laughs for the first time. Although Smith's powers derive from his alien heritage, he yearns to understand and improve the human condition, and his libertarian elitism is tempered by a genuine desire for things to be better for everyone: "There's no *need* for them to be so unhappy." At its best, *Stranger in a Strange Land* remains a vivid argument for the possibility of radical change and social **progress**.

Bibliography

Russell Blackford. "Heinlein's Martian Named Smith." *New York Review of Science Fiction*, No. 181 (September, 2003), 1, 6–8.

Russell Blackford. "Neo-Bible and Ur-Text." *Foundation*, No. 53 (Autumn, 1991), 70–80.

Tim Blackmore. "Talking with Strangers." *Extrapolation*, 36 (Summer, 1995), 136–150.

R.L. Cansler. "*Stranger in a Strange Land*." *Journal of Popular Culture*, 5 (Spring, 1972), 944–954.

William H. Patterson, Jr. and Andrew Thronton. *The Martian Named Smith*. Citrus Heights, CA: Nutrosyncretic Press, 2001.

Robert Plank. "Omnipotent Cannibals in *Stranger in a Strange Land*." Joseph D. Olander and Martin H. Greenberg, eds., *Robert A. Heinlein*. New York: Taplinger, 1978, 83–106.

Shaun Reno. "The Zuni Indian Tribe: A Model for *Stranger in a Strange Land*'s Martian Culture." *Extrapolation*, 36 (Summer, 1995), 151–158.

David N. Samuelson. "Stranger in the Sixties" Dick Riley, ed., *Critical Encounters*. New York: Ungar, 1978, 144–175.

—*F. Brett Cox*

SUPERMAN (1978)

■

Faster than a speeding bullet! More powerful than a locomotive! Able to leap tall buildings at a single bound! This amazing stranger from the planet Krypton, the Man of Steel, Superman! Possessing remarkable physical strength, Superman fights a never-ending battle for truth and justice, disguised as a mild-mannered newspaper reporter, Clark Kent.

—Jay Morton
Billion Dollar Limited (1941)

Summary

After Superman's 1938 debut in *Action Comics*, his saga was developed and perfected in subsequent comic books. As a **baby**, Superman is rocketed from Krypton by parents Jor-El and La-Ra before the doomed planet explodes; on **Earth**, he develops super powers, including super strength and invulnerability. He is adopted by the Kents, who name him Clark and train him to someday use his powers to benefit **humanity**. After his parents die, the adult Clark moves to Metropolis and becomes a reporter for the newspaper *The Daily Planet*, working alongside star reporter and romantic interest Lois Lane (see **Romance**), gruff editor Perry White, and cub reporter Jimmy Olsen while periodically slipping away to remove street clothes, combat evildoers, and assist persons in need. This story is retold in the 1978 film starring Christopher Reeve, with a focus on two menaces drawn from comic books: three Kryptonian criminals, exiled by Jor-El into the Phantom Zone, who survive Krypton's destruction and return in the film's sequel *Superman II* (1981) as super-powered opponents, and scientific mastermind Lex Luthor, maniacally scheming to destroy California. When Lois is killed due to Luthor's machinations, Superman reverses the Earth's spin to turn **time** backward and restore her to life.

Discussion

In early adventures, Superman was a **superhero** with limited abilities who mainly fought ordinary **villains** and combated social injustices. This Superman moved into radio and the George Reeves television series *The Adventures of Superman* (1951–1957); to emphasize Superman as a crimefighter (see **Crime and Punishment**), a new character was introduced, Inspector Henderson, who works with Superman to apprehend criminals. In the comics, however, both Superman's powers and those of his opponents were expanding: instead of tremendous leaps, he develops the ability of flying as well as amazing powers of vision (to see through walls, see great distances, and emit heat rays) (see **Vision and Blindness**), super breath, and super **speed**; he can even fly faster than **light** to engage in **time travel**. Enemies became **mad scientists** like Luthor with fabulous **inventions**, aliens, **monsters**, and super-powered villains. This more extravagant Superman figures in the Max Fleischer cartoons of the 1940s and the Reeve films.

Comics also placed more emphasis on Superman's status as an **alien on Earth**, with stories involving trips to Krypton via time travel, preserved artifacts from Krypton, and encounters with surviving Kryptonians, including super **dog** Krypto and Superman's cousin Supergirl, also featured in a 1984 film. A fascination with Superman's Kryptonian origins influenced the first two Reeve films, which introduce holograms of Jor-El and La-Ra (see **Virtual Reality**), projected by crystals sent with him to Earth, to advise their son in his Fortress of Solitude at the North Pole (see **Polar Regions**).

However, making Superman predominantly a figure of science fiction threatened to distance him from everyday people and concerns, and revisions of the comic book character in the 1970s, 1980s, and 1990s sought to make Superman more vulnerable, strip away vestiges of his Kryptonian heritage (like Supergirl and the deadly **element** kryptonite), and emphasize his **secret identity** Clark Kent, who becomes less the awkward performance enacted by Reeve and more a genuine person who even woos Lois on his own. In other media, while the spectacularly heroic Superman carried on in two additional Reeve films, *Superman III* (1983) and *Superman IV: The Quest for Peace* (1989), and the television series *Superboy* (1988–1992), a more down-to-Earth Superman emerged in the Dean Cain series *Lois and Clark: The New Adventures of Superman* (1993–1997), which centers on the characters' romantic relationship and is also the first Superman story to realistically portray the profession of **journalism**. In this series, as in more recent comics, Luthor is refashioned as a scheming corporate tycoon (see **Business**), and Clark's parents (see **Fathers; Mothers**) remain alive to help their adult son. Another series, *Smallville* (2001–), also depicts Superman in more human terms while presenting the **Bildungsroman** of a young alien struggling to understand his powers and his proper role, the story touched upon in the 1978 film as a brief sequence featuring Jeff East as a teenage Superman.

In the 1990s, the comic-book Superman experiences a dramatic **death** and **rebirth** and, as in *Lois and Clark*, finally marries Lois (see **Marriage**). Still, despite these and other changes, Superman has remained a remarkably consistent icon. He battles for and represents, in the words of the introduction to the 1950s series, "truth, justice, and the American way" (see **America**), and reflects an untroubled altruism untainted by the inner conflicts that bedevil his sometimes-colleague *Batman*. In casting Superman, directors must seek as the performer's key quality the ability to project not strength and determination, but friendliness and appealing modesty. Reeves in the 1950s and Cain in the 1990s both did this well, but Christopher Reeve best defined the essentially soft-spoken, understated character of Superman, so it is appropriate that he became, after a paralyzing accident, a beloved American icon in his own right whose untimely death in 2004 was widely mourned.

Bibliography

Brian Attebery. "Super Men." *Science-Fiction Studies*, 25 (March, 1998), 61–76.
Les Daniels. *Superman*. San Francisco: Chronicle, 1998.

Dennis Dooley and Gary Engle, eds. *Superman at Fifty*. Cleveland: Octavia, 1987.

Michael L. Fleischer, with Janet E. Lincoln. *The Great Superman Book*. New York: Warner, 1978.

Gary Grossman. *Superman*. New York: Popular Library, 1976.

Sam Moskowitz. "Superman." Moskowitz, *Seekers of Tomorrow*. Cleveland: World, 1963, 101–117.

David Michael Petrou. *The Making of Superman the Movie*. New York: Warner, 1978.

Gary Westfahl. "The Three Lives of Superman—And Everybody Else." Westfahl, *Science Fiction, Children's Literature, and Popular Culture*. Westport, CT: Greenwood Press, 2000, 13–17.

Rhonda V. Wilcox. "Lois's Locks." Elyce Rae Helford, ed., *Fantasy Girls*. Lanham, MD: Rowman and Littlefield, 2000, 91–114.

—*Gary Westfahl*

THE SWORD OF SHANNARA
BY TERRY BROOKS (1977)

Summary

Shea Ohmsford, half-human, half-elven adopted son of an innkeeper (see **Taverns and Inns**), lives in peaceful Shady Vale and knows little of the troubles that plague the rest of the world. Then into his life comes a **giant**, forbidding Druid (see **Wizards**), Allanon, who reveals that the **evil** Warlock Lord is plotting to destroy the world. The sole **weapon** that can defeat this Power of Darkness is the Sword of Shannara, which can only be wielded by a true heir of Shannara. Shea is the last of the bloodline, and all hope rests with him. Soon a Skull Bearer, dread minion of the Warlock Lord, flies into the Vale, seeking to kill him. Rather than risk the Vale's destruction, Shea and his cynical half-brother Flick flee. They follow Allanon's cryptic orders to embark on a **quest** to find the Sword and bring it to the ravaged Northland. Along the way they meet up with **elves** and **dwarfs** and battle against gnomes and trolls. Somehow they make it through, despite opposition from false **kings**, **supernatural creatures**, and other **monsters**. In the end, Shea alone confronts the Warlock Lord, a dead wizard holding on to a lie that is shattered by the truth that the Sword of Shannara reveals.

Discussion

Despite *The Sword of Shannara*'s huge success, most readers, and Terry Brooks himself, cite the sequel, *The Elfstones of Shannara* (1982), as their favorite of the series. After *Elfstones* came *The Wishsong of Shannara* (1985), completing the first bestselling trilogy. Over the years, Brooks has worked on other books, like the humorous Magic Kingdom series (see **Humor**), beginning with *Magic Kingdom for Sale—Sold!* (1986); the **dark fantasy** series The Word and The Void, beginning with *Running with the Demon* (1997); and novelizations of the **Peter and Wendy** sequel *Hook* (1991), and the **Star Wars** prequel *Star Wars, Episode I: The Phantom Menace*

(1999). But he has regularly returned to the series that made him famous, creating the four-book Heritage of Shannara series, *The Scions of Shannara* (1990), *The Druid of Shannara* (1991), *The Elf Queen of Shannara* (1992), and *The Talismans of Shannara* (1993); *The First King of Shannara* (1996), a prequel set 500 years before the events of *The Sword of Shannara* revealing how the Sword came to be; and The Voyage of the Jerle Shannara trilogy, *Ilse Witch* (2000), *Antrax* (2001), and *Morgawr* (2002). These straightforward **heroic fantasy** tales of **sword and sorcery** do not break new ground, but nonetheless do not leave Shannara fans disappointed, and that is why more sequels to *The Sword of Shannara* continue to be written.

According to Brooks, *The Sword of Shannara* was born from a need to escape the rigors of studying law. It is unsurprising, then, that the book features one harrowing **escape** after another. Brooks developed characters that people can care about and placed them in circumstances that are seemingly impossible to escape from, only to pull them out without drawing too heavily on **magic** or the might of their medieval-style **swords**, choosing rather to display how the characters respond on an emotional level and use their **wisdom** to get out of tough situations.

The influence of J.R.R. Tolkien's *The Lord of the Rings* can be seen throughout the Shannara series, as exemplified by the **clichés** of the peaceful village with an unassuming man who is approached by a strange wandering wizard telling him that the **destiny** of the world rests on him and he must stop the great evil. The similarities continue throughout, right down to the titular Sword of Shannara, which, like Tolkien's One Ring, is a weapon of unparalleled magic (see **Magical Objects**) whose ownership determines the balance of power between good and evil. What sets the Shannara series apart from other Tolkien emulations is Brooks's knack for creating complex, unforgettable characters, whether they are humans, druids, gnomes, or elves. The vivid detail of the locales each of the **heroes** visit, the believable turmoil they endure in **race relations**, and the challenges they face engender a strong sense of affinity with fans. Readers identify with the Ohmsfords, the Shannara series' ubiquitous Everyman figures, because everyone can relate to the plights of people struggling with misfortunes wrought by others or by circumstance, people who want to get out of whatever dilemmas they find themselves in (see **Freedom**).

The Shannara series is set in a world that is timeless and placeless, yet nevertheless hints strongly of **Earth**. This world is a result of great **future wars** that have destroyed our present **knowledge**, and science has been replaced by magic. It is hardly likely that after a **nuclear war**, folkloric **mutation** and **psychic powers** would rise from the ashes of human **disaster**, but the stories are fantasy, not **hard science fiction**. Whether the world of Shannara derives from ours or not, there are definite parallels between their past and our present. For instance, **nuclear power** is alluded to in *Elfstones of Shannara*, and in *Wishsong of Shannara*, a subway system is described. And Brooks offers an explanation for the existence of clichéd fantasy races rather than simply having the reader accept them as part of his **imaginary world**. In the post-apocalyptical (see **Apocalypse**) world, remaining populations are spread out across the globe and unable to contact one another. Because of nuclear fallout, humans evolve (see **Evolution**) differently: some into thin and dexterous elves, some into short and strong dwarfs, some into huge trolls, some into squat gnomes, and some remain normal humans.

The Sword of Shannara is an attractive **fairy tale**. It embodies the classic tale of good versus evil, along with other **philosophies**, ideas, and emotions which, portrayed with fantastical creatures of **mythology**, make the novel and its sequels memorable.

Bibliography

Thomas Arndt. "Swords, Sales and Magic Kingdoms." *Starlog*, No. 107 (June, 1986), 72–73.

Jayme Lynn Blaschke. "An Interview with Terry Brooks." *Chronicle*, No. 230 (November, 2002), 40–42.

Charles Brown. "An Online Interview with *Star Wars* Writer, Terry Brooks." *Locus*, 46 (February, 2001), 6, 85.

Ellen Cheshire. "Return to Shannara." *Vector*, No. 215 (January/February, 2001), 14–17.

Robert Dahlin. "Ballantine and Random House Join Their Imaginations to Publish a Fantasy of Epic Size." *Publishers Weekly*, 211 (January 3, 1977), 38–39.

Stan Nicholls. "Terry Brooks Majors in Myth." Nicholls, *Wordsmiths of Wonder*. London: Orbit, 1993, 303–310.

Stan Nicholls. "The Nature of the Beast." *Interzone*, No. 60 (June, 1992), 40–42.

J.B. Post. "The Four Lands." Post, *An Atlas of Fantasy*. Revised Ed. New York: Ballantine Books, 1979, 204–205.

—Nick Aires

T

TARZAN OF THE APES
BY EDGAR RICE BURROUGHS (1914)

*I had this story from one who had no
business to tell it to me, or to any other.*

—Edgar Rice Burroughs
Tarzan of the Apes (1914)

Summary

When England's Lord Greystoke and his wife die while lost in the African **jungle**, their abandoned **baby** son is adopted and raised by a compassionate female **ape**. Named "Tarzan," or "white skin," the boy grows up learning the language of apes and other jungle creatures, but also figures out how to read written English from **books** left by his **father** (see **Language and Linguistics; Reading**). Eventually, after his ape **mother** dies, Tarzan leaves his tribe of apes and strikes out on his own, encountering a shipwrecked Professor Archimedes Q. Porter and his daughter Jane, with whom Tarzan immediately falls in **love**; he also meets a Frenchman, d'Arnot, who teaches him how to speak French and later brings him back to **Europe** to learn the ways of **civilization**. Upon learning that Jane, due to financial problems, has agreed to marry another man, Tarzan declines to claim his title of Lord Greystoke and returns to **Africa**.

When *Tarzan of the Apes* proved amazingly popular with readers, Burroughs quickly wrote a sequel, *The Return of Tarzan* (1915), essentially a retelling of the first novel's second half—including another coincidental shipwreck involving the Porters—but with a happy ending, as Tarzan is finally recognized as Lord Greystoke and marries Jane. Tarzan went on to further adventures in twenty-two additional Burroughs novels, novels by other authors, numerous films, a comic strip, comic books, and two television series, becoming one of literature's most famous characters.

Discussion

The **youth** and adolescence of Tarzan invite consideration as a unique **Bildungsroman** of a boy raised by animals who nonetheless must learn to be human. The tale was anticipated in part by Rudyard Kipling's *The Jungle Book* (1894) but explored more interestingly by Burroughs in both *Tarzan of the Apes* and *Jungle Tales of Tarzan* (1919), a series of charming stories about young Tarzan playing with animals, falling in love with a girl ape, seeing a human for the first time, and "rescuing" the **Moon** from being devoured during a lunar eclipse.

Although films often present the adult Tarzan as an uncouth, ignorant **barbarian**, Burroughs's Tarzan was a sophisticated, articulate English aristocrat who spent most of his time dressed in European clothes on his African plantation and occasionally visited England to make speeches in the House of Lords. Far from representing a noble savage schooled by rugged **nature** and thus superior to effete civilization, this Tarzan instead validates the traditional British **class system**, demonstrating the innate superiority of upper-class nobles who are destined to succeed even if placed in inauspicious circumstances (see **Destiny**). Still, Burroughs does speak of Tarzan's happiness whenever a crisis requires him to strip off his clothing (see **Nudity**) and return to the **freedom** of the jungle, suggesting that civilized society and its stifling requirements are best regarded as a necessary **evil**.

In addition to great strength and fighting ability, Tarzan was said to have superior eyesight and a keen sense of smell, and he enjoyed a unique rapport with the jungle animals, able to speak their language and persuade them to follow his commands. In *Tarzan's Quest* (1936), Tarzan also drinks an immortality potion (see **Immortality and Longevity**), allowing Burroughs to explain how his perpetually youthful **hero** was able to fight in both World War I and World War II.

Tarzan—and evidently Burroughs—had trouble reconciling his adventurous lifestyle with his **family** life. Burroughs was visibly unsure about how to handle Jane: after experimentally killing Jane in *Tarzan the Untamed* (1920), then resurrecting her as a jungle hero in her own right in *Tarzan the Terrible* (1921), he made her into a housewife figure, content to stay at **home** whenever her husband went off on a mission. Tarzan always remained faithful to Jane, though he was attracted to the exotic priestess La and other **temptresses**. He also had a son, Korak, who grew to young adulthood in *The Son of Tarzan* (1917) but later faded into the background. Somehow, this iconic jungle hero seemed best suited to be a solitary figure, communing more with nature than with other people and **communities**.

Knowing little about the continent and its inhabitants, Burroughs filled Tarzan's Africa with exotic **lost worlds** usually inhabited by Caucasian representatives of ancient cultures, like the outpost of the Roman Empire discovered in *Tarzan and the Lost Empire* (1929). Burroughs's stories often focus, then, on the white Tarzan's interactions with other white heroes and **villains** in African jungles, with no African natives in sight. It is this marginalization of Africa's indigenous peoples, more so than emphatic stereotyping or condescension, that can make the Tarzan novels seem racist to modern readers (see **Race Relations**).

Tarzan's most fantastic adventures involved traveling into a **hollow Earth** in *Tarzan at the Earth's Core* (1930) and shrinking to mingle with a race of tiny men in *Tarzan and the Ant Men* (1924) (see **Miniaturization**). The Tarzan films of the 1930s, 1940s, and 1950s, which reduced Burroughs's hero to a grunting simpleton who lived in a treehouse, removed these fantasy elements from the Tarzan saga, pitting the lord of the jungle against routine menaces like conniving villains, stampeding elephants, and hostile tribes. But later films, most notably *Greystoke: The Legend of Tarzan, Lord of the Apes* (1984), at least restored the dignity of Tarzan, if not the **magic** of Burroughs's classic novels.

Bibliography

William J. Boerst. *Edgar Rice Burroughs, Creator of Tarzan*. Greensboro, NC: Morgan Reynolds, 2000.
Clark A. Brady. *The Burroughs Cyclopaedia*. Jefferson, NC: McFarland, 1996.
Philip José Farmer. *Tarzan Alive*. New York: Popular Library, 1972.
David Fury. *Kings of the Jungle*. Jefferson, NC: McFarland, 1994.
Erling B. Holtsmark. *Tarzan and Tradition*. Westport, CT: Greenwood Press, 1981.
Richard A. Lupoff. *Edgar Rice Burroughs: Master of Adventure*. Revised Edition. New York: Ace Books, 1968.
Irwin Porges. *Edgar Rice Burroughs*. Provo, UT: Brigham Young University Press, 1975.
John Taliaferro. *Tarzan Forever*. New York: Scribner's, 1999.
David A. Ullery. *The Tarzan Novels of Edgar Rice Burroughs*. Jefferson, NC: McFarland, 2001.

—*Gary Westfahl*

THE TERMINATOR (1984)

∎

Summary

James Cameron's *The Terminator* portrays a struggle between humans and computerized machines (see **Computers; Machines and Mechanization**). The story continues in two sequels: *Terminator 2: Judgment Day* (1991), also directed by Cameron, and *Terminator 3: Rise of the Machines* (2003), directed by Jonathan Mostow.

As described in the first two movies, an American military computer called Skynet became self-aware in 1997. When its creators attempted to shut it down, it responded by triggering a **nuclear war** and attempting to exterminate the remaining humans, using a variety of robotic devices, some designed to imitate human beings (see **Androids; Cyborgs; Robots**). In the aftermath of the war, John Connor led the human Resistance and broke through Skynet's defenses in a final battle in 2029 (see **Future Wars; Post-Holocaust Societies; Rebellion**). Skynet retaliated at the last minute by sending a humanoid machine known as a Terminator back in time to kill Connor's **mother** in 1984, before she could give **birth** to her son (see **Time Travel**). In *Terminator 2*, it transpires that *two* Terminators were sent back by Skynet. A more advanced model was sent to kill Connor himself if the first Terminator's mission failed. In what seems to be 1994, it attacks Connor, who is still a boy, but he is successfully protected by a Terminator sent back by rebels.

As a result of events in *Terminator 2*, it appears that Skynet will not be built and nuclear war will be prevented. In *Terminator 3*, however, it becomes clear that the creation of Skynet has only been delayed. A decade after the events of *Terminator 2*, a third Terminator sent by Skynet kills some of Connor's future lieutenants and attempts to kill Connor himself.

Discussion

All three Terminator movies tell much the same story. They depict the human protagonists' struggles to **escape**, or somehow stop, near-indestructible Terminators that pursue them like **personifications** of **death**. Indeed, each sequel is almost a remake of its predecessor, with new twists to the basic plot.

The narrative, then, is essentially one of **survival**. In *The Terminator*, John's mother, Sarah Connor, must survive attempts on her life if her son is to be born and grow up to be **humanity**'s **messiah**. Similarly, John himself must survive as a child (in *Terminator 2*) and a young man (in *Terminator 3*), if humanity is to endure the nuclear war and its aftermath (see **Children; Youth**).

In each movie, the Resistance has sent a protector from the future to assist Sarah and/or John. In *The Terminator*, it is a soldier, Kyle Reese, who briefly becomes Sarah's lover and **fathers** John. In *Terminator 2* and *Terminator 3*, the protectors are reprogrammed Terminators of the same appearance and "model" as the one that almost killed Sarah in the first movie (all portrayed by Arnold Schwarzenegger). With their assistance, Sarah and John stay alive, but their triumphs come at terrible personal cost: Sarah is visibly ravaged by her experiences in *Terminator 2* and has died at an early age by the time of *Terminator 3*; young John in the third film has become a vagrant and **drug** user who is nevertheless still committed to his terrible **destiny**.

As *Terminator 3* ends, Skynet finally initiates the delayed war while John, now an adult, awaits his own fate, secure in a deep military bunker. The Terminator that most recently tried to kill him was presumably sent back from a "new" future, though one in which events must have followed a similar course to that made familiar in the first two movies. Since some of Connor's future lieutenants are dead by this point, the future has "changed" again, and final victory is not certain.

The complex set-up requires that humans and Terminators travel naked through time—facilitating a visual emphasis on the dramatic "build" or toned bodies of actors (see **Nudity**). Little **weaponry** can be brought from the future (none at all in the first two movies), which makes the story told by Kyle and Sarah less plausible to the authorities—where is their proof?

The movies generally avoid the complications that would ensue if the characters opposed each other with unfamiliar weapons, tools, or equipment (though Terminators have extraordinary capabilities built into them). For their running battles, the antagonists use firearms from several eras, plus anything else that comes to hand, particularly factory machines, **automobiles**, and an assortment of ground and air vehicles. Much of what goes on minute-by-minute is gun-blasting, metal-crunching **violence**.

The Terminator movies display a pessimistic attitude to **technology** (see **Optimism and Pessimism**), which is shown to be ubiquitous. However, the pessimism is relieved somewhat in the sequels, confirming that seemingly anti-technological science fiction often finds a place in its value system for what it initially rejects. In *Terminator 2*, the "good" Terminator comes to resemble a benign version of a **Frankenstein monster**. Both here and in *Terminator 3*, the reprogrammed killing machines ultimately **sacrifice** themselves for the sake of humanity just as Kyle did in the first movie.

Bibliography

Thomas B. Byers. "Terminating the Postmodern." *Modern Fiction Studies*, 41 (Spring, 1995), 5–33.

James Cameron and William Wisher. *Terminator 2: Judgment Day*. New York: Applause Books, 1991.

Sean French. *The Terminator*. London: British Film Institute, 1996.

Jonathan Goldberg. "Recalling Totalities." Chris Hables Gray., ed., *The Cyborg Handbook*. New York and London: Routledge, 1995, 233–254.

Howard V. Hendrix. "The Body Apocalyptic." Gary Westfahl and George Slusser, ed., *No Cure for the Future*. Westport, CT: Greenwood Press, 2002, 141–150.

Gary Kern. "The Triumph of Teen-Prop." Gary Westfahl and George Slusser, eds., *Nursery Realms*. Athens: University of Georgia Press, 1999, 48–69.

Hanna M. Roisman. "Predestination in Greek Literature and the Terminator Films." *Classical and Modern Literature*, 21 (Fall, 2001), 99–107.

Janice Hocker Rushing and Thomas S. Frentz. *"The Terminator"* and *"Terminator 2: Judgment Day."* Rushing and Frentz, *Projecting the Shadow*. Chicago: University of Chicago Press, 1995, 164–201.

J.P. Telotte. "The Exposed Modern Body." Telotte, *Replications*. Urbana: University of Illinois Press, 1995, 169–185.

—*Russell Blackford*

THE THING (FROM ANOTHER WORLD) (1951)

■

An intellectual carrot. The mind boggles.

—Charles Lederer
The Thing (from Another World) (1951)

Captain Hendry and his aircrew are dispatched from Anchorage, Alaska to a base 2000 miles north (see **Polar Regions**), to investigate **scientists**' claim that an airplane crashed nearby. Hendry is happy to return because his last date with Nikki, Dr. Carrington's assistant, ended badly, and he wants to see her again. After discovering a flying saucer (see **UFOs**) buried in the ice but accidentally destroying it, they recover an alien embedded in a block of ice (see **Suspended Animation and Cryonics**). At the base, conflict develops between Hendry, who wants instructions from superiors, and Carrington, who wants to study this **alien on Earth**. Nikki and Hendry's **romance** blossoms. Unintentionally thawed out, the alien goes on a murderous rampage, feeding on **blood** (see **Vampires**). The base is isolated by bad weather, preventing **communication** with the outside world. Carrington begins growing more aliens from seeds, watering them with plasma. He tries to sabotage their trap for the alien and then to communicate with it. It brushes him aside but is electrocuted in a death-trap. Once the alien dies, communications are restored.

Discussion

Based on John W. Campbell, Jr.'s "Who Goes There?" (1938), *The Thing (from Another World)* is an early entry in the 1950s cycle of movies about **invasion** from space, including *Invaders from Mars* and *The War of the Worlds* (1953). Like the latter's Martians, the alien never communicates its motives, making it difficult to read it as embodying any particular **anxiety** of the period. The movie contains scattered references to the Soviet Union, and the alien's uniform bears the symbol of the atom, suggesting two concerns usually evoked in discussions of 1950s American science fiction. A military–scientific expedition to a northern **wilderness**, in which airmen and scientists are forced to effectively draw their wagons into a circle to fight off an alien threat, recalls many **westerns** and other imperialist-colonialist adventures like *King Kong*, *Island of Lost Souls*, Robert A. Heinlein's *Starship Troopers*, and various *Star Trek* series; and as in these there is a clear racial subtext, ambiguously manifested here in passing references to thieving, cowardly Eskimos and lynchings (see **Race Relations**).

As with *Buffy the Vampire Slayer* and countless **horror** movies, there seems to be some connection between the **monster** and sexual desire (see **Sexuality**), with the alien thawing as the romance between Hendry and Nikki is rekindled. Along with John Wyndham's *The Day of the Triffids* and *The Quatermass Experiment*, it is one of several 1950s science fiction texts featuring vegetable monsters (see **Plants**). Carrington's experiments with the Thing's seeds emphasize the peculiarities of reproduction—a significant parallel with the vegetable-**horrors** of *Invasion of the Body Snatchers*, which attempt to prevent the union of its sexually active leads.

Like Morbius in *Forbidden Planet*, Carrington represents reason pushed to such an extreme that it becomes oblivious to consequences, and his otherness is emphasized by his costume and appearance, which simultaneously recalls stereotypes of Soviet officials, Jewish intellectuals, and wealthy homosexuals (see **Homosexuality**). While this range of possibilities might seem to indicate a confused and confusing movie, it is this very variety of potential meanings, and the irreducibility of its meaning, which places *The Thing (from Another World)* at the core of 1950s science fiction cinema and still lends it potency 50 years on.

Who actually directed *The Thing (from Another World)* has been long debated, although it seems that producer Howard Hawks rehearsed the cast and crew each day then oversaw the direction of his former editor, Christian Nyby, the credited director. Certainly the film bears many hallmarks of Hawks's movies: the strong sense of camaraderie between male professionals doing a tough job in difficult circumstances; the hardboiled romance with an intelligent, courageous dame; the blend of **humor** and adventure; and snappy, overlapping dialogue, uncomplicated camerawork, and crisp editing. The opposition between the natural–instinctual and the socialized–rational—manifested not so much in disagreements between Hendry and Carrington as in the **love** scene in which Nikki ties Hendry to a chair—is also a recurring theme in Hawks's movies, most obviously in the marginally science-fictional *Monkey Business* (1952).

Ironically, then, it is only in John Carpenter's remake, *The Thing* (1982), that notions of **identity**, replication, and simulation come to the fore. More faithful to Campbell's original story, it reintroduces the shapeshifting alien capable of consuming as a raw material, and taking on the form of, any being it encounters (see **Shapeshifters**)—although disturbingly, unlike Campbell's alien, it does not seem to have an original form. In the absence of female characters, it is tempting to read this fleshy eruption as signalling the period's misogyny and homophobia—and it is perhaps significant that the movie closes with a confrontation between a black character and white character, both uncertain of the other. These articulations of 1980s anxieties about race, **gender**, and sexuality reward comparison with *Alien*, itself undoubtedly indebted to *The Thing (from Another World)*.

While the legacy of the New Deal and experience of World War II enabled the original movie to envision a cooperative, communitarian **politics**—despite problematic valorizations of hierarchy and a close interrelationship between the military, science, and the press (see **Journalism**)—the remake seems incapable of imagining a social world that is not fragmented, alienated, and atomized (see **Paranoia**). This is hardly surprising, inasmuch as the preceding decades' limited social and economic gains were attacked, undermined, retrenched, and replaced by a politics of atomized consumerist individualism.

Bibliography

Anne Billson. *The Thing*. London: British Film Institute, 1997.

Michael A. Katovich and Patrick T. Kinkade. "The Stories Told in Science Fiction and Social Science." *Sociological Quarterly*, 34 (1993), 619–651.

Brooks Landon. *The Aesthetics of Ambivalence*. Westport, CT: Greenwood Press, 1992.

Stephen Prince. "Dread, Taboo and *The Thing*." *Wide Angle*, 10 (1988), 19–29.

Steven J. Schneider. "Toward an Aesthetics of Cinematic Horror." Stephen Prince, ed., *The Horror Film*. New Brunswick: Rutgers University Press, 2004, 131–149.

Margaret Tarrat. "Monsters from the Id." Barry Keith Grant, ed., *Film Genre Reader II*. Austin: University of Texas Press, 1995, 330–349.

John Trushell. "*The Thing*." *Foundation*, No. 76 (Summer, 1999), 76–89.

Errol Vieth. *Screening Science*. Lanham, MD: Scarecrow, 2001.

Eric White. "The Erotics of Becoming." *Science-Fiction Studies*, 20 (November, 1993), 394–408.

—Mark Bould

THINGS TO COME (1936)

■

[Raymond Passworthy:] Oh, God, is there ever to be any age of happiness? Is there never to be any rest?

[Oswald Cabal:] Rest enough for the individual man—too much, and too soon—and we call it death. But for Man, no rest and no ending. He must go on, conquest beyond conquest. First this little planet with its winds and ways, and then all the laws of mind and matter that restrain him. Then the planets about him and at last out across immensity to the stars. And when he has conquered all the deeps of space and all the mysteries of time, still he will be beginning.

[Passworthy:] But . . . we're such little creatures. Poor humanity's so fragile, so weak. Little . . . little animals.

[Cabal:] Little animals. If we're no more than animals, we must snatch each little scrap of happiness and live and suffer and pass, mattering no more than all the other animals do or have done. It is this, or that. All the universe, or nothingness. Which shall it be, Passworthy? Which shall it be?

—H.G. Wells
Things to Come (1936)

Summary

During **Christmas** in Everytown, newspaper headlines warn of approaching **war**, and a **family**'s members are divided between fear (John Cabal) and hope (Pippa Passworthy). With war comes the total destruction of **civilization**. Small tribal states emerge under egotistical dictators who govern by force. Pestilence is rife and warfare among small states continual. The only exception to this world of pre-industrial barbarism (see **Barbarians**) is "Wings Over the World," a union of aeronauts formed from all the disputing nations of the world. The union monopolizes flight and introduces a world state governed from Basra by functional agencies that rebuild the world along advanced technocratic lines (see **Governance Systems**). The final scenes of the film see the world orderly and pacified, though still restless. The great-grandsons of the characters in the opening scene, Oswald Cabal and Raymond Passworthy, discuss the next stage for **humanity**—space **exploration** (see **Space Travel**)—while a group of artistic conservatives (see **Art**), led by Theotocopulos, attempt to prevent a space launch, though they arrive too late at the giant space gun to stop its occurrence. As Cabal's daughter and Passworthy's son are fired moonward (see **Astronauts; Moon**), Passworthy bemoans the continued pursuit of scientific advance, but Cabal insists that it must be, asking "All the universe or nothingness. Which shall it be?"

Discussion

Things to Come was arguably the first science fiction film in sound, produced by Alexander Korda's London Films and directed by William Cameron Menzies. The screenplay was essentially scripted by H.G. Wells, though finessed for the screen by Korda and Menzies. Originally titled "Whither Mankind?," Wells's script was born of his novel *The Shape of Things to Come* (1933) and, according to Thomas C. Renzi, is a visual representation of the original's abstract proposals. The film condenses the expansive scope of the novel, omitting the historical perspective and limiting the span of **time** to just under 100 years (1940 to 2036) (see **Near Future**).

According to Patrick Parrinder, what is implicit in *Things to Come* is nothing less than the whole tragic political **history** of the first half of the twentieth century. Several broad themes are present in the film—concerns such as civilization, **cultures,** politics, **progress**, and **technology**. Frank McConnell points to the scene at the end of the film, when humankind launches the space gun despite the violent protests of a reactionary crowd led by Theotocopulos, as a broad but accurate **allegory** of Wells's hopes for the infinitely expansive future and his suspicion of those whose aesthetics led them to undervalue the contributions of science.

In technological terms, *Things to Come* is often seen as utopian (see **Utopia**), though opinion on its prophetic aspects is divided. Leon Stover, for instance, claims that the space gun is a ridiculous contraption in technological terms, important instead as a political symbol demonstrating the conversion of **weaponry** into technology for human progress. George Zebrowski, on the other hand, claims that the electric cannon that launches the spacecraft is a sophisticated **invention**. Far from being a simple Vernian cannon, which would compress the astronauts into pulp with the sudden acceleration of firing, it is a "graduated electric catapult" in the shape of a cannon within a cannon, which would accelerate the vehicle by stages. It was designed by Willy Ley, an expert on **rockets**, and foreshadowed research by both the United States and the Soviet Union into similarly ground-based, powered booster systems.

In different ways, Christopher Frayling and Allan Asherman comment upon the cultural impact of *Things to Come*. For Asherman, there is a feminist ending to an otherwise male-dominated story; Cabal's daughter, Catherine, is working with society (see **Feminism**). She has become a part of it to the extent that she is one of the first two space explorers. The onlooker gets the impression that the next generation will probably consist of men and women working together, each enjoying the reciprocal respect of each other (see **Work and Leisure**). By postponing **gender** equality until as late as 2036, Wells was acknowledging the cultural distance that humanity had to travel before equality could be achieved, rather than dismissing equality altogether. Frayling sees the cultural inheritance of the film in terms of its influence on later filmmakers. It has become a cult film on the art school circuit and as such has entered the bloodstream of contemporary visual culture through the work of countless graphic, **fashion**, and product designers. Indeed, Frayling goes so far as to say that *Things to Come* is to modernism as *Blade Runner* is to **postmodernism**.

While critics like Stover have invested a lot of time and energy in close readings of *Things to Come*, Zebrowski has argued persuasively that in the case of Wells, the specific details of the film should be secondary considerations: Wells wanted his audience to accept not his specifics, which belong only to the world of the film's story, but his general constructive attitudes—the idea that the future must be an object of creative concern, that futures are to be made, invented, and not passively predicted (see **Predictions**).

Bibliography

Allan Asherman. "Introduction." H.G. Wells, *Things to Come*. Boston: Gregg, 1975, vii–xiv.

Christopher Frayling. *Things to Come*. London: British Film Institute, 1995.

Frank McConnell. *The Science Fiction of H.G. Wells*. Oxford: Oxford University Press, 1981.

Patrick Parrinder. *Shadows of the Future*. Liverpool: Liverpool University Press, 1995.

Thomas C. Renzi. *H.G. Wells: Six Scientific Romances Adapted for Film*. Second Ed. Lanham, MD: Scarecrow, 2004.

Jeffrey Richards. "*Things to Come* and Science Fiction in the 1930s." I.Q. Hunter, ed., *British Science Fiction Cinema*. New York: Routledge, 1999, 16–32.

Leon Stover. *The Prophetic Soul*. Jefferson, NC: McFarland, 1987.

J.P. Telotte. "So Big: The Monumental Technology of *Things to Come*." *Science Fiction Studies*, 25 (March, 1998), 77–86.

George Zebrowski. "Introduction." H.G. Wells, *Things to Come*. Boston: Gregg, 1975, xxxiii–xxxix.

—John S. Partington

THE TIME MACHINE BY H.G. WELLS (1895)

∎

"Upon that machine," said the Time Traveller, holding the lamp aloft, "I intend to explore time."

—H.G. Wells
The Time Machine (1895)

Summary

H.G. Wells's most famous story explores the concept of the fourth **dimension** as time. After inventing a machine able to range through time, the unnamed Time Traveller departs for the year 802,701 when England has become "two nations." The effete, pleasure-loving Eloi inhabit an idyllic **Arcadia**, eat only fruit, and fear **darkness**. When night falls he learns why: they are preyed upon by a subterranean, carnivorous race, the Morlocks, who keep the Eloi as their food source. Working in underground factories, Morlocks are blinded by **light**, so the Eloi are safe to roam during daylight. At first enchanted by the Eloi, especially the girl Weena, the Time Traveller discovers that their leisure is dependent on the mechanization developed by the Morlocks, former slaves of the Eloi (see **Machines and Mechanization**).

The Time Traveller repeatedly has his confidence as a **scientist** shattered: his machine is stolen (see **Theft**), he wastes precious matches, and he unwittingly starts a forest **fire**, thereby becoming disoriented and causing Weena's death. He then travels on thirty million years to observe a cold, dying **Earth**. His final journey, from which he fails to return, is intended to produce tangible proof of his **time travel** for skeptical friends.

Discussion

A reworking of Wells's earlier story "The Chronic Argonauts" (1888), *The Time Machine* is a complex depiction of scientific optimism, embodied in the notion of time travel as **exploration**, and **fin de siècle** pessimism (see **Optimism and Pessimism**). It reflects Wells's own reservations about **technology** and fears that the contemporary social order was tottering. Thus, the Time Traveller is both attractive in his enthusiastic search for **knowledge** and inadequate in emergencies that threaten his rationalism. In 802,701 he misunderstands the **race relations** of the binary **class system**, defending the Eloi whose existence actually involves hedonistic **decadence**. Their museums and **libraries** are ruins and, living only for the present, they have no sense of **history** or **progress**. The strange, wilted **flowers** the Traveller brings back symbolize the Eloi—beautiful, useless, and moribund. The Morlocks in their sub-terranean **labyrinth** of machines provide powerful visual imagery of technological **dystopia**. In this sociological **allegory** Wells interrogates **social Darwinism** and warns of how **humanity** might evolve if exploitation of the working class continues on a capitalist rationale. Unable to respect the Eloi or endorse the Morlocks, the Traveller in his predicament reflects Wells, renouncing the pre-industrial **dreams** of Ruskin and Morris but rejecting a **culture** focused solely on technology. The literary power of *The Time Machine* lies in its opposition between paradisal and demonic imagery, pastoralism and technology, aestheticism and utilitarianism.

The Time Traveller is sympathetic but essentially powerless, a victim of shifting paradoxes. Having invented a time machine to overcome restrictions of time, he repeatedly finds himself its prisoner, in a more inimical time. The further he travels into the future, the more it resembles the remote past. Bored by the childish Eloi and revolted by cannibal Morlocks, he nevertheless returns to London craving meat. Though enthusiastic in the cause of science, he "thought but cheerlessly of the Advancement of Mankind." The other great visual image of *The Time Machine* is the Traveller as the **last man** observing the **apocalypse** of the dying Earth, dark, cold, and almost lifeless, with giant crustaceans moving slowly across the littoral **landscape**.

Apart from its powerful imagery *The Time Machine* is conceptually intriguing. Wells analyzes the idea of a time dimension, and once we accept the fantasy of traveling through time, he forestalls any philosophical objections. This is the more amazing when we consider that he originally wrote it seventeen years before publication of Albert Einstein's Theory of Special Relativity, the first scientific paper to address the concept of time as the fourth dimension. The descriptions of the machine's departure and arrival are wholly consistent with Einstein's illustration of the two clocks, one stationary, one moving. Wells even discusses the danger of the machine arriving in a different time at a place where a solid object occupies its space. More in doubt is the issue of chronological determinism: if the Traveller has visited the year 802,701, then in one sense he must always be in that place in that year, and his **destiny** is to be the last man alive on Earth. This difficulty is avoided in Gregory Benford's novel, *Timescape*, where a message is sent back through time to prevent Earth's destruction through pollution and social unrest.

Despite the technical difficulties of producing a visually convincing time machine, where Wells had been deliberately vague, filmmakers have been attracted to the special effects potential of the Morlocks' underworld, beautiful Eloi, and dying planet. When the threat of **nuclear war** was paramount, George Pal's film *The Time Machine* (1960) explained the Eloi and Morlocks as survivors of an atomic **apocalypse** in 1966. Time travel associated with nuclear war was also featured in films like *Beyond the Time Barrier* (1960), *The Time Travelers* (1964), **Planet of the Apes**, and **The Terminator**. In contrast, Simon Wells's film *The Time Machine* (2002) emphasized the romantic interest (see **Romance**) and concentrated on special effects.

Bibliography

Bernard Bergonzi. "*The Time Machine.*" Bergonzi, *H.G. Wells.* Upper Saddle River, NJ: Prentice Hall, 1976, 39–56.

Roslynn D. Haynes. *H.G. Wells.* London: Macmillan, 1980.

Mark M. Hennelly, Jr. "*The Time Machine.*" *Extrapolation,* 20 (Summer, 1979), 154–167.

Mark R. Hillegas. *The Future as Nightmare.* New York: Oxford University Press, 1967.

Veronica Hollinger. "Deconstructing the Time Machine." *Science-Fiction Studies,* 14 (July, 1987), 201–221.

Frank McConnell. *The Science Fiction of H.G. Wells.* Oxford: Oxford University Press, 1981.

Tom Miller. "H.G. Wells and Aldous Huxley." *The Wellsian,* 17 (1994), 3–10.

Mark Rose. "Filling the Void." *Science-Fiction Studies,* 8 (July, 1981), 121–142.

Gary Westfahl. "Partial Derivatives." Westfahl, *Science Fiction, Children's Literature, and Popular Culture.* Westport, CT: Greenwood Press, 2002, 129–141.

—*Roslynn Haynes*

TIMESCAPE BY GREGORY BENFORD (1980)

■

> Time and space were themselves players, vast lands engulfing the figures, a weave of future and past. There was no riverrun of years. The abiding loops of causality ran both forward and back. The timescape rippled with waves, roiled and flexed, a great beast in the dark sea.
>
> —Gregory Benford
> *Timescape* (1980)

Summary

The world of 1998 is bordering on chaos. Oceans are gradually being destroyed by chemical waste; skies are fouled by an airborne bacterium that turns clouds pink and causes airplanes to crash because their navigational systems are unable to function. In Great Britain, meat supplies are dubious, electricity is unreliable, and the coronation of the new **King** is indefinitely postponed because the nation cannot afford it. So, **scientists** in Britain's Cavendish Laboratory conceive the idea of using tachyons to send a message to 1963, giving scientists of that era the information they need to prevent these ecological catastrophes (see **Ecology**). This message is carefully written to ensure that the world of 1998 is not eliminated by discoveries made 35 years earlier.

In 1963, Gordon Bernstein, a struggling assistant professor of **physics**, receives the message. He tries to interpret it while maintaining his teaching load and avoiding the knives of academic **politics**. When the message is made public, unflattering press publicity ensures that Bernstein's academic career is nearly derailed, but scientists eventually use the message from 1998 to make sensational scientific discoveries. As an unanticipated side effect, a man searching for news about the message on November 22, 1963 stumbles upon Lee Harvey Oswald and thwarts President Kennedy's assassination. As we learn in a postscript set in 1974, this creates an **alternate history** with a new and greatly improved future, for both Bernstein and **humanity** as a whole.

Discussion

Gregory Benford's *Timescape* fuses several traditions. It is an ecological **disaster** novel, projecting a future that was significantly worse than the author's era. *Timescape* is also a **technothriller**, but a quiet one, in the tradition of J.G. Ballard, Brian W. Aldiss, John Wyndham, and Keith Roberts. Benford's **near future** Britain is suffering a cozy catastrophe, portrayed not with thunder but with subtlety. A poisoned sausage consumed at a pub shows problems with the British meat supply, while a fight between a scientist's wife and a long-unemployed worker begging for **money** and food shows that the British economy is on the verge of collapse. Part of the suspense in *Timescape* is that humanity's **survival** is in question, even though the future is being destroyed through a series of small forceful blows rather than one gigantic catastrophe.

Timescape is also **hard science fiction**. Readers learn quite a bit about how tachyons work, how they can be used as a severely limited form of **time travel**, and how, because of the properties of **antimatter**, they can effect one-way **communication** between the present and the past. The Cavendish scientists understand that they want to prevent disaster but not otherwise change **history**.

Timescape further combines science fiction with a realistic account of how scientists work, in the vein of C.P. Snow's *The New Men* (1954), since Benford is a professional physicist with a keen awareness of the intricacies and frustrations of academic politics. Bernstein's boss at the University of California at La Jolla, Professor Lakin (his first name is never mentioned), is not only a **mentor**, but a supervisor whose disdain could wreck a career. Benford shows us that science is not done in isolation, but is a collaborative effort in which scientists must work together if they are to succeed. How many professors should sign their names to a paper? Should they write a short note about the discoveries produced by the tachyon message for *Physical Review Letters*, or prepare a longer paper for *Physical Review*, knowing that publication would take at least nine months once the article is accepted?

Another problem professional scientists face is dealing with journalists, who often present new discoveries as wondrous breakthroughs but fail to understand that science advances by small steps, not giant leaps (see **Journalism**). But given that the central device of *Timescape*—a message from the future—would be front-page news if made public, a comic undercurrent in the novel involves Bernstein's efforts to block publicity, hoping to avoid the wrath of Professor Lakin, who fears ridicule. Like the tachyon message itself, communication between scientists and the press, as portrayed by Benford, is a one-way, error-laden transmission of information.

Finally, Benford's novel is a study in the limits of **knowledge**. Scientists of 1998 seek to change the past, but in a way that will eliminate the disaster while otherwise not altering events. Their efforts are ultimately unsuccessful because the past is altered so as to create a superior **parallel world**; but this leaves the ecological problems facing scientists in the original 1998 unresolved. Thus *Timescape* is a different— and a more realistic—sort of hard science fiction from the more optimistic works of a generation earlier (see **Optimism and Pessimism**). Instead of heroic scientists solving the world's problems through individual might, Benford's scientists muddle through, doing the best they can, after spending too much time attending committee meetings and conducting office politics. The novel's twin conclusions— continuing catastrophe for the original world, relief and comfort for the new world—convey uncertainty about whether scientific advances will ultimately be able to save the human race.

Bibliography

Gregory Benford. "On *Timescape*." Ben Bova, ed., *The Best of the Nebulas*. New York: Tor, 1989, 28–29.

———. "The Profession of Science Fiction, 22: A String of Days." *Foundation*, No. 21 (February, 1981), 5–17.

———. "Time and *Timescape*." *Science-Fiction Studies*, 20 (July, 1993), 184–190.

Russell Blackford, Gregory Benford, Damien Broderick, Alison Goodman, Sean McMullen, and Aubrey Townsend. "Time Travel, Time Scrapes, and *Timescape*." *New York Review of Science Fiction*, No. 144 (August, 2000), 1, 8–15.

Raimund Borgmeier. "Science Fiction Comes to College." Borgmeier, ed., *Gattungsprobleme in der Anglo-Amerikanischen Literatur*. Tubingen: Niemeyer, 1986, 239–253.

David Pringle. "*Timescape* by Gregory Benford (1980)." Pringle, *Science Fiction: The 100 Best Novels*. New York: Carroll and Graf, 1985, 199–200.

Norman Spinrad. "On Books." *Destinies*, 2 (Summer, 1980), 250–259.

Susan Stone-Blackburn. "Science and Humanism in Gregory Benford's *Timescape*." *Science-Fiction Studies*, 15 (November, 1988), 295–311.

—*Martin Morse Wooster*

TITUS GROAN BY MERVYN PEAKE (1946)

Summary

Mervyn Peake's *Titus Groan* is half of a tale, which continues in *Gormenghast* (1950). It is, by default, part of what is now known as the Gormenghast Trilogy— due to the author's ill health, which rendered him unable to fully complete a third volume, though a version of one eventually appeared as *Titus Alone* (1959); he also left a few notes for a fourth book. The novel, set in an **imaginary world**, involves the vast **castle** of Gormenghast where Titus, the seventy-seventh Earl, is still a small child at the end of the first novel. The place, steeped in immemorial tradition and meaningless **rituals**, is the focus of the ambitions of the rebel Steerpike, a social climber of lowly birth who by flattery, trickery, hard work, and occasional murder rises very high before he is destroyed at the end of the second volume. The first volume, taken by itself, creates a wholly self-contained world and brings Titus onstage as the object of contention; some conflicts are resolved (notably in a titanic battle between servant Flay and cook Swelter) while others are left in abeyance.

Discussion

One of the great, eccentric masterpieces of English letters, *Titus Groan* and its sequel defy easy synopsis. They are filled with magnificently poetic language, grotesque characters like something from a **Gothic** Dickens, and vivid moments of **horror** interspersed with startling wit (see **Humor**). Peake, although he seemed almost incapable of comprehending **mathematics**, was otherwise a kind of universal genius—novelist, poet, and artist of very great merit, arguably the greatest illustrator of the mid-twentieth century. The Gormenghast books are a profound meditation on life from a truly original mind, a fantasia of experience transmogrified into **dream**.

Born of missionary parents, Peake spent his first years in **China**. Gormenghast, with its musty exoticism and stifling rituals, may be a reflection of the Forbidden City in Peking at a time when the Manchu dynasty was actually over, but the boy-emperor and his courtiers continued their ancient rituals, completely divorced from reality. While Gormenghast has something of a hinterland (or at least villages clinging to its walls), it too seems disconnected. One also sees in Titus's upbringing and growing **rebellion** a dissatisfaction with the traditional English **class system**. Whereas most fantasy is conservative in its tone and backward-looking, *Titus Groan* and *Gormenghast* are radical.

Peake is often compared to J.R.R. Tolkien because the success of ***The Lord of the Rings*** led Tolkien's American publisher, Ballantine, to seek out more fantasy "trilogies" and package them similarly, including Peake's books. Thus, Peake first became popular when pitched to Tolkien's audience. While comparisons between the two are few, contrasts are intriguing. Both were writers of what might be called "life works," because they poured everything they had learned about life and everything they cared about into their books. But Tolkien is the conservative, yearning for the purer, simpler days of the past (which are equated with childhood). Unlike Peake, he is religious, ultimately offering reassurance that God is in his **Heaven** and somehow the good people will muddle through if they all do their bit (see **Religion**). There is regret that the best parts of Middle-earth must pass away, but Tolkien's characters bravely shoulder their adult responsibilities (forced upon them painfully, as adulthood is upon everyone) and soldier on.

Peake's Steerpike, almost an antihero, develops a profound contempt for the social system in which he finds himself. Wearing the false mask of **friendship** and loyalty, he betrays everyone, including himself when he finds he cannot, ultimately, sexually possess one of the noble Groan family, Titus's sister Fuchsia (see **Betrayal**). Despite everything, he is still a commoner. His mistake, even **tragedy**, is that he still wants what the aristocrats want. Even as he despises it, he has bought into their value system.

The true rebel (see **Freedom**) proves to be Titus, who at the end of the second volume, in a fit of adolescent rage, abdicates his position, leaves Gormenghast, and rides forth into the wide world and **exile**. By the end of the third volume, the now adult Titus realizes that he carries Gormenghast within him wherever he goes. He may have left the ancient walls behind, but Gormenghast has made him who he is. It is as if Frodo Baggins said, "to Hell with it," threw the **ring** away, fled Middle-earth, and came to terms with himself. It was Peake's intention to continue Titus's adventures through life into old age, but Peake's own illness (a degenerative brain condition compounded by inept surgeries) prevented this.

Not exactly an **allegory**, or fantasy in the conventional sense, lacking supernatural elements, *Titus Groan* and its sequels are Peake's main legacy. There is nothing else like them in literature, and although they have been widely admired by fantasy writers and have visibly influenced some—including Michael Moorcock, Gene Wolfe, China Miéville, and Jeff Vandermeer—we have seen only the beginnings of a "Peakean" school in his wake, and certainly not a whole publishing category devoted to cloned imitations. Peake will never be as popular as Tolkien, but he will always be admired by readers sensitive to his textures, poetic language, and amazing characters.

Bibliography

John Batchelor. *Mervyn Peake*. London: Duckworth, 1974.

Maeve Gilmore. *A World Away*. London: Gollancz, 1970.

David H. Keller. "*Titus Groan:* An Appreciation." Darrell Schweitzer, ed., *Exploring Fantasy Worlds*. San Bernardino, CA: Borgo Press, 1985, 83–88.

Edwin Morgan. "The Walls of Gormenghast." *The Chicago Review*, 14 (Autumn/Winter, 1960), 74–81.

Sebastian Peake. *A Child of Bliss*. Oxford: Lennard, 1989.

P.G. Smith. *Mervyn Peake*. London: Gollancz, 1984.

John Whatney. *Mervyn Peake*. New York: St. Martin's Press, 1976.

G. Peter Winnington. *Vast Alchemies*. London: Peter Owen, Publishers, 2000.

Malcolm Yorke. *Mine Eyes Mint Gold*. London: John Murray, 2000.

—Darrell Schweitzer

TOPPER (1937)

Summary

High-spirited, glamorous, and wealthy, George and Marion Kerby are given to drink. Their middle-aged friend, Cosmo Topper, chafes against the constraints of his regimented existence and wife Clara's mildly nagging insistence on order and decorum (see **Individualism and Conformity**). When the Kerbys die in a **automobile** crash (see **Death**), a rebellious Cosmo buys their showy, undignified car, which he crashes. The now-ghostly Kerbys (see **Ghosts and Hauntings**), convinced they must perform a good deed to get into **Heaven**, set about redeeming Cosmo, encouraging him to drink, dance, and sing. Cosmo is soon in court, and newspapers suggest he is involved with a burlesque queen, causing his social standing to skyrocket. Further comic shenanigans ensue (see **Comedy; Invisibility**). When Cosmo mops his brow with silk lingerie, Clara is convinced that their **marriage** is over. Cosmo and Marion hole up at a hotel. Their spree ends when George reappears, intent on causing chaos. George and Marion make up. Cosmo, injured in another crash, wants to depart with the Kerbys, but he is nursed back to health and reconciled to Clara.

Discussion

Based on Thorne Smith's *Topper: An Improbable Adventure* (1926), *Topper* tones down the novel's Prohibition-era emphasis on alcohol and rather saucy comedy, although inebriation and the suggestion that the invisible Marion might be nude (see **Nudity**) do play a part in the movie's light-hearted **humor**. Whereas the novel focuses on Cosmo, *Topper* places greater emphasis on its ghosts, played by stars Cary Grant and Constance Bennett. This can be seen as part of the emphasis in 1930s popular culture, most evident in screwball comedy, on companionate marriage—the sense, partially derived from developing consumer culture, that spouses should be friends and relationships fun. The spontaneity, irresponsibility, and playfulness of the Kerbys stand in for the sexual pleasure whose depiction was forbidden by the Production Code. Like the pioneering screwball comedy *It Happened One Night* (1934), *Topper* confirms this unspoken knowledge in its final frames: to please Cosmo, and because it constitutes and signifies her own **rebellion** against their straitlaced lives, a penitent Clara rolls up her dress to show him that she is wearing the silk underwear.

Whereas other comedies of the New Deal era like *My Man Godfrey* (1936) and *Sullivan's Travels* (1941) recognize the existence of a **class system,** or at least widespread impoverishment, *Topper* gives greater emphasis to Cosmo, a bank president, as victim of a system that robs his life of joy and the freedom even to listen to the **birds** sing. **Freedom**, it seems, is to be found not by changing determinate economic and social structures, but by becoming, like Cosmo's **trickster mentors**, wealthy enough to behave like children and consume. As always, Hollywood can only offer a sense of what **utopia** might feel like rather than how it might be arranged, and only indicates those deficiencies of capitalism which capitalism itself claims to be able to meet. So, although Clara's new underwear is a problematic image of revolt, it does anticipate by fifty years a post-feminist (see **Feminism**) conceptualization of bourgeois female liberation through **sexuality** and shopping.

There were two sequels. In *Topper Takes a Trip* (1939), which takes only the Riviera setting and some gags from Smith's bawdy 1932 sequel of that name, Cosmo and Marion rescue an estranged Clara from the clutches of a conman suitor. *Topper Returns* (1941), which takes nothing from Smith but Cosmo and Clara, is an old dark house **mystery** in which Topper helps the ghost of Gail Richards solve her own murder and save the life of her heiress friend, the killer's real target. The period also saw three other Smith adaptations: *The Night Life of the Gods* (1935) and *Turnabout* (1940), both based on 1931 novels with the same titles, and *I Married A Witch* (1942), based on his uncompleted *The Passionate Witch* (1941) (which can also be seen as the inspiration for *Bewitched* [1964–1972] and *I Dream of Jeannie* [1965–1970]). The TV series *Topper* (1953–1956) starred Leo G. Carroll as a more dithering Cosmo, while two later pilot movies, *Topper Returns* (1973) and *Topper* (1979), did not lead to series.

While peripheral to the 1930s screwball cycle, *Topper* and other Smith adaptations are central to a less-examined decade-long cycle of supernatural comedies and fantasies, which included *The Ghost Goes West* (1936), *The Cat and the Canary* (1939), *The Ghost Breakers* (1940), *Here Comes Mr. Jordan* (1941) (see **Heaven Can Wait**), *Hold that Ghost* (1941), *Heaven Can Wait* (1943), *The Canterville Ghost* (1944), *Blithe Spirit* (1945), *A Matter of Life and Death* (1946), *Angel on My Shoulder* (1946), *The Bishop's Wife* (1947), *Down to Earth* (1947) and *The Ghost and Mrs Muir* (1947). The supernatural comedy movie has rarely worked well since the 1940s. Where it has succeeded, it has transformed into blockbuster comedy or sentimentality, as in *Ghostbusters* (1984) and *Ghost* (1990), or into the gross-out slapstick of Sam Raimi and Peter Jackson's earlier movies—the tone of which could not be more different from Smith's novels and their adaptations.

Bibliography

Donald Deschner. *The Complete Films of Cary Grant*. Secaucus: Citadel, 1973.

Warren G. Harris. "*Topper* Turns the Trick." Harris, *Cary Grant*. New York: Doubleday, 1987, 78–86.

Peter Jordan. "Wish Fulfillment." *Studies in Popular Culture*, 8 (1985), 53–62.

Barry Putterman. *On Television and Comedy*. Jefferson, NC: McFarland, 1995.

Richard Schickel. "Bringing Up Cary." Schickel, *Cary Grant*. New York: Applause Books, 1999, 51–72.

Ted Sennett. *Lunatics and Lovers*. New Rochelle: Arlington House, 1973.

Kenneth Von Gunden. *Flights of Fancy*. Jefferson: McFarland, 1989.

Richard Ward. "Golden Age, Blue Pencils." *Media History*, 8 (June 1, 2002), 103–119.

—Mark Bould

TOTAL RECALL (1990)

—

He awoke—and wanted Mars. The valleys, he thought, what would it be like to trudge among them? Great and greater yet; the dream grew as he became fully conscious, the dream and the yearning.

—Philip K. Dick
"We Can Remember It for You Wholesale"
(1966)

Summary

Construction worker Doug Quaid dreams of a life on **Mars** and so decides to buy the **memory** of an **espionage** adventure on the red planet from Rekall, Inc. Unfortunately, it appears that he really has a **secret identity** as an agent and the person he believes is his wife only met him six weeks previously. Even more ominously, someone wants him dead. He goes to Mars to investigate and finds a former lover,

Melina, who takes him to meet Kuato, leader of the rebels who are fighting against Cohaagen's monopoly on production of air on Mars. Unfortunately, it seems that Quaid is really a man named Hauser, who works for Cohaagen and has been programmed to set a trap to capture Kuato. However, after Kuato's death Quaid is still being pursued and goes off to locate Cohaagen's secret—an alien artifact that can produce enough oxygen to give the planet an atmosphere (see **Terraforming**). When the device is triggered, Mars's atmosphere is instantly transformed, and Quaid and Melina kiss on the surface of Mars without pressure suits.

Discussion

This film bears little resemblance to Philip K. Dick's story "We Can Remember It for You Wholesale" (1966) after its first twenty minutes, descending into the **violence** and purportedly witty one-liners associated with star Arnold Schwarzenegger throughout the 1980s and 1990s. In the story, white-collar Doug Quail has false memories that turn out to be true, so the company replaces that memory with an even more bizarre one that turn outs to be true as well—culminating in the discovery that Quail actually saved **Earth** from **invasion** by mouse-like **aliens on Earth**. True, the film contains Dickian elements—like the **robot** taxi cab and mutant rebel inside another rebel—but these play second fiddle to the action. Significantly, the film changes both the lead protagonist's **name**—perhaps because Quail echoed the name of then-current American Vice President Dan Quayle, or because it seemed too unmanly for Schwarzenegger—and his profession—undoubtedly because the muscular Schwarzenegger looked more like a construction worker than an executive. Dick's name is even misspelled, as "Phillip" in the opening credits, but this was due to a mistake in a contract Dick himself had signed, so filmmakers were obliged to spell it incorrectly.

Given the credentials of two of the film's screenwriters—Dan O'Bannon and Ronald Shussett wrote *Alien*, and O'Bannon co-wrote *Dark Star* (1974)—and career of director Paul Verhoeven—he directed *RoboCop* (1987) and would direct *Starship Troopers* (1997)—the film might be regarded as a disappointment, since it contains little of the irony and **satire** that these other projects did. Any deeper reading of the film largely depends on assuming that some or all of the film is a dream. This would mirror the dream sequence at the start of the film and would also explain how a lethal planetary environment can be transformed into a human **habitat** in which **survival** is possible simply by finding a convenient piece of alien **technology**; and only in a dream, arguably, could two people placed in a vacuum that caused their eyes to expand to an alarming size survive unharmed. At one point, a psychologist appears who tells Quaid that he is still in an hallucination, a moment providing an authentic thrill of Dickian **estrangement**, but this appears to be explained away as another act of **betrayal** by those who surround Quaid and are attempting to locate the rebel leader (and is a piece of plotting that requires more convoluted application of **psychology** than anyone suffering from **paranoia** could begin to consider).

The film might have worked better in the hands of David Cronenberg, originally slated to direct the script in the early 1980s, since he has played clever games with what is real and what is **illusion** in films like *Videodrome* (1982), *Naked Lunch* (1991) and *eXistenZ* (1999). However, he pulled out of the project after a dozen rewrites of the script, which eventually passed from Dino De Laurentiis (who made *Dune* [1984]) to the Carolco Company, best known for effects-laden action movies like *Terminator 2* (1991) (see **The Terminator**) and *Universal Soldier* (1992).

There is perhaps some mileage in considering how far this **frontier** planet is dependent on Cohaagen's monopoly on oxygen and willingness to supply the **city** for a price—the privatization of essentials being a political concern in the 1980s and explored in *RoboCop* with the sale of police labor to private **business** concerns. However, it becomes increasingly unclear as to whether Quaid is standing up for a group of rebels who are being starved of oxygen (but again who recover instantly), whether he has been manipulated into this (in the process using a piece of holograph technology which enemies may have supplied him with in an attempt to convince him that he was an agent), or whether he is simply acting out of a concern for his personal survival (see **Guilt and Responsibility**). As is usually the case, the size of a film's budget (in this case, about $60 million) is inversely proportional to its intelligence.

Bibliography

Carl Brandon. "*Total Recall.*" *Cinefantastique*, 21 (April, 1991), 36–38.

R.J. Ellis. "Are You a Fucking Mutant?" *Foundation*, No. 65 (Autumn, 1995), 81–97.

Fred Glass. "Totally Recalling Arnold." *Film Quarterly*, 44 (Spring, 1990), 2–13.

Jonathan Goldberg. "Recalling Totalities." Chris Hables Gray, ed., *The Cyborg Handbook*. New York: Routledge, 1995, 233–254.

Robert Miklitsch. "*Total Recall.*" *Camera Obscura*, 32 (1994), 5–39.

Linda Mizejewski. "Total Recoil." *Post Script*, 12 (Fall, 1993), 80–87.

Donald E. Palumbo. "Inspired . . . by Philip K. Dick." *Journal of the Fantastic in the Arts*, 4 (1991), 69–80.

Johanna Schmertz. "On Reading the Politics of *Total Recall*." *Post Script*, 12 (Fall, 1993), 34–42.

Rob van Scheers. *Paul Verhoeven*. London and Boston: Faber & Faber, 1997.

—*Andrew M. Butler*

A TRIP TO THE MOON (1902)

Summary

Barbenfouillis (played by director Georges Méliès), leader of a group of astonomers who more closely resemble **wizards** than **scientists**, proposes a journey from **Earth** to the **Moon**. They tour the factory where the projectile (see **Rockets**) is being constructed and observe the casting of the cannon that will fire them into space. The projectile is launched with much ceremony (see **Space Travel**), and crashes into the Moon's right eye (see **Personification**). The unlikely **astronauts** emerge onto the lunar **landscape** and watch Earth rise above the horizon. After they bed down for the night, a comet (see **Comets and Asteroids**) crosses the sky, the seven **stars** of Ursa Major appear, and from each one a woman's face looks down at the sleeping savants. The stars are replaced by two women holding a star aloft, a woman seated on a crescent moon, and an old man looking down from Saturn (see **Jupiter and the Outer Planets**). The savants are awakened by a fall of snow and descend into the lunar interior (see **Underground Adventure**), where they find a grotto filled with giant mushrooms. One savant opens his umbrella and it takes root, transforming (see **Metamorphosis**) into a giant mushroom. A cavorting, contorting Selenite appears (see **First Contact**). A savant strikes it, and it disappears in a cloud of smoke. Another Selenite is similarly dispatched, but the savants are outnumbered and captured. They are brought before the lunar **king**. Barbenfouillis breaks free and strikes the king, and in the confusion the savants **escape**, pursued by the Selenite army. Once the savants are safely in the projectile, Barbenfouillis topples it off a cliff and it falls to Earth. It splashes down at sea and is towed into harbor.

Discussion

Of the more than 500 films Méliès made between 1896 and 1912, about 170 survive. Although he was not primarily, as is widely believed, a maker of naive **fairy tales** and fantasies, a significant proportion of his output was devoted to trick films—utilizing split-screens, dissolves, undercranked and overcranked cameras—with fantastical settings, characters, and plots. His first science fiction films were the now-lost *A Twentieth Century Surgeon* and *The Clown and the Automaton* in 1897. Of all his films, *A Trip to the Moon*, inspired by Adolphe Dennery's stage adaptation of Jules Verne's *From the Earth to the Moon* and H.G. Wells's *The First Men in the Moon* (1901), is the most famous.

Like many later science fiction movies, it often seems more concerned with spectacle than narrative, concatenating special effects and moments of physical **humor** and slapstick **comedy** against elaborate painted backdrops and repeatedly displaying female bodies—dressed in pageboy costumes (see **Androgyny**), saucy naval uniforms, and diaphanous gowns. Méliès, who made a number of erotic films, often costumed women to suggest **nudity** (see **Sexism**). His eroticization of space culminated in *The Eclipse, or the Courtship of the Sun and Moon* (1907) in which an astonomer observes female figures riding shooting stars, Saturn and **Mars** competing for the attentions of a female Moon, and a rain of female shooting stars, as well as a gay sexual encounter (see **Homosexuality**) between a flirtatious Moon and lascivious **Sun**.

Another spectacular aspect of the film was its length. At 260 meters (approximately 13 minutes), there would have been few, if any, longer films made before it, and such durations would remain uncommon for several years. A more expensive hand-tinted version was also available to exhibitors.

One reason that *A Trip to the Moon* is often considered as a sequence of scenes, not a proper narrative, is that it is usually revived without the narration written to accompany it. The narration adds narrative coherence and, by naming the savants (Nostradamus, Micromegas, Omega), further situates the film within a fantasy and science fiction tradition. Like Cyrano de Bergerac's *The Comical History of the States and Empires of the Moon and Sun* (1687), Jonathan Swift's **Gulliver's Travels** (which Méliès also adapted in 1902), and Voltaire's *Micromégas* (1752), it is a **satire**, establishing both the scientific congress and lunar court as absurd hierarchies.

As France then controlled the second largest empire, this equation between modern France, caught between superstition and reason, and the Selenites, who resemble colonialist fantasies of Africans, is not insignificant.

The Impossible Voyage (1904) is sometimes described as a sequel to *A Trip to the Moon*; and as a more elaborate and longer (374 meters or approximately 16 minutes) semi-remake, it fits the pattern of more recent film sequels. Like its precursor, it starts with a scientific congress and a visit to the factory where a fabulous vehicle is being built—this time a combination car-train-submarine-boat-with-dirigibles-and-an-icebox (see **Transportation**) intended to take its crew around the world. Instead, they land on the Sun, where they must freeze themselves to survive (see **Suspended Animation and Cryonics**). They topple off a cliff back to Earth and an extended **underwater adventure**, including an encounter with a giant octopus (see **Fish and Sea Creatures**). An explosion throws them ashore, where they receive a rapturous welcome. The film is a compendium of elements taken from Jules Verne's novels, including *Journey to the Center of the Earth* (1863), **Twenty Thousand Leagues Under the Sea**, and *Around the World in Eighty Days* (1873). Méliès later adapted *The Mysterious Island* (1875) in 1905 and *Twenty Thousand Leagues Under the Sea* in 1907; and, although it is not based on Verne's fiction, one of his last three films, made for Pathé in 1912 after his own company had collapsed, has the distinctly Verne-like title of *The Conquest of the Pole*.

Bibliography

Richard Abel. *The Ciné Goes to Town*. Berkeley: University of California Press, 1998.

Thomas Elsaesser, ed. *Early Cinema*. London: British Film Institute, 1990.

Elizabeth Ezra. *Georges Méliès*. Manchester: Manchester University Press, 2000.

John Frazer. *Artfully Arranged Scenes*. Boston: G.K. Hall, 1979.

Paul Hammond. *Georges Méliès*. London: Gordon Fraser, 1974.

David Robinson. *Georges Méliès*. London: Museum of the Moving Image, 1993.

David Sandner. "Shooting for the Moon." *Extrapolation*, 39 (Spring, 1998), 5–25.

Gary Westfahl. "Celebrating a Century of Science Fiction Columns with *A Trip to the Moon*." *Interzone*, No. 176 (February, 2002), 47–48.

Alan Williams. *Republic of Images*. Cambridge: Harvard University Press, 1992.

—*Mark Bould*

TRIPLANETARY BY E.E. "DOC" SMITH (1948)

Two thousand million or so years ago two galaxies were colliding; or, rather, were passing through each other.

—E.E. "Doc" Smith
Triplanetary (1948)

Summary

Triplanetary introduces E.E. "Doc" Smith's Lensman series—once grandiosely published as The History of Civilization—whose core books are early high points of **space opera** despite crudity and **clichés**. Most had magazine incarnations, *Triplanetary* as early as 1934 (although, first written as a standalone adventure, it was heavily revised for book publication to serve as the series' introduction). The series continues with *First Lensman* (1950), *Galactic Patrol* (1950), *Gray Lensman* (1951), *Second Stage Lensmen* (1953), *Children of the Lens* (1954), and—only tangentially related to the main storyline—*The Vortex Blaster* (1960).

The vast scale is signalled by *Triplanetary*'s famous opening sentence: "Two thousand million or so years ago, two galaxies were colliding . . . ." Planets and planetary life result. The Arisians, benevolent alien **mentors**, steer the **evolution** of human and other life-forms in readiness to resist the tyrannical designs of the Arisians' **evil** counterparts, the Eddoreans.

Galactic **civilization** is given one Arisian tool, the Lens, granting **psychic powers** including telepathy and universal translation (see **Language and Linguistics**). Only the best and brightest members of the Galactic Patrol receive Lenses. Kimball Kinnison, the top human Lensman introduced in *Galactic Patrol*, spearheads the battle against successive levels of the Eddoreans' layered organization ("Boskone"). Innovations of **technology** lead to ever more apocalyptic **weaponry** as the **space war** expands throughout and beyond our galaxy.

Discussion

Boskone proves to be behind all three assaults on civilization, which the square-dealing Patrolmen initially (in *First Lensman*) believe to be independent: dirty **politics**, **drugs**, and space **pirates**. The last, not individual raiders but advance parties of an entrenched and organized foe, come to dominate the struggle.

For both sides, **space travel** is achieved by an inertia-cancelling drive allowing incredible **speeds** limited only by the density of interstellar dust. Kinnison's first mission in *Galactic Patrol* is to steal the secret of Boskone's superior spaceship power units. From this modest beginning, both his personal array of psychic abilities and the **war**-driven advance of technology increase exponentially.

Antimatter weapons are developed in frantic haste. The possibility of cancelling and restoring the inertia of an entire world points to the grand finale of *Gray Lensman*, when the "impregnable" fortress world of the current Boskone echelon is smashed between two aimed planets on opposing courses. Thanks to the discovery of **hyperspace**, *Second Stage Lensmen* sees a counterattack as Boskone invades the solar system via a "hyper-spatial tube" with forces including (another line beloved by fans) "Planets. Seven of them. Armed and powered as only a planet can be armed and powered . . . ." Fortunately Kinnison is prepared with the gigantic, system-spanning "sunbeam" apparatus that focuses the full output of our **Sun** upon the hapless intruders. Still the technological escalation is far from complete. The final campaign exploits unthinkable energies from a tachyonic universe where nothing travels *slower* than **light**.

On the Intelligence front, there is a similar to-and-fro dance of increasingly potent mind probes and thought screens, spy-rays and spy-ray blocks, "drills" that penetrate screens and blocks, the ultimate psionic "sense of perception" that sees through opaque matter, **force** fields that can block even this . . . and so on.

In this series Smith rose above the characteristic **xenophobia** of the period and his earlier Skylark sequence, whereby all non-humanoid **aliens in space** tended to be **villains**. The Lensman universe has **monsters** aplenty, some monstrously sadistic—at one stage Boskonian **torture** leaves Kinnison salvagable only by multiple amputation and advanced tissue regeneration techniques (see **Medicine**). But there are also staunch alien allies of many shapes, including **dragon**-like Velantians; eyeless, tentacled Rigellians; and cryogenic Palainians whose bodies extend beyond three **dimensions**. One of each of these species proves worthy, like Kinnison, of advanced Arisian training to achieve the added powers and responsibilities of Second Stage Lensmen; and these nonhumans become favorite companions and mentors of three of Kinnison's highly gifted **children** in *Children of the Lens*.

These siblings, five in all, represent the culmination of an Arisian-guided eugenics program begun long before the fall of **Atlantis**. Working as a gestalt (see **Hive Minds**) backed by the pooled mental power of Arisia and the entire Galactic Patrol, they deal the final **death** blow to the Eddoreans.

An incidental feature of the series is a physiological classification system, in which (lapsing into anthropocentrism) the human form is classed AAAAAA while the most monstrous aliens register as "straight Z's to ten or twelve places." This coding was later adapted and rationalized by James White in *Hospital Station* and its sequels.

Smith's use of language hardly matched his galaxy-spanning narrative ambition. Stylistic tics include archaisms like "wight" for "person," unconvincing salutations like "QX! Hot jets and clear ether!" and carefully sanitized space-oaths: "By Klono's TUNGSTEN TEETH and CURVING CARBALLOY CLAWS!" **Love** scenes, though likewise highly restrained, tend to generate embarrassment.

Nevertheless Smith still retains an appreciative audience, thanks to his boyish exuberance of **invention**, the exhilarating black-and-white (see **Yin and Yang**) simplicities of his galactic conflict, and his gleeful piling up of technological and conceptual excesses as each "ultimate" weapon or defense is trumped by a *more* ultimate countermeasure. Many writers of more modern, sophisticated **space opera** took their impetus from Smith and his indomitable Lensmen.

Bibliography

Daniel Dickholtz. "One Hundred Most Important People in Science Fiction/Fantasy: E.E. Smith." *Starlog*, No. 100 (November, 1985), 31–32.

R.R. Eberle, "Checklist (1928–1965) of E. E. Smith." *Science Fiction Times*, No. 433 (November, 1965), 8–9.

Ron Ellik and Bill Evans. *The Universes of E. E. Smith*. Chicago, IL: Advent, 1966.

Edmond Hamilton. "Tribute to 'Doc' Smith." *Vector*, No. 36 (November, 1965), 9–10.

David A. Kyle. "The Worlds of E. E. 'Doc' Smith." *Starlog*, No. 139 (February, 1989), 45–48, 57.

Stephen C. Lucchetti. *Doc—First Galactic Roamer*. Framingham, MA: NESFA Press, 2004.

Sam Moskowitz. "Edward E. Smith, Ph.D." Moskowitz, *Seekers of Tomorrow*. Cleveland, OH: World Publishing, 1966, 9–26.

E.E. Smith. "The Epic of Space." Lloyd Arthur Eshbach, ed., *Of Worlds Beyond*. Second Ed. Chicago: Advent, 1964, 77–88.

Brian Stableford. "Creators of Science Fiction, 7: E. E. 'Doc' Smith." *Interzone*, No. 111 (September, 1996), 48–52.

—*David Langford*

TRITON BY SAMUEL R. DELANY (1976)

Summary

In 2112, colonies have been established on **Mars** and several of the larger moons of our solar system (see **Planetary Colonies**). Bron Helstrom, an intelligent, physically vigorous, but strangely self-absorbed man, has previously worked on Mars as a male prostitute. He now lives in a **city** called Tethys, on Neptune's moon Triton (see **Jupiter and the Outer Planets**), where most of the action of *Triton* takes place. Here, a kind of utopian society (see **Utopia**) has been established, characterized by advanced **technology**, a sophisticated **governance system**, and social arrangements that are designed to cater for individuals of almost any personality type, style, or **sexuality**, including **homosexuality**.

As the action unfolds, tensions among **Earth** and the various colonized worlds and moons embroil the people of Triton in an immensely destructive **war**, though this provides little more than the backdrop to the main story. On Triton, Bron meets, and seemingly falls in **love** with, a brilliant young woman who is a theatrical director known as the Spike (see **Theatre**). Their **romance** soon fails, when she sees him for what he really is. Though the **civilization** of the Outer Satellites offers extraordinary **freedom**, and everything that Bron could reasonably want is available, he is unhappy with his life, out of harmony with those around him, and continually looking for others to blame.

A trip to Earth leads to another encounter with the Spike—this one disastrous—and Bron returns to Triton, where he eventually takes the drastic step of changing sex in an attempt to solve his personal problems. However, it becomes plain to the reader, if not to Bron himself, that this is a further evasion rather than a solution: the cause of his problems lies deep within his own psyche (see **Identity; Psychology**).

Discussion

Triton has not been published in a revised edition, formally designated as such, but some revisions have been incorporated into subsequent reprints, culminating in the 1996 edition from Wesleyan University Press, *Trouble on Triton*. Though the 1996 Wesleyan version is packaged as no more than a retitling of the 1976 novel, some important changes and corrections have been made (in addition to the use of the author's preferred title). Accordingly, *Trouble on Triton* should be considered the preferred edition to be consulted by serious students of Delany's work.

The novel consists of a main narrative plus two appendices; one contains work notes and omitted pages, while the other is an essay on the life and thought of an off-stage character, Ashima Slade. The main narrative is subtitled *An Ambiguous Heterotopia*, setting up a resonance with Ursula K. Le Guin's **The Dispossessed**, first published just two years before, which is subtitled *An Ambiguous Utopia*. To what extent *Triton* is a response to *The Dispossessed* may be debated; certainly, Delany is in part reacting to the gray utilitarianism of Le Guin's world by providing his future residents with a more colorful and hedonistic lifestyle. Yet unlike Le Guin, Delany seems to be more focused on exploring personal, not political, issues.

In essence, *Triton* portrays the mind of a character who is unable to take advantage of living in an enviroment of liberty and economic plenty (see **Economics**). Bron is infuriatingly egocentric, judgmental, and concerned with appearances and proprieties. His background in the relatively conservative society of Mars has not equipped him psychologically for the freedoms of the Outer Satellites, and he displays a marked degree of racism, **sexism**, and heterosexism in his thoughts and speech, and in his general attitudes to people and events that he encounters.

Delany uses a prose style that closely follows Bron's remarkably self-conscious thought processes. The sentences bristle with italized words that break the expected rhythm of the language, while marking careful distinctions. Many parenthetical comments qualify or elaborate Bron's thinking. Bron is shown to be an individual who is almost obsessed with his own actions and responses, even while making harsh judgments about others, or dismissing their conduct insultingly, for example as that of a "crazed lesbian."

In one key scene, Bron meets up with the Spike on Earth, after previous encounters on Triton, and he attempts to impress her by organizing an elaborate meal (see **Food and Drink**) at a palatial restaurant in Mongolia. However, the more he tries to impress her, the more he reveals himself to be unspontaneous, egocentric, coarse, and bound by debilitating cultural misconceptions (see **Cultures**).

He is especially ready to cast blame on Triton's society, which he appears to see as soft and morally decadent (see **Decadence**), with its options for almost anyone—though not for him. He actually seems to crave a traditional romance in which a woman will be swept away by love for him, and will respond by sacrificing her own interests and career (see **Sacrifice**). He cannot come to terms with having to live in a time and place where this is no longer a real possibility. *Triton* is the study of a personality who cannot find happiness even in a society genuinely superior to our own.

Bibliography

Russell Blackford. "Jewels in Junk City." *Review of Contemporary Fiction* 16 (Fall, 1996), 142–147.

Neil Easterbrook. "State, Heterotopia." Donald M. Hassler and Clyde Wilcox, eds., *Political Science Fiction*. Columbia: University of South Carolina Press, 1997, 43–75.

John Fekete. "*The Dispossessed* and *Triton*." *Science-Fiction Studies*, 6 (July, 1979), 129–143.

Robert Elliott Fox. "The Politics of Desire in Delany's *Triton* and *The Tides of Lust*." James Sallis, ed., *Ash of Stars*. Jackson: University Press of Mississippi, 1996, 43–61.

Valerie Holliday. "Delany Dispossessed." *Extrapolation*, 44 (Winter, 2003), 425–436.

Michelle Massé. "All You Have to Do Is Know What You Want." George E. Slusser, Eric S. Rabkin, and Robert Scholes, eds., *Coordinates*. Carbondale and Edwardsville: Southern Illinois University Press, 1983, 49–64.

Tom Moylan. "Samuel R. Delany, *Triton*." Moylan, *Demand the Impossible*. New York and London: Methuen, 1986, 156–195.

Robert M. Philmus. "On *Triton* and Other Matters." *Science-Fiction Studies*, 17 (November, 1990), 295–324.

—*Russell Blackford*

TWENTY THOUSAND LEAGUES UNDER THE SEA BY JULES VERNE (1870)

> Look at that sea! Who can say it isn't actually alive! It expresses its anger and its tenderness! Yesterday it went to sleep as we did, and now like us it is awakening after a peaceful night.
>
> —Jules Verne
> *Twenty Thousand Leagues under the Sea*
> (1870), trans. Walter James Miller
> and Frederick Paul Walter (1993)

Summary

In this classic **underwater adventure**, Verne sends **scientist**–explorer Professor Aronnax into one of the few remaining unexplored regions on **Earth**. Responding to reports of an enormous unknown maritime object traveling with amazing rapidity, the American ship *Abraham Lincoln* starts in pursuit with Aronnax and his servant Conseil aboard. After six months they sight the object—a huge submarine, the *Nautilus*. During the chase, Aronnax, Conseil, and Canadian harpooner Ned Land are washed overboard and taken inside the *Nautilus* where its captain, Nemo, provides every comfort but keeps them prisoners. For ten months they undertake an **exploration** of the world's oceans, including a passage beneath Antarctica where the Nautilus narrowly escapes being crushed by ice, and a reconnoitering of the site of **Atlantis**. Aronnax meticulously records the sequence of marvels, including enormous cetaceans, sharks, a giant squid, and numerous wrecks on the seabed. The enigmatic Nemo has a mysterious past, which is presumed to account for his intense hatred of imperialism—specifically British imperialism—his insatiable desire for vengeance, his passion for **music**, and his compassion for members of oppressed races. Finally, after ramming an attacking ship, the *Nautilus* is destroyed in a maelstrom off the Norwegian coast, but Aronnax and his companions are miraculously rescued.

Discussion

In his early novels, collectively entitled Les Voyages Extraordinaires, Jules Verne developed his belief that scientific discovery was the greatest of all adventures and that European Man would progressively master **nature**. The marvels of science invariably overcome the dangers of nature as, with unfailing optimism (see **Optimism and Pessimism**), his scientists courageously risk their lives in a quest for **knowledge**. The stories also had a strongly didactic subtext, intended to elicit in their youthful readers bravery and belief in **technology** and **progress**.

As an engineer, Verne included scientific or quasi-scientific explanations of technological **inventions**. Here, Professor Aronnax of the Paris Museum of Natural History functions as intellectual guide, describing and cataloguing the sea creatures observed through the submarine's windows or encountered when the visitors explore the marine world as divers.

Verne's focus on novel means of **transportation** is significant. **Speed** becomes a metaphor for breaking through boundaries and asserting individual **freedom** and environmental domination, encapsulated in Nemo's motto, *mobilis in mobili*. The *Nautilus* is a **microcosm** characterized by self-sufficiency, technological ingenuity, velocity, and ornamental elegance, being equipped with an organ, a gallery of European masterpieces, and a natural **history** museum. Verne's scientists do not leave their comfort zone; they take it with them—an indication of tacit imperialism.

Like their predecessors in Francis Bacon's *The New Atlantis* (1629), Verne's scientists are compulsive collectors of facts and natural objects. Nemo is the first serious oceanographer in literature, converting the *Nautilus* into a vast museum of **fish and sea creatures**, which functions as both result and symbol of the systematizing process. Aronnax cheerfully endures imprisonment in return for the opportunity to observe, describe, and photograph underwater phenomena for the first time.

Nemo is an unusually complex character in science fiction. He owed something to several of Verne's contemporaries, including Colonel Charras and the oceanographer Albert I of Monaco, but he is also psychologically interesting. As a wandering individual, Nemo epitomized Verne's image of **humanity**, endowed with technology and attempting to create a peaceful world, but a victim of his mysterious past and his insatiable desire for vengeance against British imperialism. This anglophobia owes something to the American Robert Fulton who, in 1801, had built an actual submarine called the *Nautilus*, which he offered to Napoleon to place powder mines beneath British warships. Fulton's motto, "*Libertas maris, terrarum felicitas*," is reflected in Nemo's "*mobilis in mobili*," painted around an "N." The sequel, *The Mysterious Island* (1874–1875), reveals that Nemo was formerly an Indian Prince Dakkan, who participated in the Indian Mutiny of 1857. Dispossessed, Nemo becomes a submarine Robin Hood, distributing to oppressed races and individuals the wealth he rescues from submerged wrecks. He is the Byronic **hero** championing Greek independence.

An interesting extension of his pity for the oppressed is Nemo's advanced environmental attitude to the oceans and endangered species (see **Ecology**). He is far ahead of contemporary thinking in refusing to countenance purposeless killing of southern whales, as urged by Ned Land. Nevertheless Nemo himself exhibits the competitiveness that **postcolonialism** associates with imperialism, as when he plants his flag at the South Pole (see **Polar Regions**). In this, as in his ruthless jeopardizing of his crew's safety, he shows similarities with Captain Walton in Mary Shelley's *Frankenstein*.

The enormous popularity of Verne's writings during his lifetime indicates how competently he reflected current expectations about science, technology, and engineering. Embarked on a physical journey—a metaphor for an intellectual journey—his protagonists embody contemporary confidence in science to overcome dangers and charter the unknowable. Verne gave fantasy a new respectability by insisting on technological credibility and linking geographical travel with the discovery of new knowledge. His novels inspired scientists, inventors, and explorers as well as writers. Richard Fleischer's film for Walt Disney (1954) depicted the *Nautilus* as an atomic-powered craft sinking all warfaring ships in a bid for world peace but apocalyptically destroyed in a mushroom cloud. *The Warlords of Atlantis* (1978) and *The Abyss* (1989) owe much to Verne's sequel, *The Mysterious Island*.

Bibliography

William Butcher. *Verne's Journey to the Center of the Self*. London: Macmillan, 1990.

Peter Costello. *Jules Verne, Inventor of Science Fiction*. London: Hodder and Stoughton, 1978.

Arthur B. Evans. *Jules Verne Rediscovered*. New York: Greenwood Press, 1988.

Herbert R. Lottman. *Jules Verne*. New York: St. Martin's Press, 1996.

James W. Maertens. "Between Jules Verne and Walt Disney." *Science-Fiction Studies*, 22 (July, 1995), 209–225.

Andrew Martin. *The Mask of the Prophet*. Oxford and New York: Oxford University Press, 1990.

Walter James Miller, ed. *The Annotated Jules Verne: Twenty Thousand Leagues under the Sea*, by Jules Verne. New York: Harper and Row, 1976.

Mark Rose. "Filling the Void: Verne, Wells and Lem." *Science-Fiction Studies*, 8 (July, 1981), 121–142.

Brian Taves and Stephen Michaluk. *The Jules Verne Encyclopedia*. Lanham, MD: Scarecrow Press, 1996.

—*Roslynn Haynes*

THE TWILIGHT ZONE (1959–1964)

You're traveling through another dimension, a dimension not only of sight and sound but of mind; a journey into a wondrous land whose boundaries are that of imagination. That's the signpost up ahead—your next stop, The Twilight Zone.

—Rod Serling
The Twilight Zone (1959)

Summary

Writer Rod Serling said that he launched the anthology series *The Twilight Zone* to escape restrictive censorship by telling stories involving **magic** or **space travel** that could address controversial issues without upsetting advertisers or his television network. However, while occasional episodes reflect such an intent—like "The Monsters Are Due on Maple Street" (1960) and "I Am the Night—Color Me Black" (1964), critiques of the corrosive effects of prejudice (see **Race Relations**), and "Two" (1961), an allegorical attack on the Cold War—the series more often presented generalized **fables** about **humanity**'s vices and virtues, in tones ranging from gentle sentimentality to bitter irony. Serling himself wrote the bulk of the episodes, though other writers like Richard Matheson and Charles Beaumont made significant contributions; the series' thematic unity stemmed mostly from Serling's memorable performances as on-camera narrator—standing amidst an eerie fog, smoking the cigarettes that eventually killed him, and concluding each episode with a pithy comment to drive its point home.

Discussion

With episodes limited to twenty-two minutes in length (except for the fourth season, which experimentally expanded to hour-long episodes), writers were often restricted to stories that amounted to little more than extended jokes or elaborate setups for a surprise ending, though such episodes could be involving and effective in their own way. Many involved strange **role reversals**: in one famous episode, "The Eye of the Beholder" (1960), a bandaged woman described as deformed turns out to be a beautiful woman in a world of ugly, pig-faced people (see **Beauty**); in "A Nice Place to Visit" (1960), a man tiring of the endless pleasures of **Heaven** finally learns that he is actually in **Hell**; in "The Invaders" (1961), a woman in a farmhouse attacking aliens in a tiny flying saucer (see **UFOs**) is finally revealed as a **giant** alien herself, while the "invaders" are human **astronauts**; in "The Midnight Sun" (1961), a woman suffering in the extreme heat as **Earth** moves closer to the **Sun** turns out to be having a **dream** in an increasingly cold world actually drifting away from the Sun; and in "The Dummy" (1962), a ventriloquist ends up trading places with his **evil** dummy (see **Dolls and Puppets**).

Other episodes build up to a moment of supreme irony: in "Time Enough at Last" (1959), a man welcomes the discovery that he alone has survived a **nuclear war** because he will finally have enough time to read as much as he wants—but then breaks the glasses he depends on for reading; in "The Rip Van Winkle Caper" (1961), four criminals go into hibernation to **escape** justice (see **Suspended Animation and Cryonics**)—only to awaken in a future world in which the gold that they stole is worthless (see **Gold and Silver**); and in "The Last Night of a Jockey" (1963), a jockey tired of being small has his wish granted and becomes tall—but then is too big to ride horses. Deals with the Devil that backfire (see **Satan**) figure in "Escape Clause" (1959), "Printer's Devil" (1963), and "Of Late, I Think of Cliffordsville" (1963).

A number of episodes involve people using various forms of **time travel** to return to their own pasts—either pleasantly rediscovering their lost youth, as in "Kick the Can" (1962) and "Static" (1961); finding that it was not as pleasant as they remembered, as in "The Trouble with Templeton" (1960) and "The Incredible World of Horace Ford" (1963); or becoming victims of a cruel **destiny**, as in

"The Last Flight" (1960) and "Back There" (1961). A few episodes interestingly involve **metafiction and recursiveness**, like "The 16mm Shrine" (1959), about an actress who escapes into the world of her old movies; "A World of Difference" (1960), where a man discovers that he is only an actor in a movie; "A World of His Own" (1960), about a man who can literally bring characters to life; "Showdown with Rance McGrew" (1962), in which a cowboy actor finds himself in the real American west (see **Westerns**); and "The Bard" (1963), in which a revived William Shakespeare adjusts to the modern **business** of writing for television.

Two episodes involve machines with murderous minds of their own (see **Machines and Mechanization**): a slot machine in "The Fever" (1960), and a man's household appliances in "A Thing about Machines" (1960). Memorable episodes that defy ready categorization include "Night of the Meek" (1960), in which a fired department store Santa becomes the real Santa Claus (see **Christmas**); "It's a Good Life" (1961), involving a little boy with **psychic powers** who cruelly controls everyone in his small town; "Little Girl Lost" (1962), about a girl who slips into another **dimension**; and "Nightmare at 20,000 Feet" (1963), wherein a man on an airplane flight is the only one who sees a destructive gremlin sitting on the airplane's wing.

After cancellation of *The Twilight Zone*, Serling hosted and wrote for another anthology series, *Night Gallery* (1970–1973), but he lacked creative control and found the experience unsatisfying, as did most audiences. After his death, there were two films based on his first series—*Twilight Zone: The Movie* (1983) and *The Twilight Zone: Rod Serling's Lost Classics* (1994)—as well as two revivals of the series, running from 1985 to 1988 and from 2002 to 2003. Along with remakes of classic episodes from Serling's series, these new series did feature some striking episodes, like "Her Pilgrim Soul" (1985), about a fetus who appears in a **scientist**'s hologram and rapidly matures to adulthood, eventually revealing herself as the scientist's prematurely deceased wife in a previous life who has returned to help him find peace of mind (see **Reincarnation**), and "It's Still a Good Life" (2002), a sequel to the original episode that found the **evil** child has grown to adulthood and raised a daughter who has inherited his powers. In general, however, these later series failed to recapture the special magic of Serling's original episodes, which are still finding new audiences forty years after they first aired.

Bibliography

Linda Brevelle. "Rod Serling." *Twilight Zone*, 2 (April, 1982), 20–27.

Joel Engel. *Rod Serling*. Chicago: Contemporary Books, 1989.

Gary Gerani and Paul H. Schulman. "*The Twilight Zone*." Gerani and Schulman, *Fantastic Television*. New York: Harmony Books, 1977, 34–47.

S.T. Joshi. "The Life and Work of Rod Serling." *Studies in Weird Fiction*, No. 7 (Spring, 1990), 22–28.

Jean-Marc L'Officier and Randy L'Officier. *Into the Twilight Zone*. London: Virgin Books, 1995.

Bob Pondillo. "Rod Serling." *Television Quarterly*, 33 (Spring, 2002), 34–43.

Gordon Sander. *Serling*. New York: Penguin/Dutton, 1992.

Peter Wolfe. *In the Zone*. Bowling Green, OH: Bowling Green State University Popular Press, 1997.

Marc Scott Zicree. *The Twilight Zone Companion*. New York: Bantam Books, 1982.

—Gary Westfahl

2001: A Space Odyssey (1968)

■

I don't think there is any question about it. It can only be attributable to human error. This sort of thing has cropped up before, and it has always been due to human error.

—Stanley Kubrick and Arthur C. Clarke
2001: A Space Odyssey (1968)

Summary

In prehistoric **Africa**, on an arid plain, two groups of humanoid **apes** contend over a waterhole. The defeated group wakes to find a monolith, a perfect black slab, upright in their midst. They approach and touch it. They discover how to use bones as clubs and drive the other apes from the waterhole. Cut to 2001: Heywood Floyd is flying from **Earth** to a **space station** to the **Moon**, where a monolith has been unearthed. As the lunar day dawns, the **Sun** strikes the alien artifact, which emits a radio signal towards Jupiter (see **Jupiter and the Outer Planets**). Eighteen months later, the spaceship *Discovery* is en route to Jupiter. When HAL, the ship's **computer**, behaves erratically, **astronauts** Frank Poole and Dave Bowman debate disconnecting its higher functions. HAL (see **Frankenstein Monsters**) kills Poole and other crew members but cannot prevent Bowman from disabling it. Bowman investigates the monolith orbiting Jupiter, racing through tunnels of **light** over alien landscapes (see **Sublime**). In a room, he watches a future version of himself eat. That older Bowman watches an even older, bed-ridden Bowman, who reaches out to the monolith at the foot of his bed. He is replaced by a fetus (see **Babies**) in a womb of light, which then approaches Earth.

Discussion

Despite its many ambiguities, synopses of *2001* tend to view it as a simultaneously elliptical and relatively straightforward account of extraterrestrial intervention in human **evolution**, transforming humanoid apes into humans and, millions of years later, prompting the **rebirth** of one human into a Star Child, harbinger of the species' coming evolutionary leap into a transcendent posthumanity. As such, *2001* operates at the intersection of two related science fiction traditions: one concerned with the evolution of **humanity**, as in H.G. Wells's "A Story of the Stone Age" (1897), Jack London's *Before Adam* (1906), J.H. Rosny-Aîné's *The Quest for Fire* (1909), and Jean Auel's *The Clan of the Cave Bear* (see **Prehistoric Fiction**); and the other with humanity's future evolution into other species, as in Greg Bear's **Blood Music**, Arthur C. Clarke's **Childhood's End**, Theodore Sturgeon's **More than Human** and, more grimly, Kurt Vonnegut, Jr.'s *Galàpagos* and Wells's **The Time Machine**. Whereas these examples focus on evolution as a process driven by **mutation** and/or the development of new **technologies**, *2001* also belongs to a tradition in which human evolution has been controlled or manipulated by alien intervention (see **Uplift**), as in E.E. "Doc" Smith's **Triplanetary**, Olaf Stapledon's *Star Maker*,

Vonnegut's *The Sirens of Titan* (1959), Gregory Benford's *In the Ocean of Night* (1977), and Octavia E. Butler's **Dawn**. (Humans perform similar interventions in Wells's *The Island of Doctor Moreau* and David Brin's *Startide Rising*.) In this context, *2001* can be regarded as an as-yet incomplete species **Bildungsroman**—although such a reading has been primarily derived not from the movie but from Clarke's relatively unambiguous novelization (based on the screenplay he co-authored with director Stanley Kubrick). This interpretation was further fixed by Clarke's *2010: Odyssey Two* (1982), filmed as *2010: The Year We Make Contact* (1984), in which the monoliths transform Jupiter into a **star** to prompt the evolution of life on Europa and divert humanity from pursuing **nuclear war**.

2001, however, is also a darkly comic treatment of Clarke's **near future** near-**utopia** of an improving humanity in a universe moderated by benevolence. While a series of visual echoes, beginning with the transition from bone-club to space vehicle, signal technological **progress**, the awkward and technologically mediated conversations suggest a human failure to communicate directly, emphasized by the fact that human characters never share a conventional shot/reverse-shot sequence. While images of procreation—spaceships like ova and spermatazoa—and **birth** recur, this future disavows **sexuality**. Developing the **satire** of *Dr. Strangelove*, *2001* depicts a world of bland subordination to corporate structures (see **Individualism and Conformity**), in which even the show of **politics** has become irrelevant. This enables *2001* to capture the boring routine of **space travel**, equating it initially with international **air travel**, complete with a gendered division between pilots and cabin crew (see **Sexism**), then to varieties of stasis (see **Suspended Animation and Cryonics**) and repetition, exemplified by Poole's endless jogging around *Discovery*. Furthermore, the satire indicates that humans are dominated within both their **governance systems** and their assisted evolution; monoliths are, like Floyd (see **Fathers**), absent parents. At all levels, from **family** to nation to species, humanity seems divorced from itself and powerless within systems beyond its control, and there is nothing to indicate that the Star Child's approach to Earth is a matter for celebration.

Because it depends upon and subordinates narrative to extended special effects sequences (see **Sense of Wonder**), *2001* has been seen as the first science fiction blockbuster. It is not so much the 70mm frame and Kubrick's technological innovations as his experiments with cinematic form—carefully sectioning the film; presenting the music, rather than subordinating it to visual images; ambiguously juxtaposing shots whose discontinuity is emphasised by use of wide-angle lenses—that constitute the reinvigoration of a cinematic genre that has always been concerned with spectacle. Even critics who consider *2001*'s technical virtuosity matched by an intellectual vacuity must regret the fact that, with rare exceptions like Andrei Tarkovsky's relentless *Stalker* (1979) and Mike Hodge's ironic *Flash Gordon* (1980), subsequent cinematic science fiction spectacles have opted for *Star Wars*'s straightfaced action-adventure as a model.

Bibliography

Jerome B. Agel, ed. *The Making of Kubrick's 2001*. New York: New American Library, 1970.

Piers Bizony. *2001*. London: Aurum, 1994.

Michel Chion. *Kubrick's Cinema Odyssey*. Translated by Claudia Gorbman. London: BFI, 2001.

Arthur C. Clarke. *The Lost Worlds of 2001.* New York: New American Library, 1972.

Carl Freedman. "On Kubrick's *2001*." Freedman, *The Incomplete Projects.* Middletown: Wesleyan University Press, 2002, 91–112.

Carol L. Fry. "From Technology to Transcendence." *Extrapolation*, 44 (Fall, 2003) 331–343.

John Izod. "*2001: A Space Odyssey*." Christopher Hauke and Ian Alister, eds., *Jung & Film.* Hove: Brunner-Routledge, 2001, 129–150.

Stephanie Schwam, ed. *The Making of 2001: A Space Odyssey.* New York: Modern Library, 2000.

Leonard F. Wheat. *Kubrick's 2001.* Metuchen, NJ: Scarecrow, 2000.

—*Mark Bould*

2001: A SPACE ODYSSEY
BY ARTHUR C. CLARKE (1968)

∎

[The Star Child] waited, marshaling his thoughts and brooding over his still untested powers. For though he was master of the world, he was not quite sure what to do next.
But he would think of something.

—Arthur C. Clarke
2001: A Space Odyssey (1968)

Summary

An American expedition on the **Moon** excavates a mysterious black monolith of precise geometric proportions thirty feet below the surface of the crater Tycho. Buried millions of years ago, it is the first sign of other intelligent life in the universe. When exposed to the rays of the lunar sunrise it emits a powerful radio signal, which, **scientists** conclude, is an alarm alerting its alien creators that humans have mastered **space travel**. Indeed, unknown to modern humankind, a similar monolith left on **Earth** three million years before sparked **intelligence** in apes, endowing them with the rudimentary grasp of **technology** crucial for their **evolution** into *homo sapiens*. **America** outfits the spaceship *Discovery* with a five-man crew to pursue the radio signal like a homing beacon to Japetus, a moon of Saturn that is its apparent receiver (see **Jupiter and the Outer Planets**). En route, the mission is nearly scuttled by HAL, the malfunctioning onboard **computer**. David Bowman, the sole astronaut to survive HAL's sabotage, navigates the ship through a **star** gateway where aliens, who have perhaps evolved beyond physical form into a state of pure energy, have been waiting. After transforming Bowman physically, they return him to Earth as a Star Child who, presumably, will start humankind on the next evolutionary step toward its cosmic **destiny**.

Discussion

2001 is a tale of **first contact** and represents the culmination of a theme Arthur C. Clarke first addressed in his story "The Sentinel" (1951), about an alien artifact discovered on the Moon that alerts **humanity** to other intelligent life in the universe and communicates humanity's mastery of space travel (see **Communication**). Clarke developed the theme of human encounters with superior races in other stories, most spectacularly in *Childhood's End*, wherein a race of alien overseers assumes a parental role towards humans, helping them overcome their self-destructive tendencies and evolve into a posthuman species. As he relates in *The Lost Worlds of 2001* (1972), Clarke brainstormed these and other ideas with director Stanley Kubrick starting in 1964, resulting in the screenplay for the film *2001: A Space Odyssey* and near-simultaneous writing of the novel.

With degrees in **physics** and **mathematics**, Clarke is a leading writer of **hard science fiction**, and the novel's impact derives significantly from its balance of hard science with existential and eschatological speculations (see **Eschatology**). Clarke views evolution in terms of humanity's mastery of technology. In the opening chapters set in prehistoric **Africa** (see **Prehistoric Fiction**), the tribe of apes that first encounters the alien monolith acquire the intelligence necessary to develop the first tool: a bone that they use as a weapon (see **Weaponry**). This insures their evolutionary superiority and **survival**, and it is significant that the purpose of this first tool is to kill.

Clarke presents scientific advances of the twenty-first century as part of the same continuum of technological **progress**, especially space travel (accentuated in the film by a famous transitional scene in which the bone thrown into the air by the ape Moonwatcher morphs into the image of a space vehicle, moving the story into the **near future**). Space travel has become a common form of **transportation** and certain accommodations are now taken for granted, including orbiting **space stations** used as transportation terminuses and suspended animation (see **Suspended Animation and Cryonics**) for the long-distance flight to Saturn and other planets in the solar system. But space travel has also necessitated the **invention** of computers like HAL, which Clarke depicts as a space-age version of the **Frankenstein monster**. Created to speak and respond like its makers, HAL replicates their all-too-human flaws. Perhaps because HAL, a machine of pure logic, has been turned schizophrenic by instructions that he not reveal the truth of the mission to **astronauts** aboard the *Discovery* (as confirmed in the novel's sequel, *2010: Odyssey Two* [1982]), HAL manifests the dangerous potential of technology in the hands of fallible humans. He illustrates an innate destructive capacity that, presumably, humanity will evolve beyond through the intervention of the monolith creators.

David Bowman's **metamorphosis** and **rebirth** as the Star Child at the novel's end is an audacious moment in science fiction, one that crystallizes the novel's spirit of cosmic **mystery** and evokes a sense of near-religious uplift (see **Religion**) in its suggestion that humanity, through proper grooming and improvement, will ultimately become one with its cosmic overseer. In three sequels to the novel, however, Clarke dispels such optimism. Bowing to the film's decision to move the alien rendezvous point from Saturn to Jupiter, *2010: Odyssey Two* shows the United States and **Russia** traveling to the Jovian system to investigate the fate of the *Discovery* and, if possible, rehabilitate HAL. But the decision of monolith creators to implode Jupiter and create a sun vital for a developing species on Europa has grave implications for humanity that are borne out in *2061: Odyssey Three* (1987) and *3001: The Final Odyssey* (1997), in which humanity is forbidden from meddling with developments on Europa, and then is threatened by apparent plans by the forces behind the monolith to terminate humanity as a failed experiment.

Its theme of transcendence notwithstanding, Clarke's *2001* series offers a bittersweet appraisal of humanity. It suggests that humans are afflicted with inherent traits counterproductive to their own advancement, requiring assistance from superiors to achieve their full potential. Its final image of human evolution as merely one of countless other experiments initiated by cosmic scientists, who ultimately may be indifferent to humanity's survival, powerfully evokes science fiction's **sense of wonder**, albeit through a unique vision of **eternity** in which humanity may have no role.

Bibliography

J.H. Boylan. "Hal in *2001: A Space Odyssey*." *Journal of Popular Culture*, 18 (Spring, 1985), 53–56.

Arthur C. Clarke. *The Lost Worlds of 2001*. New York: New American Library, 1972.

———. "Valediction." Clarke, *3001: The Final Odyssey*. 1997. New York: Ballantine/Del Rey, 1999, 257–263.

John Hollow. "*2001* in Perspective." *Southwest Review*, 61 (Spring, 1976), 113–129.

Joseph D. Olander and Martin H. Greenberg, eds. *Arthur C. Clarke*. New York: Taplinger, 1977.

Robert Plank. "Sons and Father, A.D. 2001." *Hartford Studies in Literature*, 1 (1969), 26–33.

Robin A. Reid. *Arthur C. Clarke*. Westport, CT: Greenwood Press, 1997.

A.J. Richard and Philip M. Tucker. "The Alchemical Art of Arthur C. Clarke." *Foundation*, No. 41 (Winter, 1987), 30–41.

George Slusser. *The Space Odysseys of Arthur C. Clarke*. San Bernardino, CA: Borgo Press, 1978.

—*Stefan Dziemianowicz*

U

UTOPIA BY THOMAS MORE (1516)

Summary

Utopia, written in Latin, reports a colloquium among More, his friend Pieter Gillis, and the imaginary Portuguese scholar and explorer, Raphael Hythloday (Greek for "speaker of nonsense"), combining elements of Platonic symposium and travel book. In the first part the friends discuss aspects of English law, particularly mistreatment of the poor and enclosure of public lands, and other topics of no great relevance to utopian thought (see **Utopia**) or fantastic fiction. The second portion of *Utopia* is a document of great cultural significance. Hythloday, who accompanied Americo Vespucci to **America** and continued on farther south, describes Utopia (Greek for "not" and "place") as an **island** off South America, possibly in the area of the Rio de la Plata. Originally connected to the mainland, it was detached by good King Utopus, around 250 BCE, who set it up as a hermit land. In the most significant, concentrated, detailed discussion of an ideal state since Plato's *Republic* (c. 380 BCE) and *Laws* (c. 360 BCE), Hythloday goes on to describe a communist **culture** that has been called the ultimate pragmatic society based on the economic welfare of the people. There is little or no private property. Everything is held in common, as was the theoretical practice in early **Christianity**. Everyone works for the state, and the state supplies necessities of life, including food and shelter. **Money** does not exist, nor does internal **trade**. When Hythloday concludes, More ponders some objections to the society he described but also acknowledges that Utopia has many attractive features that **Europe** might consider adopting.

Discussion

In the summer of 1515, Thomas More, a brilliant young English lawyer and esteemed Renaissance humanist, was a member of a trade delegation to the Low Lands. During this time he became acquainted with Gillis, scheve of Antwerp, and began the work we now know as *Utopia* in association with Gillis. Finished after More's return to England, *Utopia* was published in late 1516 or early 1517. The book was accepted with delight by his circle and became part of the world's literary heritage, a highly influential social document.

The cultural personality of Utopia is altruistic and, on the whole, benevolent. This aspect of Utopia has proved appealing to many readers. Still, other aspects of

Utopia may sound less attractive to moderns. Life is very drab, with uniform utility clothing; there is no real room for literature, the **arts**, or other personal expression. Thought control is extensively practiced, and includes brainwashing against neighboring cultures. Sex is controlled, with severe punishment for premarital **sexuality** or adultery; much has been made of the suggestion that engaged couples should view each other nude (see **Nudity**). Although there is free time, due to the efficient work force, the chief entertainment seems to be **reading** edifying homilies (see **Work and Leisure**). All in all, as has been pointed out, it is much like a monastery.

Although the state provides housing, it may also remove dwellers arbitrarily. Populations may be shifted to meet an ideal statistical pattern, even to the point of colonizing neighboring lands by force if there is **overpopulation**. Foreign relations are conducted in a Machiavellian manner, with troops of mercenaries paid from the state treasury and by bribing and suborning foreign leaders.

Politically, Utopia is a very paternal elective oligarchy (see **Politics**), with a pyramidal structure rising from the large **family** up to a council for each of the 54 semiautonomous states and a general island legislature. While the text is cloudy, there seems to be no **king** or supreme executive, though each **city** is ruled by a prince elected for a lifetime. In **religion**, pagan Utopians are tolerant but they have squelched an overenthusiastic Christian proselytizer. Culturally, the Utopians are about on the same scientific and technological level as advanced Europe, but without firearms and printing.

Utopia, as an *imaginary land*, is More's invention, but the concept of eutopia, as *better land*, does not appear in the text. It is in "Hexastichon," one laudatory verse contributed to the book by friends: "I am deservedly to be called Eutopia." Not signed, it was probably written by Gillis, More's friend and colleague in Antwerp.

Utopia seems to have been taken as a not-too-serious flight of fancy by More's friends, but today there is considerable disagreement among scholars as to More's intention, particularly the question of whether he was advocating his Utopia as an ideal state. A modern lay reader can view it as an multimodal work, with elements of eutopia, **dystopia**, and ethnography, which is partly serious, partly jesting. More would have approved of the sections about English internal affairs, but More—who dressed richly, was a fervent religionist, and loyally supported the Tudors—probably would not have liked the drabness, paganism, and lack of a national prince. It is impossible to say why More mixed levels; he possibly did not have as clear an idea of an utopia as more recent authors have.

Utopia was first translated into English by Raphe Robynson in 1551, revised 1556; it is occasionally reprinted with modern spelling. Modern translations are generally preferable, including those by Edward Sturtz, G.C. Richard, Paul Turner, and Peter Marshall. Throughout history readers have selected those portions that fitted their situation and ignored those that did not. In addition to providing ideas, *Utopia* also supplied a superb example of how political ideas could be promulgated in an entertaining fashion.

Bibliography

Merritt Abrash. "Missing the Point in More's *Utopia*." *Extrapolation*, 19 (December, 1977), 27–38.

Peter Ackroyd. *The Life of Thomas More*. London: Catto & Windus, 1998.

Everett F. Bleiler. "Pieter Gillis and More's *Utopia*." *Extrapolation*, 27 (Winter, 1986), 304–319.

Mardelle Fortier and Robert F. Fortier. *The Utopian Thought of St. Thomas More and Its Development in Literature*. Lewiston, ME: Edwin Mellen Press, 1992.

J.H. Hexter. *More's Utopia: The Biography of an Idea*. Princeton: Princeton University Press, 1952.

Anthony Kenny. *Thomas More*. Oxford: Oxford University Press, 1983.

George Logan. *The Meaning of Thomas More's Utopia*. Princeton: Princeton University Press, 1983.

E.E. Reynolds. *Thomas More and Erasmus*. London: Burns and Oates, 1965.

E.D.S. Sullivan. *Utopian Vision*. San Diego: San Diego State University Press, 1983.

—*Everett F. Bleiler*

A Voyage to Arcturus by David Lindsay (1920)

Summary

A seance in a fashionable house is attended by a giant of a man called Maskull (see **Psychic Powers**). The medium conjures up the apparition of a young man with a beatific smile on his face, only to see a rough stranger, Krag, "kill" the apparition. Suddenly the smile is replaced by the hideous grimace of the enemy, Crystalman. Outside, Krag informs Maskull that he, another attendee of the seance called Nightspore, and Krag are to voyage to a planet of the double sun (see **Stars**) of Arcturus. They reconvene at an observatory in Scotland. From there Maskull travels to Arcturus in a crystalline "torpedo." On the planet Tormance, he undergoes a series of mystical and transformative adventures. His body acquires new sensory organs. But each stage of his **metamorphosis** is violent. He kills most people he meets, because they serve as **illusions** that prevent him from reaching Muspel, a fiery realm of ineffable transcendence. Ultimately, Maskull himself has to be cast aside like one more useless husk before Nightspore can reach Muspel. Krag, its seems, is known on **Earth** as Pain (see **Pain**). Only through suffering can transcendence be achieved.

Discussion

The fact that David Lindsay's *A Voyage to Arcturus* was accepted when first submitted to a publisher was perhaps a fluke, the consequences of which were not always best for the writer. It is a mystical novel, dense with symbolism and not, as even admirers will admit, particularly well-written. Indeed, critics tend to over-defensively explain the book's lack of broad popular appeal by the clumsiness of Lindsay's prose, which, if not exactly poetic and singing, is more or less serviceable. Certainly Lindsay could write rings around pulp writers like E.E. "Doc" Smith (see *Triplanetary*). The difficulty with the book, instead, is that it lacks or deliberately eschews identifiable emotions in its characters, as if **love**, wonder, and **courage** are but further illusions of Crystalman, to be rejected on the path to enlightenment.

Whether this was Lindsay's own view is one of the mysteries of *A Voyage to Arcturus*. When the book appeared in 1920, it was like nothing else in all of literature. There had been interplanetary novels before, those of H.G. Wells being the best known, but here was something closer to John Bunyan's *The Pilgrim's Progress* (1678), but by no means an orthodox **allegory**. It was ultimately a book that no one understood, which has been variously described as Calvinist, Gnostic, Nietzschean, or psychedelic. Its publisher Methuen took a risk in publishing it and sold 596 copies, receiving largely indifferent or hostile reviews.

Lindsay, meanwhile, buoyed by his initial "success," set out to be a full-time literary man. The rest of his career was a worsening struggle until ultimately he could no longer get published at all. As a writer, he was at war with himself, attempting to suppress the very things that made him unique. His 1923 novel *Sphinx*, for instance, has only brief mystical flashes amid endless chapters of society small-talk. Rather than learn to write his own material more compellingly, he tried to meet other people's preconceptions. He actually produced a conventional historical novel in the Dumas mode, *The Adventures of M. de Mailly* (1926), but today this is his only book which is not reprinted. A continuing audience exists for *A Voyage to Arcturus*, drawn to everything that Lindsay's later publishers must have tried to discourage in an attempt to make him "commercial." The irony is that *Arcturus* is his only commercial book, which even had several paperback printings in the early 1970s. But Lindsay knew nothing of this. He fell into despair, neglected his health, and died from rotted teeth in 1945.

The fascination with *A Voyage to Arcturus*, despite its difficulty, stems from the fact that Lindsay, in C.S. Lewis's words, was "the first writer to discover what 'other planets' in fiction are good for," which tells us nearly as much about Lewis as it does about Lindsay. Indeed, Lewis's **Out of the Silent Planet** is deeply influenced by *A Voyage to Arcturus*. It is significant that the real Arcturus known to astronomy is not the double star Lindsay says it is. A **hard science fiction** writer like Hal Clement would never make a "mistake" like that, but Lindsay, with his symbolic, colored suns, had different "uses" for astronomical objects.

Lewis was attracted to Lindsay's use of the "other planet" as a setting where mystical adventures could take place, an "otherworld" like the Celtic Fairyland where the nature of existence could be glimpsed in veiled form. Lewis, too, was writing visionary novels with vaguely science-fictional trappings. His methods are those of Lindsay, and he first saw the possibilities in *A Voyage to Arcturus*.

What, then does *A Voyage to Arcturus* mean? Was Lindsay's Calvinist upbringing showing when he rejects pleasure in favor of Krag's instructive pain? Is Muspel-fire akin to the Buddhist nirvana (see **Religion**)? Is the whole thing a psychedelic **dream**–vision in which the goal and effort at transformation are one and the same? Is the author a misogynist? A romantic? A follower of Friedrich Nietzsche or Arthur Schopenhauer? Lindsay's friend, noted Milton scholar E.H. Visiak, unpersuasively argued that the book was a relatively orthodox Christian allegory (see **Christianity**). Perhaps, even as meaning on Tormance continues to shift as one seeks Muspel-fire, so too the book represents Lindsay's struggle to express what was ultimately inexpressible.

Bibliography

Loren Eiseley. "Introduction." 1963. David Lindsay, *A Voyage to Arcturus*. New York: Ballantine Books, 1968, vii–x.

Galad Elflandsson. "David Lindsay and the Quest for Muspel-Fire." 1984. Darrell Schweitzer, ed., *Discovering Classic Fantasy Fiction*. Mercer Island, WA: Starmont House, 1996, 104–122.

J.B. Pick, with Colin Wilson and E.H. Visiak. *The Strange Genius of David Lindsay*. London: John Baker, 1970.

Joy Pohl. "Dualities in David Lindsay's *A Voyage to Arcturus*." *Extrapolation*, 22 (Summer, 1981), 164–170.

David Power. *David Lindsay's Vision*. Nottingham: Pauper's Press, 1991.

Bernard Sellin. *The Life and Works of David Lindsay*. Cambridge: Cambridge University Press, 1981.

Ian Watson. "From Pan in the Home Countries to Pain on a Far Planet." *Foundation*, No. 43 (Summer, 1988), 25–36.

Colin Wilson. *Haunted Man*. San Bernardino, CA: Borgo Press, 1979.

Gary K. Wolfe. *David Lindsay*. Mercer Island, WA: Starmont House, 1982.

—Darrell Schweitzer

THE WAR OF THE WORLDS
BY H.G. WELLS (1898)

No one would have believed, in the last years of the nineteenth century, that human affairs were being watched keenly and closely by intelligences greater than man's and yet as mortal as his own . . . . At most, terrestrial men fancied there might be other men upon Mars, perhaps inferior to themselves and ready to welcome a missionary enterprise. Yet, across the gulf of space, minds that are to our minds as ours are to those of the beasts that perish, intellects vast and cool and unsympathetic, regarded this earth with envious eyes, and slowly and surely drew their plans against us.

—H.G. Wells
The War of the Worlds (1898)

Summary

The War of the Worlds begins with earthly observations of activities on and around **Mars**: unusual **weather** patterns, surface flashes reminiscent of explosions, and the unusual nearness of **Mars** to **Earth**. These phenomena lead to speculation about conditions on the planet and the story's narrator considers what Martians might make of earthly life. It is in this mood of contemplation that the Martians arrive, landing around London in metallic cylinders. Despite local curiosity, life in England goes on as normal. It is only when the first Martian cylinder opens (see **First Contact**) and its occupants show aggressive tendencies that England is roused. The Martians use a heat ray to obliterate human plenipotentiaries and destroy everything within the range of the cylinder. This initial destruction is followed by the Martians assembling tripodal fighting-machines (see **Machines and Mechanization**) and marching towards London destroying everything in their paths, living as **vampires** on human **blood**. In addition to the heat-ray, they are equipped to spread a black smoke that poisons whole areas of the country. Just as the Martians appear unstoppable they die, killed by bacteria to which they have no immunity (see **Death; Plagues and Diseases**). Framing this Martian destructive orgy is the response of the English to the onslaught of the invaders. No longer masters of the largest empire the world has ever known, the people of London panic and stampede in a frenzied attempt to save themselves ahead of the Martians' complete conquest of their **island** kingdom.

Discussion

The novel inspired two notable adaptations: Orson Welles's 1938 Mercury Theater radio broadcast, and George Pal's 1953 film. Although both adaptations relocate the story to **America**, their re-presentations of the story line are different. Welles aims for social realism, using news intermissions during a **music** program to generate tension and ultimately cause regional panic, while Pal reduces the social breakdown and emphasizes the power of faith and providence (see **Christianity**) in the fight against the Martians. Two further film versions of the story are scheduled for release in 2005: Timothy Hines's *H.G. Wells's The War of the Worlds* attempts to be faithful to Wells's novel, setting it in London of the 1890s, while Steven Spielberg's *The War of the Worlds* is a modernization of the 1953 film, set in present-day America.

The War of the Worlds contains many science fiction themes that have influenced the development of the genre ever since. Perhaps the most important is the idea of **aliens on Earth**. According to John R. Reed, Wells endowed Martians with certain qualities that he himself admired in men; thus, the Martians' passionlessness gives them a scientific detachment which makes them superior. Patricia Kerslake argues that the narrator begins to look beyond the Martians' monstrousness and postulates the ways in which the Martians are nonetheless human. His deliberations proceed to the point where we understand that this is what **humanity** itself may become, as our species evolves away from the physical and into realms of pure intellect (see **Biology**). Frank McConnell suggests that Martians are not aliens but are ourselves, mutated beyond sympathy (see **Mutation**), though not beyond recognition. It is in this vein of interpretation that Leon Stover suggests that Wells's Martians are a demonstration of Darwinian theory (see **Social Darwinism**). Thomas C. Renzi observes that the Martians have invented **cyborgs** (see **Inventions**), living machines created by merging organic life with mechanical parts. Robert M. Philmus sees *The War of the Worlds* as challenging late-Victorian notions of human superiority, as the novel counters the idea that man is the consummation of the evolutionary process with the myth of an alien **intelligence** superior to humans and possessing more advanced **technology**.

A further theme discussed in the novel is that of **invasion**. I.F. Clarke points out that while *The War of the Worlds* is only one of many **future wars** stories of the late nineteenth century, it is the first to feature a Martian invasion of a great European power. Written at the end of a century of presumed inevitable **progress**, Reed says that the attack from beyond Earth instructs humanity that it is not safe and secure, and that it must consciously work for its future welfare. Indeed, Patrick Parrinder claims that after the Martian invasion humankind is no longer a master but an animal among animals. Stover agrees, seeing the Martians as at once an enemy and a model, recalling humanity to its need for **survival** in a universe indifferent to it.

Robert Crossley sees the human reaction to the invasion of England as more interesting than the Martians themselves, noting that when London is finally roused to the threat against it, social institutions and moral constraints collapse. Along the roads, at the railway stations, on the docks, panic is the only rule (see **Anxiety**). Rights of property are no longer recognized as refugees from London pillage rural granaries, and elementary decencies are subordinated to the cruelest expediencies of survival. The least edifying features of the human personality surface—its barbarism, selfishness, and silly parochialism.

Bibliography

I.F. Clarke. *Voices Prophesying War*. Second Ed. Oxford: Oxford University Press, 1992.

Robert Crossley. *H.G. Wells*. Mercer Island, WA: Starmont House, 1986.

Patricia Kerslake. "Moments of Empire." John S. Partington, ed., *The Wellsian: Selected Essays on H.G. Wells*. [Oss]: Equilibris, 2003, 69–83.

Frank McConnell. *The Science Fiction of H.G. Wells*. Oxford: Oxford University Press, 1981.

Patrick Parrinder. *Shadows of the Future*. Liverpool: Liverpool University Press, 1995.

Robert M. Philmus. *Into the Unknown*. Berkeley: University of California Press, 1983.

John R. Reed. *The Natural History of H.G. Wells*. Athens: Ohio University Press, 1982.

Thomas C. Renzi. *H.G. Wells*. Metuchen, NJ: Scarecrow, 1992.

Leon Stover, ed. *The War of the Worlds: A Critical Text of the 1898 London First Edition, by H.G. Wells*. Jefferson, NC: McFarland, 2001, 1–46.

—*John S. Partington*

THE WATER BABIES BY CHARLES KINGSLEY (1863)

■

Summary

Tom is a young chimney sweep who knows neither of his parents and is at the mercy of his abusive master Mr. Grimes. When Tom accidentally appears during a sweeping job in the bedroom of the local squire's young daughter, he runs away to **escape** punishment. His flight leads him to throw himself in a local stream where, instead of drowning, he becomes a tiny creature called a water **baby**. Free from the abuse, starvation, and overwork he suffered under Grimes, Tom begins his **education**. He learns about other creatures in the sea and how to help, rather than harm, them. Then, after being reunited with Ellie, the squire's daughter (who has since died and comes to the sea to teach him), Tom desires to become good enough to join Ellie in her heavenly **home**. Thus, the **fairies** Mrs. Bedonebyasyoudid and

Mrs. Doasyouwouldbedoneby send Tom on a journey to the Other-end-of-Nowhere to redeem the **evil** Mr. Grimes. Tom passes through several countries where people doom themselves by their own folly, but finally finds Grimes and, with the fairies' help, frees him. The fairies reward Tom by allowing him to go **home** with Ellie on Sundays.

Discussion

Although Charles Kingsley wrote *The Water Babies* as a **fairy tale**, the book conforms to this definition only in terms of the Victorian tradition of a long fantasy written for **children** and including magical creatures. The dedication is to Kingsley's own son and the narrator continually directs comments to him. In this way, *The Water Babies* serves not only as the story of Tom the chimney sweep, but as an education for readers in everything from child labor practices to scientific breakthroughs and **politics**. Kingsley practices what he preaches, as he argues within the book that education is not only important, but the right of all children. And because **youth** is a time of play, learning should be accomplished through entertainment and discovery as often as possible.

For Tom, both entertainment and discovery are found in the **water**. Perhaps because his work as a chimney sweep forced him to grow old before his time, he achieves a backwards **metamorphosis** as he falls into a stream, changing from child to baby. Tom's metamorphosis allows him two major benefits: he sees himself as part of, rather than separate from, the natural world (see **Nature**); and by growing down rather than up, he can find connections with several characters who act as **mothers** for him. As a water baby, Tom falls out of his chimney sweeping clothes; **nudity** helps Tom to see himself as another of the many **fish and sea creatures** that he lives with. Kingsley draws parallels between human–animal relationships and relationships among humans when Tom helps a lobster escape from his **prison** just as the old dame in Vendale helped Tom escape from those chasing him. In addition, Kingsley uses the metaphor of water as **birth** canal by having Tom travel through **rivers** before he reaches the womb of the ocean; here he meets Mother Carey who creates everything new in the world. Tom then discovers that Mother Carey is just one embodiment of the ultimate mother-figure and God who is creator, judge, and caretaker of the world; fairies Mrs. Bedonebyasyoudid and Mrs. Doasyouwouldbedoneby are two others.

Tom also learns to separate the sea creatures who aim at a higher life, either through metamorphosis to winged creatures (like dragonflies) or by traveling to the sea (as salmon do), from those who are bottom feeders with coarse manners (like trout). This **allegory** of the use and neglect of conscience and striving for improvement gives Tom strength to complete his **quest** to help redeem Grimes. Trapped in a chimney, Grimes cannot escape from his prison until he cries tears for his mother; Tom's tale of transformation helps Grimes realize that redemption is a choice it is never too late to make.

Although *The Water Babies* has elements of the **pastoral**—Tom cannot begin his redemption until he leaves the **city** for the countryside, and only completes it when he returns to the innocence of babyhood—Kingsley's creation is not antiscience. Even though he satirizes **scientists** like Charles Darwin and Carolus Linnaeus (see **Satire**), the nature of the water baby itself suggests the concepts of **evolution** and classification; like **mermaids**, water babies are half-animal, half-human, a missing link between sea and land. Humans ultimately represent the highest order of animal, partly because they have souls, but also because they have the capability to solve problems and can choose to use science and **technology** wisely. At the end of the novel, Tom does indeed get to go home with Ellie on Sundays, presumably to **Heaven**—but during the rest of the week he is a railroad-building engineer.

Bibliography

Brian Alderson. "Introduction." Charles Kingsley, *The Water-Babies*. Oxford: Oxford University Press, 1995, ix–xxix.

Humphrey Carpenter. "Parson Lot Takes a Cold Bath." Carpenter, *Secret Gardens*. Boston: Houghton Mifflin, 1985, 23–43.

Valentine Cunningham. "Soiled Fairy." *Essays in Criticism*, 35 (April, 1985), 121–148.

Arthur Johnston. "*The Water-Babies*." *English*, 12 (Autumn, 1959), 215–219.

Colin Manlove. "Charles Kingsley (1819–1875) and *The Water Babies*." Manlove, *Modern Fantasy*. Cambridge: Cambridge University Press, 1975, 13–54.

Brendan Rapple. "The Motif of Water in Charles Kingsley's *The Water Babies*." *University of Mississippi Studies in English*, 11–12 (1993–1995), 259–271.

Deborah Stevenson. "Sentiment and Significance." *Lion and the Unicorn*, 21 (1997), 112–130.

Jo-Ann Wallace. "De-Scribing *The Water Babies*." Chris Tiffin and Alan Lawson, eds., *De-Scribing Empire*. London: Routledge, 1994, 171–184.

Naomi Wood. "A Sea Green Victorian." *Lion and the Unicorn*, 19 (1995), 233–252.

—*Karen Sands-O'Connor*

WE BY YEVGENY ZAMIATIN (1924)

■

*I hope we shall conquer. More than that—
I am certain we shall conquer. Because
Reason must prevail.*

—Yevgeny Zamiatin
We (1924), transl. Mirra Ginsburg (1972)

Summary

We is narrated by D-503, builder of the first **rocket** to be launched by the Single State to spread its purportedly perfect thirtieth-century communism. Intended as propaganda, D-503's journal relates how he is seduced by I-330 so that the rebellious "Mephis" can seize the *Integral* to overthrow the regime. She disrupts his legally sanctioned **love** triangle whereby he shares O-90's sexual favors with R-13. Unbeknownst to D-503, the poet R-13 is a dissident also linked with I-330, as is the hunchbacked S-4711 who keeps D-503 under surveillance. Illicit sex causes D-503's

sleep to be disturbed by **dreams** as he rediscovers portions of the psyche concealed by 600 years of social conditioning. D-503's consciousness becomes a battleground as Mephis launch their coup d'etat on the Day of Unanimity when all "numbers" are expected to reelect the Benefactor. The Guardians order all "numbers" to undergo the excision of their fantasy and, having read D-503's journal, foil the Mephis' attempt to seize the *Integral*. The Mephis blow a hole in the Green Wall which had sealed the Single State from the outside world, but I-330 and the ringleaders are arrested and tortured (see **Torture**) as D-503, who has been subjected to the operation, watches unmoved and predicts the failure of their uprising. Nevertheless, a battle rages in the middle of the **city** and O-90 **escapes** to the outside world to bear their illegal **baby**.

Discussion

Zamiatin lived in a writer's commune during **Russia**'s civil **war** and lectured on literature while writing *We*, yet little is known about its composition. The manuscript has disappeared. This seminal **dystopia** was the first book banned in the U.S.S.R.; it appeared in English translation in 1925. Zamiatin's works were banned after publication of a bowdlerized Russian version in Czechoslovakia in 1927 and he was exiled from the Soviet Union. The complete original text was first published in 1953 in Paris; it appeared in Soviet print in 1988.

Although the Single State with its assured food, room, and social order must have presented an attractive picture during the privations of 1919 and 1920, readers readily recognized *We*'s hostility to Soviet communism. Formerly a Bolshevik, Zamiatin extrapolated incipient trends in the new socialist state: state-run cafeterias, housing in dormitories, controlled **journalism**, artist unions (see **Art**), and surveillance by secret police (see **Governance Systems**). He prophesized features of Stalinism which appeared later: show trials, "unanimous" "elections," and revering the leader as a virtual god.

We draws themes from past classics of Russian literature, especially Dostoevsky's novels which presaged individualistic and irrational resistance to regimentation (see **Identity**). "Numbers" sleep in **gender**-segregated dormitories and bear alphanumeric **names**. They live according to the Table of Hours, eat at communal meals, and even masticate to a metronome (see **Food and Drink**). Sex takes place only during Personal Hours with sanctioned partners per a state-devised schedule. **Family** life is banned: **children** are raised in factories and **education** is conducted by **robots**.

On one level, *We* is a **satire** on the nascent Soviet Union. Some readers see the bald Benefactor as Lenin. Clearly with D-503's regimented language, especially his insistence on "we," Zamiatin is lampooning Prolitkult poets who espoused depersonalized, machine-like behavior. The novel reflects the U.S.S.R.'s interest in Frederick Winslow Taylor's time and motion studies intended to effect industrial efficiency. Individuality is crushed by official conformity: "numbers" have shaved heads and wear identical clothes (see **Individualism and Conformity**).

The novel's dense, interconnected imagery embodies Zamiatin's espousal of the "mother metaphor" and is aligned with Hegelian dialectics (see **Philosophy**), the creative clash between thesis and antithesis leading to a new synthesis: the Wall between the blue Single State and yellow outside world is Green, much as exogamy between effete numbers of the city and hirsute foragers beyond the Wall will recreate whole human beings. *We* conveys a profound attack on Plato's *Republic* (c. 380 BCE), the basis of Western **utopias**. D-503's mathematical imagery (see **Mathematics**) contains numerous references to the Pythagoreanism underlying much of Platonism, shown by the way the Single State privileges integers and geometric solids. Although aligned with irrationalism, the Mephis utilize advanced concepts like infinity and non-Euclidean geometry.

Zamiatin conveys an anarchist's hostility towards all fixed ideologies. Officially atheistic like the U.S.S.R., the Single State utilizes Christian myths (see **Christianity**). The Benefactor is called a "new Jehovah" and "the Number of Numbers," the Day of Unity is compared to Easter, and the secret police are called Guardians. R-13 retells the Fall in the Garden of Eden, noting that **Adam and Eve** chose **freedom** over happiness, a choice promoted by the Mephis. Zamiatin espouses an open-ended spiral of expanding awareness and continuous change to closed circles of dogma, if only to keep sensibilities alive. The core conflict of dystopian literature is often seen as instinct (or human nature) versus social organization. Indeed, the novel valorizes disruptive innate proclivities like love, spite, sexual jealousy, and **violence** to suggest that our spirit can never be conclusively regimented.

Bibliography

Christopher Collins. *Evgenij Zamiatin*. The Hague: Mouton, 1973.

Brett Cooke. *Human Nature in Utopia*. Evanston, IL: Northwestern University Press, 2002.

S.A. Cowan. "The Crystalline Center of Zamiatin's *We*," *Extrapolation*, 29 (Summer, 1988), 160–178.

Sona S. Hoisington. "The Mismeasure of I-330." Hoisington, ed., *A Plot of Her Own*. Evanston, IL: Northwestern University Press, 1995, 81–88.

Robert Louis Jackson. *Dostoevskij's Underground Man in Russian Literature*. S'-Gravenhage: Mouton, 1958.

Gary Kern, ed. *Zamiatin's We*. Ann Arbor, MI: Ardis, 1988.

Patrick Parrinder. "Imagining the Future." *Science-Fiction Studies*, 1 (Spring, 1973), 17–26.

Gary Rosenshield. "The Imagination and the 'I' in Zamiatin's *We*." *Slavic and East European Journal*, 23 (Spring, 1979), 51–62.

Yevgeny Zamiatin. *A Soviet Heretic*. Ed. and trans. Mirra Ginsburg. Chicago: University of Chicago Press, 1970.

—*Brett Cooke*

A WIZARD OF EARTHSEA
BY URSULA K. LE GUIN (1968)

■

He believed that the wise man is one who never sets himself apart from other living things, whether they have speech

or not, and in later years he strove long
to learn what can be learned, in silence,
from the eyes of animals, the flight of
birds, the great slow gestures of trees.

—Ursula K. Le Guin
A Wizard of Earthsea (1968)

Summary

This limpid fantasy describes the boyhood, training, and early career of a **wizard** compelled to learn that **magic** power carries responsibility (see **Guilt and Responsibility**); every action is fraught with consequences. Initially written for **children**, the Earthsea sequence gathered an appreciative adult audience and critical acclaim.

Earthsea is an archipelago world of countless **islands**, dependent on **sea travel** and fair winds conjured by sorcerous **weather** control. The **hero** Ged grows up on an island noted for wizardry, uses precocious magic against **pirate** raiders, studies under a wise old **mentor** who practices a Taoist **philosophy** of minimal intervention, and pridefully sets off to learn grander magic at Roke Island wizards' school.

There Ged acquires **education**, but with boasting **hubris** attempts a spell that goes awry and releases a terrible shadow into the world. Sent into **exile**, he can master **dragons** but not this personal **Frankenstein monster**. At one point he escapes by **metamorphosis** into **bird** form, risking permanent loss of his human **identity**. Finally, after a prolonged sea **quest**, Ged confronts the shadow and—rather than fighting or fleeing—he accepts it as his own. Balance is restored (see **Yin and Yang**).

Discussion

Earthsea's intuitively satisfying system of magic is based on the "true **names**" of components of the world, as expressed in a primal language that directly maps reality. True names are shorthand for the deep **knowledge** and understanding required for enchantment; they also set the limits of magic. Even master wizards cannot bespell the entire sea, because life is too short to learn the true name of every region, wave, and current covered by our false generalization "sea." There is a great gulf between simple magical **illusions** and major spells that change a thing's true name. Le Guin conveys all this with great conviction in fine prose.

Earthsea has no actively intrusive **gods and goddesses**, and its shadowy afterlife is not **Heaven** or **Hell** but something like the Hades of Greek **mythology**: a place without **water**, containing emotionless ghosts or echoes of the dead (see **Ghosts and Hauntings**). But there are antilife powers of **Earth** and stone, one of which Ged encounters and resists in *A Wizard of Earthsea*.

The second volume, *The Tombs of Atuan* (1971), centers on another stronghold of such **evil** spirits of place, a **labyrinth**, which is the underground focus of a memorably oppressive, life-denying **religion**. The protagonist, a girl who is supposedly the **reincarnation** of an eternal priestess, is stripped of her name, denied **sexuality**, and dedicated as a metaphorical **sacrifice** to ungrateful powers of earth and **darkness**. Ged, entering the labyrinth in search of a lost **ring** that is a talisman of peace, is seen from outside as a threatening interloper. (There is also an aspect of **race relations**, since like most Earthsea folk he has darker skin than the pale people of

Atuan.) The heroine entraps him in the maze-**prison** and—in accordance with what she has been taught—decrees his slow **death**. But he restores, or recognizes by **divination**, her true name Tenar, and she is slowly won over to thoughts of **rebellion** and **escape**. Ged, like his first master, must use his power to hold back the full force of an earthquake before reaching **freedom** with Tenar.

The darkness in *The Farthest Shore* (1972) is less localized and claustrophobic. Something is going wrong throughout Earthsea, with magic and craft skills slipping from **memory**. Ged, now Archmage of Roke, voyages in search of the evil, accompanied by young prince Arren (later to be a great **king**) who is the viewpoint character. It emerges that a rogue wizard has upset the fundamental balance between life and death in his search for immortality (see **Immortality and Longevity**). The cost is too high: buyers lose their names, in effect their souls, for the promise of a return from the afterworld in a grisly parody of **birth**. Everything is soiled by this central wrongness, even Earthsea's wise, powerful dragons: "There is a hole in the world, and the light is running out of it." Another great price must be paid to heal the wounded land. Ged travels painfully through the shadowy afterworld and sacrifices all his magic to close the breach between living and dead. Only Arren's dogged efforts bring him back to the world of **light**. Ged's wizardry is over; he goes **home**.

For all their originality and power, these books conventionally show only male wizards as prime movers. Women are allowed wisdom, but **witches** are proverbially deprecated: "weak/wicked as women's magic" (see **Feminism**). Le Guin redresses this balance in *Tehanu: The Last Book of Earthsea* (1990), showing Tenar and a dismayingly dwindled Ged late in life. Women's magic, exemplified by the secret power of a dreadfully **fire**-scarred child (see **Children**), proves to have a deep, vital affinity with dragons.

Dragons recur in *The Other Wind* (2001), which rethinks and reforms Earthsea's bleak afterlife—rather as **Hell** is harrowed by human intervention in Philip Pullman's *The Amber Spyglass* (2000). Shorter stories appear in *Tales from Earthsea* (2001). Many readers prefer the initial trilogy's clear, moving resonance to Le Guin's later self-revisions.

Bibliography

Douglas Barbour. "On Ursula Le Guin's *A Wizard of Earthsea*." *Riverside Quarterly*, 6 (1974), 119–123.

Harold Bloom, ed. *Ursula K. Le Guin*. New York: Chelsea House, 1986.

Joe De Bolt, ed. *Ursula K. Le Guin*. Port Washington, NY: Kennikat, 1979.

Ursula K. Le Guin. *Earthsea Revisioned*. Madison, NJ: Children's Literature New England, 1993.

Peter Nicholls. "*The Farthest Shore*." *Foundation*, No. 5 (January, 1974), 71–80.

Joseph D. Olander and Martin H. Greenberg, eds. *Ursula K. Le Guin*. New York: Taplinger, 1979.

R.F. Patteson. "Le Guin's Earthsea Trilogy." R.A. Collins, ed., *Scope of the Fantastic*. Westport, CT: Greenwood Press, 1985, 239–248.

Norman Talbot. "'Escape!': That Dirty Word in Modern Fantasy." Kath Filmer, ed., *Twentieth-Century Fantasists*. New York: St. Martin's, 1992, 135–147.

Ann Welton. "Earthsea Revisited." *Voice of Youth Advocates*, 14 (April, 1991), 14–16.

—David Langford

THE WIZARD OF OZ (1939)

∎

Toto, I've a feeling we're not in Kansas anymore.

—Noel Langley, Florence Ryerson,
and Edgar Allan Woolf
The Wizard of Oz (1939)

Summary

The orphaned Dorothy lives with her **dog** Toto on the Kansas **farm** of her Auntie Em and Uncle Henry. A tornado whisks the farmhouse, with Dorothy and Toto inside, into the air; it lands in the Arcadian realm of Oz, where **colors** are brighter. (The black-and-white film shifts into color.) Dorothy encounters the **dwarf** Munchkins and the Good Witch of the North, Glinda; the house crushed and killed the **evil** Wicked Witch of the East, but Dorothy is advised to appropriate her ruby slippers. Glinda tells Dorothy to follow the Yellow Brick Road to the Emerald City where the Wizard of Oz will help her get back **home** to Kansas. During her **quest**, Dorothy is joined by the Scarecrow (who lacks a brain), Tin Man (who lacks a heart), and Cowardly Lion (who lacks **courage**) (see **Lions and Tigers**); they too wish to meet the **Wizard** to gain what they are missing. The Wizard—seen only as a disembodied head—says he will grant their wishes if they bring him the broomstick of the Wicked Witch of the West. In accomplishing this, Dorothy's friends discover they have the attributes they thought they were lacking, and Dorothy fortuitously kills the **witch** by spilling **water** on her. Back in the Emerald City, they discover the Wizard is a sham, achieving impressive effects through gadgetry. He proposes that Dorothy should join him in **flying** to Kansas by balloon (see **Air Travel**), but she is left behind. Glinda appears and tells Dorothy to tap her Ruby Slippers three times and say, "There's no place like home"—which leads to Dorothy waking up in her bed in Kansas, suggesting that her experience was only a **dream**.

Discussion

This beloved film is based on L. Frank Baum's *The Wonderful Wizard of Oz* but changes the story in significant ways. An expanded depiction of Dorothy's life in Kansas adds five characters—three farmhands, an evil neighbor named Miss Gulch, and a traveling showman, Professor Marvel—who are **doppelgängers** of Oz's Scarecrow, Tin Woodman, Cowardly Lion, Wicked Witch of the West, and Wizard. Her adventures in Oz can then be interpreted as Dorothy's confused dream-**memories** of recent experiences in Kansas; being rescued by farmhands from a pig trough; Miss Gulch attempting to seize Toto; and Professor Marvel giving Dorothy kindly guidance. The film conflates the Good Witch of the North and Glinda, Good Witch of the South while entirely eliminating Dorothy's extended adventures in the South after the Wizard's departure; some characters are left out—such as the field mice who save the travelers from the poppy field who are replaced by Glinda—while others are added—such as several Munchkin characters and sinister, anthropomorphic trees.

More significantly, while Baum's story and its sequels project the atmosphere of a benign **utopia**, the film offers a more Manichean vision of good and evil as balanced, equal forces battling for the upper hand, in Kansas and Oz. Dorothy's idyllic life in Kansas is darkened by Gulch, whom her parents struggle to resist; in Oz, her every movement is watched by both a Wicked Witch seeking to harm her and a Good Witch poised to protect her.

The result, by some opinions, is a more compelling story, filled with genuinely terrifying moments that balance scenes of gaiety and song. Others are discomfited by its juxtapositions of involving drama and staged musical sequences, finding the film plodding and overrated. The film's dual nature may in part stem from its two directors: the uncredited King Vidor directed the exhilarating opening sequences in black and white, while credited director Victor Fleming handled the more literal color scenes that form the bulk of the film. All can agree, however, that the film's songs are exceptional, especially "Somewhere Over the Rainbow," which may be one reason the film has become such a favorite.

There were several earlier versions of Baum's story, some produced by Baum himself, but none are of particular interest. Little cinematic attention was paid to Oz in the 1940s and 1950s, but by the 1960s, when repeated television showings had established *The Wizard of Oz* as a classic, many attempted to replicate its story and its charm, with mixed results. The animated *Journey Back to Oz* (1974) is a generally stilted affair distinguished by its voice track, with the role of Dorothy spoken and sung by Liza Minnelli, daughter of the 1939 film's Judy Garland. *The Wiz* (1978), based on a stage musical, featured an all-black cast, lots of pop **music**, and a twisted version of New York City as its setting. The 1982 Japanese-American animated film *The Wizard of Oz*, based on the novel rather than the 1939 film, is more intriguing; here the Wizard's gadgetry effectively makes him a **shapeshifter**.

Of more note is *Return to Oz* (1985), a sequel largely derived from Baum's first two sequels to his original novel, *The Marvelous Land of Oz* (1904) and *Ozma of Oz* (1907); it is primarily live action but includes some Claymation. Dorothy, along with a talking chicken (see **Talking Animals**), is swept back to Oz by a **flood**. In company with Tik Tok and Jack Pumpkinhead, she vies with the Nome King, evil Princess Mombi, and thuggish Wheelers to save the Scarecrow and enthrone rightful ruler Princess Ozma, whom Mombi has banished into a **mirror** world. Eschewing musical sequences, and framed by the dark story line of Dorothy in Kansas receiving electroshock therapy to deal with her memories of Oz, the film displeased viewers who were expecting a colorful romp, but it is in its own way a memorable fantasy, more reminiscent of 1984's *The Neverending Story* than the 1939 film.

Bibliography

Stephen Cox. *The Munchkins of Oz*. Third Ed. Nashville: Cumberland House, 2002.

Peter Glassman, ed. *Oz: The Hundredth Anniversary Celebration*. New York: HarperCollins, 2000.

Aljean Harmetz. *The Making of The Wizard of Oz*. New York: Limelight, 1984.

Doug McClelland. *Down the Yellow Brick Road*. 50th Anniversary Edition. New York: Bonanza, 1989.

Salman Rushdie. *The Wizard of Oz*. London: British Film Institute, 1992.

Jay Scarfone and William Stillman. *The Wizardry of Oz.* Second Edition. New York: Hal Leonard, 2004.

David Shipman. *Judy Garland.* New York: Hyperion, 1993.

Mark Evan Swartz. *Oz Before the Rainbow.* Baltimore: Johns Hopkins University Press, 2000.

—John Grant

WOMAN ON THE EDGE OF TIME BY MARGE PIERCY (1976)

Free. Our ancestors said that was the most beautiful word in the language.

—Marge Piercy
Woman on the Edge of Time (1976)

Summary

Because of alleged child abuse and a history of substance abuse, the authorities deem Connie Ramos, a thirty-seven-year-old Chicana, an unfit **mother** and she loses custody of her daughter Angelina. Misdiagnosed as a paranoid schizophrenic, Connie is locked up in a mental institution against her will. To cure Connie of her supposed violent fits, she is forced to undergo physical treatments. Her own story—of being the victim of domestic **violence** that led to an abortion and enforced hysterectomy—is denied. Men further dehumanize Connie when the doctors perform brain surgery on her after getting her brother's—not Connie's—written consent to subject her to this "therapy." Because Connie has an unusually high ability for empathy, she can be telepathically contacted by Luciente, a resident of the village Mattapoisett of the twenty-second century (see **Psychic Powers**). In several trips reminiscent of classic utopian **time travel** (see **Utopia**) or **dream**-induced mental travel, Connie telepathically visits Mattapoisett where the sociopolitical movements of the squalid 1970s **America** Connie lives in—**feminism, ecology**, and socialism—have led to a society that values differences, equality, cooperation, and **community**. Because the future existence of this utopia depends on actions taken or not taken in Connie's present, Luciente also takes Connie to a **dystopia**, an alternative future where women are sexually exploited and surveillance, **drugs**, crime, and class segregation prevail. This dystopian visit occurs when Connie is subjected to a brain implant. In an attempt to bring about the future utopia, Connie then poisons various staff members of the mental hospital.

Discussion

Along with a strong wave of feminist utopias that grew out of the women's liberation movement in the 1970s, Marge Piercy's *Woman on the Edge of Time* addresses female reality, **sexuality**, and distribution of power within society and **family** in patriarchy. By juxtaposing the future utopia seen through Connie's eyes with her own present seen through Luciente's eyes and with the dystopian alternative future they visit together—which represents the dreary outcome of the sociopolitical realities of Connie's present—within the same text, Piercy highlights the differences between all three societies. In particular, the comparison of Connie, Luciente, and Gildina as future versions of Connie illustrates the differing treatment of women.

Both Connie's New York and, even more so, the dystopian New York of the future are polluted, dirty, and noisy **cities**, whereas inhabitants of the village Mattapoisett live in a **pastoral** rural environment. Whereas Connie is discriminated against because of her ethnic background, **gender**, and class (see **Class System**), and Gildina—a surgically altered caricature of femininity working as a prostitute in the future New York where sexuality is generally abusive—is victimized as a sex object, Mattapoisett is a society free of **sexism** and racism (see **Race Relations**). In contrast to the authoritative and hierarchical present that silences women's voices, Mattapoisett is based on sharing and mediation. It is a nonhierarchical, classless, and decentralized society emphasizing **gender** equality, communitarian goals, consensual decision-making, cooperation, ecological issues (see **Ecology**), and the necessity to distinguish between social construction of gender and biological sexual difference. Additionally, to create a bias-free language (see **Language and Linguistics**), in Mattapoisett gender-specific terms are eliminated and the gendered pronouns "he" and "she" are replaced with "person" and "his" and "her" with "per." And while consumerism rules the 1970s, the ideal society has no use for **money** and has eradicated ownership.

Other important central themes are childcare, mothering, and reproduction. Caretaking and mothering are relegated to women and **birth** is controlled by doctors in Connie's world, and in the dystopian future women are categorized as sex toys or breeding machines. In Mattapoisett, however, natural reproduction and childrearing as exclusively female tasks are viewed as mechanisms of oppression. Thus, the nuclear family is abolished and mothering as well as its cultural background are separated from **biology**. A sophisticated breeding program of **genetic engineering** ensures that genes and offspring of various ethnic backgrounds are mixed. Human diversity is immensely valued, but cultural **identity** is thus no longer tied to genetics. Mothering is a voluntary concept based on nonpossessiveness. This parenting and nurturing concept embraces men: **children** are cared for by three "co-mothers," who can also be male. Consequently, biology no longer plays a major role, since with the help of hormones men too can breast-feed.

In the dystopian future, medical **technology** is misused as a tool for oppression, not for healing, mirroring Connie's maltreatment at the mental hospital. Due to perfected brain surgery and control, most humans are walking automatons. Mattapoisett's advanced technology is used to liberate humans from biological restraints instead of dehumanizing them.

As several critics stress, the novel's ambiguous end invites two readings: either Connie retaliates against the immense violence she has been subjected to, or the doctors were right in diagnosing her condition as **madness**. However, Connie's active attempt to change her own future implies that our future is not a historical inevitability (see **History**) but that ordinary people's actions in the present can bring about utopia.

Bibliography

Elham Afnan. "Chaos and Utopia." *Extrapolation*, 37 (Winter, 1996), 330–340.

Frances Bartkowski. *Feminist Utopias.* Lincoln: University of Nebraska, 1989.

Keith B. Booker. "Woman on the Edge of a Genre." *Science-Fiction Studies*, 21 (November, 1994), 337–350.

Maureen Devine. "*Woman on the Edge of Time* and *The Wanderground.*" Arno Heller, Walter Hölbling and Waldemar Zacharasiewicz, eds., *Utopian Thought in American Literature.* Tübingen: Narr, 1988, 131–145.

Chris Ferns. "Dreams of Freedom." *English Studies in Canada*, 14 (Winter, 1988), 453–466.

Libby Falk Jones. "Gilman, Bradley, Piercy, and the Evolving Rhetoric of Feminist Utopias." Libby Falk Jones and Sarah Webster Goodwin, eds., *Feminism, Utopia, and Narrative.* Knoxville: University of Tennessee, 1990, 116–129.

Carol Farley Kessler. "*Woman on the Edge of Time.*" *Extrapolation*, 28 (Winter, 1987), 310–318.

Elaine Orr. "Mothering as Good Fiction." *Journal of Narrative Technique*, 23 (1993), 61–79.

Kerstin W. Shands. *The Repair of the World.* Westport, CT: Greenwood Press, 1995.

—Dunja M. Mohr

THE WONDERFUL WIZARD OF OZ BY L. FRANK BAUM (1900)

■

I'm really a very good man, but I'm a very bad Wizard, I must admit.

—L. Frank Baum
The Wonderful Wizard of Oz (1900)

Summary

A house containing a little girl named Dorothy is flown by a cyclone to the magical land of Oz (see **Magic**), where it lands on and kills the Wicked Witch of the East, allowing Dorothy to claim her silver slippers. For assistance in returning to Kansas, she is advised to travel to the Emerald City on the Yellow Brick Road and seek help from the mysterious Wizard of Oz; on her journey, she meets the Scarecrow, Tin Woodman, and Cowardly Lion (see **Lions and Tigers**), who join her as they respectively seek to obtain a brain, a heart, and **courage**. The Wizard of Oz, who appears in various frightful forms, says that he will grant their requests only after they kill the Wicked Witch of the West; after hardships, they accomplish the task when Dorothy splashes **water** on the Witch and causes her to melt. Returning to the Emerald City, they discover the Wizard of Oz is really a fraud, an ordinary man from Dorothy's world, who satisfies her companions with contrivances and offers to take Dorothy **home** with him in a balloon; unfortunately, Dorothy misses the flight. She and her friends then travel to meet Glinda, Good Witch of the South, who informs

Dorothy that her silver slippers have the power to transport her back to Kansas, and she promptly returns home.

Discussion

Due to the popularity of *The Wonderful Wizard of Oz*, L. Frank Baum eventually wrote thirteen sequels to the book, as well as related minor books and compilations and several Oz films that he produced. After his death, several authors produced additional Oz books. Baum's immediate sequel *The Marvelous Land of Oz* (1904) introduced the key character of Ozma, the princess who becomes the benevolent ruler of Oz; this and later books feature other new characters as well as returning figures from the first book. Eventually, Dorothy, her Aunt Em and Uncle Henry, and the Wizard of Oz are brought back to Oz as contented residents.

The magical Ozma, who often resolves characters' problems as a sort of **deus ex machina**, and other recurring female characters like Dorothy and Glinda, have inspired the common viewpoint that Baum's Oz essentially becomes a **utopia** for little girls, dominated by women and informed by an overarching sensibility of gentleness that gradually eliminates **evil** and any genuine conflicts and perils. This is even true of the first book, which moves at a leisurely pace and has none of the sense of urgency and drama foregrounded in its famous film adaptation, *The Wizard of Oz*. All people and animals in Oz are effectively immortal (see **Immortality and Longevity**), and animals automatically have the power of speech (see **Talking Animals**).

Oz is a **color**-coded world, with four regions dominated by the colors blue, purple, red, and yellow surrounding the central Emerald City, where spectacles make everything look green; it is surrounded by a harsh **desert** that makes it impossible for people to reach it, suggesting the image of a fecund oasis in an arid **wilderness**. The original story can be regarded in various ways as an **allegory**; for example, Baum may be supporting the then-fashionable monetary policy of bimetallism (backing currency with both **gold and silver**) by having Dorothy don *silver* slippers to travel on the Yellow Brick Road (representing *gold*) to reach the Emerald City of prosperity (its green being the color of America's paper currency). There have been several ingenious explanations of the name "Oz": though Baum insisted that it came only from seeing the alphabetizing label "O-Z" on a file cabinet, some detect a reference to **Australia** or a sly nod to the two states where Baum lived, New York and Pennsylvania, commonly abbreviated "NY" and "PA," with "Oz" comprised of the letters between N and O and between Y and A (assuming a cyclical alphabet in which Z is followed again by A). Dorothy's three companions, who repeatedly display the **intelligence**, compassion, and courage that they avowedly lack, convey the uplifting message that people can draw upon their own inner resources to develop as they choose, although they may require some form of outward validation (like the *faux* brain, heart, and courage that the Wizard gives them) to recognize their own good qualities.

Baum is unfailingly imaginative in creating new characters and devices that may result from magic, **technology**, or some combination thereof. The Tin Woodman is first a **cyborg** whose mechanical parts gradually replace his human parts until he becomes a **robot**; another mechanical figure was the Tik-Tok Man introduced in *Ozma of Oz* (1906). The Powder of Life creates the Gump of *The Marvelous Land* *of Oz*, made up of an animal's head, two sofas, leaves, and a broom. Baum also delights in bringing to life familiar objects from a child's world, like Jack Pumpkin-head of *The Marvelous Land of Oz*, an ambulatory jack-o-lantern (see **Halloween**), the Raggedy Ann-like *The Patchwork Girl of Oz* (1913), and the living china dolls encountered in their own little country in *The Wonderful Wizard of Oz*.

Baum's Oz powerfully influenced later fantasy by constructing an **imaginary world** described in a **map** and repeatedly elaborated and expanded in a series of books. To pay tribute, a few later writers have reinterpreted Oz as a **parallel world** that people can visit, as in Robert A. Heinlein's *The Number of the Beast* (1980) and Philip Jose Farmer's *A Barnstormer in Oz* (1982), while Geoff Ryman's *Was* (1992) reinvents Dorothy Gale and brings her into contact with L. Frank Baum to explain the genesis of his story. Baum's major competitor as an influence is ironically the 1939 film, also explored in Ryman's *Was* and repeatedly referenced in later books and films.

Bibliography

Frank Joslyn Baum and Russell P. MacFall. *To Please a Child*. Chicago: Reilly and Lee, 1961.

Ranjit S. Dighe, ed. *The Historian's Wizard of Oz*. Westport, CT: Greenwood Press, 2002.

Neil Earle. *The Wonderful Wizard of Oz in American Popular Culture*. Lewiston, NY: E. Mellen, 1993.

Michael Patrick Hearn, ed. *The Annotated Wizard of Oz*, by L. Frank Baum. New York: Schocken Books, 1983.

Raylyn Moore. *Wonderful Wizard, Marvelous Land*. Bowling Green, OH: Bowling Green State University Popular Press, 1974.

Russel Nye and Martin Gardner, eds. *The Wizard of Oz, and Who He Was*. East Lansing: Michigan State University Press, 1957.

Michael O. Riley. *Oz and Beyond*. Lawrence: University of Kansas Press, 1997.

Katharine M. Rogers. *L. Frank Baum*. New York: St. Martin's Press, 2002.

Jack Snow. *Who's Who in Oz*. Chicago: Reilly and Lee, 1954.

—Lynne Lundquist

WONDER WOMAN (1976–1979)

At last, in a world torn by the hatreds and wars of men, appears a woman to whom the problems and feats of men are mere child's play—a woman whose identity is known to none, but whose sensational feats are outstanding in a fast-moving world! With a hundred times the agility and strength of our best male athletes and strongest wrestlers, she appears as though from nowhere to

> *avenge an injustice or right a wrong! As lovely as Aphrodite—as wise as Athena—with the speed of Mercury and the strength of Hercules—she is known only as Wonder Woman, but who she is, or whence she came, nobody knows!*
>
> —William Moulton Marston
> "Introducing Wonder Woman" (1941)

Summary

Created by William Moulton Marston, a psychologist best-known for inventing the polygraph (see **Psychology**), Wonder Woman made her 1941 debut in *All-Star Comics*. By her second appearance, her personal mythos and supporting cast were in place. Crafted from clay by her **mother, Queen** Hyppolyte, and granted the gifts of life and fantastic **beauty**, strength, and **speed** by Greek **gods and goddesses**, Princess Diana grows to adulthood among the immortal, peaceful **Amazons** of Paradise Island (see **Immortality and Longevity; Lost Worlds**), a **utopia** sheltered from the World of Men. When U.S. Army pilot Steve Trevor crashes on the **island** during World War II, Diana nurses him back to health. The goddesses Athena and Aphrodite advise Hippolyte to send an Amazon champion to escort Trevor back to **America**. To decide the champion, a contest of physical prowess is held, which is won by the Diana in **disguise**. After returning Trevor safely to America, Diana remains in the United States, devoting herself to the fight for **freedom**, democracy, and equal rights for women. This origin story is retold in the 1975 ABC television movie *The New Original Wonder Woman* starring Lynda Carter, which led to a television series chronicling her ongoing adventures.

Discussion

The popular reception of Carter's version of Wonder Woman prompted ABC to order two more one-hour specials, and finally eleven regular series episodes. Series like *Charlie's Angels* (1976–1981) and *The Bionic Woman* (1976–1978) featuring strong women in central roles often saving men (see **Role Reversals**) illustrated television's attempts to come to grips with **feminism** during the 1970s. In this environment, *Wonder Woman* was almost an inevitability. Created by Marston as a counterpart to the wildly popular *Superman*, Wonder Woman served as a heroic role model for girls (see **Heroes**). Often overlooked, however, is that Wonder Woman introduced feminist concepts to boys, who comprised as much as 90 percent of comics readership. Promoting women as independent, capable equals during the "Rosie the Riveter" era was not an accident, and thus it is unsurprising that feminists would eventually adopt Wonder Woman as an unofficial icon.

Earlier attempts to adapt Wonder Woman to television were less noteworthy. Encouraged by the success of *Batman* (1966–1968) (see **Batman**), Stan Hart and Larry Seigel scripted a campy Wonder Woman pilot in 1967, but the concept was quickly abandoned. Hollywood returned to the character with the made-for-TV movie *Wonder Woman* (1974). Played by blonde tennis pro Cathy Lee Crosby, this version of Wonder Woman dispensed with the familiar costume and owed more to Emma Peel of *The Avengers* (1961–1969) than the comics. Despite the negative audience reception, ABC was determined to try again. Titling the latest project *The New Original Wonder Woman* to avoid confusion with the Crosby telefilm, and casting the statuesque Carter, a former Miss World USA, in the lead role, yielded much better results.

Drawing heavily on the source material, the first season's episodes took place during World War II, complete with versions of Trevor, Etta Candy, Wonder Girl, and even Gestapo agent Baroness Paula Von Gunther, all transplanted from the comics. To better fight the Nazi menace, Wonder Woman adopts the **secret identity** of Diana Prince and gets a job with Army Intelligence. Aiding in her fight is an array of **magical objects**: bullet-deflecting *feminum* bracelets; an undetectable, **invisible** plane; a golden girdle that preserves her incredible strength away from Paradise Island; and an unbreakable, golden lasso that compels those bound by it to tell the truth.

Invariably, each episode featured Wonder Woman battling some improbable Nazi effort to jeopardize the American war effort. In the episode "Wonder Woman vs. Gargantua!" (1976), Nazi scientists breed an exceptionally powerful gorilla (see **Apes**) to destroy Wonder Woman. The two-parter "Judgement from Outer Space" (1977) evokes *The Day the Earth Stood Still* when Andros, an alien envoy (see **Aliens on Earth**) from an advanced **civilization**, arrives on Earth to judge the war-like human race and destroy the planet if necessary. In another two-parter, "The Feminum Mystique" (1976), Nazis invade Paradise Island to discover the secret of the titular bulletproof metal. The theme of men forcing **violence** upon Amazon society is also explored at length in Lillian Stewart Carl's fantasy novel *Sabazel* (1985) and Judith Tarr's *Queen of the Amazons* (2004).

ABC cancelled the series at the end of the season, but CBS resurrected it as *The New Adventures of Wonder Woman* (1977–1979). The re-tooled show was updated to the present, with Carter reprising her role as the ageless Amazon. Lyle Waggoner, the only other cast holdover, appears as Steve Trevor, Jr., son of his first-season character and head of a national security agency. Ironically, the "contemporary" 1970s episodes are more dated than "period" episodes and lack much of the wit and charm that marked the original. Wonder Woman's role shifted from a defender of freedom to that of a more traditional **superhero**, focused on apprehending criminals (see **Crime and Punishment**).

In the comics, Wonder Woman has remained consistent despite a major revamp in the mid-1980s, which emphasized the **mythology** and historical aspects of the character and Amazon society. A series of stand-alone graphic novels, including Paul Dini and Alex Ross's *Spirit of Truth* (2001) and Greg Rucka and J.G. Jones's *The Hiketeia* (2003), explore **gender**, **sexism**, and cultural issues from Wonder Woman's perspective.

Bibliography

Scott Beatty. *Wonder Woman*. New York: DK Publishing, Inc., 2003.
Les Daniels. *Wonder Woman*. San Francisco: Chronicle Books, 2000.
Bea Feitler, ed. *Wonder Woman*. New York: Holt, Rinehart, and Winston, 1972.
David Hoftede. *Hollywood and the Comics*. Las Vegas, NV: Zanne-3, 1991.

Sherrie A. Inness. *Tough Girls*. Philadelphia: University of Pennsylvania Press, 1999.

William Moulton Marston. "Why 100,000,000 Americans Read Comics." *The American Scholar*, 13 (Winter, 1943/1944), 35–44.

Sam Moskowitz. "Women's Liberation." Moskowitz, *Strange Horizons*. New York: Charles Scribner's Sons, 1976, 70–91.

Olive Richard. "Our Women are Our Future." *Family Circle*, (August 14, 1942), 10–11.

William Schöel. *Comic Book Heroes of the Screen*. Sacramento, CA: Citadel Press, 1991.

—*Jayme Lynn Blaschke*

THE WORM OUROBOROS BY E.R. EDDISON (1922)

Summary

The Worm Ouroboros is a self-contained fantasy that yet manages to institute a **cycle** of heroic **romance**, developing ideas of **reincarnation** that are further explored in the succeeding "Zimiamvian trilogy." Lessingham—man of action, poet, and artist—is transported in a **dream** to **Mercury**. He observes Gorice XI, King of Witchland, lay claim to Lord Juss's Demonland. A challenge to single combat between Gorice and Juss's champion Goldry Bluszco gives initial advantage to Gorice. Goldry is so infuriated by the treachery that he kills Gorice, and the king's spirit is transferred to another body. "Gorice XII" is aided by renegade Goblin Gro in his **escape** and carries off Goldry. Juss and his lords must rescue their comrade and carry on the fight. After **quests** and double-dealing, and both victories and defeats, Juss succeeds. But the Demon-lords now have no enemy worth their fighting. They look forward to being "stingless drones" until an act of **magic** reverses **time** to the arrival of the Witchland Ambassador. The eponymous symbol of the serpent that eats its own tail becomes complete.

Discussion

Eddison's "**Demons**" and "**Witches**" are warriors whose honor is based upon **chivalry** and combat. Lessingham swiftly fades as viewpoint character, to be subsumed into a narrative involving the conflict between "Honour" and "Policy" as envisaged by the High Renaissance literary texts echoed throughout. Although good and **evil** are invoked, there are no moral "sides" in the sense of modern genre fantasy's positioning of such concepts. This is underlined, perhaps, by the names of this realm's "nations," which carry none of the symbolic weight of the normal use of these terms. Awe and a **sense of wonder** are evoked by set-piece descriptions of *things*, especially **landscape** and **architecture and interior design**, but also by hints and correspondences, more fully worked out in the succeeding trilogy, in which a mental landscape of desire and refusal is laid out.

The story is in many ways the antithesis of that **sword and sorcery** which places the **barbarian** at the narrative center. Eddison's characters are magnificent and

Machiavellian, created out of literary rather than generic stock. His world is the ideal Heroic Age: it is the Homeric, the Icelandic saga-time, or the world that the Elizabethan Renaissance aspired to be. His characters quote authors—William Dunbar, John Donne, Robert Greene, Robert Herrick, John Webster—from "our" heritage, arising naturally and effectively from Eddison's cosmos. The tail-biting serpent is both the Norse symbol (the world-serpent) underlying the book's mythic quality and the key to its structure. Final victory can only be pyrrhic because it denies the very factor—**war** against an equal—which gives meaning to existence. Hence there is the time-reversal at the moment of victory so combatants can enjoy the battle again. Presumably, no one thinks to ask the spear-carriers.

The succeeding *Mistress of Mistresses* (1935), *A Fish Dinner in Memison* (1941), and the posthumous *The Mezentian Gate* (1958) show us Lessingham reincarnated in the Valhalla-like Zimamvia, glimpsed by Juss as a physical place behind a mighty **mountain** range. *Mistress of Mistresses*, in particular, shows Eddison's command of character in the **villain** Horius Parry and underling Gabriel De Flores and the construction of his fiction from the self-image and **poetry** of the Classics and Renaissance. Here, Eddison is one of the few fantasy writers to use strong female characters, like the Muse/Goddess figure Fiorinda, who is also Mary Lessingham. Her relationship with Duke Barganax—who is, like Lessingham, a "dress" of the male principle—invokes a charged, obscure **sexuality**. We learn more about the twentieth-century Lessingham, a scholar–warlord born out of his time, and, through the philosopher Vandermast, of this universe's complex erotic theology. *A Fish Dinner in Memison* reverses the structure by showing us our entire cosmos (including, presumably, the Lessingham and "Mercury" of *The Worm Ouroboros*) created and destroyed to illustrate a dinner-party argument.

Despite the deities and semi-deities who are Eddison's characters, **religion** is absent, as is any real engagement with the twentieth century other than to deny it in favor of the **romance**-world someone like Lessingham would wish to lose himself in. Despite guarded praise from C.S. Lewis and others, and Eddison's arguable attempt to do for Classical and Renaissance literary sources what J.R.R. Tolkien's *The Lord of the Rings* would do for Northern **fairy tale**, Eddison's direct popularity has been marginal. Nevertheless, he influenced many writers in similar veins. It may be true that *The Worm Ouroboros* and its sequels are as much simplistic power-fantasies as their barbarian-based cousins and that their literary borrowings dress up a sense that our universe (and we ourselves) are unreal playthings for cultured English public-school alumni like Lessingham. But the imagined cosmos conveys a sense of heroic **illusion** that we read, as Eddison wrote, for its own sake. *The Worm Ouroboros* and its sequels can also be read for the inventive echoings, mirrorings, and shadowings that highlight Eddison's saga-like plots. They are among the finest attempts to construct a literary **mythology**.

Bibliography

Lin Carter. *Imaginary Worlds*. New York: Ballantine, 1973.

Don D'Ammassa. "Villains of Necessity." Darrell Schweitzer, ed., *Discovering Fantasy Fiction*. San Bernardino, CA: Borgo Press, 1996, 49–55.

L. Sprague de Camp. *Literary Swordsmen and Sorcerers*. Sauk City, WI: Arkham House, 1976.

David A. Oakes. "The Eternal Circle." *Extrapolation*, 40 (Summer 1999), 124–128.
Helmut W. Pesch. "The Sign of the Worm." Carl B. Yoke and Donald M. Hassler, eds., *Death and the Serpent*. Westport, CT: Greenwood Press, 1985, 91–101.
Andy Sawyer. "Twice Removed From Reality." *Vector*, No. 149 (April/May, 1989), 10–15.
William M. Schuyler, Jr. "E.R. Eddison's Metaphysics of the Hero." *New York Review of Science Fiction*, No. 31 (March 1991), 12–17.
Sharon Wilson. "The Doctrine of Organic Unity." *Extrapolation*, 25 (Spring, 1984), 12–19.

—Andy Sawyer

𝒳

THE X-FILES (1993–2002)

■

I'm not going to give up. I can't give up.
Not as long as the truth is out there.

—Chris Carter
"The Erlenmeyer Flask," episode
of *The X-Files* (1994)

Summary

The X-Files, created by Chris Carter, involved FBI agents Fox Mulder and Dana Scully and their investigations of "X files," cases that do not lend themselves to conventional explanations. Mulder, obsessed with the childhood disappearance of his younger sister, is convinced that she was abducted by aliens and that the U.S. government is covering up information regarding **aliens on Earth**. His obsession has damaged his reputation within the FBI, so he is partnered with Dana Scully, a medical doctor and super-rational skeptic who is ordered to keep an eye on him and report her observations to superiors. During the series, standalone episodes in which the agents investigate cases involving paranormal activity intermix with episodes detailing a remarkably complex story arc gradually revealing a vast government conspiracy to hide not only the existence of aliens on Earth but also an ongoing program of abductions, attempts at **genetic engineering** to produce human/alien hybrids, and **war** between competing alien races. As the series progresses, Scully grows less skeptical and forms a deep, loyal, and eventually intimate bond with Mulder while herself becoming a victim of the conspiracy. When star David Duchovny left the show in its eighth season, two new agents, John Dogget and Monica Reyes, were introduced, and Scully—who by now had given **birth** to a child that would figure prominently in the "alien" story arc—became more of a background figure. By the end of the series, Scully and Mulder are reunited and the conspiracy has largely collapsed, but the aliens are still out there and are coming back soon to complete plans to colonize **Earth**.

Discussion

The X-Files has inspired to date one theatrical film, *The X-Files: Fight the Future* (1998), further developing the alien/conspiracy story arc. A companion series, *Millennium* (1996–1999), was generally well-received but never enjoyed the success of *The X-Files*; a spinoff, *The Lone Gunmen* (2001), was short-lived.

Carter's series was most obviously associated with **UFOs**, and the episodes that spun out the alien/conspiracy story arc (known to fans as "the mythology") incorporated a number of elements from the UFO **culture** of preceding decades, from mysterious "Men in Black" and alien corpses held in secret government facilities to, preeminently, alien abduction of humans. However, one of the series' strengths was the way it linked these spectacular events to the ongoing development of its main characters. Throughout the "mythology" episodes, Mulder relentlessly pursues the truth in the face of constant opposition from those in power (the X-Files division is closed down more than once) and frequent **betrayal** by his colleagues (who are part of the government conspiracy). It is a pursuit that takes a greater and greater toll on him as the line between honor and **hubris** threatens to disappear altogether into **madness**. At the same time, as Scully witnesses more and more that simply cannot be explained, and eventually is abducted herself, she must confront the possible limitations of both her own training as a **scientist** and the **religion** (Catholicism) to which she still adheres. Throughout the series, the two central characteristics of UFO culture—a desperate yearning for transcendence rooted in a pervasive **paranoia**—are consistently and vividly portrayed, reinforced by the show's twin mantras: "The Truth Is Out There" and "Trust No One."

Although the "mythology" lay at the heart of the series, many of its finest episodes were "standalones" in which Mulder and Scully investigated **mysteries** involving telepathy, telekinesis (see **Psychic Powers**), **shapeshifters, monsters, supernatural creatures,** and special **talents.** Among the most highly regarded of these episodes are "Beyond the Sea" (1994), in which Scully is deeply affected by a prisoner who claims he can help her communicate with her dead **father;** "Humbug" (1995), an early example of the show's effective use of **humor** as Mulder and Scully investigate a murder in a town of circus performers; "Clyde Bruckman's Final Repose" (1995), in which an investigation of murdered fortune tellers is aided by a man who really can foretell the future; "Jose Chung's *From Outer Space*" (1996), a semi-mythology episode that offers ironic commentary on the whole notion of alien abduction; "Home" (1996), an investigation of inbreeding in a rural **family** whose **horror** element was so strong that the Fox Network refused to rerun the episode; "Musings of a Cigarette-Smoking Man" (1996), which suggests that the series' main **villain** is, among other things, a failed novelist; "The Post-Modern Prometheus" (1997), a black-and-white retelling of *Frankenstein* and one of the series' notable forays into **metafiction and recursiveness;** "Bad Blood" (1998), another example of humor as Mulder and Scully give conflicting accounts of their encounter with an alleged **vampire;** "Monday" (1999), in which a woman caught in a **time** loop tries to prevent Mulder and Scully's murder; and "The Unnatural" (1999), another semi-mythology episode (written and directed by Duchovny) that tells of a 1940s baseball player who was, possibly, an alien.

The X-Files was not a perfect work of art. Many found the "mythology" confusing and inconsistent, and some within the science fiction community regarded the show's focus on UFO paranoia as an unwelcome glorification of irrationality. The final two seasons were disappointing, as the show was unable to either integrate its new characters fully into the established storyline or turn the show over to them altogether. Nonetheless, *The X-Files* at its best was a showcase for remarkably effective writing, direction, and performance, and the series attained a cumulative power seldom seen on television. It remains one of the most important and influential science fiction television series ever made.

Bibliography

Jan Delarsara. *PopLit, PopCult and The X-Files*. Jefferson, NC: McFarland, 2000.

N.E. Genge. *The Unofficial X-Files Companion*. New York: Crown, 1995.

James Hatfield and James Burt. *The Unauthorized X-Cyclopedia*. New York: Kensington, 1997.

David Lavery, Angela Hague, and Marla Cartwright, eds. *Deny All Knowledge*. Syracuse, NY: Syracuse University Press, 1996.

Frank Lovece. *The X-Files Declassified*. Secaucus, NJ: Carol Publishing Group, 1996.

Brian Lowry. *The Truth Is Out There*. New York: HarperCollins, 1995.

Anne Simon. *The Real Science Behind The X-Files*. New York: Simon & Schuster, 1999.

Tom Soter. *Investigating Couples*. Jefferson, NC: McFarland, 2001.

Michael White. *The Science of the X-Files*. London: Legend, 1996.

—*F. Brett Cox*

XENA: WARRIOR PRINCESS (1995–2001)

Summary

The leather-clad warrior heroine Xena was introduced in a trilogy of **Hercules: The Legendary Journeys** episodes as a fierce warlord whom Hercules converts to fighting for the good and innocent. Her spin-off series, like *Hercules*, was filmed in New Zealand and set in a **sword and sorcery** version of the ancient world. In the first episode, Xena renounces **war** and buries her **weaponry**, only to retrieve the weapons moments later to rescue peasants from slave traders. Among the peasants is Gabrielle, an innocent village girl who **dreams** of adventure. The two become friends and begin a six-year odyssey all over Greece, as well as Rome, **Egypt**, India, Germany, and the Far East. They befriend the inept warrior Joxer (see **Clowns and Fools**), **Amazons**, and the Christ-like Eli (see **Messiahs**), and feud with Julius Caesar (see **Alternate History**), the vengeful warrior woman Callisto, and the **witch** Alti. Xena's relationship with the seductive war god Ares (see **Gods and Goddesses**) provides constant intrigue as he seeks to woo her back to his service.

Among major plot points, Caesar's crucifixion of Xena and Gabrielle ("The Ides of March" [1999]) leads to their participation in a war between **Heaven** and **Hell** (see **Angels; Demons**) before being resurrected by a miracle ("Fallen Angel" [1999]). Lawless's pregnancy during the fifth season led to a story line involving a prophecy that Xena's miraculously conceived child (see **Babies**) will bring the end of the gods. In the resulting war, all major Olympians except Ares and Aphrodite perish, most at the hands of Xena herself, making way for worship of the pseudo-Christian "God of Eli" (see **Christianity**); and Xena and Gabrielle fall under a spell-induced **sleep**. Hence, the final season takes place twenty-five years after the rest of the series; Xena makes peace with her past in the series finale "A Friend in Need" (2001) by sacrificing her life (see **Sacrifice**) to redeem the souls of 40,000 Japanese whose **deaths** she caused in her warlord days.

Discussion

In some ways the successor to television action heroines like **Wonder Woman**, *The Bionic Woman* (1976–1978), and *Charlie's Angels* (1976–1981), Xena stands apart from this earlier generation of heroines who were either partnered with or under the authority of men. As a female **hero** independent of any male influence (see **Feminism**), she more nearly resembles film heroines like *Alien*'s Ripley and the conflicted female warriors of Hong Kong martial arts movies, who were the original inspiration for the character.

Central to the series' success was the **friendship** between Xena and Gabrielle. Viewers responded to the chemistry between series leads Lucy Lawless and Renee O'Connor, as well as the contrast between the archetypal jaded warrior and innocent **youth**. This friendship is always dynamic rather than static, evolving from hero and sidekick to equals, and allowing Xena and Gabrielle to quarrel and even attempt to kill each other after Gabrielle's demonic daughter murders Xena's young son. This **estrangement** is resolved in the musical episode "The Bitter Suite" (1998) in which Xena and Gabrielle journey in a **dream** world. Before *Xena*, such an in-depth exploration of friendship between two women was almost unknown in the action–adventure genre.

Because of their emotional intimacy, Xena and Gabrielle also became lesbian icons (see **Homosexuality**). While many scenes hinted at a lesbian subtext, producers and actors consistently refused to specify whether or not the relationship had a homosexual dimension, preferring to leave the issue open to viewer interpretation.

Xena's struggle to atone for her past crimes and reconcile her use of **violence** with her noble ideals is an ongoing theme, most deeply examined in the fourth season when Gabrielle adopts a Hindu-inspired pacifism. In "Seeds of Faith" (2000) Gabrielle promises Eli that she will not use violence to defend him, and then is aghast when Eli lets Ares kill him, rather than forsake his Way of Love. Xena later refuses to avenge Eli by killing Ares, thus accepting Eli's message that violence must end through individual choices. In other episodes, Eli's martyrdom is seen to foster the spread of his message; while Xena herself twice shows the miraculous power of **love**, by offering her own soul to save those of Callisto and her warlord daughter Livia.

Like the *Hercules* series, *Xena* draws on Greek and Roman **mythology** and history, as well as the traditions of **Judaism**, Germany, India, and **Japan**. In all instances, characters and events are freely adapted to serve the modern tone and the demands of the story at hand. The series also pays homage to modern film and theater with genres like **westerns**, slapstick **comedy**, and science fiction. This approach, especially in cultural borrowings, inevitably caused some controversy, most notably the Hindu-inspired episode "The Way" (1999). Conservative Hindus objected to the portrayal of Krishna, especially as his assistance to Xena and Gabrielle appeared to condone a lesbian relationship. After its initial airing, the episode was withheld from syndication for several months, then released with one shot edited out and a new disclaimer inserted to placate Hindus.

Xena is that television rarity, a spin-off that became a bigger hit than the original series. The show quickly achieved cult status while Xena herself became a pop culture icon, as recognizable as Spock (see **Star Trek**) or Darth Vader (see **Star Wars**). Her success paved the way for a generation of action-adventure series with female protagonists, most notably **Buffy the Vampire Slayer** and *Alias* (2001–).

Bibliography

K. Stoddard Hayes, *Xena: Warrior Princess*. London: Titan Books, 2003.

K. Stoddard Hayes. "Angels and Warriors." *Xena: Warrior Princess*, 1 (September, 2000), 42–48.

Elyce Rae Helford, "Feminism, Queer Studies, and the Sexual Politics of *Xena: Warrior Princess*." Helford, ed., *Fantasy Girls*. Lanham: Rowman & Littlefield, 2000, 135–162.

Jon Miller. "Working in the Sin Trade." *Xena: Warrior Princess*, 1 (November, 1999), 48–52.

Joanne Morreale, "*Xena: Warrior Princess* as Feminist Camp." *Journal of Popular Culture*, 32 (Fall, 1998), 79–86.

Jim Smith. "Twilight of the Gods." *Xena: Warrior Princess*, 1 (January, 2001), 52–57.

Eddie Summers. "Redemption Songs." *Xena: Warrior Princess*, 1 (November, 1999), 22–26.

Francis Tomaszyk. "Lunatics with Lethal Combat Skills." *Femspec*, 4 (2002), 38–46.

Robert Weisbrot, *Xena: Warrior Princess*. New York: Bantam Books, 1998.

—Karen Stoddard Hayes

THE YEARS OF RICE AND SALT
BY KIM STANLEY ROBINSON (2002)

Summary

In one of the most ambitious of **alternate histories**, Kim Stanley Robinson imagines that the fourteenth-century plague known as the Black Death did not merely decimate the population of **Europe**, as historians estimate (some put the death-rate as high as one-third), but almost completely wiped it out, at the same time more or less exterminating **Christianity** (and indeed virtually all white-skinned humans). Thereafter the shape of human **civilization** is molded not by Europe and Christianity but by people from **Africa, Asia,** and North **America,** guided by the **religions** of Buddhism and **Islam.**

Although generally described as a novel, *The Years of Rice and Salt* relates its history through a series of ten novellas, their stories separated by decades and linked by a group (*jati*) of characters who undergo a form of **reincarnation,** being reborn in different guises into each new epoch. These characters, identified by the letters B, I, K, and S, retain their general attributes of soul from one incarnation to the next, however much their positions in the world and relationships between them might change. At the end of each physical life they once again encounter and recognize each other in the *bardo*, the limbo-like place where they await the gods' judgment of their immediate past life before being sent back for the next. Thus, between each episode on **Earth** we have shorter accounts of the procedures the group members go through to successfully renew their mundane activities. This literary device gives a form of continuity to what might otherwise seem a set of unrelated tales from different time periods.

Discussion

Probably the most entertaining of the book's ten episodes is "The Alchemist"; at the same time it is the section most implausible as a fiction. It depicts an alternate version of the Renaissance, occurring in Samarkand—almost entirely in Samarkand. The central figure of this section, alchemist Khalid (K), is a sort of Super-Leonardo, although possessed of a greater practical bent. Mainly at the behest of a ruler whose sole interest is in **weaponry,** Khalid and his team invent a plethora of the technological devices to which we have become accustomed in our own world (see **Technology**) while at the same time making scientific conceptual breakthroughs that are virtually without number. This preposterous conceit makes the episode impossible to accept as "real history"; at the same time, though, it can be accepted as a sort of mythopoeized **history** in which the semi-legendary figure of Khalid is credited with **inventions** and discoveries made by the numerous individuals who contributed to the scientific and technological revolution—rather in the same way that all products of the Pythagorean School tend to be attributed to Pythagoras himself.

Although other episodes deliver a less fatal jolt to the suspension of disbelief, they are not always wholly successful. The parts of the book that deal with the interactions and **race relations** between peoples of **China** and Islam, on the one hand, and the **Native American** cultures they encounter when they make their way by **sea travel** to the Americas, are initially highly plausible; however, the Native American **culture** itself is, bizarrely, depicted as near-utopian (see **Utopia**). Whatever happened to Europe would not directly have affected the Native Americans of Robinson's **parallel world**, yet the Native American cultures of our own history were very far from utopian when Europeans encountered them. What trick of social **anthropology** could make them so different in Robinson's world? That they then take over the self-perceived role of the real world's United States, spreading **freedom**, democracy, and enlightenment wherever their influence reaches, adds a further layer of implausibility to what has already become an increasingly unpalatable substrate.

The book also contains extended discussions of the nature of history (there is even a brief discussion between two characters in which they dismiss the merits of what-if alternate-history speculation). If the version recounted in *The Years of Rice and Salt* is to be believed, then history will always converge toward the same general course, no matter what the kind or scale of events that might disrupt it: the fictional story of human **progress** quite closely parallels the real one, only the historiogeographical details differing (as per the North American influence being born from a Native American rather than European-descended culture). Perhaps human **psychology** is the true determinant of the course of human history. However, Robinson's discussions do not reflect that potentially interesting thesis, concerning themselves more with such notions as history's supposedly cyclical nature (see **Cycles**).

The Years of Rice and Salt is vast in its ambition (and indeed just plain vast); it is for the most part beautifully written, although a few passages give the impression of being stuffed in at the last moment in draft form. Many regard it as the ultimate alternate history novel, the benchmark against which all others will in future be judged; and such talk is not altogether hyperbolic. It is to be hoped, however, that its successor in this pole position will have a greater regard for history.

Bibliography

Mark Bould. "*The Years of Rice and Salt* by Kim Stanley Robinson." *Foundation*, No. 86 (Autumn, 2002), 134–136.

Paul Buhle. "Kim Stanley Robinson, Science Fiction Socialist." *Monthly Review: An Independent Socialist Magazine*, 54 (July, 2002), 87–90.

Edgar L. Chapman and Carl B. Yoke, eds. *Classic and Iconoclastic Alternate History Science Fiction*. Lewiston: Edwin Mellen Press, 2003.

Amy Clarke. "Like a Japanese Paper Flower in Water: An Interview with Kim Stanley Robinson." *Writing on the Edge*, 12 (Fall/Winter, 2001), 5–14.

Nick Gevers. "The Spin of a Coin, An Anthology of Souls: Kim Stanley Robinson Interviewed." *Interzone*, No. 177 (March, 2002), 15–19.

Matt Hills. "Resurrections and Reincarnations." *Interzone*, No. 181 (August, 2002), 58–60.

Farah Mendlesohn. "*The Years of Rice and Salt.*" *SFRA Review*, No. 257 (March/April, 2002), 24–27.

Amy J. Ransom. "Alternate History and Uchronia." *Foundation*, No. 87 (Spring, 2003), 58–72.

—*John Grant*

Bibliography

This bibliography lists secondary resources on science fiction and fantasy that are likely to be accessible and useful to a broad range of readers and scholars. They are classified as Reference Works, Histories, General Studies, and Subgenre and Thematic Studies.

REFERENCE WORKS

Brian Ash, ed. *The Visual Encyclopedia of Science Fiction*. New York: Harmony Books, 1977.

Neil Barron, ed. *Anatomy of Wonder*. Fourth Ed. New Providence, NJ: Bowker, 1995.

————, ed. *Fantasy and Horror: A Critical and Historical Guide to Literature, Illustration, Film, TV, Radio, and the Internet*. Lanham, MD: Scarecrow Press, 1999.

Everett F. Bleiler. *Science-Fiction: The Early Years*. Kent, OH: Kent State University Press, 1990.

Everett F. Bleiler with Richard Bleiler. *Science-Fiction: The Gernsback Years*. Kent, OH: Kent State University Press, 1998.

Richard Bleiler, ed. *Science Fiction Writers*. Second Ed. New York: Scribner's, 1999.

————, ed. *Supernatural Fiction Writers*. Second Ed. 2 vols. New York: Scribner's, 2003.

John Clute. *SF: The Illustrated Encyclopedia*. London, New York, and Stuttgart: Dorling Kindersley, 1995.

John Clute and John Grant, eds. *The Encyclopedia of Fantasy*. New York: St. Martin's Press, 1997.

John Clute and Peter Nicholls, eds. *The Encyclopedia of Science Fiction*. New York: St. Martin's Press, 1993.

Roger Fulton and John Betancourt. *The Sci-Fi Channel Encyclopedia of TV Science Fiction*. New York: Warner Books, 1998.

Philip B. Gove. *The Imaginary Voyage in Prose Fiction: A History of its Criticism and a Guide for Its Study, with an Annotated Checklist of 215 Imaginary Voyages from 1700 to 1800*. New York: Columbia University Press, 1941.

James Gunn, ed. *The New Encyclopedia of Science Fiction*. New York: Viking, 1988.

Phil Hardy, ed. *The Encyclopedia of Science Fiction Movies*. Minneapolis: Woodbury, 1986.

Robert Holdstock, ed. *Encyclopedia of Science Fiction*. London: Octopus Books, 1978.

Frank N. Magill, ed. *Survey of Science Fiction Literature*. 5 volumes. Englewood Cliffs, NJ: Salem Press, 1979.

Sam Moskowitz. *Explorers of the Infinite: Shapers of Science Fiction.* Cleveland: World Publishing Company, 1963.

———. *Seekers of Tomorrow: Masters of Modern Science Fiction.* Cleveland: World Publishing Company, 1966.

Jay P. Peterson, ed. *St. James Guide to Science Fiction Writers.* Detroit: Gale Research, 1996.

David Pringle. *Modern Fantasy: The Hundred Best Novels.* London: Grafton, 1988.

———. *Science Fiction: The 100 Best Novels.* London: Xanadu, 1985.

———, ed. *St. James Guide to Fantasy Writers.* Detroit: Gale Research, 1996.

———, ed. *St. James Guide to Horror, Ghost and Gothic Writers.* Detroit: Gale Research, 1998.

Robert Reginald, ed. *Contemporary Science Fiction Authors.* New York: Arno Press, 1975.

———, ed. *Science Fiction and Fantasy Literature: A Checklist, 1700–1974.* Detroit: Gale Research, 1979.

———, ed. *Science Fiction and Fantasy Literature, 1975–1991.* Detroit: Gale Research, 1992.

Baird Searles, Martin Last, Beth Meacham, and Michael Franklin. *A Reader's Guide to Science Fiction.* New York: Avon Books, 1979.

T.A. Shippey, consulting ed. A.J. Sobchak, project ed. *Magill's Guide to Science Fiction and Fantasy Literature.* 4 vols. Pasadena, CA: Salem Press, 1996.

Donald H. Tuck. *The Encyclopedia of Science Fiction and Fantasy through 1968.* 3 vols. Second ed. Chicago: Advent, 1982.

Marhsall B. Tymn, ed. *The Science Fiction Reference Book.* Mercer Island, WA: Starmont House, 1981.

David Wingrove, ed. *Science Fiction Film Source Book.* Harlow, Essex, England: Longman, 1985.

———, ed. *The Science Fiction Source Book.* Harlow, Essex, England: Longman, 1984.

Gary K. Wolfe. *Critical Terms for Science Fiction and Fantasy: A Glossary and Guide to Scholarship.* Westport, CT: Greenwood Press, 1986.

HISTORIES

Brian W. Aldiss with David Wingrove. *Trillion Year Spree: The History of Science Fiction.* New York: Atheneum, 1986.

Paul Alkon. *Origins of Futuristic Fiction.* Athens: University of Georgia Press, 1987.

———. *Science Fiction before 1900.* New York: Twayne, 1994.

Randy Broecker. *Fantasy of the 20th Century.* Portland, OR: Collectors Press, 2001.

Paul Carter. *The Creation of Tomorrow: Fifty Years of Magazine Science Fiction.* New York: Columbia University Press, 1977.

James Gunn. *Alternate Worlds: The Illustrated History of Science Fiction.* New York: A & W Visual Library, 1975.

David Kyle. *A Pictorial History of Science Fiction.* London: Hamlyn Publishing, 1976.

Brooks Landon. *Science Fiction after 1900.* Boston: Twayne Publishers, 1997.

Sam J. Lundwall. *Science Fiction: An Illustrated History.* 1977. New York: Grosset & Dunlap, 1978.

Marjorie Hope Nicolson. *Voyages to the Moon*. New York: Macmillan, 1948.

Alexei Panshin and Cory Panshin. *The World Beyond the Hill: Science Fiction and the Quest for Transcendence*. Los Angeles: Jeremy P. Tarcher, 1989.

Frank M. Robinson. *Science Fiction of the 20th Century*. Portland, OR: Collectors Press, 1999.

Franz Rottensteiner. *The Science Fiction Book: An Illustrated History*. London: Thames and Hudson, 1975.

Brian Stableford. *Scientific Romance in Britain, 1890–1950*. London: Fourth Estate, 1985.

Robert Weinberg. *Horror of the 20th Century*. Portland, OR: Collectors Press, 2000.

Dieter Wuckel and Bruce Cassiday. *The Illustrated History of Science Fiction*. New York: Ungar, 1989.

GENERAL STUDIES

Kingsley Amis. *New Maps of Hell*. New York: Ballantine Books, 1960.

Brian Attebery. *Strategies of Fantasy*. Bloomington: Indiana University Press, 1992.

J.O. Bailey. *Pilgrims through Time and Space: Trends and Patterns in Scientific and Utopian Fiction*. New York: Argus Books, 1947.

William Sims Bainbridge. *Dimensions of Science Fiction*. Cambridge, MA: Harvard University Press, 1986.

Marleen Barr. *Alien to Femininity*. New York: Greenwood Press, 1987.

James Blish. *The Issues at Hand*. Chicago: Advent Publishers, 1964.

———. *More Issues at Hand*. Chicago: Advent Publishers, 1970.

Christine Brooke-Rose. *A Rhetoric of the Unreal*. New York: Cambridge University Press, 1981.

John Clute. *Look at the Evidence: Essays and Reviews*. New York: Serconia, 1995.

———. *Scores: Reviews 1993–2003*. Harold Wood, UK: Beccon, 2003.

———. *Strokes: Essays and Reviews, 1966–1986*. Seattle: Serconia, 1988.

Basil Davenport, ed. *The Science Fiction Novel: Imagination and Social Criticism*. Chicago: Advent, 1959.

L. Sprague de Camp and Catherine Crook de Camp. *Science Fiction Handbook, Revised*. New York: McGraw-Hill, 1975.

Samuel R. Delany. *Starboard Wine: More Notes on the Language of Science Fiction*. Pleasantville, NY: Dragon, 1984.

———. *Silent Interviews: On Language, Race, Sex, Science Fiction, and Some Comics*. Hanover, NH: Wesleyan University Press, 1994.

Thomas M. Disch. *The Dreams Our Stuff Is Made Of*. New York: Free Press, 1998.

Harlan Ellison. *Sleepless Nights in the Procrustean Bed*. Ed. Marty Clark. San Bernardino, CA: Borgo Press, 1984.

Carl Freedman. *Critical Theory and Science Fiction*. Middletown, CT: Wesleyan University Press, 2000.

James Gunn. *Inside Science Fiction*. San Bernardino, CA: Borgo Press, 1992.

David G. Hartwell. *Age of Wonders*. Second Ed. New York: Tor Books, 1996.

Kathryn Hume. *Fantasy and Mimesis*. New York: Methuen, 1984.

Rosemary Jackson. *Fantasy: The Literature of Subversion*. New York: Methuen, 1981.

Edward James. *Science Fiction in the 20th Century*. Oxford and New York: Oxford University Press, 1994.

Edward James and Farah Mendlesohn, eds. *The Cambridge Companion to Science Fiction*. Cambridge: Cambridge University Press, 2003.

Gwyneth Jones. *Deconstructing the Starships: Science, Fiction, and Reality*. Liverpool: Liverpool University Press, 1999.

David Ketterer. *New Worlds for Old: The Apocalyptic Imagination, Science Fiction, and American Literature*. Bloomington, IN: Indiana University Press, 1974.

Damon Knight. *In Search of Wonder*. 1956. Revised and Enlarged. Chicago: Advent Publishers, 1967.

David Kyle. *The Illustrated Book of Science Fiction Ideas and Dreams*. New York: Hamlyn, 1977.

David Langford. *Up Through an Empty House of Stars*. Holicong, PA: Cosmos Books, 2003.

Ursula K. Le Guin, *The Language of the Night*. Ed. Susan Wood. New York: Perigee, 1980.

Stanislaw Lem. *Microworlds: Writings on Science Fiction and Fantasy*. Ed. Franz Rottensteiner. New York: Harcourt, 1984.

C.S. Lewis. *Of Other Worlds*. Ed. Walter Hooper. New York: Harcourt Brace Jovanovich, 1966.

Barry N. Malzberg. *The Engines of the Night*. 1982. New York: Bluejay Books, 1984.

Carl D. Malmgren. *Worlds Apart: Narratology of Science Fiction*. Bloomington: Indiana University Press, 1991.

Sam Moskowitz. *Strange Horizons: The Spectrum of Science Fiction*. New York: Scribner, 1976.

John J. Pierce. *Foundations of Science Fiction: A Study in Imagination and Evolution*. Westport, CT: Greenwood Press, 1987.

John J. Pierce. *When World Views Collide: A Study in Imagination and Evolution*. Westport, CT: Greenwood Press, 1989.

Eric S. Rabkin. *The Fantastic in Literature*. Princeton: Princeton University Press, 1976.

Adam Roberts. *Science Fiction*. London and New York: Routledge, 2000.

Andy Sawyer and David Seed, eds. *Speaking Science Fiction*. Liverpool: Liverpool University Press, 2000.

Robert Scholes and Eric S. Rabkin. *Science Fiction: History, Science, Vision*. Oxford and New York: Oxford University Press, 1977.

Darrell Schweitzer, ed. *Exploring Fantasy Worlds*. San Bernardino, CA: Borgo Press, 1985.

David Seed, ed. *A Companion to Science Fiction*. Oxford: Blackwell Publishers, 2005.

George Slusser, George R. Guffey, and Mark Rose, eds. *Bridges to Science Fiction*. Carbondale: Southern Illinois University Press, 1980.

Norman Spinrad. *Science Fiction in the Real World*. Carbondale: Southern Illinois University Press, 1990.

Peter Stockwell. *The Poetics of Science Fiction*. New York: Longman, 2000.

Darko Suvin. *Metamorphoses of Science Fiction*. New Haven: Yale University Press, 1979.

Tzvetan Todorov. *The Fantastic*. Trans. Richard Howard. Cleveland: Press of Case Western Reserve University, 1973.

Gary Westfahl. *The Mechanics of Wonder*. Liverpool: Liverpool University Press, 1998.

Gary K. Wolfe. *The Known and the Unknown: The Iconography of Science Fiction*. Kent, OH: Kent State University Press, 1979.

Donald A. Wollheim. *The Universe Makers*. New York: Harper, 1971.

SUBGENRE AND THEMATIC STUDIES

Brian W. Aldiss. *Science Fiction Art*. New York: Crown, 1975.

Camille Bacon-Smith. *Science Fiction Culture*. Philadelphia: University of Pennsylvania Press, 1999.

Marleen Barr. *Feminist Fabulation: Space/Postmodern Fiction*. Iowa City: University of Iowa Press, 1992.

Frances Bartkowski. *Feminist Utopias*. Lincoln: University of Nebraska Press, 1989.

John Baxter. *Science Fiction in the Cinema*. New York: Barnes, 1970.

M. Keith Booker. *Science Fiction Television*. Westport, CT: Praeger, 2004.

Paul Brians. *Nuclear Holocausts: Atomic War in Fiction, 1895–1984*. Kent, OH: Kent State University Press, 1987.

Damien Broderick. *Reading by Starlight: Postmodern Science Fiction*. New York: Routledge, 1995.

John Brosnan. *Future Tense: The Cinema of Science Fiction*. London: Macdonald, 1978.

Scott Bukatman. *Terminal Identity: The Virtual Subject in Postmodern Science Fiction*. Durham, NC: Duke University Press, 1993.

Thomas D. Clareson. *Some Kind of Paradise: The Emergence of American Science Fiction*. Westport, CT: Greenwood Press, 1985.

I.F. Clarke. *Voices Prophesying War: Future Wars, 1763–3749*. London: Oxford University Press, 1992.

Jane L. Donawerth. *Frankenstein's Daughters: Women Writing Science Fiction*. Syracuse, NY: Syracuse University Press, 1997.

H. Bruce Franklin. *War Stars: The Superweapon and the American Imagination*. Oxford: Oxford University Press, 1988.

Colin Greenland. *The Entropy Exhibition: Michael Moorcock and the British "New Wave" in Science Fiction*. London: Routledge, 1983.

N. Katherine Hayles. *How We Became Posthuman: Virtual Bodies in Cybernetics, Literature, and Infomatics*. Chicago: University of Chicago Press, 1999.

Mark R. Hillegas. *The Future as Nightmare: H.G. Wells and the Anti-Utopians*. New York: Oxford University Press, 1967.

Justine Larbalestier. *The Battle of the Sexes in Science Fiction*. Middletown, CT: Wesleyan University Press, 2002.

Rob Latham. *Consuming Youth: Vampires, Cyborgs, and the Culture of Consumption*. Chicago: University of Chicago Press, 2002.

Sarah Lefanu. *In the Chinks of the World Machine: Feminism and Science Fiction*. London: The Women's Press, 1988.

Robert Lambourne, Michael Shallis, and Michael Shortland. *Close Encounters? Science and Science Fiction*. New York: Adam Hilger, 1990.

Larry McCaffery, ed. *Storming the Reality Studio: A Casebook of Cyberpunk and Postmodern Science Fiction.* Durham, NC: Duke University Press, 1991.

Walter E. Meyers. *Aliens and Linguists: Language Study and Science Fiction.* Athens: University of Georgia Press, 1980.

Tom Moylan. *Scraps of the Untainted Sky: Science Fiction, Utopia, Dystopia.* Boulder, CO: Westview, 2000.

Peter Nicholls, David Langford, and Brian Stableford. *The Science in Science Fiction.* 1982. New York: Knopf, 1983.

Joanna Russ. *To Write Like a Woman: Essays on Feminism and Science Fiction.* Bloomington: Indiana University Press, 1995.

Vivian Sobchack. *Screening Space: The American Science Fiction Film.* New York: Ungar, 1987.

Brian M. Stableford. *The Sociology of Science Fiction.* San Bernardino, CA: Borgo Press, 1987.

Darko Suvin. *Victorian Science Fiction in the UK: The Discourses of Knowledge and of Power.* Boston: Hall, 1983.

J.P. Telotte. *Replications: A Robotic History of the Science Fiction Film.* Champaign: University of Illinois Press, 1995.

Patricia S. Warrick. *The Cybernetic Imagination in Science Fiction.* Cambridge, MA: M.I.T Press, 1980.

Gary Westfahl. *Cosmic Engineers: A Study of Hard Science Fiction.* Westport, CT: Greenwood Press, 1996.

Jenny Wolmark. *Aliens and Others: Science Fiction, Feminism and Postmodernism.* Iowa City: University of Iowa Press, 1994.

Index

Boldfaced page numbers indicate main entries in the encyclopedia.

Editors and Contributors

Darrell Schweitzer
Philadelphia, Pennsylvania

CONTRIBUTORS

Nick Aires
Port Moody, British Columbia
Canada

Patricia Altner
Columbia, Maryland

Lou Anders
Birmingham, Alabama

Alex (Sandy) Antunes
School of Computational Sciences
George Mason University
Laurel, Maryland

Neal Baker
Information Technology and Reference Librarian
Earlham College
Richmond, Indiana

Elizabeth Barrette
Charleston, Illinois

Russell Blackford
School of Philosophy and Bioethics
Monash University
Melbourne, Australia

Tim Blackmore
Associate Professor, Information and Media Studies
University of Western Ontario
London, Ontario
Canada

Daniel E. Blackston
Springfield, Illinois

Jayme Lynn Blaschke
New Braunfels, Texas

Everett F. Bleiler
Interlaken, New York

Richard Bleiler
Reference Librarian
University of Connecticut
Storrs, Connecticut

Janice M. Bogstad
Professor and Head of Collection Development
McIntyre Library
University of Wisconsin-Eau Claire
Eau Claire, Wisconsin

Mark Bould
Senior Lecturer, Film Studies
University of the West of England
Bristol, United Kingdom

Chantal Bourgault du Coudray
Lecturer, Communication Studies
University of Western Australia
Crawley, Western Australia
Australia

Wendy Bousfield
Reference Librarian
Syracuse University Library
Syracuse, New York

Paul Brians
Professor, English
Washington State University
Pullman, Washington

Charlene Brusso
Pepperell, Massachusetts

Andrew M. Butler
Senior Lecturer, Media and Cultural Studies
Canterbury Christ Church University College
Canterbury, United Kingdom

John Clute
London, United Kingdom

Frank Coffman
Associate Professor, English and Journalism
Rock Valley College
Rockford, Illinois

Brett Cooke
Professor, European and Classical Languages
Texas A&M University
College Station, Texas

F. Brett Cox
Assistant Professor, English
Norwich University
Northfield, Vermont

Jeff D'Anastasio
Instructor, Communications
Minnesota State College
Red Wing, Minnesota

Janis Dawson
Doctoral Student, English
University of Victoria
Victoria, British Columbia
Canada

Charles De Paolo
Professor, English
Manhattan Community College
New York, New York

Noreen Doyle
Gardiner, Maine

Stefan Dziemianowicz
Bloomfield, New Jersey

Neil Easterbrook
Associate Professor, English
Texas Christian University
Fort Worth, Texas

Bob Eggleton
Providence, Rhode Island

Stefan Ekman
Doctoral Student, Lund University
Lund, Sweden

Alan C. Elms
Professor Emeritus, Psychology
University of California, Davis
Davis, California

Gregory Feeley
Hamden, Connecticut

Liz Fielden
Doctoral Student, Anglia Polytechnic University
Cambridge, United Kingdom

Toiya Kristen Finley
Nashville, Tennessee

Mark Finn
Austin, Texas

Carl Freedman
Professor, English
Louisiana State University
Baton Rouge, Louisiana

Pawel Frelik
Assistant Professor, American Literature and Culture
Maria Curie Sklodowska University
Lublin, Poland

Neil Gaiman
Minneapolis, Minnesota

Lincoln Geraghty
Lecturer, Creative Arts, Film, and Media
University of Portsmouth
Portsmouth, Hampshire
United Kingdom

Alan Gibbs
Lecturer, American and Canadian Studies
University of Nottingham
Nottingham, United Kingdom

Stephen L. Gillett
Research Associate, Mackay School of Mines
University of Nevada, Reno
Reno, Nevada

Alexander Graf
Senior Lecturer, Film and Moving Image Studies
University of Wales
Newport, United Kingdom

Charles Gramlich
Professor, Psychology
Xavier University of Louisiana
New Orleans, Louisiana

John Grant
Hewitt, New Jersey

Glenn R. Gray
Archivist/Assistant Special Collections Librarian
Henry Madden Library
California State University, Fresno
Fresno, California

James Gunn
Professor Emeritus, English
University of Kansas
Lawrence, Kansas

Stefan Hall
Doctoral Student, American Cultural Studies
Bowling Green State University
Bowling Green, Ohio

Darren Harris-Fain
Associate Professor, English and Humanities
Shawnee State University
Portsmouth, Ohio

Donald M. Hassler
Professor, English
Kent State University
Kent, Ohio

Karen Stoddard Hayes
Narragansett, Rhode Island

Roslynn Haynes
Adjunct Associate Professor, English
University of New South Wales
Sydney, New South Wales
Australia

Elyce Rae Helford
Professor, English
Director and Affiliate Faculty, Women's Studies
Middle Tennessee State University
Murfreesboro, Tennessee

Derek Hill
Portland, Oregon

Kenneth Hite
Chicago, Illinois

Veronica Hollinger
Professor, Cultural Studies
Trent University
Peterborough, Ontario
Canada

James Craig Holte
Professor, English
East Carolina University
Greenville, North Carolina

Martin Horstkotte
Librarian
University of Osnabruck
Osnabruck, Germany

Frederick A. Jandt
Milwaukee, Wisconsin

Beverley Jansen
Doctoral Student, English
University of Nottingham
Nottingham, United Kingdom

Paula Johanson
Legal, Alberta
Canada

Nancy Johnston
Lecturer, English
McMaster University
Hamilton, Ontario
Canada

Fiona Kelleghan
Associate Professor and Librarian
Otto G. Richter Library
University of Miami
Coral Gables, Florida

Patricia Kerslake
Postgraduate Program Facilitator
Central Queensland University
Melbourne, Australia

Leigh Kimmel
Indianapolis, Indiana

Paul Kincaid
Folkestone, Kent
United Kingdom

Rick Klaw
Austin, Texas

Jay Lake
Portland, Oregon

David Langford
Reading, Berkshire
United Kingdom

Rob Latham
Professor, English
University of Iowa
Iowa City, Iowa

Michelle Le Blanc
Coventry, United Kingdom

Marissa Lingen
Eagan, Minnesota

James Lowder
New Berlin, Wisconsin

Lynne Lundquist
Lecturer, Theatre and Dance Department
California State University, Fullerton
Fullerton, California

Brad Lyau
San Mateo, California

Christine Mains
University of Calgary
Calgary, Alberta
Canada

Tom Marcinko
Queen Creek, Arizona

Richard L. McKinney
Librarian, Human Ecology
Lund University
Lund, Sweden

Ed McKnight
Assistant Professor, English
Anderson College
Anderson, South Carolina

Joseph Milicia
Professor, English
University of Wisconsin-Sheboygan
Sheboygan, Wisconsin

Dunja M. Mohr
Assistant Professor, English Literature
University of Erfurt
Erfurt, Germany

Derryl Murphy
Prince George, British Columbia
Canada

Ian Nichols
Doubeview, Western Australia
Australia

Terry O'Brien
Fort Wayne, Indiana

Colin Odell
Coventry, United Kingdom

Shannan Palma
Doctoral Student, Women's Studies
Emory University
Atlanta, Georgia

John S. Partington
Reading, United Kingdom

Wendy Pearson
Postdoctoral Fellow, English
University of Western Ontario
London, Ontario
Canada

Michael Penncavage
Oak Ridge, New Jersey

Jefferson Peters
Professor, English
Fukuoka University
Fukuoka, Japan

A. William Pett
Adjunct Professor, English
Rhode Island College
Providence, Rhode Island

Frances Pheasant-Kelly
Senior Lecturer, Film Studies
University of Wolverhampton
Wolverhampton, United Kingdom

Kathleen Church Plummer
Lecturer Emeritus, Environmental Design
University of California, Davis
Davis, California

Don Riggs
Auxiliary Professor, English and Philosophy
Drexel University
Philadelphia, Pennsylvania

Chris Roberson
Austin, Texas

Adam Roberts
Professor, Nineteenth-Century Literature
Royal Holloway University of London
London, United Kingdom

Stephen D. Rogers
Buzzards Bay, Massachusetts

Michael Saler
Associate Professor, History
University of California, Davis
Davis, California

Karen Sands-O'Connor
Associate Professor, English
Buffalo State College
Buffalo, New York

Andy Sawyer
Science Fiction Librarian
Special Collections and Archives
University of Liverpool Library
Liverpool, United Kingdom

Sandra Martina Schwab
Johannes Gutenberg University
Mainz, Germany

Darrell Schweitzer
Philadelphia, Pennsylvania

Joyce Scrivner
Minneapolis, Minnesota

Laura Scuriatti
Assistant Professor, English
European College of Liberal Arts
Berlin, Germany

Michael Sharp
Assistant Professor, English
Binghamton University
Binghamton, New York

Bruce Shaw
Doctoral Student, University of South Australia
Adelaide, South Australia
Australia

Nisi Shawl
Seattle, Washington

Theodore James Sherman
Professor, English
Middle Tennessee State University
Murfreesboro, Tennessee

M.J. Simpson
Visiting Lecturer, Communications Studies
University of Lincoln
Lincoln, United Kingdom

Alison Sinclair
Victoria, British Columbia
Canada

George Slusser
Professor, Comparative Literature and Foreign Languages
University of California, Riverside
Riverside, California

Kevin P. Smith
Sheffield, South Yorkshire
United Kingdom

Lucy A. Snyder
Systems Specialist, Office of Information Technology
Ohio State University
Columbus, Ohio

David Soyka
Faculty Practitioner, Business Writing
University of Phoenix
Nogales, Arizona

Maureen Kincaid Speller
University of Kent
Canterbury, United Kingdom

C.W. Sullivan III
Professor, English
East Carolina University
Greenville, North Carolina

Éva Tettenborn
Assistant Professor, English
Penn State Worthington-Scranton
Scranton, Pennsylvania

William Thompson
Mesilla, New Mexico

Trent Walters
Omaha, Nebraska

Batya Weinbaum
Cleveland Heights, Ohio

Gary Westfahl
Instructor, Learning Center
University of California, Riverside
Riverside, California

D. Harlan Wilson
Grand Rapids, Michigan
East Lansing, Michigan

Gina Wisker
Coordinator and Professor, Women's Studies
Anglia Polytechnic University
Cambridge, United Kingdom

Matthew Wolf-Meyer
Doctoral Student, Anthropology
University of Minnesota, Twin Cities
Minneapolis, Minnesota

Martin Morse Wooster
Silver Spring, Maryland

Cat Yampell
Doctoral Student, English
Wayne State University
Detroit, Michigan

About the Editor

GARY WESTFAHL teaches at the University of California, Riverside. His previous books include *No Cure for the Future* (2002), *Unearthly Visions* (2002), *Worlds Enough and Time* (2002), *Science Fiction, Canonization, Marginalization, and the Academy* (2002), *Science Fiction, Children's Literature, and Popular Culture* (2002), *Space and Beyond* (2000), and *Cosmic Engineers* (1996), all available from Greenwood Press.